THE BASIC WRITINGS
OF C. G. JUNG

from

The Collected Works of C. G. Jung

VOLUMES 3, 5, 6, 7, 8, 9i, 11, 12, 16, 17

BOLLINGEN SERIES XX

THE BASIC
WRITINGS
OF C. G. JUNG

TRANSLATED BY R.F.C. HULL

Selected and Introduced by
Violet S. de Laszlo

BOLLINGEN SERIES
PRINCETON UNIVERSITY PRESS

EDITORIAL NOTE

In the mid-1950s, the Bollingen Foundation was approached by two New York publishers, each offering the idea of an anthology of C. G. Jung's writings. General interest in Jung's work was growing, and no selection was then available which presented his entire thought, and particularly that of his later years. The Foundation enlisted a distinguished analytical psychologist and scholar of Jung, Dr. Violet de Laszlo, who undertook to organize two separate collections, each representing the Jungian corpus in a different way and of value to the general reader as well as the student. At the time, only a half-dozen volumes of the Collected Works had been published, and Dr. de Laszlo drew translations from other sources or from R.F.C. Hull's translations in preparation. For the present edition, the text of the Collected Works has been substituted. Dr. de Laszlo's introduction has been retained.

Psyche and Symbol was published in 1958, one of the earliest volumes in the pioneering Doubleday Anchor paperback series. The editor's intention was to select writings "which would illustrate in convincing fashion the objects of [Jung's] symbol research and the manner of his approach, as well as a synopsis of the conclusions to which he was led." Professor Jung, who followed Dr. de Laszlo's projects with close interest, contributed a preface, written in August 1957. *The Basic Writings of C. G. Jung* was published in 1959 in the Modern Library (Random House). The editor aimed "to present as fully as possible some of the most important areas of Jung's conception of the nature and functioning of the human psyche."*

Violet Staub de Laszlo was born in Zurich in 1900 and completed her medical studies at the University of Zurich. She was a pupil of Jung's while beginning her practice in Switzerland, and during the 1930s she lived in London, playing a central role in the first organization of analytical psychologists in England. In 1940 she settled in the United States, practicing, teaching, and writing during a twenty-five year residence. Violet de Laszlo was recog-

---

* *Psyche and Symbol* is also published as a Princeton/Bollingen paperback.

nized as one of the leading exponents of the Jungian school. In 1965 she returned to Zurich, continuing an active life until her death in 1988. For the paperback edition the paragraph and footnote numbers of the *Collected Works* have been retained to facilitate reference, as well as the original figure numbers for the illustrations in "Introduction to the Religious and Psychological Problems of Alchemy."

In her introduction, written for publication in 1959, Dr. de Laszlo explains the principles that governed her selection and the occasional abridgments that she made. (In the present edition, it has been possible to restore some of the abridged passages.)

W. McG./D.T.

TABLE OF CONTENTS

TABLE OF CONTENTS

EDITOR'S INTRODUCTION

by Violet S. de Laszlo

There is, in short, a comparative anatomy of the mind as well as of the body, and it promises to be no less fruitful of far-reaching consequences, not merely speculative but practical, for the future of humanity.

—Sir James Frazer: *Folklore in the Old Testament*
(Abridged Edition, New York, 1923)

This volume is intended to present as fully as possible some of the most important areas of Jung's conception of the nature and functioning of the human psyche. It is intended as a basic reader for those who wish to acquaint themselves with the original structure of his conception.

It has not been possible until recently for the English-speaking public to form an adequate opinion of Jung's work because publication of the translations had not kept pace with the Swiss editions. Now, however, publication of the Collected Works in English has begun to remedy the deficit. Since it will do so without regard for the chronological sequence of the volumes, some of the important recent writings are being made available sooner. These later works, written in the seventh and eighth decades of Jung's life, represent the culmination of his achievement. Their focal area is occupied by the symbolic expressions of man's spiritual experience. In observing, describing, and collating its manifestations in the imaginative activities of the individual, in the formation of mythologies and of religious symbolism in various cultures, Jung has laid the groundwork for a psychology of the *spirit*.¹ These studies in turn rest upon the underpinnings of Jung's earlier work and can therefore be fairly grasped and evaluated only with the aid of a comprehensive knowledge of the earlier premises. Since spiritual life is indissolubly linked with religious life and experience ("religious" as distinct from any particular dogma or church), Jung's attention has been increasingly focused upon the spontaneous spiritual and religious activities of the psyche. These activities have been observed to originate in those regions of the psyche which, for want of a more positively descriptive word, have come to be named the *unconscious*. The reader will find in this volume ample evidence of Jung's concept of the unconscious. It is the central pillar of his life's work, which began shortly after the turn of the century with his experimental researches and clinical investigations at the Zurich psychiatric clinic in his native Switzerland.

In his essay *The Spirit of Psychology*, later entitled *On the Nature of the Psyche*, Jung speaks of the significance of the unconscious in psychology as follows: "The hypothesis of the unconscious puts a large question mark after the idea of the psyche. The soul, as hitherto postulated by the philosophical intellect and equipped with all the necessary faculties, threatened to emerge from its chrysalis as something with unexpected and uninvestigated properties. It no longer represented anything immediately known, about which nothing more remained to be discovered except a few more or less satisfying definitions. Rather, it now appeared in strangely double guise, as both known and unknown. In consequence, the old psychology was thoroughly unseated and as much revolutionized as classical physics had been by the discovery of radioactivity." Indeed, Jung's entire work constitutes a multidimensional research project into the nature of the *unconscious*, more particularly of the *collective unconscious*. The latter comprises the sum total of all the psychic areas which lie beyond the limits of the *personal unconscious*, this in turn being approximately identical with the area discovered and investigated by Freud under the single designation of the *unconscious*. It is essential for the understanding of Jung's work to bear in mind these distinctions, without which ideological and semantic confusion becomes inevitable. Jung's *collective unconscious* designates all the structural and functional areas which are com-

¹ *Spirit*: "The animating or vital principle in man, the immaterial intelligent or sentient part of a person." (Definition from the *Oxford English Dictionary*.)

mon to the human psyche *per se*, the outline of all its general features which in a manner of speaking might be equated with the general build and features of the human body. Each individuality, both psychically and somatically speaking, presents a unique mosaic within the framework of the general features.

A science of psychology must concern itself with many partial aspects of the total psychic structure and functioning. First of all, it needs to make a distinction between consciousness and the unconscious. The investigation of consciousness will result in a series of observations leading to a psychology of the *ego* with its range of individual variations. Since conscious behavior and strivings rest upon the immediate subsoil of the personal unconscious, no ego psychology can avoid paying attention to the latter. In regard to both motivation and perception the marginal and submarginal regions below the threshold of consciousness have to be taken into account. It is the network of half or totally forgotten impressions and reactions, of partially realized or wholly suppressed emotions, of critically rejected thoughts and feelings which in their totality make up the shadow region of the personal unconscious. This, then, is a product of the individual's personal existence and biography. Much of it can be remembered and assimilated into consciousness with the help of the techniques of association used by the various schools of depth analysis. This brings about an increase of self-understanding which is experienced as a psychic growth. Jung's early contribution in this field consisted in devising and perfecting the association method, which later became known as the word-association test. He made extensive studies of the verbal responses of his experimental subjects to a given set of stimulus words. The observations included the reaction-time intervals as well as the disturbances in reproduction regarding the stimulus. The association experiments were bound to be of considerable significance in psychopathology.[2] At this point, evidently, the unconscious had already become the object of investigation.

Since this research was undertaken during the years which Jung spent at the Zurich psychiatric clinic under Professor Eugen Bleuler, he was naturally led to observe the state of the unconscious in the mentally diseased. Whereas Freud's discovery of the unconscious took place chiefly through his observation of a case of hysteria, Jung's attention became mainly directed towards the uncon-

2 "The Association Method" and "Studies in Word Association," *Collected Works*, Vol. 2.

scious contents of the schizophrenic psychoses. One of the papers written at that time in co-authorship with Professor Bleuler bore the title *Complexes and the Cause of Illness in Dementia Praecox*.[3] (I am, of course, translating these originally German titles.) Out of this work later developed Jung's theory of the complexes, in which he came to regard the complexes as the smallest energic entities of the psychic dynamism, each invested with a certain amount of energy and functioning with varying degrees of relative independence and interdependence. In this context the complex loses its pathological connotation and is regarded as the normal basic constituent of psychic life. Consequently, its pathology, if any, is derived from a particular malfunctioning and relative distortion, disproportion, or displacement somewhat analogous to the dysfunctions in the realm of the body. Another avenue which began to open up at the time of these researches was to lead directly into what soon became Jung's chief field of interest: symbolic content and language of the unconscious psyche.

During these same years, contact was made between the Zurich workers and the imaginatively creative group that had begun to gather in Vienna—Freud, Adler, Rank, Stekel, to name but a few. The mutual stimulation resulting from these intensive exchanges led to the publication, beginning in 1909, of the *Yearbook for Psychoanalytical and Psychopathological Researches*, under the general direction of Bleuler and Freud and the editorship of Jung. Many of the most important papers and studies made during those years were published in the *Yearbook*, which, unfortunately, came to an end in 1914. To leaf through these rich volumes today leaves the reader sorrowing over the sudden demise of the *Yearbook* because of the external disruptive forces of World War I and their internal equivalent of scientific dissension.

In the 1912 volume of the *Yearbook*, Jung published his first major work under the title *Transformations and Symbols of the Libido*. The different concept of the libido on the one hand, and on the other hand the concept of the unconscious extended here far beyond the confines of the personal individualistic biography, were unacceptable to Freud and became the ideological-spiritual reason for his subsequent rejection of Jung. The work itself represents a milestone in the pursuit of the psychological understanding of the dynamics of the unconscious. It has been extensively revised by

Jung in recent years in order to relate it more directly to the advances in his studies and research in symbolism of the past two decades. It was republished under the title *Symbols of Transformation* in 1956. Its opening chapter, "Two Kinds of Thinking," explains in essence Jung's approach to the unconscious in terms of the nature of the unconscious itself, that is, as the spontaneous activity of the living psyche. The two kinds of thinking are: the directed thinking in logical sequences commonly understood in the use of the term, and regarded as a phylogenetically more recent acquisition, in contrast to the spontaneous, imaginative, largely non-verbal and non-logical processes which can be said to form the raw material of all creative activity. It is important that the reader should familiarize himself thoroughly with this distinction, and particularly with the nondirected, more archaic, more "natural" nature of the imaginative processes. Without such an understanding the body and intent of Jung's work cannot be properly grasped, because his work is predicated precisely on these processes and on the contents which they reveal. It is, one might say, based on the logical use of an empiricism which comes to grips with its material through an empathic rather than an analytical approach. In other words, Jung approaches the unconscious in its own terms. His reader in turn should use the same approach in exposing himself at first as fully and as uncritically as his reader training (or mistraining) will permit. Since the logically directed and the spontaneous mental and psychic activities mutually exclude each other to a considerable degree, no live relationship can be established with the unconscious through the directed pathways of thought. However, this is not to deny the value nor the place of the thinking function, which in its turn is needed to comprehend this relationship analytically and intellectually—but only after the relationship has been experienced. If it has not been given a chance to come to life, then, after all, nothing is there which might be analyzed.

To familiarize the reader as fully as possible with Jung's concept of the unconscious, his illuminating paper *On the Nature of the Psyche* has been made the second selection of the present volume. This is followed by three chapters from Part One and two chapters from Part Two of *The Relations Between the Ego and the Unconscious*, taken from the volume *Two Essays on Analytical Psychology*. The sum of this material represents a clear introduction to the impressive and convincing evidence of certain major aspects of the nature and functioning of the unconscious which Jung has elaborated during more than five decades of painstaking observation, research, and analytical thought. *On the Nature of the Psyche*, originally written in 1946, represents a relatively recent résumé of his observations and conclusions on the nature of the psyche.

Of all Jung's works, these "Two Essays" have undergone the most frequent re-editing, revision, and expansion, together with changes in titles indicating shifts in emphasis and in presentation. In his preface to the second edition (1934), Jung speaks of his essay on the *Relations Between the Ego and the Unconscious* as "the expression of a long-standing endeavour to grasp and—at least in its essential features—to depict the strange character and course of the *drame intérieur*, the transformation process of the unconscious psyche. This idea of the independence of the unconscious, which distinguishes my views so radically from those of Freud, came to me as far back as 1902, when I was engaged in studying the psychic history of a young girl somnambulist (*On the Psychology and Pathology of So-Called Occult Phenomena*, *Collected Works*, Volume 1). In a lecture which I delivered in Zurich in 1908 on the content of the psychoses (*Collected Works*, Volume 3), I approached this idea from another side. In 1912, I illustrated some of the main points of the process in an individual case and at the same time I indicated the historical and ethnological parallels to these seemingly universal psychic events."

The data we have presented, though perhaps confusing in their interweaving, are of great importance for the understanding of the evolution of Jung's thought. It must be borne in mind that a body of thought so vast and intricate cannot be comprehended through a brief and superficial acquaintance, but can only reveal its significance to a perseveringly receptive mind. To make matters still more complex, the same decade that witnessed the publication of *Transformation and Symbols of the Libido* was also the decade of travail for the *Psychological Types*. To quote from Jung's own foreword (1920): "This book is the fruit of nearly twenty years' work in the domain of practical psychology. It is a gradual intellectual structure, equally compounded of numberless impressions and experiences in the practice of psychiatry and nervous maladies, and of intercourse with men of all social levels; it is a product, therefore, of my personal dealings with friend and with foe; and finally it has a further source in the criticism of my own psychological particularity."

Psychological Types is represented in the present volume by (a) Jung's own Introduction, preceded by the significant motto taken from Heine on the characteristic traits in the natures of Plato and Aristotle elevated to the prototypes of two distinct human natures; (b) an abridged rendering of Jung's chapter entitled "General Description of the Types"; (c) an abridged rendering of the chapter of "Definitions." These definitions relate to a number of expressions in the language of psychology which have been used by various authors with widely different connotations, and which Jung has used throughout his writings in certain specific senses discussed by him in this chapter.

The original edition of *Psychological Types*, apart from the definitions, was composed of ten chapters, each of which illuminates a certain historical aspect. The chapter headings and subtitles speak for themselves:

Chapter I. "The Problem of Types in the History of Classical and Medieval Thought," divided into (1) Psychology in the Classical Age: The Gnostics, Tertullian, and Origen; (2) The Theological Disputes of the Ancient Church; (3) The Problem of Transubstantiation; (4) Nominalism and Realism; (5) The Holy Communion Controversy between Luther and Zwingli.

Chapter II. Jung discusses "Schiller's Ideas upon the Type Problem" based upon Schiller's *Letters on the Aesthetic Education of Man* and his ideas on *Naive and Sentimental Poetry*.

Chapter III. "The Apollonian and the Dionysian" takes as its basis Nietzsche's *Birth of Tragedy*.

Chapter IV. "The Type Problem in the Discernment of Human Character" was written in reference to a book by the English surgeon, F. Jordan, entitled *Character as seen in Body and Parentage.*

The subsequent chapter is devoted to the "Problem of Types in Poetry," based on the narrative *Prometheus and Epimetheus* by the Swiss poet Carl Spitteler, and leads to a comparison between the epic of Spitteler and Goethe's *Prometheus*. It also includes an extensive discussion of the psychologic-philosophical problem of the opposites in Brahmanic and in Chinese Taoist philosophy.

The final chapters are devoted to the Type problem in psychiatry, in aesthetics, and in modern philosophy, with particular reference to William James's types.

This brief glimpse of the elaboration of the Type problem may serve to assist the reader in locating the territory in which the tenth chapter, the "General Description of the Types," lies embedded.

xv

Its structure has been editorially simplified for presentation in this volume through the omission of alternating subsections, which it is hoped will clarify the pattern without unduly curtailing its meaning.

Jung speaks of *attitude types*, which are distinguished by the general direction of the individual's interest or "libido" movement. In regard to the attitude types he has designated as *extraverted* the person whose interest flows naturally outward towards the surrounding objects, be they of a concrete or an abstract nature: factual, ideological, or emotional, engaging and holding his interest through whatever appropriate channels may be available to him. Conversely, the interest of the *introverted* person is mainly directed towards his inner life and internal reactions, be they his own responses to stimuli from the environment, or the spontaneously arising thoughts, images, and feelings from within himself, that is to say, out of the unconscious. The attitude type is therefore characterized by his relation with the external and the internal object respectively, since the endopsychic processes can be regarded as an objective inner existence capable of being consciously experienced, observed, and registered. The life of the extravert is lived mainly through his direct attention, frequently to the point of identification, to the object of his interest. The life of the introvert derives its value from his internal assimilation of whatever material enters into his experience. The dynamics of both types are, therefore, opposite and compensatory. This is not to say that any given person reacts exclusively in one or the other fashion, but rather that the possibility exists for anyone to observe the predominance of one reaction pattern over the other in large numbers of persons as well as within himself.

In addition to the attitude types, Jung distinguishes a number of *function types*. We are here confronted with a special use of the general term *function*. Jung defines it as follows: "By psychological function I understand a certain form of psychic activity that remains theoretically the same under varying circumstances." He goes on to enumerate what he considers to be the four basic psychological functions, namely, *thinking* and *feeling*, designated as the two rational functions because they are evaluative, and *sensation* and *intuition*, designated as irrational because of their immediate perceptive character.

Of these four basic functions it can further be observed that each of them appears to be developed in varying degrees in every individual, and that one or at most two functions predominate over the remaining ones in each person. "Developed" here means accessible to conscious use and accordingly perfected as an adaptive tool with which a person masters the tasks and problems which he encounters in the course of his life. Anyone engaged in an intellectual pursuit will use and develop primarily his thinking function. A painter or sculptor on the other hand is likely to achieve his work primarily through the channels of feeling and sensation, the latter referring to the sum total of his sensory perceptions and including his assimilation of ideational elements. The paintings of Paul Klee could be taken to illustrate this conception. This is not to say that thought and intuition are excluded from the artist's reactions—far from it. Conversely, a mechanic or engineer must needs possess a good factual and analytical mind, and so must the scientist—thereby using a combination of sensation and thought. There again, the role of intuition will be the greater the more creative the personality. In reference to the degree of development of each function Jung speaks of the "superior" or the more differentiated in contrast to the "inferior" or the less differentiated one. By this no value judgment is expressed about any particular function except as regards its state of differentiation or development.

These introductory remarks can barely indicate the general scope of Jung's conception of the types and its vast practical and scientific potential. To recognize oneself or another as an introvert or extravert, possessed of a sound and reliable feeling or thinking function as the case may be, has obvious values and advantages of a practical, theoretical, and spiritual nature. This becomes clear when one reads the far-reaching conclusions at which Jung arrived in his studies on the attitude and function types. It has been briefly mentioned that they are conceived of as relating to each other in an opposite yet compensatory manner. This holds true for the attitudes of extraversion and introversion as well as for the functional opposites of thinking/feeling and sensation/intuition. Since each individual is regarded as being potentially capable of developing both attitudes and all of the four functions, the relatively less developed attitudes and functions must of necessity be the ones of which he is unaware—in other words, the ones that lie unused and submerged in the unconscious. If they can be lifted into consciousness, and thus made available, his mode of experiencing will thereby gain correspondingly in breadth and depth. The introvert who can establish a fuller relationship with his environment and the extravert who can discover the reality and wealth of his inner life will both be immensely richer than before, and so will the thinking man who gains access to his formerly unknown feeling values, or the factual sensation person who previously found himself excluded from the sphere of the intuitive imagination. This increase in the modes of experience and of comprehension represents psychological growth. Jung considers that this *growth potential is inherent in every human psyche*, and that whereas the first half of life is normally devoted to learning and to adapting to life's demands in terms of the natively given primary attitudes, the second half finds its fulfillment through the assimilation of the hitherto unconscious potential. Evidently, this equals a greater degree of "wholeness" and of maturity of judgment and experience.

The process of growth and maturation during the individual life span Jung has designated by the term *individuation*. This is a concept—or more than a concept: the statement of a fact observed and experienced innumerable times—which in the course of the years became the main focus of Jung's thought and studies, culminating in his stupendous contribution to what might be described as a psychology of the spirit. Growth at all levels must include spiritual development as its most subtle and valuable aspect. The life of the spirit, manifest in the psyche, must evolve in accordance with certain principles and forms, which, in turn, must be related to all the other levels of human existence. If they were totally incommensurate or dissociated, life could not continue. To designate these principles and forms Jung has adopted the term *archetypes*. Rather than devote his time to the peculiarities of many individual life histories, he was led to concentrate his energies upon the observation of the common matrix of psychic existence which he decided to designate as the *collective unconscious*. In this context the archetypes represent the basic forms and pathways in which our psychic existence is being enacted and which at any stage of our individual development exert their powerful influence. It is the archetypes which from times immemorial and in true recognition of their ever-present dominance have been elevated to the ranks of deities and heroes. The sequences of events which constitute the life histories of these beings are the stuff which is woven into the patterns of our mythologies. Such mythologies, therefore, reflect in an immediate and spontaneous manner the inner distinctive life of the psyche of any given culture or any religious belief. Jung has written widely on the archetypes and the collective unconscious—indeed, a comprehensive double volume of the Collected Works, the ninth, is devoted to twelve specialized papers and a long monograph on these dominant concepts. We have chosen two of these for the present volume. *Archetypes of the Collective Unconscious*, a more general survey, was first published in 1934 and was recently revised by Jung. *Psychological Aspects of the Mother Archetype* (1938, later revised), a fascinating and extensive treatment of what many will consider—along with its counterpart, the father archetype—the most significant and surely the most compelling archetype of all, has not been generally available in English before. Jung has written special studies also of the self, the primordial child, the *kore* or maiden, the anima, rebirth, the spirit, the shadow, and the mandala, and has treated these and other archetypes elsewhere in his writings.

Part Two of the present volume is assigned to questions of psychopathology and of therapy. The paper *On the Nature of Dreams* is of comparatively recent date (1945) and sums up Jung's point of view regarding their significance and value and his approach to their interpretation in an admirably concise manner. After paying homage to Freud for having established a valid method of dream interpretation, Jung describes his own differing procedure as a "survey of the context." In this approach no use is made of free association. In its place a careful investigation is made of all the elements which the dreamer is able to assemble around each component of the dream: reminiscences, similarities to objects, persons, and events encountered in his life, spontaneous attempts at interpretation, etc. These elements enlarge the tissue of the dream itself and the dreamer is not encouraged to stray far from its natural center. Thus, a certain amount of conscious understanding is directed towards that area of the unconscious whence the dream in question originated. Here again, as in the *Types*, Jung emphasizes the complementary nature of consciousness and the unconscious. It is important, therefore, to try to understand the message of the dream in its own language, without any assumption as to a fixed meaning of any given element, at least in regard to the personal aspects of the dream. However, where the dream presents recognizable mythological themes and archetypal figures, the interpretation must take into account their claim to general validity. The contact with the deeper regions of the unconscious forms an essential part of the individuation process to which Jung refers also as the "spontaneous realization of the whole person."

Turning now to psychopathology, the paper *On the Psychogenesis of Schizophrenia* has been included here in preference to any other works presenting Jung's point of view and understanding of the psychoses and neuroses. Discussions of neurosis are difficult to isolate from their context in his writings, but fortunately this paper contains much illuminating material regarding psychosis. These are in step with Jung's central point regarding schizophrenia, that is, that a lowering of the level of psychic functioning (referred to throughout this paper in the original French designation coined by Pierre Janet—"abaissement du niveau mental") opens the floodgates for an invasion of the conscious mind by the unconscious. In this inundation, as it were, no possibility exists for a gradual assimilation of the unconscious contents, which erupt in the form of archaic fantasies, of fears and desires in their crude instinctual nakedness. Thus, the unconscious is experienced not in its creative but in its destructive power.

Obviously, it is at the point of conflict and imbalance in the relation between the conscious personality and the unconscious psyche that the question of therapy arises. The following section of the present volume is Jung's introductory chapter to his *Psychology of the Transference*, which was published in Zurich in 1946. At the time when *Psychology of the Transference* was being written, its author had long been deeply engaged in his studies of the symbolism contained in the writings of the medieval alchemists. Their treatises had revealed themselves to be a rich stream of symbolic lore which drew its nourishment from many sources ranging from Greek mythology to the Old and the New Testaments, the Christian Church Fathers and other even more distant tributaries. This stream welled up from its subterranean unconscious existence, prompting the alchemists into undertaking their experiments and cogitations, which appear to our modern rational thought like a strange intermingling of practical experiment with astute philosophical musings and endless chains of visionary dreams. Having been forcefully struck by the similarities of a number of symbols in the dreams of his patients to the multifarious symbols found in the alchemical literature, Jung made himself thoroughly at home in the alchemical texts, which he studied in their Latin and Greek intricacies of thought and of symbol. He came to the conclusion that these symbols belong to what he had already come to describe as the collective unconscious. Since the archetypal symbols of the deeper psyche in their entirety are the carriers of the process of *individuation*, it became clear why the alchemists were so fascinated by the upsurge of the images which they experienced in the course of their work, and upon which they meditated at such length.

What, one must ask, have these interesting observations got to do with the transference in psychotherapy? The common denominator is to be found in the *symbols of individuation*. In fact, the first paper in which Jung established the parallels between certain symbols in modern dreams and their counterparts in alchemical literature bore the title *Dream Symbols of the Process of Individuation*.[4] This study was later expanded into a major work entitled *Psychology and Alchemy*, the introductory chapter of which is included in this volume. The inner experience of psychic growth is frequently reflected in a series of symbolic images made manifest in dreams. This can be ascertained in cases where a careful record of the dreams is kept over a long period of time. It then becomes apparent that certain elements and motifs keep recurring in different modulations, thus proving a continuity which would have remained unobserved in the absence of a sustained interest. Likewise, the ancient and medieval alchemical literature abounds in sequences of symbolic images which upon closer study revealed striking parallels to a number of recorded series of dreams from certain patients. One such particularly striking dream sequence became the material upon which Jung based his comparative study of alchemical symbolism and the integrative symbols in the modern psyche. This indicates a validity of certain symbols in the sense of their being operative in vastly different epochs and circumstances. It also indicates a validity of the respective sequences as portraying a psychic evolution within the life span of an individual existence.

The considerations on the theme of the transference swing between the two poles of the patient-doctor relationship (subsequently developed into a general theory of the unconscious dynamics of interpersonal relationships) and the inner psychic development from a state of conflict towards one of greater inner freedom and unity, which is symbolized in the idea of the mystic marriage or union; for this the Greek expression *hieros gamos* is frequently used by Jung. In contradistinction to Freud, Jung assigns an actively participating role to the analyst, whose empathy and carefully self-observant supportive attitude combined with his

4 First published in English in *The Integration of the Personality*, New York, 1939.

knowledge of the archetypal dynamics should enable him to assist the patient in establishing the much-needed contact with the deeper self. Jung develops these thoughts by means of analyzing a sequence of images from an alchemical treatise, *Rosarium philosophorum*, published in the year 1550. They depict the union of male and female figures called the King and Queen, also the Sun and Moon (Sol and Luna), and the new birth resulting therefrom, interpreted by Jung as symbolic of the renewal of the inner personality and as the fruit of the therapeutic contact with the eternal realm of the archetypes.

This theme, in turn, forms the core of the work *Psychology and Alchemy*. It heralds the final and most lofty of Jung's concerns: his study of the religious function of the soul. He says: "I have been accused of 'deifying the soul.' Not I, but God Himself has deified it! I did not attribute a religious function to the soul, I merely produced the facts which prove that the soul is *naturaliter religiosa*, i.e., possesses a religious function. . . . For it is obvious that far too many people are incapable of establishing a connection between the sacred figures and their own psyche: that is to say, they cannot see to what extent the equivalent images lie dormant in their own unconscious." In this perspective the secular preoccupations have been laid aside and the soul is being viewed *sub specie aeternitatis*: the archetypes reveal the essence of their immortal character which is being refashioned ever anew in the "sacred images." The city of God or of the gods, and the sacred personages dwelling therein with their attendants and their animal companions, are present in one form or another in every main religion. Their existence is convincingly proclaimed by the initiator of each religion. Their images are carried along the path of each tradition by the priests, the artists, and by the multitudes of believers whose unconscious receives and re-emits their resonance. Participation in the religious experience can take place through the inward assent given to the traditionally validated symbols, or in contrast, through the immediate contact with the religious symbols which can arise spontaneously from the religious depths of the psyche. This immediate experience constitutes the true meaning of mysticism. The more familiar the reader becomes with the life work of Jung, the more awed will he find himself—provided he can allow himself to respond at these levels—by the singlemindedness amidst the diversity of interest and of subject matter with which Jung's thought and energies have revolved around the soul which is *"naturaliter religiosa."*

For this reason, the following section of the present volume consists of the first two of the three chapters of *Psychology and Religion*, originally written in English for delivery as the Terry Lectures at Yale in 1937. The present version is the revised one published in the *Collected Works*. Here again, the titles sum up the content: "The Autonomy of the Unconscious" and "Dogma and Natural Symbols." The independent and purposive functioning of the unconscious is difficult to accept, both theoretically and experientially, for the Western-educated mind, in whose opinion consciousness has reigned supreme since the epoch of enlightenment. In the place of an unconscious occupying a limited area we are here presented with the concept of a virtually limitless sphere within which large numbers of meaningful operations take place. "Meaning" here assumes a psychological-spiritual-religious significance in which the unconscious as well as consciousness participate: the former as the "ground of being" (to borrow Paul Tillich's expression), the latter as the perceiving agent without whom the stream of images could run on endlessly and ineffectually, as can be observed in cases of insanity. The conscious ego's need and desire to comprehend the contents of the unconscious play a vital part in any therapeutic procedure which hopes not only to resolve the paralyzing tangles of a neurosis, but also and above all to assist in the maturation or individuation of the personality.

Indeed, the urge towards creative self-fulfilment is regarded by Jung as so universal as to deserve the designation of an instinct, regardless of the mode of life within which it expresses itself. Since both instinct and archetype designate innate and purposeful modes of behavior and of experience, this "instinct" of individuation, in turn, is closely related to the archetype of wholeness, of the psyche in the totality of its conscious plus its unconscious components. This totality Jung has designated as the *self*. The *self* by definition comprises the full scope of a personality from its most individual traits to its most generic attitudes and experiences, actual as well as potential. Hence, it transcends the existing personality. The archetype of wholeness or of the self can therefore be regarded as the dominant of psychic growth. The inherent plan of an individual integrative psychic process can thus be likened to the biological plan inherent in the seed of any living organism. This process can be experienced existentially in the personal life history, and symbolically wherever the image of wholeness or of the self is present. Indeed, the individuation process can be said to lie at the core of all spiritual experience, since it is coequal with a creative transformation of the inner person, and hence reflects the archetypal experience of an inner rebirth. In this context the impact of the symbol becomes the experience of "meaning" itself, and the archetypal image becomes an ultimate psychic truth and reality. Here then would seem to lie the central connecting link between psychology and religion.

In the last section of the present volume, out of the numerous essays written by Jung on the development of the personality, *Marriage as a Psychological Relationship* has been selected because the practical importance of the topic makes it especially worthy of being presented once again to a wider public. Considering how vast an amount of literature on human development is now available to the general reader, it seems appropriate to reconsider Jung's essay on marriage, with its pertinent distinctions concerning the conscious and unconscious factors which contribute to the relative harmony or disharmony in this, the most important of human relationships.

I have tried to provide here as representative as possible a selection of writings from the seminal work of C. G. Jung. I shall be deeply pleased if this book stimulates a number of its readers to a closer study of Jung's immense contribution to the understanding of the human psyche.

I

ON THE NATURE AND FUNCTIONING
OF THE PSYCHE

FROM *SYMBOLS OF TRANSFORMATION*

FOREWORD TO THE FOURTH (SWISS) EDITION [1]

I have long been conscious of the fact that this book, which was written thirty-seven years ago, stood in urgent need of revision, but my professional obligations and my scientific work never left me sufficient leisure to settle down in comfort to this unpleasant and difficult task. Old age and illness released me at last from my professional duties and gave me the necessary time to contemplate the sins of my youth. I have never felt happy about this book, much less satisfied with it: it was written at top speed, amid the rush and press of my medical practice, without regard to time or method. I had to fling my material hastily together, just as I found it. There was no opportunity to let my thoughts mature. The whole thing came upon me like a landslide that cannot be stopped. The urgency that lay behind it became clear to me only later: it was the explosion of all those psychic contents which could find no room, no breathing-space, in the constricting atmosphere of Freudian psychology and its narrow outlook. I have no wish to denigrate Freud, or to detract from the extraordinary merits of his investigation of the individual psyche. But the conceptual framework into which he fitted the psychic phenomenon seemed to me unendurably narrow. I am not thinking here of his theory of neurosis, which can be as narrow as it pleases if only it is adequate to the empirical facts, or of his theory of dreams, about which different views may be held in all good faith; I am thinking more of the reductive causalism of his whole outlook, and the almost complete disregard of the teleological directedness which is so characteristic of everything psychic. Although Freud's book *The Future of an Illusion* dates from his later years, it gives the best possible account of his earlier views, which move within the confines of the outmoded rationalism and scientific materialism of the late nineteenth century.

As might be expected, my book, born under such conditions, consisted of larger or smaller fragments which I could only string together in an unsatisfying manner. It was an attempt,

[1] [The edition here translated.—EDITORS.]

only partially successful, to create a wider setting for medical psychology and to bring the whole of the psychic phenomenon within its purview. One of my principal aims was to free medical psychology from the subjective and personalistic bias that characterized its outlook at that time, and to make it possible to understand the unconscious as an objective and collective psyche. The personalism in the views of Freud and Adler that went hand in hand with the individualism of the nineteenth century failed to satisfy me because, except in the case of instinctive dynamisms (which actually have too little place in Adler), it left no room for objective, impersonal facts. Freud, accordingly, could see no objective justification for my attempt, but suspected personal motives.

Thus this book became a landmark, set up on the spot where two ways divided. Because of its imperfections and its incompleteness it laid down the programme to be followed for the next few decades of my life. Hardly had I finished the manuscript when it struck me what it means to live with a myth, and what it means to live without one. Myth, says a Church Father, is "what is believed always, everywhere, by everybody"; hence the man who thinks he can live without myth, or outside it, is an exception. He is like one uprooted, having no true link either with the past, or with the ancestral life which continues within him, or yet with contemporary human society. He does not live in a house like other men, does not eat and drink like other men, but lives a life of his own, sunk in a subjective mania of his own devising, which he believes to be the newly discovered truth. This plaything of his reason never grips his vitals. It may occasionally lie heavy on his stomach, for that organ is apt to reject the products of reason as indigestible. The psyche is not of today; its ancestry goes back many millions of years. Individual consciousness is only the flower and the fruit of a season, sprung from the perennial rhizome beneath the earth; and it would find itself in better accord with the truth if it took the existence of the rhizome into its calculations. For the root matter is the mother of all things.

So I suspected that myth had a meaning which I was sure to miss if I lived outside it in the haze of my own speculations. I was driven to ask myself in all seriousness: "What is the myth you are living?" I found no answer to this question, and had to admit that I was not living with a myth, or even in a myth, but rather in an uncertain cloud of theoretical possibilities which I was beginning to regard with increasing distrust. I did not know that I was living a myth, and even if I had known it, I would not have known what sort of myth was ordering my life without my knowledge. So, in the most natural way, I took it upon myself to get to know "my" myth, and I regarded this as the task of tasks, for—so I told myself—how could I, when treating my patients, make due allowance for the personal factor, for my personal equation, which is yet so necessary for a knowledge of the other person, if I was unconscious of it? I simply had to know what unconscious or preconscious myth was forming me, from what rhizome I sprang. This resolve led me to devote many years of my life to investigating the subjective contents which are the products of unconscious processes, and to work out methods which would enable us, or at any rate help us, to explore the manifestations of the unconscious. Here I discovered, bit by bit, the connecting links that I should have known about before if I was to join up the fragments of my book. I do not know whether I have succeeded in this task now, after a lapse of thirty-seven years. Much pruning had to be done, many gaps filled. It has proved impossible to preserve the style of 1912, for I had to incorporate many things that I found out only many years later. Nevertheless I have tried, despite a number of radical interventions, to leave as much of the original edifice standing as possible, for the sake of continuity with previous editions. And although the alterations are considerable, I do not think one could say that it has turned into a different book. There can be no question of that because the whole thing is really only an extended commentary on a practical analysis of the prodromal stages of schizophrenia. The symptoms of the case form the Ariadne thread to guide us through the labyrinth of symbolistic parallels, that is, through the amplifications which are absolutely essential if we wish to establish the meaning of the archetypal context. As soon as these parallels come to be worked out they take up an incredible amount of space, which is why expositions of case histories are such an arduous task. But that is only to be expected: the deeper you go, the broader the base becomes. It certainly does not become narrower, and it never by any chance ends in a point—in a psychic trauma, for instance. Any such theory presupposes a knowledge of the traumatically affected psyche which no human being possesses, and which can only be laboriously acquired by investigating the workings of the unconscious. For this a great deal of comparative material is needed, and it cannot be dispensed with any more than in comparative anatomy. Knowledge of the subjective contents of consciousness means very little, for it tells us next to nothing about the real, subterranean life of the psyche. In psychology as in every science a fairly wide knowledge of other subjects is among the requisites for research work. A nodding acquaintance with the theory and pathology of neurosis is totally inadequate, because medical knowledge of this kind is merely information about an illness, but not knowledge of the soul that is ill. I wanted, so far as lay within my power, to redress that evil with this book—then as now.

This book was written in 1911, in my thirty-sixth year. The time is a critical one, for it marks the beginning of the second half of life, when a metanoia, a mental transformation, not infrequently occurs. I was acutely conscious, then, of the loss of friendly relations with Freud and of the lost comradeship of our work together. The practical and moral support which my wife gave me at that difficult period is something I shall always hold in grateful remembrance.

September, 1950

C. G. Jung

Therefore theory, which gives facts their value and significance, is often very useful, even if it is partially false, because it throws light on phenomena which no one has observed, it forces an examination, from many angles, of facts which no one has hitherto studied, and provides the impulse for more extensive and more productive researches. . . .

Hence it is a moral duty for the man of science to expose himself to the risk of committing error, and to submit to criticism in order that science may continue to progress. A writer . . . has launched a vigorous attack on the author, saying that this is a scientific ideal which is very limited and very paltry. . . . But those who are endowed with a mind serious and impersonal enough not to believe that everything they write is the expression of absolute and eternal truth will approve of this theory, which puts the aims of science well above the miserable vanity and paltry *amour propre* of the scientist.

—Ferrero, *Les Lois psychologiques du symbolisme*, p. viii

INTRODUCTION

I

1   Anyone who can read Freud's *Interpretation of Dreams* without being outraged by the novelty and seemingly unjustified boldness of his procedure, and without waxing morally indignant over the stark nakedness of his dream-interpretations, but can let this extraordinary book work upon his imagination calmly and without prejudice, will not fail to be deeply impressed at that point [1] where Freud reminds us that an individual conflict, which he calls the incest fantasy, lies at the root of that monumental drama of the ancient world, the Oedipus legend. The impression made by this simple remark may be likened to the uncanny feeling which would steal over us if, amid the noise and bustle of a modern city street, we were suddenly to come upon an ancient relic—say the Corinthian capital of a long-immured column, or a fragment of an inscription. A moment ago, and we were completely absorbed in the hectic, ephemeral life of the present; then, the next moment, something very remote and strange flashes upon us, which directs our gaze to a different order of things. We turn away from the vast confusion of the present to glimpse the higher continuity of history. Suddenly we remember that on this spot where we now hasten to and fro about our business a similar scene of life and activity prevailed two thousand years ago in slightly different forms; similar passions moved mankind, and people were just as convinced as we are of the uniqueness of their lives. This is the impression that may very easily be left behind by a first acquaintance with the monuments of antiquity, and it seems to me that Freud's reference to the Oedipus legend is in every way comparable. While still struggling with the confusing impressions of the infinite variability of the individual psyche, we suddenly catch a glimpse of the simplicity and grandeur of the

1 *The Interpretation of Dreams*, pp. 260–61.

8

Oedipus tragedy, that perennial highlight of the Greek theatre. This broadening of our vision has about it something of a revelation. For our psychology, the ancient world has long since been sunk in the shadows of the past; in the schoolroom one could scarcely repress a sceptical smile when one indiscreetly calculated the matronly age of Penelope or pictured to oneself the comfortable middle-aged appearance of Jocasta, and comically compared the result with the tragic tempests of eroticism that agitate the legend and drama. We did not know then—and who knows even today?—that a man can have an unconscious, all-consuming passion for his mother which may undermine and tragically complicate his whole life, so that the monstrous fate of Oedipus seems not one whit overdrawn. Rare and pathological cases like that of Ninon de Lenclos and her son [2] are too remote from most of us to convey a living impression. But when we follow the paths traced out by Freud we gain a living knowledge of the existence of these possibilities, which, although too weak to compel actual incest, are yet sufficiently strong to cause very considerable psychic disturbances. We cannot, to begin with, admit such possibilities in ourselves without a feeling of moral revulsion, and without resistances which are only too likely to blind the intellect and render self-knowledge impossible. But if we can succeed in discriminating between objective knowledge and emotional value-judgments, then the gulf that separates our age from antiquity is bridged over, and we realize with astonishment that Oedipus is still alive for us. The importance of this realization should not be underestimated, for it teaches us that there is an identity of fundamental human conflicts which is independent of time and place. What aroused a feeling of horror in the Greeks still remains true, but it is true for us only if we give up the vain illusion that we are *different*, i.e., morally better, than the ancients. We have merely succeeded in forgetting that an indissoluble link binds us to the men of antiquity. This truth opens the way to an understanding of the classical spirit such as has never existed before—the way of inner sympathy on the one hand and of intellectual comprehension on the other. By penetrating into the blocked subterranean passages of our own psyches we grasp the living meaning

[2] He is supposed to have killed himself when he heard that his adored Ninon was really his mother.

of classical civilization, and at the same time we establish a firm foothold outside our own culture from which alone it is possible to gain an objective understanding of its foundations. That at least is the hope we draw from the rediscovery of the immortality of the Oedipus problem.

This line of inquiry has already yielded fruitful results: to it we owe a number of successful advances into the territory of the human mind and its history. These are the works of Riklin,[3] Abraham,[4] Rank,[5] Maeder,[6] and Jones,[7] to which there has now been added Silberer's valuable study entitled "Phantasie und Mythos." Another work which cannot be overlooked is Pfister's contribution to Christian religious psychology.[8] The *leitmotiv* of all these works is to find a clue to historical problems through the application of insights derived from the activity of the unconscious psyche in modern man. I must refer the reader to the works specified if he wishes to inform himself of the extent and nature of the insights already achieved. The interpretations are sometimes uncertain in particulars, but that does not materially detract from the total result. It would be significant enough if this merely demonstrated the far-reaching analogy between the psychological structure of the historical products and those of modern individuals. But the analogy applies with particular force to the symbolism, as Riklin, Rank, Maeder, and Abraham have shown, and also to the individual mechanisms governing the unconscious elaboration of motifs.

3   Psychological investigators have hitherto turned their attention mainly to the analysis of individual problems. But, as things are at present, it seems to me imperative that they should broaden the basis of this analysis by a comparative study of the historical material, as Freud has already tried to do in his study of Leonardo da Vinci.[9] For, just as psychological knowledge furthers our understanding of the historical material, so, conversely, the historical material can throw new light on individual psychological problems. These considerations have led me to direct my attention more to the historical side of the picture, in the hope of gaining fresh insight into the foundations of

---

3 *Wishfulfilment and Symbolism in Fairy Tales.*   4 *Dreams and Myths.*
5 *The Myth of the Birth of the Hero.*   6 "Die Symbolik in den Legenden."
7 *On the Nightmare.*   8 *Die Frömmigkeit des Grafen Ludwig von Zinzendorf.*
9 Also Rank, "Ein Traum, der sich selbst deutet."

psychology. In my later writings [10] I have concerned myself chiefly with the question of historical and ethnological parallels, and here the researches of Erich Neumann have made a massive contribution towards solving the countless difficult problems that crop up everywhere in this hitherto little explored territory. I would mention above all his key work, *The Origins and History of Consciousness*,[11] which carries forward the ideas that originally impelled me to write this book, and places them in the broad perspective of the evolution of human consciousness in general.

10 [I.e., after 1912, the date of the original publication of the present work.—EDITORS.]

11 His subsequent publications, *Umkreisung der Mitte* and *The Great Mother*, may also be included in this category. [Three of the essays in the former work were translated in *Art and the Creative Unconscious*.—EDITORS.]

TWO KINDS OF THINKING

4   As most people know, one of the basic principles of
analytical psychology is that dream-images are to be understood
symbolically; that is to say, one must not take them literally,
but must surmise a hidden meaning in them. This ancient idea
of dream symbolism has aroused not only criticism, but the
strongest opposition. That dreams should have a meaning, and
should therefore be capable of interpretation, is certainly
neither a strange nor an extraordinary idea. It has been known
to mankind for thousands of years; indeed it has become something of a truism. One remembers having heard even at school
of Egyptian and Chaldaean dream-interpreters. Everyone knows
the story of Joseph, who interpreted Pharaoh's dreams, and of
Daniel and the dream of King Nebuchadnezzar; and the dream-
book of Artemidorus is familiar to many of us. From the written
records of all times and peoples we learn of significant and
prophetic dreams, of warning dreams and of healing dreams sent
by the gods. When an idea is so old and so generally believed,
it must be true in some way, by which I mean that it is *psychologically true.*

5   For modern man it is hardly conceivable that a God
existing outside ourselves should cause us to dream, or that the
dream foretells the future prophetically. But if we translate this
into the language of psychology, the ancient idea becomes much
more comprehensible. The dream, we would say, originates in
an unknown part of the psyche and prepares the dreamer for
the events of the following day.

6   According to the old belief, a god or demon spoke to the
sleeper in symbolic language, and the dream-interpreter had to
solve the riddle. In modern speech we would say that the dream
is a series of images which are apparently contradictory and
meaningless, but that it contains material which yields a clear
meaning when properly translated.

7   Were I to suppose my readers to be entirely ignorant of dream-analysis, I should be obliged to document this statement with numerous examples. Today, however, these things are so well known that one must be sparing in the use of case-histories so as not to bore the public. It is an especial inconvenience that one cannot recount a dream without having to add the history of half a lifetime in order to represent the individual foundations of the dream. Certainly there are typical dreams and dream-motifs whose meaning appears to be simple enough if they are regarded from the point of view of sexual symbolism. One can apply this point of view without jumping to the conclusion that the content so expressed must also be sexual in origin. Common speech, as we know, is full of erotic metaphors which are applied to matters that have nothing to do with sex; and conversely, sexual symbolism by no means implies that the interests making use of it are by nature erotic. Sex, as one of the most important instincts, is the prime cause of numerous affects that exert an abiding influence on our speech. But affects cannot be identified with sexuality inasmuch as they may easily spring from conflict situations—for instance, many emotions spring from the instinct of self-preservation.

8   It is true that many dream-images have a sexual aspect or express erotic conflicts. This is particularly clear in the motif of *assault*. Burglars, thieves, murderers, and sexual maniacs figure prominently in the erotic dreams of women. It is a theme with countless variations. The instrument of murder may be a lance, a sword, a dagger, a revolver, a rifle, a cannon, a fire-hydrant, a watering-can; and the assault may take the form of a burglary, a pursuit, a robbery, or it may be someone hidden in the cupboard or under the bed. Again, the danger may be represented by wild animals, for instance by a horse that throws the dreamer to the ground and kicks her in the stomach with his hind leg; by lions, tigers, elephants with threatening trunks, and finally by snakes in endless variety. Sometimes the snake creeps into the mouth, sometimes it bites the breast like Cleopatra's legendary asp, sometimes it appears in the role of the paradisal serpent, or in one of the variations of Franz Stuck, whose snake-pictures bear significant titles like "Vice," "Sin," or "Lust" (cf. pl. x). The mixture of anxiety and lust is perfectly

expressed in the sultry atmosphere of these pictures, and far more crudely than in Mörike's piquant little poem:

Girl's First Love Song

What's in the net? I feel
Frightened and shaken!
Is it a sweet-slipping eel
Or a snake that I've taken?

Love's a blind fisherman,
Love cannot see;
Whisper the child, then,
What would love of me?

It leaps in my hands! This is
Anguish unguessed.
With cunning and kisses
It creeps to my breast.

It bites me, O wonder!
Worms under my skin.
My heart bursts asunder,
I tremble within.

Where go and where hide me?
The shuddersome thing
Rages inside me,
Then sinks in a ring.

What poison can this be?
O that spasm again!
It burrows in ecstasy
Till I am slain.[1]

9   All these things seem simple and need no explanation to be intelligible. Somewhat more complicated is the following dream of a young woman. She dreamt that she saw *the triumphal Arch of Constantine. Before it stood a cannon, to the right a bird, to the left a man. A cannon-ball shot out of the muzzle and hit her; it went into her pocket, into her purse. There it remained, and she held the purse as if there were something very precious inside it. Then the picture faded, and all she could see was the*

[1] Mörike, *Werke*, I, p. 33.

14

stock of the cannon, with Constantine's motto above it: "*In hoc signo vinces.*" The sexual symbolism of this dream is sufficiently obvious to justify the indignant surprise of all innocent-minded people. If it so happens that this kind of realization is entirely new to the dreamer, thus filling a gap in her conscious orientation, we can say that the dream has in effect been interpreted. But if the dreamer has known this interpretation all along, then it is nothing more than a repetition whose purpose we cannot ascertain. Dreams and dream-motifs of this nature can repeat themselves in a never-ending series without our being able to discover—at any rate from the sexual side—anything in them except what we know already and are sick and tired of knowing. This kind of approach inevitably leads to that "monotony" of interpretation of which Freud himself complained. In these cases we may justly suspect that the sexual symbolism is as good a *façon de parler* as any other and is being used as a dream-language. "*Canis panem somniat, piscator pisces.*" Even dream-language ultimately degenerates into jargon. The only exception to this is in cases where a particular motif or a whole dream repeats itself because it has never been properly understood, and because it is necessary for the conscious mind to reorient itself by recognizing the compensation which the motif or dream expresses. In the above dream it is certainly a case either of ordinary unconsciousness, or of repression. One can therefore interpret it sexually and leave it at that, without going into all the niceties of the symbolism. The words with which the dream ends—"In hoc signo vinces"—point to a deeper meaning, but this level could only be reached if the dreamer became conscious enough to admit the existence of an erotic conflict.

10   These few references to the symbolic nature of dreams must suffice. We must accept dream symbolism as an accomplished fact if we wish to treat this astonishing truth with the necessary degree of seriousness. It is indeed astonishing that the conscious activity of the psyche should be influenced by products which seem to obey quite other laws and to follow purposes very different from those of the conscious mind.

11   How is it that dreams are symbolical at all? In other words, whence comes this capacity for symbolic representation, of which we can discover no trace in our conscious thinking? Let us examine the matter a little more closely. If we analyse a train of thought, we find that we begin with an "initial" idea, or a

"leading" idea, and then, without thinking back to it each time, but merely guided by a sense of direction, we pass on to a series of separate ideas that all hang together. There is nothing symbolical in this, and our whole conscious thinking proceeds along these lines.[1a] If we scrutinize our thinking more closely still and follow out an intensive train of thought—the solution of a difficult problem, for instance—we suddenly notice that we are *thinking in words*, that in very intensive thinking we begin talking to ourselves, or that we occasionally write down the problem or make a drawing of it, so as to be absolutely clear. Anyone who has lived for some time in a foreign country will certainly have noticed that after a while he begins to think in the language of that country. Any very intensive train of thought works itself out more or less in verbal form—if, that is to say, one wants to express it, or teach it, or convince someone of it. It is evidently directed *outwards*, to the outside world. To that extent, directed or logical thinking is reality-thinking,[2] a thinking that is adapted to reality,[3] by means of which we imitate the successiveness of objectively real things, so that the images inside our mind follow one another in the same strictly causal sequence as the events taking place outside it.[4] We also call this "thinking with directed attention." It has in addition the peculiarity of causing fatigue, and is for that reason brought

---

1a Cf. Liepmann, *Über Ideenflucht*; also my "Studies in Word Association" (1918/-19 edn., p. 124). For thinking as subordination to a ruling idea, cf. Ebbinghaus, in *Kultur der Gegenwart*, pp. 221ff. Kuelpe (*Outlines of Psychology*, p. 447) expresses himself in a similar manner: in thinking "we find an anticipatory apperception, which covers a more or less extensive circle of individual reproductions, and differs from a group of accidental incentives to reproduction only in the consistency with which all ideas outside the circle are checked or suppressed."

2 In his *Psychologia empirica*, ch. II, § 23, p. 16, Christian Wolff says simply and precisely: "Cogitatio est actus animae quo sibi sui rerumque aliarum extra se conscia est." (Thinking is an act of the soul whereby it becomes conscious of itself and of other things outside itself.)

3 The element of adaptation is particularly stressed by William James in his definition of logical thinking (*Principles of Psychology*, II, p. 330): "Let us make this ability to deal with *novel* data the technical differentia of reasoning. This will sufficiently mark it out from common associative thinking."

4 "Thoughts are shadows of our feelings, always darker, emptier, and simpler than these," says Nietzsche. Lotze (*Logik*, p. 552) remarks in this connection: "Thinking, if left to the logical laws of its own movement, coincides once more at the end of its correct trajectory with the behaviour of objectively real things."

into play for short periods only. The whole laborious achievement of our lives is adaptation to reality, part of which consists in directed thinking. In biological terms it is simply a process of psychic assimilation that leaves behind a corresponding state of exhaustion, like any other vital achievement.

The material with which we think is *language* and *verbal concepts*—something which from time immemorial has been directed outwards and used as a bridge, and which has but a single purpose, namely that of communication. So long as we think directedly, we think *for* others and speak *to* others.[5] Language was originally a system of emotive and imitative sounds—sounds which express terror, fear, anger, love, etc., and sounds which imitate the noises of the elements: the rushing and gurgling of water, the rolling of thunder, the roaring of the wind, the cries of the animal world, and so on; and lastly, those which represent a combination of the sound perceived and the emotional reaction to it.[6] A large number of onomatopoeic vestiges remain even in the more modern languages; note, for instance, the sounds for running water: *rauschen, rieseln, rüschen, rinnen, rennen, rush, river, ruscello, ruisseau, Rhein*. And note *Wasser, wissen, wissern, pissen, piscis, Fisch*.

Thus, language, in its origin and essence, is simply a system of signs or symbols that denote real occurrences or their echo in the human soul.[7] We must emphatically agree with Anatole France when he says:

What is thinking? And how does one think? We think with words; that in itself is sensual and brings us back to nature. Think of it! a metaphysician has nothing with which to build his world system except the perfected cries of monkeys and dogs. What he calls profound speculation and transcendental method is merely the stringing together, in an arbitrary order, of onomatopoeic cries of hunger,

---

5 Cf. Baldwin's remarks quoted below. The eccentric philosopher Johann Georg Hamann (1730–88) actually equates reason with language. (See Hamann's writings, pub. 1821–43.) With Nietzsche reason fares even worse as "linguistic metaphysics." Friedrich Mauthner goes the furthest in this direction (*Sprache und Psychologie*), for him there is absolutely no thought without speech, and only speaking is thinking. His idea of the "word fetishism" that dominates science is worth noting.   6 Cf. Kleinpaul, *Das Leben der Sprache*.

7 My small son gave me an explicit example of the subjectivity of such symbols, which originally seem to belong entirely to the subject: He described everything he wanted to take or eat with an energetic "stò lòi" (Swiss-German for "leave it!").

fear, and love from the primeval forests, to which have become attached, little by little, meanings that are believed to be abstract merely because they are loosely used. Have no fear that the succession of little cries, extinct or enfeebled, that composes a book of philosophy will teach us so much about the universe that we can no longer go on living in it.[8]

14 So our directed thinking, even though we be the loneliest thinkers in the world, is nothing but the first stirrings of a cry to our companions that water has been found, or the bear been killed, or that a storm is approaching, or that wolves are prowling round the camp. There is a striking paradox of Abelard's which intuitively expresses the human limitations of our complicated thought-process: "Speech is generated by the intellect and in turn generates intellect." The most abstract system of philosophy is, in its method and purpose, nothing more than an extremely ingenious combination of natural sounds.[9] Hence the craving of a Schopenhauer or a Nietzsche for recognition and understanding, and the despair and bitterness of their loneliness. One might expect, perhaps, that a man of genius would luxuriate in the greatness of his own thoughts and renounce the cheap approbation of the rabble he despises; yet he succumbs to the more powerful impulse of the herd instinct. His seeking and his finding, his heart's cry, are meant for the herd and must be heeded by them. When I said just now that directed thinking is really thinking in words, and quoted that amusing testimony of Anatole France as drastic proof, this might easily give rise to the misunderstanding that directed thinking is after all "only a matter of words." That would certainly be going too far. Language must be taken in a wider sense than speech, for speech is only the outward flow of thoughts formulated for communication. Were it otherwise, the

8 *Le Jardin d'Épicure*, p. 80.
9 It is difficult to estimate how great is the seductive influence of primitive word meanings on our thinking. "Everything that has ever been in consciousness remains as an active element in the unconscious," says Hermann Paul (*Prinzipien der Sprachgeschichte*, p. 25). The old word-meanings continue to have an effect which is imperceptible at first and proceeds "from that dark chamber of the unconscious in the soul" (ibid.). Hamann states emphatically (*Schriften*, VII, p. 8): "Metaphysics misuses all the verbal signs and figures of speech based on empirical knowledge and reduces them to empty hieroglyphs and types of ideal relationships." Kant is supposed to have learnt a thing or two from Hamann.

deaf-mute would be extremely limited in his thinking capacity, which is not the case at all. Without any knowledge of the spoken word, he too has his "language." Historically speaking, this ideal language, this directed thinking, is derived from primitive words, as Wundt has explained:

A further important consequence of the interaction of sound and meaning is that many words come to lose their original concrete significance altogether, and turn into signs for general ideas expressive of the apperceptive functions of relating and comparing, and their products. In this way abstract thought develops, which, because it would not be possible without the underlying changes of meaning, is itself the product of those psychic and psychophysical interchanges in which the development of language consists.[10]

15   Jodl [11] rejects the identity of language and thought on the ground that the same psychic fact can be expressed in different ways in different languages. From this he infers the existence of a "supra-linguistic" type of thinking. No doubt there is such a thing, whether one elects to call it "supra-linguistic" with Jodl or "hypological" with Erdmann. Only, it is not logical thinking. My views coincide with those of Baldwin, who says:

The transition from pre-judgmental to judgmental meaning is just that from knowledge which has social confirmation to that which gets along without it. The meanings utilized for judgment are those already developed in their presuppositions and implications through the confirmations of social intercourse. Thus the personal judgment, trained in the methods of social rendering, and disciplined by the interaction of its social world, projects its content into that world again. In other words, the platform for all movement into the assertion of individual judgment—the level from which new experience is utilized—is *already and always socialized*; and it is just this movement that we find reflected in the actual result as the sense of the "appropriateness" or synnomic character of the meaning rendered. . . .

Now the development of thought, as we are to see in more detail, is by a method essentially of trial and error, of experimentation, of *the use of meanings as worth more than they are as yet recognized to be worth*. The individual must use his old thoughts, his established knowledge, his grounded judgments, for the embodiment of

10 *Grundriss der Psychologie*, pp. 363–64.
11 *Lehrbuch aer Psychologie*, II, ch. 10, par. 26, p. 260.

18   This brings us to a further question: What happens when we do not think directly? Well, our thinking then lacks all leading ideas and the sense of direction emanating from them.[16] We no longer compel our thoughts along a definite track, but let them float, sink or rise according to their specific gravity. In Kuelpe's view,[17] thinking is a sort of "inner act of the will," and its absence necessarily leads to an "automatic play of ideas." William James regards non-directed thinking, or "merely associative" thinking, as the ordinary kind. He expresses himself as follows:

Much of our thinking consists of trains of images suggested one by another, of a sort of spontaneous revery of which it seems likely enough that the higher brutes should be capable. This sort of thinking leads nevertheless to rational conclusions both practical and theoretical.

As a rule, in this sort of irresponsible thinking the terms which come to be coupled together are empirical concretes, not abstractions.[18]

19   We can supplement James's definitions by saying that this sort of thinking does not tire us, that it leads away from reality into fantasies of the past or future. At this point thinking in verbal form ceases, image piles on image, feeling on feeling,[19]

16 So at least it appears to the conscious mind. Freud (*The Interpretation of Dreams*, II, p. 528) says in this connection: "For it is demonstrably untrue that we are being carried along a purposeless stream of ideas when, in the process of interpreting a dream, we abandon reflection and allow involuntary ideas to emerge. It can be shown that all we can ever get rid of are purposive ideas that are *known* to us; as soon as we have done this, *unknown*—or, as we inaccurately say, 'unconscious'—purposive ideas take charge and thereafter determine the course of the involuntary ideas. No influence that we can bring to bear upon our mental processes can ever enable us to think without purposive ideas; nor am I aware of any states of psychical confusion which can do so."

17 *Outlines*, p. 448.

18 *Principles*, II, p. 325.

19 This statement is based primarily on experiences derived from the field of normal psychology. Indefinite thinking is very far removed from "reflection," particularly where readiness of speech is concerned. In psychological experiments I have frequently found that subjects—I am speaking only of cultivated and intelligent people—whom I allowed to indulge in reveries, as though unintentionally and without previous instruction, exhibited affects which could be registered experimentally, but that with the best will in the world they could express the underlying thought only very imperfectly or not at all. More instructive are experiences

and there is an ever-increasing tendency to shuffle things about and arrange them not as they are in reality but as one would like them to be. Naturally enough, the stuff of this thinking which shies away from reality can only be the past with its thousand-and-one memory images. Common speech calls this kind of thinking "dreaming."

[20]   Anyone who observes himself attentively will find that the idioms of common speech are very much to the point, for almost every day we can see for ourselves, when falling asleep, how our fantasies get woven into our dreams, so that between day-dreaming and night-dreaming there is not much difference. We have, therefore, two kinds of thinking: directed thinking, and dreaming or fantasy-thinking. The former operates with speech elements for the purpose of communication, and is difficult and exhausting; the latter is effortless, working as it were spon-taneously, with the contents ready to hand, and guided by unconscious motives. The one produces innovations and adapta-tion, copies reality, and tries to act upon it; the other turns away from reality, sets free subjective tendencies, and, as regards adaptation, is unproductive.[20]

of a pathological nature, not so much those arising in the field of hysteria and the various neuroses, which are characterized by an overwhelming transference tendency, as experiences connected with introversion neurosis or psychosis, which must be regarded as constituting by far the greater number of mental disturb-ances, at any rate the whole of Bleuler's schizophrenic group. As already indi-cated by the term "introversion" (which I cursorily introduced in 1910, in my "Psychic Conflicts in a Child," pp. 13 and 16 [*Coll. Works*, Vol. 17]), this type of neurosis leads to an isolated inner life. And here we meet with that "supra-linguistic" or pure "fantasy thinking," which moves in "inexpressible" images and feelings. You get some idea of this when you try to find out the meaning of the pitiful and muddled expressions used by these people. As I have often observed, it costs these patients endless trouble and effort to put their fantasies into ordi-nary human speech. A highly intelligent patient, who "translated" such a fantasy system for me piecemeal, used to say to me: "I know quite well what it's all about, I can see and feel everything, but it is quite impossible for me to find the right words for it."

[20] Similarly James, *Principles*, II, pp. 325–26. Reasoning is productive, whereas "empirical" (merely associative) thinking is only reproductive. This opinion, how-ever, is not altogether satisfying. It is no doubt true that fantasy-thinking is not immediately productive, i.e., is unadapted and therefore useless for all practical purposes. But in the long run the play of fantasy uncovers creative forces and contents, just as dreams do. Such contents cannot as a rule be realized except through passive, associative, and fantasy-thinking.

As I have indicated above, history shows that directed thinking was not always as developed as it is today. The clearest
expression of modern directed thinking is science and the techniques fostered by it. Both owe their existence simply and solely
to energetic training in directed thinking. Yet at the time when
the forerunners of our present-day culture, such as the poet
Petrarch, were just beginning to approach nature in a spirit of
understanding,[21] an equivalent of our science already existed
in scholasticism.[22] This took its subjects from fantasies of the
past, but it gave the mind a dialectical training in directed
thinking. The one goal of success that shone before the thinker
was rhetorical victory in disputation, and not the visible transformation of reality. The subjects he thought about were often
unbelievably fantastic; for instance, it was debated how many
angels could stand on the point of a needle, whether Christ
could have performed his work of redemption had he come into
the world in the shape of a pea, etc. The fact that these
problems could be posed at all—and the stock metaphysical
problem of how to know the unknowable comes into this category—proves how peculiar the medieval mind must have been,
that it could contrive questions which for us are the height of

[21] Cf. the impressive description of Petrarch's ascent of Mt. Ventoux, in Burckhardt, *The Civilization of the Renaissance in Italy*, pp. 180–81: "A description
of the view from the summit would be looked for in vain, not because the poet
was insensible to it, but, on the contrary, because the impression was too overwhelming. His whole past life, with all its follies, rose before his mind; he remembered that ten years ago that day he had quitted Bologna a young man,
and turned a longing gaze towards his native country; he opened a book which
was then his constant companion, the 'Confessions of St. Augustine,' and his eye
fell on the passage in the tenth chapter: 'and men go forth, and admire lofty
mountains and broad seas, and roaring torrents, and the ocean, and the course
of the stars, and turn away from themselves while doing so.' His brother, to whom
he read these words, could not understand why he closed the book and said
no more."

[22] Wundt gives a short account of the scholastic method in his *Philosophische
Studien* (XIII, p. 345). The method consisted "firstly, in regarding as the chief
aim of scientific investigation the discovery of a firmly established conceptual
scheme capable of being applied in a uniform manner to the most varied problems; secondly, in laying an inordinate value upon certain general concepts, and
consequently upon the verbal symbols designating these concepts, as a result of
which an analysis of the meanings of words or, in extreme cases, a vapid intellectual subtlety and splitting of hairs comes to replace an investigation of the real
facts from which the concepts are abstracted."

absurdity. Nietzsche glimpsed something of the background of this phenomenon when he spoke of the "glorious tension of mind," which the Middle Ages produced.

22   On a historical view, the scholastic spirit in which men of the intellectual calibre of St. Thomas Aquinas, Duns Scotus, Abelard, William of Ockham, and others worked is the mother of our modern scientific method, and future generations will see clearly how far scholasticism still nourishes the science of today with living undercurrents. It consisted essentially in a dialectical gymnastics which gave the symbol of speech, the word, an absolute meaning, so that words came in the end to have a substantiality with which the ancients could invest their Logos only by attributing to it a mystical value. The great achievement of scholasticism was that it laid the foundations of a solidly built intellectual function, the *sine qua non* of modern science and technology.

23   If we go still further back into history, we find what we call science dissolving in an indistinct mist. The culture-creating mind is ceaselessly employed in stripping experience of everything subjective, and in devising formulas to harness the forces of nature and express them in the best way possible. It would be a ridiculous and unwarranted presumption on our part if we imagined that we were more energetic or more intelligent than the men of the past—our material knowledge has increased, but not our intelligence. This means that we are just as bigoted in regard to new ideas, and just as impervious to them, as people were in the darkest days of antiquity. We have become rich in knowledge, but poor in wisdom. The centre of gravity of our interest has switched over to the materialistic side, whereas the ancients preferred a mode of thought nearer to the fantastic type. To the classical mind everything was still saturated with mythology, even though classical philosophy and the beginnings of natural science undeniably prepared the way for the work of "enlightenment."

24   Unfortunately, we get at school only a very feeble idea of the richness and tremendous vitality of Greek mythology. All the creative power that modern man pours into science and technics the man of antiquity devoted to his myths. This creative urge explains the bewildering confusion, the kaleidoscopic changes and syncretistic regroupings, the continual rejuvenation, of

myths in Greek culture. We move in a world of fantasies which, untroubled by the outward course of things, well up from an inner source to produce an ever-changing succession of plastic or phantasmal forms. This activity of the early classical mind was in the highest degree artistic: the goal of its interest does not seem to have been how to understand the real world as objectively and accurately as possible, but how to adapt it aesthetically to subjective fantasies and expectations. There was very little room among the ancients for that coldness and disillusionment which Giordano Bruno's vision of infinite worlds and Kepler's discoveries brought to mankind. The naïve man of antiquity saw the sun as the great Father of heaven and earth, and the moon as the fruitful Mother. Everything had its demon, was animated like a human being, or like his brothers the animals. Everything was conceived anthropomorphically or theriomorphically, in the likeness of man or beast. Even the sun's disc was given wings or little feet to illustrate its motion (pl. 1*b*). Thus there arose a picture of the universe which was completely removed from reality, but which corresponded exactly to man's subjective fantasies. It needs no very elaborate proof to show that children think in much the same way. They too animate their dolls and toys, and with imaginative children it is easy to see that they inhabit a world of marvels.

We also know that the same kind of thinking is exhibited in dreams. The most heterogeneous things are brought together regardless of the actual conditions, and a world of impossibilities takes the place of reality. Freud finds that the hallmark of waking thought is *progression*: the advance of the thought stimulus from the systems of inner or outer perception through the endopsychic work of association to its motor end, i.e., innervation. In dreams he finds the reverse: regression of the thought stimulus from the pre-conscious or unconscious sphere to the perceptual system, which gives the dream its peculiar atmosphere of sensuous clarity, rising at times to almost hallucinatory vividness. Dream-thinking thus regresses back to the raw material of memory. As Freud says: "In regression the fabric of the dream-thoughts is resolved into its raw material."[23] The reactivation of original perceptions is, however, only one side of regression. The other side is regression to infantile memories,

23 *The Interpretation of Dreams*, II, p. 543.

and though this might equally well be called regression to the original perceptions, it nevertheless deserves special mention because it has an importance of its own. It might even be considered as an "historical" regression. In this sense the dream can, with Freud, be described as a modified memory—modified through being projected into the present. The original scene of the memory is unable to effect its own revival, so has to be content with returning as a dream.[24] In Freud's view it is an essential characteristic of dreams to "elaborate" memories that mostly go back to early childhood, that is, to bring them nearer to the present and recast them in its language. But, in so far as infantile psychic life cannot deny its archaic character, the latter quality is the especial peculiarity of dreams. Freud expressly draws attention to this:

Dreams, which fulfil their wishes along the short path of regression, have merely preserved for us in that respect a sample of the psychical apparatus's primary method of working, a method which was abandoned as being inefficient. What once dominated waking life, while the mind was still young and incompetent, seems now to have been banished into the night—just as the primitive weapons, the bows and arrows, that have been abandoned by adult men, turn up once more in the nursery.[25]

26   These considerations [26] tempt us to draw a parallel between the mythological thinking of ancient man and the similar think-

24 Ibid., p. 546.   25 Ibid., p. 567.

26 The passage in *The Interpretation of Dreams* that follows immediately afterwards has since been confirmed through investigation of the psychoses. "These methods of working on the part of the psychical apparatus, which are normally suppressed in waking hours, become current once more in psychosis and then reveal their incapacity for satisfying our needs in relation to the external world" (ibid., p. 567). The importance of this sentence is borne out by the views of Pierre Janet, which were developed independently of Freud and deserve mention here because they confirm it from an entirely different angle, namely the biological side. Janet distinguishes in the function a firmly organized "inferior" part and a "superior" part that is in a state of continuous transformation: "It is precisely on this 'superior' part of the functions, on their adaptation to existing circumstances, that the neuroses depend. . . . Neuroses are maladies dependent on the various functions of the organism and are characterized by an alteration in the superior parts of these functions, which are checked in their evolution, in their adaptation to the present moment and the existing state of the external world and

ing found in children,[27] primitives, and in dreams. This idea is not at all strange; we know it quite well from comparative anatomy and from evolution, which show that the structure and function of the human body are the result of a series of embryonic mutations corresponding to similar mutations in our racial history. The supposition that there may also be in psychology a correspondence between ontogenesis and phylogenesis therefore seems justified. If this is so, it would mean that infantile thinking [28] and dream-thinking are simply a recapitulation of earlier evolutionary stages.

In this regard, Nietzsche takes up an attitude well worth noting:

In sleep and in dreams we pass through the whole thought of earlier humanity. . . . What I mean is this: as man now reasons in dreams, so humanity also reasoned for many thousands of years when awake; the first cause which occurred to the mind as an explanation of anything that required explanation was sufficient and passed for truth. . . . This atavistic element in man's nature still manifests itself in our dreams, for it is the foundation upon which the higher reason has developed and still develops in every individual. Dreams carry us back to remote conditions of human culture and give us a ready means of understanding them better. Dream thinking comes so easily to us now because this form of fantastic and facile explanation in terms of the first random idea has been drilled

of the individual, while there is no deterioration in the older parts of these same functions. . . . In place of these superior operations some degree of physical and mental disturbance develops—above all, emotionality. This is nothing but the tendency to replace the superior operations by an exaggeration of certain inferior operations, and particularly by gross visceral disturbances." (Les Névroses, pp. 386ff.) The "older parts" are the same as the "inferior parts" of the functions, and they replace the abortive attempts at adaptation. Similar views concerning the nature of neurotic symptoms are expressed by Claparède (p. 169). He regards the hysterogenic mechanism as a "tendance à la reversion," a kind of atavistic reaction.

27 I am indebted to Dr. Abraham for the following story: "A small girl of three and a half had been presented with a baby brother, who soon became the object of well-known childish jealousy. One day she said to her mother: 'You are two Mamas. You are my Mama, and your breast is little brother's Mama.'" She had just been observing with great interest the act of suckling. It is characteristic of the archaic thinking of the child to call the breast "Mama" [so in the original—EDITORS]. Mamma is Latin for 'breast.'

28 Cf. particularly Freud's "Analysis of a Phobia in a Five-year-old Boy" and my "Psychic Conflicts in a Child."

into us for immense periods of time. To that extent dreaming is a recreation for the brain, which by day has to satisfy the stern demands of thought imposed by a higher culture. . . .

From this we can see how *lately* the more acute logical thinking, the strict discrimination of cause and effect, has been developed, since our rational and intellectual faculties still involuntarily hark back to those primitive forms of reasoning, and we pass about half our lives in this condition.[29]

28   Freud, as we have seen, reached similar conclusions regarding the archaic nature of dream-thinking on the basis of dream-analysis. It is therefore not such a great step to the view that myths are dreamlike structures. Freud himself puts it as follows: "The study of constructions of folk-psychology such as these is far from being complete, but it is extremely probable that myths, for instance, are distorted vestiges of the wishful phantasies of whole nations, the [age-long] dreams of youthful humanity."[30] In the same way Rank[31] regards myth as the collective dream of a whole people.[32]

29   Riklin has drawn attention to the dream mechanism in fairy-tales,[33] and Abraham has done the same for myths. He says: "The myth is a fragment of the superseded infantile psychic life of the race"; and again: "The myth is therefore a fragment preserved from the infantile psychic life of the race, and dreams are the myths of the individual."[34] The conclusion that the myth-makers thought in much the same way as we still think in dreams is almost self-evident. The first attempts at myth-making can, of course, be observed in children, whose games of make-believe often contain historical echoes. But one must certainly put a large question-mark after the assertion that myths spring from the "infantile" psychic life of the race. They are on the contrary the most mature product of that young humanity. Just as those first fishy ancestors of man, with their gill-slits, were not embryos, but fully developed creatures, so the myth-making and myth-inhabiting man was a grown reality and not a four-year-old child. Myth is certainly not an infantile

29 *Human, All-Too Human*, trans. by Zimmern and Cohn, I, pp. 24–27, modified.   31 *Der Künstler*, p. 36.
30 "Creative Writers and Day-Dreaming," p. 152, mod.
32 Cf. also Rank, *The Birth of the Hero.*
33 *Wishfulfilment and Symbolism in Fairy Tales.*
34 Abraham, *Dreams and Myths*, pp. 36 and 72, modified.

phantasm, but one of the most important requisites of primitive life.

30   It might be objected that the mythological proclivities of children are implanted by education. This objection is futile. Has mankind ever really got away from myths? Everyone who has his eyes and wits about him can see that the world is dead, cold, and unending. Never yet has he beheld a God, or been compelled to require the existence of such a God from the evidence of his senses. On the contrary, it needed the strongest inner compulsion, which can only be explained by the irrational force of instinct, for man to invent those religious beliefs whose absurdity was long since pointed out by Tertullian. In the same way one can withhold the material content of primitive myths from a child but not take from him the need for mythology, and still less his ability to manufacture it for himself. One could almost say that if all the world's traditions were cut off at a single blow, the whole of mythology and the whole history of religion would start all over again with the next generation. Only a very few individuals succeed in throwing off mythology in epochs of exceptional intellectual exuberance—the masses never. Enlightenment avails nothing, it merely destroys a transitory manifestation, but not the creative impulse.

31   Let us now turn back to our earlier reflections.

32   We were speaking of the ontogenetic recapitulation of phylogenetic psychology in children, and we saw that archaic thinking is a peculiarity of children and primitives. We now know that this same thinking also occupies a large place in modern man and appears as soon as directed thinking ceases. Any lessening of interest, or the slightest fatigue, is enough to put an end to the delicate psychological adaptation to reality which is expressed through directed thinking, and to replace it by fantasies. We wander from the subject and let our thoughts go their own way; if the slackening of attention continues, we gradually lose all sense of the present, and fantasy gains the upper hand.

33   At this point the important question arises: How are fantasies made, and what is their nature? From the poets we learn much, from scientists little. It was the psychotherapists who first began to throw light on the subject. They showed that fantasies go in typical cycles. The stammerer fancies himself a great

orator, which actually came true in the case of Demosthenes, thanks to his enormous energy; the poor man fancies himself a millionaire, the child a grown-up. The oppressed wage victorious war on the oppressor, the failure torments or amuses himself with ambitious schemes. All seek compensation through fantasy.

34   But just where do the fantasies get their material? Let us take as an example a typical adolescent fantasy. Faced by the vast uncertainty of the future, the adolescent puts the blame for it on the past, saying to himself: "If only I were not the child of my very ordinary parents, but the child of a rich and elegant count and had merely been brought up by foster-parents, then one day a golden coach would come and the count would take his long-lost child back with him to his wonderful castle," and so on, just as in a Grimms' fairy-story which a mother tells to her children. With a normal child the fantasy stops short at the fleeting idea, which is soon over and forgotten. There was a time, however, in the ancient world, when the fantasy was a legitimate truth that enjoyed universal recognition. The heroes—Romulus and Remus (pl. II), Moses, Semiramis, and many others—were foundlings whose real parents had lost them.[35] Others were directly descended from the gods, and the noble families traced their descent from the heroes and gods of old. Hence the fantasy of our adolescent is simply a re-echo of an ancient folk-belief which was once very widespread. The fantasy of ambition therefore chooses, among other things, a classical form which at one time had real validity. The same is true of certain erotic fantasies. Earlier on we mentioned the dream of sexual assault: the robber who breaks in and does something dangerous. That too is a mythological theme and in days gone by was undoubtedly a reality.[36] Quite apart from the fact that rape was a common occurrence in prehistoric times, it was also a popular theme of mythology in more civilized epochs. One has only to think of the rape of Persephone, of Deïanira, Europa, and of the Sabine women. Nor should we forget that in many parts of the earth there are

[35] Rank, *The Birth of the Hero*; also Kerényi, "The Primordial Child," in Jung and Kerényi, *Science of Mythology*, pp. 38f. (1963 edn., pp. 27ff.).

[36] For the mythological rape of the bride, cf. id., "Kore," pp. 170ff. (122ff.).

35 marriage customs existing today which recall the ancient marriage by capture.

One could give countless examples of this kind. They would all prove the same thing, namely that what, with us, is a subterranean fantasy was once open to the light of day. What, with us, crops up only in dreams and fantasies was once either a conscious custom or a general belief. But what was once strong enough to mould the spiritual life of a highly developed people will not have vanished without trace from the human soul in the course of a few generations. We must remember that a mere eighty generations separate us from the Golden Age of Greek culture. And what are eighty generations? They shrink to an almost imperceptible span when compared with the enormous stretch of time that separates us from Neanderthal or Heidelberg man. I would like in this connection to call attention to the pointed remarks of the great historian Ferrero:

36 It is a very common belief that the further man is separated from the present in time, the more he differs from us in his thoughts and feelings; that the psychology of humanity changes from century to century, like fashions or literature. Therefore, no sooner do we find in past history an institution, a custom, a law, or a belief a little different from those with which we are familiar, than we immediately search for all manner of complicated explanations, which more often than not resolve themselves into phrases of no very precise significance. And indeed, man does not change so quickly; his psychology at bottom remains the same, and even if his culture varies much from one epoch to another, it does not change the functioning of his mind. The fundamental laws of the mind remain the same, at least during the short historical periods of which we have knowledge; and nearly all the phenomena, even the most strange, must be capable of explanation by those common laws of the mind which we can recognize in ourselves.[37]

The psychologist should accept this view without qualification. The Dionysian phallagogies, the chthonic mysteries of classical Athens, have vanished from our civilization, and the theriomorphic representations of the gods have dwindled to mere vestiges, like the Dove, the Lamb, and the Cock adorning our church towers. Yet all this does not alter the fact that in childhood we go through a phase when archaic thinking and

37 Ferrero, *Les Lois psychologiques*, p. vii.

37   feeling once more rise up in us, and that all through our lives we possess, side by side with our newly acquired directed and adapted thinking, a fantasy-thinking which corresponds to the antique state of mind. Just as our bodies still retain vestiges of obsolete functions and conditions in many of their organs, so our minds, which have apparently outgrown those archaic impulses, still bear the marks of the evolutionary stages we have traversed, and re-echo the dim bygone in dreams and fantasies.

The question of where the mind's aptitude for symbolical expression comes from brings us to the distinction between the two kinds of thinking—the directed and adapted on the one hand, and the subjective, which is actuated by inner motives, on the other. The latter form, if not constantly corrected by adapted thinking, is bound to produce an overwhelmingly subjective and distorted picture of the world. This state of mind has been described in the first place as infantile and autoerotic, or, with Bleuler, as "autistic," which clearly expresses the view that the subjective picture, judged from the standpoint of adaptation, is inferior to that of directed thinking. The ideal instance of autism is found in schizophrenia, whereas infantile autoeroticism is more characteristic of neurosis. Such a view brings a perfectly normal process like non-directed fantasy-thinking dangerously close to the pathological, and this must be ascribed less to the cynicism of doctors than to the circumstance that it was the doctors who were the first to evaluate this type of thinking. Non-directed thinking is in the main subjectively motivated, and not so much by conscious motives as—far more —by unconscious ones. It certainly produces a world-picture very different from that of conscious, directed thinking. But there is no real ground for assuming that it is nothing more than a distortion of the objective world-picture, for it remains to be asked whether the mainly unconscious inner motive which guides these fantasy-processes is not itself an *objective fact.* Freud himself has pointed out on more than one occasion how much unconscious motives are grounded on instinct, which is certainly an objective fact. Equally, he half admitted their archaic nature.

38   The unconscious bases of dreams and fantasies are only apparently infantile reminiscences. In reality we are concerned with primitive or archaic thought-forms, based on instinct,

which naturally emerge more clearly in childhood than they do later. But they are not in themselves infantile, much less pathological. To characterize them, we ought therefore not to use expressions borrowed from pathology. So also the myth, which is likewise based on unconscious fantasy-processes, is, in meaning, substance, and form, far from being infantile or the expression of an autoerotic or autistic attitude, even though it produces a world-picture which is scarcely consistent with our rational and objective view of things. The instinctive, archaic basis of the mind is a matter of plain objective fact and is no more dependent upon individual experience or personal choice than is the inherited structure and functioning of the brain or any other organ. Just as the body has its evolutionary history and shows clear traces of the various evolutionary stages, so too does the psyche.[38]

39   Whereas directed thinking is an altogether conscious phenomenon,[39] the same cannot be said of fantasy-thinking. Much of it belongs to the conscious sphere, but at least as much goes on in the half-shadow, or entirely in the unconscious, and can therefore be inferred only indirectly.[40] Through fantasy-thinking, directed thinking is brought into contact with the oldest layers of the human mind, long buried beneath the threshold of consciousness. The fantasy-products directly engaging the conscious mind are, first of all, waking dreams or daydreams, to which Freud, Flournoy, Pick, and others have devoted special attention; then ordinary dreams, which present to the conscious mind a baffling exterior and only make sense on the basis of indirectly inferred unconscious contents. Finally, in split-off complexes there are completely unconscious fantasy-systems that have a marked tendency to constitute themselves as separate personalities.[41]

[38] See my paper "On the Nature of the Psyche," pars. 398ff.
[39] Except for the fact that the contents entering consciousness are already in a high state of complexity, as Wundt has pointed out.
[40] Schelling (Philosophie der Mythologie, II) regards the "preconscious" as the creative source, just as Fichte (Psychologie, I, pp. 508ff.) regards the "preconscious region," as the birthplace of important dream contents.
[41] Cf. Flournoy, From India to the Planet Mars. Also my "On the Psychology and Pathology of So-called Occult Phenomena," "The Psychology of Dementia Praecox," and "A Review of the Complex Theory." Excellent examples are to be found in Schreber, Memoirs of My Nervous Illness.

40   All this shows how much the products of the unconscious have in common with mythology. We should therefore have to conclude that any introversion occurring in later life regresses back to infantile reminiscences which, though derived from the individual's past, generally have a slight archaic tinge. With stronger introversion and regression the archaic features become more pronounced.

41   This problem merits further discussion. Let us take as a concrete example Anatole France's story of the pious Abbé Oegger.[42] This priest was something of a dreamer, and much given to speculative musings, particularly in regard to the fate of Judas: whether he was really condemned to everlasting punishment, as the teaching of the Church declares, or whether God pardoned him after all. Oegger took up the very understandable attitude that God, in his supreme wisdom, had chosen Judas as an instrument for the completion of Christ's work of redemption.[43] This necessary instrument, without whose help humanity would never have had a share in salvation, could not possibly be damned by the all-good God. In order to put an end to his doubts, Oegger betook himself one night to the church and implored God to give him a sign that Judas was saved. Thereupon he felt a heavenly touch on his shoulder. The next day he went to the archbishop and told him that he was resolved to go out into the world to preach the gospel of God's unending mercy.

42   Here we have a well-developed fantasy-system dealing with the ticklish and eternally unresolved question of whether the legendary figure of Judas was damned or not. The Judas legend is itself a typical motif, namely that of the mischievous betrayal of the hero. One is reminded of Siegfried and Hagen, Baldur and Loki: Siegfried and Baldur were both murdered by a perfidious traitor from among their closest associates. This myth is moving and tragic, because the noble hero is not felled in a fair fight, but through treachery. At the same time it is an event that was repeated many times in history, for instance in the case of Caesar and Brutus. Though the myth is extremely old it is still

[42] *Le Jardin d'Épicure.*
[43] The Judas-figure assumes great psychological significance as the sacrificer of the Lamb of God, who by this act sacrifices himself at the same time (suicide). See Part II.

a subject for repetition, as it expresses the simple fact that envy does not let mankind sleep in peace. This rule can be applied to the mythological tradition in general: it does not perpetuate accounts of ordinary everyday events in the past, but only of those which express the universal and ever-renewed thoughts of mankind. Thus the lives and deeds of the culture-heroes and founders of religions are the purest condensations of typical mythological motifs, behind which the individual figures entirely disappear.[44]

43 But why should our pious Abbé worry about the old Judas legend? We are told that he went out into the world to preach the gospel of God's unending mercy. Not long afterwards he left the Catholic Church and became a Swedenborgian. Now we understand his Judas fantasy: *he* was the Judas who betrayed his Lord. Therefore he had first of all to assure himself of God's mercy in order to play the role of Judas undisturbed.

44 Oegger's case throws light on the mechanism of fantasies in general. The conscious fantasy may be woven of mythological or any other material; it should not be taken literally, but must be interpreted according to its meaning. If it is taken too literally it remains unintelligible, and makes one despair of the meaning and purpose of the psychic function. But the case of the Abbé Oegger shows that his doubts and his hopes are only apparently concerned with the historical person of Judas, but in reality revolve round his own personality, which was seeking a way to freedom through the solution of the Judas problem.

45 Conscious fantasies therefore illustrate, through the use of

44 Cf. Drews' remarks in *The Christ Myth*. Intelligent theologians, like Kalthoff (*The Rise of Christianity*), are of the same opinion as Drews. Thus Kalthoff says: "The documents that give us our information about the origin of Christianity are of such a nature that in the present state of historical science no student would venture to use them for the purpose of compiling a biography of an historical Jesus" (ibid., p. 10). "To look behind these evangelical narratives for the life of a natural historical human being would not occur to any thoughtful men today if it were not for the influence of the earlier rationalistic theologians" (p. 13). "In Christ the divine is always most intimately one with the human. From the God-man of the Church there is a straight line back, through the Epistles and Gospels of the New Testament, to the apocalypse of Daniel, in which the ecclesiastical conception of Christ makes its first appearance. But at every single point in this line Christ has superhuman features; he is never what critical theology would make him—a mere natural man, an historical individual" (p. 11). Cf. also Schweitzer, *The Quest of the Historical Jesus*.

mythological material, certain tendencies in the personality which are either not yet recognized or are recognized no longer. It will readily be understood that a tendency which we fail to recognize and which we treat as non-existent can hardly contain anything that would fit in with our conscious character. Hence it is mostly a question of things which we regard as immoral or impossible, and whose conscious realization meets with the strongest resistances. What would Oegger have said had one told him in confidence that he was preparing himself for the role of Judas? Because he found the damnation of Judas incompatible with God's goodness, he proceeded to think about this conflict. That is the *conscious* causal sequence. Hand in hand with this goes the *unconscious* sequence: because he wanted to be Judas, or had to be Judas, he first made sure of God's goodness. For him Judas was the symbol of his own unconscious tendency, and he made use of this symbol in order to reflect on his own situation—its direct realization would have been too painful for him. There must, then, be typical myths which serve to work out our racial and national complexes. Jacob Burckhardt seems to have glimpsed this truth when he said that every Greek of the classical period carries in himself a little bit of Oedipus, and every German a little bit of Faust.[45]

46   The problems with which the simple tale of the Abbé Oegger confronts us will meet us again when we examine another set of fantasies, which owe their existence this time to the exclusive activity of the unconscious. We are indebted to a young American woman, known to us by the pseudonym of Miss Frank Miller, for a series of fantasies, partly poetical in form, which

[45] Cf. Burckhardt's letter (1855) to his student Albert Brenner (trans. by Dru, p. 116, modified): "I have no special explanation of *Faust* ready prepared and filed away. And in any case you are well provided with commentaries of every kind. Listen: take all those second-hand wares back to the library from which they originally came! (Perhaps in the meanwhile you have already done so.) What you are destined to discover in *Faust*, you will have to discover intuitively (*N.B.* I am only speaking of the first part). *Faust* is a genuine myth, i.e., a great primordial image, in which every man has to discover *his* own being and destiny in his own way. Let me make a comparison: whatever would the Greeks have said if a commentator had planted himself between them and the Oedipus saga? There was an Oedipus chord in every Greek that longed to be directly touched and to vibrate after its own fashion. The same is true of *Faust* and the German nation."

Théodore Flournoy made available to the public in 1906, in the *Archives de psychologie* (Geneva), under the title "Quelques faits d'imagination créatrice subconsciente."

*

The Significance of the Unconscious in Psychology

356   The hypothesis of the unconscious puts a large question-mark after the idea of the psyche. The soul, as hitherto postulated by the philosophical intellect and equipped with all the necessary faculties, threatened to emerge from its chrysalis as something with unexpected and uninvestigated properties. It no longer represented anything immediately known, about which nothing more remained to be discovered except a few more or less satisfying definitions. Rather it now appeared in strangely double guise, as both known and unknown. In consequence, the old psychology was thoroughly unseated and as much revolutionized [23] as classical physics had been by the discovery of radioactivity. These first experimental psychologists were in the same predicament as the mythical discoverer of the numerical sequence, who strung peas together in a row and

1 [Originally published as "Der Geist der Psychologie," *Eranos-Jahrbuch 1946* (Zurich, 1947), pp. 385–490. This essay, revised and augmented, was republished as "Theoretische Überlegungen zum Wesen des Psychischen" In *Von den Wurzeln des Bewusstseins* (Psychologische Abhandlungen, IX; Zurich, 1954), pp. 497–608. The former version was translated by R. F. C. Hull as "The Spirit of Psychology" and published in *Spirit and Nature* (Papers from the Eranos Yearbooks, 1; New York, 1954; London, 1955), pp. 371–444. That translation is now further revised to bring it into conformity with the 1954 German version.—EDITORS.]

23 I reproduce here what William James says about the importance of the discovery of the unconscious psyche (*Varieties of Religious Experience*, p. 233): "I cannot but think that the most important step forward that has occurred in psychology since I have been a student of that science is the discovery, first made in 1886, that . . . there is not only the consciousness of the ordinary field, with its usual center and margin, but an addition thereto in the shape of a set of memories, thoughts, and feelings which are extramarginal and outside of the primary consciousness altogether, but yet must be classed as conscious facts of some sort, able to reveal their presence by unmistakable signs. I call this the most important step forward because, unlike the other advances which psychology has made, this discovery has revealed to us an entirely unsuspected peculiarity in the constitution of human nature. No other step forward which psychology has made can proffer any such claim as this." The discovery of 1886 to which James refers is the positing of a "subliminal consciousness" by Frederic W. H. Myers. See n. 47, infra.

357

simply went on adding another unit to those already present. When he contemplated the result, it looked as if there were nothing but a hundred identical units; but the numbers he had thought of only as names unexpectedly turned out to be peculiar entities with irreducible properties. For instance, there were even, uneven, and primary numbers; positive, negative, irrational, and imaginary numbers, etc.[24] So it is with psychology: if the soul is really only an idea, this idea has an alarming air of unpredictability about it—something with qualities no one would ever have imagined. One can go on asserting that the psyche is consciousness and its contents, but that does not prevent, in fact it hastens, the discovery of a background not previously suspected, a true matrix of all conscious phenomena, a preconsciousness and a postconsciousness, a superconsciousness and a subconsciousness. The moment one forms an idea of a thing and successfully catches one of its aspects, one invariably succumbs to the illusion of having caught the whole. One never considers that a total apprehension is right out of the question. Not even an idea posited as total is total, for it is still an entity on its own with unpredictable qualities. This self-deception certainly promotes peace of mind: the unknown is named, the far has been brought near, so that one can lay one's finger on it. One has taken possession of it, and it has become an inalienable piece of property, like a slain creature of the wild that can no longer run away. It is a magical procedure such as the primitive practises upon objects and the psychologist upon the psyche. He is no longer at its mercy, but he never suspects that the very fact of grasping the object conceptually gives it a golden opportunity to display all those qualities which would never have made their appearance had it not been imprisoned in a concept (remember the numbers!).

The attempts that have been made, during the last three hundred years, to grasp the psyche are all part and parcel of that tremendous expansion of knowledge which has brought the universe nearer to us in a way that staggers the imagination. The thousandfold magnifications made possible by the electron-microscope vie with the five hundred million light-year distances which the telescope travels. Psychology is still a long way from the kind of development which other sciences have attained; moreover, it has been much less able to free itself from the grip of philosophy. To be sure, every science

24 A mathematician once remarked that everything in science was man-made except numbers, which had been created by God himself.

40

a development similar to that which the other natural sciences have undergone; also, as we have seen, it has been much less able to shake off the trammels of philosophy. All the same, every science is a function of the psyche, and all knowledge is rooted in it. The psyche is the greatest of all cosmic wonders and the *sine qua non* of the world as an object. It is in the highest degree odd that Western man, with but very few—and ever fewer—exceptions, apparently pays so little regard to this fact. Swamped by the knowledge of external objects, the subject of all knowledge has been temporarily eclipsed to the point of seeming non-existence.

358   The soul was a tacit assumption that seemed to be known in every detail. With the discovery of a possible unconscious psychic realm, man had the opportunity to embark upon a great adventure of the spirit, and one might have expected that a passionate interest would be turned in this direction. Not only was this not the case at all, but there arose on all sides an outcry against such an hypothesis. Nobody drew the conclusion that if the subject of knowledge, the psyche, were in fact a veiled form of existence not immediately accessible to consciousness, then all our knowledge must be incomplete, and moreover to a degree that we cannot determine. The validity of conscious knowledge was questioned in an altogether different and more menacing way than it had ever been by the critical procedures of epistemology. The latter put certain bounds to human knowledge in general, from which post-Kantian German Idealism struggled to emancipate itself; but natural science and common sense accommodated themselves to it without much difficulty, if they condescended to notice it at all. Philosophy fought against it in the interests of an antiquated pretension of the human mind to be able to pull itself up by its own bootstraps and know things that were right outside the range of human understanding. The victory of Hegel over Kant dealt the gravest blow to reason and to the further development of the German and, ultimately, of the European mind, all the more dangerous as Hegel was a psychologist in disguise who projected great truths out of the subjective sphere into a cosmos he himself had created. We know how far Hegel's influence extends today. The forces compensating this calamitous development personified themselves partly in the later Schelling, partly in Schopenhauer and Carus,

while on the other hand that unbridled "bacchantic God" whom Hegel had already scented in nature finally burst upon us in Nietzsche.

359   Carus' hypothesis of the unconscious was bound to hit the then prevailing trend of German philosophy all the harder, as the latter had apparently just got the better of Kantian criticism and had restored, or rather reinstated, the well-nigh godlike sovereignty of the human spirit—Spirit with a capital S. The spirit of medieval man was, in good and bad alike, still the spirit of the God whom he served. Epistemological criticism was on the one hand an expression of the modesty of medieval man, and on the other a renunciation of, or abdication from, the spirit of God, and consequently a modern extension and reinforcement of human consciousness within the limits of reason. Wherever the spirit of God is extruded from our human calculations, an unconscious substitute takes its place. In Schopenhauer we find the unconscious Will as the new definition of God, in Carus the unconscious, and in Hegel identification and inflation, the practical equation of philosophical reason with Spirit, thus making possible that intellectual juggling with the object which achieved such a horrid brilliance in his philosophy of the State. Hegel offered a solution of the problem raised by epistemological criticism in that he gave ideas a chance to prove their unknown power of autonomy. They induced that hybris of reason which led to Nietzsche's superman and hence to the catastrophe that bears the name of Germany. Not only artists, but philosophers too, are sometimes prophets.

360   I think it is obvious that all philosophical statements which transgress the bounds of reason are anthropomorphic and have no validity beyond that which falls to psychically conditioned statements. A philosophy like Hegel's is a self-revelation of the psychic background and, philosophically, a presumption. Psychologically, it amounts to an invasion by the unconscious. The peculiar high-flown language Hegel uses bears out this view: it is reminiscent of the megalomanic language of schizophrenics, who use terrific spellbinding words to reduce the transcendent to subjective form, to give banalities the charm of novelty, or pass off commonplaces as searching wisdom. So bombastic a terminology is a symptom of weakness, ineptitude, and lack of substance. But that does not prevent the latest German philos-

361 ophy from using the same crackpot power-words and pretending that it is not unintentional psychology.

In the face of this elemental inrush of the unconscious into the Western sphere of human reason, Schopenhauer and Carus had no solid ground under them from which to develop and apply their compensatory effect. Man's salutary submission to a benevolent Deity, and the *cordon sanitaire* between him and the demon of darkness—the great legacy of the past—remained unimpaired with Schopenhauer, at any rate in principle, while with Carus it was hardly touched at all, since he sought to tackle the problem at the root by leading it away from the over-presumptuous philosophical standpoint towards that of psychology. We have to close our eyes to his philosophical allure if we wish to give full weight to his essentially psychological hypothesis. He had at least come a step nearer to the conclusion we mentioned earlier, by trying to construct a world-picture that included the dark part of the soul. This structure still lacked something whose unprecedented importance I would like to bring home to the reader.

362 For this purpose we must first make it quite clear to ourselves that all knowledge is the result of imposing some kind of order upon the reactions of the psychic system as they flow into our consciousness—an order which reflects the behaviour of a *meta-psychic* reality, of that which is in itself real. If, as certain modern points of view, too, would have it, the psychic system coincides and is identical with our conscious mind, then, in principle, we are in a position to know everything that is capable of being known, i.e., everything that lies within the limits of the theory of knowledge. In that case there is no cause for disquiet, beyond that felt by anatomists and physiologists when contemplating the function of the eye or the organ of hearing. But should it turn out that the psyche does *not* coincide with consciousness, and, what is more, that it functions unconsciously in a way similar to, or *different* from, the conscious portion of it, then our disquiet must rise to the point of agitation. For it is then no longer a question of general epistemological limits, but of a flimsy threshold that separates us from the unconscious contents of the psyche. The hypothesis of the threshold and of the unconscious means that the indispensable raw material of all knowledge—namely psychic reactions—and perhaps even uncon-

363   scious "thoughts" and "insights" lie close beside, above, or below consciousness, separated from us by the merest "threshold" and yet apparently unattainable. We have no knowledge of how this unconscious functions, but since it is conjectured to be a psychic system it may possibly have everything that consciousness has, including perception, apperception, memory, imagination, will, affectivity, feeling, reflection, judgment, etc., all in subliminal form.[25]

Here we are faced with Wundt's objection that one cannot possibly speak of unconscious "perceptions," "representations," "feelings," much less of "volitional actions," seeing that none of these phenomena can be represented without an experiencing subject. Moreover, the idea of a threshold presupposes a mode of observation in terms of energy, according to which consciousness of psychic contents is essentially dependent upon their intensity, that is, their energy. Just as only a stimulus of a certain intensity is powerful enough to cross the threshold, so it may with some justice be assumed that other psychic contents too must possess a higher energy-potential if they are to get across. If they possess only a small amount of energy they remain subliminal, like the corresponding sense-perceptions.

364   As Lipps has already pointed out, the first objection is nullified by the fact that the psychic process remains essentially the same whether it is "represented" or not. Anyone who takes the view that the phenomena of consciousness comprise the whole psyche must go a step further and say that "representations which we do not have"[26] can hardly be described as "representa-

[25] G. H. Lewes in *The Physical Basis of Mind* takes all this for granted. For instance, on p. 358, he says: "Sentience has various modes and degrees, such as Perception, Ideation, Emotion, Volition, which may be conscious, subconscious, or unconscious." On p. 363: "Consciousness and Unconsciousness are correlatives, both belonging to the sphere of Sentience. Every one of the unconscious processes is operant, changes the general state of the organism, and is capable of at once issuing in a discriminated sensation when the force which balances it is disturbed." On p. 367: "There are many involuntary actions of which we are distinctly conscious, and many voluntary actions of which we are at times subconscious and unconscious. . . . Just as the thought which at one moment passes unconsciously, at another consciously, is in itself the same thought . . . so the action which at one moment is voluntary, and at another involuntary, is itself the same action." Lewes certainly goes too far when he says (p. 373): "There is no real and essential distinction between voluntary and involuntary actions." Occasionally there is a world of difference.

[26] Fechner, II, pp. 438f.

tions." He must also deny any psychic quality to what is left over. For this rigorous point of view the psyche can only have the phantasmagoric existence that pertains to the ephemeral phenomena of consciousness. This view does not square with common experience, which speaks in favour of a possible psychic activity without consciousness. Lipps' idea of the existence of psychic processes *an sich* does more justice to the facts. I do not wish to waste time in proving this point, but will content myself with saying that never yet has any reasonable person doubted the existence of psychic processes in a dog, although no dog has, to our knowledge, ever expressed consciousness of its psychic contents.[27]

3. *The Dissociability of the Psyche*

365   There is no *a priori* reason for assuming that unconscious processes must inevitably have a subject, any more than there is for doubting the reality of psychic processes. Admittedly the problem becomes difficult when we suppose unconscious acts of the will. If this is not to be just a matter of "instincts" and "inclinations," but rather of considered "choice" and "decision" which are peculiar to the will, then one cannot very well get round the need for a controlling subject to whom something is "represented." But that, by definition, would be to lodge a consciousness in the unconscious, though this is a conceptual operation which presents no great difficulties to the psychopathologist. He is familiar with a psychic phenomenon that seems to be quite unknown to "academic" psychology, namely the dissociation or dissociability of the psyche. This peculiarity arises from the fact that the connecting link between the psychic processes themselves is a very conditional one. Not only are unconscious processes sometimes strangely independent of the experiences of the conscious mind, but the conscious processes, too, show a distinct loosening or discreteness. We all know of the absurdities which are caused by complexes and are to be observed with the greatest accuracy in the association experiment. Just as the cases of double consciousness doubted by Wundt really do happen, so the cases where not the whole personality is split in half, but

27 I am not counting "Clever Hans" [but cf. D. Katz, *Animals and Men*, 13ff.— EDITORS] and the dog who talked about the "primordial soul."

only smaller fragments are broken off, are much more probable and in fact more common. This is an age-old experience of mankind which is reflected in the universal supposition of a plurality of souls in one and the same individual. As the plurality of psychic components at the primitive level shows, the original state is one in which the psychic processes are very loosely knit and by no means form a self-contained unity. Moreover, psychiatric experience indicates that it often takes only a little to shatter the unity of consciousness so laboriously built up in the course of development and to resolve it back into its original elements.

This dissociability also enables us to set aside the difficulties that flow from the logically necessary assumption of a threshold of consciousness. If it is correct to say that conscious contents become subliminal, and therefore unconscious, through loss of energy, and conversely that unconscious processes become conscious through accretion of energy, then, if unconscious acts of volition are to be possible, it follows that these must possess an energy which enables them to achieve consciousness, or at any rate to achieve a state of secondary consciousness which consists in the unconscious process being "represented" to a subliminal subject who chooses and decides. This process must necessarily possess the amount of energy required for it to achieve such a consciousness; in other words, it is bound eventually to reach its "bursting point." [28] If that is so, the question arises as to why the unconscious process does not go right over the threshold and become perceptible to the ego. Since it obviously does not do this, but apparently remains suspended in the domain of a subliminal secondary subject, we must now explain why this subject, which is *ex hypothesi* charged with sufficient energy to become conscious, does not in its turn push over the threshold and articulate with the primary ego-consciousness. Psychopathology has the material needed to answer this question. This secondary consciousness represents a personality-component which has not been separated from ego-consciousness by mere accident, but which owes its separation to definite causes. Such a dissociation has two distinct aspects: in the one case, there is

366

28 James, *Varieties of Religious Experience*, p. 232.

an originally conscious content that became subliminal because it was repressed on account of its incompatible nature: in the other case, the secondary subject consists essentially in a process that never entered into consciousness at all because no possibilities exist there of apperceiving it. That is to say, ego-consciousness cannot accept it for lack of understanding, and in consequence it remains for the most part subliminal, although, from the energy point of view, it is quite capable of becoming conscious. It owes its existence not to repression, but to subliminal processes that were never themselves conscious. Yet because there is in both cases sufficient energy to make it potentially conscious, the secondary subject does in fact have an effect upon ego-consciousness—indirectly or, as we say, "symbolically," though the expression is not a particularly happy one. The point is that the contents that appear in consciousness are at first *symptomatic*. In so far as we know, or think we know, what they refer to or are based on, they are *semiotic*, even though Freudian literature constantly uses the term "symbolic," regardless of the fact that in reality symbols always express something we do *not* know. The symptomatic contents are in part truly symbolic, being the indirect representatives of unconscious states or processes whose nature can be only imperfectly inferred and realized from the contents that appear in consciousness. It is therefore possible that the unconscious harbours contents so powered with energy that under other conditions they would be bound to become perceptible to the ego. In the majority of cases they are *not yet* repressed contents, but simply contents that are *not yet conscious* and have not been subjectively realized, like the demons and gods of the primitives or the "isms" so fanatically believed in by modern man. This state is neither pathological nor in any way peculiar; it is on the contrary the original norm, whereas the psychic wholeness comprehended in the unity of consciousness is an ideal goal that has never yet been reached.

367   Not without justice we connect consciousness, by analogy, with the sense functions, from the physiology of which the whole idea of a "threshold" is derived. The sound-frequencies perceptible to the human ear range from 20 to 20,000 vibrations per second; the wave-lengths of light visible to the eye range from 7700 to 3900 angstrom-units. This analogy makes it

368

conceivable that there is a lower as well as an upper threshold for psychic events, and that consciousness, the perceptual system par excellence, may therefore be compared with the perceptible scale of sound or light, having like them a lower and upper limit. Maybe this comparison could be extended to the psyche in general, which would not be an impossibility if there were "psychoid" processes at both ends of the psychic scale. In accordance with the principle "natura non facit saltus," such an hypothesis would not be altogether out of place.

In using the term "psychoid" I am aware that it comes into collision with the concept of the same name postulated by Driesch. By "the psychoid" he understands the directing principle, the "reaction determinant," the "prospective potency" of the germinal element. It is "the elemental agent discovered in action," [29] the "entelechy of real acting." [30] As Eugen Bleuler has aptly pointed out, Driesch's concept is more philosophical than scientific. Bleuler, on the other hand, uses the expression "die Psychoide" [31] as a collective term chiefly for the subcortical processes, so far as they are concerned with biological "adaptive functions." Among these Bleuler lists "reflexes and the development of species." He defines it as follows: "The *Psychoide* is the sum of all the purposive, mnemonic, and life-preserving functions of the body and central nervous system, with the exception of those cortical functions which we have always been accustomed to regard as psychic." [32] Elsewhere he says: "The body-psyche of the individual and the phylo-psyche together form a unity which, for the purposes of our present study, can most usefully be designated by the name *Psychoide*. Common to both *Psychoide* and psyche are . . . conation and the utilization of previous experiences . . . in order to reach the goal. This would include memory (engraphy and ecphoria) and association, hence something analogous to thinking." [33] Although it is clear what is meant by the "Psychoide," in practice it often gets confused with "psyche," as the above passage shows. But it is not at all clear why the subcortical functions it is supposed to

29 Hans A. E. Driesch, *The Science and Philosophy of the Organism*, 1929, p. 221.
30 Ibid., p. 281.
31 In *Die Psychoide als Prinzip der organischen Entwicklung*, p. 11. A fem. sing. noun derived from *Psyche* (ψυχοειδής = 'soul-like')
32 Ibid., p. 11.
33 Ibid., p. 33.

designate should then be described as "quasi-psychic." The confusion obviously springs from the organological standpoint, still observable in Bleuler, which operates with concepts like "cortical soul" and "medullary soul" and has a distinct tendency to derive the corresponding psychic functions from these parts of the brain, although it is always the function that creates its own organ, and maintains or modifies it. The organological standpoint has the disadvantage that all the purposeful activities inherent in living matter ultimately count as "psychic," with the result that "life" and "psyche" are equated, as in Bleuler's use of the words "phylo-psyche" and "reflexes." It is extremely difficult, if not impossible, to think of a psychic function as independent of its organ, although in actual fact we experience the psychic process apart from its relation to the organic substrate. For the psychologist, however, it is the totality of these experiences that constitutes the object of investigation, and for this reason he must abjure a terminology borrowed from the anatomist. If I make use of the term "psychoid" [34] I do so with three reservations: firstly, I use it as an adjective, not as a noun; secondly, no psychic quality in the proper sense of the word is implied, but only a "quasi-psychic" one such as the reflex-processes possess; and thirdly, it is meant to distinguish a category of events from merely vitalistic phenomena on the one hand and from specifically psychic processes on the other. The latter distinction also obliges us to define more closely the nature and extent of the psyche, and of the unconscious psyche in particular.

369   If the unconscious can contain everything that is known to be a function of consciousness, then we are faced with the possibility that it too, like consciousness, possesses a subject, a sort of ego. This conclusion finds expression in the common and ever-recurring use of the term "subconsciousness." The latter term is certainly open to misunderstanding, as either it means what is "below consciousness," or it postulates a "lower" and

[34] I can avail myself of the word "psychoid" all the more legitimately because, although my use of the term derives from a different field of perception, it nevertheless seeks to delineate roughly the same group of phenomena that Bleuler had in mind. A. Busemann, in his book *Die Einheit der Psychologie* (p. 31), calls this non-differentiated psyche the "micropsychic."

370 secondary consciousness. At the same time this hypothetical "subconsciousness," which immediately becomes associated with a "superconsciousness,"[35] brings out the real point of my argument: the fact, namely, that a second psychic system coexisting with consciousness—no matter what qualities we suspect it of possessing—is of absolutely revolutionary significance in that it could radically alter our view of the world. Even if no more than the perceptions taking place in such a second psychic system were carried over into ego-consciousness, we should have the possibility of enormously extending the bounds of our mental horizon.

371 Once we give serious consideration to the hypothesis of the unconscious, it follows that our view of the world can be but a provisional one; for if we effect so radical an alteration in the subject of perception and cognition as this dual focus implies, the result must be a world view very different from any known before. This holds true only if the hypothesis of the unconscious holds true, which in turn can be verified only if unconscious contents can be changed into conscious ones—if, that is to say, the disturbances emanating from the unconscious, the effects of spontaneous manifestations, of dreams, fantasies, and complexes, can successfully be integrated into consciousness by the interpretative method.

4. *Instinct and Will*

Whereas, in the course of the nineteenth century, the main concern was to put the unconscious on a philosophical footing,[36] towards the end of the century various attempts were made in different parts of Europe, more or less simultaneously and independently of one another, to understand the unconscious experimentally or empirically. The pioneers in this field were

35 Especial exception is taken to this "superconsciousness" by people who have come under the influence of Indian philosophy. They usually fail to appreciate that their objection only applies to the hypothesis of a "subconsciousness," which ambiguous term I avoid using. On the other hand my concept of the *unconscious* leaves the question of "above" or "below" completely open, as it embraces both aspects of the psyche.

36 Cf. in particular Eduard von Hartmann, *Philosophie des Unbewussten* (1869).

372 Pierre Janet [37] in France and Sigmund Freud [38] in the old Austria. Janet made himself famous for his investigation of the formal aspect, Freud for his researches into the content of psychogenic symptoms.

I am not in a position here to describe in detail the transformation of unconscious contents into conscious ones, so must content myself with hints. In the first place, the structure of psychogenic symptoms was successfully explained on the hypothesis of unconscious processes. Freud, starting from the symptomatology of the neuroses, also made out a plausible case for dreams as the mediators of unconscious contents. What he elicited as contents of the unconscious seemed, on the face of it, to consist of elements of a personal nature that were quite capable of consciousness and had therefore been conscious under other conditions. It seemed to him that they had "got repressed" on account of their morally incompatible nature. Hence, like forgotten contents, they had once been conscious and had become subliminal, and more or less irrecoverable, owing to a counter-effect exerted by the attitude of the conscious mind. By suitably concentrating the attention and letting oneself be guided by associations—that is, by the pointers still existing in consciousness—the associative recovery of lost contents went forward as in a mnemo-technical exercise. But whereas forgotten contents were irrecoverable because of their lowered threshold-value, repressed contents owed their relative irrecoverability to a check exercised by the conscious mind.

373 This initial discovery logically led to the interpretation of the unconscious as a phenomenon of repression which could be understood in personalistic terms. Its contents were lost elements that had once been conscious. Freud later acknowledged the continued existence of archaic vestiges in the form of primitive modes of functioning, though even these were explained personalistically. On this view the unconscious psyche appears as a subliminal appendix to the conscious mind.

37 An appreciation of his work is to be found in Jean Paulus, *Le Problème de l'hallucination et l'évolution de la psychologie d'Esquirol à Pierre Janet.*
38 In this connection we should also mention the important Swiss psychologist Théodore Flournoy and his chef d'œuvre *Des Indes à la Planète Mars* (1900). Other pioneers were W. B. Carpenter (*Principles of Mental Physiology*, 1874) and G. H. Lewes (*Problems of Life and Mind*, 1873–79). For Frederic W. H. Myers see nn. 23 and 47.

374 The contents that Freud raised to consciousness are those which are the most easily recoverable because they have the capacity to become conscious and were originally conscious. The only thing they prove with respect to the unconscious psyche is that there is a psychic limbo somewhere beyond consciousness. Forgotten contents which are still recoverable prove the same. This would tell us next to nothing about the nature of the unconscious psyche did there not exist an undoubted link between these contents and the instinctual sphere. We think of the latter as physiological, as in the main a function of the glands. The modern theory of internal secretions and hormones lends the strongest support to this view. But the theory of human instincts finds itself in a rather delicate situation, because it is uncommonly difficult not only to define the instincts conceptually, but even to establish their number and their limitations.[39] In this matter opinions diverge. All that can be ascertained with any certainty is that the instincts have a physiological and a psychological aspect.[40] Of great use for descriptive purposes is Pierre Janet's view of the "partie supérieure et inférieure d'une fonction."[41]

375 The fact that all the psychic processes accessible to our observation and experience are somehow bound to an organic substrate indicates that they are articulated with the life of the organism as a whole and therefore partake of its dynamism—in other words, they must have a share in its instincts or be in a certain sense the results of the action of those instincts. This is not to say that the psyche derives exclusively from the instinctual sphere and hence from its organic substrate. The psyche as such cannot be explained in terms of physiological chemistry, if only because, together with "life" itself, it is the only "natural factor" capable of converting statistical organizations which are

39 This indistinctness and blurring of the instincts may, as E. N. Marais has shown in his experiments with apes (*The Soul of the White Ant*, P. 429), have something to do with the superior learning-capacity prevailing over the instincts, as is obviously the case with man too. On the question of instincts see L. Szondi, *Experimentelle Triebdiagnostik* and *Triebpathologie*.

40 "The instincts are physiological and psychic dispositions which . . . cause the organism to move in a clearly defined direction" (W. Jerusalem, *Lehrbuch der Psychologie*, P. 188). From another point of view Oswald Külpe describes instinct as "a fusion of feelings and organ sensations" (*Outlines of Psychology*, P. 322, modified).

41 *Les Névroses*, pp. 384ff.

376

subject to natural law into "higher" or "unnatural" states, in opposition to the rule of entropy that runs throughout the inorganic realm. How life produces complex organic systems from the inorganic we do not know, though we have direct experience of how the psyche does it. Life therefore has a specific law of its own which cannot be deduced from the known physical laws of nature. Even so, the psyche is to some extent dependent upon processes in the organic substrate. At all events, it is highly probable that this is so. The instinctual base governs the *partie inférieure* of the function, while the *partie supérieure* corresponds to its predominantly "psychic" component. The *partie inférieure* proves to be the relatively unalterable, automatic part of the function, and the *partie supérieure* the voluntary and alterable part.[42]

377

The question now arises: when are we entitled to speak of "psychic," and how in general do we define the "psychic" as distinct from the "physiological"? Both are life-phenomena, but they differ in that the functional component characterized as the *partie inférieure* has an unmistakably physiological aspect. Its existence or nonexistence seems to be bound up with the hormones. Its functioning has a compulsive character: hence the designation "drive." Rivers asserts that the "all-or-none reaction"[43] is natural to it, i.e., the function acts altogether or not at all, which is specific of compulsion. On the other hand the *partie supérieure*, which is best described as psychic and is moreover sensed as such, has lost its compulsive character, can be subjected to the will[44] and even applied in a manner contrary to the original instinct.

From these reflections it appears that the psychic is an

[42] Janet says (p. 384): "It seems that we must distinguish in every function inferior and superior parts. When a function has been in use for a long time it contains parts which are very old, work very easily, and are represented by very distinct and specialized organs. . . . these are the inferior parts of the function. But it is my opinion that in every function there are also superior parts which consist in the function's adaptation to more recent and much less usual circumstances, and are represented by organs which are differentiated in a markedly lesser degree." But the highest part of the function consists "in its adaptation to the particular circumstances of the present moment, the moment at which we have to use it."   [43] W. H. R. Rivers, "Instinct and the Unconscious."

[44] This formulation is purely psychological and has nothing to do with the philosophical problem of indeterminism.

emancipation of function from its instinctual form and so from the compulsiveness which, as sole determinant of the function, causes it to harden into a mechanism. The psychic condition or quality begins where the function loses its outer and inner determinism and becomes capable of more extensive and freer application, that is, where it begins to show itself accessible to a will motivated from other sources. At the risk of anticipating my programme, I cannot refrain from pointing out that if we delimit the psyche from the physiological sphere of instinct at the bottom, so to speak, a similar delimitation imposes itself at the top. For, with increasing freedom from sheer instinct the *partie supérieure* will ultimately reach a point at which the intrinsic energy of the function ceases altogether to be oriented by instinct in the original sense, and attains a so-called "spiritual" form. This does not imply a substantial alteration of the motive power of instinct, but merely a different mode of its application. The meaning or purpose of the instinct is not unambiguous, as the instinct may easily mask a sense of direction other than biological, which only becomes apparent in the course of development.

378 Within the psychic sphere the function can be deflected through the action of the will and modified in a great variety of ways. This is possible because the system of instincts is not truly harmonious in composition and is exposed to numerous internal collisions. One instinct disturbs and displaces the other, and, although taken as a whole it is the instincts that make individual life possible, their blind compulsive character affords frequent occasion for mutual injury. Differentiation of function from compulsive instinctuality, and its voluntary application, are of paramount importance in the maintenance of life. But this increases the possibility of collision and produces cleavages—the very dissociations which are forever putting the unity of consciousness in jeopardy.

379 In the psychic sphere, as we have seen, the will influences the function. It does this by virtue of the fact that it is itself a form of energy and has the power to overcome another form. In this sphere which I define as psychic, the will is in the last resort motivated by instincts—not, of course, absolutely, otherwise it would not be a will, which by definition must have a certain freedom of choice. "Will" implies a certain amount of energy

freely disposable by the psyche. There must be such amounts of disposable libido (or energy), or modifications of the functions would be impossible, since the latter would then be chained to the instincts—which are in themselves extremely conservative and correspondingly unalterable—so exclusively that no variations could take place, unless it were organic variations. As we have already said, the motivation of the will must in the first place be regarded as essentially biological. But at the (permitting such an expression) upper limit of the psyche, where the function breaks free from its original goal, the instincts lose their influence as movers of the will. Through having its form altered, the function is pressed into the service of other determinants or motivations, which apparently have nothing further to do with the instincts. What I am trying to make clear is the remarkable fact that the will cannot transgress the bounds of the psychic sphere: it cannot coerce the instinct, nor has it power over the spirit, in so far as we understand by this something more than the intellect. Spirit and instinct are by nature autonomous and both limit in equal measure the applied field of the will. Later I shall show what seems to me to constitute the relation of spirit to instinct.

380   Just as, in its lower reaches, the psyche loses itself in the organic-material substrate, so in its upper reaches it resolves itself into a "spiritual" form about which we know as little as we do about the functional basis of instinct. What I would call the psyche proper extends to all functions which can be brought under the influence of a will. Pure instinctuality allows no consciousness to be conjectured and needs none. But because of its empirical freedom of choice, the will needs a supraordinate authority, something like a consciousness of itself, in order to modify the function. It must "know" of a goal different from the goal of the function. Otherwise it would coincide with the driving force of the function. Driesch rightly emphasizes: "There is no willing without knowing." [45] Volition presupposes a choosing subject who envisages different possibilities. Looked at from this angle, psyche is essentially conflict between blind instinct and will (freedom of choice). Where instinct predominates, *psychoid*

[45] *Die "Seele" als elementarer Naturfaktor*, p. 80. "Individualized stimuli inform . . . the 'primary knower' of the abnormal state, and now this 'knower' not only *wants* a remedy but *knows* what it is" (p. 82).

processes set in which pertain to the sphere of the unconscious as elements incapable of consciousness. The psychoid process is not the unconscious as such, for this has a far greater extension. Apart from psychoid processes, there are in the unconscious ideas and volitional acts, hence something akin to conscious processes;[46] but in the instinctual sphere these phenomena retire so far into the background that the term "psychoid" is probably justified. If, however, we restrict the psyche to acts of the will, we arrive at the conclusion that psyche is more or less identical with consciousness, for we can hardly conceive of will and freedom of choice without consciousness. This apparently brings us back to where we always stood, to the axiom *psyche = consciousness.* What, then, has happened to the postulated psychic nature of the unconscious?

5. *Conscious and Unconscious*

381   This question, regarding the nature of the unconscious, brings with it the extraordinary intellectual difficulties with which the psychology of the unconscious confronts us. Such difficulties must inevitably arise whenever the mind launches forth boldly into the unknown and invisible. Our philosopher sets about it very cleverly, since, by his flat denial of the unconscious, he clears all complications out of his way at one sweep. A similar quandary faced the physicist of the old school, who believed exclusively in the wave theory of light and was then led to the discovery that there are phenomena which can be explained only by the particle theory. Happily, modern physics has shown the psychologist that it can cope with an apparent *contradictio in adiecto.* Encouraged by this example, the psychologist may be emboldened to tackle this controversial problem without having the feeling that he has dropped out of the world of natural science altogether. It is not a question of his *asserting* anything, but of constructing a *model* which opens up a promising and useful field of inquiry. A model does not assert that something *is* so, it simply illustrates a particular mode of observation.

382   Before we scrutinize our dilemma more closely, I would like

46 Cf. sec. 6 below, "The Unconscious as a Multiple Consciousness."

to clarify one aspect of the concept of the unconscious. The unconscious is not simply the unknown, it is rather the *unknown psychic*; and this we define on the one hand as all those things in us which, if they came to consciousness, would presumably differ in no respect from the known psychic contents, with the addition, on the other hand, of the psychoid system, of which nothing is known directly. So defined, the unconscious depicts an extremely fluid state of affairs: everything of which I know, but of which I am not at the moment thinking; everything of which I was once conscious but have now forgotten; everything perceived by my senses, but not noted by my conscious mind; everything which, involuntarily and without paying attention to it, I feel, think, remember, want, and do; all the future things that are taking shape in me and will sometime come to consciousness: all this is the content of the unconscious. These contents are all more or less capable, so to speak, of consciousness, or were once conscious and may become conscious again the next moment. Thus far the unconscious is "a fringe of consciousness," as William James put it.[47] To this marginal phenomenon, which is born of alternating shades of light and darkness, there also belong the Freudian findings we have already noted. But, as I say, we must also include in the unconscious the psychoid functions that are not capable of consciousness and of whose existence we have only indirect knowledge.

383   We now come to the question: in what state do psychic

[47] James speaks also of a "transmarginal field" of consciousness and identifies it with the "subliminal consciousness" of F. W. H. Myers, one of the founders of the British Society for Psychical Research (cf. *Proceedings S.P.R.*, VII, 1892, pp. 298ff., and William James, "Frederic Myers' Service to Psychology," ibid., XVII, 1901, pp. 13ff.). Concerning the "field of consciousness" James says (*Varieties of Religious Experience*, p. 232): "The important fact which this 'field' formula commemorates is the indetermination of the margin. Inattentively realized as is the matter which the margin contains, it is nevertheless there, and helps both to guide our behavior and to determine the next movement of our attention. It lies around us like a 'magnetic field' inside of which our center of energy turns like a compass needle as the present phase of consciousness alters into its successor. Our whole past store of memories floats beyond this margin, ready at a touch to come in; and the entire mass of residual powers, impulses, and knowledges that constitute our empirical self stretches continuously beyond it. So vaguely drawn are the outlines between what is actual and what is only potential at any moment of our conscious life, that it is always hard to say of certain mental elements whether we are conscious of them or not."

384   contents find themselves when not related to the conscious ego? (This relation constitutes all that can be called consciousness.) In accordance with "Occam's razor," *entia praeter necessitatem non sunt multiplicanda* ("principles are not to be multiplied beyond the necessary"), the most cautious conclusion would be that, except for the relation to the conscious ego, nothing is changed when a content becomes unconscious. For this reason I reject the view that momentarily unconscious contents are only physiological. The evidence is lacking, and apart from that the psychology of neurosis provides striking proofs to the contrary. One has only to think of the cases of double personality, *automatisme ambulatoire*, etc. Both Janet's and Freud's findings indicate that everything goes on functioning in the unconscious state just as though it were conscious. There is perception, thinking, feeling, volition, and intention, just as though a subject were present; indeed, there are not a few cases—e.g., the double personality above mentioned—where a second ego actually appears and vies with the first. Such findings seem to show that the unconscious is in fact a "subconscious." But from certain experiences—some of them known already to Freud—it is clear that the state of unconscious contents is not quite the same as the conscious state. For instance, feeling-toned complexes in the unconscious do not change in the same way that they do in consciousness. Although they may be enriched by associations, they are not corrected, but are conserved in their original form, as can easily be ascertained from the continuous and uniform effect they have upon the conscious mind. Similarly, they take on the uninfluenceable and compulsive character of an automatism, of which they can be divested only if they are made conscious. This latter procedure is rightly regarded as one of the most important therapeutic factors. In the end such complexes—presumably in proportion to their distance from consciousness—assume, by self-amplification, an archaic and mythological character and hence a certain numinosity, as is perfectly clear in schizophrenic dissociations. Numinosity, however, is wholly outside conscious volition, for it transports the subject into the state of rapture, which is a state of will-less surrender.

These peculiarities of the unconscious state contrast very strongly with the way complexes behave in the conscious mind. Here they can be corrected: they lose their automatic character and can be substantially transformed. They slough off their mythological envelope, and, by entering into the adaptive process going forward in consciousness, they personalize and rationalize themselves to the point where a dialectical discussion becomes possible.[48] Evidently the unconscious state is different after all from the conscious. Although at first sight the process continues in the unconscious as though it were conscious, it seems, with increasing dissociation, to sink back to a more primitive (archaic-mythological) level, to approximate in character to the underlying instinctual pattern, and to assume the qualities which are the hallmarks of instinct: automatism, non-susceptibility to influence, all-or-none reaction, and so forth. Using the analogy of the spectrum, we could compare the lowering of unconscious contents to a displacement towards the red end of the colour band, a comparison which is especially edifying in that red, the blood colour, has always signified emotion and instinct.[49]

385   The unconscious is accordingly a different medium from the conscious. In the near-conscious areas there is not much change, because here the alternation of light and shadow is too rapid. But it is just this no man's land which is of the greatest value in supplying the answer to the burning question of whether psyche = consciousness. It shows us how relative the unconscious state is, so relative, indeed, that one feels tempted to make use of a concept like "the subconscious" in order to define the darker part of the psyche. But consciousness is equally relative, for it embraces not only consciousness as such, but a whole scale of intensities of consciousness. Between "I do this" and "I am conscious of doing this" there is a world of difference, amounting sometimes to outright contradiction. Consequently there is a consciousness in which unconsciousness predominates, as well as a consciousness in which self-consciousness predominates. This paradox becomes immediately intelligible when we realize that there is no conscious content which can with absolute certainty

[48] In schizophrenic dissociation there is no such change in the conscious state, because the complexes are received not into a complete but into a fragmentary consciousness. That is why they so often appear in the original archaic state.

[49] Red had a *spiritual* significance for Goethe, but that was in accord with his creed of feeling. Here we may conjecture the alchemical and Rosicrucian background, e.g., the red tincture and the carbuncle. Cf. *Psychology and Alchemy*, pars. 335, 454, 552.

386

be said to be totally conscious,[50] for that would necessitate an unimaginable totality of consciousness, and that in turn would presuppose an equally unimaginable wholeness and perfection of the human mind. So we come to the paradoxical conclusion that there is no conscious content which is not in some other respect unconscious. Maybe, too, there is no unconscious psychism which is not at the same time conscious.[51] The latter proposition is more difficult to prove than the first, because our ego, which alone could verify such an assertion, is the point of reference for all consciousness and has no such association with unconscious contents as would enable it to say anything about their nature. So far as the ego is concerned, they are, for all practical purposes, unconscious: which is not to say that they are not conscious to it in another respect, for the ego may know these contents under one aspect but not know them under another aspect, when they cause disturbances of consciousness. Besides, there are processes with regard to which no relation to the conscious ego can be demonstrated and which yet seem to be "represented" or "quasi-conscious." Finally, there are cases where an unconscious ego and hence a second consciousness are present, as we have already seen, though these are the exceptions.[52]

In the psychic sphere, the compulsive pattern of behaviour gives way to variations of behaviour which are conditioned by experience and by volitional acts, that is, by conscious processes. With respect to the psychoid, reflex-instinctual state, therefore, the psyche implies a loosening of bonds and a steady recession of mechanical processes in favour of "selected" modifications. This selective activity takes place partly inside consciousness and

50 As already pointed out by E. Bleuler: *Naturgeschichte der Seele und ihres Bewusstwerdens*, pp. 300f.

51 With the explicit exception of the psychoid unconscious, as this includes things which are not capable of consciousness and are only "quasi-psychic."

52 In this connection I would mention that C. A. Meier associates observations of this kind with similar phenomena in physics. He says: "The relationship of complementary between conscious and unconscious urges upon us yet another physical parallel, namely the need for a strict application of the 'principle of correspondence.' This might provide the key to the 'strict logic' of the unconscious (the logic of probability) which we so often experience in analytical psychology and which makes us think of an 'extended state of consciousness.'"— "Moderne Physik—Moderne Psychologie," p. 360.

partly outside it, i.e., without reference to the conscious ego, and hence unconsciously. In the latter case the process is "quasi-conscious," *as if* it were "represented" and conscious.

387 As there are no sufficient grounds for assuming that a second ego exists in every individual or that everyone suffers from dissociation of personality, we have to discount the idea of a second ego-consciousness as a source of voluntary decisions. But since the existence of highly complex, quasi-conscious processes in the unconscious has been shown, by the study of psychopathology and dream psychology, to be uncommonly probable, we are for better or worse driven to the conclusion that although the state of unconscious contents is not identical with that of conscious ones, it is somehow very "like" it. In these circumstances there is nothing for it but to suppose something midway between the conscious and unconscious state, namely an approximative consciousness. As we have immediate experience only of a reflected state, which is *ipso facto* conscious and known because it consists essentially in relating ideas or other contents to an ego-complex that represents our empirical personality, it follows that any other kind of consciousness—either without an ego or without contents—is virtually unthinkable. But there is no need to frame the question so absolutely. On a somewhat more primitive human level, ego-consciousness loses much of its meaning, and consciousness is accordingly modified in a characteristic way. Above all, it ceases to be reflected. And when we observe the psychic processes in the higher vertebrates and particularly in domestic animals, we find phenomena resembling consciousness which nevertheless do not allow us to conjecture the existence of an ego. As we know from direct experience, the light of consciousness has many degrees of brightness, and the ego-complex many gradations of emphasis. On the animal and primitive level there is a mere "luminosity," differing hardly at all from the glancing fragments of a dissociated ego. Here, as on the infantile level, consciousness is not a unity, being as yet uncentred by a firmly-knit ego-complex, and just flickering into life here and there wherever outer or inner events, instincts, and affects happen to call it awake. At this stage it is still like a chain of islands or an archipelago. Nor is it a fully integrated whole even at the higher and highest stages; rather, it is capable of indefinite expansion. Gleaming islands, indeed whole continents,

388

can still add themselves to our modern consciousness—a phenomenon that has become the daily experience of the psychotherapist. Therefore we would do well to think of ego-consciousness as being surrounded by a multitude of little luminosities.

6. The Unconscious as a Multiple Consciousness

The hypothesis of multiple luminosities rests partly, as we have seen, on the quasi-conscious state of unconscious contents and partly on the incidence of certain images which must be regarded as symbolical. These are to be found in the dreams and visual fantasies of modern individuals, and can also be traced in historical records. As the reader may be aware, one of the most important sources for symbolical ideas in the past is alchemy. From this I take, first and foremost, the idea of the *scintillae*—sparks—which appear as visual illusions in the "arcane substance." [53] Thus the *Aurora consurgens*, Part II, says: "Scito quod terra foetida cito recipit scintillulas albas" (Know that the foul earth quickly receives white sparks). [54] These sparks Khunrath explains as "radii atque scintillae" of the "anima catholica," the world-soul, which is identical with the spirit of God. [55] From this interpretation it is clear that certain of these luminosities had already divined the psychic nature of these luminosities. They were seeds of light broadcast in the chaos, which Khunrath calls "mundi futuri seminarium" (the seed plot of a world to come). [56]

53 *Psychology and Alchemy*, pars. 352, 472. [And *Myst. Coniunctionis*, pars. 42ff.]

54 *Artis auriferae* (1593), I, p. 208. Said to be a quotation from Morienus (cf. infra, par. 394), repeated by Mylius, *Philosophia reformata* (1622), p. 146. On p. 149 he adds "scintillas aureas."

55 "Variae eius radii atque scintillae, per totius ingentem materiei primae massae molem hinc inde dispersae ac dissipatae: inque mundi partibus disiunctis etiam et loco et corporis mole, necnon circumscriptione, postea separatis . . . unius Animae universalis scintillae nunc etiam inhabitantes" (Its divers rays and sparks are dispersed and dissipated throughout the immense bulk of the whole mass of the *prima materia*: the sparks of the one universal soul now inhabiting those disunited parts of the world which were later separated from the place and mass of the body, and even from its circumference). Khunrath, *Amphitheatrum sapientiae aeternae solius verae* (1604), pp. 195f., 198.

56 Ibid., p. 197. Cf. the Gnostic doctrine of the Seeds of Light harvested by the Virgin of Light, and the Manichaean doctrine of the light-particles which have to

One such spark is the human mind.[57] The arcane substance—the watery earth or earthy water (*limus*: mud) of the World Essence—is "universally animated" by the "fiery spark of the soul of the world," in accordance with the Wisdom of Solomon 1 : 7: "For the Spirit of the Lord filleth the world." [58] In the "Water of the Art," in "our Water," which is also the chaos,[59] there are to be found the "fiery sparks of the soul of the world as pure *Formae Rerum essentiales*." [60] These *formae* [61] correspond to the Platonic Ideas, from which one could equate the *scintillae* with the archetypes on the assumption that the Forms "stored up in a supracelestial place" are a philosophical version of the latter. One would have to conclude from these alchemical visions that the archetypes have about them a certain effulgence or quasi-consciousness, and that numinosity entails luminosity. Paracelsus seems to have had an inkling of this. The following is taken from his *Philosophia sagax*: "And as little as aught can exist in man without the divine numen, so little can aught exist in man without the natural lumen. A man is made perfect by numen and lumen and these two alone. Everything springs from these two, and these two are in man, but without them man is nothing, though they can be without man." [62] In confirmation of this Khunrath writes: "There be . . . *Scintillae Animae Mundi igneae, Luminis nimirum Naturae*, fiery sparks of the world soul, i.e., of the light of nature . . . dispersed or sprinkled in and throughout the structure of the great world

57 "Mens humani animi scintilla altior et lucidior" (The mind of the human soul is a higher and more luminous spark). *Amphitheatrum*, p. 63.

58 Khunrath, *Von hylealischen . . . Chaos* (1597), p. 63.

59 As synonyms, Khunrath mentions (p. 216) "forma aquina, pontica, limus terrae Adamae, Azoth, Mercurius" (a form watery and sea-like, the slime of the earth of Adama, etc.). [*Adama* is Hebrew for 'earth.'—EDITORS.]   60 Ibid., p. 216.

61 The "formae scintillaeve Animae Mundi" (forms or sparks of the world soul) are also called by Khunrath (p. 189) "rationes seminariae Naturae specificae" (the seed-ideas of Nature, the origin of species), thus reproducing an ancient idea. In the same way he calls the *scintilla* "*Entelechia*" (p. 65).

62 *Paracelsus: Sämtliche Werke*, ed. by Karl Sudhoff, XII, p. 231; *Bücher und Schrifften . . . Paracelsi . . .*, ed. by Johannes Huser, X, p. 206.

be taken into one's body as ritual food, at a sort of Eucharist when melons were eaten. The earliest mention of this idea seems to be the καρπιστής (Irenaeus, *Contra haereses*, I, 2, 4). Concerning the melons see M.-L. von Franz, "Der Traum des Descartes."

389   The sparks have a clear psychological meaning for Dorn. He says: "Thus little by little he will come to see with his mental eyes a number of sparks shining day by day and more and more and growing into such a great light that thereafter all things needful to him will be made known."[67] This light is the *lumen naturae* which illuminates consciousness, and the *scintillae* are germinal luminosities shining forth from the darkness of the unconscious. Dorn, like Khunrath, owes much to Paracelsus, with whom he concurs when he supposes an "invisible sun unknown to many).[68] Of this natural light innate in man Dorn says: "For the life, the light of men,[69] shineth in us, albeit dimly, and as into all fruits of the elements everywhere."[63] The sparks come from the "Ruach Elohim," the Spirit of God.[64] Among the *scintillae* he distinguishes a "scintilla perfecta Unici Potentis ac Fortis," which is the elixir and hence the arcane substance itself.[65] If we may compare the sparks to the archetypes, it is evident that Khunrath lays particular stress on one of them. This One is also described as the Monad and the Sun, and they both indicate the Deity. A similar image is to be found in the letter of Ignatius of Antioch to the Ephesians, where he writes of the coming of Christ: "How, then, was he manifested to the world? A star shone in heaven beyond the stars, and its light was unspeakable, and its newness caused astonishment, and all the other stars, with the sun and moon, gathered in chorus round this star. . . ."[66] Psychologically, the One Scintilla or Monad is to be regarded as a symbol of the self—an aspect I mention only in passing.

63 *Von hyleatischen Chaos*, p. 94.   64 Ibid., p. 249.

65 Ibid., p. 54. In this he agrees with Paracelsus, who calls the *lumen naturae* the Quintessence, extracted from the four elements by God himself. (Sudhof, XII, pp. 36, 304.)

66 Ch. XIX, 1ff. (trans. by Lake in *The Apostolic Fathers*, I, p. 193).

67 "Sic paulatim scintillas aliquot magis ac magis indies perlucere suis oculis mentalibus percipiet, ac in tantam excrescere lucem, ut successivo tempore quaevis innotescant, quae sibi necessaria fuerint." Gerhard Dorn, "Speculativae philosophiae," in *Theatrum chemicum*, I (1602), p. 275.

68 "Sol est invisibilis in hominibus, in terra vero visibilis, tamen ex uno et eodem sole sunt ambo" (The sun is invisible in men, but visible in the world, yet both are of one and the same sun). Ibid., p. 308.

69 "Et vita erat lux hominum. Et lux in tenebris lucet" (And the life was the light of men. And the light shineth in the darkness). John 1 : 4, 5.

though in darkness. It is not to be extracted from us, yet it is in us and not of us, but of Him to Whom it belongs, Who deigns to make us his dwelling-place. . . . He has implanted that light in us that we may see in its light the light of Him Who dwells in inaccessible light, and that we may excel His other creatures; in this wise we are made like unto Him, that He has given us a spark of His light. Thus the truth is to be sought not in ourselves, but in the image of God which is within us." [70]

390   Thus the one archetype emphasized by Khunrath is known also to Dorn as the *sol invisibilis* or *imago Dei*. In Paracelsus the *lumen naturae* comes primarily from the "astrum" or "sydus," the "firmament" (a synonym for the star) is the "star" in man.[71] The "corner-stone" of all truth is the natural light.[72] Hence "Astronomia," which is "a mother to all the other arts. . . . After her beginneth the divine wisdom, after her beginneth the light of nature," [73] even the "most excellent Religiones" hang upon Astronomia.[74] For the star "desireth to drive man toward great wisdom . . . that he may appear wondrous in the light of nature, and the mysteria of God's wondrous work be discovered and revealed in their grandeur." [75] Indeed, man himself is an "Astrum": "not by himself alone, but for ever and ever with all apostles and saints; each and every one is an astrum, the heaven a star . . . therefore saith also the Scripture: ye are lights of the world." [76] "Now as in the star lieth the whole natural light, and from it man taketh the same like food from the earth into which he is born, so too must he be born into the star." [77] Also the

---

[70] "Lucet in nobis licet obscure vita lux hominum tanquam in tenebris, quae non ex nobis quaerenda, tamen in et non a nobis, sed ab eo cuius est, qui etiam in nobis habitationem facere dignatur. . . . Hic eam lucem plantavit in nobis, ut in eius lumine qui lucem inaccessibilem inhabitat, videremus lumen; hoc ipso quoque caeteras eius praecelleremus creaturas; illi nimirum similes hac ratione facti, quod scintillam sui luminis dederit nobis. Est igitur veritas non in nobis quaerenda, sed in imagine Dei quae in nobis est." "Philosophia meditativa," *Theatrum chemicum*, I, p. 460.

[71] Sudhoff, XII, p. 23: "That which is in the light of nature, the same is the working of the star." (Huser, X, p. 19.)

[72] *Philosophia sagax*, Huser, X, p. 1 (Sudhoff, XII, p. 3).

[73] Ibid., pp. 3f. (pp. 5f.).

[74] The apostles are "Astrologi": ibid., p. 23 (p. 27).   [75] Ibid., p. 54 (p. 62).

[76] Ibid., p. 344 (p. 386). The last sentence refers to Matthew 5 : 14: "Vos estis lux mundi."   [77] Ibid., p. 409 (pp. 456f.).

391

animals have the natural light which is an "inborn spirit."[78] Man at his birth is "endowed with the perfect light of nature."[79] Paracelsus calls it "primum ac optimum thesaurum, quem naturae Monarchia in se claudit"[80] (the first and best treasure which the monarchy of nature hides within itself), in this concurring with the world-wide descriptions of the One as the pearl of great price, the hidden treasure, the "treasure hard to attain," etc. The light is given to the "inner man" or the inner body (*corpus subtile*, breath-body), as the following passage makes clear:

A man may come forth with sublimity and wisdom from his outer body, because the same wisdom and understanding which he needeth for this are coeval with this body and are the inner man; thus he may live and not as an outer man. For such an inner man is eternally transfigured and true, and if in the mortal body he appeareth not perfect, yet he appeareth perfect after the separation of the same. That which we now tell of is called *lumen naturae* and is eternal. God hath given it to the inner body, that it may be ruled by the inner body and in accordance with reason . . . for the light of nature alone is reason and no other thing . . . the light is that which giveth faith . . . to each man God hath given sufficient predestined light that he err not. . . . But if we are to describe the origin of the inner man or body, mark that all inner bodies be but one body and one single thing in all men, albeit divided in accordance with the well-disposed numbers of the body, each one different. And should they all come together, it is but one light, and one reason.[82]

"Moreover, the light of nature is a light that is lit from the Holy Ghost and goeth not out, for it is well lit . . . and the light is of a kind that desireth to burn,[83] and the longer [it burns][78] " . . . like the cocks which crow the coming weather and the peacocks the death of their master . . . all this is of the inborn spirit and is the light of nature."

---

[78] " . . . like the cocks which crow the coming weather and the peacocks the death of their master . . . all this is of the inborn spirit and is the light of nature." *Fragmenta medica*, cap. "De morbis somnii." Huser, V, p. 130 (Sudhoff, IX, p. 361).

[79] *Liber de generatione hominis*, VIII, p. 172 (I, p. 300).

[80] *De vita longa*, ed. by Adam von Bodenstein (1562), Lib. V, c. ii.

[81] *Philosophia sagax*, X, p. 341 (XII, p. 382): "Now it is clear that all the human wisdom of the earthly body lieth in the light of nature." It is "man's light of eternal wisdom": ibid., p. 395 (p. 441).

[82] *Liber de generatione hominis*, VIII, pp. 171f., (I, pp. 299f.).

[83] "I am come to send fire on the earth; and what will I, if it be already kindled?" Luke (AV) 12 : 49.

to shine the more, and the longer the greater . . . therefore in the light of nature is a fiery longing to enkindle."[84] It is an "invisible" light: "Now it follows that in the invisible alone hath man his wisdom, his art from the light of nature."[85] Man is "a prophet of the natural light."[86] He "learns" the *lumen naturae* through dreams,[87] among other things. "As the light of nature cannot speak, it buildeth shapes in sleep from the power of the word" (of God).[88]

392 I have allowed myself to dwell at some length on Paracelsus and to cite a number of authentic texts, because I wanted to give the reader a rough idea of the way in which this author conceives the *lumen naturae*. It strikes me as significant, particularly in regard to our hypothesis of a multiple consciousness and its phenomena, that the characteristic alchemical vision of sparks scintillating in the blackness of the arcane substance should, for Paracelsus, change into the spectacle of the "interior firmament" and its stars. He beholds the darksome psyche as a star-strewn night sky, whose planets and fixed constellations represent the archetypes in all their luminosity and numinosity.[89] The starry vault of heaven is in truth the open book of cosmic projection, in which are reflected the mythologems, i.e., the archetypes. In this vision astrology and alchemy, the two classical functionaries of the psychology of the collective unconscious, join hands.

393 Paracelsus was directly influenced by Agrippa von Nettesheim,[90] who supposes a "luminositas sensus naturae." From this "gleams of prophecy came down to the four-footed beasts, the birds, and other living creatures," and enabled them to foretell future things.[91] He bases the *sensus naturae* on the authority of

84 *Fragmenta cum libro de fundamento sapientiae*, IX, p. 448 (XIII, pp. 325f.).
85 *Philosophia sagax*, X, p. 46 (XII, p. 53).   86 Ibid., p. 79 (p. 94).
87 *Practica in scientiam divinationis*, X, p. 438 (XII, p. 488).
88 *Liber de Caducis*, IV, p. 274 (VIII, p. 298).
89 In the *Hieroglyphica* of Horapollo the starry sky signifies God as ultimate Fate, symbolized by a "5," presumably a quincunx. [Trans. by George Boas, p. 66.—Editors.]   90 *Alchemical Studies*, index, *s.v.* "Agrippa."
91 Cornelius Heinrich Agrippa von Nettesheim, *De occulta philosophia* (1533), p. lxix: "Nam iuxta Platonicorum doctrinam, est rebus inferioribus vis quaedam insita, per quam magna ex parte cum superioribus conveniunt, unde etiam animalium taciti consensus cum divinis corporibus consentire videntur, atque his viribus eorum corpora et affectus affici." (For according to the doctrine of the

394 Gulielmus Parisiensis, who is none other than William of Auvergne (G. Alvernus; d. 1249), bishop of Paris from about 1228, author of many works, which influenced Albertus Magnus among others. Alvernus says that the *sensus naturae* is superior to the perceptive faculty in man, and he insists that animals also possess it.[92] The doctrine of the *sensus naturae* is developed from the idea of the all-pervading world-soul with which another Gulielmus Parisiensis was much concerned, a predecessor of Alvernus by name of Guillaume de Conches[93] (1080–1154), a Platonist scholastic who taught in Paris. He identified the *anima mundi*, this same *sensus naturae*, with the Holy Ghost, just as Abelard did. The world-soul is a natural force which is responsible for all the phenomena of life and the psyche. As I have shown elsewhere, this view of the *anima mundi* ran through the whole tradition of alchemy in so far as Mercurius was interpreted now as *anima mundi* and now as the Holy Ghost.[94] In view of the importance of alchemical ideas for the psychology of the unconscious, it may be worth our while to devote a little time to a very illuminating variant of this spark symbolism.

Even more common than the spark-motif is that of the fish's eyes, which have the same significance. I said above that a Morienus passage is given by the authors as the source for the "doctrine" of the *scintillae*. This passage is, indeed, to be found in the treatise of Morienus Romanus. But it reads: ". . . Purus laton tamdiu decoquitur, donec veluti oculi piscium elucescat . . ."[95] Here too the saying seems to be a citation from a still earlier source. In later authors these fish's eyes are always cropping up. There is a variant in Sir George Ripley, stating that on the "desiccation of the sea" a substance is left behind

---

Platonists there is in the lower things a certain virtue through which they agree in large measure with the higher; whence it would seem that the tacit consent of animals is in agreement with divine bodies, and that their bodies and affections are touched by these virtues), etc.

[92] Lynn Thorndike, *History of Magic and Experimental Science*, II, pp. 348f.

[93] François Picavet, *Essais sur l'histoire générale et comparée des théologies et des philosophies médiévales*, p. 207.

[94] Cf. *Psychology and Alchemy*, pars. 172, 265, 506, and pars. 446, 518.

[95] "Liber de compositione Alchemiae," in *Artis auriferae*, II, p. 32: "The pure lato is cooked until it has the lustre of fish's eyes." Thus, by the authors themselves, the *oculi piscium* are interpreted as *scintillae*.

which "glitters like a fish's eye"[96]—an obvious allusion to the gold and the sun (God's eye). Hence it is not to be wondered at if an alchemist[97] of the seventeenth century uses the words of Nicholas Flamel: Zacharias 4 : 10 as a motto for his edition of Nicholas Flamel: "Et videbunt lapidem stanneum in manu Zorobabel. Septem isti oculi sunt Domini, qui discurrunt in universam terram" (And . . . they shall see the tin plummet in the hand of Zorobabel. These are the seven eyes of the Lord that run to and fro through the whole earth).[98] These seven eyes are evidently the seven planets which, like the sun and moon, are the eyes of God, never resting, ubiquitous and all-seeing. The same motif is probably at the bottom of the many eyed giant Argus. He is nicknamed Πανόπτης, 'the All-Seeing,' and is supposed to symbolize the starry heavens. Sometimes he is one-eyed, sometimes four-eyed, sometimes hundred-eyed, and even myriad-eyed (μυριωπός). Besides which he never sleeps. Hera transferred the eyes of Argus Panoptes to the peacock's tail.[99] Like the guardian Argus, the constellation of the Dragon is also given an all-surveying position in the Aratus citations of Hippolytus. He is there described as the one "who from the height of the Pole looks down upon all things and sees all things, so that nothing that happens shall be hidden from him."[100] This dragon is sleepless, because the Pole "never sets." Often he appears to be confused with the sun's serpentine passage through the sky: "C'est pour ce motif qu'on dispose parfois les signes du zodiaque entre les circonvolutions du reptile," says Cumont.[101] Sometimes the serpent bears six signs of the zodiac upon his back.[102] As Eisler has remarked, on account of the time symbolism the all-seeing quality of the dragon

---

[96] *Opera omnia chemica* (1649), p. 159.

[97] Eirenaeus Orandus, *Nicholas Flamel: His Exposition of the Hieroglyphicall Figures etc.* (1624).

[98] Zach. 3 : 9 is also relevant: ". . . upon one stone there are seven eyes." (Both DV.)

[99] This mythologem is of importance in interpreting the "cauda pavonis."

[100] "Τετάχθαι γὰρ νομίζουσι κατὰ τὸν ἀρκτικὸν πόλον τὸν Δράκοντα, τὸν ὄφιν, ἀπὸ τοῦ ὑψηλοτάτου πόλον πάντα ἐπιβλέποντα καὶ πάντα ἐφορῶντα, ἵνα μηδὲν τῶν πραττομένων αὐτὸν λάθῃ." *Elenchos*, IV, 47, 2, 3. Cf. Legge, I, p. 109.

[101] F. Cumont, *Textes et monuments figurés relatifs aux mystères de Mithra*, I, p. 80.

[102] "Προσέταξε τὸν αὐτὸν δράκοντα βαστάξειν ἐξ ζῴδια ἐπὶ τοῦ νώτου αὐτοῦ."—Pitra, ed., *Analecta sacra*, V, p. 300. Quoted in Robert Eisler, *Weltenmantel und Himmelszelt* (1910), II, p. 389, 5.

is transferred to Chronos, whom Sophocles names "ὁ πάντ᾽ ὁρῶν Χρόνος," while in the memorial tablet for those who fell at Chaeronea he is called "παντεπίσκοπος δαίμων."[103] The Uroboros has the meaning of eternity (αἰών) and cosmos in Horapollo. The identification of the All-Seeing with Time probably explains the eyes on the wheels in Ezekiel's vision (A.V., 1:18: "As for their rings, they were so high that they were dreadful; and their rings were full of eyes round about them four"). We mention this identification because of its special importance: it indicates the relation between the *mundus archetypus* of the unconscious and the "phenomenon" of Time—in other words, it points to the *synchronicity* of archetypal events, of which I shall have more to say towards the end of this paper.

395   From Ignatius Loyola's autobiography, which he dictated to Loys Gonzales,[104] we learn that he used to see a bright light, and sometimes this apparition seemed to him to have the form of a serpent. It appeared to be full of shining eyes, which were yet no eyes. At first he was greatly comforted by the beauty of the vision, but later he recognized it to be an evil spirit.[105] This vision sums up all the aspects of our optic theme and presents a most impressive picture of the unconscious with its disseminated luminosities. One can easily imagine the perplexity which a medieval man would be bound to feel when confronted by such an eminently "psychological" intuition, especially as he had no dogmatic symbol and no adequate patristic allegory to come to his rescue. But, as a matter of fact, Ignatius was not so very wide of the mark, for multiple eyes are also a characteristic of Purusha, the Hindu Cosmic Man. The Rig-Veda (10. 90) says: "Thousand-headed is Purusha, thousand-eyed, thousand-footed. He encompasses the earth on every side and rules over the ten-finger space."[106] Monoïmos the Arabian, according to Hip-

103 Eisler, p. 388. "The All-seeing Chronos" and "the all-beholding daemon."
104 *The Testament of Ignatius Loyola,* trans. by E. M. Rix, p. 72.
105 Ignatius also had the vision of a "res quaedam rotunda tanquam ex auro et magna" that floated before his eyes: a thing round, as if made of gold, and great. He interpreted it as Christ appearing to him like a *sun.* Philipp Funk, *Ignatius von Loyola,* pp. 57, 65, 74, 112.
106 [Trans. derived from various sources. As Coomaraswamy explains in the *Journal of the American Oriental Society,* LVI (1946), 145–61, "the ten-finger space" (lit. "the ten-fingered") refers "macrocosmically to the distance between sky and earth and microcosmically to the space between the top of the head and

396   polytus, taught that the First Man ("Ανθρωπος) was a single Monad (μία μονάς), not composed (ἀσύνθετος), indivisible (ἀδιαίρετος), and at the same time composed (συνθέτη) and divisible (διαρετή). This Monad is the iota or dot (μία κεραία), and this tiniest of units which corresponds to Khunrath's one *scintilla* has "many faces" (πολυπρόσωπος) and "many eyes" (πολυόμματος).[107] Monoïmos bases himself here mainly on the prologue to the Gospel of St. John! Like Purusha, his First Man is the universe (ἄνθρωπος εἶναι τὸ πᾶν).[108]

Such visions must be understood as introspective intuitions that somehow capture the state of the unconscious and, at the same time, as assimilations of the central Christian idea. Naturally enough, the motif has the same meaning in modern dreams and fantasies, where it appears as the star-strewn heavens, as stars reflected in dark water, as nuggets of gold or golden sand scattered in black earth,[109] as a regatta at night, with lanterns on the dark surface of the sea, as a solitary eye in the depths of the sea or earth, as a parapsychic vision of luminous globes, and so on. Since consciousness has always been described in terms derived from the behaviour of light, it is in my view not too much to assume that these multiple luminosities correspond to tiny conscious phenomena. If the luminosity appears in monadic form as a single star, sun, or eye, it readily assumes the shape of a mandala and must then be interpreted as the self. It has nothing whatever to do with "double consciousness," because there is no indication of a dissociated personality. On the contrary, the symbols of the self have a "uniting" character.[110]

---

the chin" of a man. He continues: "I therefore consider it shown that what RV 10. 90. 1 . . . means is that Purusha, making the whole earth his footstool, fills the entire universe, and rules over it by means of the powers of vision, etc., that proceed from his face, and to which man's own powers of vision, etc., are analogous; this face, whether of God or man, being . . . itself an image of the whole threefold universe."—TRANS.]

[107] *Elenchos*, VIII, 12, 5. [Cf. *Aion*, pars. 340ff.—EDITORS.]

[108] Ibid, VIII, 12, 2.

[109] Cf. the alchemical dictum: "Seminate aurum in terram albam foliatam" (Sow the gold in white foliated earth).

[110] Cf. my remarks on the "uniting symbol" in *Psychological Types*, ch. V, sections 3 and 5.

7. *Patterns of Behaviour and Archetypes*

397   We have stated that the lower reaches of the psyche begin where the function emancipates itself from the compulsive force of instinct and becomes amenable to the will, and we have defined the will as disposable energy. But that, as said, presupposes a disposing subject, capable of judgment and endowed with consciousness. In this way we arrived at the position of proving, as it were, the very thing that we started by rejecting, namely the identification of psyche with consciousness. This dilemma resolves itself once we realize how very relative consciousness is, since its contents are conscious and unconscious at the same time, i.e., conscious under one aspect and unconscious under another. As is the way of paradoxes, this statement is not immediately comprehensible.[111] We must, however, accustom ourselves to the thought that conscious and unconscious have no clear demarcations, the one beginning where the other leaves off. It is rather the case that the psyche is a conscious-unconscious whole. As to the no man's land which I have called the "personal unconscious," it is fairly easy to prove that its contents correspond exactly to our definition of the psychic. But—as we define "psychic"—is there a psychic unconscious that is not a "fringe of consciousness" and not personal?

398   I have already mentioned that Freud established the existence of archaic vestiges and primitive modes of functioning in the unconscious. Subsequent investigations have confirmed this result and brought together a wealth of observational material. In view of the structure of the body, it would be astonishing if the psyche were the only biological phenomenon not to show clear traces of its evolutionary history, and it is altogether probable that these marks are closely connected with the instinctual base. Instinct and the archaic mode meet in the bio-

[111] Freud also arrived at similar paradoxical conclusions. Thus, in his article "The Unconscious" (p. 177) he says: "An instinct can never become an object of consciousness—only the idea that represents the instinct can. *Even in the unconscious, moreover, an instinct cannot be represented otherwise than by an idea.*" (My italics.) As in my above account we were left asking, "Who is the subject of the unconscious will?" so we must ask here, "Exactly *who* has the idea of the instinct in the unconscious state?" For "unconscious" ideation is a *contradictio in adjecto.*

399

logical conception of the "pattern of behaviour." There are, in fact, no amorphous instincts, as every instinct bears in itself the pattern of its situation. Always it fulfils an image, and the image has fixed qualities. The instinct of the leaf-cutting ant fulfils the image of ant, tree, leaf, cutting, transport, and the little ant-garden of fungi.[112] If any one of these conditions is lacking, the instinct does not function, because it cannot exist without its total pattern, without its image. Such an image is an *a priori* type. It is inborn in the ant prior to any activity, for there can be no activity at all unless an instinct of corresponding pattern initiates and makes it possible. This schema holds true of all instincts and is found in identical form in all individuals of the same species. The same is true also of man: he has in him these *a priori* instinct types which provide the occasion and the pattern for his activities, in so far as he functions instinctively. As a biological being he has no choice but to act in a specifically human way and fulfil his pattern of behaviour. This sets narrow limits to his possible range of volition, the more narrow the more primitive he is, and the more his consciousness is dependent upon the instinctual sphere. Although from one point of view it is quite correct to speak of the pattern of behaviour as a still-existing archaic vestige, as Nietzsche did in respect of the function of dreams, such an attitude does scant justice to the biological and psychological meaning of these types. They are not just relics or vestiges of earlier modes of functioning; they are the ever-present and biologically necessary regulators of the instinctual sphere, whose range of action covers the whole realm of the psyche and only loses its absoluteness when limited by the relative freedom of the will. We may say that the image represents the *meaning* of the instinct.

Although the existence of an instinctual pattern in human biology is probable, it seems very difficult to prove the existence of distinct types empirically. For the organ with which we might apprehend them—consciousness—is not only itself a transformation of the original instinctual image, but also its transformer. It is therefore not surprising that the human mind finds it impossible to specify precise types for man similar to those we know in the animal kingdom. I must confess that I can see no

112 For details see C. Lloyd Morgan, *Habit and Instinct.*

400

direct way to solve this problem. And yet I have succeeded, or so I believe, in finding at least an indirect way of approach to the instinctual image.

In what follows, I would like to give a brief description of how this discovery took place. I had often observed patients whose dreams pointed to a rich store of fantasy-material. Equally, from the patients themselves, I got the impression that they were stuffed full of fantasies, without their being able to tell me just where the inner pressure lay. I therefore took up a dream-image or an association of the patient's, and, with this as a point of departure, set him the task of elaborating or developing his theme by giving free rein to his fantasy. This, according to individual taste and talent, could be done in any number of ways, dramatic, dialectic, visual, acoustic, or in the form of dancing, painting, drawing, or modelling. The result of this technique was a vast number of complicated designs whose diversity puzzled me for years, until I was able to recognize that in this method I was witnessing the spontaneous manifestation of an unconscious process which was merely assisted by the technical ability of the patient, and to which I later gave the name "individuation process." But, long before this recognition dawned upon me, I had made the discovery that this method often diminished, to a considerable degree, the frequency and intensity of the dreams, thus reducing the inexplicable pressure exerted by the unconscious. In many cases, this brought a large measure of therapeutic success, which encouraged both myself and the patient to press forward despite the baffling nature of the results.[113] I felt bound to insist that they were baffling, if only to stop myself from framing, on the basis of certain theoretical assumptions, interpretations which I felt were not only inadequate but liable to prejudice the ingenuous productions of the patient. The more I suspected these configurations of harbouring a certain purposefulness, the less inclined I was to risk any theories about them. This reticence was not made easy for me, since in many cases I was dealing with patients who needed an intellectual *point d'appui* if they were not to get totally lost in the darkness. I had to try to give provisional interpretations at least, so far as I was able, interspersing them with innumer-

113 Cf. "The Aims of Psychotherapy," pars. 101ff.; and *Two Essays on Analytical Psychology*, pars. 343ff. [Also "The Transcendent Function," pars. 166ff.]

able "perhapses" and "ifs" and "buts" and never stepping beyond the bounds of the picture lying before me. I always took good care to let the interpretation of each image tail off into a question whose answer was left to the free fantasy-activity of the patient.

401   The chaotic assortment of images that at first confronted me reduced itself in the course of the work to certain well-defined themes and formal elements, which repeated themselves in identical or analogous form with the most varied individuals. I mention, as the most salient characteristics, chaotic multiplicity and order; duality; the opposition of light and dark, upper and lower, right and left; the union of opposites in a third; the quaternity (square, cross); rotation (circle, sphere); and finally the centring process and a radial arrangement that usually followed some quaternary system. Triadic formations, apart from the *complexio oppositorum* in a third, were relatively rare and formed notable exceptions which could be explained by special conditions.[114] The centring process is, in my experience, the never-to-be-surpassed climax of the whole development,[115] and is characterized as such by the fact that it brings with it the greatest possible therapeutic effect. The typical features listed above go to the limits of abstraction, yet at the same time they are the simplest expressions of the formative principles here at work. In actual reality, the patterns are infinitely more variegated and far more concrete than this would suggest. Their variety defies description. I can only say that there is probably no motif in any known mythology that does not at some time appear in these configurations. If there was any conscious knowledge of mythological motifs worth mentioning in my patients, it is left far behind by the ingenuities of creative fantasy. In general, my patients had only a minimal knowledge of mythology.

402   These facts show in an unmistakable manner how fantasies guided by unconscious regulators coincide with the records of man's mental activity as known to us from tradition and ethnological research. All the abstract features I have mentioned are in a certain sense conscious: everyone can count up to four and knows what a circle is and a square; but, as formative principles, they are unconscious, and by the same token their psychological

114 The same applies to the pentadic figures.
115 So far as the development can be ascertained from the objective material.

406   its numinosity, and it has a corresponding effect upon the emotions. It mobilizes philosophical and religious convictions in the very people who deemed themselves miles above any such fits of weakness. Often it drives with unexampled passion and remorseless logic towards its goal and draws the subject under its spell, from which despite the most desperate resistance he is unable, and finally no longer even willing, to break free, because the experience brings with it a depth and fulness of meaning that was unthinkable before. I fully appreciate the resistance that all rooted convictions are bound to put up against psychological discoveries of this kind. With more foreboding than real knowledge, most people feel afraid of the menacing power that lies fettered in each of us, only waiting for the magic word to release it from the spell. This magic word, which always ends in "ism," works most successfully with those who have the least access to their interior selves and have strayed the furthest from their instinctual roots into the truly chaotic world of *collective consciousness.*

In spite or perhaps because of its affinity with instinct, the archetype represents the authentic element of spirit, but a spirit which is not to be identified with the human intellect, since it is the latter's *spiritus rector.* The essential content of all mythologies and all religions and all isms is archetypal. The archetype is spirit or pseudo-spirit: what it ultimately proves to be depends on the attitude of the human mind. Archetype and instinct are the most polar opposites imaginable, as can easily be seen when one compares a man who is seized by the spirit with a man who is ruled by his instinctual drives. But, just as between all opposites there obtains so close a bond that no position can be established or even thought of without its corresponding negation, so in this case also "les extrêmes se touchent." They belong together as correspondences, which is not to say that the one is derivable from the other, but that they subsist side by side as reflections in our own minds of the opposition that underlies all psychic energy. Man finds himself simultaneously driven to act and free to reflect. This contrariety in his nature has no moral significance, for instinct is not in itself bad any more than spirit is good. Both can be both. Negative electricity is as good as positive electricity: first and foremost it is electricity. The psychological opposites, too, must be regarded from a scientific

407   standpoint. True opposites are never incommensurables; if they were they could never unite. All contrariety notwithstanding, they do show a constant propensity to union, and Nicholas of Cusa defined God himself as a *complexio oppositorum*.

Opposites are extreme qualities in any state, by virtue of which that state is perceived to be real, for they form a potential. The psyche is made up of processes whose energy springs from the equilibrium of all kinds of opposites. The spirit / instinct antithesis is only one of the commonest formulations, but it has the advantage of reducing the greatest number of the most important and most complex psychic processes to a common denominator. So regarded, psychic processes seem to be balances of energy flowing between spirit and instinct, though the question of whether a process is to be described as spiritual or as instinctual remains shrouded in darkness. Such evaluation or interpretation depends entirely upon the standpoint or state of the conscious mind. A poorly developed consciousness, for instance, which because of massed projections is inordinately impressed by concrete or apparently concrete things and states, will naturally see in the instinctual drives the source of all reality. It remains blissfully unaware of the spirituality of such a philosophical surmise, and is convinced that with this opinion it has established the essential instinctuality of all psychic processes. Conversely, a consciousness that finds itself in opposition to the instincts can, in consequence of the enormous influence then exerted by the archetypes, so subordinate instinct to spirit that the most grotesque "spiritual" complications may arise out of what are undoubtedly biological happenings. Here the instinctuality of the fanaticism needed for such an operation is ignored.

408   Psychic processes therefore behave like a scale along which consciousness "slides." At one moment it finds itself in the vicinity of instinct, and falls under its influence; at another, it slides along to the other end where spirit predominates and even assimilates the instinctual processes most opposed to it. These counter-positions, so fruitful of illusion, are by no means symptoms of the abnormal; on the contrary, they form the twin poles of that psychic one-sidedness which is typical of the normal man of today. Naturally this does not manifest itself only in the

409   spirit / instinct antithesis; it assumes many other forms, as I have shown in my *Psychological Types*.

410   This "sliding" consciousness is thoroughly characteristic of modern man. But the one-sidedness it causes can be removed by what I have called the "realization of the shadow." A less "poetic" and more scientific-looking Greco-Latin neologism could easily have been coined for this operation. In psychology, however, one is to be dissuaded from ventures of this sort, at least when dealing with eminently practical problems. Among these is the "realization of the shadow," the growing awareness of the inferior part of the personality, which should not be twisted into an intellectual activity, for it has far more the meaning of a suffering and a passion that implicate the whole man. The essence of that which has to be realized and assimilated has been expressed so trenchantly and so plastically in poetic language by the word "shadow" that it would be almost presumptuous not to avail oneself of this linguistic heritage. Even the term "inferior part of the personality" is inadequate and misleading, whereas "shadow" presumes nothing that would rigidly fix its content. The "man without a shadow" is statistically the commonest human type, one who imagines he actually *is* only what he cares to know about himself. Unfortunately neither the so-called religious man nor the man of scientific pretensions forms any exception to this rule.

   Confrontation with an archetype or instinct is an *ethical* problem of the first magnitude, the urgency of which is felt only by people who find themselves faced with the need to assimilate the unconscious and integrate their personalities. This only falls to the lot of the man who realizes that he has a neurosis or that all is not well with his psychic constitution. These are certainly not the majority. The "common man," who is preponderantly a mass man, acts on the principle of realizing nothing, nor does he need to, because for him the only thing that commits mistakes is that vast anonymity conventionally known as "State" or "Society." But once a man knows that he is, or should be, responsible, he feels responsible also for his psychic constitution, the more so the more clearly he sees what he would have to be in order to become healthier, more stable, and more efficient. Once he is on the way to assimilating the unconscious he can be certain that he will escape no difficulty that is an integral part of his nature. The mass man, on the other hand, has the privilege of being at all times "not guilty" of the social and political catastrophes in which the whole world is engulfed. His final calculation is thrown out accordingly; whereas the other at least has the possibility of finding a spiritual point of vantage, a kingdom that "is not of this world."

411 It would be an unpardonable sin of omission were one to overlook the *feeling-value* of the archetype. This is extremely important both theoretically and therapeutically. As a numinous factor, the archetype determines the nature of the configurational process and the course it will follow, with seeming foreknowledge, or as though it were already in possession of the goal to be circumscribed by the centring process.[119] I would like to make the way in which the archetype functions clear from this simple example. While sojourning in equatorial east Africa, on the southern slopes of Mount Elgon, I found that the natives used to step out of their huts at sunrise, hold their hands before their mouths, and spit or blow into them vigorously. Then they lifted their arms and held their hands with the palms toward the sun. I asked them the meaning of what they did, but nobody could give me an explanation. They had always done it like that, they said, and had learnt it from their parents. The medicine-man, he knew as little as the others, but assured me that his grandfather had still known. It was just what people did at every sunrise, and at the first phase of the new moon. For these people, as I was able to show, the moment when the sun or the new moon appeared was "mungu," which corresponds to the Melanesian words "mana" or "mulungu"[120] and is translated by the missionaries as "God." Actually the word *adhista* in Elgonyi means sun as well as God, although they deny that the sun is God. Only the moment when it rises is *mungu* or *adhista.* Spittle and breath mean soul-substance. Hence they offer their soul to God, but do not know what they are doing and never have known. They do it, motivated by the same preconscious archetype which the ancient Egyptians, on their monuments, also ascribed to the sun-worshipping dog-headed baboon, albeit in

---

[119] Cf. *Psychology and Alchemy*, Part II, for evidence of this.

[120] [*Mulungu* = 'spirit, soul, daemonism, magic, prestige': *Two Essays*, par. 108, and the first paper in this volume, pars. 117, 123f.—EDITORS.]

full knowledge that this ritual gesture was in honour of God. The behaviour of the Elgonyi certainly strikes us as exceedingly primitive, but we forget that the educated Westerner behaves no differently. What the meaning of the Christmas-tree might be our forefathers knew even less than ourselves, and it is only quite recently that we have bothered to find out at all.

412   The archetype is pure, unvitiated nature,[121] and it is nature that causes man to utter words and perform actions whose meaning is unconscious to him, so unconscious that he no longer gives it a thought. A later, more conscious humanity, faced with such meaningful things whose meaning none could declare, hit upon the idea that these must be the last vestiges of a Golden Age, when there were men who knew all things and taught wisdom to the nations. In the degenerate days that followed, these teachings were forgotten and were now only repeated as mindless mechanical gestures. In view of the findings of modern psychology it cannot be doubted that there are preconscious archetypes which were never conscious and can be established only indirectly through their effects upon the conscious contents. There is in my opinion no tenable argument against the hypothesis that all the psychic functions which today seem conscious to us were once unconscious and yet worked as if they *were* conscious. We could also say that all the psychic phenomena to be found in man were already present in the natural unconscious state. To this it might be objected that it would then be far from clear why there is such a thing as consciousness at all. I would, however, remind the reader that, as we have already seen, all unconscious functioning has the automatic character of an instinct, and that the instincts are always coming into collision or, because of their compulsiveness, pursuing their courses unaltered by any influence even under conditions that may positively endanger the life of the individual. As against this, consciousness enables him to adapt in an orderly way and to check the instincts, and consequently it cannot be dispensed with. Man's capacity for consciousness alone makes him man.

413   The achievement of a synthesis of conscious and unconscious contents, and the conscious realization of the archetype's effects upon the conscious contents, represents the climax of a con-

121 "Nature" here means simply that which is, and always was, given.

centrated spiritual and psychic effort, in so far as this is under-taken consciously and of set purpose. That is to say, the synthesis can also be prepared in advance and brought to a certain point—James's "bursting point"—unconsciously, whereupon it irrupts into consciousness of its own volition and confronts the latter with the formidable task of assimilating the contents that have burst in upon it, yet without damaging the viability of the two systems, i.e., of ego-consciousness on the one hand and the irrupted complex on the other. Classical examples of this process are Paul's conversion and the Trinity vision of Nicholas of Flüe.

414   By means of "active imagination" we are put in a position of advantage, for we can then make the discovery of the archetype without sinking back into the instinctual sphere, which would only lead to blank unconsciousness or, worse still, to some kind of intellectual substitute for instinct. This means—to employ once more the simile of the spectrum—that the instinctual image is to be located not at the red end but at the violet end of the colour band. The dynamism of instinct is lodged as it were in the infra-red part of the spectrum, whereas the instinctual image lies in the ultra-violet part. If we remember our colour sym-bolism, then, as I have said, red is not such a bad match for instinct. But for spirit, as might be expected,[122] blue would be a better match than violet. Violet is the "mystic" colour, and it certainly reflects the indubitably "mystic" or paradoxical qual-ity of the archetype in a most satisfactory way. Violet is a com-pound of blue and red, although in the spectrum it is a colour in its own right. Now, it is, as it happens, rather more than just an edifying thought if we feel bound to emphasize that the archetype is more accurately characterized by violet, for, as well as being an image in its own right, it is at the same time a *dynamism* which makes itself felt in the numinosity and fascinat-ing power of the archetypal image. The realization and assimila-tion of instinct never take place at the red end, i.e., by absorption into the instinctual sphere, but only through integration of the image which signifies and at the same time evokes the instinct, although in a form quite different from the one we meet on the

122 This expectation is based on the experience that blue, the colour of air and sky, is most readily used for depicting spiritual contents, whereas red, the "warm" colour, is used for feelings and emotions.

biological level. When Faust remarks to Wagner: "You are conscious only of the single urge / O may you never learn to know the other!" this is a saying that could equally well be applied to instinct in general. It has two aspects: on the one hand it is experienced as physiological dynamism, while on the other hand its multitudinous forms enter into consciousness as images and groups of images, where they develop numinous effects which offer, or appear to offer, the strictest possible contrast to instinct physiologically regarded. For anyone acquainted with religious phenomenology it is an open secret that although physical and spiritual passion are deadly enemies, they are nevertheless brothers-in-arms, for which reason it often needs the merest touch to convert the one into the other. Both are real, and together they form a pair of opposites, which is one of the most fruitful sources of psychic energy. There is no point in deriving one from the other in order to give primacy to one of them. Even if we know only one at first, and do not notice the other until much later, that does not prove that the other was not there all the time. Hot cannot be derived from cold, nor high from low. An opposition either exists in its binary form or it does not exist at all, and a being without opposites is completely unthinkable, as it would be impossible to establish its existence.

416   Absorption into the instinctual sphere, therefore, does not and cannot lead to conscious realization and assimilation of instinct, because consciousness struggles in a regular panic against being swallowed up in the primitivity and unconsciousness of sheer instinctuality. This fear is the eternal burden of the hero-myth and the theme of countless taboos. The closer one comes to the instinct-world, the more violent is the urge to shy away from it and to rescue the light of consciousness from the murks of the sultry abyss. Psychologically, however, the archetype as an image of instinct is a spiritual goal toward which the whole nature of man strives; it is the sea to which all rivers wend their way, the prize which the hero wrests from the fight with the dragon.

    Because the archetype is a formative principle of instinctual power, its blue is contaminated with red: it appears to be violet, or again, we could interpret the simile as an apocatastasis of instinct raised to a higher frequency, just as we could easily

417 derive instinct from a latent (i.e., transcendent) archetype that manifests itself on a longer wave-length.[123] Although it can admittedly be no more than an analogy, I nevertheless feel tempted to recommend this violet image to my reader as an illustrative hint of the archetype's affinity with its own opposite. The creative fantasy of the alchemists sought to express this abstruse secret of nature by means of another, no less concrete, symbol: the Uroboros, or tail-eating serpent.

I do not want to work this simile to death, but, as the reader will understand, one is always delighted, when discussing difficult problems, to find support in a helpful analogy. In addition this simile helps to throw light on a question we have not yet asked ourselves, much less answered, the question regarding the *nature* of the archetype. The archetypal representations (images and ideas) mediated to us by the unconscious should not be confused with the archetype as such. They are very varied structures which all point back to one essentially "irrepresentable" basic form. The latter is characterized by certain formal elements and by certain fundamental meanings, although these can be grasped only approximately. The archetype as such is a psychoid factor that belongs, as it were, to the invisible, ultraviolet end of the psychic spectrum. It does not appear, in itself, to be capable of reaching consciousness. I venture this hypothesis because everything archetypal which is perceived by consciousness seems to represent a set of variations on a ground theme. One is most impressed by this act when one studies the endless variations of the mandala motif. This is a relatively simple ground form whose meaning can be said to be "central." But although it looks like the structure of a centre, it is still uncertain whether within that structure the centre or the periphery, division or non-division, is the more accentuated. Since other archetypes give rise to similar doubts, it seems to me probable that the real nature of the archetype is not capable of being made conscious, that it is transcendent, on which account I call it psychoid. Moreover every archetype, when represented to the mind, is already conscious and therefore differs to an indeterminable extent from that which caused the representation. As

123 Sir James Jeans (*Physics and Philosophy*, p. 193) points out that the shadows on the wall of Plato's cave are just as real as the invisible figures that cast them and whose existence can only be inferred mathematically.

Theodor Lipps has stressed, the nature of the psychic is unconscious. Anything conscious is part of the phenomenal world which—so modern physics teaches—does not supply explanations of the kind that objective reality requires. Objective reality requires a mathematical model, and experience shows that this is based on invisible and irrepresentable factors. Psychology cannot evade the universal validity of this fact, the less so as the observing psyche is already included in any formulation of objective reality. Nor can psychological theory be formulated mathematically, because we have no measuring rod with which to measure psychic quantities. We have to rely solely upon qualities, that is, upon perceptible phenomena. Consequently psychology is incapacitated from making any valid statement about unconscious states, or to put it another way, there is no hope that the validity of any statement about unconscious states or processes will ever be verified scientifically. Whatever we say about the archetypes, they remain visualizations or concretizations which pertain to the field of consciousness. But—we cannot speak about archetypes in any other way. We must, however, constantly bear in mind that what we mean by "archetype" is in itself irrepresentable, but has effects which make visualizations of it possible, namely, the archetypal images and ideas. We meet with a similar situation in physics: there the smallest particles are themselves irrepresentable but have effects from the nature of which we can build up a model. The archetypal image, the motif or mythologem, is a construction of this kind. When the existence of two or more irrepresentables is assumed, there is always the possibility—which we tend to overlook—that it may not be a question of two or more factors but of one only. The identity or non-identity of two irrepresentable quantities is something that cannot be proved. If on the basis of its observations psychology assumes the existence of certain irrepresentable psychoid factors, it is doing the same thing in principle as physics does when the physicist constructs an atomic model. And it is not only psychology that suffers from the misfortune of having to give its object, the unconscious, a name that has often been criticized because it is merely negative; the same thing happened in physics, since it could not avoid using the ancient term "atom" (meaning "indivisible") for the smallest particle of matter. Just as the atom is not indivisible, so, as we shall see, the unconscious is not merely unconscious. And just as physics in its psychological aspect can do no more than establish the existence of an observer without being able to assert anything about the nature of that observer, so psychology can only indicate the relation of psyche to matter without being able to make out the least thing about its nature.

418 Since psyche and matter are contained in one and the same world, and moreover are in continuous contact with one another and ultimately rest on irrepresentable, transcendental factors, it is not only possible but fairly probable, even, that psyche and matter are two different aspects of one and the same thing. The synchronicity phenomena point, it seems to me, in this direction, for they show that the nonpsychic can behave like the psychic, and vice versa, without there being any causal connection between them. Our present knowledge does not allow us to do much more than compare the relation of the psychic to the material world with two cones, whose apices, meeting in a point without extension—a real zero-point—touch and do not touch.

419 In my previous writings I have always treated archetypal phenomena as psychic, because the material to be expounded or investigated was concerned solely with ideas and images. The psychoid nature of the archetype, as put forward here, does not contradict these earlier formulations; it only means a further degree of conceptual differentiation, which became inevitable as soon as I saw myself obliged to undertake a more general analysis of the nature of the psyche and to clarify the empirical concepts concerning it, and their relation to one another.

420 Just as the "psychic infra-red," the biological instinctual psyche, gradually passes over into the physiology of the organism and thus merges with its chemical and physical conditions, so the "psychic ultra-violet," the archetype, describes a field which exhibits none of the peculiarities of the physiological and yet, in the last analysis, can no longer be regarded as psychic, although it manifests itself psychically. But physiological processes behave in the same way, without on that account being declared psychic. Although there is no form of existence that is not mediated to us psychically and only psychically, it would hardly do to say that everything is merely psychic. We must apply this argument logically to the archetypes as well. Since their essential being is unconscious to us, and still they are

experienced as spontaneous agencies, there is probably no alternative now but to describe their nature, in accordance with their chiefest effect, as "spirit," in the sense which I attempted to make plain in my paper "The Phenomenology of the Spirit in Fairytales." If so, the position of the archetype would be located beyond the psychic sphere, analogous to the position of physiological instinct, which is immediately rooted in the stuff of the organism and, with its psychoid nature, forms the bridge to matter in general. In archetypal conceptions and instinctual perceptions, spirit and matter confront one another on the psychic plane. Matter and spirit both appear in the psychic realm as distinctive qualities of conscious contents. The ultimate nature of both is transcendental, that is, irrepresentable, since the psyche and its contents are the only reality which is given to us *without a medium.*

8. *General Considerations and Prospects*

421   The problems of analytical psychology, as I have tried to outline them here, led to conclusions that astonished even me. I fancied I was working along the best scientific lines, establishing facts, observing, classifying, describing causal and functional relations, only to discover in the end that I had involved myself in a net of reflections which extend far beyond natural science and ramify into the fields of philosophy, theology, comparative religion, and the humane sciences in general. This transgression, as inevitable as it was suspect, has caused me no little worry. Quite apart from my personal incompetence in these fields, it seemed to me that my reflections were suspect also in principle, because I am profoundly convinced that the "personal equation" has a telling effect upon the results of psychological observation. The tragic thing is that psychology has no self-consistent mathematics at its disposal, but only a calculus of subjective prejudices. Also, it lacks the immense advantage of an Archimedean point such as physics enjoys. The latter observes the physical world from the psychic standpoint and can translate it into psychic terms. The psyche, on the other hand, observes itself and can only translate the psychic back into the psychic. Were physics in this position, it could do nothing except leave the physical process to its own devices, because in that way

it would be most plainly itself. There is no medium for psychology to reflect itself in: it can only portray itself in itself, and describe itself. That, logically, is also the principle of my own method: it is, at bottom, a purely experiential process in which hit and miss, interpretation and error, theory and speculation, doctor and patient, form a *symptosis* (σύμπτωσις) or a *symptoma* (σύμπτωμα)—a coming together—and at the same time are symptoms of a certain process or run of events. What I am describing, therefore, is basically no more than an outline of psychic happenings which exhibit a certain statistical frequency. We have not, scientifically speaking, removed ourselves to a plane in any way "above" the psychic process, nor have we translated it into another medium. Physics, on the other hand, is in a position to detonate mathematical formulae—the product of pure psychic activity—and kill seventy-eight thousand persons at one blow.

422   This literally "devastating" argument is calculated to reduce psychology to silence. But we can, in all modesty, point out that mathematical thinking is also a psychic function, thanks to which matter can be organized in such a way as to burst asunder the mighty forces that bind the atoms together—which it would never occur to them to do in the natural course of things, at least not upon this earth. The psyche is a disturber of the natural laws of the cosmos, and should we ever succeed in doing something to Mars with the aid of atomic fission, this too will have been brought to pass by the psyche.

423   The psyche is the world's pivot: not only is it the one great condition for the existence of a world at all, it is also an intervention in the existing natural order, and no one can say with certainty where this intervention will finally end. It is hardly necessary to stress the dignity of the psyche as an object of natural science. With all the more urgency, then, we must emphasize that the smallest alteration in the psychic factor, if it be an alteration of principle, is of the utmost significance as regards our knowledge of the world and the picture we make of it. The integration of unconscious contents into consciousness, which is the main endeavour of analytical psychology, is just such an alteration of principle, in that it does away with the sovereignty of the subjective ego-consciousness and confronts it with unconscious collective contents. Accordingly ego-consciousness seems to be dependent on two factors: firstly, on the

conditions of the collective, i.e., the social, consciousness; and secondly, on the archetypes, or dominants, of the collective unconscious. The latter fall phenomenologically into two categories: instinctual and archetypal. The first includes the natural impulses, the second the dominants that emerge into consciousness as universal ideas. Between the contents of collective consciousness, which purport to be generally accepted truths, and those of the collective unconscious there is so pronounced a contrast that the latter are rejected as totally irrational, not to say meaningless, and are most unjustifiably excluded from the scientific purview as though they did not exist. However, psychic phenomena of this kind exist with a vengeance, and if they appear nonsensical to us, that only proves that we do not understand them. Once their existence is recognized they can no longer be banished from our world-picture, even though the prevailing conscious *Weltanschauung* proves to be incapable of grasping the phenomena in question. A conscientious study of these phenomena quickly reveals their uncommon significance, and we can hardly avoid the conclusion that between collective consciousness and the collective unconscious there is an almost unbridgeable gulf over which the subject finds himself suspended.

424   As a rule, collective consciousness wins hands down with its "reasonable" generalities that cause the average intelligence no difficulty whatever. It still believes in the necessary connection of cause and effect and has scarcely taken note of the fact that causality has become relative. The shortest distance between two points is still, for it, a straight line, although physics has to reckon with innumerable shortest distances, which strikes the educated Philistine of today as exquisitely absurd. Nevertheless the impressive explosion at Hiroshima has induced an awestruck respect for even the most abstruse alembications of modern physics. The explosion which we recently had occasion to witness in Europe, though far more terrible in its repercussions, was recognized as an unmitigated psychic disaster only by the few. Rather than do this, people prefer the most preposterous political and economic theories, which are about as useful as explaining the Hiroshima explosion as the chance hit of a large meteorite.

425   If the subjective consciousness prefers the ideas and opinions of collective consciousness and identifies with them, then the contents of the collective unconscious are repressed. The repression has typical consequences: the energy-charge of the repressed contents adds itself, in some measure,[124] to that of the repressing factor, whose effectiveness is increased accordingly. The higher its charge mounts, the more the repressive attitude acquires a fanatical character and the nearer it comes to conversion into its opposite, i.e., an enantiodromia. And the more highly charged the collective consciousness, the more the ego forfeits its practical importance. It is, as it were, absorbed by the opinions and tendencies of collective consciousness, and the result of that is the mass man, the ever-ready victim of some wretched "ism." The ego keeps its integrity only if it does not identify with one of the opposites, and if it understands how to hold the balance between them. This is possible only if it remains conscious of both at once. However, the necessary insight is made exceedingly difficult not by one's social and political leaders alone, but also by one's religious mentors. They all want decision in favour of one thing, and therefore the utter identification of the individual with a necessarily one-sided "truth." Even if it were a question of some great truth, identification with it would still be a catastrophe, as it arrests all further spiritual development. Instead of knowledge one then has only belief, and sometimes that is more convenient and therefore more attractive.

426   If, on the other hand, the content of the collective unconscious is realized, if the existence and efficacy of archetypal representations are acknowledged, then a violent conflict usually breaks out between what Fechner has called the "day-time and the night-time view." Medieval man (and modern man too, in so far as he has kept the attitude of the past) lived fully conscious of the discord between worldliness, which was subject to

[124] It is very probable that the archetypes, as instincts, possess a specific energy which cannot be taken away from them in the long run. The energy peculiar to the archetype is normally not sufficient to raise it into consciousness. For this it needs a definite quantum of energy flowing into the unconscious from consciousness, whether because consciousness is not using this energy or because the archetype attracts it to itself. The archetype can be deprived of its supplementary charge, but not of its specific energy.

the *princeps huius mundi* (St. John 12 : 31 and 16 : 11 [125]), and the will of God. For centuries this contradiction was demonstrated before his very eyes by the struggle between imperial and papal power. On the moral plane the conflict swelled to the everlasting cosmic tug of war between good and evil in which man was implicated on account of original sin. The medieval man had not yet fallen such a helpless victim to worldliness as the contemporary mass man, for, to offset the notorious and, so to speak, tangible powers of this world, he still acknowledged the equally influential metaphysical potencies which demanded to be taken into account. Although in one respect he was politically and socially unfree and without rights—e.g., as a serf—and also found himself in the extremely disagreeable situation of being tyrannized over by black superstition, he was at least biologically nearer to that unconscious wholeness which primitive man enjoys in even larger measure, and the wild animal possesses to perfection. Looked at from the standpoint of modern consciousness, the position of medieval man seems as deplorable as it is in need of improvement. But the much needed broadening of the mind by science has only replaced medieval one-sidedness—namely, that age-old unconsciousness which once predominated and has gradually become defunctive—by a new one-sidedness, the overvaluation of "scientifically" attested views. These each and all relate to knowledge of the external object and in a chronically one-sided way, so that nowadays the backwardness of psychic development in general and of self-knowledge in particular has become one of the most pressing contemporary problems. As a result of the prevailing one-sidedness, and in spite of the terrifying optical demonstration of an unconscious that has become alienated from the conscious, there are still vast numbers of people who are the blind and helpless victims of these conflicts, and who apply their scientific scrupulosity only to external objects, never to their own psychic condition. Yet the psychic facts are as much in need of objective scrutiny and acknowledgment. There are objective psychic factors which are every bit as important as radios and automobiles. Ultimately everything (particularly in the case of the atom-

---

[125] Although both passages hint that the devil was cast out during the life-time of Jesus, in the Apocalypse the business of rendering him harmless is deferred until Doomsday (Rev. 20 : 2ff.).

bomb) depends on the uses to which these factors are put, and that is always conditioned by one's state of mind. The current "isms" are the most serious threat in this respect, because they are nothing but dangerous identifications of the subjective with the collective consciousness. Such an identity infallibly produces a mass psyche with its irresistible urge to catastrophe. Subjective consciousness must, in order to escape this doom, avoid identification with collective consciousness by recognizing its shadow as well as the existence and the importance of the archetypes. These latter are an effective defence against the brute force of collective consciousness and the mass psyche that goes with it. In point of effectiveness, the religious outlook of medieval man corresponds roughly to the attitude induced in the ego by the integration of unconscious contents, with the difference that in the latter case susceptibility to environmental influences and unconsciousness are replaced by scientific objectivity and conscious knowledge. But so far as religion, for the contemporary consciousness, still means, if anything, a creed, and hence a collectively accepted system of religious statements neatly codified as dogmatic precepts, it has closer affinities with collective consciousness even though its symbols express the once-operative archetypes. So long as the communal consciousness presided over by the Church is objectively present, the psyche, as said, continues to enjoy a certain equilibrium. At all events, it constitutes a sufficiently effective defence against inflation of the ego. But once Mother Church and her motherly Eros fall into abeyance, the individual is at the mercy of any passing collectivism and the attendant mass psyche. He succumbs to social or national inflation, and the tragedy is that he does so with the same psychic attitude which had once bound him to a church.

427   But if he is independent enough to recognize the bigotedness of the social "ism," he may then be threatened with subjective inflation, for usually he is not capable of seeing that religious ideas do not, in psychological reality, rest solely upon tradition and faith, but originate with the archetypes, the "careful consideration" of which—*religere!*—constitutes the essence of religion. The archetypes are continuously present and active; as such they need no believing in, but only an intuition of their meaning and a certain sapient awe, a δεισιδαιμονία, which never

428 loses sight of their import. A consciousness sharpened by experience knows the catastrophic consequences that disregard of this entails for the individual as well as for society. Just as the archetype is partly a spiritual factor, and partly like a hidden meaning immanent in the instincts, so the spirit, as I have shown,[126] is two-faced and paradoxical: a great help and an equally great danger.[127] It seems as if man were destined to play a decisive role in solving this uncertainty, and to solve it moreover by virtue of his consciousness, which once started up like a light in the murk of the primeval world. Nowhere do we know for sure about these matters, but least of all where "isms" flourish, for they are only a sophisticated substitute for the lost link with psychic reality. The mass psyche that infallibly results destroys the meaning of the individual and of culture generally.

From this it is clear that the psyche not only disturbs the natural order but, if it loses its balance, actually destroys its own creation. Therefore the careful consideration of psychic factors is of importance in restoring not merely the individual's balance, but society's as well, otherwise the destructive tendencies easily gain the upper hand. In the same way that the atom-bomb is an unparalleled means of physical mass destruction, so the misguided development of the soul must lead to psychic mass destruction. The present situation is so sinister that one cannot suppress the suspicion that the Creator is planning another deluge that will finally exterminate the existing race of men. But if anyone imagines that a healthy belief in the existence of archetypes can be inculcated from outside, he is as simple as the people who want to outlaw war or the atom-bomb. Such measures remind one of the bishop who excommunicated the cockchafers for their unseemly proliferation. Change of consciousness begins at home; it is an age-long process that depends entirely on how far the psyche's capacity for development extends. All we know at present is that there are single individuals who are capable of developing. How great their total number is we do not know, just as we do not know what the suggestive power of an extended consciousness may be, or what influence it may

126 Cf. "The Phenomenology of the Spirit in Fairytales."
127 Aptly expressed in the logion cited by Origen (*Homiliae in Jeremiam*, XX, 3): "He who is near unto me is near unto the fire. He who is far from me is far from the kingdom." This "unclaimed saying of the Master" refers to Isaiah 33 : 14.

have upon the world at large. Effects of this kind never depend on the reasonableness of an idea, but far more on the question (which can only be answered *ex effectu*): is the time ripe for change, or not?

*

429   As I have said, the psychology of complex phenomena finds itself in an uncomfortable situation compared with the other natural sciences because it lacks a base outside its object. It can only translate itself back into its own language, or fashion itself in its own image. The more it extends its field of research and the more complicated its objects become, the more it feels the lack of a point which is distinct from those objects. And once the complexity has reached that of the empirical man, his psychology inevitably merges with the psychic process itself. It can no longer be distinguished from the latter, and so turns into it. But the effect of this is that the process attains to consciousness. In this way, psychology actualizes the unconscious urge to consciousness. It is, in fact, the coming to consciousness of the psychic process, but it is not, in the deeper sense, an explanation of this process, for no explanation of the psychic can be anything other than the living process of the psyche itself. Psychology is doomed to cancel itself out as a science and therein precisely it reaches its scientific goal. Every other science has so to speak an outside; not so psychology, whose object is the inside subject of all science.

430   Psychology therefore culminates of necessity in a developmental process which is peculiar to the psyche and consists in integrating the unconscious contents into consciousness. This means that the psychic human being becomes a whole, and becoming whole has remarkable effects on ego-consciousness which are extremely difficult to describe. I doubt my ability to give a proper account of the change that comes over the subject under the influence of the individuation process; it is a relatively rare occurrence, which is experienced only by those who have gone through the wearisome but, if the unconscious is to be integrated, indispensable business of coming to terms with the unconscious components of the personality. Once these unconscious components are made conscious, it results not only in

their assimilation to the already existing ego-personality, but in a transformation of the latter. The main difficulty is to describe the manner of this transformation. Generally speaking the ego is a hard-and-fast complex which, because tied to consciousness and its continuity, cannot easily be altered, and should not be altered unless one wants to bring on pathological disturbances. The closest analogies to an alteration of the ego are to be found in the field of psychopathology, where we meet not only with neurotic dissociations but also with the schizophrenic fragmentation, or even dissolution, of the ego. In this field, too, we can observe pathological attempts at integration—if such an expression be permitted. These consist in more or less violent irruptions of unconscious contents into consciousness, the ego proving itself incapable of assimilating the intruders. But if the structure of the ego-complex is strong enough to withstand their assault without having its framework fatally dislocated, then assimilation can take place. In that event there is an alteration of the ego as well as of the unconscious contents. Although it is able to preserve its structure, the ego is ousted from its central and dominating position and thus finds itself in the role of a passive observer who lacks the power to assert his will under all circumstances, not so much because it has been weakened in any way, as because certain considerations give it pause. That is, the ego cannot help discovering that the afflux of unconscious contents has vitalized the personality, enriched it and created a figure that somehow dwarfs the ego in scope and intensity. This experience paralyzes an over-egocentric will and convinces the ego that in spite of all difficulties it is better to be taken down a peg than to get involved in a hopeless struggle in which one is invariably handed the dirty end of the stick. In this way the will, as disposable energy, gradually subordinates itself to the stronger factor, namely to the new totality-figure I call the *self*. Naturally, in these circumstances there is the greatest temptation simply to follow the power-instinct and to identify the ego with the self outright, in order to keep up the illusion of the ego's mastery. In other cases the ego proves too weak to offer the necessary resistance to the influx of unconscious contents and is thereupon assimilated by the unconscious, which produces a blurring or darkening of ego-consciousness and its identification with a preconscious wholeness.[128] Both these developments make the realization of the self impossible, and at the same time are fatal to the maintenance of ego-consciousness. They amount, therefore, to pathological effects. The psychic phenomena recently observable in Germany fall into this category. It is abundantly clear that such an *abaissement du niveau mental*, i.e., the overpowering of the ego by unconscious contents and the consequent identification with a preconscious wholeness, possesses a prodigious psychic virulence, or power of contagion, and is capable of the most disastrous results. Developments of this kind should, therefore, be watched very carefully; they require the closest control. I would recommend anyone who feels himself threatened by such tendencies to hang a picture of St. Christopher on the wall and to meditate upon it. For the self has a functional meaning only when it can act compensatorily to ego-consciousness. If the ego is dissolved in identification with the self, it gives rise to a sort of nebulous superman with a puffed-up ego and a deflated self. Such a personage, however saviourlike or baleful his demeanour, lacks the *scintilla*, the soul-spark, the little wisp of divine light that never burns more brightly than when it has to struggle against the invading darkness. What would the rainbow be were it not limned against the lowering cloud?

431 This simile is intended to remind the reader that pathological analogies of the individuation process are not the only ones. There are spiritual monuments of quite another kind, and they are positive illustrations of our process. Above all I would mention the *koans* of Zen Buddhism, those sublime paradoxes that light up, as with a flash of lightning, the inscrutable interrelations between ego and self. In very different language, St. John of the Cross has made the same problem more readily accessible to the Westerner in his account of the "dark night of the soul." That we find it needful to draw analogies from psychopathology and from both Eastern and Western mysticism is only to be expected: the individuation process is, psychically, a border-line

128 Conscious wholeness consists in a successful union of ego and self, so that both preserve their intrinsic qualities. If, instead of this union, the ego is overpowered by the self, then the self too does not attain the form it ought to have, but remains fixed on a primitive level and can express itself only through archaic symbols.

432   phenomenon which needs special conditions in order to become conscious. Perhaps it is the first step along a path of development to be trodden by the men of the future—a path which, for the time being, has taken a pathological turn and landed Europe in catastrophe.

    To one familiar with our psychology, it may seem a waste of time to keep harping on the long-established difference between becoming conscious and the coming-to-be of the self (individuation). But again and again I note that the individuation process is confused with the coming of the ego into consciousness and that the ego is in consequence identified with the self, which naturally produces a hopeless conceptual muddle. Individuation is then nothing but ego-centredness and autoeroticism. But the self comprises infinitely more than a mere ego, as the symbolism has shown from of old. It is as much one's self, and all other selves, as the ego. Individuation does not shut one out from the world, but gathers the world to oneself.

433   With this I would like to bring my exposition to an end. I have tried to sketch out the development and basic problems of our psychology and to communicate the quintessence, the very spirit, of this science. In view of the unusual difficulties of my theme, the reader may pardon the undue demands I have made upon his good-will and attention. Fundamental discussions are among the things that mould a science into shape, but they are seldom entertaining.

Supplement

434   As the points of view that have to be considered in elucidating the unconscious are often misunderstood, I would like, in connection with the foregoing discussions of principle, to examine at least two of the main prejudices somewhat more closely.

435   What above all stultifies understanding is the arrant assumption that "archetype" means an inborn idea. No biologist would ever dream of assuming that each individual acquires his general mode of behaviour afresh each time. It is much more probable that the young weaver-bird builds his characteristic nest because he is a weaver-bird and not a rabbit. Similarly, it is more probable that man is born with a specifically human mode

of behaviour and not with that of a hippopotamus or with none at all. Integral to his characteristic behaviour is his psychic phenomenology, which differs from that of a bird or quadruped. Archetypes are typical forms of behaviour which, once they become conscious, naturally present themselves *as ideas and images*, like everything else that becomes a content of consciousness. Because it is a question of characteristically human modes, it is hardly to be wondered at that we can find psychic forms in the individual which occur not only at the antipodes but also in other epochs with which archaeology provides the only link.

436   Now if we wish to prove that a certain psychic form is not a unique but a typical occurrence, this can be done only if I myself testify that, having taken the necessary precautions, I have observed the same thing in different individuals. Then other observers, too, must confirm that they have made the same or similar observations. Finally we have to establish that the same or similar phenomena can be shown to occur in the folklore of other peoples and races and in the texts that have come down to us from earlier centuries and epochs. My method and whole outlook, therefore, begin with individual psychic facts which not I alone have established, but other observers as well. The material brought forward—folkloristic, mythological, or historical—serves in the first place to demonstrate the uniformity of psychic events in time and space. But, since the meaning and substance of the typical individual forms are of the utmost importance in practice, and knowledge of them plays a considerable role in each individual case, it is inevitable that the mythologem and its content will also be drawn into the limelight. This is not to say that the purpose of the investigation is to interpret the mythologem. But, precisely in this connection, a widespread prejudice reigns that the psychology of unconscious processes is a sort of *philosophy* designed to explain mythologems. This unfortunately rather common prejudice assiduously overlooks the crucial point, namely, that our psychology starts with observable facts and not with philosophical speculations. If, for instance, we study the mandala structures that are always cropping up in dreams and fantasies, ill-considered criticism might raise, and indeed has raised, the objection that we are reading Indian or Chinese philosophy into the psyche. But in reality all we have done is to compare individual

psychic occurrences with obviously related collective phenomena. The introspective trend of Eastern philosophy has brought to light material which all introspective attitudes bring to light all over the world, at all times and places. The great snag so far as the critic is concerned is that he has no personal experience of the facts in question, any more than he has of the state of mind of a lama engaged in "constructing" a mandala. These two prejudices render any access to modern psychology impossible for not a few heads with scientific pretensions. There are in addition many other stumbling-blocks that cannot be overcome by reason. We shall therefore refrain from discussing them.

437   Inability to understand, or the ignorance of the public, cannot however prevent the scientist from employing certain calculations of probability, of whose treacherous nature he is sufficiently well informed. We are fully aware that we have no more knowledge of the various states and processes of the unconscious as such than the physicist has of the process underlying physical phenomena. Of what lies beyond the phenomenal world we can have absolutely no idea, for there is no idea that could have any other source than the phenomenal world. If we are to engage in fundamental reflections about the nature of the psychic, we need an Archimedean point which alone makes a judgment possible. This can only be the nonpsychic, for, as a living phenomenon, the psychic lies embedded in something that appears to be of a nonpsychic nature. Although we perceive the latter as a psychic datum only, there are sufficient reasons for believing in its objective reality. This reality, so far as it lies outside our body's limits, is mediated to us chiefly by particles of light impinging on the retina of the eye. The organization of these particles produces a picture of the phenomenal world which depends essentially upon the constitution of the apperceiving psyche on the one hand, and upon that of the light medium on the other. The apperceiving consciousness has proved capable of a high degree of development, and constructs instruments with the help of which our range of seeing and hearing has been extended by many octaves. Consequently the postulated reality of the phenomenal world as well as the subjective world of consciousness have undergone an unparalleled expansion. The existence of this remarkable correlation be-

438   tween consciousness and the phenomenal world, between subjective perception and objectively real processes, i.e., their energic effects, requires no further proof.

As the phenomenal world is an aggregate of processes of atomic magnitude, it is naturally of the greatest importance to find out whether, and if so how, the photons (shall we say) enable us to gain a definite knowledge of the reality underlying the mediative energy processes. Experience has shown that light and matter both behave like separate particles and also like waves. This paradoxical conclusion obliged us to abandon, on the plane of atomic magnitudes, a causal description of nature in the ordinary space-time system, and in its place to set up invisible fields of probability in multidimensional spaces, which do in fact represent the state of our knowledge at present. Basic to this abstract scheme of explanation is a conception of reality that takes account of the uncontrollable effects the observer has upon the system observed, the result being that reality forfeits something of its objective character and that a subjective element attaches to the physicist's picture of the world.[129]

439   The application of statistical laws to processes of atomic magnitude in physics has a noteworthy correspondence in psychology, so far as psychology investigates the bases of consciousness by pursuing the conscious processes until they lose themselves in darkness and unintelligibility, and nothing more can be seen but effects which have an *organizing* influence on the contents of consciousness.[130] Investigation of these effects

[129] I owe this formulation to the kind help of Professor W. Pauli.

[130] It may interest the reader to hear the opinion of a physicist on this point. Professor Pauli, who was good enough to glance through the ms. of this supplement, writes: "As a matter of fact the physicist would expect a psychological correspondence at this point, because the epistemological situation with regard to the concepts 'conscious' and 'unconscious' seems to offer a pretty close analogy to the undermentioned 'complementarity' situation in physics. On the one hand the unconscious can only be inferred indirectly from its (organizing) effects on conscious contents. On the other hand every 'observation of the unconscious,' i.e., every conscious realization of unconscious contents, has an uncontrollable reactive effect on these same contents (which as we know precludes in principle the possibility of 'exhausting' the unconscious by making it conscious). Thus the physicist will conclude *per analogiam* that this uncontrollable reactive effect of the observing subject on the unconscious limits the objective character of the latter's reality and lends it at the same time a certain subjectivity. Although the

yields the singular fact that they proceed from an unconscious, i.e., objective, reality which behaves at the same time like a subjective one—in other words, like a consciousness. Hence the reality underlying the unconscious effects includes the observing subject and is therefore constituted in a way that we cannot conceive. It is, at one and the same time, absolute subjectivity and universal truth, for in principle it can be shown to be present everywhere, which certainly cannot be said of conscious contents of a personalistic nature. The elusiveness, capriciousness, haziness, and uniqueness that the lay mind always associates with the idea of the psyche applies only to consciousness, and not to the absolute unconscious. The qualitatively rather than quantitatively definable units with which the unconscious works, namely the archetypes, therefore have a nature that *cannot with certainty be designated as psychic.*

440   Although I have been led by purely psychological considerations to doubt the exclusively psychic nature of the archetypes, psychology sees itself obliged to revise its "only psychic" assumptions in the light of the physical findings too. Physics has demonstrated, as plainly as could be wished, that in the realm of atomic magnitudes an observer is postulated in objective reality, and that only on this condition is a satisfactory scheme of explanation possible. This means that a subjective element attaches to the physicist's world picture, and secondly that a connection necessarily exists between the psyche to be explained and the objective space-time continuum. Since the physical continuum is inconceivable it follows that we can form no picture of its

position of the 'cut' between conscious and unconscious is (at least up to a point) left to the free choice of the 'psychological experimen\ter', the *existence* of this 'cut' remains an unavoidable necessity. Accordingly, from the standpoint of the psychologist, the 'observed system' would consist not of physical objects only, but would also include the unconscious, while consciousness would be assigned the role of 'observing medium.' It is undeniable that the development of 'microphysics' has brought the way in which nature is described in this science very much closer to that of the newer psychology: but whereas the former, on account of the basic 'complementarity' situation, is faced with the impossibility of eliminating the effects of the observer by determinable correctives, and has therefore to abandon in principle any objective understanding of physical phenomena, the latter can supplement the purely subjective psychology of consciousness by postulating the existence of an unconscious that possesses a large measure of objective reality."

psychic aspect either, which also necessarily exists. Nevertheless, the relative or partial identity of psyche and physical continuum is of the greatest importance theoretically, because it brings with it a tremendous simplification by bridging over the seeming incommensurability between the physical world and the psychic, not of course in any concrete way, but from the physical side by means of mathematical equations, and from the psychological side by means of empirically derived postulates—archetypes—whose content, if any, cannot be represented to the mind. Archetypes, so far as we can observe and experience them at all, manifest themselves only through their ability to *organize* images and ideas, and this is always an unconscious process which cannot be detected until afterwards. By assimilating ideational material whose provenance in the phenomenal world is not to be contested, they become visible and *psychic*. Therefore they are recognized at first only as psychic entities and are conceived as such, with the same right with which we base the physical phenomena of immediate perception on Euclidean space. Only when it comes to explaining psychic phenomena of a minimal degree of clarity are we driven to assume that archetypes must have a nonpsychic aspect. Grounds for such a conclusion are supplied by the phenomena of synchronicity, which are associated with the activity of unconscious operators and have hitherto been regarded, or repudiated, as "telepathy," etc.[131] Scepticism should, however, be levelled only at incorrect theories and not at facts which exist in their own right. No unbiased observer can deny them. Resistance to the recognition of such facts rests principally on the repugnance people feel for an allegedly supernatural faculty tacked on to the psyche, like "clairvoyance." The very diverse and confusing aspects of these phenomena are, so far as I can see at present, completely explicable on the assumption of a psychically relative space-time continuum. As soon as a psychic content crosses the threshold of consciousness, the synchronistic marginal phenomena disappear, time and space resume their accustomed sway, and consciousness is once more isolated in its subjectivity. We have here one of those instances which can best be understood in terms of

131 The physicist Pascual Jordan ("Positivistische Bemerkungen über die parapsychischen Erscheinungen," 14ff.) has already used the idea of relative space to explain telepathic phenomena.

the physicist's idea of "complementarity." When an unconscious content passes over into consciousness its synchronistic manifestation ceases; conversely, synchronistic phenomena can be evoked by putting the subject into an unconscious state (trance). The same relationship of complementarity can be observed just as easily in all those extremely common medical cases in which certain clinical symptoms disappear when the corresponding unconscious contents are made conscious. We also know that a number of psychosomatic phenomena which are otherwise outside the control of the will can be induced by hypnosis, that is, by this same restriction of consciousness. Professor Pauli formulates the physical side of the complementarity relationship here expressed, as follows: "It rests with the free choice of the experimenter (or observer) to decide . . . which insights he will gain and which he will lose; or, to put it in popular language, whether he will measure A and ruin B or ruin A and measure B. It does *not* rest with him, however, to gain only insights and not lose any." This is particularly true of the relation between the physical standpoint and the psychological. Physics determines quantities and their relation to one another; psychology determines qualities without being able to measure quantities. Despite that, both sciences arrive at ideas which come significantly close to one another. The parallelism of psychological and physical explanations has already been pointed out by C. A. Meier in his essay "Moderne Physik—Moderne Psychologie." [132] He says: "Both sciences have, in the course of many years of independent work, amassed observations and systems of thought to match them. Both sciences have come up against certain barriers which . . . display similar basic characteristics. The object to be investigated, and the human investigator with his organs of sense and knowledge and their extensions (measuring instruments and procedures), are indissolubly bound together. That is complementarity in physics as well as in psychology." Between physics and psychology there is in fact "a genuine and authentic relationship of complementarity."

441   Once we can rid ourselves of the highly unscientific pretence that it is merely a question of chance coincidence, we shall see that synchronistic phenomena are not unusual occurrences at

132 *Die kulturelle Bedeutung der komplexen Psychologie*, p. 362.

all, but are relatively common. This fact is in entire agreement with Rhine's "probability-exceeding" results. The psyche is not a chaos made up of random whims and accidents, but is an objective reality to which the investigator can gain access by the methods of natural science. There are indications that psychic processes stand in some sort of energy relation to the physiological substrate. In so far as they are objective events, they can hardly be interpreted as anything but energy processes,[133] or to put it another way: in spite of the nonmeasurability of psychic processes, the perceptible changes effected by the psyche cannot possibly be understood except as a phenomenon of energy. This places the psychologist in a situation which is highly repugnant to the physicist: the psychologist also talks of energy although he has nothing measurable to manipulate, besides which the concept of energy is a strictly defined mathematical quantity which cannot be applied as such to anything psychic. The formula for kinetic energy, $E = \dfrac{mv^2}{2}$, contains the factors m (mass) and v (velocity), and these would appear to be incommensurable with the nature of the empirical psyche. If psychology nevertheless insists on employing its own concept of energy for the purpose of expressing the activity ($\dot{\epsilon}\nu\dot{\epsilon}\rho\gamma\epsilon\iota\alpha$) of the psyche, it is not of course being used as a mathematical formula, but only as its analogy. But note: the analogy is itself an older intuitive idea from which the concept of physical energy originally developed. The latter rests on earlier applications of an $\dot{\epsilon}\nu\dot{\epsilon}\rho\gamma\epsilon\iota\alpha$ not mathematically defined, which can be traced back to the primitive or archaic idea of the "extraordinarily potent." This mana concept is not confined to Melanesia, but can also be found in Indonesia and on the east coast of Africa; and it still echoes in the Latin *numen* and, more faintly, in *genius* (e.g., *genius loci*). The use of the term *libido* in the newer medical psychology has surprising affinities with the primitive mana.[134] This archetypal idea is therefore far from being only primitive, but differs from the physicist's conception of energy by the fact that it is essentially qualitative and not quantitative. In psychology the

133 By this I only mean that psychic phenomena have an energic aspect by virtue of which they can be described as "phenomena." I do not mean that the energic aspect embraces or explains the whole of the psyche.
134 Cf. the first paper in this volume.

442   exact measurement of quantities is replaced by an approximate determination of intensities, for which purpose, in strictest contrast to *physics*, we enlist the function of *feeling* (valuation). The latter takes the place, in psychology, of concrete measurement in physics. The psychic intensities and their graduated differences point to quantitative processes which are inaccessible to direct observation and measurement. While psychological data are essentially qualitative, they also have a sort of latent physical energy, since psychic phenomena exhibit a certain quantitative aspect. Could these quantities be measured the psyche would be bound to appear as having motion in space, something to which the energy formula would be applicable. Therefore, since mass and energy are of the same nature, mass and velocity would be adequate concepts for characterizing the psyche so far as it has any observable effects in space: in other words, it must have an aspect under which it would appear as mass in motion. If one is unwilling to postulate a pre-established harmony of physical and psychic events, then they can only be in a state of interaction. But the latter hypothesis requires a psyche that touches matter at some point, and, conversely, a matter with a latent psyche, a postulate not so very far removed from certain formulations of modern physics (Eddington, Jeans, and others). In this connection I would remind the reader of the existence of parapsychic phenomena whose reality value can only be appreciated by those who have had occasion to satisfy themselves by personal observation.

If these reflections are justified, they must have weighty consequences with regard to the nature of the psyche, since as an objective fact it would then be intimately connected not only with physiological and biological phenomena but with physical events too—and, so it would appear, most intimately of all with those that pertain to the realm of atomic physics. As my remarks may have made clear, we are concerned first and foremost to establish certain analogies, and no more than that; the existence of such analogies does not entitle us to conclude that the connection is already proven. We must, in the present state of our physical and psychological knowledge, be content with the mere resemblance to one another of certain basic reflections. The existing analogies, however, are significant enough in themselves to warrant the prominence we have given them.

FROM *RELATIONS BETWEEN THE EGO AND THE UNCONSCIOUS*

PREFACE TO THE SECOND EDITION (1935)

This little book is the outcome of a lecture which was originally published in 1916 under the title "La Structure de l'inconscient."[1] This same lecture later appeared in English under the title "The Conception of the Unconscious," in my *Collected Papers on Analytical Psychology*.[2] I mention these facts because I wish to place it on record that the present essay is not making its first appearance, but is rather the expression of a long-standing endeavour to grasp and—at least in its essential features—to depict the strange character and course of that *drame intérieur*, the transformation process of the unconscious psyche. This idea of the independence of the unconscious, which distinguishes my views so radically from those of Freud, came to me as far back as 1902, when I was engaged in studying the psychic history of a young girl somnambulist.[3] In a lecture given in Zurich [1908] on "The Content of the Psychoses," I approached this idea from another side. In 1912, I illustrated some of the main points of the process in an individual case and at the same time I indicated the historical and ethnological parallels to these seemingly universal psychic events.[4] In the above-mentioned essay, "La

1 Cf. below, pars. 442ff.: "The Structure of the Unconscious."

2 2nd edn., London, 1917; New York, 1920.

3 "On the Psychology and Pathology of So-called Occult Phenomena."

4 *Wandlungen und Symbole der Libido* (Leipzig and Vienna, 1912); trans. by Beatrice M. Hinkle as *Psychology of the Unconscious* (New York, 1916; London, 1917). [Rewritten as *Symbole der Wandlung* (Zurich, 1952), trans. in *Coll. Works*, Vol. 5: *Symbols of Transformation*.—EDITORS.]

Structure de l'inconscient," I attempted for the first time to give a comprehensive account of the whole process. It was a mere attempt, of whose inadequacy I was painfully aware. The difficulties presented by the material were so great that I could not hope to do them anything like justice in a single essay. I therefore let it rest at the stage of an "interim report," with the firm intention of returning to this theme at a later opportunity. Twelve years of further experience enabled me, in 1928, to undertake a thorough revision of my formulations of 1916, and the result of these labours was the little book *Die Beziehungen zwischen dem Ich und dem Unbewussten.* [5] This time I tried to describe chiefly the relation of the ego-consciousness to the unconscious process. Following this intention, I concerned myself more particularly with those phenomena which are to be regarded as the reactive symptoms of the conscious personality to the influences of the unconscious. In this way I tried to effect an indirect approach to the unconscious process itself. These investigations have not yet come to a satisfactory conclusion, for the answer to the crucial problem of the nature and essence of the unconscious process has still to be found. I would not venture upon this exceedingly difficult task without the fullest possible experience. Its solution is reserved for the future.

I trust the reader of this book will bear with me if I beg him to regard it—should he persevere—as an earnest attempt on my part to form an intellectual conception of a new and hitherto unexplored field of experience. It is not concerned with a clever system of thought, but with the formulation of complex psychic experiences which have never yet been the subject of scientific study. Since the psyche is an irrational datum and cannot, in accordance with the old picture, be equated with a more or less divine Reason, it should not surprise us if in the course of psychological experience we come across, with extreme frequency, processes and happenings which run counter to our rational expectations and are therefore rejected by the rationalistic attitude of our conscious mind. Such an attitude is naturally not very skilled at psychological observation because it is in the highest degree unscientific. We must not attempt to tell nature what to do if we want to observe her operations undisturbed.

5 [Trans. by H. G. and C. F. Baynes as "The Relations Between the Ego and the Unconscious" in *Two Essays on Analytical Psychology* (London and New York, 1928).]

It is twenty-eight years of psychological and psychiatric experience that I am trying to sum up here, so perhaps my little book may lay some claim to serious consideration. Naturally I could not say everything in this single exposition. The reader will find a development of the last chapter, [with reference to the concept of the self], in my commentary to *The Secret of the Golden Flower*, the book I brought out in collaboration with my friend Richard Wilhelm. I did not wish to omit reference to this publication, because Oriental philosophy has been concerned with these interior psychic processes for many hundreds of years and is therefore, in view of the great need for comparative material, of inestimable value in psychological research.

October 1934

C. C. JUNG

PART ONE

THE EFFECTS OF THE UNCONSCIOUS
UPON CONSCIOUSNESS

THE PERSONAL AND THE COLLECTIVE
UNCONSCIOUS

202   In Freud's view, as most people know, the contents of the unconscious are reducible to infantile tendencies which are repressed because of their incompatible character. Repression is a process that begins in early childhood under the moral influence of the environment and continues throughout life. By means of analysis the repressions are removed and the repressed wishes made conscious.

203   According to this theory, the unconscious contains only those parts of the personality which could just as well be conscious, and have been suppressed only through the process of education. Although from one point of view the infantile tendencies of the unconscious are the most conspicuous, it would nonetheless be a mistake to define or evaluate the unconscious entirely in these terms. The unconscious has still another side to it: it includes not only repressed contents, but all psychic material that lies below the threshold of consciousness. It is impossible to explain the subliminal nature of all this material on the principle of repression, for in that case the removal of repression ought to endow a person with a prodigious memory which would thenceforth forget nothing.

204   We therefore emphatically affirm that in addition to the repressed material the unconscious contains all those psychic components that have fallen below the threshold, as well as sub-

liminal sense-perceptions. Moreover we know, from abundant experience as well as for theoretical reasons, that the unconscious also contains all the material that has *not yet* reached the threshold of consciousness. These are the seeds of future conscious contents. Equally we have reason to suppose that the unconscious is never quiescent in the sense of being inactive, but is ceaselessly engaged in grouping and regrouping its contents. This activity should be thought of as completely autonomous only in pathological cases; normally it is co-ordinated with the conscious mind in a compensatory relationship.

205   It is to be assumed that all these contents are of a personal nature in so far as they are acquired during the individual's life. Since this life is limited, the number of acquired contents in the unconscious must also be limited. This being so, it might be thought possible to empty the unconscious either by analysis or by making a complete inventory of the unconscious contents, on the ground that the unconscious cannot produce anything more than what is already known and assimilated into consciousness. We should also have to suppose, as already said, that if one could arrest the descent of conscious contents into the unconscious by doing away with repression, unconscious productivity would be paralysed. This is possible only to a very limited extent, as we know from experience. We urge our patients to hold fast to repressed contents that have been re-associated with consciousness, and to assimilate them into their plan of life. But this procedure, as we may daily convince ourselves, makes no impression on the unconscious, since it calmly goes on producing dreams and fantasies which, according to Freud's original theory, must arise from personal repressions. If in such cases we pursue our observations systematically and without prejudice, we shall find material which, although similar in form to the previous personal contents, yet seems to contain allusions that go far beyond the personal sphere.

206   Casting about in my mind for an example to illustrate what I have just said, I have a particularly vivid memory of a woman patient with a mild hysterical neurosis which, as we expressed it in those days [about 1910], had its principal cause in a "father-complex." By this we wanted to denote the fact that the patient's peculiar relationship to her father stood in her way. She had been on very good terms with her father, who had since

died. It was a relationship chiefly of feeling. In such cases it is usually the intellectual function that is developed, and this later becomes the bridge to the world. Accordingly our patient became a student of philosophy. Her energetic pursuit of knowledge was motivated by her need to extricate herself from the emotional entanglement with her father. This operation may succeed if her feelings can find an outlet on the new intellectual level, perhaps in the formation of an emotional tie with a suitable man, equivalent to the former tie. In this particular case, however, the transition refused to take place, because the patient's feelings remained suspended, oscillating between her father and a man who was not altogether suitable. The progress of her life was thus held up, and that inner disunity so characteristic of a neurosis promptly made its appearance. The so-called normal person would probably be able to break the emotional bond in one or the other direction by a powerful act of will, or else—and this is perhaps the more usual thing—he would come through the difficulty unconsciously, on the smooth path of instinct, without ever being aware of the sort of conflict that lay behind his headaches or other physical discomforts. But any weakness of instinct (which may have many causes) is enough to hinder a smooth unconscious transition. Then all progress is delayed by conflict, and the resulting stasis of life is equivalent to a neurosis. In consequence of the standstill, psychic energy flows off in every conceivable direction, apparently quite uselessly. For instance, there are excessive innervations of the sympathetic system, which lead to nervous disorders of the stomach and intestines; or the vagus (and consequently the heart) is stimulated; or fantasies and memories, uninteresting enough in themselves, become overvalued and prey on the conscious mind (mountains out of molehills). In this state a new motive is needed to put an end to the morbid suspension. Nature herself paves the way for this, unconsciously and indirectly, through the phenomenon of the transference (Freud). In the course of treatment the patient transfers the father imago to the doctor, thus making him, in a sense, the father, and in the sense that he is *not* the father, also making him a substitute for the man she cannot reach. The doctor therefore becomes both a father and a kind of lover—in other words, an object of conflict. In him the opposites are united, and for this reason he stands for a quasi-ideal solution of the conflict. Without in the least wishing it, he draws upon himself an over-valuation that is almost incredible to the outsider, for to the patient he seems like a saviour or a god. This way of speaking is not altogether so laughable as it sounds. It is indeed a bit much to be a father and lover at once. Nobody could possibly stand up to it in the long run, precisely because it is too much of a good thing. One would have to be a demigod at least to sustain such a role without a break, for all the time one would have to be the giver. To the patient in the state of transference, this provisional solution naturally seems ideal, but only at first; in the end she comes to a standstill that is just as bad as the neurotic conflict was. Fundamentally, nothing has yet happened that might lead to a real solution. The conflict has merely been transferred. Nevertheless a successful transference can—at least temporarily—cause the whole neurosis to disappear, and for this reason it has been very rightly recognized by Freud as a healing factor of first-rate importance, but, at the same time, as a provisional state only, for although it holds out the possibility of a cure, it is far from being the cure itself.

207   This somewhat lengthy discussion seemed to me essential if my example was to be understood, for my patient had arrived at the state of transference and had already reached the upper limit where the standstill begins to make itself disagreeable. The question now arose: what next? I had of course become the complete saviour, and the thought of having to give me up was not only exceedingly distasteful to the patient, but positively terrifying. In such a situation "sound common sense" generally comes out with a whole repertory of admonitions: "you simply must," "you really ought," "you just cannot," etc. So far as sound common sense is, happily, not too rare and not entirely without effect (pessimists, I know, exist), a rational motive can, in the exuberant feeling of buoyancy you get from the transference, release so much enthusiasm that a painful sacrifice can be risked with a mighty effort of will. If successful—and these things sometimes are—the sacrifice bears blessed fruit, and the erstwhile patient leaps at one bound into the state of being practically cured. The doctor is generally so delighted that he fails to tackle the theoretical difficulties connected with this little miracle.

208   If the leap does not succeed—and it did not succeed with my patient—one is then faced with the problem of resolving the

209   transference. Here "psychoanalytic" theory shrouds itself in a thick darkness. Apparently we are to fall back on some nebulous trust in fate: somehow or other the matter will settle itself. "The transference stops automatically when the patient runs out of money," as a slightly cynical colleague once remarked to me. Or the ineluctable demands of life make it impossible for the patient to linger on in the transference—demands which compel the involuntary sacrifice, sometimes with a more or less complete relapse as a result. (One may look in vain for accounts of such cases in the books that sing the praises of psychoanalysis!)

210   To be sure, there are hopeless cases where nothing helps; but there are also cases that do not get stuck and do not inevitably leave the transference situation with bitter hearts and sore heads. I told myself, at this juncture with my patient, that there must be a clear and respectable way out of the impasse. My patient had long since run out of money—if indeed she ever possessed any—but I was curious to know what means nature would devise for a satisfactory way out of the transference deadlock. Since I never imagined that I was blessed with that "sound common sense" which always knows exactly what to do in every quandary, and since my patient knew as little as I, I suggested to her that we could at least keep an eye open for any movements coming from a sphere of the psyche uncontaminated by our superior wisdom and our conscious plannings. That meant first and foremost her dreams.

211   Dreams contain images and thought-associations which we do not create with conscious intent. They arise spontaneously without our assistance and are representatives of a psychic activity withdrawn from our arbitrary will. Therefore the dream is, properly speaking, a highly objective, natural product of the psyche, from which we might expect indications, or at least hints, about certain basic trends in the psychic process. Now, since the psychic process, like any other life-process, is not just a causal sequence, but is also a process with a teleological orientation, we might expect dreams to give us certain *indicia* about the objective causality as well as about the objective tendencies, precisely because dreams are nothing less than self-representations of the psychic life-process.

    On the basis of these reflections, then, we subjected the dreams to a careful examination. It would lead too far to quote

212 word for word all the dreams that now followed. Let it suffice to sketch their main character: the majority referred to the person of the doctor, that is to say, the actors were unmistakably the dreamer herself and her doctor. The latter, however, seldom appeared in his natural shape, but was generally distorted in a remarkable way. Sometimes his figure was of supernatural size, sometimes he seemed to be extremely aged, then again he resembled her father, but was at the same time curiously woven into nature, as in the following dream: *Her father (who in reality was of small stature) was standing with her on a hill that was covered with wheat-fields. She was quite tiny beside him, and he seemed to her like a giant. He lifted her up from the ground and held her in his arms like a little child. The wind swept over the wheat-fields, and as the wheat swayed in the wind, he rocked her in his arms.*

213 From this dream and from others like it I could discern various things. Above all I got the impression that her unconscious was holding unshakably to the idea of my being the father-lover, so that the fatal tie we were trying to undo appeared to be doubly strengthened. Moreover one could hardly avoid seeing that the unconscious placed a special emphasis on the supernatural, almost "divine" nature of the father-lover, thus accentuating still further the over-valuation occasioned by the transference. I therefore asked myself whether the patient had still not understood the wholly fantastic character of her transference, or whether perhaps the unconscious could never be reached by understanding at all, but must blindly and idiotically pursue some nonsensical chimera. Freud's idea that the unconscious can "do nothing but wish," Schopenhauer's blind and aimless Will, the gnostic demiurge who in his vanity deems himself perfect and then in the blindness of his limitation creates something lamentably imperfect—all these pessimistic suspicions of an essentially negative background to the world and the soul came threateningly near. And there would indeed be nothing to set against this except a well-meaning "you ought," reinforced by a stroke of the axe that would cut down the whole phantasmagoria for good and all.

But, as I turned the dreams over and over in my mind, there dawned on me another possibility. I said to myself: it cannot be denied that the dreams continue to speak in the same old metaphors with which our conversations have made the patient as well as myself sickeningly familiar. But the patient has an undoubted understanding of her transference fantasy. She knows that I appear to her as a semi-divine father-lover, and she can, at least intellectually, distinguish this from my factual reality. Therefore the dreams are obviously reiterating the conscious standpoint minus the conscious criticism, which they completely ignore. They reiterate the conscious contents, not *in toto*, but insist on the fantastic standpoint as opposed to "sound common sense."

214   I naturally asked myself what was the source of this obstinacy and what was its purpose? That it must have some purposive meaning I was convinced, for there is no truly living thing that does not have a final meaning, that can in other words be explained as a mere left-over from antecedent facts. But the energy of the transference is so strong that it gives one the impression of such fantasies? That being so, what is the purpose of such fantasies? A careful examination and analysis of the dreams, especially of the one just quoted, revealed a very marked tendency—in contrast to conscious criticism, which always seeks to reduce things to human proportions—to endow the person of the doctor with superhuman attributes. He had to be gigantic, primordial, huger than the father, like the wind that sweeps over the earth—was he then to be made into a god? Or, I said to myself, was it rather the case that the unconscious was trying to *create* a god out of the person of the doctor, as it were to free a vision of God from the veils of the personal, so that the transference to the person of the doctor was no more than a misunderstanding on the part of the conscious mind, a stupid trick played by "sound common sense"? Was the urge of the unconscious perhaps only apparently reaching out towards the person, but in a deeper sense towards a god? Could the longing for a god be a *passion* welling up from our darkest, instinctual nature, a passion unswayed by any outside influences, deeper and stronger perhaps than the love for a human person? Or was it perhaps the highest and truest meaning of that inappropriate love we call "transference," a little bit of real *Gottesminne*, that has been lost to consciousness ever since the fifteenth century?

215   No one will doubt the reality of a passionate longing for a human person; but that a fragment of religious psychology, an

historical anachronism, indeed something of a medieval curiosity—we are reminded of Mechtild of Magdeburg—should come to light as an immediate living reality in the middle of the consulting-room, and be expressed in the prosaic figure of the doctor, seems almost too fantastic to be taken seriously.

216 A genuinely scientific attitude must be unprejudiced. The sole criterion for the validity of an hypothesis is whether or not it possesses an heuristic—i.e., explanatory—value. The question now is, can we regard the possibilities set forth above as a valid hypothesis? There is no *a priori* reason why it should not be just as possible that the unconscious tendencies have a goal beyond the human person, as that the unconscious can "do nothing but wish." Experience alone can decide which is the more suitable hypothesis. This new hypothesis was not entirely plausible to my very critical patient. The earlier view that I was the father-lover, and as such presented an ideal solution of the conflict, was incomparably more attractive to her way of feeling. Nevertheless her intellect was sufficiently keen to appreciate the theoretical possibility of the new hypothesis. Meanwhile the dreams continued to disintegrate the person of the doctor and swell him to ever vaster proportions. Concurrently with this there now occurred something which at first I alone perceived, and with the utmost astonishment, namely a kind of subterranean undermining of the transference. Her relations with a certain friend deepened perceptibly, notwithstanding the fact that consciously she still clung to the transference. So that when the time came for leaving me, it was no catastrophe, but a perfectly reasonable parting. I had the privilege of being the only witness during the process of severance. I saw how the transpersonal control-point developed—I cannot call it anything else—a *guiding function* and step by step gathered to itself all the former personal over-valuations; how, with this afflux of energy, it gained influence over the resisting conscious mind without the patient's consciously noticing what was happening. From this I realized that the dreams were not just fantasies, but self-representations of unconscious developments which allowed the psyche of the patient gradually to grow out of the pointless personal tie.[1]

217 This change took place, as I showed, through the unconscious development of a transpersonal control-point; a virtual

[1] Cf. the "transcendent function" in *Psychological Types*, Def. 51, "Symbol."

218 goal, as it were, that expressed itself symbolically in a form which can only be described as a vision of God. The dreams swelled the human person of the doctor to superhuman proportions, making him a gigantic primordial father who is at the same time the wind, and in whose protecting arms the dreamer rests like an infant. If we try to make the patient's conscious, and traditionally Christian, idea of God responsible for the divine image in the dreams, we would still have to lay stress on the distortion. In religious matters the patient had a critical and agnostic attitude, and her idea of a possible deity had long since passed into the realm of the inconceivable, i.e., had dwindled into a complete abstraction. In contrast to this, the god-image of the dreams corresponded to the archaic conception of a naturedaemon, something like Wotan. Θεὸς τὸ πνεῦμα, 'God is spirit,' is here translated back into its original form where πνεῦμα means 'wind': God is the wind, stronger and mightier than man, an invisible breath-spirit. As in Hebrew *ruah*, so in Arabic *ruh* means breath and spirit.[2] Out of the purely personal form the dreams develop an archaic god-image that is infinitely far from the conscious idea of God. It might be objected that this is simply an infantile image, a childhood memory. I would have no quarrel with this assumption if we were dealing with an old man sitting on a golden throne in heaven. But there is no trace of any sentimentality of that kind; instead, we have a primordial idea that can correspond only to an archaic mentality.

These primordial ideas, of which I have given a great many examples in my *Symbols of Transformation*, oblige one to make, in regard to unconscious material, a distinction of quite a different character from that between "preconscious" and "unconscious" or "subconscious" and "unconscious." The justification for these distinctions need not be discussed here. They have their specific value and are worth elaborating further as points of view. The fundamental distinction which experience has forced upon me claims to be no more than that. It should be evident from the foregoing that we have to distinguish in the unconscious a layer which we may call the *personal unconscious*. The materials contained in this layer are of a personal nature in so far as they have the character partly of acquisitions derived

2 For a fuller elaboration of this theme see *Symbols of Transformation*, index, s.v. "wind."

from the individual's life and partly of psychological factors which could just as well be conscious. It can readily be understood that incompatible psychological elements are liable to repression and therefore become unconscious. But on the other hand this implies the possibility of making and keeping the repressed contents conscious once they have been recognized. We recognize them as personal contents because their effects, or their partial manifestation, or their source can be discovered in our personal past. They are the integral components of the personality, they belong to its inventory, and their loss to consciousness produces an inferiority in one respect or another—an inferiority, moreover, that has the psychological character not so much of an organic lesion or an inborn defect as of a lack which gives rise to a feeling of moral resentment. The sense of moral inferiority always indicates that the missing element is something which, to judge by this feeling about it, really ought not be missing, or which could be made conscious if only one took sufficient trouble. The moral inferiority does not come from a collision with the generally accepted and, in a sense, arbitrary moral law, but from the conflict with one's own self which, for reasons of psychic equilibrium, demands that the deficit be redressed. Whenever a sense of moral inferiority appears, it indicates not only a need to assimilate an unconscious component, but also the possibility of such assimilation. In the last resort it is a man's moral qualities which force him, either through direct recognition of the need or indirectly through a painful neurosis, to assimilate his unconscious self and to keep himself fully conscious. Whoever progresses along this road of self-realization must inevitably bring into consciousness the contents of the personal unconscious, thus enlarging the scope of his personality. I should add at once that this enlargement has to do primarily with one's moral consciousness, one's knowledge of oneself, for the unconscious contents that are released and brought into consciousness by analysis are usually unpleasant—which is precisely why these wishes, memories, tendencies, plans, etc. were repressed. These are the contents that are brought to light in much the same way by a thorough confession, though to a much more limited extent. The rest comes out as a rule in dream analysis. It is often very interesting to watch how the dreams fetch up the essential points, bit by bit and with the nicest choice.

The total material that is added to consciousness causes a considerable widening of the horizon, a deepened self-knowledge which, more than anything else, is calculated to humanize a man and make him modest. But even self-knowledge, assumed by all wise men to be the best and most efficacious, has different effects on different characters. We make very remarkable discoveries in this respect in practical analysis, but I shall deal with this question in the next chapter.

219   As my example of the archaic idea of God shows, the unconscious seems to contain other things besides personal acquisitions and belongings. My patient was quite unconscious of the derivation of "spirit" from "wind," or of the parallelism between the two. This content was not the product of her thinking, nor had she ever been taught it. The critical passage in the New Testament was inaccessible to her—τὸ πνεῦμα πνεῖ ὅπου θέλει —since she knew no Greek. It we must take it as a wholly personal acquisition, it might be a case of so-called cryptomnesia,[3] the unconscious recollection of a thought which the dreamer had once read somewhere. I have nothing against such a possibility in this particular case; but I have seen a sufficient number of other cases—many of them are to be found in the book mentioned above—where cryptomnesia can be excluded with certainty. Even if it were a case of cryptomnesia, which seems to me very improbable, we should still have to explain what the predisposition was that caused just this image to be retained and later, as Semon puts it, "ecphorated" (ἐκφορεῖν, Latin efferre, 'to produce'). In any case, cryptomnesia or no cryptomnesia, we are dealing with a genuine and thoroughly primitive god-image that grew up in the unconscious of a civilized person and produced a living effect—an effect which might well give the psychologist of religion food for reflection. There is nothing about this image that could be called personal: it is a wholly collective image, the ethnic origin of which has long been known to us. Here is an historical image of world-wide distribution that has come into existence again through a natural psychic function. This is not so very surprising, since my patient was born into the

3 Cf. Flournoy, Des Indes à la planète Mars: Étude sur un cas de somnambulisme avec glossolalie (trans. by D. B. Vermilye as From India to the Planet Mars), and Jung, "Psychology and Pathology of So-called Occult Phenomena," pars. 138ff.

world with a human brain which presumably still functions today much as it did of old. We are dealing with a reactivated *archetype*, as I have elsewhere called these primordial images.[4] These ancient images are restored to life by the primitive, analogical mode of thinking peculiar to dreams. It is not a question of inherited ideas, but of inherited thought-patterns.[5]

220   In view of these facts we must assume that the unconscious contains not only personal, but also impersonal collective components in the form of inherited categories[6] or archetypes. I have therefore advanced the hypothesis that at its deeper levels the unconscious possesses collective contents in a relatively active state. That is why I speak of a collective unconscious.

[4] Cf. *Psychological Types*, Def. 26.
[5] Consequently, the accusation of "fanciful mysticism" levelled at my ideas is lacking in foundation.
[6] Hubert and Mauss, *Mélanges d'histoire des religions*, p. xxix.

II

PHENOMENA RESULTING FROM
THE ASSIMILATION OF
THE UNCONSCIOUS

221   The process of assimilating the unconscious leads to some very remarkable phenomena. It produces in some patients an unmistakable and often unpleasant increase of self-confidence and conceit: they are full of themselves, they know everything, they imagine themselves to be fully informed of everything concerning their unconscious, and are persuaded that they understand perfectly everything that comes out of it. At every interview with the doctor they get more and more above themselves. Others on the contrary feel themselves more and more crushed under the contents of the unconscious, they lose their self-confidence and abandon themselves with dull resignation to all the extraordinary things that the unconscious produces. The former, overflowing with feelings of their own importance, assume a responsibility for the unconscious that goes much too far, beyond all reasonable bounds; the others finally give up all sense of responsibility, overcome by a sense of the powerlessness of the ego against the fate working through the unconscious.

222   If we analyse these two modes of reaction more deeply, we find that the optimistic self-confidence of the first conceals a profound sense of impotence, for which their conscious optimism acts as an unsuccessful compensation; while the pessimistic resignation of the others masks a defiant will to power, far surpassing in cocksureness the conscious optimism of the first type.

223   With these two modes of reaction I have sketched only two crude extremes. A finer shading would have been truer to reality. As I have said elsewhere, every analysand starts by unconsciously misusing his newly won knowledge in the interests of his abnormal, neurotic attitude, unless he is sufficiently freed from his symptoms in the early stages to be able to dispense with further treatment altogether. A very important contributory

factor is that in the early stages everything is still understood on the objective level, i.e., without distinction between imago and object, so that everything is referred directly to the object. Hence the man for whom "other people" are the objects of prime importance will conclude from any self-knowledge he may have imbibed at this stage of the analysis: "Aha! so that is what other people are like!" He will therefore feel it his duty, according to his nature, tolerant or otherwise, to enlighten the world. But the other man, who feels himself to be more the object of his fellows than their subject, will be weighed down by this self-knowledge and become correspondingly depressed. (I am naturally leaving out of account those numerous and more superficial natures who experience these problems only by the way.) In both cases the relation to the object is reinforced—in the first case in an active, in the second case in a reactive sense. The collective element is markedly accentuated. The one extends the sphere of his action, the other the sphere of his suffering.

224 Adler has employed the term "godlikeness" to characterize certain basic features of neurotic power psychology. If I likewise borrow the same term from *Faust*, I use it here more in the sense of that well-known passage where Mephisto writes "Eritis sicut Deus, scientes bonum et malum" in the student's album, and makes the following aside:

Just follow the old advice
And my cousin the snake.
There'll come a time when your godlikeness
Will make you quiver and quake.[1]

The godlikeness evidently refers to knowledge, the knowledge of good and evil. The analysis and conscious realization of unconscious contents engender a certain superior tolerance, thanks to which even relatively indigestible portions of one's unconscious characterology can be accepted. This tolerance may look very wise and superior, but often it is no more than a grand gesture that brings all sorts of consequences in its train. Two spheres have been brought together which before were kept anxiously apart. After considerable resistances have been overcome, the union of opposites is successfully achieved, at least to

1 *Faust*, Part I, 3rd scene in Faust's study.

all appearances. The deeper understanding thus gained, the juxtaposition of what was before separated, and hence the apparent overcoming of the moral conflict, give rise to a feeling of superiority that may well be expressed by the term "godlikeness." But this same juxtaposition of good and evil can have a very different effect on a different kind of temperament. Not everyone will feel himself a superman, holding in his hands the scales of good and evil. It may also seem as though he were a helpless object caught between hammer and anvil; not in the least a Hercules at the parting of the ways, but rather a rudderless ship buffeted between Scylla and Charybdis. For without knowing it, he is caught up in perhaps the greatest and most ancient of human conflicts, experiencing the throes of eternal principles in collision. Well might he feel himself like a Prometheus chained to the Caucasus, or as one crucified. This would be a "godlikeness" in suffering. Godlikeness is certainly not a scientific concept, although it aptly characterizes the psychological state in question. Nor do I imagine that every reader will immediately grasp the peculiar state of mind implied by "godlikeness." The term belongs too exclusively to the sphere of *belles-lettres*. So I should probably be better advised to give a more circumspect description of this state. The insight and understanding, then, gained by the analysand usually reveal much to him that was before unconscious. He naturally applies this knowledge to his environment; in consequence he sees, or thinks he sees, many things that before were invisible. Since his knowledge was helpful to him, he readily assumes that it would be useful also to others. In this way he is liable to become arrogant; it may be well meant, but it is nonetheless annoying to other people. He feels as though he possesses a key that opens many, perhaps even all, doors. Psychoanalysis itself has this same bland unconsciousness of its limitations, as can clearly be seen from the way it meddles with works of art.

Since human nature is not compounded wholly of light, but also abounds in shadows, the insight gained in practical analysis is often somewhat painful, the more so if, as is generally the case, one has previously neglected the other side. Hence there are people who take their newly won insight very much to heart, far too much in fact, quite forgetting that they are not unique in having a shadow-side. They allow themselves to get unduly de-

225

pressed and are then inclined to doubt everything, finding nothing right anywhere. That is why many excellent analysts with very good ideas can never bring themselves to publish them, because the psychic problem, as they see it, is so overwhelmingly vast that it seems to them almost impossible to tackle it scientifically. One man's optimism makes him overweening, while another's pessimism makes him over-anxious and despondent. Such are the forms which the great conflict takes when reduced to a smaller scale. But even in these lesser proportions the essence of the conflict is easily recognized: the arrogance of the one and the despondency of the other share a common uncertainty as to their boundaries. The one is excessively expanded, the other excessively contracted. Their individual boundaries are in some way obliterated. If we now consider the fact that, as a result of psychic compensation, great humility stands very close to pride, and that "pride goeth before a fall," we can easily discover behind the haughtiness certain traits of an anxious sense of inferiority. In fact we shall see clearly how his uncertainty forces the enthusiast to puff up his truths, of which he feels none too sure, and to win proselytes to his side in order that his followers may prove to himself the value and trustworthiness of his own convictions. Nor is he altogether so happy in his fund of knowledge as to be able to hold out alone; at bottom he feels isolated by it, and the secret fear of being left alone with it induces him to trot out his opinions and interpretations in and out of season, because only when convincing someone else does he feel safe from gnawing doubts.

226   It is just the reverse with our despondent friend. The more he withdraws and hides himself, the greater becomes his secret need to be understood and recognized. Although he speaks of his inferiority he does not really believe it. There arises within him a defiant conviction of his unrecognized merits, and in consequence he is sensitive to the slightest disapprobation, always wearing the stricken air of one who is misunderstood and deprived of his rightful due. In this way he nurses a morbid pride and an insolent discontent—which is the very last thing he wants and for which his environment has to pay all the more dearly.

227   Both are at once too small and too big; their individual mean, never very secure, now becomes shakier than ever. It

126

228   sounds almost grotesque to describe such a state as "godlike." But since each in his way steps beyond his human proportions, both of them are a little "superhuman" and therefore, figuratively speaking, godlike. If we wish to avoid the use of this metaphor, I would suggest that we speak instead of "psychic inflation." The term seems to me appropriate in so far as the state we are discussing involves an extension of the personality beyond individual limits, in other words, a state of being puffed up. In such a state a man fills a space which normally he cannot fill. He can only fill it by appropriating to himself contents and qualities which properly exist for themselves alone and should therefore remain outside our bounds. What lies outside ourselves belongs either to someone else, or to everyone, or to no one. Since psychic inflation is by no means a phenomenon induced exclusively by analysis, but occurs just as often in ordinary life, we can investigate it equally well in other cases. A very common instance is the humourless way in which many men identify themselves with their business or their titles. The office I hold is certainly my special activity; but it is also a collective factor that has come into existence historically through the cooperation of many people and whose dignity rests solely on collective approval. When, therefore, I identify myself with my office or title, I behave as though I myself were the whole complex of social factors of which that office consists, or as though I were not only the bearer of the office, but also and at the same time the approval of society. I have made an extraordinary extension of myself and have usurped qualities which are not in me but outside me. *L'état c'est moi* is the motto for such people.

In the case of inflation through knowledge we are dealing with something similar in principle, though psychologically more subtle. Here it is not the dignity of an office that causes the inflation, but very significant fantasies. I will explain what I mean by a practical example, choosing a mental case whom I happened to know personally and who is also mentioned in a publication by Maeder.[2] The case is characterized by a high degree of inflation. (In mental cases we can observe all the phenomena that are present only fleetingly in normal people, in a

2 Maeder, "Psychologische Untersuchungen an Dementia-Praecox-Kranken" (1910), pp. 209ff.

cruder and enlarged form.)³ The patient suffered from paranoid dementia with megalomania. He was in telephonic communication with the Mother of God and other great ones. In human reality he was a wretched locksmith's apprentice who at the age of nineteen had become incurably insane. He had never been blessed with intelligence, but he had, among other things, hit upon the magnificent idea that the world was his picture-book, the pages of which he could turn at will. The proof was quite simple: he had only to turn round, and there was a new page for him to see.

229   This is Schopenhauer's "world as will and idea" in unadorned, primitive concreteness of vision. A shattering idea indeed, born of extreme alienation and seclusion from the world, but so naïvely and simply expressed that at first one can only smile at the grotesqueness of it. And yet this primitive way of looking lies at the very heart of Schopenhauer's brilliant vision of the world. Only a genius or a madman could so disentangle himself from the bonds of reality as to see the world as his picture-book. Did the patient actually work out or build up such a vision, or did it just befall him? Or did he perhaps fall into it? His pathological disintegration and inflation point rather to the latter. It is no longer *he* that thinks and speaks, but *it* thinks and speaks within him: he hears voices. So the difference between him and Schopenhauer is that, in him, the vision remained at the stage of a mere spontaneous growth, while Schopenhauer abstracted it and expressed it in language of universal validity. In so doing he raised it out of its subterranean beginnings into the clear light of collective consciousness. But it would be quite wrong to suppose that the patient's vision had a purely personal character or value, as though it were something that belonged to him. If that were so, he would be a philosopher. A man is a philosopher of genius only when he succeeds in transmuting the primitive and merely natural vision into an abstract idea be-

³ When I was still a doctor at the psychiatric clinic in Zurich, I once took an intelligent layman through the sick-wards. He had never seen a lunatic asylum from the inside before. When we had finished our round, he exclaimed, "I tell you, it's just like Zurich in miniature! A quintessence of the population. It is as though all the types one meets every day on the streets had been assembled here in their classical purity. Nothing but oddities and picked specimens from top to bottom of society!" I had never looked at it from this angle before, but my friend was not far wrong.

longing to the common stock of consciousness. This achievement, and this alone, constitutes his personal value, for which he may take credit without necessarily succumbing to inflation. But the sick man's vision is an impersonal value, a natural growth against which he is powerless to defend himself, by which he is actually swallowed up and "wafted" clean out of the world. Far from *his* mastering the idea and expanding *it* into a philosophical view of the world, it is truer to say that the undoubted grandeur of his vision blew *him* up to pathological proportions. The personal value lies entirely in the philosophical achievement, not in the primary vision. To the philosopher as well this vision comes as so much increment, and is simply a part of the common property of mankind, in which, in principle, everyone has a share. The golden apples drop from the same tree, whether they be gathered by an imbecile locksmith's apprentice or by a Schopenhauer.

230   There is, however, yet another thing to be learnt from this example, namely, that these transpersonal contents are not just inert or dead matter that can be annexed at will. Rather they are living entities which exert an attractive force upon the conscious mind. Identification with one's office or one's title is very attractive indeed, which is precisely why so many men are nothing more than the decorum accorded to them by society. In vain would one look for a personality behind the husk. Underneath all the padding one would find a very pitiable little creature. That is why the office—or whatever this outer husk may be—is so attractive: it offers easy compensation for personal deficiencies.

231   Outer attractions, such as offices, titles, and other social regalia are not the only things that cause inflation. These are simply impersonal quantities that lie outside in society, in the collective consciousness. But just as there is a society outside the individual, so there is a collective psyche outside the personal psyche, namely the collective unconscious, concealing, as the above example shows, elements that are no whit less attractive. And just as a man may suddenly step into the world on his professional dignity ("Messieurs, à présent je suis Roy"), so another may disappear out of it equally suddenly when it is his lot to behold one of those mighty images that put a new face upon the world. These are the magical *représentations collectives* which underlie the slogan, the catchword, and, on a higher level, the lan-

guage of the poet and mystic. I am reminded of another mental case who was neither a poet nor anything very outstanding, just a naturally quiet and rather sentimental youth. He had fallen in love with a girl and, as so often happens, had failed to ascertain whether his love was requited. His primitive *participation mystique* took it for granted that his agitations were plainly the agitations of the other, which on the lower levels of human psychology is naturally very often the case. Thus he built up a sentimental love-fantasy which precipitately collapsed when he discovered that the girl would have none of him. He was so desperate that he went straight to the river to drown himself. It was late at night, and the stars gleamed up at him from the dark water. It seemed to him that the stars were swimming two by two down the river, and a wonderful feeling came over him. He forgot his suicidal intentions and gazed fascinated at the strange, sweet drama. And gradually he became aware that every star was a face, and that all these pairs were lovers, who were carried along locked in a dreaming embrace. An entirely new understanding came to him: all had changed—his fate, his disappointment, even his love, receded and fell away. The memory of the girl grew distant, blurred; but instead, he felt with complete certainty that untold riches were promised him. He knew that an immense treasure lay hidden for him in the neighbouring observatory. The result was that he was arrested by the police at four o'clock in the morning, attempting to break into the observatory.

What had happened? His poor head had glimpsed a Dantesque vision, whose loveliness he could never have grasped had he read it in a poem. But he saw it, and it transformed him. What had hurt him most was now far away; a new and undreamed-of world of stars, tracing their silent courses far beyond this grievous earth, had opened out to him the moment he crossed "Proserpine's threshold." The intuition of untold wealth—and could any fail to be touched by this thought?—came to him like a revelation. For his poor turnip-head it was too much. He did not drown in the river, but in an eternal image, and its beauty perished with him.

Just as one man may disappear in his social role, so another may be engulfed in an inner vision and be lost to his surroundings. Many fathomless transformations of personality, like sudden conversions and other far-reaching changes of mind, originate in the attractive power of a collective image,[4] which, as the present example shows, can cause such a high degree of inflation that the entire personality is disintegrated. This disintegration is a mental disease, of a transitory or a permanent nature, a "splitting of the mind" or "schizophrenia," in Bleuler's term.[5] The pathological inflation naturally depends on some innate weakness of the personality against the autonomy of collective unconscious contents.

234   We shall probably get nearest to the truth if we think of the conscious and personal psyche as resting upon the broad basis of an inherited and universal psychic disposition which is as such unconscious, and that our personal psyche bears the same relation to the collective psyche as the individual to society.

235   But equally, just as the individual is not merely a unique and separate being, but is also a social being, so the human psyche is not a self-contained and wholly individual phenomenon, but also a collective one. And just as certain social functions or instincts are opposed to the interests of single individuals, so the human psyche exhibits certain functions or tendencies which, on account of their collective nature, are opposed to individual needs. The reason for this is that every man is born with a highly differentiated brain and is thus assured of a wide range of mental functioning which is neither developed ontogenetically nor acquired. But, to the degree that human brains are uniformly differentiated, the mental functioning thereby made possible is also collective and universal. This explains, for example, the interesting fact that the unconscious processes of the most widely separated peoples and races show a quite remarkable correspondence, which displays itself, among other things, in the extraordinary but well-authenticated analogies between the forms and motifs of autochthonous myths. The universal similarity of human brains leads to the universal possibility of a uniform mental functioning. This functioning is the *collective psyche*. Inasmuch as there are differentiations corresponding to race, tribe, and even family, there is also a collective psyche lim-

4 Cf. *Psychological Types*, Def. 26, "Image." Léon Daudet, in *L'Hérédo*, calls this process "autofécondation intérieure," by which he means the reawakening of an ancestral soul.

5 Bleuler, *Dementia Praecox or the Group of Schizophrenias* (orig. 1911).

236

ited to race, tribe, and family over and above the "universal" collective psyche. To borrow an expression from Pierre Janet,[6] the collective psyche comprises the *parties inférieures* of the psychic functions, that is to say those deep-rooted, well-nigh automatic portions of the individual psyche which are inherited and are to be found everywhere, and are thus impersonal or suprapersonal. Consciousness plus the personal unconscious constitutes the *parties supérieures* of the psychic functions, those portions, therefore, that are developed ontogenetically and acquired. Consequently, the individual who annexes the unconscious heritage of the collective psyche to what has accrued to him in the course of his ontogenetic development, as though it were part of the latter, enlarges the scope of his personality in an illegitimate way and suffers the consequences. In so far as the collective psyche comprises the *parties inférieures* of the psychic functions and thus forms the basis of every personality, it has the effect of crushing and devaluing the personality. This shows itself either in the aforementioned stifling of self-confidence or else in an unconscious heightening of the ego's importance to the point of a pathological will to power.

By raising the personal unconscious to consciousness, the analysis makes the subject aware of things which he is generally aware of in others, but never in himself. This discovery makes him therefore less individually unique, and more collective. His collectivization is not always a step to the bad; it may sometimes be a step to the good. There are people who repress their good qualities and consciously give free rein to their infantile desires. The lifting of personal repressions at first brings purely personal contents into consciousness; but attached to them are the collective elements of the unconscious, the ever-present instincts, qualities, and ideas (images) as well as all those "statistical" quotas of average virtue and average vice which we recognize when we say, "Everyone has in him something of the criminal, the genius, and the saint." Thus a living picture emerges, containing pretty well everything that moves upon the checkerboard of the world, the good and the bad, the fair and the foul. A sense of solidarity with the world is gradually built up, which is felt by many natures as something very positive and in certain cases actually is the deciding factor in the treatment of neurosis.

6 *Les Névroses* (1898).

I have myself seen cases who, in this condition, managed for the first time in their lives to arouse love, and even to experience it themselves; or, by daring to leap into the unknown, they get involved in the very fate for which they were suited. I have seen not a few who, taking this condition as final, remained for years in a state of enterprising euphoria. I have often heard such cases referred to as shining examples of analytical therapy. But I must point out that cases of this euphoric and enterprising type are so utterly lacking in differentiation from the world that nobody could pass them as fundamentally cured. To my way of thinking they are as much cured as not cured. I have had occasion to follow up the lives of such patients, and it must be owned that many of them showed symptoms of maladjustment, which, if persisted in, gradually leads to the sterility and monotony so characteristic of those who have divested themselves of their egos. Here too I am speaking of the border-line cases, and not of the less valuable, normal, average folk for whom the question of adaptation is more technical than problematical. If I were more of a therapist than an investigator, I would naturally be unable to check a certain optimism of judgment, because my eyes would then be glued to the number of cures. But my conscience as an investigator is concerned not with quantity but with quality. Nature is aristocratic, and one person of value outweighs ten lesser ones. My eye followed the valuable people, and from them I learned the dubiousness of the results of a purely personal analysis, and also to understand the reasons for this dubiousness.

237   If, through assimilation of the unconscious, we make the mistake of including the collective psyche in the inventory of personal psychic functions, a dissolution of the personality into its paired opposites inevitably follows. Besides the pair of opposites already discussed, megalomania and the sense of inferiority, which are so painfully evident in neurosis, there are many others, from which I will single out only the specifically moral pair of opposites, namely good and evil. The specific virtues and vices of humanity are contained in the collective psyche like everything else. One man arrogates collective virtue to himself as his personal merit, another takes collective vice as his personal guilt. Both are as illusory as the megalomania and the inferiority, because the imaginary virtues and the imaginary wickednesses are simply the moral pair of opposites contained in the

collective psyche, which have become perceptible or have been rendered conscious artificially. How much these paired opposites are contained in the collective psyche is exemplified by primitives: one observer will extol the greatest virtues in them, while another will record the very worst impressions of the self-same tribe. For the primitive, whose personal differentiation is, as we know, only just beginning, both judgments are true, because his psyche is essentially collective and therefore for the most part unconscious. He is still more or less identical with the collective psyche, and for that reason shares equally in the collective virtues and vices, without any personal attribution and without inner contradiction. The contradiction arises only when the personal development of the psyche begins, and when reason discovers the irreconcilable nature of the opposites. The consequence of this discovery is the conflict of repression. We want to be good, and therefore must repress evil; and with that the paradise of the collective psyche comes to an end. Repression of the collective psyche was absolutely necessary for the development of personality. In primitives, development of personality, or more accurately, development of the person, is a question of magical prestige. The figure of the medicine-man or chief leads the way: both make themselves conspicuous by the singularity of their ornaments and their mode of life, expressive of their social roles. The singularity of his outward tokens marks the individual off from the rest, and the segregation is still further enhanced by the possession of special ritual secrets. By these and similar means the primitive creates around him a shell, which might be called a persona (mask). Masks, as we know, are actually used among primitives in totem ceremonies—for instance, as a means of enhancing or changing the personality. In this way the outstanding individual is apparently removed from the sphere of the collective psyche, and to the degree that he succeeds in identifying himself with his persona, he actually is removed. This removal means magical prestige. One could easily assert that the impelling motive in this development is the will to power. But that would be to forget that the building up of prestige is always a product of collective compromise: not only must there be one who wants prestige, there must also be a public seeking somebody on whom to confer prestige. That being so, it would be incorrect to say that a man creates prestige for him-

134

238 self out of his individual will to power; it is on the contrary an entirely collective affair. Since society as a whole needs the magically effective figure, it uses this need of the will to power in the individual, and the will to submit in the mass, as a vehicle, and thus brings about the creation of personal prestige. The latter is a phenomenon which, as the history of political institutions shows, is of the utmost importance for the comity of nations.

The importance of personal prestige can hardly be overestimated, because the possibility of regressive dissolution in the collective psyche is a very real danger, not only for the outstanding individual but also for his followers. This possibility is most likely to occur when the goal of prestige—universal recognition—has been reached. The person then becomes a collective truth, and that is always the beginning of the end. To gain prestige is a positive achievement not only for the outstanding individual but also for the clan. The individual distinguishes himself by his deeds, the many by their renunciation of power. So long as this attitude needs to be fought for and defended against hostile influences, the achievement remains positive; but as soon as there are no more obstacles and universal recognition has been attained, prestige loses its positive value and usually becomes a dead letter. A schismatic movement then sets in, and the whole process begins again from the beginning.

239 Because personality is of such paramount importance for the life of the community, everything likely to disturb its development is sensed as a danger. But the greatest danger of all is the premature dissolution of prestige by an invasion of the collective psyche. Absolute secrecy is one of the best known primitive means of exorcising this danger. Collective thinking and feeling and collective effort are far less of a strain than individual functioning and effort; hence there is always a great temptation to allow collective functioning to take the place of individual differentiation of the personality. Once the personality has been differentiated and safeguarded by magical prestige, its levelling down and eventual dissolution in the collective psyche (e.g., Peter's denial) occasion a "loss of soul" in the individual, because an important personal achievement has been either neglected or allowed to slip into regression. For this reason taboo infringements are followed by Draconian punishments altogether in keeping with the seriousness of the situation. So long as we re-

gard these things from the causal point of view, as mere historical survivals and metastases of the incest taboo,[7] it is impossible
to understand what all these measures are for. If, however, we
approach the problem from the teleological point of view, much
that was quite inexplicable becomes clear.

240   For the development of personality, then, strict differentiation from the collective psyche is absolutely necessary, since partial or blurred differentiation leads to an immediate melting
away of the individual in the collective. There is now a danger
that in the analysis of the unconscious the collective and the personal psyche may be fused together, with, as I have intimated,
highly unfortunate results. These results are injurious both to
the patient's life-feeling and to his fellow men, if he has any influence at all on his environment. Through his identification
with the collective psyche he will infallibly try to force the demands of his unconscious upon others, for identity with the collective psyche always brings with it a feeling of universal validity—"godlikeness"—which completely ignores all differences in
the personal psyche of his fellows. (The feeling of universal validity comes, of course, from the universality of the collective
psyche.) A collective attitude naturally presupposes this same
collective psyche in others. But that means a ruthless disregard
not only of individual differences but also of differences of a
more general kind within the collective psyche itself, as for example differences of race.[8] This disregard for individuality obviously means the suffocation of the single individual, as a consequence of which the element of differentiation is obliterated
from the community. The element of differentiation is the individual. All the highest achievements of virtue, as well as the

7 Freud, *Totem and Taboo.*

8 Thus it is a quite unpardonable mistake to accept the conclusions of a Jewish
psychology as generally valid. Nobody would dream of taking Chinese or Indian
psychology as binding upon ourselves. The cheap accusation of anti-Semitism
that has been levelled at me on the ground of this criticism is about as intelligent
as accusing me of an anti-Chinese prejudice. No doubt, on an earlier and deeper
level of psychic development, where it is still impossible to distinguish between
an Aryan, Semitic, Hamitic, or Mongolian mentality, all human races have a
common collective psyche. But with the beginning of racial differentiation
essential differences are developed in the collective psyche as well. For this reason
we cannot transplant the spirit of a foreign race *in globo* into our own mentality
without sensible injury to the latter, a fact which does not, however, deter sun-
dry natures of feeble instinct from affecting Indian philosophy and the like.

136

blackest villainies, are individual. The larger a community is, and the more the sum total of collective factors peculiar to every large community rests on conservative prejudices detrimental to individuality, the more will the individual be morally and spiritually crushed, and, as a result, the one source of moral and spiritual progress for society is choked up. Naturally the only thing that can thrive in such an atmosphere is sociality and whatever is collective in the individual. Everything individual in him goes under, i.e., is doomed to repression. The individual elements lapse into the unconscious, where, by the law of necessity, they are transformed into something essentially baleful, destructive, and anarchical. Socially, this civil principle shows itself in the spectacular crimes—regicide and the like—perpetrated by certain prophetically-inclined individuals; but in the great mass of the community it remains in the background, and only manifests itself indirectly in the inexorable moral degeneration of society. It is a notorious fact that the morality of society as a whole is in inverse ratio to its size; for the greater the aggregation of individuals, the more the individual factors are blotted out, and with them morality, which rests entirely on the moral sense of the individual and the freedom necessary for this. Hence every man is, in a certain sense, unconsciously a worse man when he is in society than when acting alone; for he is carried by society and to that extent relieved of his individual responsibility. Any large company composed of wholly admirable persons has the morality and intelligence of an unwieldy, stupid, and violent animal. The bigger the organization, the more unavoidable is its immorality and blind stupidity (*Senatus bestia, senatores boni viri*). Society, by automatically stressing all the collective qualities in its individual representatives, puts a premium on mediocrity, on everything that settles down to vegetate in an easy, irresponsible way. Individuality will inevitably be driven to the wall. This process begins in school, continues at the university, and rules all departments in which the State has a hand. In a small social body, the individuality of its members is better safeguarded, and the greater is their relative freedom and the possibility of conscious responsibility. Without freedom there can be no morality. Our admiration for great organizations dwindles when once we become aware of the other side of the wonder: the tremendous piling up and accentuation of all that is primitive

137

241 in man, and the unavoidable destruction of his individuality in the interests of the monstrosity that every great organization in fact is. The man of today, who resembles more or less the collective ideal, has made his heart into a den of murderers, as can easily be proved by the analysis of his unconscious, even though he himself is not in the least disturbed by it. And in so far as he is normally "adapted" [9] to his environment, it is true that the greatest infamy on the part of his group will not disturb him, so long as the majority of his fellows steadfastly believe in the exalted morality of their social organization. Now, all that I have said here about the influence of society upon the individual is identically true of the influence of the collective unconscious upon the individual psyche. But, as is apparent from my examples, the latter influence is as invisible as the former is visible. Hence it is not surprising that its inner effects are not understood, and that those to whom such things happen are called pathological freaks and treated as crazy. If one of them happened to be a real genius, the fact would not be noted until the next generation or the one after. So obvious does it seem to us that a man should drown in his own dignity, so utterly incomprehensible that he should seek anything other than what the mob wants, and that he should vanish permanently from view in this other. One could wish both of them a sense of humour, that —according to Schopenhauer—truly "divine" attribute of man which alone befits him to maintain his soul in freedom.

The collective instincts and fundamental forms of thinking and feeling whose activity is revealed by the analysis of the unconscious constitute, for the conscious personality, an acquisition which it cannot assimilate without considerable disturbance. It is therefore of the utmost importance in practical treatment to keep the integrity of the personality constantly in mind. For, if the collective psyche is taken to be the personal possession of the individual, it will result in a distortion or an overloading of the personality which is very difficult to deal with. Hence it is imperative to make a clear distinction between personal contents and those of the collective psyche. This distinction is far from easy, because the personal grows out of the collective psyche and is intimately bound up with it. So it is difficult to say exactly what contents are to be called personal and what collective.

9 Cf. "adjustment" and "adaptation" in *Psychological Types*, par. 564.

There is no doubt, for instance, that archaic symbolisms such as we frequently find in fantasies and dreams are collective factors. All basic instincts and basic forms of thinking and feeling are collective. Everything that all men agree in regarding as universal is collective, likewise everything that is universally understood, universally found, universally said and done. On closer examination one is always astonished to see how much of our so-called individual psychology is really collective. So much, indeed, that the individual traits are completely overshadowed by it. Since, however, individuation[10] is an ineluctable psychological necessity, we can see from the ascendancy of the collective what very special attention must be paid to this delicate plant "individuality" if it is not to be completely smothered.

242   Human beings have one faculty which, though it is of the greatest utility for collective purposes, is most pernicious for individuation, and that is the faculty of imitation. Collective psychology cannot dispense with imitation, for without it all mass organizations, the State and the social order, are impossible. Society is organized, indeed, less by law than by the propensity to imitation, implying equally suggestibility, suggestion, and mental contagion. But we see every day how people use, or rather abuse, the mechanism of imitation for the purpose of personal differentiation: they are content to ape some eminent personality, some striking characteristic or mode of behaviour, thereby achieving an outward distinction from the circle in which they move. We could almost say that as a punishment for this the uniformity of their minds with those of their neighbours, already real enough, is intensified into an unconscious, compulsive bondage to the environment. As a rule these specious attempts at individual differentiation stiffen into a pose, and the imitator remains at the same level as he always was, only several degrees more sterile than before. To find out what is truly individual in ourselves, profound reflection is needed; and suddenly we realize how uncommonly difficult the discovery of individuality is.

10 Ibid., Def. 29: "Individuation is a process of differentiation, having for its goal the development of the individual personality."—"As the individual is not just a single, separate being, but by his very existence presupposes a collective relationship, it follows that the process of individuation must lead to more intense and broader collective relationships and not to isolation."

246 When we analyse the persona we strip off the mask, and discover that what seemed to be individual is at bottom collective; in other words, that the persona was only a mask of the collective psyche. Fundamentally the persona is nothing real: it is a compromise between individual and society as to what a man should appear to be. He takes a name, earns a title, exercises a function, he is this or that. In a certain sense all this is real, yet in relation to the essential individuality of the person concerned it is only a secondary reality, a compromise formation, in making which others often have a greater share than he. The persona is a semblance, a two-dimensional reality, to give it a nickname.

247 It would be wrong to leave the matter as it stands without at the same time recognizing that there is, after all, something individual in the peculiar choice and delineation of the persona, and that despite the exclusive identity of the ego-consciousness with the persona the unconscious self, one's real individuality, is always present and makes itself felt indirectly if not directly. Although the ego-consciousness is at first identical with the persona—that compromise role in which we parade before the community—yet the unconscious self can never be repressed to the point of extinction. Its influence is chiefly manifest in the special nature of the contrasting and compensating contents of the unconscious. The purely personal attitude of the conscious mind evokes reactions on the part of the unconscious, and these, together with personal repressions, contain the seeds of individual development in the guise of collective fantasies. Through the analysis of the personal unconscious, the conscious mind becomes suffused with collective material which brings with it the elements of individuality. I am well aware that this conclusion must be almost unintelligible to anyone not familiar with my views and technique, and particularly so to those who habitually regard the unconscious from the standpoint of Freudian theory. But if the reader will recall my example of the philosophy student, he can form a rough idea of what I mean. At the beginning of the treatment the patient was quite unconscious of the fact that her relation to her father was a fixation, and that she was therefore seeking a man like her father, whom she could then meet with her intellect. This in itself would not have been a mistake if her intellect had not had that peculiarly protesting

character such as is unfortunately often encountered in intellectual women. Such an intellect is always trying to point out mistakes in others; it is pre-eminently critical, with a dis-agreeably personal undertone, yet it always wants to be considered objective. This invariably makes a man bad-tempered, particularly if, as so often happens, the criticism touches on some weak spot which, in the interests of fruitful discussion, were better avoided. But far from wishing the discussion to be fruitful, it is the unfortunate peculiarity of this feminine intellect to seek out a man's weak spots, fasten on them, and exasperate him. This is not usually a conscious aim, but rather has the unconscious purpose of forcing a man into a superior position and thus making him an object of admiration. The man does not as a rule notice that he is having the role of the hero thrust upon him; he merely finds her taunts so odious that in future he will go a long way to avoid meeting the lady. In the end the only man who can stand her is the one who gives in at the start, and therefore has nothing wonderful about him.

248   My patient naturally found much to reflect upon in all this, for she had no notion of the game she was playing. Moreover she still had to gain insight into the regular romance that had been enacted between her and her father ever since childhood. It would lead us too far to describe in detail how, from her earliest years, with unconscious sympathy, she had played upon the shadow-side of her father which her mother never saw, and how, far in advance of her years, she became her mother's rival. All this came to light in the analysis of the personal unconscious. Since, if only for professional reasons, I could not allow myself to be irritated, I inevitably became the hero and father-lover. The transference too consisted at first of contents from the personal unconscious. My role as a hero was just a sham, and so, as it turned me into the merest phantom, she was able to play her traditional role of the supremely wise, very grown-up, all-understanding mother-daughter-beloved—an empty role, a persona behind which her real and authentic being, her individual self, lay hidden. Indeed, to the extent that she at first completely identified herself with her role, she was altogether unconscious of her real self. She was still in her nebulous infantile world and had not yet discovered the real world at all. But as, through pro-gressive analysis, she became conscious of the nature of her

249   transference, the dreams I spoke of in Chapter I began to mate-
rialize. They brought up bits of the collective unconscious, and
that was the end of her infantile world and of all the heroics. She
came to herself and to her own real potentialities. This is
roughly the way things go in most cases, if the analysis is carried
far enough. That the consciousness of her individuality should
coincide exactly with the reactivation of an archaic god-image is
not just an isolated coincidence, but a very frequent occurrence
which, in my view, corresponds to an unconscious law.

After this digression, let us turn back to our earlier reflections.

250   Once the personal repressions are lifted, the individuality
and the collective psyche begin to emerge in a coalescent state,
thus releasing the hitherto repressed personal fantasies. The fantasies and dreams which now appear assume a somewhat different aspect. An infallible sign of collective images seems to be the
appearance of the "cosmic" element, i.e., the images in the
dream or fantasy are connected with cosmic qualities, such as
temporal and spatial infinity, enormous speed and extension of
movement, "astrological" associations, telluric, lunar, and solar
analogies, changes in the proportions of the body, etc. The obvious occurrence of mythological and religious motifs in a dream
also points to the activity of the collective unconscious. The collective element is very often announced by peculiar symptoms,[2]
as for example by dreams where the dreamer is flying through
space like a comet, or feels that he is the earth, or the sun, or a
star; or else is of immense size, or dwarfishly small; or that he is
dead, is in a strange place, is a stranger to himself, confused,
mad, etc. Similarly, feelings of disorientation, of dizziness and
the like, may appear along with symptoms of inflation.

251   The forces that burst out of the collective psyche have a confusing and blinding effect. One result of the dissolution of the
persona is a release of involuntary fantasy, which is apparently
nothing else than the specific activity of the collective psyche.
This activity throws up contents whose existence one had never
suspected before. But as the influence of the collective uncon-

2 It may not be superfluous to note that collective elements in dreams are not
restricted to this stage of the analytical treatment. There are many psychological
situations in which the activity of the collective unconscious can come to the
surface. But this is not the place to enlarge upon these conditions.

144

scious increases, so the conscious mind loses its power of leadership. Imperceptibly it becomes the led, while an unconscious and impersonal process gradually takes control. Thus, without noticing it, the conscious personality is pushed about like a figure on a chess-board by an invisible player. It is this player who decides the game of fate, not the conscious mind and its plans. This is how the resolution of the transference, apparently so impossible to the conscious mind, was brought about in my earlier example.

252   The plunge into this process becomes unavoidable whenever the necessity arises of overcoming an apparently insuperable difficulty. It goes without saying that this necessity does not occur in every case of neurosis, since perhaps in the majority the prime consideration is only the removal of temporary difficulties of adaptation. Certainly severe cases cannot be cured without a far-reaching change of character or of attitude. In by far the greater number, adaptation to external reality demands so much work that inner adaptation to the collective unconscious cannot be considered for a very long time. But when this inner adaptation becomes a problem, a strange, irresistible attraction proceeds from the unconscious and exerts a powerful influence on the conscious direction of life. The predominance of unconscious influences, together with the associated disintegration of the persona and the deposition of the conscious mind from power, constitute a state of psychic disequilibrium which, in analytical treatment, is artificially induced for the therapeutic purpose of resolving a difficulty that might block further development. There are of course innumerable obstacles that can be overcome with good advice and a little moral support, aided by goodwill and understanding on the part of the patient. Excellent curative results can be obtained in this way. Cases are not uncommon where there is no need to breathe a word about the unconscious. But again, there are difficulties for which one can foresee no satisfactory solution. If in these cases the psychic equilibrium is not already disturbed before treatment begins, it will certainly be upset during the analysis, and sometimes without any interference by the doctor. It often seems as though these patients had only been waiting to find a trustworthy person in order to give up and collapse. Such a loss of balance is similar in principle to a psychotic disturbance; that is, it differs from the

initial stages of mental illness only by the fact that it leads in the end to greater health, while the latter leads to yet greater destruction. It is a condition of panic, a letting go in face of apparently hopeless complications. Mostly it was preceded by desperate efforts to master the difficulty by force of will; then came the collapse, and the once guiding will crumbles completely. The energy thus freed disappears from consciousness and falls into the unconscious. As a matter of fact, it is at these moments that the first signs of unconscious activity appear. (I am thinking of the example of that young man who was weak in the head.) Obviously the energy that fell away from consciousness has activated the unconscious. The immediate result is a change of attitude. One can easily imagine that a stronger head would have taken that vision of the stars as a healing apparition, and would have looked upon human suffering *sub specie aeternitatis*, in which case his senses would have been restored.[3]

253   Had this happened, an apparently insurmountable obstacle would have been removed. Hence I regard the loss of balance as purposive, since it replaces a defective consciousness by the automatic and instinctive activity of the unconscious, which is aiming all the time at the creation of a new balance and will moreover achieve this aim, provided that the conscious mind is capable of assimilating the contents produced by the unconscious, i.e., of understanding and digesting them. If the unconscious simply rides roughshod over the conscious mind, a psychotic condition develops. If it can neither completely prevail nor yet be understood, the result is a conflict that cripples all further advance. But with this question, namely the understanding of the collective unconscious, we come to a formidable difficulty which I have made the theme of my next chapter.

3 Cf. Flournoy, "Automatisme téléologique antisuicide: un cas de suicide empêché par une hallucination" (1907), 113–37; and Jung, "The Psychology of Dementia Praecox," pars. 304ff.

PART TWO

INDIVIDUATION

I

THE FUNCTION OF THE UNCONSCIOUS

266   There is a destination, a possible goal, beyond the alternative stages dealt with in our last chapter. That is the way of individuation. Individuation means becoming an "in-dividual," and, in so far as "individuality" embraces our innermost, last, and incomparable uniqueness, it also implies becoming one's own self. We could therefore translate individuation as "coming to selfhood" or "self-realization."

267   The possibilities of development discussed in the preceding chapters were, at bottom, alienations of the self, ways of divesting the self of its reality in favour of an external role or in favour of an imagined meaning. In the former case the self retires into the background and gives place to social recognition; in the latter, to the auto-suggestive meaning of a primordial image. In both cases the collective has the upper hand. Self-alienation in favour of the collective corresponds to a social ideal; it even passes for social duty and virtue, although it can also be misused for egotistical purposes. Egoists are called "selfish," but this, naturally, has nothing to do with the concept of "self" as I am using it here. On the other hand, self-realization seems to stand in opposition to self-alienation. This misunderstanding is quite general, because we do not sufficiently distinguish between individualism and individuation. Individualism means deliberately stressing and giving prominence to some supposed peculiarity rather than to collective considerations and obligations. But individuation means precisely the better and more complete ful-

filament of the collective qualities of the human being, since adequate consideration of the peculiarity of the individual is more conducive to a better social performance than when the peculiarity is neglected or suppressed. The idiosyncrasy of an individual is not to be understood as any strangeness in his substance or in his components, but rather as a unique combination, or gradual differentiation, of functions and faculties which in themselves are universal. Every human face has a nose, two eyes, etc., but these universal factors are variable, and it is this variability which makes individual peculiarities possible. Individuation, therefore, can only mean a process of psychological development that fulfils the individual qualities given; in other words, it is a process by which a man becomes the definite, unique being he in fact is. In so doing he does not become "selfish" in the ordinary sense of the word, but is merely fulfilling the peculiarity of his nature, and this, as we have said, is vastly different from egotism or individualism.

268   Now in so far as the human individual, as a living unit, is composed of purely universal factors, he is wholly collective and therefore in no sense opposed to collectivity. Hence the individualistic emphasis on one's own peculiarity is a contradiction of this basic fact of the living being. Individuation, on the other hand, aims at a living co-operation of all factors. But since the universal factors always appear only in individual form, a full consideration of them will also produce an individual effect, and one which cannot be surpassed by anything else, least of all by individualism.

269   The aim of individuation is nothing less than to divest the self of the false wrappings of the persona on the one hand, and of the suggestive power of primordial images on the other. From what has been said in the previous chapters it should be sufficiently clear what the persona means psychologically. But when we turn to the other side, namely to the influence of the collective unconscious, we find we are moving in a dark interior world that is vastly more difficult to understand than the psychology of the persona, which is accessible to everyone. Everyone knows what is meant by "putting on official airs" or "playing a social role." Through the persona a man tries to appear as this or that, or he hides behind a mask, or he may even build up a definite persona as a barricade. So the problem of the persona should

148

present no great intellectual difficulties.

270 It is, however, another thing to describe, in a way that can be generally understood, those subtle inner processes which invade the conscious mind with such suggestive force. Perhaps we can best portray these influences with the help of examples of mental illness, creative inspiration, and religious conversion. A most excellent account—taken from life, so to speak—of such an inner transformation is to be found in H. G. Wells' *Christina Alberta's Father*.[a] Changes of a similar kind are described in Léon Daudet's eminently readable *L'Hérédo*. A wide range of material is contained in William James' *Varieties of Religious Experience*. Although in many cases of this kind there are certain external factors which either directly condition the change, or at least provide the occasion for it, yet it is not always the case that the external factor offers a sufficient explanation of these changes of personality. We must recognize the fact that they can also arise from subjective inner causes, opinions, convictions, where external stimuli play no part at all, or a very insignificant one. In pathological changes of personality this can even be said to be the rule. The cases of psychosis that present a clear and simple reaction to some overwhelming outside event belong to the exceptions. Hence, for psychiatry, the essential aetiological factor is the inherited or acquired pathological disposition. The same is probably true of most creative intuitions, for we are hardly likely to suppose a purely causal connection between the falling apple and Newton's theory of gravitation. Similarly all religious conversions that cannot be traced back directly to suggestion and contagious example rest upon independent interior processes culminating in a change of personality. As a rule these processes have the peculiarity of being subliminal, i.e., uncorscious, in the first place and of reaching consciousness only gradually. The moment of irruption can, however, be very sudden, so that consciousness is instantaneously flooded with extremely strange and apparently quite unsuspected contents. That is how it looks to the layman and even to the person concerned, but the experienced observer knows that psychological events are never sudden. In reality the irruption has been preparing for many years, often for half a lifetime, and already in childhood all sorts

[a] [Concerning the origin of this novel in a conversation between Wells and Jung, cf. Bennet, *What Jung Really Said*, p. 93.—EDITORS.]

of remarkable signs could have been detected which, in more or less symbolic fashion, hinted at abnormal future developments. I am reminded, for instance, of a mental case who refused all nourishment and created quite extraordinary difficulties in connection with nasal feeding. In fact an anaesthetic was necessary before the tube could be inserted. The patient was able in some remarkable way to swallow his tongue by pressing it back into the throat, a fact that was quite new and unknown to me at the time. In a lucid interval I obtained the following history from the man. As a boy he had often revolved in his mind the idea of how he could take his life, even if every conceivable measure were employed to prevent him. He first tried to do it by holding his breath, until he found that by the time he was in a semiconscious state he had already begun to breathe again. So he gave up these attempts and thought: perhaps it would work if he refused food. This fantasy satisfied him until he discovered that food could be poured into him through the nasal cavity. He therefore considered how this entrance might be closed, and thus it was that he hit upon the idea of pressing his tongue backwards. At first he was unsuccessful, and so he began a regular training, until at last he succeeded in swallowing his tongue in much the same way as sometimes happens accidentally during anaesthesia, evidently in his case by artificially relaxing the muscles at the root of the tongue.

271   In this strange manner the boy paved the way for his future psychosis. After the second attack he became incurably insane. This is only one example among many others, but it suffices to show how the subsequent, apparently sudden irruption of alien contents is really not sudden at all, but is rather the result of an unconscious development that has been going on for years.

272   The great question now is: in what do these unconscious processes consist? And how are they constituted? Naturally, so long as they are unconscious, nothing can be said about them. But sometimes they manifest themselves, partly through symptoms, partly through actions, opinions, affects, fantasies, and dreams. Aided by such observational material we can draw indirect conclusions as to the momentary state and constitution of the unconscious processes and their development. We should not, however, labour under the illusion that we have now dis-

273 covered the real nature of the unconscious processes. We never succeed in getting further than the hypothetical "as if."

"No mortal mind can plumb the depths of nature"—nor even the depths of the unconscious. We do know, however, that the unconscious never rests. It seems to be always at work, for even when asleep we dream. There are many people who declare that they never dream, but the probability is that they simply do not remember their dreams. It is significant that people who talk in their sleep mostly have no recollection either of the dream which started them talking, or even of the fact that they dreamed at all. Not a day passes but we make some slip of the tongue, or something slips our memory which at other times we know perfectly well, or we are seized by a mood whose cause we cannot trace, etc. These things are all symptoms of some consistent unconscious activity which becomes directly visible at night in dreams, but only occasionally breaks through the inhibitions imposed by our daytime consciousness.

274 So far as our present experience goes, we can lay it down that the unconscious processes stand in a compensatory relation to the conscious mind. I expressly use the word "compensatory" and not the word "contrary" because conscious and unconscious are not necessarily in opposition to one another, but complement one another to form a totality, which is the *self*. According to this definition the self is a quantity that is supraordinate to the conscious ego. It embraces not only the conscious but also the unconscious psyche, and is therefore, so to speak, a personality which we *also* are. It is easy enough to think of ourselves as possessing part-souls. Thus we can, for instance, see ourselves as a persona without too much difficulty. But it transcends our powers of imagination to form a clear picture of what we are as a self, for in this operation the part would have to comprehend the whole. There is little hope of our ever being able to reach even approximate consciousness of the self, since however much we may make conscious there will always exist an indeterminate and indeterminable amount of unconscious material which belongs to the totality of the self. Hence the self will always remain a supraordinate quantity.

275 The unconscious processes that compensate the conscious ego contain all those elements that are necessary for the self-

151

regulation of the psyche as a whole. On the personal level, these are the not consciously recognized personal motives which appear in dreams, or the meanings of daily situations which we have overlooked, or conclusions we have failed to draw, or affects we have not permitted, or criticisms we have spared ourselves. But the more we become conscious of ourselves through self-knowledge, and act accordingly, the more the layer of the personal unconscious that is superimposed on the collective unconscious will be diminished. In this way there arises a consciousness which is no longer imprisoned in the petty, oversensitive, personal world of the ego, but participates freely in the wider world of objective interests. This widened consciousness is no longer that touchy, egotistical bundle of personal wishes, fears, hopes, and ambitions which always has to be compensated or corrected by unconscious counter-tendencies; instead, it is a function of relationship to the world of objects, bringing the individual into absolute, binding, and indissoluble communion with the world at large. The complications arising at this stage are no longer egotistical wish-conflicts, but difficulties that concern others as much as oneself. At this stage it is fundamentally a question of collective problems, which have activated the collective unconscious because they require collective rather than personal compensation. We can now see that the unconscious produces contents which are valid not only for the person concerned, but for others as well, in fact for a great many people and possibly for all.

276   The Elgonyi, natives of the Elgon forests, of central Africa, explained to me that there are two kinds of dreams: the ordinary dream of the little man, and the "big vision" that only the great man has, e.g., the medicine-man or chief. Little dreams are of no account, but if a man has a "big dream" he summons the whole tribe in order to tell it to everybody.

277   How is a man to know whether his dream is a "big" or a "little" one? He knows it by an instinctive feeling of significance. He feels so overwhelmed by the impression it makes that he would never think of keeping the dream to himself. He *has* to tell it, on the psychologically correct assumption that it is of general significance. Even with us the collective dream has a feeling of importance about it that impels communication. It springs from a conflict of relationship and must therefore be

278 built into our conscious relations, because it compensates these and not just some inner personal quirk.

The processes of the collective unconscious are concerned not only with the more or less personal relations of an individual to his family or to a wider social group, but with his relations to society and to the human community in general. The more general and impersonal the condition that releases the unconscious reaction, the more significant, bizarre, and overwhelming will be the compensatory manifestation. It impels not just private communication, but drives people to revelations and confessions, and even to a dramatic representation of their fantasies.

279 I will explain by an example how the unconscious manages to compensate relationships. A somewhat arrogant gentleman once came to me for treatment. He ran a business in partnership with his younger brother. Relations between the two brothers were very strained, and this was one of the essential causes of my patient's neurosis. From the information he gave me, the real reason for the tension was not altogether clear. He had all kinds of criticisms to make of his brother, whose gifts he certainly did not show in a very favourable light. The brother frequently came into his dreams, always in the role of a Bismarck, Napoleon, or Julius Caesar. His house looked like the Vatican or Yildiz Kiosk. My patient's unconscious evidently had the need to exalt the rank of the younger brother. From this I concluded that he was setting himself too high and his brother too low. The further course of analysis entirely justified this inference.

280 Another patient, a young woman who clung to her mother in an extremely sentimental way, always had very sinister dreams about her. She appeared in the dreams as a witch, as a ghost, as a pursuing demon. The mother had spoilt her beyond all reason and had so blinded her by tenderness that the daughter had no conscious idea of her mother's harmful influence. Hence the compensatory criticism exercised by the unconscious.

281 I myself once happened to put too low a value on a patient, both intellectually and morally. In a dream I saw a castle perched on a high cliff, and on the topmost tower was a balcony, and there sat my patient. I did not hesitate to tell her this dream at once, naturally with the best results.

282 We all know how apt we are to make fools of ourselves in front of the very people we have unjustly underrated. Naturally

153

the case can also be reversed, as once happened to a friend of mine. While still a callow student he had written to Virchow, the pathologist, craving an audience with "His Excellency." When, quaking with fear, he presented himself and tried to give his name, he blurted out, "My name is Virchow." Whereupon His Excellency, smiling mischievously, said, "Ah! So your name is Virchow too?" The feeling of his own nullity was evidently too much for the unconscious of my friend, and in consequence it instantly prompted him to present himself as equal to Virchow in grandeur.

283   In these more personal relations there is of course no need for any very collective compensations. On the other hand, the figures employed by the unconscious in our first case are of a definitely collective nature: they are universally recognized heroes. Here there are two possible interpretations: either my patient's younger brother is a man of acknowledged and far-reaching collective importance, or my patient is overestimating his own importance not merely in relation to his brother but in relation to everybody else as well. For the first assumption there was no support at all, while for the second there was the evidence of one's own eyes. Since the man's extreme arrogance affected not only himself, but a far wider social group, the compensation availed itself of a collective image.

284   The same is true of the second case. The "witch" is a collective image; hence we must conclude that the blind dependence of the young woman applied as much to the wider social group as it did to her mother personally. This was indeed the case, in so far as she was still living in an exclusively infantile world, where the world was identical with her parents. These examples deal with relations within the personal orbit. There are, however, impersonal relations which occasionally need unconscious compensation. In such cases collective images appear with a more or less mythological character. Moral, philosophical, and religious problems are, on account of their universal validity, the most likely to call for mythological compensation. In the aforementioned novel by H. G. Wells we find a classical type of compensation: Mr. Preemby, a midget personality, discovers that he is really a reincarnation of Sargon, King of Kings. Happily, the genius of the author rescues poor old Sargon from pathological absurdity, and even gives the reader a chance to appre-

285   ciate the tragic and eternal meaning in this lamentable affray. Mr. Preemby, a complete nonentity, recognizes himself as the point of intersection of all ages past and future. This knowledge is not too dearly bought at the cost of a little madness, provided that Preemby is not in the end devoured by that monster of a primordial image—which is in fact what nearly happens to him.

286   The universal problem of evil and sin is another aspect of our impersonal relations to the world. Almost more than any other, therefore, this problem produces collective compensations. One of my patients, aged sixteen, had as the initial symptom of a severe compulsion neurosis the following dream: *He is walking along an unfamiliar street. It is dark, and he hears steps coming behind him. With a feeling of fear he quickens his pace. The footsteps come nearer, and his fear increases. He begins to run. But the footsteps seem to be overtaking him. Finally he turns round, and there he sees the devil. In deathly terror he leaps into the air and hangs there suspended.* This dream was repeated twice, a sign of its special urgency.

287   It is a notorious fact that the compulsion neuroses, by reason of their meticulousness and ceremonial punctilio, not only have the surface appearance of a moral problem but are indeed brimful of inhuman beastliness and ruthless evil, against the integration of which the very delicately organized personality puts up a desperate struggle. This explains why so many things have to be performed in ceremonially "correct" style, as though to counteract the evil hovering in the background. After this dream the neurosis started, and its essential feature was that the patient had, as he put it, to keep himself in a "provisional" or "uncontaminated" state of purity. For this purpose he either severed or made "invalid" all contact with the world and with everything that reminded him of the transitoriness of human existence, by means of lunatic formalities, scrupulous cleansing ceremonies, and the anxious observance of innumerable rules and regulations of an unbelievable complexity. Even before the patient had any suspicion of the hellish existence that lay before him, the dream showed him that if he wanted to come down to earth again there would have to be a pact with evil.

288   Elsewhere I have described a dream that illustrates the compensation of a religious problem in a young theological student.[1]

[1] "Archetypes of the Collective Unconscious," par. 71.

He was involved in all sorts of difficulties of belief, a not uncommon occurrence in the man of today. In his dream he was the pupil of the "white magician," who, however, was dressed in black. After having instructed him up to a certain point, the white magician told him that they now needed the "black magician." The black magician appeared, but clad in a white robe. He declared that he had found the keys of paradise, but needed the wisdom of the white magician in order to understand how to use them. This dream obviously contains the problem of opposites which, as we know, has found in Taoist philosophy a solution very different from the views prevailing in the West. The figures employed by the dream are impersonal collective images corresponding to the nature of the impersonal religious problem. In contrast to the Christian view, the dream stresses the relativity of good and evil in a way that immediately calls to mind the Taoist symbol of Yin and Yang.

288   We should certainly not conclude from these compensations that, as the conscious mind becomes more deeply engrossed in universal problems, the unconscious will bring forth correspondingly far-reaching compensations. There is what one might call a legitimate and an illegitimate interest in impersonal problems. Excursions of this kind are legitimate only when they arise from the deepest and truest needs of the individual; illegitimate when they are either mere intellectual curiosity or a flight from unpleasant reality. In the latter case the unconscious produces all too human and purely personal compensations, whose manifest aim is to bring the conscious mind back to ordinary reality. People who go illegitimately mooning after the infinite often have absurdly banal dreams which endeavour to damp down their ebullience. Thus, from the nature of the compensation, we can at once draw conclusions as to the seriousness and rightness of the conscious strivings.

289   There are certainly not a few people who are afraid to admit that the unconscious could ever have "big" ideas. They will object, "But do you really believe that the unconscious is capable of offering anything like a constructive criticism of our Western mentality?" Of course, if we take the problem intellectually and impute rational intentions to the unconscious, the thing becomes absurd. But it would never do to foist our conscious psychology upon the unconscious. Its mentality is an instinctive

one; it has no differentiated functions, and it does not "think" as we understand "thinking." It simply creates an image that answers to the conscious situation. This image contains as much thought as feeling, and is anything rather than a product of rationalistic reflection. Such an image would be better described as an artist's vision. We tend to forget that a problem like the one which underlies the dream last mentioned cannot, even to the conscious mind of the dreamer, be an intellectual problem, but is profoundly emotional. For a moral man the ethical problem is a passionate question which has its roots in the deepest instinctual processes as well as in his most idealistic aspirations. The problem for him is devastatingly real. It is not surprising, therefore, that the answer likewise springs from the depths of his nature. The fact that everyone thinks his psychology is the measure of all things, and, if he also happens to be a fool, will inevitably think that such a problem is beneath his notice, should not trouble the psychologist in the least, for he has to take things objectively, as he finds them, without twisting them to fit his subjective suppositions. The richer and more capacious natures may legitimately be gripped by an impersonal problem, and to the extent that this is so, their unconscious can answer in the same style. And just as the conscious mind can put the question, "Why is there this frightful conflict between good and evil?," so the unconscious can reply, "Look closer! Each needs the other. The best, just because it is the best, holds the seed of evil, and there is nothing so bad but good can come of it."

290   It might then dawn on the dreamer that the apparently insoluble conflict is, perhaps, a prejudice, a frame of mind conditioned by time and place. The seemingly complex dream-image might easily reveal itself as plain, instinctive common sense, as the tiny germ of a rational idea, which a maturer mind could just as well have thought consciously. At all events Chinese philosophy thought of it ages ago. The singularly apt, plastic configuration of thought is the prerogative of that primitive, natural spirit which is alive in all of us and is only obscured by a one-sided conscious development. If we consider the unconscious compensations from this angle, we might justifiably be accused of judging the unconscious too much from the conscious standpoint. And indeed, in pursuing these reflections, I have always started from the view that the unconscious simply reacts to the

conscious contents, albeit in a very significant way, but that it lacks initiative. It is, however, far from my intention to give the impression that the unconscious is merely reactive in all cases. On the contrary, there is a host of experiences which seem to prove that the unconscious is not only spontaneous but can actually take the lead. There are innumerable cases of people who lingered on in a pettifogging unconsciousness, only to become neurotic in the end. Thanks to the neurosis contrived by the unconscious, they are shaken out of their apathy, and this in spite of their own laziness and often desperate resistance.

Yet it would, in my view, be wrong to suppose that in such cases the unconscious is working to a deliberate and concerted plan and is striving to realize certain definite ends. I have found nothing to support this assumption. The driving force, so far as it is possible for us to grasp it, seems to be in essence only an urge towards self-realization. If it were a matter of some general teleological plan, then all individuals who enjoy a surplus of unconsciousness would necessarily be driven towards higher consciousness by an irresistible urge. That is plainly not the case. There are vast masses of the population who, despite their notorious unconsciousness, never get anywhere near a neurosis. The few who are smitten by such a fate are really persons of the "higher" type who, for one reason or another, have remained too long on a primitive level. Their nature does not in the long run tolerate persistence in what is for them an unnatural torpor. As a result of their narrow conscious outlook and their cramped existence they save energy; bit by bit it accumulates in the unconscious and finally explodes in the form of a more or less acute neurosis. This simple mechanism does not necessarily conceal a "plan." A perfectly understandable urge towards self-realization would provide a quite satisfactory explanation. We could also speak of a retarded maturation of the personality.

Since it is highly probable that we are still a long way from the summit of absolute consciousness, presumably everyone is capable of wider consciousness, and we may assume accordingly that the unconscious processes are constantly supplying us with contents which, if consciously recognized, would extend the range of consciousness. Looked at in this way, the unconscious appears as a field of experience of unlimited extent. If it were merely reactive to the conscious mind, we might aptly call it a psychic mirror-world. In that case, the real source of all contents and activities would lie in the conscious mind, and there would be absolutely nothing in the unconscious except the distorted reflections of conscious contents. The creative process would be shut up in the conscious mind, and anything new would be nothing but conscious invention or cleverness. The empirical facts give the lie to this. Every creative man knows that spontaneity is the very essence of creative thought. Because the unconscious is not just a reactive mirror-reflection, but an independent, productive activity, its realm of experience is a self-contained world, having its own reality, of which we can only say that it affects us as we affect it—precisely what we say about our experience of the outer world. And just as material objects are the constituent elements of this world, so psychic factors constitute the objects of that other world.

293   The idea of psychic objectivity is by no means a new discovery. It is in fact one of the earliest and most universal acquisitions of humanity: it is nothing less than the conviction as to the concrete existence of a spirit-world. The spirit-world was certainly never an invention in the sense that fire-boring was an invention; it was far rather the experience, the conscious acceptance of a reality in no way inferior to that of the material world. I doubt whether primitives exist anywhere who are not acquainted with magical influence or a magical substance. ("Magical" is simply another word for "psychic.") It would also appear that practically all primitives are aware of the existence of spirits.[2] "Spirit" is a psychic fact. Just as we distinguish our own bodiliness from bodies that are strange to us, so primitives—if they have any notion of "souls" at all—distinguish between their own souls and the spirits, which are felt as strange and as "not belonging." They are objects of outward perception, whereas their own soul (or one of several souls where a plurality is assumed), though believed to be essentially akin to the spirits, is not usually an object of so-called sensible perception. After death the soul (or one of the plurality of souls) becomes a spirit which survives the dead man, and often it shows a marked dete-

[2] In cases of reports to the contrary, it must always be borne in mind that the fear of spirits is sometimes so great that people will actually deny that there are any spirits to fear. I have come across this myself among the dwellers on Mount Elgon.

rioration of character that partly contradicts the notion of personal immortality. The Bataks,[3] of Sumatra, go so far as to assert that the people who were good in this life turn into malign and dangerous spirits. Nearly everything that the primitives say about the tricks which the spirits play on the living, and the general picture they give of the *revenants*, corresponds down to the last detail with the phenomena established by spiritualistic experience. And just as the communications from the "Beyond" can be seen to be the activities of broken-off bits of the psyche, so these primitive spirits are manifestations of unconscious complexes.[4] The importance that modern psychology attaches to the 'parental complex' is a direct continuation of primitive man's experience of the dangerous power of the ancestral spirits. Even the error of judgment which leads him unthinkingly to assume that the spirits are realities of the external world is carried on in our assumption (which is only partially correct) that the real parents are responsible for the parental complex. In the old trauma theory of Freudian psychoanalysis, and in other quarters as well, this assumption even passed for a scientific explanation. (It was in order to avoid this confusion that I advocated the term "parental imago."[5])

294   The simple soul is of course quite unaware of the fact that his nearest relations, who exercise immediate influence over him, create in him an image which is only partly a replica of themselves, while its other part is compounded of elements derived from himself. The imago is built up of parental influences plus the specific reactions of the child; it is therefore an image that reflects the object with very considerable qualifications. Naturally, the simple soul believes that his parents are as he sees them. The image is unconsciously projected, and when the parents die, the projected image goes on working as though it were a spirit existing on its own. The primitive then speaks of parental spirits who return by night (*revenants*), while the modern man calls it a father or mother complex.

295   The more limited a man's field of consciousness is, the more

---

3 Warnecke, *Die Religion der Batak* (1909).

4 Cf. "The Psychological Foundations of Belief in Spirits."

5 [This term was taken up by psychoanalysis, but in analytical psychology it has been largely replaced by "primordial image of the parent" or "parental archetype."—EDITORS.]

numerous the psychic contents (imagos) which meet him as quasi-external apparitions, either in the form of spirits, or as magical potencies projected upon living people (magicians, witches, etc.). At a rather higher stage of development, where the idea of the soul already exists, not all the imagos continue to be projected (where this happens, even trees and stones talk), but one or the other complex has come near enough to consciousness to be felt as no longer strange, but as somehow "belonging." Nevertheless, the feeling that it "belongs" is not at first sufficiently strong for the complex to be sensed as a subjective content of consciousness. It remains in a sort of no man's land between conscious and unconscious, in the half-shadow, in part belonging or akin to the conscious subject, in part an autonomous being, and meeting consciousness as such. At all events it is not necessarily obedient to the subject's intentions, it may even be of a higher order, more often than not a source of inspiration or warning, or of "supernatural" information. Psychologically such a content could be explained as a partly autonomous complex that is not yet fully integrated. The archaic souls, the *ba* and *ka* of the Egyptians, are complexes of this kind. At a still higher level, and particularly among the civilized peoples of the West, this complex is invariably of the feminine gender—anima and ψυχή—a fact for which deeper and cogent reasons are not lacking.

296 Among all possible spirits the spirits of the parents are in practice the most important; hence the universal incidence of the ancestor cult. In its original form it served to conciliate the *revenants*, but on a higher level of culture it became an essentially moral and educational institution, as in China. For the child, the parents are his closest and most influential relations. But as he grows older this influence is split off; consequently the parental imagos become increasingly shut away from consciousness, and on account of the restrictive influence they sometimes continue to exert, they easily acquire a negative aspect. In this way the parental imagos remain as alien elements somewhere "outside," the psyche. In place of the parents, woman now takes up her position as the most immediate environmental influence in the life of the adult man. She becomes his companion, she belongs to him in so far as she shares his life and is more or less of the same age. She is not of a superior order, either by virtue of age, authority, or physical strength. She is, however, a very influential factor and, like the parents, she produces an imago of a relatively autonomous nature—not an imago to be split off like that of the parents, but one that has to be kept associated with consciousness. Woman, with her very dissimilar psychology, is and always has been a source of information about things for which a man has no eyes. She can be his inspiration; her intuitive capacity, often superior to man's, can give him timely warning, and her feeling, always directed towards the personal, can show him ways which his own less personally accented feeling would never have discovered. What Tacitus says about the Germanic women is exactly to the point in this respect.[1]

297 Here, without a doubt, is one of the main sources for the feminine quality of the soul. But it does not seem to be the only

[1] *Germania* (Loeb edn.), pars. 18, 19.

162

298 source. No man is so entirely masculine that he has nothing feminine in him. The fact is, rather, that very masculine men have—carefully guarded and hidden—a very soft emotional life, often incorrectly described as "feminine." A man counts it a virtue to repress his feminine traits as much as possible, just as a woman, at least until recently, considered it unbecoming to be "mannish." The repression of feminine traits and inclinations naturally causes these contrasexual demands to accumulate in the unconscious. No less naturally, the imago of woman (the soul-image) becomes a receptacle for these demands, which is why a man, in his love-choice, is strongly tempted to win the woman who best corresponds to his own unconscious femininity—a woman, in short, who can unhesitatingly receive the projection of his soul. Although such a choice is often regarded and felt as altogether ideal, it may turn out that the man has manifestly married his own worst weakness. This would explain some highly remarkable conjunctions.

299 It seems to me, therefore, that apart from the influence of woman there is also the man's own femininity to explain the feminine nature of the soul-complex. There is no question here of any linguistic "accident," of the kind that makes the sun feminine in German and masculine in other languages. We have, in this matter, the testimony of art from all ages, and besides that the famous question: *habet mulier animam?* Most men, probably, who have any psychological insight at all will know what Rider Haggard means by "She-who-must-be-obeyed," and will also recognize the chord that is struck when they read Benoît's description of Antinéa.[2] Moreover they know at once the kind of woman who most readily embodies this mysterious factor, of which they have so vivid a premonition.

The wide recognition accorded to such books shows that there must be some supra-individual quality in this image of the anima,[3] something that does not owe a fleeting existence simply to its individual uniqueness, but is far more typical, with roots that go deeper than the obvious surface attachments I have pointed out. Both Rider Haggard and Benoît give unmistak-

2 Cf. Rider Haggard, *She*; Benoît, *L'Atlantide*.
3 Cf. *Psychological Types*, Def. 48. "Soul." [Also "Concerning the Archetypes, with Special Reference to the Anima Concept" and "The Psychological Aspects of the Kore."—EDITORS.]

able utterance to this supposition in the *historical* aspect of their anima figures.

300 As we know, there is no human experience, nor would experience be possible at all, without the intervention of a subjective aptitude. What is this subjective aptitude? Ultimately it consists in an innate psychic structure which allows man to have experiences of this kind. Thus the whole nature of man presupposes woman, both physically and spiritually. His system is tuned in to woman from the start, just as it is prepared for a quite definite world where there is water, light, air, salt, carbohydrates, etc. The form of the world into which he is born is already inborn in him as a virtual image. Likewise parents, wife, children, birth, and death are inborn in him as virtual images, as psychic aptitudes. These *a priori* categories have by nature a collective character; they are images of parents, wife, and children in general, and are not individual predestinations. We must therefore think of these images as lacking in solid content, hence as unconscious. They only acquire solidity, influence, and eventual consciousness in the encounter with empirical facts, which touch the unconscious aptitude and quicken it to life. They are in a sense the deposits of all our ancestral experiences, but they are not the experiences themselves. So at least it seems to us, in the present limited state of our knowledge. (I must confess that I have never yet found infallible evidence for the inheritance of memory images, but I do not regard it as positively precluded that in addition to these collective deposits which contain nothing specifically individual, there may also be inherited memories that are individually determined.)

301 An inherited collective image of woman exists in a man's unconscious, with the help of which he apprehends the nature of woman. This inherited image is the third important source for the femininity of the soul.

302 As the reader will have grasped, we are not concerned here with a philosophical, much less a religious, concept of the soul, but with the psychological recognition of the existence of a semiconscious psychic complex, having partial autonomy of function. Clearly, this recognition has as much or as little to do with philosophical or religious conceptions of the soul, as psychology has as much or as little to do with philosophy or religion. I have no wish to embark here on a "battle of the facul-

ties," nor do I seek to demonstrate either to the philosopher or to the theologian what exactly he means by "soul." I must, however, restrain both of them from prescribing what the psychologist *ought* to mean by "soul." The quality of personal immortality so fondly attributed to the soul by religion is, for science, no more than a psychological *indicium* which is already included in the idea of autonomy. The quality of personal immortality is by no means a constant attribute of the soul as the primitive sees it, nor even immortality as such. But setting this view aside as altogether inaccessible to science, the immediate meaning of "immortality" is simply a psychic activity that transcends the limits of consciousness. "Beyond the grave" or "on the other side of death" means, psychologically, "beyond consciousness." There is positively nothing else it could mean, since statements about immortality can only be made by the living, who, as such, are not exactly in a position to pontificate about conditions "beyond the grave."

303   The autonomy of the soul-complex naturally lends support to the notion of an invisible, personal entity that apparently lives in a world very different from ours. Consequently, once the activity of the soul is felt to be that of an autonomous entity having no ties with our mortal substance, it is but a step to imagining that this entity must lead an entirely independent existence, perhaps in a world of invisible things. Yet it is not immediately clear why the *invisibility* of this independent entity should simultaneously imply its *immortality*. The quality of immortality might easily derive from another fact to which I have already alluded, namely the characteristically historical aspect of the soul. Rider Haggard has given one of the best descriptions of this in *She*. When the Buddhists say that progressive perfection through meditation awakens memories of former incarnations, they are no doubt referring to the same psychological reality, the only difference being that they ascribe the historical factor not to the soul but to the Self (*atman*). It is altogether in keeping with the thoroughly extraverted attitude of the Western mind so far, that immortality should be ascribed, both by feeling and by tradition, to a soul which we distinguish more or less from our ego, and which also differs from the ego on account of its feminine qualities. It would be entirely logical if, by deepening that neglected, introverted side of our spiritual culture, there

were to take place in us a transformation more akin to the Eastern frame of mind, where the quality of immortality would transfer itself from the ambiguous figure of the soul (*anima*) to the self. For it is essentially the overvaluation of the material object without that constellates a spiritual and immortal figure within (obviously for the purpose of compensation and self-regulation). Fundamentally, the historical factor does not attach only to the archetype of the feminine, but to all archetypes whatsoever, i.e., to every inherited unit, mental as well as physical. Our life is indeed the same as it ever was. At all events, in our sense of the word it is not transitory; for the same physiological and psychological processes that have been man's for hundreds of thousands of years still endure, instilling into our inmost hearts this profound intuition of the "eternal" continuity of the living. But the self, as an inclusive term that embraces our whole living organism, not only contains the deposit and totality of all past life, but is also a point of departure, the fertile soil from which all future life will spring. This premonition of futurity is as clearly impressed upon our innermost feelings as is the historical aspect. The idea of immortality follows legitimately from these psychological premises.

305   The persona is a complicated system of relations between the individual consciousness and society, fittingly enough a kind of mask, designed on the one hand to make a definite impression upon others, and, on the other, to conceal the true nature of the individual. That the latter function is superfluous could be maintained only by one who is so identified with his persona that he no longer knows himself; and that the former is unnecessary could only occur to one who is quite unconscious of the true nature of his fellows. Society expects, and indeed must expect, every individual to play the part assigned to him as perfectly as possible, so that a man who is a parson must not only carry out his official functions objectively, but must at all times and in all circumstances play the role of parson in a flawless manner. Society demands this as a kind of surety; each must stand at his

304   In the Eastern view the concept of the anima, as we have stated it here, is lacking, and so, logically, is the concept of a persona. This is certainly no accident, for, as I have already indicated, a compensatory relationship exists between persona and anima.

post, here a cobbler, there a poet. No man is expected to be both. Nor is it advisable to be both, for that would be "odd." Such a man would be "different" from other people, not quite reliable. In the academic world he would be a dilettante, in politics an "unpredictable" quantity, in religion a free-thinker—in short, he would always be suspected of unreliability and incompetence, because society is persuaded that only the cobbler who is not a poet can supply workmanlike shoes. To present an unequivocal face to the world is a matter of practical importance: the average man—the only kind society knows anything about— must keep his nose to one thing in order to achieve anything worth while; two would be too much. Our society is undoubtedly set on such an ideal. It is therefore not surprising that everyone who wants to get on must take these expectations into account. Obviously no one could completely submerge his individuality in these expectations; hence the construction of an artificial personality becomes an unavoidable necessity. The demands of propriety and good manners are an added inducement to assume a becoming mask. What goes on behind the mask is then called "private life." This painfully familiar division of consciousness into two figures, often preposterously different, is an incisive psychological operation that is bound to have repercussions on the unconscious.

306   The construction of a collectively suitable persona means a formidable concession to the external world, a genuine self-sacrifice which drives the ego straight into identification with the persona, so that people really do exist who believe they are what they pretend to be. The "soullessness" of such an attitude is, however, only apparent, for under no circumstances will the unconscious tolerate this shifting of the centre of gravity. When we examine such cases critically, we find that the excellence of the mask is compensated by the "private life" going on behind it. The pious Drummond once lamented that "bad temper is the vice of the virtuous." Whoever builds up too good a persona for himself naturally has to pay for it with irritability. Bismarck had hysterical weeping fits, Wagner indulged in correspondence about the belts of silk dressing-gowns, Nietzsche wrote letters to his "dear lama," Goethe held conversations with Eckermann, etc. But there are subtler things than the banal lapses of heroes. I once made the acquaintance of a very venerable personage—in

fact, one might easily call him a saint. I stalked round him for three whole days, but never a mortal failing did I find in him. My feeling of inferiority grew ominous, and I was beginning to think seriously of how I might better myself. Then, on the fourth day, his wife came to consult me. . . . Well, nothing of the sort has ever happened to me since. But this I did learn: that any man who becomes one with his persona can cheerfully let all disturbances manifest themselves through his wife without her noticing it, though she pays for her self-sacrifice with a bad neurosis.

307   These identifications with a social role are a very fruitful source of neuroses. A man cannot get rid of himself in favour of an artificial personality without punishment. Even the attempt to do so brings on, in all ordinary cases, unconscious reactions in the form of bad moods, affects, phobias, obsessive ideas, backslidings, vices, etc. The social "strong man" is in his private life often a mere child where his own states of feeling are concerned; his discipline in public (which he demands quite particularly of others) goes miserably to pieces in private. His "happiness in his work" assumes a woeful countenance at home; his "spotless" public morality looks strange indeed behind the mask—we will not mention deeds, but only fantasies, and the wives of such men would have a pretty tale to tell. As to his selfless altruism, his children have decided views about that.

308   To the degree that the world invites the individual to identify with the mask, he is delivered over to influences from within. "High rests on low," says Lao-tzu. An opposite forces its way up from inside; it is exactly as though the unconscious suppressed the ego with the very same power which drew the ego into the persona. The absence of resistance outwardly against the lure of the persona means a similar weakness inwardly against the influence of the unconscious. Outwardly an effective and powerful role is played, while inwardly an effeminate weakness develops in face of every influence coming from the unconscious. Moods, vagaries, timidity, even a limp sexuality (culminating in impotence) gradually gain the upper hand.

309   The persona, the ideal picture of a man as he should be, is inwardly compensated by feminine weakness, and as the individual outwardly plays the strong man, so he becomes inwardly a woman, i.e., the anima, for it is the anima that reacts to the

persona. But because the inner world is dark and invisible to the extraverted consciousness, and because a man is all the less capable of conceiving his weaknesses the more he is identified with the persona, the persona's counterpart, the anima, remains completely in the dark and is at once projected, so that our hero comes under the heel of his wife's slipper. If this results in a considerable increase of her power, she will acquit herself none too well. She becomes inferior, thus providing her husband with the welcome proof that it is not he, the hero, who is inferior in private, but his wife. In return the wife can cherish the illusion, so attractive to many, that at least she has married a hero, unperturbed by her own uselessness. This little game of illusion is often taken to be the whole meaning of life.

310   Just as, for the purpose of individuation, or self-realization, it is essential for a man to distinguish between what he is and how he appears to himself and to others, so it is also necessary for the same purpose that he should become conscious of his invisible system of relations to the unconscious, and especially of the anima, so as to be able to distinguish himself from her. One cannot of course distinguish oneself from something unconscious. In the matter of the persona it is easy enough to make it clear to a man that he and his office are two different things. But it is very difficult for a man to distinguish himself from his anima, the more so because she is invisible. Indeed, he has first to contend with the prejudice that everything coming from inside him springs from the truest depths of his being. The "strong man" will perhaps concede that in private life he is singularly undisciplined, but that, he says, is just his "weakness" with which, as it were, he proclaims his solidarity. Now there is in this tendency a cultural legacy that is not to be despised; for when a man recognizes that his ideal persona is responsible for his anything but ideal anima, his ideals are shattered, the world becomes ambiguous, he becomes ambiguous even to himself. He is seized by doubts about goodness, and what is worse, he doubts his own good intentions. When one considers how much our private idea of good intentions is bound up with vast historical assumptions, it will readily be understood that it is pleasanter and more in keeping with our present view of the world to deplore a personal weakness than to shatter ideals.

311   But since the unconscious factors act as determinants no less

than the factors that regulate the life of society, and are no less collective, I might just as well learn to distinguish between what I want and what the unconscious thrusts upon me, as to see what my office demands of me and what I myself desire. At first the only thing that is at all clear is the incompatibility of the demands coming from without and from within, with the ego standing between them, as between hammer and anvil. But over against this ego, tossed like a shuttlecock between the outer and inner demands, there stands some scarcely definable arbiter, which I would on no account label with the deceptive name "conscience," although, taken in its best sense, the word fits that arbiter very aptly indeed. What we have made of this "conscience" Spitteler has described with unsurpassable humour.[4] Hence we should do far better to realize that the tragic counterplay between inside and outside (depicted in Job and *Faust* as the wager with God) represents, at bottom, the energetics of the life process, the polar tension that is necessary for self-regulation. However different, to all intents and purposes, these opposing forces may be, their fundamental meaning and desire is the life of the individual: they always fluctuate round this centre of balance. Just because they are inseparably related through opposition, they also unite in a mediatory meaning, which, willingly or unwillingly, is born out of the individual and is therefore divined by him. He has a strong feeling of what should be and what could be. To depart from this divination means error, aberration, illness.

It is probably no accident that our modern notions of "personal" and "personality" derive from the word *persona*. I can assert that my ego is personal or a personality, and in exactly the same sense I can say that my persona is a personality with which I identify myself more or less. The fact that I then possess two personalities is not so remarkable, since every autonomous or even relatively autonomous complex has the peculiarity of appearing as a personality, i.e., of being personified. This can be observed most readily in the so-called spiritualistic manifestations of automatic writing and the like. The sentences produced are always personal statements and are propounded in the first person singular, as though behind every utterance there stood

4 *Psychological Types*, pars. 282ff.

170

an actual personality. A naïve intelligence at once thinks of spirits. The same sort of thing is also observable in the hallucinations of the insane, although these, more clearly than the first, can often be recognized as mere thoughts or fragments of thoughts whose connection with the conscious personality is immediately apparent to everyone.

313   The tendency of the relatively autonomous complex to direct personification also explains why the persona exercises such a "personal" effect that the ego is all too easily deceived as to which is the "true" personality.

314   Now, everything that is true of the persona and of all autonomous complexes in general also holds true of the anima. She likewise is a personality, and this is why she is so easily projected upon a woman. So long as the anima is unconscious she is always projected, for everything unconscious is projected. The first bearer of the soul-image is always the mother; later it is borne by those women who arouse the man's feelings, whether in a positive or a negative sense. Because the mother is the first bearer of the soul-image, separation from her is a delicate and important matter of the greatest educational significance. Accordingly among primitives we find a large number of rites designed to organize this separation. The mere fact of becoming adult, and of outward separation, is not enough; impressive initiations into the "men's house" and ceremonies of rebirth are still needed in order to make the separation from the mother (and hence from childhood) entirely effective.

315   Just as the father acts as a protection against the dangers of the external world and thus serves his son as a model persona, so the mother protects him against the dangers that threaten from the darkness of his psyche. In the puberty rites, therefore, the initiate receives instruction about these things of "the other side," so that he is put in a position to dispense with his mother's protection.

316   The modern civilized man has to forgo this primitive but nonetheless admirable system of education. The consequence is that the anima, in the form of the mother-imago, is transferred to the wife; and the man, as soon as he marries, becomes childish, sentimental, dependent, and subservient, or else truculent, tyrannical, hypersensitive, always thinking about the prestige of his superior masculinity. The last is of course merely the reverse

of the first. The safeguard against the unconscious, which is what his mother meant to him, is not replaced by anything in the modern man's education; unconsciously, therefore, his ideal of marriage is so arranged that his wife has to take over the magical role of the mother. Under the cloak of the ideally exclusive marriage he is really seeking his mother's protection, and thus he plays into the hands of his wife's possessive instincts. His fear of the dark incalculable power of the unconscious gives his wife an illegitimate authority over him, and forges such a dangerously close union that the marriage is permanently on the brink of explosion from internal tension—or else, out of protest, he flies to the other extreme, with the same results.

317   I am of the opinion that it is absolutely essential for a certain type of modern man to recognize his distinction not only from the persona, but from the anima as well. For the most part our consciousness, in true Western style, looks outwards, and the inner world remains in darkness. But this difficulty can be overcome easily enough, if only we will make the effort to apply the same concentration and criticism to the psychic material which manifests itself, not outside, but in our private lives. So accustomed are we to keep a shamefaced silence about this other side —we even tremble before our wives, lest they betray us!—and, if found out, to make rueful confessions of "weakness," that there would seem to be only one method of education, namely, to crush or repress the weaknesses as much as possible or at least hide them from the public. But that gets us nowhere.

318   Perhaps I can best explain what has to be done if I use the persona as an example. Here everything is plain and straightforward, whereas with the anima all is dark, to Western eyes anyway. When the anima continually thwarts the good intentions of the conscious mind, by contriving a private life that stands in sorry contrast to the dazzling persona, it is exactly the same as when a naive individual, who has not the ghost of a persona, encounters the most painful difficulties in his passage through the world. There are indeed people who lack a developed persona— "Canadians who know not Europe's sham politeness"—blundering from one social solecism to the next, perfectly harmless and innocent, soulful bores or appealing children, or, if they are women, spectral Cassandras dreaded for their tactlessness, eternally misunderstood, never knowing what they are about, al-

ways taking forgiveness for granted, blind to the world, hopeless dreamers. From them we can see how a neglected persona works, and what one must do to remedy the evil. Such people can avoid disappointments and an infinity of sufferings, scenes, and social catastrophes only by learning to see how men behave in the world. They must learn to understand what society expects of them; they must realize that there are factors and persons in the world far above them; they must know that what they do has a meaning for others, and so forth. Naturally all this is child's play for one who has a properly developed persona. But if we reverse the picture and confront the man who possesses a brilliant persona with the anima, and, for the sake of comparison, set him beside the man with no persona, then we shall see that the latter is just as well informed about the anima and her affairs as the former is about the world. The use which either makes of his knowledge can just as easily be abused, in fact it is more than likely that it will be.

319   The man with the persona is blind to the existence of inner realities, just as the other is blind to the reality of the world, which for him has merely the value of an amusing or fantastic playground. But the fact of inner realities and their unqualified recognition is obviously the *sine qua non* for a serious consideration of the anima problem. If the external world is, for me, simply a phantasm, how should I take the trouble to establish a complicated system of relationship and adaptation to it? Equally, the "nothing but fantasy" attitude will never persuade me to regard my anima manifestations as anything more than fatuous weakness. If, however, I take the line that the world is outside *and* inside, that reality falls to the share of both, I must logically accept the upsets and annoyances that come to me from inside as symptoms of faulty adaptation to the conditions of that inner world. No more than the blows rained on the innocent abroad can be healed by moral repression will it help him resignedly to catalogue his "weaknesses." Here are reasons, intentions, consequences, which can be tackled by will and understanding. Take, for example, the "spotless" man of honour and public benefactor, whose tantrums and explosive moodiness terrify his wife and children. What is the anima doing here?

320   We can see it at once if we just allow things to take their natural course. Wife and children will become estranged; a vac-

uum will form about him. At first he will bewail the hard-heartedness of his family, and will behave if possible even more vilely than before. That will make the estrangement absolute. If the good spirits have not utterly forsaken him, he will after a time notice his isolation, and in his loneliness he will begin to understand how he caused the estrangement. Perhaps, aghast at himself, he will ask, "What sort of devil has got into me?"—without of course seeing the meaning of this metaphor. Then follow remorse, reconciliation, oblivion, repression, and, in next to no time, a new explosion. Clearly, the anima is trying to enforce a separation. This tendency is in nobody's interest. The anima comes between them like a jealous mistress who tries to alienate the man from his family. An official post or any other advantageous social position can do the same thing, but there we can understand the force of the attraction. Whence does the anima obtain the power to wield such enchantment? On the analogy with the persona there must be values or some other important and influential factors lying in the background like seductive promises. In such matters we must guard against rationalizations. Our first thought is that the man of honour is on the look-out for another woman. That might be—it might even be arranged by the anima as the most effective means to the desired end. Such an arrangement should not be misconstrued as an end in itself, for the blameless gentleman who is correctly married according to the law can be just as correctly divorced according to the law, which does not alter his fundamental attitude one iota. The old picture has merely received a new frame.

321   As a matter of fact, this arrangement is a very common method of implementing a separation—and of hampering a final solution. Therefore it is more reasonable not to assume that such an obvious possibility is the end-purpose of the separation. We would be better advised to investigate what is behind the tendencies of the anima. The first step is what I would call the objectivation of the anima, that is, the strict refusal to regard the trend towards separation as a weakness of one's own. Only when this has been done can one face the anima with the question, "Why do you want this separation?" To put the question in this personal way has the great advantage of recognizing the anima as a personality, and of making a relationship possible. The more personally she is taken the better.

322   To anyone accustomed to proceed purely intellectually and rationally, this may seem altogether too ridiculous. It would indeed be the height of absurdity if a man tried to have a conversation with his persona, which he recognized merely as a psychological means of relationship. But it is absurd only for the man who *has* a persona. If he has none, he is in this point no different from the primitive who, as we know, has only one foot in what we commonly call reality. With the other foot he stands in a world of spirits, which is quite real to him. Our model case behaves, in the world, like a modern European; but in the world of spirits he is the child of a troglodyte. He must therefore submit to living in a kind of prehistoric kindergarten until he has got the right idea of the powers and factors which rule that other world. Hence he is quite right to treat the anima as an autonomous personality and to address personal questions to her.

323   I mean this as an actual technique. We know that practically every one has not only the peculiarity, but also the faculty, of holding a conversation with himself. Whenever we are in a predicament we ask ourselves (or whom else?), "What shall I do?" either aloud or beneath our breath, and we (or who else?) supply the answer. Since it is our intention to learn what we can about the foundations of our being, this little matter of living in a metaphor should not bother us. We have to accept it as a symbol of our primitive backwardness (or of such naturalness as is still, mercifully, left to us) that we can, like the Negro, discourse personally with our "snake." The psyche not being a unity but a contradictory multiplicity of complexes, the dissociation required for our dialectics with the anima is not so terribly difficult. The art of it consists only in allowing our invisible partner to make herself heard, in putting the mechanism of expression momentarily at her disposal, without being overcome by the distaste one naturally feels at playing such an apparently ludicrous game with oneself, or by doubts as to the genuineness of the voice of one's interlocutor. This latter point is technically very important: we are so in the habit of identifying ourselves with the thoughts that come to us that we invariably assume we have made them. Curiously enough, it is precisely the most impossible thoughts for which we feel the greatest subjective responsibility. If we were more conscious of the inflexible universal laws that govern even the wildest and most wanton fantasy, we

might perhaps be in a better position to see these thoughts above all others as objective occurrences, just as we see dreams, which nobody supposes to be deliberate or arbitrary inventions. It certainly requires the greatest objectivity and absence of prejudice to give the "other side" the opportunity for perceptible psychic activity. As a result of the repressive attitude of the conscious mind, the other side is driven into indirect and purely symptomatic manifestations, mostly of an emotional kind, and only in moments of overwhelming affectivity can fragments of the unconscious come to the surface in the form of thoughts or images. The inevitable accompanying symptom is that the ego momentarily identifies with these utterances, only to revoke them in the same breath. And, indeed, the things one says when in the grip of an affect sometimes seem very strange and daring. But they are easily forgotten, or wholly denied. This mechanism of deprecation and denial naturally has to be reckoned with if one wants to adopt an objective attitude. The habit of rushing in to correct and criticize is already strong enough in our tradition, and it is as a rule further reinforced by fear—a fear that can be confessed neither to oneself nor to others, a fear of insidious truths, of dangerous knowledge, of disagreeable verifications, in a word, fear of all those things that cause so many of us to flee from being alone with ourselves as from the plague. We say that it is egoistic or "morbid" to be preoccupied with oneself; one's own company is the worst, "it makes you melancholy"—such are the glowing testimonials accorded to our human make-up. They are evidently deeply ingrained in our Western minds. Whoever thinks in this way has obviously never asked himself what possible pleasure other people could find in the company of such a miserable coward. Starting from the fact that in a state of affect one often surrenders involuntarily to the truths of the other side, would it not be far better to make use of an affect so as to give the other side an opportunity to speak? It could therefore be said just as truly that one should cultivate the art of conversing with oneself in the setting provided by an affect, as though the affect itself were speaking without regard to our rational criticism. So long as the affect is speaking, criticism must be withheld. But once it has presented its case, we should begin criticizing as conscientiously as though a real person closely connected with us were our interlocutor. Nor should the matter

324 rest there, but statement and answer must follow one another until a satisfactory end to the discussion is reached. Whether the result is satisfactory or not, only subjective feeling can decide. Any humbug is of course quite useless. Scrupulous honesty with oneself and no rash anticipation of what the other side might conceivably say are the indispensable conditions of this technique for educating the anima.

324 There is, however, something to be said for this characteristically Western fear of the other side. It is not entirely without justification, quite apart from the fact that it is real. We can understand at once the fear that the child and the primitive have of the great unknown. We have the same childish fear of our inner side, where we likewise touch upon a great unknown world. All we have is the affect, the fear, without knowing that this is a world-fear—for the world of affects is invisible. We have either purely theoretical prejudices against it, or superstitious ideas. One cannot even talk about the unconscious before many educated people without being accused of mysticism. The fear is legitimate in so far as our rational *Weltanschauung* with its scientific and moral certitudes—so hotly believed in because so deeply questionable—is shattered by the facts of the other side. If only one could avoid them, then the emphatic advice of the Philistine to "let sleeping dogs lie" would be the only truth worth advocating. And here I would expressly point out that I am not recommending the above technique as either necessary or even useful to any person not driven to it by necessity. The stages, as I said, are many, and there are greybeards who die as innocent as babes in arms, and in this year of grace troglodytes are still being born. There are truths which belong to the future, truths which belong to the past, and truths which belong to no time.

325 I can imagine someone using this technique out of a kind of holy inquisitiveness, some youth, perhaps, who would like to set wings to his feet, not because of lameness, but because he yearns for the sun. But a grown man, with too many illusions dissipated, will submit to this inner humiliation and surrender only if forced, for why should he let the terrors of childhood again have their way with him? It is no light matter to stand between a day-world of exploded ideals and discredited values, and a nightmare-world of apparently senseless fantasy. The weirdness of this

326   standpoint is in fact so great that there is probably nobody who does not reach out for security, even though it be a reaching back to the mother who shielded his childhood from the terrors of night. Whoever is afraid must needs be dependent; a weak thing needs support. That is why the primitive mind, from deep psychological necessity, begot religious instruction and embodied it in magician and priest. *Extra ecclesiam nulla salus* is still a valid truth today—for those who can go back to it. For the few who cannot, there is only dependence upon a human being, a humbler and a prouder dependence, a weaker and a stronger support, so it seems to me, than any other. What can one say of the Protestant? He has neither church nor priest, but only God— and even God becomes doubtful.

The reader may ask in some consternation, "But what on earth does the anima do, that such double insurances are needed before one can come to terms with her?" I would recommend my reader to study the comparative history of religion so intently as to fill these dead chronicles with the emotional life of those who lived these religions. Then he will get some idea of what lives on the other side. The old religions with their sublime and ridiculous, their friendly and fiendish symbols did not drop from the blue, but were born of this human soul that dwells within us at this moment. All those things, their primal forms, live on in us and may at any time burst in upon us with annihilating force, in the guise of mass-suggestions against which the individual is defenceless. Our fearsome gods have only changed their names: they now rhyme with *ism*. Or has anyone the nerve to claim that the World War or Bolshevism was an ingenious invention? Just as outwardly we live in a world where a whole continent may be submerged at any moment, or a pole be shifted, or a new pestilence break out, so inwardly we live in a world where at any moment something similar may occur, albeit in the form of an idea, but no less dangerous and untrustworthy for that. Failure to adapt to this inner world is a negligence entailing just as serious consequences as ignorance and ineptitude in the outer world. It is after all only a tiny fraction of humanity, living mainly on that thickly populated peninsula of Asia which juts out into the Atlantic Ocean, and calling themselves "cultured," who, because they lack all contact with nature, have hit upon the idea that religion is a peculiar kind of

327 mental disturbance of undiscoverable purport. Viewed from a safe distance, say from central Africa or Tibet, it would certainly look as if this fraction had projected its own unconscious mental derangements upon nations still possessed of healthy instincts.

Because the things of the inner world influence us all the more powerfully for being unconscious, it is essential for anyone who intends to make progress in self-culture (and does not all culture begin with the individual?) to objectivate the effects of the anima and then try to understand what contents underlie those effects. In this way he adapts to, and is protected against, the invisible. No adaptation can result without concessions to both worlds. From a consideration of the claims of the inner and outer worlds, or rather, from the conflict between them, the possible and the necessary follows. Unfortunately our Western mind, lacking all culture in this respect, has never yet devised a concept, nor even a name, for the *union of opposites through the middle path*, that most fundamental item of inward experience, which could respectably be set against the Chinese concept of Tao. It is at once the most individual fact and the most universal, the most legitimate fulfilment of the meaning of the individual's life.

328 In the course of my exposition so far, I have kept exclusively to *masculine* psychology. The anima, being of feminine gender, is exclusively a figure that compensates the masculine consciousness. In woman the compensating figure is of a masculine character, and can therefore appropriately be termed the *animus*. If it was no easy task to describe what is meant by the anima, the difficulties become almost insuperable when we set out to describe the psychology of the animus.

329 The fact that a man naïvely ascribes his anima reactions to himself, without seeing that he really cannot identify himself with an autonomous complex, is repeated in feminine psychology, though if possible in even more marked form. This identification with an autonomous complex is the essential reason why it is so difficult to understand and describe the problem, quite apart from its inherent obscurity and strangeness. We always start with the naïve assumption that we are masters in our own house. Hence we must first accustom ourselves to the thought that, in our most intimate psychic life as well, we live in a kind of house which has doors and windows to the world, but that,

although the objects or contents of this world act upon us, they do not belong to us. For many people this hypothesis is by no means easy to conceive, just as they do not find it at all easy to understand and to accept the fact that their neighbour's psychology is not necessarily identical with their own. My reader may think that the last remark is something of an exaggeration, since in general one is aware of individual differences. But it must be remembered that our individual conscious psychology develops out of an original state of unconsciousness and therefore of non-differentiation (termed by Lévy-Bruhl *participation mystique*). Consequently, consciousness of differentiation is a relatively late achievement of mankind, and presumably but a relatively small sector of the indefinitely large field of original identity. Differentiation is the essence, the *sine qua non* of consciousness. Everything unconscious is undifferentiated, and everything that happens unconsciously proceeds on the basis of non-differentiation—that is to say, there is no determining whether it belongs or does not belong to oneself. It cannot be established *a priori* whether it concerns me, or another, or both. Nor does feeling give us any sure clues in this respect.

331 An inferior consciousness cannot *eo ipso* be ascribed to women; it is merely different from masculine consciousness. But, just as a woman is often clearly conscious of things which a man is still groping for in the dark, so there are naturally fields of experience in a man which, for woman, are still wrapped in the shadows of non-differentiation, chiefly things in which she has little interest. Personal relations are as a rule more important and interesting to her than objective facts and their interconnections. The wide fields of commerce, politics, technology, and science, the whole realm of the applied masculine mind, she relegates to the penumbra of consciousness; while, on the other hand, she develops a minute consciousness of personal relationships, the infinite nuances of which usually escape the man entirely.

We must therefore expect the unconscious of woman to show aspects essentially different from those found in man. If I were to attempt to put in a nutshell the difference between man and woman in this respect, i.e., what it is that characterizes the animus as opposed to the anima, I could only say this: as the anima produces *moods*, so the animus produces *opinions*; and as the moods of a man issue from a shadowy background, so the opinions of a woman rest on equally unconscious prior assumptions. Animus opinions very often have the character of solid convictions that are not lightly shaken, or of principles whose validity is seemingly unassailable. If we analyse these opinions, we immediately come upon unconscious assumptions whose existence must first be inferred; that is to say, the opinions are apparently conceived *as though* such assumptions existed. But in reality the opinions are not thought out at all; they exist ready made, and they are held so positively and with so much conviction that the woman never has the shadow of a doubt about them.

332   One would be inclined to suppose that the animus, like the anima, personifies itself in a single figure. But this, as experience shows, is true only up to a point, because another factor unexpectedly makes its appearance, which brings about an essentially different situation from that existing in a man. The animus does not appear as one person, but as a plurality of persons. In II. G. Wells' novel *Christina Alberta's Father*, the heroine, in all that she does or does not do, is constantly under the surveillance of a supreme moral authority, which tells her with remorseless precision and dry matter-of-factness what she is doing and for what motives. Wells calls this authority a "Court of Conscience." This collection of condemnatory judges, a sort of College of Preceptors, corresponds to a personification of the animus. The animus is rather like an assembly of fathers or dignitaries of some kind who lay down incontestable, "rational," *ex cathedra* judgments. On closer examination these exacting judgments turn out to be largely sayings and opinions scraped together more or less unconsciously from childhood on, and compressed into a canon of average truth, justice, and reasonableness, a compendium of preconceptions which, whenever a conscious and competent judgment is lacking (as not infrequently happens), instantly obliges with an opinion. Sometimes these opinions take the form of so-called sound common sense, sometimes they appear as principles which are like a travesty of education: "People have always done it like this," or "Everybody says it is like that."

333   It goes without saying that the animus is just as often projected as the anima. The men who are particularly suited to these projections are either walking replicas of God himself, who know all about everything, or else they are misunderstood

word-addicts with a vast and windy vocabulary at their command, who translate common or garden reality into the terminology of the sublime. It would be insufficient to characterize the animus merely as a conservative, collective conscience; he is also a neologist who, in flagrant contradiction to his correct opinions, has an extraordinary weakness for difficult and unfamiliar words which act as a pleasant substitute for the odious task of reflection.

334   Like the anima, the animus is a jealous lover. He is an adept at putting, in place of the real man, an opinion about him, the exceedingly disputable grounds for which are never submitted to criticism. Animus opinions are invariably collective, and they override individuals and individual judgments in exactly the same way as the anima thrusts her emotional anticipations and projections between man and wife. If the woman happens to be pretty, these animus opinions have for the man something rather touching and childlike about them, which makes him adopt a benevolent, fatherly, professorial manner. But if the woman does not stir his sentimental side, and competence is expected of her rather than appealing helplessness and stupidity, then her animus opinions irritate the man to death, chiefly because they are based on nothing but opinion for opinion's sake, and "everybody has a right to his own opinions." Men can be pretty venomous here, for it is an inescapable fact that the animus always plays up the anima—and *vice versa*, of course—so that all further discussion becomes pointless.

335   In intellectual women the animus encourages a critical disputatiousness and would-be highbrowism, which, however, consists essentially in harping on some irrelevant weak point and nonsensically making it the main one. Or a perfectly lucid discussion gets tangled up in the most maddening way through the introduction of a quite different and if possible perverse point of view. Without knowing it, such women are solely intent upon exasperating the man and are, in consequence, the more completely at the mercy of the animus. "Unfortunately I am always right," one of these creatures once confessed to me.

336   However, all these traits, as familiar as they are unsavoury, are simply and solely due to the extraversion of the animus. The animus does not belong to the function of conscious relationship; his function is rather to facilitate relations with the uncon-

scious. Instead of the woman merely associating opinions with external situations—situations which she ought to think about consciously—the animus, as an associative function, should be directed inwards, where it could associate the contents of the unconscious. The technique of coming to terms with the animus is the same in principle as in the case of the anima; only here the woman must learn to criticize and hold her opinions at a distance; not in order to repress them, but, by investigating their origins, to penetrate more deeply into the background, where she will then discover the primordial images, just as the man does in his dealings with the anima. The animus is the deposit, as it were, of all woman's ancestral experiences of man—and not only that, he is also a creative and procreative being, not in the sense of masculine creativity, but in the sense that he brings forth something we might call the λόγος σπερματικός, the spermatic word. Just as a man brings forth his work as a complete creation out of his inner feminine nature, so the inner masculine side of a woman brings forth creative seeds which have the power to fertilize the feminine side of the man. This would be the *femme inspiratrice* who, if falsely cultivated, can turn into the worst kind of dogmatist and high-handed pedagogue—a regular "animus hound," as one of my women patients aptly expressed it.

337 A woman possessed by the animus is always in danger of losing her femininity, her adapted feminine persona, just as a man in like circumstances runs the risk of effeminacy. These psychic changes of sex are due entirely to the fact that a function which belongs inside has been turned outside. The reason for this perversion is clearly the failure to give adequate recognition to an inner world which stands autonomously opposed to the outer world, and makes just as serious demands on our capacity for adaptation.

338 With regard to the plurality of the animus as distinguished from what we might call the "uni-personality" of the anima, this remarkable fact seems to me to be a correlate of the conscious attitude. The conscious attitude of woman is in general far more exclusively personal than that of man. Her world is made up of fathers and mothers, brothers and sisters, husbands and children. The rest of the world consists likewise of families, who nod to each other but are, in the main, interested essentially in

themselves. The man's world is the nation, the state, business concerns, etc. His family is simply a means to an end, one of the foundations of the state, and his wife is not necessarily *the* woman for him (at any rate not as the woman means it when she says "my man"). The general means more to him than the personal; his world consists of a multitude of co-ordinated factors, whereas her world, outside her husband, terminates in a sort of cosmic mist. A passionate exclusiveness therefore attaches to the man's anima, and an indefinite variety to the woman's animus. Whereas the man has, floating before him, in clear outlines, the alluring form of a Circe or a Calypso, the animus is better expressed as a bevy of Flying Dutchmen or unknown wanderers from over the sea, never quite clearly grasped, protean, given to persistent and violent motion. These personifications appear especially in dreams, though in concrete reality they can be famous tenors, boxing champions, or great men in far-away, unknown cities.

339   These two crepuscular figures from the dark hinterland of the psyche—truly the semi-grotesque "guardians of the threshold," to use the pompous jargon of theosophy—can assume an almost inexhaustible number of shapes, enough to fill whole volumes. Their complicated transformations are as rich and strange as the world itself, as manifold as the limitless variety of their conscious correlate, the persona. They inhabit the twilight sphere, and we can just make out that the autonomous complex of anima and animus is essentially a psychological function that has usurped, or rather retained, a "personality" only because this function is itself autonomous and undeveloped. But already we can see how it is possible to break up the personifications, since by making them conscious we convert them into bridges to the unconscious. It is because we are not using them purposefully as functions that they remain personified complexes. So long as they are in this state they must be accepted as relatively independent personalities. They cannot be integrated into consciousness while their contents remain unknown. The purpose of the dialectical process is to bring these contents into the light; and only when this task has been completed, and the conscious mind has become sufficiently familiar with the unconscious processes reflected in the anima, will the anima be felt simply as a function.

340 I do not expect every reader to grasp right away what is meant by animus and anima. But I hope he will at least have gained the impression that it is not a question of anything "metaphysical," but far rather of empirical facts which could equally well be expressed in rational and abstract language. I have purposely avoided too abstract a terminology because, in matters of this kind, which hitherto have been so inaccessible to our experience, it is useless to present the reader with an intellectual formulation. It is far more to the point to give him some conception of what the actual possibilities of experience are. Nobody can really understand these things unless he has experienced them himself. I am therefore much more interested in pointing out the possible ways to such experience than in devising intellectual formulae which, for lack of experience, must necessarily remain an empty web of words. Unfortunately there are all too many who learn the words by heart and add the experiences in their heads, thereafter abandoning themselves, according to temperament, either to credulity or to criticism. We are concerned here with a new—and yet age-old—field of psychological experience. We shall be able to establish relatively valid theories about it only when the corresponding psychological facts are known to a sufficient number of people. The first things to be discovered are always facts, not theories. Theory-building is the outcome of discussion among many.

Plato and Aristotle! These are not merely two systems, they are types of two distinct human natures, which from time immemorial, under every sort of disguise, stand more or less inimically opposed. The whole medieval world in particular was riven by this conflict, which persists down to the present day, and which forms the most essential content of the history of the Christian Church. Although under other names, it is always of Plato and Aristotle that we speak. Visionary, mystical, Platonic natures disclose Christian ideas and the corresponding symbols from the fathomless depths of their souls. Practical, orderly, Aristotelian natures build out of these ideas and symbols a fixed system, a dogma and a cult. Finally the Church embraces both natures, one of them entrenched in the clergy and the other in monasticism, but both keeping up a constant feud.

—Heine, *Deutschland*, I

FROM *PSYCHOLOGICAL TYPES*

INTRODUCTION

1 In my practical medical work with nervous patients I have long been struck by the fact that besides the many individual differences in human psychology there are also typical differences. Two types especially become clear to me; I have termed them the introverted and the extraverted types.

2 When we consider the course of human life, we see how the fate of one individual is determined more by the objects of his interest, while in another it is determined more by his own inner self, by the subject. Since we all swerve rather more towards one side or the other, we naturally tend to understand everything in terms of our own type.

3 I mention this circumstance at once in order to avoid possible misunderstandings. It will be apparent that it is one which considerably aggravates the difficulty of a general description of types. I must presume unduly upon the goodwill of the reader if I may hope to be rightly understood. It would be relatively simple if every reader knew to which category he belonged. But it is often very difficult to find out whether a person belongs to one type or the other, especially in regard to oneself. In respect of one's own personality one's judgment is as a rule extraordinarily clouded. This subjective clouding of judgment is particularly common because in every pronounced type there is a special tendency to compensate the one-sidedness of that type, a tendency which is biologically purposive since it strives constantly to maintain the psychic equilibrium. The compensation gives rise to secondary characteristics, or secondary types, which present a picture that is extremely difficult to interpret, so difficult that one is inclined to deny the existence of types altogether and to believe only in individual differences.

4 I must emphasize this difficulty in order to justify certain peculiarities in my presentation. It might seem as if the simplest way would be to describe two concrete cases and to dis-

sect them side by side. But everyone possesses both mechanisms, extraversion as well as introversion, and only the relative predominance of one or the other determines the type. Hence, in order to throw the picture into the necessary relief, one would have to retouch it rather vigorously, and this would amount to a more or less pious fraud. Moreover, the psychological reactions of a human being are so complicated that my powers of description would hardly suffice to draw an absolutely correct picture. From sheer necessity, therefore, I must confine myself to a presentation of principles which I have abstracted from a wealth of facts observed in many different individuals. In this there is no question of a *deductio a priori*, as it might appear; it is rather a deductive presentation of empirically gained insights. These insights will, I hope, help to clarify a dilemma which, not only in analytical psychology but in other branches of science as well, and especially in the personal relations of human beings with one another, has led and still continues to lead to misunderstanding and discord. For they explain how the existence of two distinct types is actually a fact that has long been known: a fact that in one form or another has struck the observer of human nature or dawned upon the brooding reflection of the thinker, presenting itself to Goethe's intuition, for instance, as the all-embracing principle of systole and diastole. The names and concepts by which the mechanisms of extraversion and introversion have been grasped are extremely varied, and each of them is adapted to the standpoint of the observer in question. But despite the diversity of the formulations the fundamental idea common to them all constantly shines through: in one case an outward movement of interest towards the object, and in the other a movement of interest away from the object to the subject and his own psychological processes. In the first case the object works like a magnet upon the tendencies of the subject; it determines the subject to a large extent and even alienates him from himself. His qualities may become so transformed by assimilation to the object that one might think it possessed some higher and decisive significance for him. It might almost seem as if it were an absolute determinant, a special purpose of life or fate that he should abandon himself wholly to the object. But in the second case the subject is and remains the

188

centre of every interest. It looks, one might say, as though all the life-energy were ultimately seeking the subject, and thus continually prevented the object from exercising any overpowering influence. It is as though the energy were flowing away from the object, and the subject were a magnet drawing the object to itself.

5   It is not easy to give a clear and intelligible description of this two-way relationship to the object without running the risk of paradoxical formulations which would create more confusion than clarity. But in general one could say that the introverted standpoint is one which sets the ego and the subjective psychological process above the object and the objective process, or at any rate seeks to hold its ground against the object. This attitude, therefore, gives the subject a higher value than the object, and the object accordingly has a lower value. It is of secondary importance; indeed, sometimes the object represents no more than an outward token of a subjective content, the embodiment of an idea, the idea being the essential thing. If it is the embodiment of a feeling, then again the feeling is the main thing and not the object in its own right. The extraverted standpoint, on the contrary, subordinates the subject to the object, so that the object has the higher value. In this case the subject is of secondary importance, the subjective process appearing at times as no more than a disturbing or superfluous appendage of objective events. It is clear that the psychology resulting from these contrary standpoints must be classed as two totally different orientations. The one sees everything in terms of his own situation, the other in terms of the objective event.

6   These contrary attitudes are in themselves no more than correlative mechanisms: a diastolic going out and seizing of the object, and a systolic concentration and detachment of energy from the object seized. Every human being possesses both mechanisms as an expression of his natural life-rhythm, a rhythm which Goethe, surely not by chance, described physiologically in terms of the heart's activity. A rhythmical alternation of both forms of psychic activity would perhaps correspond to the normal course of life. But the complicated outer conditions under which we live and the even more complicated conditions of our individual psychic make-up seldom permit

a completely undisturbed flow of psychic energy. Outer circumstances and inner disposition frequently favour one mechanism and restrict or hinder the other. One mechanism will naturally predominate, and if this condition becomes in any way chronic a *type* will be produced; that is, an habitual attitude in which one mechanism predominates permanently, although the other can never be completely suppressed since it is an integral part of the psychic economy. Hence there can never be a pure type in the sense that it possesses only one mechanism with the complete atrophy of the other. A typical attitude always means merely the relative predominance of one mechanism.

7   The hypothesis of introversion and extraversion allows us, first of all, to distinguish two large groups of psychological individuals. Yet this grouping is of such a superficial and general nature that it permits no more than this very general distinction. Closer investigation of the individual psychologies that fall into one group or the other will at once show great differences between individuals who nevertheless belong to the same group. If, therefore, we wish to determine wherein lie the differences between individuals belonging to a definite group, we must take a further step. Experience has taught me that in general individuals can be distinguished not only according to the broad distinction between introversion and extraversion, but also according to their basic psychological functions. For in the same measure as outer circumstances and inner disposition cause either introversion or extraversion to predominate, they also favour the predominance of one definite basic function in the individual. I have found from experience that the basic psychological functions, that is, functions which are genuinely as well as essentially different from other functions, prove to be *thinking, feeling, sensation,* and *intuition.* If one of these functions habitually predominates, a corresponding type results. I therefore distinguish a thinking, a feeling, a sensation, and an intuitive type. *Each of these types may moreover be either introverted or extraverted,* depending on its relation to the object as we have described above. In my preliminary work on psychological types[1] I did not carry out

[1] "A Contribution to the Study of Psychological Types" (1913), *infra,* Appendix, pars. 858ff., and "The Psychology of the Unconscious Processes," *Collected Papers*

this differentiation, but identified the thinking type with the introvert and the feeling type with the extravert. A deeper study of the problem has shown this equation to be untenable. In order to avoid misunderstandings, I would ask the reader to bear in mind the differentiation I have developed here. For the sake of clarity, which is essential in such complicated matters, I have devoted the last chapter of this book to the definition of my psychological concepts.

---

on *Analytical Psychology* (2nd edn., 1917), pp. 391ff. [The latter section, on types, was subsequently revised and appears as ch. IV ("The Problem of the Attitude-Type") of the first of the *Two Essays on Analytical Psychology*. Cf. also "The Structure of the Unconscious" (1916), in ibid., pars. 462, n. 8, and 482.—EDITORS.]

GENERAL DESCRIPTION OF THE TYPES

[abridged]

1. INTRODUCTION

556   In the following pages I shall attempt a general description of the psychology of the types, starting with the two basic types I have termed introverted and extraverted. This will be followed by a description of those more special types whose peculiarities are due to the fact that the individual adapts and orients himself chiefly by means of his most differentiated function. The former I would call *attitude-types*, distinguished by the direction of their interest, or of the movement of libido; the latter I would call *function-types*.

557   The attitude-types, as I have repeatedly emphasized in the preceding chapters, are distinguished by their attitude to the object. The introvert's attitude is an abstracting one; at bottom, he is always intent on withdrawing libido from the object, as though he had to prevent the object from gaining power over him. The extravert, on the contrary, has a positive relation to the object. He affirms its importance to such an extent that his subjective attitude is constantly related to and oriented by the object. The object can never have enough value for him, and its importance must always be increased. The two types are so different and present such a striking contrast that their existence becomes quite obvious even to the layman once it has been pointed out. Everyone knows those reserved, inscrutable, rather shy people who form the strongest possible contrast to the open, sociable, jovial, or at least friendly and approachable characters who are on good terms with everybody, or quarrel with everybody, but always relate to them in some way and in turn are affected by them.

558   One is naturally inclined, at first, to regard such differences as mere idiosyncrasies of character peculiar to individ-

559 uals. But anyone with a thorough knowledge of human nature will soon discover that the contrast is by no means a matter of isolated individual instances but of typical attitudes which are far more common than one with limited psychological experience would assume. Indeed, as the preceding chapters may have shown, it is a fundamental contrast, sometimes quite clear, sometimes obscured, but always apparent when one is dealing with individuals whose personality is in any way pronounced. Such people are found not merely among the educated, but in all ranks of society, so that our types can be discovered among labourers and peasants no less than among the most highly differentiated members of a community. Sex makes no difference either; one finds the same contrast among women of all classes. Such a widespread distribution could hardly have come about if it were merely a question of a conscious and deliberate choice of attitude. In that case, one would surely find one particular attitude in one particular class of people linked together by a common education and background and localized accordingly. But that is not so at all; on the contrary, the types seem to be distributed quite at random. In the same family one child is introverted, the other extraverted. Since the facts show that the attitude-type is a general phenomenon having an apparently random distribution, it cannot be a matter of conscious judgment or conscious intention, but must be due to some unconscious, instinctive cause. As a general psychological phenomenon, therefore, the type antithesis must have some kind of biological foundation.

The relation between subject and object, biologically considered, is always one of adaptation, since every relation between subject and object presupposes the modification of one by the other through reciprocal influence. Adaptation consists in these constant modifications. The typical attitudes to the object, therefore, are processes of adaptation. There are in nature two fundamentally different modes of adaptation which ensure the continued existence of the living organism. The one consists in a high rate of fertility, with low powers of defence and short duration of life for the single individual; the other consists in equipping the individual with numerous means of self-preservation plus a low fertility rate. This biological difference, it seems to me, is not merely analogous to, but the actual foundation of, our two psychological modes of adaptation. I must content myself with this broad hint. It is sufficient to note that the peculiar nature of the extravert constantly urges him to expend and propagate himself in every way, while the tendency of the introvert is to defend himself against all demands from outside, to conserve his energy by withdrawing it from objects, thereby consolidating his own position. Blake's intuition did not err when he described the two classes of men as "prolific" and "devouring."[1] Just as, biologically, the two modes of adaptation work equally well and are successful in their own way, so too with the typical attitudes. The one achieves its end by a multiplicity of relationships, the other by monopoly.

The fact that children often exhibit a typical attitude quite unmistakably even in their earliest years forces us to assume that it cannot be the struggle for existence in the ordinary sense that determines a particular attitude. It might be objected, cogently enough, that even the infant at the breast has to perform an unconscious act of psychological adaptation, in that the mother's influence leads to specific reactions in the child. This argument, while supported by incontestable evidence, becomes rather flimsy in face of the equally incontestable fact that two children of the same mother may exhibit contrary attitudes at an early age, though no change in the mother's attitude can be demonstrated. Although nothing would induce me to underrate the incalculable importance of parental influence, this familiar experience compels me to conclude that the decisive factor must be looked for in the disposition of the child. Ultimately, it must be the individual disposition which decides whether the child will belong to this or that type despite the constancy of external conditions. Naturally I am thinking only of normal cases. Under abnormal conditions, i.e., when the mother's own attitude is extreme, a similar attitude can be forced on the children too, thus violating their individual disposition, which might have opted for another type if no abnormal external influences had intervened. As a rule, whenever such a falsification of type takes place as a result of parental influence, the individual becomes neurotic later, and can be cured only by developing the attitude consonant with his nature.

[1] William Blake, *The Marriage of Heaven and Hell.*

194

561   As to the individual disposition, I have nothing to say except that there are obviously individuals who have a greater capacity, or to whom it is more congenial, to adapt in one way and not in another. It may well be that physiological causes of which we have no knowledge play a part in this. I do not think it improbable, in view of one's experience that a reversal of type often proves exceedingly harmful to the physiological well-being of the organism, usually causing acute exhaustion.

2. THE EXTRAVERTED TYPE

562   In our description of this and the following types it is necessary, for the sake of clarity, to distinguish between the psychology of consciousness and the psychology of the unconscious. We shall first describe the phenomena of consciousness.

a. The General Attitude of Consciousness

563   Although it is true that everyone orients himself in accordance with the data supplied by the outside world, we see every day that the data in themselves are only relatively decisive. The fact that it is cold outside prompts one man to put on his overcoat, while another, who wants to get hardened, finds this superfluous. One man admires the latest tenor because everybody else does, another refuses to do so, not because he dislikes him, but because in his view the subject of universal admiration is far from having been proved admirable. One man resigns himself to circumstances because experience has shown him that nothing else is possible, another is convinced that though things have gone the same way a thousand times before, the thousand and first time will be different. The one allows himself to be oriented by the given facts, the other holds in reserve a view which interposes itself between him and the objective data. Now, when orientation by the object predominates in such a way that decisions and actions are determined not by subjective views but by objective conditions, we speak of an extraverted attitude. When this is habitual, we speak of an extraverted type. If a man thinks, feels, acts, and actually lives in a way that is *directly* correlated with the objective conditions and their demands, he is extraverted. His life makes it

perfectly clear that it is the object and not this subjective view that plays the determining role in his consciousness. Naturally he has subjective views too, but their determining value is less than that of the objective conditions. Consequently, he never expects to find any absolute factors in his own inner life, since the only ones he knows are outside himself. Like Epimetheus, his inner life is subordinated to external necessity, though not without a struggle; but it is always the objective determinant that wins in the end. His whole consciousness looks outward, because the essential and decisive determination always comes from outside. But it comes from outside only because that is where he expects it to come from. All the peculiarities of his psychology, except those that depend on the primacy of one particular psychological function or on idiosyncrasies of character, follow from this basic attitude. His interest and attention are directed to objective happenings, particularly those in his immediate environment. Not only people but things seize and rivet his attention. Accordingly, they also determine his actions, which are fully explicable on those grounds. The actions of the extravert are recognizably related to external conditions. In so far as they are not merely reactive to environmental stimuli, they have a character that is always adapted to the actual circumstances, and they find sufficient play within the limits of the objective situation. No serious effort is made to transcend these bounds. It is the same with his interest: objective happenings have an almost inexhaustible fascination for him, so that ordinarily he never looks for anything else.

564
The moral laws governing his actions coincide with the demands of society, that is, with the prevailing moral standpoint. If this were to change, the extravert's subjective moral guidelines would change accordingly, without this altering his general psychological habits in any way. This strict determination by objective factors does not mean, as one might suppose, a complete let alone ideal adaptation to the general conditions of life. In the eyes of the extravert, of course, an *adjustment of* this kind to the objective situation must seem like complete adaptation, since for him no other criterion exists. But from a higher point of view it by no means follows that the objective situation is in all circumstances a normal one. It can quite well

be temporarily or locally abnormal. An individual who adjusts himself to it is admittedly conforming to the style of his environment, but together with his whole surroundings he is in an abnormal situation with respect to the universally valid laws of life. He may indeed thrive in such surroundings, but only up to the point where he and his milieu meet with disaster for transgressing these laws. He will share the general collapse to exactly the same extent as he was adjusted to the previous situation. Adjustment is not adaptation; adaptation requires far more than merely going along smoothly with the conditions of the moment. (Once again I would remind the reader of Spitteler's Epimetheus.) It requires observance of laws more universal than the immediate conditions of time and place. The very adjustment of the normal extraverted type is his limitation. He owes his normality on the one hand to his ability to fit into existing conditions with comparative ease. His requirements are limited to the objectively possible, for instance to the career that holds out good prospects at this particular moment; he does what is needed of him, or what is expected of him, and refrains from all innovations that are not entirely self-evident or that in any way exceed the expectations of those around him. On the other hand, his normality must also depend essentially on whether he takes account of his subjective needs and requirements, and this is just his weak point, for the tendency of his type is so outer-directed that even the most obvious of all subjective facts, the condition of his own body, receives scant attention. The body is not sufficiently objective or "outside," so that the satisfaction of elementary needs which are indispensable to physical well-being is no longer given its due. The body accordingly suffers, to say nothing of the psyche. The extravert is usually unaware of this latter fact, but it is all the more apparent to his household. He feels his loss of equilibrium only when it announces itself in abnormal body sensations. These he cannot ignore. It is quite natural that he should regard them as concrete and "objective," since with his type of mentality they cannot be anything else—for him. In others he at once sees "imagination" at work. A too extraverted attitude can also become so oblivious of the subject that the latter is sacrificed completely to so-called objective demands—to the

565 demands, for instance, of a continually expanding business, because orders are piling up and profitable opportunities have to be exploited.

This is the extravert's danger: he gets sucked into objects and completely loses himself in them. The resultant functional disorders, nervous or physical, have a compensatory value, as they force him into an involuntary self-restraint. Should the symptoms be functional, their peculiar character may express his psychological situation in symbolic form; for instance, a singer whose fame has risen to dangerous heights that tempt him to expend too much energy suddenly finds he cannot sing high notes because of some nervous inhibition. Or a man of modest beginnings who rapidly reaches a social position of great influence with wide prospects is suddenly afflicted with all the symptoms of a mountain sickness.[2] Again, a man about to marry a woman of doubtful character whom he adores and vastly overestimates is seized with a nervous spasm of the oesophagus and has to restrict himself to two cups of milk a day, each of which takes him three hours to consume. All visits to the adored are effectively stopped, and he has no choice but to devote himself to the nourishment of his body. Or a man who can no longer carry the weight of the huge business he has built up is afflicted with nervous attacks of thirst and speedily falls a victim to hysterical alcoholism.

566 Hysteria is, in my view, by far the most frequent neurosis of the extraverted type. The hallmark of classic hysteria is an exaggerated rapport with persons in the immediate environment and an adjustment to surrounding conditions that amounts to imitation. A constant tendency to make himself interesting and to produce an impression is a basic feature of the hysteric. The corollary of this is his proverbial suggestibility, his proneness to another person's influence. Another unmistakable sign of the extraverted hysteric is his effusiveness, which occasionally carries him into the realm of fantasy, so that he is accused of the "hysterical lie." The hysterical character begins as an exaggeration of the normal attitude; it is then complicated by compensatory reactions from the uncon-

2 [For a detailed discussion of this case, see "The Tavistock Lectures," *Coll. Works*, vol. 18, pars. 161ff.—Editors.]

567 scious, which counteract the exaggerated extraversion by means of physical symptoms that force the libido to introvert. The reaction of the unconscious produces another class of symptoms having a more introverted character, one of the most typical being a morbid intensification of fantasy activity.

After this general outline of the extraverted attitude we shall now turn to a description of the modifications which the basic psychological functions undergo as a result of this attitude.

b. The Attitude of the Unconscious

568 It may perhaps seem odd that I should speak of an "attitude of the unconscious." As I have repeatedly indicated, I regard the attitude of the unconscious as compensatory to consciousness. According to this view, the unconscious has as good a claim to an "attitude" as the latter.

569 In the preceding section I emphasized the tendency to one-sidedness in the extraverted attitude, due to the ascendency of the object over the course of psychic events. The extraverted type is constantly tempted to expend himself for the apparent benefit of the object, to assimilate subject to object. I have discussed in some detail the harmful consequences of an exaggeration of the extraverted attitude, namely, the suppression of the subjective factor. It is only to be expected, therefore, that the psychic compensation of the conscious extraverted attitude will lay special weight on the subjective factor, and that we shall find a markedly egocentric tendency in the unconscious. Practical experience proves this to be the case. I do not wish to cite case material at this point, so must refer my readers to the ensuing sections, where I try to present the characteristic attitude of the unconscious in each function-type. In this section we are concerned simply with the compensation of the extraverted attitude in general, so I shall confine myself to describing the attitude of the unconscious in equally general terms.

570 The attitude of the unconscious as an effective complement to the conscious extraverted attitude has a definitely introverting character. It concentrates the libido on the subjective factor, that is, on all those needs and demands that are

stifled or repressed by the conscious attitude. As may be gathered from what was said in the previous section, a purely objective orientation does violence to a multitude of subjective impulses, intentions, needs, and desires and deprives them of the libido that is their natural right. Man is not a machine that can be remodelled for quite other purposes as occasion demands, in the hope that it will go on functioning as regularly as before but in a quite different way. He carries his whole history with him; in his very structure is written the history of mankind. This historical element in man represents a vital need to which a wise psychic economy must respond. Somehow the past must come alive and participate in the present. Total assimilation to the object will always arouse the protest of the suppressed minority of those elements that belong to the past and have existed from the very beginning.

571   From these general considerations it is easy to see why the unconscious demands of the extravert have an essentially primitive, infantile, egocentric character. When Freud says that the unconscious "can do nothing but wish" this is very largely true of the unconscious of the extravert. His adjustment to the objective situation and his assimilation to the object prevent low-powered subjective impulses from reaching consciousness. These impulses (thoughts, wishes, affects, needs, feelings, etc.) take on a regressive character according to the degree of repression; the less they are acknowledged, the more infantile and archaic they become. The conscious attitude robs them of all energy that is readily disposable, only leaving them the energy of which it cannot deprive them. This residue, which still possesses a potency not to be underestimated, can be described only as primordial instinct. Instinct can never be eradicated in an individual by arbitrary measures; it requires the slow, organic transformation of many generations to effect a radical change, for instinct is the energic expression of the organism's make-up.

572   Thus with every repressed impulse a considerable amount of energy ultimately remains, of an instinctive character, and preserves its potency despite the deprivation that made it unconscious. The more complete the conscious attitude of extraversion is, the more infantile and archaic the unconscious atti-

tude will be. The egoism which characterizes the extravert's unconscious attitude goes far beyond mere childish selfishness; it verges on the ruthless and the brutal. Here we find in full flower the incest-wish described by Freud. It goes without saying that these things are entirely unconscious and remain hidden from the layman so long as the extraversion of the conscious attitude is not extreme. But whenever it is exaggerated, the unconscious comes to light in symptomatic form; its egoism, infantilism, and archaism lose their original compensatory character and appear in more or less open opposition to the conscious attitude. This begins as an absurd exaggeration of conscious standpoint, aiming at a further repression of the unconscious, but usually it ends in a *reductio ad absurdum* of the conscious attitude and hence in catastrophe. The catastrophe may take an objective form, since the objective aims gradually become falsified by the subjective. I remember the case of a printer who, starting as a mere employee, worked his way up after years of hard struggle till at last he became the owner of a flourishing business. The more it expanded, the more it tightened its hold on him, until finally it swallowed up all his other interests. This proved his ruin. As an unconscious compensation of his exclusive interest in the business, certain memories of his childhood came to life. As a child he had taken great delight in painting and drawing. But instead of renewing this capacity for its own sake as a compensating hobby, he channelled it into his business and began wondering how he might embellish his products in an "artistic" way. Unfortunately his fantasies materialized: he actually turned out stuff that suited his own primitive and infantile taste, with the result that after a very few years his business went to pieces. He acted in accordance with one of our "cultural ideals," which says that any enterprising person has to concentrate everything on the one aim in view. But he went too far, and merely fell a victim to the power of his infantile demands.

573   The catastrophe can, however, also be subjective and take the form of a nervous breakdown. This invariably happens when the influence of the unconscious finally paralyzes all conscious action. The demands of the unconscious then force themselves imperiously on consciousness and bring about a

574 disastrous split which shows itself in one of two ways: either the subject no longer knows what he really wants and nothing interests him, or he wants too much at once and has too many interests, but in impossible things. The suppression of infantile and primitive demands for cultural reasons easily leads to a neurosis or to the abuse of narcotics such as alcohol, morphine, cocaine, etc. In more extreme cases the split ends in suicide.

It is an outstanding peculiarity of unconscious impulses that, when deprived of energy by lack of conscious recognition, they take on a destructive character, and this happens as soon as they cease to be compensatory. Their compensatory function ceases as soon as they reach a depth corresponding to a cultural level absolutely incompatible with our own. From this moment the unconscious impulses form a block in every way opposed to the conscious attitude, and its very existence leads to open conflict.

575 Generally speaking, the compensating attitude of the unconscious finds expression in the maintenance of the psychic equilibrium. A normal extraverted attitude does not, of course, mean that the individual invariably behaves in accordance with the extraverted schema. Even in the same individual many psychological processes may be observed that involve the mechanism of introversion. We call a mode of behaviour extraverted only when the mechanism of extraversion predominates. In these cases the most differentiated function is always employed in an extraverted way, whereas the inferior functions are introverted; in other words, the superior function is the most conscious one and completely under conscious control, whereas the less differentiated functions are in part unconscious and far less under the control of consciousness. The superior function is always an expression of the conscious personality, of its aims, will, and general performance, whereas the less differentiated functions fall into the category of things that simply "happen" to one. These things need not be mere slips of the tongue or pen and other such oversights, they can equally well be half or three-quarters intended, for the less differentiated functions also possess a slight degree of consciousness. A classic example of this is the extraverted feeling type, who enjoys an excellent feeling rapport with the people

576   around him, yet occasionally "happens" to express opinions of unsurpassable tactlessness. These opinions spring from his inferior and half-conscious thinking, which, being only partly under his control and insufficiently related to the object, can be quite ruthless in its effects.

    The less differentiated functions of the extravert always show a highly subjective colouring with pronounced egocentricity and personal bias, thus revealing their close connection with the unconscious. The unconscious is continually coming to light through them. It should not be imagined that the unconscious lies permanently buried under so many overlying strata that it can only be uncovered, so to speak, by a laborious process of excavation. On the contrary, there is a constant influx of unconscious contents into the conscious psychological process, to such a degree that at times it is hard for the observer to decide which character traits belong to the conscious and which to the unconscious personality. This difficulty is met with mainly in people who are given to express themselves more profusely than others. Naturally it also depends very largely on the attitude of the observer whether he seizes hold of the conscious or the unconscious character of the personality. Generally speaking, a judging observer will tend to seize on the conscious character, while a perceptive observer will be more influenced by the unconscious character, since judgment is chiefly concerned with the conscious motivation of the psychic process, while perception registers the process itself. But in so far as we apply judgment and perception in equal measure, it may easily happen that a personality appears to us as both introverted and extraverted, so that we cannot decide at first to which attitude the superior function belongs. In such cases only a thorough analysis of the qualities of each function can help us to form a valid judgment. We must observe which function is completely under conscious control, and which functions have a haphazard and spontaneous character. The former is always more highly differentiated than the latter, which also possess infantile and primitive traits. Occasionally the superior function gives the impression of normality, while the others have something abnormal or pathological about them.

c. The Peculiarities of the Basic Psychological Functions in the Extraverted Attitude

Thinking

577 As a consequence of the general attitude of extraversion, thinking is oriented by the object and objective data. This gives rise to a noticeable peculiarity. Thinking in general is fed on the one hand from subjective and in the last resort unconscious sources, and on the other hand from objective data transmitted by sense-perception. Extraverted thinking is conditioned in a larger measure by the latter than by the former. Judgment always presupposes a criterion; for the extraverted judgment, the criterion supplied by external conditions is the valid and determining one, no matter whether it be represented directly by an objective, perceptible fact or by an objective idea; for an objective idea is equally determined by external data or borrowed from outside even when it is subjectively sanctioned. Extraverted thinking, therefore, need not necessarily be purely concretistic thinking; it can just as well be purely ideal thinking, if for instance it can be shown that the ideas it operates with are largely borrowed from outside, i.e., have been transmitted by tradition and education. So in judging whether a particular thinking is extraverted or not we must first ask: by what criterion does it judge—does it come from outside, or is its origin subjective? A further criterion is the direction the thinking takes in drawing conclusions—whether it is principally directed outwards or not. It is no proof of its extraverted nature that it is preoccupied with concrete objects, since my thinking may be preoccupied with a concrete object either because I am abstracting my thought from it or because I am concretizing my thought through it. Even when my thinking is preoccupied with concrete things and could be described as extraverted to that extent, the direction it will take still remains an essential characteristic and an open question—namely, whether or not in its further course it leads back again to objective data, external facts, or generally accepted ideas. So far as the practical thinking of the business man, the technician, or the scientific investigator is concerned, its outer-directedness is obvious enough. But in the

case of the philosopher it remains open to doubt when his thinking is directed to ideas. We then have to inquire whether these ideas are simply abstractions from objective experience, in which case they would represent higher collective concepts comprising a sum of objective facts, or whether (if they are clearly not abstractions from immediate experience) they may not be derived from tradition or borrowed from the intellectual atmosphere of the time. In the latter case, they fall into the category of objective data, and accordingly this thinking should be called extraverted.

578   Although I do not propose to discuss the nature of introverted thinking at this point, reserving it for a later section (pars. 628–31), it is essential that I should say a few words about it before proceeding further. For if one reflects on what I have just said about extraverted thinking, one might easily conclude that this covers everything that is ordinarily understood as thinking. A thinking that is directed neither to objective facts nor to general ideas, one might argue, scarcely deserves the name "thinking" at all. I am fully aware that our age and its most eminent representatives know and acknowledge only the extraverted type of thinking. This is largely because all the thinking that appears visibly on the surface in the form of science or philosophy or even art either derives directly from objects or else flows into general ideas. For both these reasons it appears essentially understandable, even though it may not always be self-evident, and it is therefore regarded as valid. In this sense it might be said that the extraverted intellect oriented by objective data is actually the only one that is recognized. But—and now I come to the question of the introverted intellect—there also exists an entirely different kind of thinking, to which the term "thinking" can hardly be denied: it is a kind that is oriented neither by immediate experience of objects nor by traditional ideas. I reach this other kind of thinking in the following manner: when my thoughts are preoccupied with a concrete object or a general idea, in such a way that the course of my thinking eventually leads me back to my starting-point, this intellectual process is not the only psychic process that is going on in me. I will disregard all those sensations and feelings which become noticeable as a more or less disturbing accompaniment to my train of thought, and will

merely point out that this very thinking process which starts from the object and returns to the object also stands in a constant relation to the subject. This relation is a *sine qua non,* without which no thinking process whatsoever could take place. Even though my thinking process is directed, as far as possible, to objective data, it is still *my* subjective process, and it can neither avoid nor dispense with this admixture of subjectivity. Struggle as I may to give an objective orientation to my train of thought, I cannot shut out the parallel subjective process and its running accompaniment without extinguishing the very spark of life from my thought. This parallel process has a natural and hardly avoidable tendency to subjectify the objective data and assimilate them to the subject.

579   Now when the main accent lies on the subjective process, that other kind of thinking arises which is opposed to extraverted thinking, namely, that purely subjective orientation which I call introverted. This thinking is neither determined by objective data nor directed to them; it is a thinking that starts from the subject and is directed to subjective ideas or subjective facts. I do not wish to enter more fully into this kind of thinking here; I have merely established its existence as the necessary complement of extraverted thinking and brought it into clearer focus.

580   Extraverted thinking, then, comes into existence only when the objective orientation predominates. This fact does nothing to alter the logic of thinking; it merely constitutes that difference between thinkers which James considered a matter of temperament. Orientation to the object, as already explained, makes no essential change in the thinking function; only its appearance is altered. It has the appearance of being captivated by the object, as though without the external orientation it simply could not exist. It almost seems as though it were a mere sequela of external facts, or as though it could reach its highest point only when flowing into some general idea. It seems to be constantly affected by the objective data and to draw conclusions only with their consent. Hence it gives one the impression of a certain lack of freedom, of occasional short-sightedness, in spite of all its adroitness within the area circumscribed by the object. What I am describing is simply the impression this sort of thinking makes on the observer, who

206

must himself have a different standpoint, otherwise it would be impossible for him to observe the phenomenon of extraverted thinking at all. But because of his different standpoint he sees only its outward aspect, not its essence, whereas the thinker himself can apprehend its essence but not its outward aspect. Judging by appearances can never do justice to the essence of the thing, hence the verdict is in most cases depreciatory.

581 In its essence this thinking is no less fruitful and creative than introverted thinking, it merely serves other ends. This difference becomes quite palpable when extraverted thinking appropriates material that is the special province of introverted thinking; when, for instance, a subjective conviction is explained analytically in terms of objective data or as being derived from objective ideas. For our scientific consciousness, however, the difference becomes even more obvious when introverted thinking attempts to bring objective data into connections not warranted by the object—in other words, to subordinate them to a subjective idea. Each type of thinking senses the other as an encroachment on its own province, and hence a sort of shadow effect is produced, each revealing to the other its least favourable aspect. Introverted thinking then appears as something quite arbitrary, while extraverted thinking seems dull and banal. Thus the two orientations are incessantly at war.

582 One might think it easy enough to put an end to this conflict by making a clear distinction between objective and subjective data. Unfortunately, this is impossible, though not a few have attempted it. And even if it were possible it would be a disastrous proceeding, since in themselves both orientations are one-sided and of limited validity, so that each needs the influence of the other. When objective data predominate over thinking to any great extent, thinking is sterilized, becoming a mere appendage of the object and no longer capable of abstracting itself into an independent concept. It is then reduced to a kind of "after-thought," by which I do not mean "reflection" but a purely imitative thinking which affirms nothing beyond what was visibly and immediately present in the objective data in the first place. This thinking naturally leads directly back to the object, but never beyond it, not even to a

583   When extraverted thinking is subordinated to objective data as a result of over-determination by the object, it engrosses itself entirely in the individual experience and accumulates a mass of undigested empirical material. The oppressive weight of individual experiences having little or no connection with one another produces a dissociation of thought which usually requires psychological compensation. This must consist in some simple, general idea that gives coherence to the disordered whole, or at least affords the possibility of such. Ideas like "matter" or "energy" serve this purpose. But when the thinking depends primarily not on objective data but on some second-hand idea, the very poverty of this thinking is compensated by an all the more impressive accumulation of facts congregating round a narrow and sterile point of view, with the result that many valuable and meaningful aspects are completely lost sight of. Many of the allegedly scientific outpourings of our own day owe their existence to this wrong orientation.

   · · ·

Feeling

595   Feeling in the extraverted attitude is likewise oriented by objective data, the object being the indispensable determinant of the quality of feeling. The extravert's feeling is always in harmony with objective values. For anyone who has known feeling only as something subjective, the nature of extraverted feeling will be difficult to grasp, because it has detached itself as much as possible from the subjective factor and subordinated itself entirely to the influence of the object. Even when it appears not to be qualified by a concrete object, it is none the less still under the spell of traditional or generally accepted

values of some kind. I may feel moved, for instance, to say that something is "beautiful" or "good," not because I find it "beautiful" or "good" from my own subjective feeling about it, but because it is fitting and politic to call it so, since a contrary judgment would upset the general feeling situation. A feeling judgment of this kind is not by any means a pretence or a lie, it is simply an act of adjustment. A painting, for instance, is called "beautiful" because a painting hung in a drawing room and bearing a well-known signature is generally assumed to be beautiful, or because to call it "hideous" would presumably offend the family of its fortunate possessor, or because the visitor wants to create a pleasant feeling atmosphere, for which purpose everything must be felt as agreeable. These feelings are governed by an objective criterion. As such they are genuine, and represent the feeling function as a whole.

596   In precisely the same way as extraverted thinking strives to rid itself of subjective influences, extraverted feeling has to undergo a process of differentiation before it is finally denuded of every subjective trimming. The valuations resulting from the act of feeling either correspond directly with objective values or accord with traditional and generally accepted standards. This kind of feeling is very largely responsible for the fact that so many people flock to the theatre or to concerts, or go to church, and do so moreover with their feelings correctly adjusted. Fashions, too, owe their whole existence to it, and, what is far more valuable, the positive support of social, philanthropic, and other such cultural institutions. In these matters extraverted feeling proves itself a creative factor. Without it, a harmonious social life would be impossible. To that extent extraverted feeling is just as beneficial and sweetly reasonable in its effects as extraverted thinking. But these salutary effects are lost as soon as the object gains ascendency. The force of extraverted feeling then pulls the personality into the object, the object assimilates him, whereupon the personal quality of the feeling, which constitutes its chief charm, disappears. It becomes cold, "unfeeling," untrustworthy. It has ulterior motives, or at least makes an impartial observer suspect them. It no longer makes that agreeable and refreshing impression which invariably accompanies genuine feeling; instead, one suspects a pose, or that the person is acting, even though he

may be quite unconscious of any egocentric motives. Over-extraverted feeling may satisfy aesthetic expectations, but it does not speak to the heart; it appeals merely to the senses or—worse still—only to reason. It can provide the aesthetic padding for a situation, but there it stops, and beyond that its effect is nil. It has become sterile. If this process goes any further, a curiously contradictory dissociation of feeling results: everything becomes an object of feeling valuations, and innumerable relationships are entered into which are all at variance with each other. As this situation would become quite impossible if the subject received anything like due emphasis, even the last vestiges of a real personal standpoint are suppressed. The subject becomes so enmeshed in the network of individual feeling processes that to the observer it seems as though there were merely a feeling process and no longer a subject of feeling. Feeling in this state has lost all human warmth; it gives the impression of being put on, fickle, unreliable, and in the worst cases hysterical.

Summary of the Extraverted Rational Types

601   I call the two preceding types rational or judging types because they are characterized by the supremacy of the reasoning and judging functions. It is a general distinguishing mark of both types that their life is, to a great extent, subordinated to rational judgment. But we have to consider whether by "rational" we are speaking from the standpoint of the individual's subjective psychology or from that of the observer, who perceives and judges from without. This observer could easily arrive at a contrary judgment, especially if he intuitively apprehended merely the outward behaviour of the person observed and judged accordingly. On the whole, the life of this type is never dependent on rational judgment alone; it is influenced in almost equal degree by unconscious irrationality. If observation is restricted to outward behaviour, without any concern for the internal economy of the individual's conscious-

210

ness, one may get an even stronger impression of the irrational and fortuitous nature of certain unconscious manifestations than of the reasonableness of his conscious intentions and motivations. I therefore base my judgment on what the individual feels to be his conscious psychology. But I am willing to grant that one could equally well conceive and present such a psychology from precisely the opposite angle. I am also convinced that, had I myself chanced to possess a different psychology, I would have described the rational types in the reverse way, from the standpoint of the unconscious—as irrational, therefore. This aggravates the difficulty of a lucid presentation of psychological matters and immeasurably increases the possibility of misunderstandings. The arguments provoked by these misunderstandings are, as a rule, quite hopeless because each side is speaking at cross purposes. This experience is one reason the more for basing my presentation on the conscious psychology of the individual, since there at least we have a definite objective footing, which completely drops away the moment we try to base our psychological rationale on the unconscious. For in that case the observed object would have no voice in the matter at all, because there is nothing about which he is more uninformed than his own unconscious. The judgment is then left entirely to the subjective observer—a sure guarantee that it will be based on his own individual psychology, which would be forcibly imposed on the observed. To my mind, this is the case with the psychologies of both Freud and Adler. The individual is completely at the mercy of the judging observer, which can never be the case when the conscious psychology of the observed is accepted as a basis. He after all is the only competent judge, since he alone knows his conscious motives.

602   The rationality that characterizes the conscious conduct of life in both these types involves a deliberate exclusion of everything irrational and accidental. Rational judgment, in such a psychology, is a force that coerces the untidiness and fortuitousness of life into a definite pattern, or at least tries to do so. A definite choice is made from among all the possibilities it offers, only the rational ones being accepted; but on the other hand the independence and influence of the psychic functions which aid the perception of life's happenings are con-

sequently restricted. Naturally this restriction of sensation and intuition is not absolute. These functions exist as before, but their products are subject to the choice made by rational judgment. It is not the intensity of a sensation as such that decides action, for instance, but judgment. Thus, in a sense, the functions of perception share the same fate as feeling in the case of the first type, or thinking in that of the second. They are relatively repressed, and therefore in an inferior state of differentiation. This gives a peculiar stamp to the unconscious of both our types: what they consciously and intentionally do accords with reason (*their* reason, of course), but what happens to them accords with the nature of infantile, primitive sensations and intuitions. At all events, what happens to these types is irrational (from their standpoint). But since there are vast numbers of people whose lives consist more of what happens to them than of actions governed by rational intentions, such a person, after observing them closely, might easily describe both our types as irrational. And one has to admit that only too often a man's unconscious makes a far stronger impression on an observer than his consciousness does, and that his actions are of considerably more importance than his rational intentions.

603

The rationality of both types is object-oriented and dependent on objective data. It accords with what is collectively considered to be rational. For them, nothing is rational save what is generally considered as such. Reason, however, is in large part subjective and individual. In our types this part is repressed, and increasingly so as the object gains in importance. Both the subject and his subjective reason, therefore, are in constant danger of repression, and when they succumb to it they fall under the tyranny of the unconscious, which in this case possesses very unpleasant qualities. Of its peculiar thinking we have already spoken. But, besides that, there are primitive sensations that express themselves compulsively, for instance in the form of compulsive pleasure-seeking in every conceivable form; there are also primitive intuitions that can become a positive torture to the person concerned and to everybody in his vicinity. Everything that is unpleasant and painful, everything that is disgusting, hateful, and evil, is sniffed out or suspected, and in most cases it is a half-truth calculated to provoke misunderstandings of the most poisonous

212

kind. The antagonistic unconscious elements are so strong that they frequently disrupt the conscious rule of reason; the individual becomes the victim of chance happenings, which exercise a compulsive influence over him either because they pander to his sensations or because he intuits their unconscious significance.

Sensation

604   Sensation, in the extraverted attitude, is pre-eminently conditioned by the object. As sense perception, sensation is naturally dependent on objects. But, just as naturally, it is also dependent on the subject, for which reason there is subjective sensation of a kind entirely different from objective sensation. In the extraverted attitude the subjective component of sensation, so far as its conscious application is concerned, is either inhibited or repressed. Similarly, as an irrational function, sensation is largely repressed when thinking or feeling holds prior place; that is to say, it is a conscious function only to the extent that the rational attitude of consciousness permits accidental perceptions to become conscious contents—in a word, registers them. The sensory function is, of course, absolute in the stricter sense; everything is seen or heard, for instance, to the physiological limit, but not everything attains the threshold value a perception must have in order to be apperceived. It is different when sensation itself is paramount instead of merely seconding another function. In this case no element of objective sensation is excluded and nothing is repressed (except the subjective component already mentioned).

605   As sensation is chiefly conditioned by the object, those objects that excite the strongest sensations will be decisive for the individual's psychology. The result is a strong sensuous tie to the object. Sensation is therefore a vital function equipped with the strongest vital instinct. Objects are valued in so far as they excite sensations, and, so far as lies within the power of sensation, they are fully accepted into consciousness whether they are compatible with rational judgments or not. The sole criterion of their value is the intensity of the sensation produced by their objective qualities. Accordingly, all objective processes which excite any sensations at all make their appearance in consciousness. However, it is only concrete, sensuously

perceived objects or processes that excite sensations for the extravert; those, exclusively, which everyone everywhere would sense as concrete. Hence the orientation of such an individual accords with purely sensuous reality. The judging, rational functions are subordinated to the concrete facts of sensation, and thus have all the qualities of the less differentiated functions, exhibiting negative, infantile, and archaic traits. The function most repressed is naturally the opposite of sensation —intuition, the function of unconscious perception.

Intuition

. . .

610   In the extraverted attitude, intuition as the function of unconscious perception is wholly directed to external objects. Because intuition is in the main an unconscious process, its nature is very difficult to grasp. The intuitive function is represented in consciousness by an attitude of expectancy, by vision and penetration; but only from the subsequent result can it be established how much of what was "seen" was actually in the object, and how much was "read into" it. Just as sensation, when it is the dominant function, is not a mere reactive process of no further significance for the object, but an activity that seizes and shapes its object, so intuition is not mere perception, or vision, but an active, creative process that puts into the object just as much as it takes out. Since it does this unconsciously, it also has an unconscious effect on the object.

611   The primary function of intuition, however, is simply to transmit images, or perceptions of relations between things, which could not be transmitted by the other functions or only in a very roundabout way. These images have the value of specific insights which have a decisive influence on action whenever intuition is given priority. In this case, psychic adaptation will be grounded almost entirely on intuitions. Thinking, feeling, and sensation are then largely repressed, sensation being the one most affected, because, as the conscious sense function, it offers the greatest obstacle to intuition. Sensation is a hindrance to clear, unbiased, naïve perception; its intrusive sensory stimuli direct attention to the physical surface, to the

very things round and beyond which intuition tries to peer. But since extraverted intuition is directed predominantly to objects, it actually comes very close to sensation; indeed, the expectant attitude to external objects is just as likely to make use of sensation. Hence, if intuition is to function properly, sensation must to a large extent be suppressed. By sensation I mean in this instance the simple and immediate sense-impression understood as a clearly defined physiological and psychic datum. This must be expressly established beforehand because, if I ask an intuitive how he orients himself, he will speak of things that are almost indistinguishable from sense-impressions. Very often he will even use the word "sensation." He does have sensations, of course, but he is not guided by them as such; he uses them merely as starting-points for his perceptions. He selects them by unconscious predilection. It is not the strongest sensation, in the physiological sense, that is accorded the chief value, but any sensation whatsoever whose value is enhanced by the intuitive's unconscious attitude. In this way it may eventually come to acquire the chief value, and to his conscious mind it appears to be pure sensation. But actually it is not so.

612   Just as extraverted sensation strives to reach the highest pitch of actuality, because this alone can give the appearance of a full life, so intuition tries to apprehend the widest range of *possibilities*, since only through envisioning possibilities is intuition fully satisfied. It seeks to discover what possibilities the objective situation holds in store; hence, as a subordinate function (i.e., when not in the position of priority), it is the auxiliary that automatically comes into play when no other function can find a way out of a hopelessly blocked situation. When it is the dominant function, every ordinary situation in life seems like a locked room which intuition has to open. It is constantly seeking fresh outlets and new possibilities in external life. In a very short time every existing situation becomes a prison for the intuitive, a chain that has to be broken. For a time objects appear to have an exaggerated value, if they should serve to bring about a solution, a deliverance, or lead to the discovery of a new possibility. Yet no sooner have they served their purpose as stepping-stones or bridges than they lose their value altogether and are discarded as burdensome

appendages. Facts are acknowledged only if they open new possibilities of advancing beyond them and delivering the individual from their power. Nascent possibilities are compelling motives from which intuition cannot escape and to which all else must be sacrificed.

. . .

Summary of the Extraverted Irrational Types

616

I call the two preceding types irrational for the reasons previously discussed, namely that whatever they do or do not do is based not on rational judgment but on the sheer intensity of perception. Their perception is directed simply and solely to events as they happen, no selection being made by judgment. In this respect they have a decided advantage over the two judging types. Objective events both conform to law and are accidental. In so far as they conform to law, they are accessible to reason; in so far as they are accidental, they are not. Conversely, we might also say that an event conforms to law when it presents an aspect accessible to reason, and that when it presents an aspect for which we can find no law we call it accidental. The postulate of universal lawfulness is a postulate of reason alone, but in no sense is it a postulate of our perceptive functions. Since these are in no way based on the principle of reason and its postulates, they are by their very nature irrational. That is why I call the perception types "irrational" by nature. But merely because they subordinate judgment to perception, it would be quite wrong to regard them as "unreasonable." It would be truer to say that they are in the highest degree *empirical*. They base themselves exclusively on experience—so exclusively that, as a rule, their judgment cannot keep pace with their experience. But the judging functions are none the less present, although they eke out a largely unconscious existence. Since the unconscious, in spite of its separation from the conscious subject, is always appearing on the scene, we notice in the actual life of the irrational types striking judgments and acts of choice, but they take the form of apparent sophistries, cold-hearted criticisms, and a seemingly calculating choice of persons and situations. These traits have a rather infantile and even primitive character; both types can on occasion be astonishingly naïve, as well as ruthless, brusque, and violent. To the rational types the real character of these people might well appear rationalistic and calculating in the worst sense. But this judgment would be valid only for their unconscious, and therefore quite incorrect for their conscious psychology, which is entirely oriented by perception, and because of its irrational nature is quite unintelligible to any rational judgment. To the rational mind it might even seem that such a hodge-podge of accidentals hardly deserves the name "psychology," at all. The irrational type ripostes with an equally contemptuous opinion of his opposite number: he sees him as something only half alive, whose sole aim is to fasten the fetters of reason on everything living and strangle it with judgments. These are crass extremes, but they nevertheless occur.

617 From the standpoint of the rational type, the other might easily be represented as an inferior kind of rationalist—when, that is to say, he is judged by what happens to him. For what happens to him is not accidental—here he is the master—instead, the accidents that befall him take the form of rational judgments and rational intentions, and these are the things he stumbles over. To the rational mind this is something almost unthinkable, but its unthinkableness merely equals the astonishment of the irrational type when he comes up against someone who puts rational ideas above actual and living happenings. Such a thing seems to him scarcely credible. As a rule it is quite hopeless to discuss these things with him as questions of principle, for all rational communication is just as alien and repellent to him as it would be unthinkable for the rationalist to enter into a contract without mutual consultation and obligation.

618 This brings me to the problem of the psychic relationship between the two types. Following the terminology of the French school of hypnotists, psychic relationship is known in modern psychiatry as "rapport." Rapport consists essentially in a feeling of agreement in spite of acknowledged differences. Indeed, the recognition of existing differences, if it be mutual, is itself a rapport, a feeling of agreement. If in a given case we make this feeling conscious to a higher degree than usual, we discover that it is not just a feeling whose nature cannot be

analysed further, but at the same time an insight or a content of cognition which presents the point of agreement in conceptual form. This rational presentation is valid only for the rational types, but not for the irrational, whose rapport is based not on judgment but on the parallelism of living events. His feeling of agreement comes from the common perception of a sensation or intuition. The rational type would say that rapport with the irrational depends purely on chance. If, by some accident, the objective situations are exactly in tune, something like a human relationship takes place, but nobody can tell how valid it is or how long it will last. To the rational type it is often a painful thought that the relationship will last just as long as external circumstances and chance provide a common interest. This does not seem to him particularly human, whereas it is precisely in this that the irrational type sees a human situation of particular beauty. The result is that each regards the other as a man destitute of relationships, who cannot be relied upon, and with whom one can never get on decent terms. This unhappy outcome, however, is reached only when one makes a conscious effort to assess the nature of one's relationships with others. But since this kind of psychological conscientiousness is not very common, it frequently happens that despite an absolute difference of standpoint a rapport nevertheless comes about, and in the following way: one party, by unspoken projection, assumes that the other is, in all essentials, of the same opinion as himself, while the other divines or senses an objective community of interest, of which, however, the former has no conscious inkling and whose existence he would at once dispute, just as it would never occur to the other that his relationship should be based on a common point of view. A rapport of this kind is by far the most frequent; it rests on mutual projection, which later becomes the source of many misunderstandings.

619   Psychic relationship, in the extraverted attitude, is always governed by objective factors and external determinants. What a man is within himself is never of any decisive significance. For our present-day culture the extraverted attitude to the problem of human relationships is the principle that counts; naturally the introverted principle occurs too, but it is still the exception and has to appeal to the tolerance of the age.

3. THE INTROVERTED TYPE

a. The General Attitude of Consciousness

620   As I have already explained in the previous section, the introvert is distinguished from the extravert by the fact that he does not, like the latter, orient himself by the object and by objective data, but by subjective factors. I also mentioned[4] that the introvert interposes a subjective view between the perception of the object and his own action, which prevents the action from assuming a character that fits the objective situation. Naturally this is a special instance, mentioned by way of example and intended to serve only as a simple illustration. We must now attempt a formulation on a broader basis.

621   Although the introverted consciousness is naturally aware of external conditions, it selects the subjective determinants as the decisive ones. It is therefore oriented by the factor in perception and cognition which responds to the sense stimulus in accordance with the individual's subjective disposition. For example, two people see the same object, but they never see it in such a way that the images they receive are absolutely identical. Quite apart from the variable acuteness of the sense organs and the personal equation, there often exists a radical difference, both in kind and in degree, in the psychic assimilation of the perceptual image. Whereas the extravert continually appeals to what comes to him from the object, the introvert relies principally on what the sense impression constellates in the subject. The difference in the case of a single apperception may, of course, be very delicate, but in the total psychic economy it makes itself felt in the highest degree, particularly in the effect it has on the ego. If I may anticipate, I consider the viewpoint which inclines, with Weininger, to describe the introverted attitude as philautic, autoerotic, egocentric, subjectivistic, egotistic, etc., to be misleading in principle and thoroughly depreciatory. It reflects the normal bias of the extraverted attitude in regard to the nature of the introvert. We must not forget—although the extravert is only too prone to do so—that perception and cognition are not purely objective, but are also subjectively conditioned. The world exists not

4 Supra, par. 563.

622

merely in itself, but also as it appears to me. Indeed, at bottom, we have absolutely no criterion that could help us to form a judgment of a world which was unassimilable by the subject. If we were to ignore the subjective factor, it would be a complete denial of the great doubt as to the possibility of absolute cognition. And this would mean a relapse into the stale and hollow positivism that marred the turn of the century—an attitude of intellectual arrogance accompanied by crudeness of feeling, a violation of life as stupid as it is presumptuous. By overvaluing our capacity for objective cognition we repress the importance of the subjective factor, which simply means a denial of the subject. But what is the subject? The subject is man himself—we are the subject. Only a sick mind could forget that cognition must have a subject, and that there is no knowledge whatever and therefore no world at all unless "I know" has been said, though with this statement one has already expressed the subjective limitation of all knowledge.

This applies to all the psychic functions: they have a subject which is just as indispensable as the object. It is characteristic of our present extraverted sense of values that the word "subjective" usually sounds like a reproof; at all events the epithet "merely subjective" is brandished like a weapon over the head of anyone who is not boundlessly convinced of the absolute superiority of the object. We must therefore be quite clear as to what "subjective" means in this inquiry. By the subjective factor I understand that psychological action or reaction which merges with the effect produced by the object and so gives rise to a new psychic datum. In so far as the subjective factor has, from the earliest times and among all peoples, remained in large measure constant, elementary perceptions and cognitions being almost universally the same, it is a reality that is just as firmly established as the external object. If this were not so, any sort of permanent and essentially unchanging reality would be simply inconceivable, and any understanding of the past would be impossible. In this sense, therefore, the subjective factor is as ineluctable a datum as the extent of the sea and the radius of the earth. By the same token, the subjective factor has all the value of a co-determinant of the world we live in, a factor that can on no account be left out of our calculations. It is another universal law, and

220

whoever bases himself on it has a foundation as secure, as permanent, and as valid as the man who relies on the object. But just as the object and objective data do not remain permanently the same, being perishable and subject to chance, so too the subjective factor is subject to variation and individual hazards. For this reason its value is also merely relative. That is to say, the excessive development of the introverted standpoint does not lead to a better and sounder use of the subjective factor, but rather to an artificial subjectivizing of consciousness which can hardly escape the reproach "merely subjective." This is then counterbalanced by a de-subjectivization which takes the form of an exaggerated extraverted attitude, an attitude aptly described by Weininger as "misautic." But since the introverted attitude is based on the ever-present, extremely real, and absolutely indispensable fact of psychic adaptation, expressions like "philautic," "egocentric," and so on are out of place and objectionable because they arouse the prejudice that it is always a question of the beloved ego. Nothing could be more mistaken than such an assumption. Yet one is continually meeting it in the judgments of the extravert on the introvert. Not, of course, that I wish to ascribe this error to individual extraverts; it is rather to be put down to the generally accepted extraverted view which is by no means restricted to the extraverted type, for it has just as many representatives among introverts, very much to their own detriment. The reproach of being untrue to their own nature can justly be levelled at the latter, whereas this at least cannot be held against the former.

623   The introverted attitude is normally oriented by the psychic structure, which is in principle hereditary and is inborn in the subject. This must not be assumed, however, to be simply identical with the subject's ego, as is implied by the above designations of Weininger; it is rather the psychic structure of the subject prior to any ego-development. The really fundamental subject, the self, is far more comprehensive than the ego, since the former includes the unconscious whereas the latter is essentially the focal point of consciousness. Were the ego identical with the self, it would be inconceivable how we could sometimes see ourselves in dreams in quite different forms and with entirely different meanings. But it is a charac-

624 teristic peculiarity of the introvert, which is as much in keeping with his own inclination as with the general bias, to confuse his ego with the self, and to exalt it as the subject of the psychic process, thus bringing about the aforementioned subjectivization of consciousness which alienates him from the object.

625 The psychic structure is the same as what Semon calls "mneme"[5] and what I call the "collective unconscious." The individual self is a portion or segment or representative of something present in all living creatures, an exponent of the specific mode of psychological behaviour, which varies from species to species and is inborn in each of its members. The inborn mode of *acting* has long been known as *instinct*, and for the inborn mode of psychic apprehension I have proposed the term *archetype*.[6] I may assume that what is understood by instinct is familiar to everyone. It is another matter with the archetype. What I understand by it is identical with the "primordial image,"[7] a term borrowed from Jacob Burckhardt,[7] and I describe it as such in the Definitions that conclude this book. I must here refer the reader to the definition "Image."[8]

The archetype is a symbolic formula which always begins to function when there are no conscious ideas present, or when conscious ideas are inhibited for internal or external reasons. The contents of the collective unconscious are represented in consciousness in the form of pronounced preferences and definite ways of looking at things. These subjective tendencies and views are generally regarded by the individual as being determined by the object—incorrectly, since they have their source in the unconscious structure of the psyche and are merely released by the effect of the object. They are stronger than the object's influence, their psychic value is higher, so that they superimpose themselves on all impressions. Thus, just as it seems incomprehensible to the introvert that the object should always be the decisive factor, it remains an enigma to the extravert how a subjective standpoint can be superior to the objective situation. He inevitably comes to the conclusion that

5 *Die Mneme als erhaltendes Prinzip im Wechsel des organischen Geschehens* (trans. by L. Simon: *The Mneme*).
6 "Instinct and the Unconscious," pars. 270ff.
7 [Cf. *Symbols of Transformation*, par. 45. n. 45—Editors.]
8 [Especially pars. 746ff.—Editors.]

the introvert is either a conceited egoist or crack-brained bigot. Today he would be suspected of harbouring an unconscious power-complex. The introvert certainly lays himself open to these suspicions, for his positive, highly generalizing manner of expression, which appears to rule out every other opinion from the start, lends countenance to all the extravert's prejudices. Moreover the inflexibility of his subjective judgment, setting itself above all objective data, is sufficient in itself to create the impression of marked egocentricity. Faced with this prejudice the introvert is usually at a loss for the right argument, for he is quite unaware of the unconscious but generally quite valid assumptions on which his subjective judgment and his subjective perceptions are based. In the fashion of the times he looks outside for an answer, instead of seeking it behind his own consciousness. Should he become neurotic, it is the sign of an almost complete identity of the ego with the self; the importance of the self is reduced to nil, while the ego is inflated beyond measure. The whole world-creating force of the subjective factor becomes concentrated in the ego, producing a boundless power-complex and a fatuous egocentricity. Every psychology which reduces the essence of man to the unconscious power drive springs from this kind of disposition. Many of Nietzsche's lapses in taste, for example, are due to this subjectivization of consciousness.

b. *The Attitude of the Unconscious*

626   The predominance of the subjective factor in consciousness naturally involves a devaluation of the object. The object is not given the importance that belongs to it by right. Just as it plays too great a role in the extraverted attitude, it has too little meaning for the introvert. To the extent that his consciousness is subjectivized and excessive importance attached to the ego, the object is put in a position which in the end becomes untenable. The object is a factor whose power cannot be denied, whereas the ego is a very limited and fragile thing. It would be a very different matter if the self opposed the object. Self and world are commensurable factors; hence a normal introverted attitude is as justifiable and valid as a normal extraverted attitude. But if the ego has usurped the claims

of the subject, this naturally produces, by way of compensation, an unconscious reinforcement of the influence of the object. In spite of positively convulsive efforts to ensure the superiority of the ego, the object comes to exert an overwhelming influence, which is all the more invincible because it seizes on the individual unawares and forcibly obtrudes itself on his consciousness. As a result of the ego's unadapted relation to the object—for a desire to dominate it is not adaptation—a compensatory relation arises in the unconscious which makes itself felt as an absolute and irrepressible tie to the object. The more the ego struggles to preserve its independence, freedom from obligation, and superiority, the more it becomes enslaved to the objective data. The individual's freedom of mind is fettered by the ignominy of his financial dependence, his freedom of action trembles in the face of public opinion, his moral superiority collapses in a morass of inferior relationships, and his desire to dominate ends in a pitiful craving to be loved. It is now the unconscious that takes care of the relation to the object, and it does so in a way that is calculated to bring the illusion of power and the fantasy of superiority to utter ruin. The object assumes terrifying proportions in spite of the conscious attempt to degrade it. In consequence, the ego's efforts to detach itself from the object and get it under control become all the more violent. In the end it surrounds itself with a regular system of defences (aptly described by Adler) for the purpose of preserving at least the illusion of superiority. The introvert's alienation from the object is now complete; he wears himself out with defence measures on the one hand, while on the other he makes fruitless attempts to impose his will on the object and assert himself. These efforts are constantly being frustrated by the overwhelming impressions received from the object. It continually imposes itself on him against his will, it arouses in him the most disagreeable and intractable affects and persecutes him at every step. A tremendous inner struggle is needed all the time in order to "keep going." The typical form his neurosis takes is psychasthenia, a malady characterized on the one hand by extreme sensitivity and on the other by great proneness to exhaustion and chronic fatigue.

An analysis of the personal unconscious reveals a mass of

power fantasies coupled with fear of objects which he himself has forcibly activated, and of which he is often enough the victim. His fear of objects develops into a peculiar kind of cowardliness; he shrinks from making himself or his opinions felt, fearing that this will only increase the object's power. He is terrified of strong affects in others, and is hardly ever free from the dread of falling under hostile influences. Objects possess puissant and terrifying qualities for him—qualities he cannot consciously discern in them, but which he imagines he sees through his unconscious perception. As his relation to the object is very largely repressed, it takes place via the unconscious, where it becomes charged with the latter's qualities. These qualities are mostly infantile and archaic, so that the relation to the object becomes primitive too, and the object seems endowed with magical powers. Anything strange and new arouses fear and mistrust, as though concealing unknown perils; heirlooms and suchlike are attached to his soul as by invisible threads; any change is upsetting, if not positively dangerous, as it seems to denote a magical animation of the object. His ideal is a lonely island where nothing moves except what he permits to move. Vischer's novel, *Auch Einer*, affords deep insight into this side of the introvert's psychology, and also into the underlying symbolism of the collective unconscious. But this latter question I must leave to one side, since it is not specific to a description of types but is a general phenomenon.

c. *The Peculiarities of the Basic Psychological Functions in the Introverted Attitude*

Thinking

628   In the section on extraverted thinking I gave a brief description of introverted thinking (pars. 578–79) and must refer to it again here. Introverted thinking is primarily oriented by the subjective factor. At the very least the subjective factor expresses itself as a feeling of guidance which ultimately determines judgment. Sometimes it appears as a more or less complete image which serves as a criterion. But whether introverted thinking is concerned with concrete or with abstract objects, always at the decisive points it is oriented by subjective data. It does not lead from concrete experience back

again to the object, but always to the subjective content. External facts are not the aim and origin of this thinking, though the introvert would often like to make his thinking appear so. It begins with the subject and leads back to the subject, far though it may range into the realm of actual reality. With regard to the establishment of new facts it is only indirectly of value, since new views rather than knowledge of new facts are its main concern. It formulates questions and creates theories, it opens up new prospects and insights, but with regard to facts its attitude is one of reserve. They are all very well as illustrative examples, but they must not be allowed to predominate. Facts are collected as evidence for a theory, never for their own sake. If ever this happens, it is merely a concession to the extraverted style. Facts are of secondary importance for this kind of thinking; what seems to it of paramount importance is the development and presentation of the subjective idea, of the initial symbolic image hovering darkly before the mind's eye. Its aim is never an intellectual reconstruction of the concrete fact, but a shaping of that dark image into a luminous idea. It wants to reach reality, to see how the external fact will fit into and fill the framework of the idea, and the creative power of this thinking shows itself when it actually creates an idea which, though not inherent in the concrete fact, is yet the most suitable abstract expression of it. Its task is completed when the idea it has fashioned seems to emerge so inevitably from the external facts that they actually prove its validity.

But no more than extraverted thinking can wrest a sound empirical concept from concrete facts or create new ones can introverted thinking translate the initial image into an idea adequately adapted to the facts. For, as in the former case the purely empirical accumulation of facts paralyzes thought and smothers their meaning, so in the latter case introverted thinking shows a dangerous tendency to force the facts into the shape of its image, or to ignore them altogether in order to give fantasy free play. In that event it will be impossible for the finished product—the idea—to repudiate its derivation from the dim archaic image. It will have a mythological streak which one is apt to interpret as "originality" or, in more pronounced cases, as mere whimsicality, since its archaic character is not immediately apparent to specialists unfamiliar with

629

mythological motifs. The subjective power of conviction exerted by an idea of this kind is usually very great, and it is all the greater the less it comes into contact with external facts. Although it may seem to the originator of the idea that his meagre store of facts is the actual source of its truth and validity, in reality this is not so, for the idea derives its convincing power from the unconscious archetype, which, as such, is eternally valid and true. But this truth is so universal and so symbolic that it must first be assimilated to the recognized and recognizable knowledge of the time before it can become a practical truth of any value for life. What would causality be, for instance, if it could nowhere be recognized in practical causes and practical effects?

630   This kind of thinking easily gets lost in the immense truth of the subjective factor. It creates theories for their own sake, apparently with an eye to real or at least possible facts, but always with a distinct tendency to slip over from the world of ideas into mere imagery. Accordingly, visions of numerous possibilities appear on the scene, but none of them ever becomes a reality, until finally images are produced which no longer express anything externally real, being mere symbols of the ineffable and unknowable. It is now merely a mystical thinking and quite as unfruitful as thinking that remains bound to objective data. Whereas the latter sinks to the level of a mere representation of facts, the former evaporates into a representation of the irrepresentable, far beyond anything that could be expressed in an image. The representation of facts has an incontestable truth because the subjective factor is excluded and the facts speak for themselves. Similarly, the representation of the irrepresentable has an immediate, subjective power of conviction because it demonstrates its own existence. The one says "Est, ergo est"; the other says "Cogito, ergo cogito." Introverted thinking carried to extremes arrives at the evidence of its own subjective existence, and extraverted thinking at the evidence of its complete identity with the objective fact. Just as the latter abnegates itself by evaporating into the object, the former empties itself of each and every content and has to be satisfied with merely existing. In both cases the further development of life is crowded out of the thinking function into the domain of the other psychic functions, which till then had

227

631 existed in a state of relative unconsciousness. The extraordinary impoverishment of introverted thinking is compensated by a wealth of unconscious facts. The more consciousness is impelled by the thinking function to confine itself within the smallest and emptiest circle—which seems, however, to contain all the riches of the gods—the more the unconscious fantasies will be enriched by a multitude of archaic contents, a veritable "pandaemonium" of irrational and magical figures, whose physiognomy will accord with the nature of the function that will supersede the thinking function as the vehicle of life. If it should be the intuitive function, then the "other side" will be viewed through the eyes of a Kubin or a Meyrink.[9] If it is the feeling function, then quite unheard-of and fantastic feeling relationships will be formed, coupled with contradictory and unintelligible value judgments. If it is the sensation function, the senses will nose up something new, and never experienced before, in and outside the body. Closer examination of these permutations will easily demonstrate a recrudescence of primitive psychology with all its characteristic features. Naturally, such experiences are not merely primitive, they are also symbolic; in fact, the more primordial and aboriginal they are, the more they represent a future truth. For everything old in the unconscious hints at something coming.

Under ordinary circumstances, not even the attempt to get to the "other side" will be successful—and still less the redeeming journey through the unconscious. The passage across is usually blocked by conscious resistance to any subjection of the ego to the realities of the unconscious and their determining power. It is a state of dissociation, in other words a neurosis characterized by inner debility and increasing cerebral exhaustion—the symptoms of psychasthenia.

. . .

Feeling

638 Introverted feeling is determined principally by the subjective factor. It differs quite as essentially from extraverted feeling as introverted from extraverted thinking. It is extremely difficult to give an intellectual account of the intro-

[9] Kubin, *The Other Side,* and Meyrink, *Das grüne Gesicht.*

228

639 verted feeling process, or even an approximate description of it, although the peculiar nature of this kind of feeling is very noticeable once one has become aware of it. Since it is conditioned subjectively and is only secondarily concerned with the object, it seldom appears on the surface and is generally misunderstood. It is a feeling which seems to devalue the object, and it therefore manifests itself for the most part negatively. The existence of positive feeling can be inferred only indirectly. Its aim is not to adjust itself to the object, but to subordinate it in an unconscious effort to realize the underlying images. It is continually seeking an image which has no existence in reality, but which it has seen in a kind of vision. It glides unheedingly over all objects that do not fit in with its aim. It strives after inner intensity, for which the objects serve at most as a stimulus. The depth of this feeling can only be guessed—it can never be clearly grasped. It makes people silent and difficult of access; it shrinks back like a violet from the brute nature of the object in order to fill the depths of the subject. It comes out with negative judgments or assumes an air of profound indifference as a means of defence.

The primordial images are, of course, just as much ideas as feelings. Fundamental ideas, ideas like God, freedom, and immortality, are just as much feeling-values as they are significant ideas. Everything, therefore, that we have said about introverted thinking is equally true of introverted feeling, only here everything is felt while there it was thought. But the very fact that thoughts can generally be expressed more intelligibly than feelings demands a more than ordinary descriptive or artistic ability before the real wealth of this feeling can be even approximately presented or communicated to the world. If subjective thinking can be understood only with difficulty because of its unrelatedness, this is true in even higher degree of subjective feeling. In order to communicate with others, it has to find an external form not only acceptable to itself, but capable also of arousing a parallel feeling in them. Thanks to the relatively great inner (as well as outer) uniformity of human beings, it is actually possible to do this, though the form acceptable to feeling is extraordinarily difficult to find so long as it is still mainly oriented to the fathomless store of primordial images. If, however, feeling is falsified by an egocentric atti-

229

tude, it at once becomes unsympathetic, because it is then concerned mainly with the ego. It inevitably creates the impression of sentimental self-love, of trying to make itself interesting, and even of morbid self-admiration. Just as the subjectivized consciousness of the introverted thinker, striving after abstraction to the nth degree, only succeeds in intensifying a thought-process that is in itself empty, the intensification of egocentric feeling only leads to inane transports of feeling for their own sake. This is the mystical, ecstatic stage which opens the way for the extraverted functions that feeling has repressed. Just as introverted thinking is counterbalanced by a primitive feeling, to which objects attach themselves with magical force, introverted feeling is counterbalanced by a primitive thinking, whose concretism and slavery to facts surpass all bounds. Feeling progressively emancipates itself from the object and creates for itself a freedom of action and conscience that is purely subjective, and may even renounce all traditional values. But so much the more does unconscious thinking fall a victim to the power of objective reality.

*

Summary of the Introverted Rational Types

644 Both the foregoing types may be termed rational, since they are grounded on the functions of rational judgment. Rational judgment is based not merely on objective but also on subjective data. The predominance of one or the other factor, however, as a result of a psychic disposition often existing from early youth, will give the judgment a corresponding bias. A judgment that is truly rational will appeal to the objective and the subjective factor equally and do justice to both. But that would be an ideal case and would presuppose an equal development of both extraversion and introversion. In practice, however, either movement excludes the other, and, so long as this dilemma remains, they cannot exist side by side but at best successively. Under ordinary conditions, therefore, an ideal rationality is impossible. The rationality of a rational type always has a typical bias. Thus, the judgment of the introverted rational types is undoubtedly rational, only it is ori-

ented more by the subjective factor. This does not necessarily imply any logical bias, since the bias lies in the premise. The premise consists in the predominance of the subjective factor prior to all conclusions and judgments. The superior value of the subjective as compared with the objective factor appears self-evident from the beginning. It is not a question of *assigning* this value, but, as we have said, of a natural disposition existing before all rational valuation. Hence, to the introvert, rational judgment has many nuances which differentiate it from that of the extravert. To mention only the most general instance, the chain of reasoning that leads to the subjective factor seems to the introvert somewhat more rational than the one that leads to the object. This difference, though slight and practically unnoticeable in individual cases, builds up in the end to unbridgeable discrepancies which are the more irritating the less one is aware of the minimal shift of standpoint occasioned by the psychological premise. A capital error regularly creeps in here, for instead of recognizing the difference in the premise one tries to demonstrate a fallacy in the conclusion. This recognition is a difficult matter for every rational type, since it undermines the apparently absolute validity of his own principle and delivers him over to its antithesis, which for him amounts to a catastrophe.

645   The introvert is far more subject to misunderstanding than the extravert, not so much because the extravert is a more merciless or critical adversary than he himself might be, but because the style of the times which he himself imitates works against him. He finds himself in the minority, not in numerical relation to the extravert, but in relation to the general Western view of the world as judged by his feeling. In so far as he is a convinced participator in the general style, he undermines his own foundations; for the general style, acknowledging as it does only the visible and tangible values, is opposed to his specific principle. Because of its invisibility, he is obliged to depreciate the subjective factor, and must force himself to join in the extraverted overvaluation of the object. He himself sets the subjective factor at too low a value, and his feelings of inferiority are his chastisement for this sin. Little wonder, therefore, that it is precisely in the present epoch, and particularly in those movements which are somewhat ahead of the time,

646   that the subjective factor reveals itself in exaggerated, tasteless forms of expression bordering on caricature. I refer to the art of the present day.

    The undervaluation of his own principle makes the introvert egotistical and forces on him the psychology of the underdog. The more egotistical he becomes, the more it seems to him that the others, who are apparently able, without qualms, to conform to the general style, are the oppressors against whom he must defend himself. He generally does not see that his chief error lies in not depending on the subjective factor with the same trust and devotion with which the extravert relies on the object. His undervaluation of his own principle makes his leanings towards egotism unavoidable, and because of this he fully deserves the censure of the extravert. If he remained true to his own principle, the charge of egotism would be altogether false, for his attitude would be justified by its effects in general, and the misunderstanding would be dissipated.

Sensation

647   Sensation, which by its very nature is dependent on the object and on objective stimuli, undergoes considerable modification in the introverted attitude. It, too, has a subjective factor, for besides the sensed object there is a sensing subject who adds his subjective disposition to the objective stimulus. In the introverted attitude sensation is based predominantly on the subjective component of perception. What I mean by this is best illustrated by works of art which reproduce external objects. If, for instance, several painters were to paint the same landscape, each trying to reproduce it faithfully, each painting will be different from the others, not merely because of differences in ability, but chiefly because of different ways of seeing; indeed, in some of the paintings there will be a distinct psychic difference in mood and the treatment of colour and form. These qualities betray the influence of the subjective factor. The subjective factor in sensation is essentially the same as in the other functions we have discussed. It is an unconscious disposition which alters the sense-perception at its source, thus depriving it of the character of a purely objective influence. In this case, sensation is related primarily to the subject and only secondarily to the object. How extraordinarily

strong the subjective factor can be is shown most clearly in art. Its predominance sometimes amounts to a complete suppression of the object's influence, and yet the sensation remains sensation even though it has become a perception of the subjective factor and the object has sunk to the level of a mere stimulus. Introverted sensation is oriented accordingly. True sense-perception certainly exists, but it always looks as though the object did not penetrate into the subject in its own right, but as though the subject were seeing it quite differently, or saw quite other things than other people see. Actually, he perceives the same things as everybody else, only he does not stop at the purely objective influence, but concerns himself with the subjective perception excited by the objective stimulus.

648 Subjective perception is markedly different from the objective. What is perceived is either not found at all in the object, or is, at most, merely suggested by it. That is, although the perception can be similar to that of other men, it is not immediately derived from the objective behaviour of things. It does not impress one as a mere product of consciousness—it is too genuine for that. But it makes a definite psychic impression because elements of a higher psychic order are discernible in it. This order, however, does not coincide with the contents of consciousness. It has to do with presuppositions or dispositions of the collective unconscious, with mythological images, with primordial possibilities of ideas. Subjective perception is characterized by the meaning that clings to it. It means more than the mere image of the object, though naturally only to one for whom the subjective factor means anything at all. To another, the reproduced subjective impression seems to suffer from the defect of not being sufficiently like the object and therefore to have failed in its purpose.

649 Introverted sensation apprehends the background of the physical world rather than its surface. The decisive thing is not the reality of the object, but the reality of the subjective factor, of the primordial images which, in their totality, constitute a psychic mirror-world. It is a mirror with the peculiar faculty of reflecting the existing contents of consciousness not in their known and customary form but, as it were, *sub specie aeternitatis*, somewhat as a million-year-old consciousness might see them. Such a consciousness would see the becoming and pass-

ing away of things simultaneously with their momentary existence in the present, and not only that, it would also see what was before their becoming and will be after their passing hence. Naturally this is only a figure of speech, but one that I needed in order to illustrate in some way the peculiar nature of introverted sensation. We could say that introverted sensation transmits an image which does not so much reproduce the object as spread over it the patina of age-old subjective experience and the shimmer of events still unborn. The bare sense impression develops in depth, reaching into the past and future, while extraverted sensation seizes on the momentary existence of things open to the light of day.

Intuition

. . .

655 Introverted intuition is directed to the inner object, a term that might justly be applied to the contents of the unconscious. The relation of inner objects to consciousness is entirely analogous to that of outer objects, though their reality is not physical but psychic. They appear to intuitive perception as subjective images of things which, though not to be met with in the outside world, constitute the contents of the unconscious, and of the collective unconscious in particular. These contents *per se* are naturally not accessible to experience, a quality they have in common with external objects. For just as external objects correspond only relatively to our perception of them, so the phenomenal forms of the inner objects are also relative—products of their (to us) inaccessible essence and of the peculiar nature of the intuitive function.

656 Like sensation, intuition has its subjective factor, which is suppressed as much as possible in the extraverted attitude but is the decisive factor in the intuition of the introvert. Although his intuition may be stimulated by external objects, it does not concern itself with external possibilities but with what the external object has released within him. Whereas introverted sensation is mainly restricted to the perception, via the unconscious, of the phenomena of innervation and is arrested there, introverted intuition suppresses this side of the subjective fac-

tor and perceives the image that caused the innervation. Supposing, for instance, a man is overtaken by an attack of psychogenic vertigo. Sensation is arrested by the peculiar nature of this disturbance of innervation, perceiving all its qualities, its intensity, its course, how it arose and how it passed, but not advancing beyond that to its content, to the thing that caused the disturbance. Intuition, on the other hand, receives from sensation only the impetus to its own immediate activity; it peers behind the scenes, quickly perceiving the inner image that gave rise to this particular form of expression—the attack of vertigo. It sees the image of a tottering man pierced through the heart by an arrow. This image fascinates the intuitive activity; it is arrested by it, and seeks to explore every detail of it. It holds fast to the vision, observing with the liveliest interest how the picture changes, unfolds, and finally fades.

657   In this way introverted intuition perceives all the background processes of consciousness with almost the same distinctness as extraverted sensation registers external objects. For intuition, therefore, unconscious images acquire the dignity of things. But, because intuition excludes the co-operation of sensation, it obtains little or no knowledge of the disturbances of innervation or of the physical effects produced by the unconscious images. The images appear as though detached from the subject, as though existing in themselves without any relation to him. Consequently, in the above-mentioned example, the introverted intuitive, if attacked by vertigo, would never imagine that the image he perceived might in some way refer to himself. To a judging type this naturally seems almost inconceivable, but it is none the less a fact which I have often come across in my dealings with intuitives.

658   The remarkable indifference of the extraverted intuitive to external objects is shared by the introverted intuitive in relation to inner objects. Just as the extraverted intuitive is continually scenting out new possibilities, which he pursues with equal unconcern for his own welfare and for that of others, pressing on quite heedless of human considerations and tearing down what has just been built in his everlasting search for change, so the introverted intuitive moves from image to image, chasing after every possibility in the teeming womb of the unconscious, without establishing any connection between

them and himself. Just as the world of appearances can never become a moral problem for the man who merely senses it, the world of inner images is never a moral problem for the intuitive. For both of them it is an aesthetic problem, a matter of perception, a "sensation." Because of this, the introverted intuitive has little consciousness of his own bodily existence or of its effect on others. The extravert would say: "Reality does not exist for him, he gives himself up to fruitless fantasies." The perception of the images of the unconscious, produced in such inexhaustible abundance by the creative energy of life, is of course fruitless from the standpoint of immediate utility. But since these images represent possible views of the world which may give life a new potential, this function, which to the outside world is the strangest of all, is as indispensable to the total psychic economy as is the corresponding human type to the psychic life of a people. Had this type not existed, there would have been no prophets in Israel.

659   Introverted intuition apprehends the images arising from the *a priori* inherited foundations of the unconscious. These archetypes, whose innermost nature is inaccessible to experience, are the precipitate of the psychic functioning of the whole ancestral line; the accumulated experiences of organic life in general, a million times repeated, and condensed into types. In these archetypes, therefore, all experiences are represented which have happened on this planet since primeval times. The more frequent and the more intense they were, the more clearly focussed they become in the archetype. The archetype would thus be, to borrow from Kant, the noumenon of the image which intuition perceives and, in perceiving, creates.

660   Since the unconscious is not just something that lies there like a psychic *caput mortuum*, but coexists with us and is constantly undergoing transformations which are inwardly connected with the general run of events, introverted intuition, through its perception of these inner processes, can supply certain data which may be of the utmost importance for understanding what is going on in the world. It can even foresee new possibilities in more or less clear outline, as well as events which later actually do happen. Its prophetic foresight is ex-

plained by its relation to the archetypes, which represent the laws governing the course of all experienceable things.

. . .

Summary of the Introverted Irrational Types

664   The two types just described are almost inaccessible to judgment from outside. Being introverted, and having in consequence little capacity or desire for expression, they offer but a frail handle in this respect. As their main activity is directed inwards, nothing is outwardly visible but reserve, secretiveness, lack of sympathy, uncertainty, and an apparently groundless embarrassment. When anything does come to the surface, it is generally an indirect manifestation of the inferior and relatively unconscious functions. Such manifestations naturally arouse all the current prejudices against this type. Accordingly they are mostly underestimated, or at least misunderstood. To the extent that they do not understand themselves—because they very largely lack judgment—they are also powerless to understand why they are so constantly underestimated by the public. They cannot see that their efforts to be forthcoming are, as a matter of fact, of an inferior character. Their vision is enthralled by the richness of subjective events. What is going on inside them is so captivating, and of such inexhaustible charm, that they simply do not notice that the little they do manage to communicate contains hardly anything of what they themselves have experienced. The fragmentary and episodic character of their communications makes too great a demand on the understanding and good will of those around them; also, their communications are without the personal warmth that alone carries the power of conviction. On the contrary, these types have very often a harsh, repelling manner, though of this they are quite unaware and did not intend it. We shall form a fairer judgment of such people, and show them greater forbearance, when we begin to realize how hard it is to translate into intelligible language what is perceived within. Yet this for-

bearance must not go so far as to exempt them altogether from the need to communicate. This would only do them the greatest harm. Fate itself prepares for them, perhaps even more than for other men, overwhelming external difficulties which have a very sobering effect on those intoxicated by the inner vision. Often it is only an intense personal need that can wring from them a human confession.

665 From an extraverted and rationalistic standpoint, these types are indeed the most useless of men. But, viewed from a higher standpoint, they are living evidence that this rich and varied world with its overflowing and intoxicating life is not purely external, but also exists within. These types are admittedly one-sided specimens of nature, but they are an object-lesson for the man who refuses to be blinded by the intellectual fashion of the day. In their own way, they are educators and promoters of culture. Their life teaches more than their words. From their lives, and not least from their greatest fault—their inability to communicate—we may understand one of the greatest errors of our civilization, that is, the superstitious belief in verbal statements, the boundless overestimation of instruction by means of words and methods. A child certainly allows himself to be impressed by the grand talk of his parents, but do they really imagine he is educated by it? Actually it is the parents' lives that educate the child—what they add by word and gesture at best serves only to confuse him. The same holds good for the teacher. But we have such a belief in method that, if only the method be good, the practice of it seems to sanctify the teacher. An inferior man is never a good teacher. But he can conceal his pernicious inferiority, which secretly poisons the pupil, behind an excellent method or an equally brilliant gift of gab. Naturally the pupil of riper years desires nothing better than the knowledge of useful methods, because he is already defeated by the general attitude, which believes in the all-conquering method. He has learned that the emptiest head, correctly parroting a method, is the best pupil. His whole environment is an optical demonstration that all success and all happiness are outside, and that only the right method is needed to attain the haven of one's desires. Or does, perchance, the life of his religious instructor demonstrate the happiness which radiates from the treasure of the inner vi-

sion? The irrational introverted types are certainly no teachers of a more perfect humanity; they lack reason and the ethics of reason. But their lives teach the other possibility, the interior life which is so painfully wanting in our civilization.

d. The Principal and Auxiliary Functions

666 In the foregoing descriptions I have no desire to give my readers the impression that these types occur at all frequently in such pure form in actual life. They are, as it were, only Galtonesque family portraits, which single out the common and therefore typical features, stressing them disproportionately, while the individual features are just as disproportionately effaced. Closer investigation shows with great regularity that, besides the most differentiated function, another, less differentiated function of secondary importance is invariably present in consciousness and exerts a co-determining influence.

667 To recapitulate for the sake of clarity: the products of all functions can be conscious, but we speak of the "consciousness" of a function only when its use is under the control of the will and, at the same time, its governing principle is the decisive one for the orientation of consciousness. This is true when, for instance, thinking is not a mere afterthought, or rumination, and when its conclusions possess an absolute validity, so that the logical result holds good both as a motive and as a guarantee of practical action without the backing of any further evidence. This absolute sovereignty always belongs, empirically, to one function alone, and *can* belong only to one function, because the equally independent intervention of another function would necessarily produce a different orientation which, partially at least, would contradict the first. But since it is a vital condition for the conscious process of adaptation always to have clear and unambiguous aims, the presence of a second function of equal power is naturally ruled out. This other function, therefore, can have only a secondary importance, as has been found to be the case in practice. Its secondary importance is due to the fact that it is not, like the primary function, valid in its own right as an absolutely reliable and decisive factor, but comes into play more as an auxiliary or complementary function. Naturally only those functions can appear as auxiliary whose nature is not opposed to the dominant

239

668 function. For instance, feeling can never act as the second function alongside thinking, because it is by its very nature too strongly opposed to thinking. Thinking, if it is to be real thinking and true to its own principle, must rigorously exclude feeling. This, of course, does not do away with the fact that there are individuals whose thinking and feeling are on the same level, both being of equal motive power for consciousness. But in these cases there is also no question of a differentiated type, but merely of relatively undeveloped thinking and feeling. The uniformly conscious or uniformly unconscious state of the functions is, therefore, the mark of a primitive mentality.

669 Experience shows that the secondary function is always one whose nature is different from, though not antagonistic to, the primary function. Thus, thinking as the primary function can readily pair with intuition as the auxiliary, or indeed equally well with sensation, but, as already observed, never with feeling. Neither intuition nor sensation is antagonistic to thinking; they need not be absolutely excluded, for they are not of a nature equal and opposite to thinking, as feeling is—which, as a judging function, successfully competes with thinking—but are functions of perception, affording welcome assistance to thought. But as soon as they reached the same level of differentiation as thinking, they would bring about a change of attitude which would contradict the whole trend of thinking. They would change the judging attitude into a perceiving one; whereupon the principle of rationality indispensable to thought would be suppressed in favour of the irrationality of perception. Hence the auxiliary function is possible and useful only in so far as it *serves* the dominant function, without making any claim to the autonomy of its own principle.

For all the types met with in practice, the rule holds good that besides the conscious, primary function there is a relatively unconscious, auxiliary function which is in every respect different from the nature of the primary function. The resulting combinations present the familiar picture of, for instance, practical thinking allied with sensation, speculative thinking forging ahead with intuition, artistic intuition selecting and presenting its images with the help of feeling-values, philosophical intuition systematizing its vision into comprehensible thought by means of a powerful intellect, and so on.

670   The unconscious functions likewise group themselves in patterns correlated with the conscious ones. Thus, the correlative of conscious, practical thinking may be an unconscious, intuitive-feeling attitude, with feeling under a stronger inhibition than intuition. These peculiarities are of interest only for one who is concerned with the practical treatment of such cases, but it is important that he should know about them. I have frequently observed how an analyst, confronted with a terrific thinking type, for instance, will do his utmost to develop the feeling function directly out of the unconscious. Such an attempt is foredoomed to failure, because it involves too great a violation of the conscious standpoint. Should the violation nevertheless be successful, a really compulsive dependence of the patient on the analyst ensues, a transference that can only be brutally terminated, because, having been left without a standpoint, the patient has made his standpoint the analyst. But the approach to the unconscious and to the most repressed function is disclosed, as it were, of its own accord, and with adequate protection of the conscious standpoint, when the way of development proceeds via the auxiliary function—in the case of a rational type via one of the irrational functions. This gives the patient a broader view of what is happening, and of what is possible, so that his consciousness is sufficiently protected against the inroads of the unconscious. Conversely, in order to cushion the impact of the unconscious, an irrational type needs a stronger development of the rational auxiliary function present in consciousness.

671   The unconscious functions exist in an archaic, animal state. Hence their symbolic appearance in dreams and fantasies is usually represented as the battle or encounter between two animals or monsters.

681   2. AFFECT. By the term affect I mean a state of feeling characterized by marked physical innervation on the one hand and a peculiar disturbance of the ideational process on the other.[5] I use *emotion* as synonymous with affect. I distinguish —in contrast to Bleuler (v. *Affectivity*)—*feeling* (q.v.) from affect, in spite of the fact that the dividing line is fluid, since every feeling, after attaining a certain strength, releases physical innervations, thus becoming an affect. For practical reasons, however, it is advisable to distinguish affect from feeling, since feeling can be a voluntarily disposable function, whereas affect is usually not. Similarly, affect is clearly distinguished from feeling by quite perceptible physical innervations, while feeling for the most part lacks them, or else their intensity is so slight that they can be demonstrated only by the most delicate instruments, as in the case of psychogalvanic phenomena.[6] Affect becomes cumulative through the sensation of the physical innervations released by it. This observation gave rise to the James-Lange theory of affect, which derives affect causally from physical innervations. As against this extreme view, I regard affect on the one hand as a psychic feeling-state and on the other as a physiological innervation-state, each of which has a cumulative, reciprocal effect on the other. That is to say, a component of sensation allies itself with the intensified feel-

5 Wundt, *Grundzüge der physiologischen Psychologie*, pp. 209ff.
6 Féré, "Note sur des modifications de la résistance électrique," pp. 217ff.; Veraguth, "Das psychogalvanische Reflexphänomen," pp. 387ff.; Binswanger, "On the Psychogalvanic Phenomenon in Association Experiments," in *Studies in Word-Association*, pp. 446ff.; Jung, "On the Psychophysical Relations of the Association Experiment."

ing, so that the affect is approximated more to *sensation* (q.v.) and essentially differentiated from the feeling-state. Pronounced affects, i.e., affects accompanied by violent physical innervations, I do not assign to the province of feeling but to that of the sensation function.

682 3. AFFECTIVITY is a term coined by Bleuler. It designates and comprises "not only the affects proper, but also the slight feelings or feeling-tones of pain and pleasure."[7] Bleuler distinguishes affectivity from the sense-perceptions and physical sensations as well as from "feelings" that may be regarded as inner perception processes (e.g., the "feeling" of certainty, of probability, etc.) or vague thoughts or discernments.[8]

4. ANIMA/ANIMUS, v. SOUL; SOUL-IMAGE.

. . .

684 6. ARCHAISM is a term by which I designate the "oldness" of psychic contents or *functions* (q.v.). By this I do not mean qualities that are "archaistic" in the sense of being pseudo-antique or copied, as in later Roman sculpture or nineteenth-century Gothic, but qualities that have the character of *relics*. We may describe as archaic all psychological traits that exhibit the qualities of the primitive mentality. It is clear that archaism attaches primarily to the *fantasies* (q.v.) of the unconscious, i.e., to the products of unconscious fantasy activity which reach consciousness. An *image* (q.v.) has an archaic quality when it possesses unmistakable mythological parallels.[10] Archaic, too, are the associations-by-analogy of unconscious fantasy, and so is their symbolism (v. *Symbol*). The relation of *identity* (q.v.) with an object, or *participation mystique* (q.v.), is likewise archaic. *Concretism* (q.v.) of thought and feeling is archaic; also compulsion and inability to control oneself (ecstatic or trance states, possession, etc.). Fusion of the psychological functions (v. *Differentiation*), of thinking with feeling, feeling with sensation, feeling with intuition, and so on, is archaic, as

7 Bleuler, *Affektivität, Suggestibilität, Paranoia*, p. 6.
8 Ibid., pp. 13f.
10 Jung, *Symbols of Transformation*.

is also the fusion of part of a function with its counterpart, e.g., positive with negative feeling, or what Bleuler calls ambitendency and ambivalence, and such phenomena as *colour hearing*.

. . . .

687   8. ATTITUDE. This concept is a relatively recent addition to psychology. It originated with Müller and Schumann.[15] Whereas Külpe[16] defines attitude as a predisposition of the sensory or motor centres to react to a particular stimulus or constant impulse, Ebbinghaus[17] conceives it in a wider sense as an effect of training which introduces the factor of habit into individual acts that deviate from the habitual. Our use of the concept derives from Ebbinghaus's. For us, attitude is a readiness of the psyche to act or react in a certain way. The concept is of particular importance for the psychology of complex psychic processes because it expresses the peculiar fact that certain psychic stimuli have too strong an effect on some occasions, and little or no effect on others. To have an attitude means to be ready for something definite, even though this something is unconscious; for having an attitude is synonymous with an *a priori* orientation to a definite thing, no matter whether this be represented in consciousness or not. The state of readiness, which I conceive attitude to be, consists in the presence of a certain subjective constellation, a definite combination of psychic factors or contents, which will either determine action in this or that definite direction, or react to an external stimulus in a definite way. Active *apperception* (q.v.) is impossible without an attitude. An attitude always has a point of reference; this can be either conscious or unconscious, for in the act of apperceiving a new content an already constellated combination of contents will inevitably accentuate those qualities or elements that appear to belong to the subjective content. Hence a selection or judgment takes place which excludes anything irrelevant. As to what is or is not relevant, this is decided by the already constellated combination of contents. Whether

15 "Ueber die psychologischen Grundlagen der Vergleichung gehobener Gewichte," pp. 37ff.
16 *Grundriss der Psychologie*, p. 44.
17 *Grundzüge der Psychologie*, I, pp. 681f.

the point of reference is conscious or unconscious does not affect the selectivity of the attitude, since the selection is implicit in the attitude and takes place automatically. It is useful, however, to distinguish between the two, because the presence of two attitudes is extremely frequent, one conscious and the other unconscious. This means that consciousness has a constellation of contents different from that of the unconscious, a duality particularly evident in neurosis.

688   The concept of attitude has some affinity with Wundt's concept of *apperception*, with the difference that apperception includes the process of relating the already constellated contents to the new content to be apperceived, whereas attitude relates exclusively to the subjectively constellated content. Apperception is, as it were, the bridge which connects the already existing, constellated contents with the new one, whereas attitude would be the support or abutment of the bridge on the one bank, and the new content the abutment on the other bank. Attitude signifies *expectation*, and expectation always operates selectively and with a sense of direction. The presence of a strongly feeling-toned content in the conscious field of vision forms (maybe with other contents) a particular constellation that is equivalent to a definite attitude, because such a content promotes the perception and apperception of everything similar to itself and blacks out the dissimilar. It creates an attitude that corresponds to it. This automatic phenomenon is an essential cause of the one-sidedness of conscious *orientation* (q.v.). It would lead to a complete loss of equilibrium if there were no self-regulating, compensatory (v. *Compensation*) function in the psyche to correct the conscious attitude. In this sense, therefore, the duality of attitude is a normal phenomenon, and it plays a disturbing role only when the one-sidedness is excessive.

689   Attitude in the sense of ordinary *attention* can be a relatively unimportant subsidiary phenomenon, but it can also be a general principle governing the whole psyche. Depending on environmental influences and on the individual's education, general experience of life, and personal convictions, a subjective constellation of contents may be habitually present, continually moulding a certain attitude that may affect the minutest details of his life. Every man who is particularly aware

of the seamy side of existence, for instance, will naturally have an attitude that is constantly on the look-out for something unpleasant. This conscious imbalance is compensated by an unconscious expectation of pleasure. Again, an oppressed person has a conscious attitude that always anticipates oppression; he selects this factor from the general run of experience and scents it out everywhere. His unconscious attitude, therefore, aims at power and superiority.

690 The whole psychology of an individual even in its most fundamental features is oriented in accordance with his habitual attitude. Although the general psychological laws operate in every individual, they cannot be said to be characteristic of a particular individual, since the way they operate varies in accordance with his habitual attitude. The habitual attitude is always a resultant of all the factors that exert a decisive influence on the psyche, such as innate disposition, environmental influences, experience of life, insights and convictions gained through *differentiation* (q.v.), *collective* (q.v.) views, etc. Were it not for the absolutely fundamental importance of attitude, the existence of an individual psychology would be out of the question. But the habitual attitude brings about such great displacements of energy, and so modifies the relations between the individual *functions* (q.v.), that effects are produced which often cast doubt on the validity of general psychological laws. In spite of the fact, for instance, that some measure of sexual activity is held to be indispensable on physiological and psychological grounds, there are individuals who, without loss to themselves, i.e., without pathological effects or any demonstrable restriction of their powers, can, to a very great extent, dispense with it, while in other cases quite insignificant disturbances in this area can have far-reaching consequences. How enormous the individual differences are can be seen most clearly, perhaps, in the question of likes and dislikes. Here practically all rules go by the board. What is there, in the last resort, that has not at some time given man pleasure, and what is there that has not caused him pain? Every instinct, every function can be subordinated to another. The ego instinct or power instinct can make sexuality its servant, or sexuality can exploit the ego. Thinking may overrun everything else, or feeling swallow up thinking and sensation, all depending on the attitude.

691   At bottom, attitude is an individual phenomenon that eludes scientific investigation. In actual experience, however, certain typical attitudes can be distinguished in so far as certain psychic functions can be distinguished. When a function habitually predominates, a typical attitude is produced. According to the nature of the differentiated function, there will be constellations of contents that create a corresponding attitude. There is thus a typical thinking, feeling, sensation, and intuitive attitude. Besides these purely psychological attitudes, whose number might very well be increased, there are also social attitudes, namely, those on which a collective idea has set its stamp. They are characterized by the various "-isms." These collective attitudes are very important, in some cases even outweighing the importance of the individual attitude.

692   9. COLLECTIVE. I term *collective* all psychic contents that belong not to one individual but to many, i.e., to a society, a people, or to mankind in general. Such contents are what Lévy-Bruhl[18] calls the *représentations collectives* of primitives, as well as general concepts of justice, the state, religion, science, etc., current among civilized man. It is not only concepts and ways of looking at things, however, that must be termed collective, but also *feelings*. Among primitives, the *représentations collectives* are at the same time collective feelings, as Lévy-Bruhl has shown. Because of this collective feeling-value he calls the *représentations collectives* "mystical,"[19] since they are not merely intellectual but emotional. Among civilized peoples, too, certain collective ideas—God, justice, fatherland, etc.—are bound up with collective feelings. This collective quality adheres not only to particular psychic elements or contents but to whole *functions* (q.v.). Thus the thinking function as a whole can have a collective quality, when it possesses general validity and accords with the laws of logic. Similarly, the feeling function as a whole can be collective, when it is identical with the general feeling and accords with general expectations, the general moral consciousness, etc. In the same way, sensation and intuition are collective when they are at the same time characteristic of a large group of men. The antithesis of collective is *individual* (q.v.).

. . .

[18] *How Natives Think*, pp. 35ff.

[19] Ibid., pp. 36f.

700   12. CONSCIOUSNESS. By consciousness I understand the relation of psychic contents to the *ego* (q.v.), in so far as this relation is perceived as such by the ego.[25] Relations to the ego that are not perceived as such are *unconscious* (q.v.). Consciousness is the function or activity[26] which maintains the relation of psychic contents to the ego. Consciousness is not identical with the *psyche* (v. *Soul*), because the psyche represents the totality of all psychic contents, and these are not necessarily all directly connected with the ego, i.e., related to it in such a way that they take on the quality of consciousness. A great many psychic complexes exist which are not necessarily connected with the ego.[27]

701   13. CONSTRUCTIVE. This concept is used by me in an equivalent sense to *synthetic*, almost in fact as an illustration of it. Constructive means "building up." I use *constructive* and *synthetic* to designate a method that is the antithesis of the *reductive* (q.v.).[28] The constructive method is concerned with the elaboration of the products of the unconscious (dreams, fantasies, etc.; v. *Fantasy*). It takes the unconscious product as a symbolic expression (v. *Symbol*) which anticipates a coming phase of psychological development.[29] Maeder actually speaks of a *prospective function* of the *unconscious* (q.v.), which half playfully anticipates future developments.[30] Adler, too, recognizes an anticipatory function of the unconscious.[31] It is certain that the product of the unconscious cannot be regarded as a finished thing, as a sort of end-product, for that would be to deny it any purposive significance. Freud himself allows the dream a teleological role at least as the "guardian of sleep,"[32] though for him its prospective function is essentially restricted

25 Natorp, *Einleitung in die Psychologie nach kritischer Methode*, p. 11. Cf. also Lipps, *Leitfaden der Psychologie*, p. 3.

26 Riehl, *Zur Einführung in die Philosophie der Gegenwart*, p. 161. Riehl considers consciousness an "activity" or "process."

27 Jung, "The Psychology of Dementia Praecox." [See also "A Review of the Complex Theory."—EDITORS.]

28 Jung, *Two Essays on Analytical Psychology*, pars. 121ff.

29 For a detailed example of this see my "On the Psychology and Pathology of So-called Occult Phenomena," esp. par. 136.

30 *The Dream Problem*, p. 30.

31 *The Neurotic Constitution.*

32 *The Interpretation of Dreams* (Standard Edition, vol. 4), p. 233.

to "wishing." The purposive character of unconscious tendencies cannot be contested *a priori* if we are to accept their analogy with other psychological or physiological functions. We conceive the product of the unconscious, therefore, as an expression oriented to a goal or purpose, but characterizing its objective in symbolic language.[33]

702 In accordance with this conception, the constructive method of interpretation is not so much concerned with the primary sources of the unconscious product, with its raw materials, so to speak, as with bringing its symbolism to a general and comprehensible expression. The "free associations" of the subject are considered with respect to their aim and not with respect to their derivation. They are viewed from the angle of future action or inaction: at the same time, their relation to the conscious situation is carefully taken into account, for, according to the *compensation* (q.v.) theory, the activity of the unconscious has an essentially complementary significance for the conscious situation. Since it is a question of an anticipatory *orientation* (q.v.), the actual relation to the object does not loom so large as in the reductive procedure, which is concerned with actual relations to the object in the past. It is more a question of the subjective *attitude* (q.v.), the object being little more than a signpost pointing to the tendencies of the subject. The aim of the constructive method, therefore, is to elicit from the unconscious product a meaning that relates to the subject's future attitude. Since, as a rule, the unconscious can create only symbolic expressions, the constructive method seeks to elucidate the symbolically expressed meaning in such a way as to indicate how the conscious orientation may be corrected, and how the subject may act in harmony with the unconscious.

703 Thus, just as no psychological method of interpretation relies exclusively on the associative material supplied by the analysand, the constructive method also makes use of comparative material. And just as reductive interpretation employs parallels drawn from biology, physiology, folklore, literature, and other sources, the constructive treatment of an intellectual problem will make use of philosophical parallels,

[33] Silberer (*Problems of Mysticism and Its Symbolism*, pp. 241ff.) expresses himself in a similar way in his formulation of *anagogic* significance.

704 while the treatment of an intuitive problem will depend more on parallels from mythology and the history of religion.

The constructive method is necessarily *individualistic*, since a future collective attitude can develop only through the individual. The reductive method, on the contrary, is *collective* (q.v.), since it leads back from the individual to basic collective attitudes or facts. The constructive method can also be directly applied by the subject to his own material, in which case it is an *intuitive* method, employed to elucidate the general meaning of an unconscious product. This elucidation is the result of an *associative* (as distinct from actively *apperceptive*, q.v.) addition of further material, which so enriches the symbolic product (e.g., a dream) that it eventually attains a degree of clarity sufficient for conscious comprehension. It becomes interwoven with more general associations and is thereby assimilated.

705 14. DIFFERENTIATION means the development of differences, the separation of parts from a whole. In this work I employ the concept of differentiation chiefly with respect to the psychological *functions* (q.v.). So long as a function is still so fused with one or more other functions—thinking with feeling, feeling with sensation, etc.—that it is unable to operate on its own, it is in an *archaic* (q.v.) condition, i.e., not differentiated, not separated from the whole as a special part and existing by itself. Undifferentiated thinking is incapable of thinking apart from other functions; it is continually mixed up with sensations, feelings, intuitions, just as undifferentiated feeling is mixed up with sensations and fantasies, as for instance in the sexualization (Freud) of feeling and thinking in neurosis. As a rule, the undifferentiated function is also characterized by ambivalence and ambitendency,[34] i.e., every position entails its own negation, and this leads to characteristic inhibitions in the use of the undifferentiated function. Another feature is the fusing together of its separate components; thus, undifferentiated sensation is vitiated by the coalescence of different

34 Bleuler, "Die negative Suggestibilität," *Psychiatrisch-neurologische Wochenschrift*, vol. 6, pp. 249ff.; *The Theory of Schizophrenic Negativism* (orig. in ibid., vol. 12, pp. 171, 189, 195); *Textbook of Psychiatry*, pp. 130, 382. [See also supra, par. 684.—EDITORS.]

sensory spheres (colour-hearing), and undifferentiated feeling by confounding hate with love. To the extent that a function is largely or wholly unconscious, it is also undifferentiated; it is not only fused together in its parts but also merged with other functions. Differentiation consists in the separation of the function from other functions, and in the separation of its individual parts from each other. Without differentiation direction is impossible, since the direction of a function towards a goal depends on the elimination of anything irrelevant. Fusion with the irrelevant precludes direction; only a differentiated function is *capable* of being directed.

. . .

706   10. EGO. By ego I understand a complex of ideas which constitutes the centre of my field of consciousness and appears to possess a high degree of continuity and identity. Hence I also speak of an *ego-complex*.[35] The ego-complex is as much a content as a condition of *consciousness* (q.v.), for a psychic element is conscious to me only in so far as it is related to my ego-complex. But inasmuch as the ego is only the centre of my field of consciousness, it is not identical with the totality of my psyche, being merely one complex among other complexes. I therefore distinguish between the ego and the *self* (q.v.), since the ego is only the subject of my consciousness, while the self is the subject of my total psyche, which also includes the unconscious. In this sense the self would be an ideal entity which embraces the ego. In unconscious *fantasies* (q.v.) the self often appears as supraordinate or ideal personality, having somewhat the relationship of Faust to Goethe or Zarathustra to Nietzsche. For the sake of idealization the archaic features of the self are represented as being separate from the "higher" self, as for instance Mephistopheles in Goethe, Epimetheus in Spitteler, and in Christian psychology the devil or Antichrist. In Nietzsche, Zarathustra discovered his shadow in the "Ugliest Man."

. . .

35 "The Psychology of Dementia Praecox," *Psychiatric Studies*, index, s.v., "ego-complex."

708   18. ENANTIODROMIA means a "running counter to." In the philosophy of Heraclitus[37] it is used to designate the play of opposites in the course of events—the view that everything that exists turns into its opposite. "From the living comes death and from the dead life, from the young old age and from the old youth; from waking, sleep, and from sleep, waking; the stream of generation and decay never stands still."[38] "Construction and destruction, destruction and construction—this is the principle which governs all the cycles of natural life, from the smallest to the greatest. Just as the cosmos itself arose from the primal fire, so must it return once more into the same—a dual process running its measured course through vast periods of time, a drama eternally re-enacted."[39]

· · ·

709   I use the term enantiodromia for the emergence of the unconscious opposite in the course of time. This characteristic phenomenon practically always occurs when an extreme, one-sided tendency dominates conscious life; in time an equally powerful counterposition is built up, which first inhibits the conscious performance and subsequently breaks through the conscious control. Good examples of enantiodromia are: the conversion of St. Paul and of Raymund Lully,[41] the self-identification of the sick Nietzsche with Christ, and his deification and subsequent hatred of Wagner, the transformation of Swedenborg from an erudite scholar into a seer, and so on.

710   19. EXTRAVERSION is an outward-turning of *libido* (q.v.). I use this concept to denote a manifest relation of subject to object, a positive movement of subjective interest towards the object. Everyone in the extraverted state thinks, feels, and acts in relation to the object, and moreover in a direct and clearly observable fashion, so that no doubt can remain about his posi-

37 Stobaeus, *Eclogae physicae*, 1, 60: εἱμαρμένη δὲ λόγου ἐκ τῆς ἐναντιοδρομίας δημιουργὸν τῶν ὄντων. ("Fate is the logical product of enantiodromia, creator of all things.")
38 Zeller, *A History of Greek Philosophy*, II, p. 17.
39 Cf. Gomperz, *Greek Thinkers*, I, p. 64.
41 [Ramon Llull, 1234-1315. Cf. "The Psychology of Dementia Praecox," par. 89.—EDITORS.]

252

tive dependence on the object. In a sense, therefore, extraversion is a transfer of interest from subject to object. If it is an extraversion of thinking, the subject thinks himself into the object; if an extraversion of feeling, he feels himself into it. In extraversion there is a strong, if not exclusive, determination by the object. Extraversion is *active* when it is intentional, and *passive* when the object compels it, i.e., when the object attracts the subject's interest of its own accord, even against his will. When extraversion is habitual, we speak of the *extraverted type* (q.v.).

711   20. FANTASY.[42] By fantasy I understand two different things: 1. a *fantasm*, and 2. *imaginative activity*. In the present work the context always shows which of these meanings is intended. By fantasy in the sense of *fantasm* I mean a complex of ideas that is distinguished from other such complexes by the fact that it has no objective referent. Although it may originally be based on memory-images of actual experiences, its content refers to no external reality; it is merely the output of creative psychic activity, a manifestation or product of a combination of energized psychic elements. In so far as psychic energy can be voluntarily directed, a fantasy can be consciously and intentionally produced, either as a whole or at least in part. In the former case it is nothing but a combination of *conscious* elements, an artificial experiment of purely theoretical interest. In actual everyday psychological experience, fantasy is either set in motion by an intuitive attitude of expectation, or it is an irruption of *unconscious* contents into consciousness.

712   We can distinguish between *active* and *passive* fantasy. *Active* fantasies are the product of *intuition* (q.v.), i.e., they are evoked by an *attitude* (q.v.) directed to the perception of unconscious contents, as a result of which the *libido* (q.v.) immediately invests all the elements emerging from the unconscious and, by association with parallel material, brings them into clear focus in visual form. *Passive* fantasies appear in visual form at the outset, neither preceded nor accompanied by intuitive expectation, the attitude of the subject being wholly passive. Such fantasies belong to the category of

42 [This appeared as Def. 41, PHANTASY, in the Baynes translation.—EDITORS]

psychic *automatisms* (Janet). Naturally, they can appear only as a result of a relative dissociation of the psyche, since they presuppose a withdrawal of energy from conscious control and a corresponding activation of unconscious material. Thus the vision of St. Paul[43] presupposes that unconsciously he was already a Christian, though this fact had escaped his conscious insight.

713 It is probable that passive fantasies always have their origin in an unconscious process that is antithetical to consciousness, but invested with approximately the same amount of energy as the conscious attitude, and therefore capable of breaking through the latter's resistance. Active fantasies, on the other hand, owe their existence not so much to this unconscious process as to a conscious propensity to assimilate hints or fragments of lightly-toned unconscious complexes and, by associating them with parallel elements, to elaborate them in clearly visual form. It is not necessarily a question of a dissociated psychic state, but rather of a positive participation of consciousness.

714 Whereas passive fantasy not infrequently bears a morbid stamp or at least shows some trace of abnormality, active fantasy is one of the highest forms of psychic activity. For here the conscious and the unconscious personality of the subject flow together into a common product in which both are united. Such a fantasy can be the highest expression of the unity of a man's *individuality* (q.v.), and it may even create that individuality by giving perfect expression to its unity. As a general rule, passive fantasy is never the expression of a unified individuality since, as already observed, it presupposes a considerable degree of dissociation based in turn on a marked conscious/unconscious opposition. Hence the fantasy that irrupts into consciousness from such a state can never be the perfect expression of a unified individuality, but will represent mainly the standpoint of the unconscious personality. The life of St. Paul affords a good example of this: his conversion to Christianity signified an acceptance of the hitherto unconscious standpoint and a repression of the hitherto anti-Christian one, which then made itself felt in his hysterical attacks. Passive fantasy, therefore, is always in need of conscious *criticism*, lest

43 Acts 9:3ff.

it merely reinforce the standpoint of the unconscious opposite. Whereas active fantasy, as the product of a conscious attitude *not* opposed to the unconscious, and of unconscious processes not opposed but merely compensatory to consciousness, does not require criticism so much as *understanding*.

. . .

720 To sum up, we might say that a fantasy needs to be understood both causally and purposively. Causally interpreted, it seems like a *symptom* of a physiological or personal state, the outcome of antecedent events. Purposively interpreted, it seems like a *symbol*, seeking to characterize a definite goal with the help of the material at hand, or trace out a line of future psychological development. Because active fantasy is the chief mark of the artistic mentality, the artist is not just a *re-producer* of appearances but a creator and educator, for his works have the value of symbols that adumbrate lines of future development.

. . .

722 This brings us to the second connotation of fantasy, namely *imaginative activity*. Imagination is the reproductive or creative activity of the mind in general. It is not a special faculty, since it can come into play in all the basic forms of psychic activity, whether *thinking, feeling, sensation,* or *intuition* (qq.v.). Fantasy as imaginative activity is, in my view, simply the direct expression of psychic life,[45] of psychic energy which cannot appear in consciousness except in the form of images or contents, just as physical energy cannot manifest itself except as a definite physical state stimulating the sense

[45] [Imaginative activity is therefore not to be confused with "active imagination," a psychotherapeutic method developed by Jung himself. Active imagination corresponds to the definitions of *active fantasy* in pars. 712–14. The method of active imagination (though not called by that name) may be found in "The Aims of Psychotherapy," pars. 101–6, "The Transcendent Function," pars. 166ff., "On the Nature of the Psyche," pars. 400–2, and *Two Essays on Analytical Psychology,* pars. 343ff., 366. The term "active imagination" was used for the first time in "The Tavistock Lectures" (delivered in London, 1935), first published as *Analytical Psychology: Its Theory and Practice* (1968), now in *Coll. Works,* vol. 18. The method is described there in pars. 391ff. Further descriptions occur in *Mysterium Coniunctionis,* esp. pars. 706, 749–54.—EDITORS.]

organs in physical ways. For as every physical state, from the energic standpoint, is a dynamic system, so from the same standpoint a psychic content is a dynamic system manifesting itself in consciousness. We could therefore say that fantasy in the sense of a fantasm is a definite sum of libido that cannot appear in consciousness in any other way than in the form of an image. A fantasm is an *idée-force*. Fantasy as imaginative activity is identical with the flow of psychic energy.

723   21. FEELING.[46] I count feeling among the four basic psychological *functions* (q.v.).

. . .

724   Feeling is primarily a process that takes place between the *ego* (q.v.) and a given content, a process, moreover, that imparts to the content a definite *value* in the sense of acceptance or rejection ("like" or "dislike"). The process can also appear isolated, as it were, in the form of a "mood," regardless of the momentary contents of consciousness or momentary sensations. The mood may be causally related to earlier conscious contents, though not necessarily so, since, as psychopathology amply proves, it may equally well arise from unconscious contents. But even a mood, whether it be a general or only a partial feeling, implies a valuation; not of one definite, individual conscious content, but of the whole conscious situation at the moment, and, once again, with special reference to the question of acceptance or rejection.

725   Feeling, therefore, is an entirely *subjective* process, which may be in every respect independent of external stimuli, though it allies itself with every sensation.[48] Even an "indifferent" sensation possesses a feeling-tone, namely that of indifference, which again expresses some sort of valuation. Hence feeling is a kind of *judgment*, differing from intellectual judgment in that its aim is not to establish conceptual relations but to set up a subjective criterion of acceptance or rejection. Valuation by feeling extends to *every* content of consciousness, of

46 [This appeared as Def. 20 in the Baynes translation.—EDITORS.]
48 For the distinction between feeling and sensation, see Wundt, *Grundzüge der physiologischen Psychologie*, I, pp. 350ff.

whatever kind it may be. When the intensity of feeling increases, it turns into an *affect* (q.v.), i.e., a feeling-state accompanied by marked physical innervations. Feeling is distinguished from affect by the fact that it produces no perceptible physical innervations, i.e., neither more nor less than an ordinary thinking process.

726 Ordinary, "simple" feeling is *concrete* (q.v.), that is, it is mixed up with other functional elements, more particularly with sensations. In this case we can call it *affective* or, as I have done in this book, *feeling-sensation,* by which I mean an almost inseparable amalgam of feeling and sensation elements. This characteristic amalgamation is found wherever feeling is still an undifferentiated function, and is most evident in the psyche of a neurotic with differentiated thinking. Although feeling is, in itself, an independent function, it can easily become dependent on another function—thinking, for instance; it is then a mere concomitant of thinking, and is not repressed only in so far as it accommodates itself to the thinking processes.

727 It is important to distinguish *abstract* feeling from ordinary concrete feeling. Just as the abstract concept (v. *Thinking*) abolishes the differences between things it apprehends, abstract feeling rises above the differences of the individual contents it evaluates, and produces a "mood" or feeling-state which embraces the different individual valuations and thereby abolishes them. In the same way that thinking organizes the contents of consciousness under concepts, feeling arranges them according to their value. The more concrete it is, the more subjective and personal is the value conferred upon them; but the more abstract it is, the more universal and objective the value will be. Just as a completely abstract concept no longer coincides with the singularity and discreteness of things, but only with their universality and non-differentiation, so completely abstract feeling no longer coincides with a particular content and its feeling-value, but with the undifferentiated totality of all contents. Feeling, like thinking, is a *rational* (q.v.) function, since values in general are assigned according to the laws of reason, just as concepts in general are formed according to these laws.

728 Naturally the above definitions do not give the essence of feeling—they only describe it from outside. The intellect

729   proves incapable of formulating the real nature of feeling in conceptual terms, since thinking belongs to a category incommensurable with feeling; in fact, no basic psychological function can ever be completely expressed by another. That being so, it is impossible for an intellectual definition to reproduce the specific character of feeling at all adequately. The mere classification of feelings adds nothing to an understanding of their nature, because even the most exact classification will be able to indicate only the content of feeling which the intellect can apprehend, without grasping its specific nature. Only as many classes of feelings can be discriminated as there are classes of contents that can be intellectually apprehended, but feeling *per se* can never be exhaustively classified because, beyond every possible class of contents accessible to the intellect, there still exist feelings which resist intellectual classification. The very notion of classification is intellectual and therefore incompatible with the nature of feeling. We must therefore be content to indicate the limits of the concept.

  The nature of valuation by feeling may be compared with intellectual *apperception* (q.v.) as an *apperception of value*. We can distinguish *active* and *passive* apperception by feeling. Passive feeling allows itself to be attracted or excited by a particular content, which then forces the feelings of the subject to participate. Active feeling is a transfer of value from the subject; it is an intentional valuation of the content in accordance with feeling and not in accordance with the intellect. Hence active feeling is a *directed* function, an act of the *will* (q.v.), as for instance loving as opposed to being in love. The latter would be *undirected*, passive feeling, as these expressions themselves show: the one is an activity, the other a passive state. Undirected feeling is *feeling-intuition*. Strictly speaking, therefore, only active, directed feeling should be termed *rational*, whereas passive feeling is *irrational* (q.v.) in so far as it confers values without the participation or even against the intentions of the subject. When the subject's attitude as a whole is oriented by the feeling function, we speak of a *feeling type* (v. *Type*).

731   22. FUNCTION (v. also INFERIOR FUNCTION). By a psychological function I mean a particular form of psychic activity

· · ·

732 that remains the same in principle under varying conditions. From the energic standpoint a function is a manifestation of *libido* (q.v.), which likewise remains constant in principle, in much the same way as a physical force can be considered a specific form or manifestation of physical energy. I distinguish four basic functions in all, two rational and two irrational (qq.v.): *thinking* and *feeling, sensation* and *intuition* (qq.v.). I can give no *a priori* reason for selecting these four as basic functions, and can only point out that this conception has shaped itself out of many years' experience. I distinguish these functions from one another because they cannot be related or reduced to one another. The principle of thinking, for instance, is absolutely different from the principle of feeling, and so forth. I make a cardinal distinction between these functions and *fantasies* (q.v.), because fantasy is a characteristic form of activity that can manifest itself in all four functions. Volition or *will* (q.v.) seems to me an entirely secondary phenomenon, and so does *attention*.

733 23. IDEA. In this work the concept "idea" is sometimes used to designate a certain psychological element which is closely connected with what I term *image* (q.v.). The image may be either *personal* or *impersonal* in origin. In the latter case it is *collective* (q.v.) and is also distinguished by mythological qualities. I then term it a *primordial image*. When, on the other hand, it has no mythological character, i.e., is lacking in visual qualities and merely collective, I speak of an *idea*. Accordingly, I use the term idea to express the *meaning* of a primordial image, a meaning that has been abstracted from the *concretism* (q.v.) of the image. In so far as an idea is an *abstraction* (q.v.), it has the appearance of something derived, or developed, from elementary factors, a product of thought. This is the sense in which it is conceived by Wundt[49] and many others.

    In so far, however, as an idea is the formulated meaning of a primordial image by which it was represented *symbolically* (v. *Symbol*), its essence is not just something derived or developed, but, psychologically speaking, exists *a priori*, as a given possibility for thought-combinations in general. Hence,

[49] "Was soll uns Kant nicht sein?," *Philosophische Studien*, VII, p. 13.

in accordance with its essence (but not with its formulation), the idea is a psychological determinant having an *a priori* existence. In this sense Plato sees the idea as a prototype of things, while Kant defines it as the "archetype [*Urbild*] of all practical employment of reason," a transcendental concept which as such exceeds the bounds of the experienceable,[50] "a rational concept whose object is not to be found in experience."[51]

. . .

736   I do not want to pile up evidence for the primary nature of the idea. These quotations should suffice to show that it can be conceived as a fundamental, *a priori* factor. It derives this quality from its precursor—the primordial, symbolic image. Its secondary nature as something abstract and derived is a result of the rational elaboration to which the primordial image is subjected to fit it for rational use. The primordial image is an autochthonous psychological factor constantly repeating itself at all times and places, and the same might be said of the idea, although, on account of its rational nature, it is much more subject to modification by rational elaboration and formulations corresponding to local conditions and the spirit of the time.

. . .

738   24. IDENTIFICATION. By this I mean a psychological process in which the personality is partially or totally *dissimilated* (v. *Assimilation*). Identification is an alienation of the subject from himself for the sake of the object, in which he is, so to speak, disguised. For example, identification with the father means, in practice, adopting all the father's ways of behaving, as though the son were the same as the father and not a separate individuality. Identification differs from *imitation* in that it is an *unconscious* imitation, whereas imitation is a conscious copying.

50 Cf. Kant, *Critique of Pure Reason* (trans. Kemp Smith) p. 319.
51 *Logik*, I, sec. 1, par. 3 (*Werke*, ed. Cassirer, VIII, p. 400). [Cf. supra, par. 519, n. 11.]

741   25. IDENTITY. I use the term *identity* to denote a psychological conformity. It is always an unconscious phenomenon since a conscious conformity would necessarily involve a consciousness of two dissimilar things, and, consequently, a separation of subject and object, in which case the identity would already have been abolished. Psychological identity presupposes that it is unconscious. It is a characteristic of the primitive mentality and the real foundation of *participation mystique* (q.v.), which is nothing but a relic of the original non-differentiation of subject and object, and hence of the primordial unconscious state. It is also a characteristic of the mental state of early infancy, and, finally, of the unconscious of the civilized adult, which, in so far as it has not become a content of consciousness, remains in a permanent state of identity with objects. Identity with the parents provides the basis for subsequent *identification* (q.v.) with them; on it also depends the possibility of *projection* (q.v.) and *introjection* (q.v.).

742   Identity is primarily an unconscious conformity with objects. It is not an *equation*, but an *a priori likeness* which was never the object of consciousness. Identity is responsible for the naive assumption that the psychology of one man is like that of another, that the same motives occur everywhere, that what is agreeable to me must obviously be pleasurable for others, that what I find immoral must also be immoral for them, and so on. It is also responsible for the almost universal desire to correct in others what most needs correcting in oneself. Identity, too, forms the basis of suggestion and psychic infection. Identity is particularly evident in pathological cases, for instance in paranoic ideas of reference, where one's own subjective contents are taken for granted in others. But identity also makes possible a consciously *collective* (q.v.), social *attitude* (q.v.), which found its highest expression in the Christian ideal of brotherly love.

743   26. IMAGE. When I speak of "image" in this book, I do not mean the psychic reflection of an external object, but a concept derived from poetic usage, namely, a figure of fancy or *fantasy-image*, which is related only indirectly to the perception of an external object. This image depends much more on

unconscious fantasy activity, and as the product of such activity it appears more or less abruptly in consciousness, somewhat in the manner of a vision or hallucination, but without possessing the morbid traits that are found in a clinical picture. The image has the psychological character of a fantasy idea and never the quasi-real character of an hallucination, i.e., it never takes the place of reality, and can always be distinguished from sensuous reality by the fact that it is an "inner" image. As a rule, it is not a projection in space, although in exceptional cases it can appear in exteriorized form. This mode of manifestation must be termed *archaic* (q.v.) when it is not primarily pathological, though that would not by any means do away with its archaic character. On the primitive level, however, the inner image can easily be projected in space as a vision or an auditory hallucination without being a pathological phenomenon.

744   Although, as a rule, no reality-value attaches to the image, this can at times actually increase its importance for psychic life, since it then has a greater *psychological* value, representing an inner reality which often far outweighs the importance of external reality. In this case the *orientation* (q.v.) of the individual is concerned less with adaptation to reality than with adaptation to inner demands.

745   The inner image is a complex structure made up of the most varied material from the most varied sources. It is no conglomerate, however, but a homogeneous product with a meaning of its own. The image is a *condensed expression of the psychic situation as a whole*, and not merely, nor even predominately, of unconscious contents pure and simple. It undoubtedly does express unconscious contents, but not the whole of them, only those that are momentarily constellated. This constellation is the result of the spontaneous activity of the unconscious on the one hand and of the momentary conscious situation on the other, which always stimulates the activity of relevant subliminal material and at the same time inhibits the irrelevant. Accordingly the image is an expression of the unconscious as well as the conscious situation of the moment. The interpretation of its meaning, therefore, can start neither from the conscious alone nor from the unconscious alone, but only from their reciprocal relationship.

746 I call the image *primordial* when it possesses an *archaic* (q.v.) character.[60] I speak of its archaic character when the image is in striking accord with familiar mythological motifs. It then expresses material primarily derived from the *collective unconscious* (q.v.), and indicates at the same time that the factors influencing the conscious situation of the moment are *collective* (q.v.) rather than personal. A *personal* image has neither an archaic character nor a collective significance, but expresses contents of the *personal unconscious* (q.v.) and a personally conditioned conscious situation.

747 The primordial image, elsewhere also termed *archetype*,[61] is always collective, i.e., it is at least common to entire peoples or epochs. In all probability the most important mythological motifs are common to all times and races; I have, in fact, been able to demonstrate a whole series of motifs from Greek mythology in the dreams and fantasies of pure-bred Negroes suffering from mental disorders.[62]

748 From[63] the scientific, causal standpoint the primordial image can be conceived as a mnemic deposit, an imprint or *engram* (Semon), which has arisen through the condensation of countless processes of a similar kind. In this respect it is a precipitate and, therefore, a typical basic form, of certain everrecurring psychic experiences. As a mythological motif, it is a continually effective and recurrent expression that reawakens certain psychic experiences or else formulates them in an appropriate way. From this standpoint it is a psychic expression of the physiological and anatomical disposition. If one holds the view that a particular anatomical structure is a product of

---

[60] A striking example of an archaic image is that of the solar phallus, *Symbols of Transformation*, pars. 151ff.

[61] Jung, "Instinct and the Unconscious," pars. 270ff. See also supra, par. 624.

[62] [In a letter to Freud, Nov. 11, 1912, reporting on a recent visit to the United States, Jung wrote: "I analyzed fifteen Negroes in Washington, with demonstrations." He did this at St. Elizabeths Hospital (a government facility) through the cooperation of its director, Dr. William Alanson White; see *Symbols of Transformation*, par. 154 and n. 52. In late 1912 Jung had already written and partially published *Wandlungen und Symbole der Libido*, and he mentioned the research on Negroes only in its revision, *Symbols of Transformation* (orig. 1952). Cf. also "The Tavistock Lectures," par. 79.—EDITORS.]

[63] [This paragraph has been somewhat revised in *Gesammelte Werke*, vol. 6, and the translation reproduces the revisions.—EDITORS.]

environmental conditions working on living matter, then the primordial image, in its constant and universal distribution, would be the product of equally constant and universal influences from without, which must, therefore, act like a natural law. One could in this way relate myths to nature, as for instance solar myths to the daily rising and setting of the sun, or to the equally obvious change of the seasons, and this has in fact been done by many mythologists, and still is. But that leaves the question unanswered why the sun and its apparent motions do not appear direct and undisguised as a content of the myths. The fact that the sun or the moon or the meteorological processes appear, at the very least, in allegorized form points to an independent collaboration of the psyche, which in that case cannot be merely a product or stereotype of environmental conditions. For whence would it draw the capacity to adopt a standpoint outside sense perception? How, for that matter, could it be at all capable of any performance more or other than the mere corroboration of the evidence of the senses? In view of such questions Semon's naturalistic and causalistic engram theory no longer suffices. We are forced to assume that the given structure of the brain does not owe its peculiar nature merely to the influence of surrounding conditions, but also and just as much to the peculiar and autonomous quality of living matter, i.e., to a law inherent in life itself. The given constitution of the organism, therefore, is on the one hand a product of external conditions, while on the other it is determined by the intrinsic nature of living matter. Accordingly, the primordial image is related just as much to certain palpable, self-perpetuating, and continually operative natural processes as it is to certain inner determinants of psychic life and of life in general. The organism confronts light with a new structure, the eye, and the psyche confronts the natural process with a symbolic image, which apprehends it in the same way as the eye catches the light. And just as the eye bears witness to the peculiar and spontaneous creative activity of living matter, the primordial image expresses the unique and unconditioned creative power of the psyche.

749   The primordial image is thus a condensation of the living process. It gives a co-ordinating and coherent meaning both to sensuous and to inner perceptions, which at first appear with-

750   out order or connection, and in this way frees psychic energy from its bondage to sheer uncomprehended perception. At the same time, it links the energies released by the perception of stimuli to a definite meaning, which then guides action along paths corresponding to this meaning. It releases unavailable, dammed-up energy by leading the mind back to nature and canalizing sheer instinct into mental forms.

The primordial image is the precursor of the *idea* (q.v.), and its matrix. By detaching it from the *concretism* (q.v.) peculiar and necessary to the primordial image, reason develops it into a concept—i.e., an idea which differs from all other concepts in that it is not a datum of experience but is actually the underlying principle of all experience. The idea derives this quality from the primordial image, which, as an expression of the specific structure of the brain, gives every experience a definite form.

754   The primordial image has one great advantage over the clarity of the idea, and that is its vitality. It is a self-activating organism, "endowed with generative power." The primordial image is an inherited organization of psychic energy, an ingrained system, which not only gives expression to the energic process but facilitates its operation. It shows how the energic process has run its unvarying course from time immemorial, while simultaneously allowing a perpetual repetition of it by means of an apprehension or psychic grasp of situations so that life can continue into the future. It is thus the necessary counterpart of *instinct* (q.v.), which is a purposive mode of action presupposing an equally purposive and meaningful grasp of the momentary situation. This apprehension is guaranteed by the pre-existent primordial image. It represents the practical formula without which the apprehension of a new situation would be impossible.

. . .

755   27. INDIVIDUAL. The psychological individual is characterized by a peculiar and in some respects unique psychology.

The peculiar nature of the individual psyche appears less in its elements than in its complex formations. The psychological individual, or his *individuality* (q.v.), has an *a priori* unconscious existence, but exists consciously only so far as a conscious of his peculiar nature is present, i.e., so far as there exists a conscious distinction from other individuals. The psychic individuality is given *a priori* as a correlate of the physical individuality, although, as observed, it is at first unconscious. A conscious process of *differentiation* (q.v.), or *individuation* (q.v.), is needed to bring the individuality to consciousness, i.e., to raise it out of the state of *identity* (q.v.) with the object. The identity of the individuality with the object is synonymous with its unconsciousness. If the individuality is unconscious, there is no psychological individual but merely a collective psychology of consciousness. The unconscious individuality is then projected on the object, and the object, in consequence, possesses too great a value and acts as too powerful a determinant.

756   28. INDIVIDUALITY. By individuality I mean the peculiarity and singularity of the individual in every psychological respect. Everything that is not *collective* (q.v.) is individual, everything in fact that pertains only to one individual and not to a larger group of individuals. Individuality can hardly be said to pertain to the psychic elements themselves, but only to their peculiar and unique grouping and combination (v. *Individual*).

757   29. INDIVIDUATION. The concept of individuation plays a large role in our psychology. In general, it is the process by which individual beings are formed and differentiated; in particular, it is the development of the psychological *individual* (q.v.) as a being distinct from the general, collective psychology. Individuation, therefore, is a process of *differentiation* (q.v.), having for its goal the development of the individual personality.

758   Individuation is a natural necessity inasmuch as its prevention by a levelling down to collective standards is injurious to the vital activity of the individual. Since *individuality* (q.v.) is a prior psychological and physiological datum, it also expresses itself in psychological and physiological ways. Any serious check to in-

dividuality, therefore, is an artificial stunting. It is obvious that a social group consisting of stunted individuals cannot be a healthy and viable institution; only a society that can preserve its internal cohesion and collective values, while at the same time granting the individual the greatest possible freedom, has any prospect of enduring vitality. As the individual is not just a single, separate being, but by his very existence presupposes a collective relationship, it follows that the process of individuation must lead to more intense and broader collective relationships and not to isolation.

759   Individuation is closely connected with the *transcendent function* (v. *Symbol*, par. 828), since this function creates individual lines of development which could never be reached by keeping to the path prescribed by collective norms.

760   Under no circumstances can individuation be the sole aim of psychological education. Before it can be taken as a goal, the educational aim of adaptation to the necessary minimum of collective norms must first be attained. If a plant is to unfold its specific nature to the full, it must first be able to grow in the soil in which it is planted.

761   Individuation is always to some extent opposed to collective norms, since it means separation and differentiation from the general and a building up of the particular—not a particularity that is *sought out*, but one that is already ingrained in the psychic constitution. The opposition to the collective norm, however, is only apparent, since closer examination shows that the individual standpoint is not *antagonistic* to it, but only *differently oriented*. The individual way can never be directly opposed to the collective norm, because the opposite of the collective norm could only be another, but contrary, norm. But the individual way can, by definition, never be a norm. A norm is the product of the totality of individual ways, and its justification and beneficial effect are contingent upon the existence of individual ways that need from time to time to orient to a norm. A norm serves no purpose when it possesses absolute validity. A real conflict with the collective norm arises only when an individual way is raised to a norm, which is the actual aim of extreme individualism. Naturally this aim is pathological and inimical to life. It has, accordingly, nothing to do with individuation, which, though it may strike out on an individual

bypath, precisely on that account needs the norm for its *orientation* (q.v.) to society and for the vitally necessary relationship of the individual to society. Individuation, therefore, leads to a natural esteem for the collective norm, but if the orientation is exclusively collective the norm becomes increasingly superfluous and morality goes to pieces. The more a man's life is shaped by the collective norm, the greater is his individual immorality.

762   Individuation is practically the same as the development of consciousness out of the original state of *identity* (q.v.). It is thus an extension of the sphere of consciousness, an enriching of conscious psychological life.

· · ·

765   31. INSTINCT. When I speak of instinct in this work or elsewhere, I mean what is commonly understood by this word, namely, an *impulsion* towards certain activities. The impulsion can come from an inner or outer stimulus which triggers off the mechanism of instinct psychically, or from organic sources which lie outside the sphere of psychic causality. Every psychic phenomenon is instinctive that does not arise from voluntary causation but from dynamic impulsion, irrespective of whether this impulsion comes directly from organic, extrapsychic sources, or from energies that are merely released by voluntary intention—in the latter case with the qualification that the end-result exceeds the effect voluntarily intended. In my view, all psychic processes whose energies are not under conscious control are instinctive. Thus *affects* (q.v.) are as much instinctive processes as they are *feeling* (q.v.) processes. Psychic processes which under ordinary circumstances are functions of the *will* (q.v.), and thus entirely under conscious control, can, in abnormal circumstances, become instinctive processes when supplied with unconscious energy. This phenomenon occurs whenever the sphere of consciousness is restricted by the repression of incompatible contents, or when, as a result of fatigue, intoxication, or morbid cerebral conditions in general, an *abaissement du niveau mental* (Janet) ensues—when, in a word, the most strongly feeling-toned proc-

268

esses are no longer, or not yet, under conscious control. Processes that were once conscious but in time have become *automatized* I would reckon among the automatic processes rather than the instinctive. Nor do they normally behave like instincts, since in normal circumstances they never appear as impulsions. They do so only when supplied with an energy which is foreign to them.

. . .

769   34. INTROVERSION means an inward-turning of *libido* (q.v.), in the sense of a negative relation of subject to object. Interest does not move towards the object but withdraws from it into the subject. Everyone whose attitude is introverted thinks, feels, and acts in a way that clearly demonstrates that the subject is the prime motivating factor and that the object is of secondary importance. Introversion may be intellectual or emotional, just as it can be characterized by *sensation* or *intuition* (qq.v.). It is *active* when the subject *voluntarily* shuts himself off from the object, *passive* when he is unable to restore to the object the libido streaming back from it. When introversion is habitual, we speak of an *introverted type* (q.v.).

770   35. INTUITION (L. *intueri*, 'to look at or into'). I regard intuition as a basic psychological *function* (q.v.). It is the function that mediates perceptions in an *unconscious way*. Everything, whether outer or inner objects or their relationships, can be the focus of this perception. The peculiarity of intuition is that it is neither sense perception, nor feeling, nor intellectual inference, although it may also appear in these forms. In intuition a content presents itself whole and complete, without our being able to explain or discover how this content came into existence. Intuition is a kind of instinctive apprehension, no matter of what contents. Like *sensation* (q.v.), it is an *irrational* (q.v.) function of perception. As with sensation, its contents have the character of being "given," in contrast to the "derived" or "produced" character of *thinking and feeling* (qq.v.).

269

771   Intuition may be *subjective* or *objective*: the first is a perception of unconscious psychic data originating in the subject, the second is a perception of data dependent on subliminal perceptions of the object and on the feelings and thoughts they evoke. We may also distinguish *concrete* and *abstract* forms of intuition, according to the degree of participation on the part of sensation. Concrete intuition mediates perceptions concerned with the actuality of things, abstract intuition mediates perceptions of ideational connections. Concrete intuition is a reactive process, since it responds directly to the given facts; abstract intuition, like abstract sensation, needs a certain element of direction, an act of the will, or an aim.

772   Like sensation, intuition is a characteristic of infantile and primitive psychology. It counterbalances the powerful sense impressions of the child and the primitive by mediating perceptions of mythological images, the precursors of *ideas* (q.v.). It stands in a compensatory relationship to sensation and, like it, is the matrix out of which thinking and feeling develop as rational functions. Although intuition is an irrational function, many intuitions can afterwards be broken down into their component elements and their origin thus brought into harmony with the laws of reason.

773   Everyone whose general *attitude* (q.v.) is oriented by intuition belongs to the intuitive *type* (q.v.).[68] Introverted and extraverted intuitives may be distinguished according to whether intuition is directed inwards, to the inner vision, or outwards, to action and achievement. In abnormal cases intui-

contents. Intuitive knowledge possesses an intrinsic certainty and conviction, which enabled Spinoza (and Bergson) to uphold the *scientia intuitiva* as the highest form of knowledge. Intuition shares this quality with *sensation* (q.v.), whose certainty rests on its physical foundation. The certainty of intuition rests equally on a definite state of psychic "alertness" of whose origin the subject is unconscious.

[68] The credit for having discovered the existence of this type belongs to Miss M. Moltzer. [Mary Moltzer, daughter of a Netherlands distiller, took up nursing as a personal gesture against alcoholic abuse and moved to Zurich. She studied under Jung, became an analytical psychologist, and was joint translator of his *The Theory of Psychoanalysis* (see vol. 4, p. 83 and par. 458). She attended the international congress of psychoanalysts at Weimar, 1911.—EDITORS.]

tion is in large measure fused together with the contents of the *collective unconscious* (q.v.) and determined by them, and this may make the intuitive type appear extremely irrational and beyond comprehension.

774   36. IRRATIONAL. I use this term not as denoting something *contrary* to reason, but something *beyond* reason, something, therefore, not grounded on reason. Elementary facts come into this category; the fact, for example, that the earth has a moon, that chlorine is an element, that water reaches its greatest density at four degrees centigrade, etc. Another irrational fact is *chance*, even though it may be possible to demonstrate a rational causation after the event.[69]

775   The irrational is an existential factor which, though it may be pushed further and further out of sight by an increasingly elaborate rational explanation, finally makes the explanation so complicated that it passes our powers of comprehension, the limits of rational thought being reached long before the whole of the world could be encompassed by the laws of reason. A completely rational explanation of an object that actually exists (not one that is merely posited) is a Utopian ideal. Only an object that is posited can be completely explained on rational grounds, since it does not contain anything beyond what has been posited by rational thinking. Empirical science, too, posits objects that are confined within rational bounds, because by deliberately excluding the accidental it does not consider the actual object as a whole, but only that part of it which has been singled out for rational observation.

776   In this sense *thinking* is a *directed function*, and so is *feeling* (qq.v.). When these functions are concerned not with a rational choice of objects, or with the qualities and interrelations of objects, but with the perception of accidentals which the actual object never lacks, they at once lose the attribute of directedness and, with it, something of their rational character, because they then accept the accidental. They begin to be irrational. The kind of thinking or feeling that is directed to the perception of accidentals, and is therefore irrational, is either *intuitive* or *sensational*. Both *intuition and sensation* (qq.v.) are functions that find fulfilment in the *absolute perception of*

[69] Jung, "Synchronicity: An Acausal Connecting Principle."

the flux of events. Hence, by their very nature, they will react to every possible occurrence and be attuned to the absolutely contingent, and must therefore lack all rational direction. For this reason I call them irrational functions, as opposed to thinking and feeling, which find fulfilment only when they are in complete harmony with the laws of reason.

777   Although the irrational as such can never become the object of science, it is of the greatest importance for a practical psychology that the irrational factor should be correctly appraised. Practical psychology stirs up many problems that are not susceptible of a rational solution, but can only be settled irrationally, in a way not in accord with the laws of reason. The expectation or exclusive conviction that there must be a rational way of settling every conflict can be an insurmountable obstacle to finding a solution of an irrational nature.

778   37. LIBIDO. By libido I mean *psychic energy*.[70] Psychic energy is the *intensity* of a psychic process, its *psychological value*. This does not imply an assignment of value, whether moral, aesthetic, or intellectual; the psychological value is already implicit in its *determining* power, which expresses itself in definite psychic effects. Neither do I understand libido as a psychic *force*, a misconception that has led many critics astray. I do not hypostatize the concept of energy, but use it to denote intensities or values. The question as to whether or not a specific psychic force exists has nothing to do with the concept of libido. I often use "libido" promiscuously with "energy." The justification for calling psychic energy libido is fully gone into in the works cited in the footnote.

779   38. OBJECTIVE LEVEL. When I speak of interpreting a dream or fantasy on the objective level, I mean that the persons or situations appearing in it are referred to objectively real persons or situations, in contrast to interpretation on the *subjective level* (q.v.), where the persons or situations refer exclusively to subjective factors. Freud's interpretation of dreams is almost entirely on the objective level, since the dream wishes refer to real objects, or to sexual processes which fall within the physiological, extra-psychological sphere.

[70] *Symbols of Transformation*, Part II, chs. II and III, and "On Psychic Energy," pars. 7ff.

780

39. ORIENTATION. I use this term to denote the general principle governing an *attitude* (q.v.). Every attitude is oriented by a certain viewpoint, no matter whether this viewpoint is conscious or not. A power attitude (v. *Power-complex*) is oriented by the power of the *ego* (q.v.) to hold its own against unfavourable influences and conditions. A thinking attitude is oriented by the principle of logic as its supreme law; a sensation attitude is oriented by the sensuous perception of given facts.

781

40. PARTICIPATION MYSTIQUE is a term derived from Lévy-Bruhl.[71] It denotes a peculiar kind of psychological connection with objects, and consists in the fact that the subject cannot clearly distinguish himself from the object but is bound to it by a direct relationship which amounts to *partial identity* (q.v.). This identity results from an *a priori* oneness of subject and object. *Participation mystique* is a vestige of this primitive condition. It does not apply to the whole subject-object relationship, in which the object (as a rule) obtains a sort of magical—i.e. absolute—influence over the subject. In the second case there is a similar influence on the part of the thing, or else an *identification* (q.v.) with a thing or the idea of a thing.

. . .

785

44. RATIONAL. The rational is the reasonable, that which accords with reason. I conceive reason as an *attitude* (q.v.) whose principle it is to conform thought, feeling, and action to objective values. Objective values are established by the everyday experience of external facts on the one hand, and of inner, psychological facts on the other. Such experiences, however, could not represent objective "values" if they were "valued" as such by the subject, for that would already amount to an act

[71] *How Natives Think.*

of reason. The rational attitude which permits us to declare objective values as valid at all is not the work of the individual subject, but the product of human history.

. . . .

788   45. REDUCTIVE means "leading back." I use this term to denote a method of psychological interpretation which regards the unconscious product not as a *symbol* (q.v.) but *semiotically*, as a *sign* or *symptom* of an underlying process. Accordingly, the reductive method traces the unconscious product back to its elements, no matter whether these be reminiscences of events that actually took place, or elementary psychic processes. The reductive method is oriented backwards, in contrast to the *constructive* (q.v.) method, whether in the purely historical sense or in the figurative sense of tracing complex, differentiated factors back to something more general and more elementary. The interpretive methods of both Freud and Adler are reductive, since in both cases there is a reduction to the elementary processes of wishing or striving, which in the last resort are of an infantile or physiological nature. Hence the unconscious product necessarily acquires the character of an inauthentic expression to which the term "symbol" is not properly applicable. Reduction has a disintegrative effect on the real significance of the unconscious product, since this is either traced back to its historical antecedents and thereby annihilated, or integrated once again with the same elementary process from which it arose.

789   46. SELF.[72] As an empirical concept, the self designates the whole range of psychic phenomena in man. It expresses the unity of the personality as a whole. But in so far as the total personality, on account of its unconscious component, can be only in part conscious, the concept of the self is, in part, only

[72] [This definition was written for the *Gesammelte Werke* edition. It may be of interest to note that the definition here given of the self as "the whole range of psychic phenomena in man" is almost identical with the definition of the psyche as "the totality of all psychic processes, conscious as well as unconscious" (par. 797). The inference would seem to be that every individual, by virtue of having, or being, a psyche, is potentially the self. It is only a question of "realizing" it. But the realization, if ever achieved, is the work of a lifetime.—EDITORS.]

potentially empirical and is to that extent a *postulate*. In other words, it encompasses both the experienceable and the inexperienceable (or the not yet experienced). It has these qualities in common with very many scientific concepts that are more names than ideas. In so far as psychic totality, consisting of both conscious and unconscious contents, is a postulate, it is a *transcendental* concept, for it presupposes the existence of unconscious factors on empirical grounds and thus characterizes an entity that can be described only in part but, for the other part, remains at present unknowable and illimitable.

790 Just as conscious as well as unconscious phenomena are to be met with in practice, the self as psychic totality also has a conscious as well as an unconscious aspect. Empirically, the self appears in dreams, myths, and fairytales in the figure of the "supraordinate personality" (V. EGO), such as a king, hero, prophet, saviour, etc., or in the form of a totality symbol, such as the circle, square, *quadratura circuli*, cross, etc. When it represents a *complexio oppositorum*, a union of opposites, it can also appear as a united duality, in the form, for instance, of *tao* as the interplay of *yang* and *yin*, or of the hostile brothers, or of the hero and his adversary (arch-enemy, dragon), Faust and Mephistopheles, etc. Empirically, therefore, the self appears as a play of light and shadow, although conceived as a totality and unity in which the opposites are united. Since such a concept is irrepresentable—*tertium non datur*—it is transcendental on this account also. It would, logically considered, be a vain speculation were it not for the fact that it designates symbols of unity that are found to occur empirically.

791 The self is not a philosophical idea, since it does not predicate its own existence, i.e., does not hypostatize itself. From the intellectual point of view it is only a working hypothesis. Its empirical symbols, on the other hand, very often possess a distinct *numinosity*, i.e., an *a priori* emotional value, as in the case of the mandala,[73] "Deus est circulus . . . ,"[74] the Pythagorean

[73] [Jung, "A Study in the Process of Individuation" and "Concerning Mandala Symbolism."—EDITORS.]

[74] [The full quotation is "Deus est circulus cuius centrum est ubique, circumferentia vero nusquam" (God is a circle whose centre is everywhere and the circumference nowhere); see "A Psychological Approach to the Dogma of the Trinity," par. 229, n. 6. In this form the saying is a variant of one attributed

792 tetraktys,[75] the quaternity,[76] etc. It thus proves to be an *archetypal idea* (v. *Idea; Image*), which differs from other ideas of the kind in that it occupies a central position befitting the significance of its content and its numinosity.

47. SENSATION. I regard sensation as one of the basic psychological *functions* (q.v.). Wundt likewise reckons it among the elementary psychic phenomena.[77] Sensation is the psychological function that mediates the perception of a physical stimulus. It is, therefore, identical with perception. Sensation must be strictly distinguished from *feeling* (q.v.), since the latter is an entirely different process, although it may associate itself with sensation as "feeling-tone." Sensation is related not only to external stimuli but to inner ones, i.e., to changes in the internal organic processes.

793 Primarily, therefore, sensation is *sense perception*—perception mediated by the sense organs and "body-senses" (kinaesthetic, vasomotor sensation, etc.). It is, on the one hand, an element of ideation, since it conveys to the mind the perceptual image of the external object; and on the other hand, it is an element of feeling, since through the perception of bodily changes it gives feeling the character of an *affect* (q.v.). Because sensation conveys bodily changes to consciousness, it is also a representative of physiological impulses. It is not identical with them, being merely a perceptive function.

794 A distinction must be made between sensuous or *concrete* (q.v.) sensation and *abstract* (q.v.) sensation. The first includes all the above-mentioned forms of sensation, whereas the sec-

---

[75] [Concerning the *tetraktys* see *Psychology and Alchemy*, par. 189; "Commentary on The Secret of the Golden Flower," par. 31; *Psychology and Religion: West and East*, pars. 61, 90, 246.—EDITORS.]

[76] [The quaternity figures so largely in Jung's later writings that the reader who is interested in its numerous significations, including that of a symbol of the self, should consult the indexes (s.v. "quaternity," "self") of *Coll. Works*, vols. 9, Parts I and II, 11, 12, 13, 14.—EDITORS.]

[77] For the history of the concept of sensation see Wundt, *Grundzüge der physiologischen Psychologie*, I, pp. 350ff.; Dessoir, *Geschichte der neueren Psychologie*; Villa, *Contemporary Psychology*; Hartmann, *Die moderne Psychologie.*

to St. Bonaventure (*Itinerarium mentis in Deum*, 5): "Deus est figura intellectualis cuius centrum . . ." (God is an intelligible sphere whose centre . . .); see *Mysterium Coniunctionis*, par. 41, n. 42. For more documentation see Borges, "Pascal's Sphere."—EDITORS.]

ond is a sensation that is abstracted or separated from the other psychic elements. Concrete sensation never appears in "pure" form, but is always mixed up with ideas, feelings, thoughts. Abstract sensation is a differentiated kind of perception, which might be termed "aesthetic" in so far as, obeying its own principle, it detaches itself from all contamination with the different elements in the perceived object and from all admixtures of thought and feeling, and thus attains a degree of purity beyond the reach of concrete sensation. The concrete sensation of a flower, on the one hand, conveys a perception not only of the flower as such, but also of the stem, leaves, habitat, and so on. It is also instantly mingled with feelings of pleasure or dislike which the sight of the flower evokes, or with simultaneous olfactory perceptions, or with thoughts about its botanical classification, etc. But abstract sensation immediately picks out the most salient sensuous attribute of the flower, its brilliant redness, for instance, and makes this the sole or at least the principal content of consciousness, entirely detached from all other admixtures. Abstract sensation is found chiefly among artists. Like every abstraction, it is a product of functional *differentiation* (q.v.), and there is nothing primitive about it. The primitive form of a function is always concrete, i.e., contaminated (v. *Archaism; Concretism*). Concrete sensation is a reactive phenomenon, while abstract sensation, like every abstraction, is always associated with the *will* (q.v.), i.e., with a sense of direction. The will that is directed to abstract sensation is an expression and application of the *aesthetic sensation attitude.*

795 Sensation is strongly developed in children and primitives, since in both cases it predominates over thinking and feeling, though not necessarily over *intuition* (q.v.). I regard sensation as conscious, and intuition as unconscious, perception. For me sensation and intuition represent a pair of opposites, or two mutually compensating functions, like thinking and feeling. Thinking and feeling are independent functions are developed, both ontogenetically and phylogenetically, from sensation (and equally, of course, from intuition as the necessary counterpart of sensation). A person whose whole *attitude* (q.v.) is oriented by sensation belongs to the *sensation type* (q.v.).

796 Since sensation is an elementary phenomenon, it is given *a priori*, and, unlike thinking and feeling, is not subject to ra-

277

tional laws. I therefore call it an *irrational* (q.v.) function, although reason contrives to assimilate a great many sensations into a rational context. Normal sensations are proportionate, i.e., they correspond approximately to the intensity of the physical stimulus. Pathological sensations are disproportionate, i.e., either abnormally weak or abnormally strong. In the former case they are inhibited, in the latter exaggerated. The inhibition is due to the predominance of another function; the exaggeration is the result of an abnormal fusion with another function, for instance with undifferentiated thinking or feeling. It ceases as soon as the function with which sensation is fused is differentiated in its own right. The psychology of the neuroses affords instructive examples of this, since we often find a strong *sexualization* (Freud) of other functions, i.e., their fusion with sexual sensations.

48. SOUL. [Psyche, personality, persona, anima.] I have been compelled, in my investigations into the structure of the unconscious, to make a conceptual distinction between *soul* and *psyche*. By psyche I understand the totality of all psychic processes, conscious as well as unconscious. By soul, on the other hand, I understand a clearly demarcated functional complex that can best be described as a "personality." In order to make clear what I mean by this, I must introduce some further points of view. It is, in particular, the phenomena of somnambulism, double consciousness, split personality, etc., whose investigation we owe primarily to the French school,[78] that have enabled us to accept the possibility of a plurality of personalities in one and the same individual.

[*Soul as a functional complex or "personality"*]

It is at once evident that such a plurality of personalities can never appear in a normal individual. But, as the above-mentioned phenomena show, the possibility of a dissociation of personality must exist, at least in the germ, within the range

797

798

[78] Azam, *Hypnotisme, double conscience, et altérations de la personnalité*; Prince, *The Dissociation of a Personality*; Landmann, *Die Mehrheit geistiger Persönlichkeiten in einem Individuum*; Ribot, *Die Persönlichkeit*; Flournoy, *From India to the Planet Mars*; Jung, "On the Psychology and Pathology of So-called Occult Phenomena."

of the normal. And, as a matter of fact, any moderately acute psychological observer will be able to demonstrate, without much difficulty, traces of character-splitting in normal individuals. One has only to observe a man rather closely, under varying conditions, to see that a change from one milieu to another brings about a striking alteration of personality, and on each occasion a clearly defined character emerges that is noticeably different from the previous one. "Angel abroad, devil at home" is a formulation of the phenomenon of character-splitting derived from everyday experience. A particular milieu necessitates a particular *attitude* (q.v.). The longer this attitude lasts, and the more often it is required, the more habitual it becomes. Very many people from the educated classes have to move in two totally different milieus—the domestic circle and the world of affairs. These two totally different environments demand two totally different attitudes, which, depending on the degree of the ego's *identification* (q.v.) with the attitude of the moment, produce a duplication of character. In accordance with social conditions and requirements, the social character is oriented on the one hand by the expectations and demands of society, and on the other by the social aims and aspirations of the individual. The domestic character is, as a rule, moulded by emotional demands and an easy-going acquiescence for the sake of comfort and convenience; whence it frequently happens that men who in public life are extremely energetic, spirited, obstinate, wilful and ruthless appear good-natured, mild, compliant, even weak, when at home and in the bosom of the family. Which is the true character, the real personality? This question is often impossible to answer.

799   These reflections show that even in normal individuals character-splitting is by no means an impossibility. We are, therefore, fully justified in treating personality dissociation as a problem of normal psychology. In my view the answer to the above question should be that such a man has no real character at all: he is not *individual* (q.v.) but *collective* (q.v.), the plaything of circumstance and general expectations. Were he individual, he would have the same character despite the variation of attitude. He would not be identical with the attitude of the moment, and he neither would nor could prevent his *individuality* (q.v.) from expressing itself just as clearly in

one state as in another. Naturally he is individual, like every living being, but unconsciously so. Because of his more or less complete identification with the attitude of the moment, he deceives others, and often himself, as to his real character. He puts on a *mask*, which he knows is in keeping with his conscious intentions, while it also meets the requirements and fits the opinions of society, first one motive and then the other gaining the upper hand.

800   This mask, i.e., the *ad hoc* adopted attitude, I have called the *persona*,[79] which was the name for the masks worn by actors in antiquity. The man who identifies with this mask I would call "personal" as opposed to "individual."

801   The two above-mentioned attitudes represent two collective personalities, which may be summed up quite simply under the name "personae." I have already suggested that the real individuality is different from both. The persona is thus a functional complex that comes into existence for reasons of adaptation or personal convenience, but is by no means identical with the individuality. The persona is exclusively concerned with the relation to objects. The relation of the individual to the object must be sharply distinguished from the relation to the subject. By the "subject" I mean first of all those vague, dim stirrings, feelings, thoughts, and sensations which flow in on us not from any demonstrable continuity of conscious experience of the object, but well up like a disturbing, inhibiting, or at times helpful, influence from the dark inner depths, from the background and underground vaults of consciousness, and constitute, in their totality, our perception of the life of the unconscious. The subject, conceived as the "inner object," *is* the unconscious. Just as there is a relation to the outer object, an outer attitude, there is a relation to the inner object, an inner attitude. It is readily understandable that this inner attitude, by reason of its extremely intimate and inaccessible nature, is far more difficult to discern than the outer attitude, which is immediately perceived by everyone. Nevertheless, it does not seem to me impossible to formulate it as a

[Soul as persona]

79 *Two Essays on Analytical Psychology*, pars. 243ff.

concept. All those allegedly accidental inhibitions, fancies, moods, vague feelings, and scraps of fantasy that hinder concentration and disturb the peace of mind even of the most normal man, and that are rationalized away as being due to bodily causes and suchlike, usually have their origin, not in the reasons consciously ascribed to them, but in perceptions of unconscious processes. Dreams naturally belong to this class of phenomena, and, as we all know, are often traced back to such external and superficial causes as indigestion, sleeping on one's back, and so forth, in spite of the fact that these explanations can never stand up to searching criticism. The attitude of the individual in these matters is extremely varied. One man will not allow himself to be disturbed in the slightest by his inner processes—he can ignore them completely; another man is just as completely at their mercy—as soon as he wakes up some fantasy or other, or a disagreeable feeling, spoils his mood for the whole day; a vaguely unpleasant sensation puts the idea into his head that he is suffering from a secret disease, a dream fills him with gloomy forebodings, although ordinarily he is not superstitious. Others, again, have only periodic access to these unconscious stirrings, or only to a certain category of them. For one man they may never have reached consciousness at all as anything worth thinking about, for another they are a worrying problem he broods on daily. One man takes them as physiological, another attributes them to the behaviour of his neighbours, another finds in them a religious revelation.

These entirely different ways of dealing with the stirrings of the unconscious are just as habitual as the attitudes to the outer object. The inner attitude, therefore, is correlated with just as definite a functional complex as the outer attitude. People who, it would seem, no more lack a typical inner attitude than the people who constantly overlook the outer object and the reality of facts lack a typical outer one. In all the latter cases, which are by no means uncommon, the persona is characterized by a lack of relatedness, at times even a blind inconsiderateness, that yields only to the harshest blows of fate. Not infrequently, it is just these people with a rigid persona who possess an attitude to the unconscious processes which is extremely susceptible and open to influence. Inwardly they are as weak, malleable, and "soft-centered" as they are inflexible and unapproachable outwardly. Their inner attitude, therefore, corresponds to a personality that is diametrically opposed to the outer personality. I know a man, for instance, who blindly and pitilessly destroyed the happiness of those nearest to him, and yet would interrupt important business journeys just to enjoy the beauty of a forest scene glimpsed from the carriage window. Cases of this kind are doubtless familiar to everyone, so I need not give further examples.

[Soul as anima]

803   We can, therefore, speak of an inner personality with as much justification as, on the grounds of daily experience, we speak of an outer personality. The inner personality is the way one behaves in relation to one's inner psychic processes; it is the inner attitude, the characteristic face, that is turned towards the unconscious. I call the outer attitude, the outward face, the *persona*; the inner attitude, the inward face, I call the *anima*.[80] To the degree that an attitude is habitual, it is a well-knit functional complex with which the ego can identify itself more or less. Common speech expresses this very graphically: when a man has an habitual attitude to certain situations, an habitual way of doing things, we say he is quite *another man* when doing this or that. This is a practical demonstration of the autonomy of the functional complex represented by the habitual attitude: it is as though another personality had taken possession of the individual, as though "another spirit had got into him." The same autonomy that very often characterizes the outer attitude is also claimed by the inner attitude, the

[80] [In the German text the word *Anima* is used only twice: here and at the beginning of par. 805. Everywhere else the word used is *Seele* (soul). In this translation *anima* is substituted for "soul" when it refers specifically to the feminine component in a man, just as in Def. 49 (SOUL-IMAGE) *animus* is substituted for "soul" when it refers specifically to the masculine component in a woman. "Soul" is retained only when it refers to the psychic factor common to both sexes. The distinction is not always easy to make, and the reader may prefer to translate *anima/animus* back into "soul" on occasions when this would help to clarify Jung's argument. For a discussion of this question and the problems involved in translating *Seele* see *Psychology and Alchemy*, pars. 296ff., for the relations between *anima/animus* and persona.—EDITORS.]

anima. It is one of the most difficult educational feats to change the persona, the outer attitude, and it is just as difficult to change the anima, since its structure is usually quite as well-knit as the persona's. Just as the persona is an entity that often seems to constitute the whole character of a man, and may even accompany him unaltered throughout his entire life, the anima is a clearly defined entity with a character that, very often, is autonomous and immutable. It therefore lends itself very readily to characterization and description.

804 As to the character of the anima, my experience confirms the rule that it is, by and large, *complementary* to the character of the persona. The anima usually contains all those common human qualities which the conscious attitude lacks. The tyrant tormented by bad dreams, gloomy forebodings, and inner fears is a typical figure. Outwardly ruthless, harsh, and unapproachable, he jumps inwardly at every shadow, is at the mercy of every mood, as though he were the feeblest and most impressionable of men. Thus his anima contains all those fallible human qualities his persona lacks. If the persona is intellectual, the anima will quite certainly be sentimental. The complementary character of the anima also affects the sexual character, as I have proved to myself beyond a doubt. A very feminine woman has a masculine soul, and a very masculine man has a feminine soul. This contrast is due to the fact that a man is not in all things wholly masculine, but also has certain feminine traits. The more masculine his outer attitude is, the more his feminine traits are obliterated: instead, they appear in his unconscious. This explains why it is just those very virile men who are most subject to characteristic weaknesses; their attitude to the unconscious has a womanish weakness and impressionability. Conversely, it is often just the most feminine women who, in their inner lives, display an intractability, an obstinacy, and a wilfulness that are to be found with comparable intensity only in a man's outer attitude. These are masculine traits which, excluded from the womanly outer attitude, have become qualities of her soul.

805 If, therefore, we speak of the *anima* of a man, we must logically speak of the *animus* of a woman, if we are to give the soul of a woman its right name. Whereas logic and objectivity are usually the predominant features of a man's outer attitude,

or are at least regarded as ideals, in the case of a woman it is feeling. But in the soul it is the other way round: inwardly it is the man who feels, and the woman who reflects. Hence a man's greater liability to total despair, while a woman can always find comfort and hope; accordingly a man is more likely to put an end to himself than a woman. However much a victim of social circumstances a woman may be, as a prostitute for instance, a man is no less a victim of impulses from the unconscious, taking the form of alcoholism and other vices.

806
As to its common human qualities, the character of the anima can be deduced from that of the persona. Everything that should normally be in the outer attitude, but is conspicuously absent, will invariably be found in the inner attitude. This is a fundamental rule which my experience has borne out over and over again. But as regards its individual qualities, nothing can be deduced about them in this way. We can only be certain that when a man is identical with his persona, his individual qualities will be associated with the anima. This association frequently gives rise in dreams to the symbol of psychic pregnancy, a symbol that goes back to the *primordial image* (q.v.) of the hero's birth. The child that is to be born signifies the individuality, which, though present, is not yet conscious. For in the same way as the persona, the instrument of adaptation to the environment, is strongly influenced by environmental conditions, the anima is shaped by the unconscious and its qualities. In a primitive milieu the persona necessarily takes on primitive features, and the anima similarly takes over the *archaic* (q.v.) features of the unconscious as well as its symbolic, prescient character. Hence the "pregnant," "creative" qualities of the inner attitude.

807
Identity (q.v.) with the persona automatically leads to an unconscious identity with the anima because, when the ego is not differentiated from the persona, it can have no conscious relation to the unconscious processes. Consequently, it *is* these processes, it is identical with them. Anyone who is himself his outward role will infallibly succumb to the inner processes; he will either frustrate his outward role by absolute inner necessity or else reduce it to absurdity, by a process of *enantiodromia* (q.v.). He can no longer keep to his individual way, and his life runs into one deadlock after another. Moreover, the

anima is inevitably projected upon a real object, with which he gets into a relation of almost total dependence. Every reaction displayed by this object has an immediate, inwardly enervating effect on the subject. Tragic ties are often formed in this way (v. *Soul-image*).

. . .

814   51. SYMBOL. The concept of a *symbol* should in my view be strictly distinguished from that of a *sign*. Symbolic and *semiotic* meanings are entirely different things. In his book on symbolism, Ferrero[82] does not speak of symbols in the strict sense, but of signs. For instance, the old custom of handing over a piece of turf at the sale of a plot of land might be described as "symbolic" in the vulgar sense of the word, but actually it is purely semiotic in character. The piece of turf is a sign, or token, standing for the whole estate. The winged wheel worn by railway officials is not a *symbol* of the railway, but a *sign* that distinguishes the personnel of the railway system. A symbol always presupposes that the chosen expression is the best possible description or formulation of a relatively unknown fact, which is none the less known to exist or is postulated as existing. Thus, when the badge of a railway official is explained as a symbol, it amounts to saying that this man has something to do with an unknown system that cannot be differently or better expressed than by a winged wheel.

815   Every view which interprets the symbolic expression as an analogue or an abbreviated designation for a *known* thing is *semiotic*. A view which interprets the symbolic expression as the best possible formulation of a relatively *unknown* thing, which for that reason cannot be more clearly or characteristically represented, is *symbolic*. A view which interprets the symbolic expression as an intentional paraphrase or transmogrification of a known thing is *allegoric*. The interpretation of the cross as a symbol of divine love is *semiotic*, because "divine love" describes the fact to be expressed better and more aptly than a cross, which can have many other meanings. On the other hand, an interpretation of the cross is *symbolic* when it puts the cross beyond all conceivable explanations, re-

82 *I simboli in rapporto alla storia e filosofia del diretto.*

garding it as expressing an as yet unknown and incomprehensible fact of a mystical or transcendent, i.e., psychological, nature, which simply finds itself most appropriately represented in the cross.

816 So long as a symbol is a living thing, it is an expression for something that cannot be characterized in any other or better way. The symbol is alive only so long as it is pregnant with meaning. But once its meaning has been born out of it, once that expression is found which formulates the thing sought, expected, or divined even better than the hitherto accepted symbol, then the symbol is *dead*, i.e., it possesses only an historical significance. We may still go on speaking of it as a symbol, on the tacit assumption that we are speaking of it as it was before the better expression was born out of it. The way in which St. Paul and the earlier speculative mystics speak of the cross shows that for them it was still a living symbol which expressed the inexpressible in unsurpassable form. For every esoteric interpretation the symbol is dead, because esotericism has already given it (at least ostensibly) a better expression, whereupon it becomes merely a conventional sign for associations that are more completely and better known elsewhere. Only from the exoteric standpoint is the symbol a living thing.

817 An expression that stands for a known thing remains a mere sign and is never a symbol. It is, therefore, quite impossible to create a living symbol, i.e., one that is pregnant with meaning, from known associations. For what is thus produced never contains more than was put into it. Every psychic product, if it is the best possible expression at the moment for a fact as yet unknown or only relatively known, may be regarded as a symbol, provided that we accept the expression as standing for something that is only divined and not yet clearly conscious. Since every scientific theory contains an hypothesis, and is therefore an anticipatory description of something still essentially unknown, it is a symbol. Furthermore, every psychological expression is a symbol if we assume that it states or signifies something more and other than itself which eludes our present knowledge. This assumption is absolutely tenable wherever a consciousness exists which is attuned to the deeper meaning of things. It is untenable only when this same consciousness has itself devised an expression which states exactly

286

what it is intended to state—a mathematical term, for instance. But for another consciousness this limitation does not exist. It can take the mathematical term as a symbol for an unknown psychic fact which the term was not intended to express but is concealed within it—a fact which is demonstrably not known to the man who devised the semiotic expression and which therefore could not have been the object of any conscious use.

818   Whether a thing is a symbol or not depends chiefly on the *attitude* (q.v.) of the observing consciousness; for instance, on whether it regards a given fact not merely as such but also as an expression for something unknown. Hence it is quite possible for a man to establish a fact which does not appear in the least symbolic to himself, but is profoundly so to another consciousness. The converse is also true. There are undoubtedly products whose symbolic character does not depend merely on the attitude of the observing consciousness, but manifests itself spontaneously in the symbolic effect they have on the observer. Such products are so constituted that they would lack any kind of meaning were we not a symbolic one conceded to them. Taken as a bare fact, a triangle with an eye enclosed in it is so meaningless that it is impossible for the observer to regard it as a merely accidental piece of foolery. Such a figure immediately conjures up a symbolic interpretation. This effect is reinforced by the widespread incidence of the same figure in identical form, or by the particular care that went into its production, which is an expression of the special value placed upon it.

819   Symbols that do not work in this way on the observer are either extinct, i.e., have been superseded by a better formulation, or are products whose symbolic nature depends entirely on the attitude of the observing consciousness. The attitude that takes a given phenomenon as symbolic may be called, for short, the *symbolic attitude*. It is only partially justified by the actual behaviour of things; for the rest, it is the outcome of a definite view of the world which *assigns meaning* to events, whether great or small, and attaches to this meaning a greater value than to bare facts. This view of things stands opposed to another view which lays the accent on sheer facts and subordinates meaning to them. For the latter attitude there can be no symbols whatever when the symbolism depends exclusively on the mode of observation. But even for such an attitude sym-

bols do exist—those, namely, that prompt the observer to conjecture a hidden meaning. A bull-headed god can certainly be explained as a man's body with a bull's head on it. But this explanation can hardly hold its own against the symbolic explanation, because the symbolism is too arresting to be overlooked. A symbol that forcibly obtrudes its symbolic nature on us need not be a *living* symbol. It may have a merely historical or philosophical significance, and simply arouses intellectual or aesthetic interest. A symbol really lives only when it is the best and highest expression for something divined but not yet known to the observer. It then compels his unconscious participation and has a life-giving and life-enhancing effect. As Faust says: "How differently this new sign works upon me!"[83]

820 The living symbol formulates an essential unconscious factor, and the more widespread this factor is, the more general is the effect of the symbol, for it touches a corresponding chord in every psyche. Since, for a given epoch, it is the best possible expression for what is still unknown, it must be the product of the most complex and differentiated minds of that age. But in order to have such an effect at all, it must embrace what is common to a large group of men. This can never be what is most differentiated, the highest attainable, for only a very few attain to that or understand it. The common factor must be something that is still so primitive that its ubiquity cannot be doubted. Only when the symbol embraces that and expresses it in the highest possible form is it of general efficacy. Herein lies the potency of the living, social symbol and its redeeming power.

821 All that I have said about the social symbol applies equally to the individual symbol. There are individual psychic products whose symbolic character is so obvious that they at once compel a symbolic interpretation. For the individual they have the same functional significance that the social symbol has for a larger human group. These products never have an exclusively conscious or an exclusively unconscious source, but arise from the equal collaboration of both. Purely unconscious products are no more convincingly symbolic *per se* than purely conscious ones; it is the symbolic attitude of the observing consciousness that endows them both with the character of a sym-

[88] [*Goethe's Faust* (trans. MacNeice), p. 22.]

bol. But they can be conceived equally well as causally determined facts, in much the same way as one might regard the red exanthema of scarlet fever as a "symbol" of the disease. In that case it is perfectly correct to speak of a "symptom" and not of a "symbol." In my view Freud is quite justified when, from his standpoint, he speaks of *symptomatic*[84] rather than symbolic actions, since for him these phenomena are not symbolic in the sense here defined, but are symptomatic signs of a definite and generally known underlying process. There are, of course, neurotics who regard their unconscious products, which are mostly morbid symptoms, as symbols of supreme importance. Generally, however, this is not what happens. On the contrary, the neurotic of today is only too prone to regard a product that may actually be full of significance as a mere "symptom."

822   The fact that there are two distinct and mutually contradictory views eagerly advocated on either side concerning the meaning or meaninglessness of things shows that processes obviously exist which express no particular meaning, being in fact mere consequences, or symptoms; and that there are other processes which bear within them a hidden meaning, processes which are not merely derived from something but which seek to become something, and are therefore symbols. It is left to our discretion and our critical judgment to decide whether the thing we are dealing with is a symptom or a symbol.

823   The symbol is always a product of an extremely complex nature, since data from every psychic function have gone into its making. It is, therefore, neither *rational* nor *irrational* (qq.v.). It certainly has a side that accords with reason, but it has another side that does not; for it is composed not only of rational but also of irrational data supplied by pure inner and outer perception. The profundity and pregnant significance of the symbol appeal just as strongly to *thinking* as to *feeling* (qq.v.), while its peculiar plastic imagery, when shaped into sensuous form, stimulates *sensation* as much as *intuition* (qq.v.). The living symbol cannot come to birth in a dull or poorly developed mind, for such a mind will be content with the already existing symbols offered by established tradition. Only the passionate yearning of a highly developed mind, for

84 *The Psychopathology of Everyday Life.*

which the traditional symbol is no longer the unified expression of the rational and the irrational, of the highest and the lowest, can create a new symbol.

824 But precisely because the new symbol is born of man's highest spiritual aspirations and must at the same time spring from the deepest roots of his being, it cannot be a onesided product of the most highly differentiated mental functions but must derive equally from the lowest and most primitive levels of the psyche. For this collaboration of opposing states to be possible at all, they must first face one another in the fullest conscious opposition. This necessarily entails a violent disunion with oneself, to the point where thesis and antithesis negate one another, while the ego is forced to acknowledge its absolute participation in both. If there is a subordination of one part, the symbol will be predominantly the product of the other part, and, to that extent, less a symbol than a symptom—a symptom of the suppressed antithesis. To the extent, however, that a symbol is merely a symptom, it also lacks a redeeming effect, since it fails to express the full right of all parts of the psyche to exist, being a constant reminder of the suppressed antithesis even though consciousness may not take this fact into account. But when there is full parity of the opposites, attested by the ego's absolute participation in both, this necessarily leads to a suspension of the *will* (q.v.), for the will can no longer operate when every motive has an equally strong countermotive. Since life cannot tolerate a standstill, a damming up of vital energy results, and this would lead to an insupportable condition did not the tension of opposites produce a new, uniting function that transcends them. This function arises quite naturally from the regression of *libido* (q.v.) caused by the blockage. All progress having been rendered temporarily impossible by the total division of the will, the libido streams backwards, as it were, to its source. In other words, the neutralization and inactivity of consciousness bring about an activity of the unconscious, where all the differentiated functions have their common, archaic root, and where all contents exist in a state of promiscuity of which the primitive mentality still shows numerous vestiges.

825 From the activity of the unconscious there now emerges a new content, constellated by thesis and antithesis in equal

measure and standing in a *compensatory* (q.v.) relation to both. It thus forms the middle ground on which the opposites can be united. If, for instance, we conceive the opposition to be sensuality versus spirituality, then the mediatory content born out of the unconscious provides a welcome means of expression for the spiritual thesis, because of its rich spiritual associations, and also for the sensual antithesis, because of its sensuous imagery. The ego, however, torn between thesis and antithesis, finds in the middle ground its own counterpart, its sole and unique means of expression, and it eagerly seizes on this in order to be delivered from its division. The energy created by the tension of opposites therefore flows into the mediatory product and protects it from the conflict which immediately breaks out again, for both the opposites are striving to get the new product on their side. Spirituality wants to make something spiritual out of it, and sensuality something sensual; the one wants to turn it into science or art, the other into sensual experience. The appropriation or dissolution of the mediatory product by either side is successful only if the ego is not completely divided but inclines more to one side or the other. But if one side succeeds in winning over and dissolving the mediatory product, the ego goes along with it, whereupon an identification of the ego with the most favoured function (v. *Inferior Function*) ensues. Consequently, the process of division will be repeated later on a higher plane.

826   If, however, as a result of the stability of the ego, neither side succeeds in dissolving the mediatory product, this is sufficient demonstration that it is superior to both. The stability of the ego and the superiority of the mediatory product to both thesis and antithesis are to my mind correlates, each conditioning the other. Sometimes it seems as though the stability of the inborn *individuality* (q.v.) were the decisive factor, sometimes as though the mediatory product possessed a superior power that determines the ego's absolute stability. In reality it may be that the stability of the one and the superior power of the other are two sides of the same coin.

827   If the mediatory product remains intact, it forms the raw material for a process not of dissolution but of construction, in which thesis and antithesis both play their part. In this way it becomes a new content that governs the whole attitude,

291

828   putting an end to the division and forcing the energy of the opposites into a common channel. The standstill is overcome and life can flow on with renewed power towards new goals.

I have called this process in its totality the *transcendent function*, "function" being here understood not as a basic function but as a complex function made up of other functions, and "transcendent" not as denoting a metaphysical quality but merely the fact that this function facilitates a transition from one attitude to another. The raw material shaped by thesis and antithesis, and in the shaping of which the opposites are united, is the living symbol. Its profundity of meaning is inherent in the raw material itself, the very stuff of the psyche, transcending time and dissolution; and its configuration by the opposites ensures its sovereign power over all the psychic functions.

829   Indications of the process of symbol-formation are to be found in the scanty records of the conflicts experienced by the founders of religion during their initiation period, e.g., the struggle between Jesus and Satan, Buddha and Mara, Luther and the devil, Zwingli and his previous worldly life; or the regeneration of Faust through the pact with the devil. In *Zarathustra* we find an excellent example of the suppressed antithesis in the "Ugliest Man."

. . .

830   53. THINKING. This I regard as one of the four basic psychological *functions* (q.v.). Thinking is the psychological function which, following its own laws, brings the contents of ideation into conceptual connection with one another. It is an *apperceptive* (q.v.) activity, and as such may be divided into *active* and *passive* thinking. Active thinking is an act of the *will* (q.v.), passive thinking is a mere occurrence. In the former case, I submit the contents of ideation to a voluntary act of judgment; in the latter, conceptual connections establish themselves of their own accord, and judgments are formed that may even contradict my intention. They are not consonant with my aim and therefore, for me, lack any sense of direction, although I may afterwards recognize their directedness through an act of active apperception. Active thinking, accordingly, would correspond to my concept of *directed thinking*.[85] Passive thinking

85 *Symbols of Transformation*, pars. 11ff.

831 was inadequately described in my previous work as "fantasy thinking."[86] Today I would call it *intuitive* thinking.

To my mind, a mere stringing together of ideas, such as is described by certain psychologists as *associative thinking*,[87] is not thinking at all, but mere ideation. The term "thinking," should, in my view, be confined to the linking up of ideas by means of a concept, in other words, to an act of judgment, no matter whether this act is intentional or not.

832 The capacity for directed thinking I call *intellect*; the capacity for passive or undirected thinking I call *intellectual intuition*. Further, I call directed thinking a *rational* (q.v.) function, because it arranges the contents of ideation under concepts in accordance with a rational norm of which I am conscious. Undirected thinking is in my view an *irrational* (q.v.) function, because it arranges and judges the contents of ideation by norms of which I am not conscious and therefore cannot recognize as being in accord with reason. Subsequently I may be able to recognize that the intuitive act of judgment accorded with reason, although it came about in a way that appears to me irrational.

833 Thinking that is governed by *feeling* (q.v.) I do not regard as intuitive thinking, but as a thinking dependent on feeling; it does not follow its own logical principle but is subordinated to the principle of feeling. In such thinking the laws of logic are only ostensibly present; in reality they are suspended in favour of the aims of feeling.

. . .

835 55. TYPE. A type is a specimen or example which reproduces in a characteristic way the character of a species or class. In the narrower sense used in this particular work, a type is a characteristic specimen of a general *attitude* (q.v.) occurring in many individual forms. From a great number of existing or possible attitudes I have singled out four; those, namely, that are primarily oriented by the four basic psychological *functions* (q.v.): *thinking, feeling, sensation, intuition* (qq.v.). When any of these attitudes is *habitual*, thus setting a definite stamp on

86 Ibid., par. 20.
87 [Cf. ibid., par. 18, citing James, *The Principles of Psychology*, II, p. 325.]

836 the character of an *individual* (q.v.), I speak of a psychological type. These *function-types*, which one can call the thinking, feeling, sensation, and intuitive types, may be divided into two classes according to the quality of the basic function, i.e., into the *rational* and the *irrational* (qq.v.): The thinking and feeling types belong to the former class, the sensation and intuitive types to the latter. A further division into two classes is permitted by the predominant trend of the movement of *libido* (q.v.), namely *introversion* and *extraversion* (qq.v.). All the basic types can belong equally well to one or the other of these classes, according to the predominance of the introverted or extraverted attitude.[88] A thinking type may belong either to the introverted or to the extraverted class, and the same holds good for the other types. The distinction between rational and irrational types is simply another point of view and has nothing to do with introversion and extraversion.

837 In my previous contributions to typology[89] I did not differentiate the thinking and feeling types from the introverted and extraverted types, but identified the thinking type with the introverted, and the feeling type with the extraverted. But a more thorough investigation of the material has shown me that we must treat the introverted and extraverted types as categories over and above the function-types. This differentiation, moreover, fully accords with experience, since, for example, there are undoubtedly two kinds of feeling types, the attitude of the one being oriented more by his feeling-experience [= introverted feeling type], the other more by the object [= extraverted feeling type].

56. UNCONSCIOUS. The concept of the *unconscious* is for me an *exclusively psychological* concept, and not a philosophical concept of a metaphysical nature. In my view the unconscious is a psychological borderline concept, which covers all psychic

88 [Hence the types belonging to the introverted or extraverted class are called *attitude-types*. Cf. supra, par. 556, and *Two Essays on Analytical Psychology*, Part I, ch. IV.—EDITORS.]

89 "A Contribution to the Study of Psychological Processes," *Collected Papers on Analytical Psychology*, pp. 391ff., 401ff.; "The Structure of the Unconscious," *Two Essays on Analytical Psychology*, pars. 462, n. 8, and 482.

838   contents or processes that are not conscious, i.e., not related to the *ego* (q.v.) in any perceptible way. My justification for speaking of the existence of unconscious processes at all is derived simply and solely from experience, and in particular from psychopathological experience, where we have undoubted proof that, in a case of hysterical amnesia, for example, the ego knows nothing of the existence of numerous psychic complexes, and the next moment a simple hypnotic procedure is sufficient to bring the lost contents back to memory.

839   Thousands of such experiences justify us in speaking of the existence of unconscious psychic contents. As to the actual state an unconscious content is in when not attached to consciousness, this is something that eludes all possibility of cognition. It is therefore quite pointless to hazard conjectures about it. Conjectures linking up the unconscious state with cerebration and physiological processes belong equally to the realm of fantasy. It is also impossible to specify the range of the unconscious, i.e., what contents it embraces. Only experience can decide such questions.

840   We know from experience that conscious contents can become unconscious through loss of their energic value. This is the normal process of "forgetting." That these contents do not simply get lost below the threshold of consciousness we know from the experience that occasionally, under suitable conditions, they can emerge from their submersion decades later, for instance in dreams, or under hypnosis, or in the form of cryptomnesia,[90] or through the revival of associations with the forgotten content. We also know that conscious contents can fall below the threshold of consciousness through "intentional forgetting," or what Freud calls the *repression* of a painful content, with no appreciable loss of value. A similar effect is produced by a dissociation of the personality, i.e., the disintegration of consciousness as the result of a violent *affect* (q.v.) or nervous shock, or through the collapse of the personality in schizophrenia (Bleuler).

841   We know from experience, too, that sense perceptions

[90] Flournoy, *From India to the Planet Mars*; Jung, "On the Psychology and Pathology of So-called Occult Phenomena," pars. 139ff., and "Cryptomnesia."

which, either because of their slight intensity or because of the deflection of attention, do not reach conscious *apperception* (q.v.), none the less become psychic contents through unconscious apperception, which again may be demonstrated by hypnosis, for example. The same thing may happen with certain judgments or other associations which remain unconscious because of their low energy charge or because of the deflection of attention. Finally, experience also teaches that there are unconscious psychic associations—mythological *images* (q.v.), for instance—which have never been the object of consciousness and must therefore be wholly the product of unconscious activity.

841   To this extent, then, experience furnishes *points d'appui* for the assumption of unconscious contents. But it can tell us nothing about what might *possibly* be an unconscious content. It is idle to speculate about this, because the range of what *could* be an unconscious content is simply illimitable. What is the lowest limit of subliminal sense perception? Is there any way of measuring the scope and subtlety of unconscious associations? When is a forgotten content totally obliterated? To these questions there is no answer.

842   Our experience so far of the nature of unconscious contents permits us, however, to make one general classification. We can distinguish a *personal unconscious*, comprising all the acquisitions of personal life, everything forgotten, repressed, subliminally perceived, thought, felt. But, in addition to these personal unconscious contents, there are other contents which do not originate in personal acquisitions but in the inherited possibility of psychic functioning in general, i.e., in the inherited structure of the brain. These are the mythological associations, the motifs and images that can spring up anew anytime anywhere, independently of historical tradition or migration. I call these contents the *collective unconscious*. Just as conscious contents are engaged in a definite activity, so too are the unconscious contents, as experience confirms. And just as conscious psychic activity creates certain products, so unconscious psychic activity produces dreams, *fantasies* (q.v.), etc. It is idle to speculate on how great a share consciousness has in dreams. A dream presents itself to us: we do not consciously create it. Conscious reproduction, or even the perception of it, certainly

alters the dream in many ways, without, however, doing away with the basic fact of the unconscious source of creative activity.

843   The functional relation of the unconscious processes to consciousness may be described as *compensatory* (q.v.), since experience shows that they bring to the surface the subliminal material that is constellated by the conscious situation, i.e., all those contents which could not be missing from the picture if everything were conscious. The compensatory function of the unconscious becomes more obvious the more one-sided the conscious *attitude* (q.v.) is; pathology furnishes numerous examples of this.

844   57. WILL. I regard the will as the amount of psychic energy at the disposal of consciousness. Volition would, accordingly, be an energic process that is released by conscious motivation. A psychic process, therefore, that is conditioned by unconscious motivation I would not include under the concept of the will. The will is a psychological phenomenon that owes its existence to culture and moral education, but is largely lacking in the primitive mentality.

ARCHETYPES OF THE COLLECTIVE UNCONSCIOUS

1 The hypothesis of a collective unconscious belongs to the class of ideas that people at first find strange but soon come to possess and use as familiar conceptions. This has been the case with the concept of the unconscious in general. After the philosophical idea of the unconscious, in the form presented chiefly by Carus and von Hartmann, had gone down under the overwhelming wave of materialism and empiricism, leaving hardly a ripple behind it, it gradually reappeared in the scientific domain of medical psychology.

2 At first the concept of the unconscious was limited to denoting the state of repressed or forgotten contents. Even with Freud, who makes the unconscious—at least metaphorically—take the stage as the acting subject, it is really nothing but the gathering place of forgotten and repressed contents, and has a functional significance thanks only to these. For Freud, accordingly, the unconscious is of an exclusively personal nature,[2] although he was aware of its archaic and mythological thought-forms.

3 A more or less superficial layer of the unconscious is undoubtedly personal. I call it the *personal unconscious*. But this personal unconscious rests upon a deeper layer, which does not derive from personal experience and is not a personal acquisition but is inborn. This deeper layer I call the *collective unconscious*. I have chosen the term "collective" because this part of the unconscious is not individual but universal; in contrast to

[1] [First published in the *Eranos-Jahrbuch 1934*, and later revised and published in *Von den Wurzeln des Bewusstseins* (Zurich, 1954), from which version the present translation is made. The translation of the original version, by Stanley Dell, in *The Integration of the Personality* (New York, 1939; London, 1940), has been freely consulted.—EDITORS.]

[2] In his later works Freud differentiated the basic view mentioned here. He called the instinctual psyche the "id," and his "super-ego" denotes the collective consciousness, of which the individual is partly conscious and partly unconscious (because it is repressed).

the personal psyche, it has contents and modes of behaviour that are more or less the same everywhere and in all individuals. It is, in other words, identical in all men and thus constitutes a common psychic substrate of a suprapersonal nature which is present in every one of us.

4   Psychic existence can be recognized only by the presence of contents that are *capable of consciousness*. We can therefore speak of an unconscious only in so far as we are able to demonstrate its contents. The contents of the personal unconscious are chiefly the *feeling-toned complexes*, as they are called; they constitute the personal and private side of psychic life. The contents of the collective unconscious, on the other hand, are known as *archetypes*.

5   The term "archetype" occurs as early as Philo Judaeus,[3] with reference to the *Imago Dei* (God-image) in man. It can also be found in Irenaeus, who says: "The creator of the world did not fashion these things directly from himself but copied them from archetypes outside himself."[4] In the *Corpus Hermeticum*,[5] God is called τὸ ἀρχέτυπον φῶς (archetypal light). The term occurs several times in Dionysius the Areopagite, as for instance in *De caelesti hierarchia*, II, 4: "immaterial Archetypes,"[6] and in *De divinis nominibus*, I, 6: "Archetypal stone."[7] The term "archetype" is not found in St. Augustine, but the idea of it is. Thus in *De diversis quaestionibus LXXXIII* he speaks of "*ideae principales*," "which are themselves not formed . . . but are contained in the divine understanding." [8] "Archetype" is an explanatory paraphrase of the Platonic εἶδος. For our purposes this term is apposite and helpful, because it tells us that so far as the col-

3 *De opificio mundi*, I, 69. Cf. Colson/Whitaker trans., I, p. 55.

4 *Adversus haereses* II, 7, 5: "Mundi fabricator non a semetipso fecit haec, sed de alienis archetypis transtulit." (Cf. Roberts/Rambaut trans., I, p. 139.)

5 Scott, *Hermetica*, I, p. 140.   6 In Migne, *P.G.*, vol. 3, col. 144.

7 Ibid., col. 595. Cf. *The Divine Names* (trans. by Rolt), pp. 62, 72.

8 Migne, *P.L.*, vol. 40, col. 30. "Archetype" is used in the same way by the alchemists, as in the "Tractatus aureus" of Hermes Trismegistus (*Theatrum chemicum*, IV, 1613, p. 718): "As God [contains] all the treasure of his godhead . . . hidden in himself as in an archetype [*in se tanquam archetypo absconditum*] . . . in like manner Saturn carries the similitudes of metallic bodies hiddenly in himself." In the "Tractatus de igne et sale" of Vigenerus (*Theatr. chem.*, VI, 1661, p. 3), the world is "ad archetypi sui similitudinem factus" (made after the likeness of its archetype) and is therefore called the "magnus homo" (the "homo maximus" of Swedenborg).

lective unconscious contents are concerned we are dealing with archaic or—I would say—primordial types, that is, with universal images that have existed since the remotest times. The term "représentations collectives," used by Lévy-Bruhl to denote the symbolic figures in the primitive view of the world, could easily be applied to unconscious contents as well, since it means practically the same thing. Primitive tribal lore is concerned with archetypes that have been modified in a special way. They are no longer contents of the unconscious, but have already been changed into conscious formulae taught according to tradition, generally in the form of esoteric teaching. This last is a typical means of expression for the transmission of collective contents originally derived from the unconscious.

6　Another well-known expression of the archetypes is myth and fairytale. But here too we are dealing with forms that have received a specific stamp and have been handed down through long periods of time. The term "archetype" thus applies only indirectly to the "représentations collectives," since it designates only those psychic contents which have not yet been submitted to conscious elaboration and are therefore an immediate datum of psychic experience. In this sense there is a considerable difference between the archetype and the historical formula that has evolved. Especially on the higher levels of esoteric teaching the archetypes appear in a form that reveals quite unmistakably the critical and evaluating influence of conscious elaboration. Their immediate manifestation, as we encounter it in dreams and visions, is much more individual, less understandable, and more naïve than in myths, for example. The archetype is essentially an unconscious content that is altered by becoming conscious and by being perceived, and it takes its colour from the individual consciousness in which it happens to appear.[9]

7　What the word "archetype" means in the nominal sense is clear enough, then, from its relations with myth, esoteric teaching, and fairytale. But if we try to establish what an archetype is *psychologically*, the matter becomes more complicated. So far mythologists have always helped themselves out with solar,

[9] One must, for the sake of accuracy, distinguish between "archetype" and "archetypal ideas." The archetype as such is a hypothetical and irrepresentable model, something like the "pattern of behaviour" in biology. Cf. "On the Nature of the Psyche," sec. 7.

lunar, meteorological, vegetal, and other ideas of the kind. The fact that myths are first and foremost psychic phenomena that reveal the nature of the soul is something they have absolutely refused to see until now. Primitive man is not much interested in objective explanations of the obvious, but he has an imperative need—or rather, his unconscious psyche has an irresistible urge—to assimilate all outer sense experiences to inner, psychic events. It is not enough for the primitive to see the sun rise and set; this external observation must at the same time be a psychic happening: the sun in its course must represent the fate of a god or hero who, in the last analysis, dwells nowhere except in the soul of man. All the mythologized processes of nature, such as summer and winter, the phases of the moon, the rainy seasons, and so forth, are in no sense allegories [10] of these objective occurrences; rather they are symbolic expressions of the inner, unconscious drama of the psyche which becomes accessible to man's consciousness by way of projection—that is, mirrored in the events of nature. The projection is so fundamental that it has taken several thousand years of civilization to detach it in some measure from its outer object. In the case of astrology, for instance, this age-old "scientia intuitiva" came to be branded as rank heresy because man had not yet succeeded in making the psychological description of character independent of the stars. Even today, people who still believe in astrology fall almost without exception for the old superstitious assumption of the influence of the stars. And yet anyone who can calculate a horoscope should know that, since the days of Hipparchus of Alexandria, the spring-point has been fixed at 0° Aries, and that the zodiac on which every horoscope is based is therefore quite arbitrary, the spring-point having gradually advanced, since then, into the first degrees of Pisces, owing to the precession of the equinoxes.

8   Primitive man impresses us so strongly with his subjectivity that we should really have guessed long ago that myths refer to something psychic. His knowledge of nature is essentially the language and outer dress of an unconscious psychic process. But the very fact that this process is unconscious gives us the reason

10 An allegory is a paraphrase of a conscious content, whereas a symbol is the best possible expression for an unconscious content whose nature can only be guessed, because it is still unknown.

why man has thought of everything except the psyche in his attempts to explain myths. He simply didn't know that the psyche contains all the images that have ever given rise to myths, and that our unconscious is an acting and suffering subject with an inner drama which primitive man rediscovers, by means of analogy, in the processes of nature both great and small.[11]

9   "The stars of thine own fate lie in thy breast,"[12] says Seni to Wallenstein—a dictum that should satisfy all astrologers if we knew even a little about the secrets of the heart. But for this, so far, men have had little understanding. Nor would I dare to assert that things are any better today.

10   Tribal lore is always sacred and dangerous. All esoteric teachings seek to apprehend the unseen happenings in the psyche, and all claim supreme authority for themselves. What is true of primitive lore is true in even higher degree of the ruling world religions. They contain a revealed knowledge that was originally hidden, and they set forth the secrets of the soul in glorious images. Their temples and their sacred writings proclaim in image and word the doctrine hallowed from of old, making it accessible to every believing heart, every sensitive vision, every farthest range of thought. Indeed, we are compelled to say that the more beautiful, the more sublime, the more comprehensive the image that has evolved and been handed down by tradition, the further removed it is from individual experience. We can just feel our way into it and sense something of it, but the original experience has been lost.

11   Why is psychology the youngest of the empirical sciences? Why have we not long since discovered the unconscious and raised up its treasure-house of eternal images? Simply because we had a religious formula for everything psychic—and one that is far more beautiful and comprehensive than immediate experience. Though the Christian view of the world has paled for many people, the symbolic treasure-rooms of the East are still full of marvels that can nourish for a long time to come the passion for show and new clothes. What is more, these images—be they Christian or Buddhist or what you will—are lovely,

11 Cf. my papers on the divine child and the Kore in the present volume, and Kerényi's complementary essays in *Essays on* [or *Introduction to*] *a Science of Mythology*. —— 12 [Schiller, *Piccolomini*, II, 6.—Editors.]

12   mysterious, richly intuitive. Naturally, the more familiar we are with them the more does constant usage polish them smooth, so that what remains is only banal superficiality and meaningless paradox. The mystery of the Virgin Birth, or the homoousia of the Son with the Father, or the Trinity which is nevertheless not a triad—these no longer lend wings to any philosophical fancy. They have stiffened into mere objects of belief. So it is not surprising if the religious need, the believing mind, and the philosophical speculations of the educated European are attracted by the symbols of the East—those grandiose conceptions of divinity in India and the abysms of Taoist philosophy in China—just as once before the heart and mind of the men of antiquity were gripped by Christian ideas. There are many Europeans who began by surrendering completely to the influence of the Christian symbol until they landed themselves in a Kierkegaardian neurosis, or whose relation to God, owing to the progressive impoverishment of symbolism, developed into an unbearably sophisticated I-You relationship—only to fall victims in their turn to the magic and novelty of Eastern symbols. This surrender is not necessarily a defeat; rather it proves the receptiveness and vitality of the religious sense. We can observe much the same thing in the educated Oriental, who not infrequently feels drawn to the Christian symbol or to the science that is so unsuited to the Oriental mind, and even develops an enviable understanding of them. That people should succumb to these eternal images is entirely normal, in fact it is what these images are for. They are meant to attract, to convince, to fascinate, and to overpower. They are created out of the primal stuff of revelation and reflect the ever-unique experience of divinity. That is why they always give man a premonition of the divine while at the same time safeguarding him from immediate experience of it. Thanks to the labours of the human spirit over the centuries, these images have become embedded in a comprehensive system of thought that ascribes an order to the world, and are at the same time represented by a mighty, far-spread, and venerable institution called the Church.

    I can best illustrate my meaning by taking as an example the Swiss mystic and hermit, Brother Nicholas of Flüe,[13] who has recently been canonized. Probably his most important re-

13 Cf. my "Brother Klaus."

304

13 ligious experience was the so-called Trinity Vision, which pre-occupied him to such an extent that he painted it, or had it painted, on the wall of his cell. The painting is still preserved in the parish church at Sachseln. It is a mandala divided into six parts, and in the centre is the crowned countenance of God. Now we know that Brother Klaus investigated the nature of his vision with the help of an illustrated devotional booklet by a German mystic, and that he struggled to get his original expe-rience into a form he could understand. He occupied himself with it for years. This is what I call the "elaboration" of the symbol. His reflections on the nature of the vision, influenced as they were by the mystic diagrams he used as a guiding thread, inevitably led him to the conclusion that he must have gazed upon the Holy Trinity itself—the *summum bonum*, eternal love. This is borne out by the "expurgated" version now in Sachseln.

The original experience, however, was entirely different. In his ecstasy there was revealed to Brother Klaus a sight so terrible that his own countenance was changed by it—so much so, in-deed, that people were terrified and felt afraid of him. What he had seen was a vision of the utmost intensity. Woelflin,[14] our oldest source, writes as follows:

All who came to him were filled with terror at the first glance. As to the cause of this, he himself used to say that he had seen a pierc-ing light resembling a human face. At the sight of it he feared that his heart would burst into little pieces. Therefore, overcome with terror, he instantly turned his face away and fell to the ground. And that was the reason why his face was now terrible to others.

14 This vision has rightly been compared[15] with the one in Revelation 1 : 13ff., that strange apocalyptic Christ-image, which for sheer gruesomeness and singularity is surpassed only by the monstrous seven-eyed lamb with seven horns (Rev. 5 : 6f.). It is certainly very difficult to see what is the relationship between this figure and the Christ of the gospels. Hence Brother Klaus's vision was interpreted in a quite definite way by the earliest sources. In 1508, the humanist Karl Bovillus (Charles de Bouelles) wrote to a friend:

[14] Heinrich Woelflin, also called by the Latin form Lupulus, born 1470, humanist and director of Latin studies at Bern. Cited in Fritz Blanke, *Bruder Klaus von Flüe*, pp. 92f.
[15] Ibid., p. 94.

I wish to tell you of a vision which appeared to him in the sky, on a night when the stars were shining and he stood in prayer and contemplation. He saw the head of a human figure with a terrifying face, full of wrath and threats.[16]

15 This interpretation agrees perfectly with the modern amplification furnished by Revelation 1 : 13.[17] Nor should we forget Brother Klaus's other visions, for instance, of Christ in the bearskin, of God the Father and God the Mother, and of himself as the Son. They exhibit features which are very undogmatic indeed.

16 Traditionally this great vision was brought into connection with the Trinity picture in the church at Sachseln, and so, likewise, was the wheel symbolism in the so-called "Pilgrim's Tract."[18] Brother Klaus, we are told, showed the picture of the wheel to a visiting pilgrim. Evidently this picture had preoccupied him for some time. Blanke is of the opinion that, contrary to tradition, there is no connection between the vision and the Trinity picture.[19] This scepticism seems to me to go too far. There must have been some reason for Brother Klaus's interest in the wheel. Visions like the one he had often cause mental confusion and disintegration (witness the heart bursting "into little pieces"). We know from experience that the protective circle, the mandala, is the traditional antidote for chaotic states of mind. It is therefore only too clear why Brother Klaus was fascinated by the symbol of the wheel. The interpretation of the terrifying vision as an experience of God need not be so wide of the mark either. The connection between the great vision and the Trinity picture, and of both with the wheel-symbol, therefore seems to me very probable on psychological grounds.

16 *Ein gesichte Bruder Clausen ynn Schweytz und seine deutunge* (Wittenberg, 1528), p. 5. Cited in Alban Stoeckli, O. M. Cap., *Die Visionen des seligen Bruder Klaus*, p. 34.

17 M. B. Lavaud, O.P. (*Vie Profonde de Nicolas de Flüe*) gives just as apt a parallel with a text from the *Horologium sapientiae* of Henry Suso, where the apocalyptic Christ appears as an infuriated and wrathful avenger, very much in contrast to the Jesus who preached the Sermon on the Mount. [Cf. Suso, *Little Book of Eternal Wisdom*, Clark trans., pp. 77–78.—EDITORS.]

18 *Ein nutzlicher und löblicher Tractat von Bruder Claus und einem Bilger* (1488).

19 Blanke, pp. 95ff.

17 This vision, undoubtedly fearful and highly perturbing, which burst like a volcano upon his religious view of the world, without any dogmatic prelude and without exegetical commentary, naturally needed a long labour of assimilation in order to fit it into the total structure of the psyche and thus restore the disturbed psychic balance. Brother Klaus came to terms with his experience on the basis of dogma, then firm as a rock; and the dogma proved its powers of assimilation by turning something horribly alive into the beautiful abstraction of the Trinity idea. But the reconciliation might have taken place on a quite different basis provided by the vision itself and its unearthly actuality—much to the disadvantage of the Christian conception of God and no doubt to the still greater disadvantage of Brother Klaus himself, who would then have become not a saint but a heretic (if not a lunatic) and would probably have ended his life at the stake.

18 This example demonstrates the use of the dogmatic symbol: it formulates a tremendous and dangerously decisive psychic experience, fittingly called an "experience of the Divine," in a way that is tolerable to our human understanding, without either limiting the scope of the experience or doing damage to its overwhelming significance. The vision of divine wrath, which we also meet in Jakob Böhme, ill accords with the God of the New Testament, the loving Father in heaven, and for this reason it might easily have become the source of an inner conflict. That would have been quite in keeping with the spirit of the age—the end of the fifteenth century, the time of Nicholas Cusanus, whose formula of the "complexio oppositorum" actually anticipated the schism that was imminent. Not long afterwards the Yahwistic conception of God went through a series of rebirths in Protestantism. Yahweh is a God-concept that contains the opposites in a still undivided state.

19 Brother Klaus put himself outside the beaten track of convention and habit by leaving his home and family, living alone for years, and gazing deep into the dark mirror, so that the wondrous and terrible boon of original experience befell him. In this situation the dogmatic image of divinity that had been developed over the centuries worked like a healing draught. It helped him to assimilate the fatal incursion of an archetypal image and so escape being torn asunder. Angelus Silesius was

not so fortunate; the inner conflict tore him to pieces, because in his day the stability of the Church that dogma guarantees was already shattered.

Jakob Böhme, too, knew a God of the "Wrath-fire," a real *Deus absconditus*. He was able to bridge the profound and agonizing contradiction on the one hand by means of the Christian formula of Father and Son and embody it speculatively in his view of the world—which, though Gnostic, was in all essential points Christian. Otherwise he would have become a dualist. On the other hand it was undoubtedly alchemy, long brewing the union of opposites in secret, that came to his aid. Nevertheless the opposition has left obvious traces in the mandala appended to his *XL Questions concerning the Soule*,[20] showing the nature of the divinity. The mandala is divided into a dark and a light half, and the semicircles that are drawn round them, instead of joining up to form a ring, are turned back to back.[21]

Dogma takes the place of the collective unconscious by formulating its contents on a grand scale. The Catholic way of life is completely unaware of psychological problems in this sense. Almost the entire life of the collective unconscious has been channelled into the dogmatic archetypal ideas and flows along like a well-controlled stream in the symbolism of creed and ritual. It manifests itself in the inwardness of the Catholic psyche. The collective unconscious, as we understand it today, was never a matter of "psychology," for before the Christian Church existed there were the antique mysteries, and these reach back into the grey mists of neolithic prehistory. Mankind has never lacked powerful images to lend magical aid against all the uncanny things that live in the depths of the psyche. Always the figures of the unconscious were expressed in protecting and healing images and in this way were expelled from the psyche into cosmic space.

The iconoclasm of the Reformation, however, quite literally made a breach in the protective wall of sacred images, and since then one image after another has crumbled away. They became dubious, for they conflicted with awakening reason. Besides, people had long since forgotten what they meant. Or had they really forgotten? Could it be that men had never really known what they meant, and that only in recent times did it occur to

20 London, 1647.　21 Cf. my "Study in the Process of Individuation," infra.

the Protestant part of mankind that actually we haven't the remotest conception of what is meant by the Virgin Birth, the divinity of Christ, and the complexities of the Trinity? It almost seems as if these images had just lived, and as if their living existence had simply been accepted without question and without reflection, much as everyone decorates Christmas trees or hides Easter eggs without ever knowing what these customs mean. The fact is that archetypal images are so packed with meaning in themselves that people never think of asking what they really do mean. That the gods die from time to time is due to man's sudden discovery that they do not mean anything, that they are made by human hands, useless idols of wood and stone. In reality, however, he has merely discovered that up till then he has never thought about his images at all. And when he starts thinking about them, he does so with the help of what he calls "reason"—which in point of fact is nothing more than the sum-total of all his prejudices and myopic views.

23   The history of Protestantism has been one of chronic iconoclasm. One wall after another fell. And the work of destruction was not too difficult once the authority of the Church had been shattered. We all know how, in large things as in small, in general as well as in particular, piece after piece collapsed, and how the alarming poverty of symbols that is now the condition of our life came about. With that the power of the Church has vanished too—a fortress robbed of its bastions and casemates, a house whose walls have been plucked away, exposed to all the winds of the world and to all dangers.

24   Although this is, properly speaking, a lamentable collapse that offends our sense of history, the disintegration of Protestantism into nearly four hundred denominations is yet a sure sign that the restlessness continues. The Protestant is cast out into a state of defencelessness that might well make the natural man shudder. His enlightened consciousness, of course, refuses to take cognizance of this fact, and is quietly looking elsewhere for what has been lost to Europe. We seek the effective images, the thought-forms that satisfy the restlessness of heart and mind, and we find the treasures of the East.

25   There is no objection to this, in and for itself. Nobody forced the Romans to import Asiatic cults in bulk. If Christianity had really been—as so often described—"alien" to the Germanic

tribes, they could easily have rejected it when the prestige of the Roman legions began to wane. But Christianity had come to stay, because it fits in with the existing archetypal pattern. In the course of the centuries, however, it turned into something its founder might well have wondered at had he lived to see it; and the Christianity of Negroes and other dark-skinned converts is certainly an occasion for historical reflections. Why, then, should the West not assimilate Eastern forms? The Romans too went to Eleusis, Samothrace, and Egypt in order to get themselves initiated. In Egypt there even seems to have been a regular tourist trade in this commodity.

26   The gods of Greece and Rome perished from the same disease as did our Christian symbols: people discovered then, as today, that they had no thoughts whatever on the subject. On the other hand, the gods of the strangers still had unexhausted mana. Their names were weird and incomprehensible and their deeds portentously dark—something altogether different from the hackneyed *chronique scandaleuse* of Olympus. At least one couldn't understand the Asiatic symbols, and for this reason they were not banal like the conventional gods. The fact that people accepted the new as unthinkingly as they had rejected the old did not become a problem at that time.

27   Is it becoming a problem today? Shall we be able to put on, like a new suit of clothes, ready-made symbols grown on foreign soil, saturated with foreign blood, spoken in a foreign tongue, nourished by a foreign culture, interwoven with foreign history, and so resemble a beggar who wraps himself in kingly raiment, a king who disguises himself as a beggar? No doubt this is possible. Or is there something in ourselves that commands us to go in for no mummeries, but perhaps even to sew our garment ourselves?

28   I am convinced that the growing impoverishment of symbols has a meaning. It is a development that has an inner consistency. Everything that we have not thought about, and that has therefore been deprived of a meaningful connection with our developing consciousness, has got lost. If we now try to cover our nakedness with the gorgeous trappings of the East, as the theosophists do, we would be playing our own history false. A man does not sink down to beggary only to pose afterwards as an Indian potentate. It seems to me that it would be far better

stoutly to avow our spiritual poverty, our symbol-lessness, instead of feigning a legacy to which we are not the legitimate heirs at all. We are, surely, the rightful heirs of Christian symbolism, but somehow we have squandered this heritage. We have let the house our fathers built fall into decay, and now we try to break into Oriental palaces that our fathers never knew. Anyone who has lost the historical symbols and cannot be satisfied with substitutes is certainly in a very difficult position today: before him there yawns the void, and he turns away from it in horror. What is worse, the vacuum gets filled with absurd political and social ideas, which one and all are distinguished by their spiritual bleakness. But if he cannot get along with these pedantic dogmatisms, he sees himself forced to be serious for once with his alleged trust in God, though it usually turns out that his fear of things going wrong if he did so is even more persuasive. This fear is far from unjustified, for where God is closest the danger seems greatest. It is dangerous to avow spiritual poverty, for the poor man has desires, and whoever has desires calls down some fatality on himself. A Swiss proverb puts it drastically: "Behind every rich man stands a devil, and behind every poor man two."

29   Just as in Christianity the vow of worldly poverty turned the mind away from the riches of this earth, so spiritual poverty seeks to renounce the false riches of the spirit in order to withdraw not only from the sorry remnants—which today call themselves the Protestant church—of a great past, but also from all the allurements of the odorous East; in order, finally, to dwell with itself alone, where, in the cold light of consciousness, the blank barrenness of the world reaches to the very stars.

30   We have inherited this poverty from our fathers. I well remember the confirmation lessons I received at the hands of my own father. The catechism bored me unspeakably. One day I was turning over the pages of my little book, in the hope of finding something interesting, when my eye fell on the paragraphs about the Trinity. This interested me at once, and I waited impatiently for the lessons to get to that section. But when the longed-for lesson arrived, my father said: "We'll skip this bit; I can't make head or tail of it myself." With that my last hope was laid in the grave. I admired my father's honesty,

but this did not alter the fact that from then on all talk of religion bored me to death.

31 Our intellect has achieved the most tremendous things, but in the meantime our spiritual dwelling has fallen into disrepair. We are absolutely convinced that even with the aid of the latest and largest reflecting telescope, now being built in America, men will discover behind the farthest nebulae no fiery empyrean; and we know that our eyes will wander despairingly through the dead emptiness of interstellar space. Nor is it any better when mathematical physics reveals to us the world of the infinitely small. In the end we dig up the wisdom of all ages and peoples, only to find that everything most dear and precious to us has already been said in the most superb language. Like greedy children we stretch out our hands and think that, if only we could grasp it, we would possess it too. But what we possess is no longer valid, and our hands grow weary from the grasping, for riches lie everywhere, as far as the eye can reach. All these possessions turn to water, and more than one sorcerer's apprentice has been drowned in the waters called up by himself—if he did not first succumb to the saving delusion that *this* wisdom was good and *that* was bad. It is from these adepts that there come those terrifying invalids who think they have a prophetic mission. For the artificial sundering of true and false wisdom creates a tension in the psyche, and from this there arises a loneliness and a craving like that of the morphine addict, who always hopes to find companions in his vice.

32 When our natural inheritance has been dissipated, then the spirit too, as Heraclitus says, has descended from its fiery heights. But when spirit becomes heavy it turns to water, and with Luciferian presumption the intellect usurps the seat where once the spirit was enthroned. The spirit may legitimately claim the *patria potestas* over the soul; not so the earth-born intellect, which is man's sword or hammer, and not a creator of spiritual worlds, a father of the soul. Hence Ludwig Klages[22] and Max Scheler[23] were moderate enough in their attempts to rehabilitate the spirit, for both were children of an age in which the spirit was no longer up above but down below, no longer fire but water.

22 [Cf. *Der Geist als Widersacher der Seele.*]
23 [Cf., e.g., *Die Stellung des Menschen im Kosmos.*—EDITORS.]

33   Therefore the way of the soul in search of its lost father—like Sophia seeking Bythos—leads to the water, to the dark mirror that reposes at its bottom. Whoever has elected for the state of spiritual poverty, the true heritage of Protestantism carried to its logical conclusion, goes the way of the soul that leads to the water. This water is no figure of speech, but a living symbol of the dark psyche. I can best illustrate this by a concrete example, one out of many:

34   A Protestant theologian often dreamed the same dream: *He stood on a mountain slope with a deep valley below, and in it a dark lake. He knew in the dream that something had always prevented him from approaching the lake. This time he resolved to go to the water. As he approached the shore, everything grew dark and uncanny, and a gust of wind suddenly rushed over the face of the water. He was seized by a panic fear, and awoke.*

35   This dream shows us the natural symbolism. The dreamer descends into his own depths, and the way leads him to the mysterious water. And now there occurs the miracle of the pool of Bethesda: an angel comes down and touches the water, endowing it with healing power. In the dream it is the wind, the pneuma, which bloweth where it listeth. Man's descent to the water is needed in order to evoke the miracle of its coming to life. But the breath of the spirit rushing over the dark water is uncanny, like everything whose cause we do not know—since it is not ourselves. It hints at an unseen presence, a numen to which neither human expectations nor the machinations of the will have given life. It lives of itself, and a shudder runs through the man who thought that "spirit" was merely what he believes, what he makes himself, what is said in books, or what people talk about. But when it happens spontaneously it is a spookish thing, and primitive fear seizes the naïve mind. The elders of the Elgonyi tribe in Kenya gave me exactly the same description of the nocturnal god whom they call the "maker of fear." "He comes to you," they said, "like a cold gust of wind, and you shudder, or he goes whistling round in the tall grass"—an African Pan who glides among the reeds in the haunted noontide hour, playing on his pipes and frightening the shepherds.

36   Thus, in the dream, the breath of the pneuma frightened another pastor, a shepherd of the flock, who in the darkness of the night trod the reed-grown shore in the deep valley of the

37 psyche. Yes, that erstwhile fiery spirit has made a descent to the realm of nature, to the trees and rocks and the waters of the psyche, like the old man in Nietzsche's *Zarathustra*, who, wearied of humankind, withdrew into the forest to growl with the bears in honour of the Creator.

We must surely go the way of the waters, which always tend downward, if we would raise up the treasure, the precious heritage of the father. In the Gnostic hymn to the soul,[24] the son is sent forth by his parents to seek the pearl that fell from the King's crown. It lies at the bottom of a deep well, guarded by a dragon, in the land of the Egyptians—that land of fleshpots and drunkenness with all its material and spiritual riches. The son and heir sets out to fetch the jewel, but forgets himself and his task in the orgies of Egyptian worldliness, until a letter from his father reminds him what his duty is. He then sets out for the water and plunges into the dark depths of the well, where he finds the pearl on the bottom, and in the end offers it to the highest divinity.

38 This hymn, ascribed to Bardesanes, dates from an age that resembled ours in more than one respect. Mankind looked and waited, and it was a *fish*—"levatus de profundo" (drawn from the deep)[25]—that became the symbol of the saviour, the bringer of healing.

39 As I wrote these lines, I received a letter from Vancouver, from a person unknown to me. The writer is puzzled by his dreams, which are always about water: "Almost every time I dream it is about water: *either I am having a bath, or the water-closet is overflowing, or a pipe is bursting, or my home has drifted down to the water's edge, or I see an acquaintance about to sink into water, or I am trying to get out of water, or I am having a bath and the tub is about to overflow*," etc.

40 Water is the commonest symbol for the unconscious. The lake in the valley is the unconscious, which lies, as it were, underneath consciousness, so that it is often referred to as the 'subconscious,' usually with the pejorative connotation of an inferior consciousness. Water is the "valley spirit," the water dragon of Tao, whose nature resembles water—a *yang* embraced in the *yin*. Psychologically, therefore, water means spirit that

24 James, *Apocryphal New Testament*, pp. 411–15.
25 Augustine, *Confessions*, Lib. XIII, cap. XXI.

has become unconscious. So the dream of the theologian is quite right in telling him that down by the water he could experience the working of the living spirit like a miracle of healing in the pool of Bethesda. The descent into the depths always seems to precede the ascent. Thus another theologian [26] dreamed that *he saw on a mountain a kind of Castle of the Grail. He went along a road that seemed to lead straight to the foot of the mountain and up it. But as he drew nearer he discovered to his great disappointment that a chasm separated him from the mountain, a deep, darksome gorge with underworldly water rushing along the bottom. A steep path led downwards and toilsomely climbed up again on the other side. But the prospect looked uninviting,* and the dreamer awoke. Here again the dreamer, thirsting for the shining heights, had first to descend into the dark depths, and this proves to be the indispensable condition for climbing any higher. The prudent man avoids the danger lurking in these depths, but he also throws away the good which a bold but imprudent venture might bring.

41   The statement made by the dream meets with violent resistance from the conscious mind, which knows "spirit" only as something to be found in the heights. "Spirit" always seems to come from above, while from below comes everything that is sordid and worthless. For people who think in this way, spirit means highest freedom, a soaring over the depths, deliverance from the prison of the chthonic world, and hence a refuge for all those timorous souls who do not want to become anything different. But water is earthy and tangible, it is also the fluid of the instinct-driven body, blood and the flowing of blood, the odour of the beast, carnality heavy with passion. The unconscious is the psyche that reaches down from the daylight of mentally and morally lucid consciousness into the nervous system that for ages has been known as the "sympathetic." This does not govern perception and muscular activity like the cerebrospinal system, and thus control the environment; but, though functioning without sense-organs, it maintains the balance of life and, through the mysterious paths of sympathetic

[26] The fact that it was another theologian who dreamed this dream is not so surprising, since priests and clergymen have a professional interest in the motif of "ascent." They have to speak of it so often that the question naturally arises as to what they are doing about their own spiritual ascent.

excitation, not only gives us knowledge of the innermost life of other beings but also has an inner effect upon them. In this sense it is an extremely collective system, the operative basis of all *participation mystique*, whereas the cerebrospinal function reaches its high point in separating off the specific qualities of the ego, and only apprehends surfaces and externals—always through the medium of space. It experiences everything as an outside, whereas the sympathetic system experiences everything as an inside.

42   The unconscious is commonly regarded as a sort of incapsulated fragment of our most personal and intimate life—something like what the Bible calls the "heart" and considers the source of all evil thoughts. In the chambers of the heart dwell the wicked blood-spirits, swift anger and sensual weakness. This is how the unconscious looks when seen from the conscious side. But consciousness appears to be essentially an affair of the cerebrum, which sees everything separately and in isolation, and therefore sees the unconscious in this way too, regarding it outright as *my* unconscious. Hence it is generally believed that anyone who descends into the unconscious gets into a suffocating atmosphere of egocentric subjectivity, and in this blind alley is exposed to the attack of all the ferocious beasts which the caverns of the psychic underworld are supposed to harbour.

43   True, whoever looks into the mirror of the water will see first of all his own face. Whoever goes to himself risks a confrontation with himself. The mirror does not flatter, it faithfully shows whatever looks into it; namely, the face we never show to the world because we cover it with the *persona*, the mask of the actor. But the mirror lies behind the mask and shows the true face.

44   This confrontation is the first test of courage on the inner way, a test sufficient to frighten off most people, for the meeting with ourselves belongs to the more unpleasant things that can be avoided so long as we can project everything negative into the environment. But if we are able to see our own shadow and can bear knowing about it, then a small part of the problem has already been solved: we have at least brought up the personal unconscious. The shadow is a living part of the personality and therefore wants to live with it in some form. It cannot be argued out of existence or rationalized into harmlessness. This problem

is exceedingly difficult, because it not only challenges the whole man, but reminds him at the same time of his helplessness and ineffectuality. Strong natures—or should one rather call them weak?—do not like to be reminded of this, but prefer to think of themselves as heroes who are beyond good and evil, and to cut the Gordian knot instead of untying it. Nevertheless, the account has to be settled sooner or later. In the end one has to admit that there are problems which one simply cannot solve on one's own resources. Such an admission has the advantage of being honest, truthful, and in accord with reality, and this prepares the ground for a compensatory reaction from the collective unconscious: you are now more inclined to give heed to a helpful idea or intuition, or to notice thoughts which had not been allowed to voice themselves before. Perhaps you will pay attention to the dreams that visit you at such moments, or will reflect on certain inner and outer occurrences that take place just at this time. If you have an attitude of this kind, then the helpful powers slumbering in the deeper strata of man's nature can come awake and intervene, for helplessness and weakness are the eternal experience and the eternal problem of mankind. To this problem there is also an eternal answer, otherwise it would have been all up with humanity long ago. When you have done everything that could possibly be done, the only thing that remains is what you could still do if only you knew it. But how much do we know of ourselves? Precious little, to judge by experience. Hence there is still a great deal of room left for the unconscious. Prayer, as we know, calls for a very similar attitude and therefore has much the same effect.

45   The necessary and needful reaction from the collective unconscious expresses itself in archetypally formed ideas. The meeting with oneself is, at first, the meeting with one's own shadow. The shadow is a tight passage, a narrow door, whose painful constriction no one is spared who goes down to the deep well. But one must learn to know oneself in order to know who one is. For what comes after the door is, surprisingly enough, a boundless expanse full of unprecedented uncertainty, with apparently no inside and no outside, no above and no below, no here and no there, no mine and no thine, no good and no bad. It is the world of water, where all life floats in suspension; where the realm of the sympathetic system, the soul of everything

living, begins; where I am indivisibly this *and* that; where I experience the other in myself and the other-than-myself experiences me.

46   No, the collective unconscious is anything but an incapsulated personal system; it is sheer objectivity, as wide as the world and open to all the world. There I am the object of every subject, in complete reversal of my ordinary consciousness, where I am always the subject that has an object. There I am utterly one with the world, so much a part of it that I forget all too easily who I really am. "Lost in oneself" is a good way of describing this state. But this self is the world, if only a consciousness could see it. That is why we must know who we are.

47   The unconscious no sooner touches us than we *are* it—we become unconscious of ourselves. That is the age-old danger, instinctively known and feared by primitive man, who himself stands so very close to this pleroma. His consciousness is still uncertain, wobbling on its feet. It is still childish, having just emerged from the primal waters. A wave of the unconscious may easily roll over it, and then he forgets who he was and does things that are strange to him. Hence primitives are afraid of uncontrolled emotions, because consciousness breaks down under them and gives way to possession. All man's strivings have therefore been directed towards the consolidation of consciousness. This was the purpose of rite and dogma; they were dams and walls to keep back the dangers of the unconscious, the "perils of the soul." Primitive rites consist accordingly in the exorcizing of spirits, the lifting of spells, the averting of the evil omen, propitiation, purification, and the production by sympathetic magic of helpful occurrences.

48   It is these barriers, erected in primitive times, that later became the foundations of the Church. It is also these barriers that collapse when the symbols become weak with age. Then the waters rise and boundless catastrophes break over mankind. The religious leader of the Taos pueblo, known as the Loco Tenente Gobernador, once said to me: "The Americans should stop meddling with our religion, for when it dies and we can no longer help the sun our Father to cross the sky, the Americans and the whole world will learn something in ten years' time, for then the sun won't rise any more." In other words, night will

318

fall, the light of consciousness is extinguished, and the dark sea of the unconscious breaks in.

49   Whether primitive or not, mankind always stands on the brink of actions it performs itself but does not control. The whole world wants peace and the whole world prepares for war, to take but one example. Mankind is powerless against mankind, and the gods, as ever, show it the ways of fate. Today we call the gods "factors," which comes from *facere*, 'to make.' The makers stand behind the wings of the world-theatre. It is so in great things as in small. In the realm of consciousness we are our own masters; we seem to be the "factors" themselves. But if we step through the door of the shadow we discover with terror that we are the objects of unseen factors. To know this is decidedly unpleasant, for nothing is more disillusioning than the discovery of our own inadequacy. It can even give rise to primitive panic, because, instead of being believed in, the anxiously guarded supremacy of consciousness—which is in truth one of the secrets of human success—is questioned in the most dangerous way. But since ignorance is no guarantee of security, and in fact only makes our insecurity still worse, it is probably better despite our fear to know where the danger lies. To ask the right question is already half the solution of a problem. At any rate we then know that the greatest danger threatening us comes from the unpredictability of the psyche's reactions. Discerning persons have realized for some time that external historical conditions, of whatever kind, are only occasions, jumping-off grounds, for the real dangers that threaten our lives. These are the present politico-social delusional systems. We should not regard them causally, as necessary consequences of external conditions, but as decisions precipitated by the collective unconscious.

50   This is a new problem. All ages before us have believed in gods in some form or other. Only an unparalleled impoverishment of symbolism could enable us to rediscover the gods as psychic factors, that is, as archetypes of the unconscious. No doubt this discovery is hardly credible at present. To be convinced, we need to have the experience pictured in the dream of the theologian, for only then do we experience the self-activity of the spirit moving over the waters. Since the stars have fallen from heaven and our highest symbols have paled, a secret life holds sway in the unconscious. That is why we have a psychology

today, and why we speak of the unconscious. All this would be quite superfluous in an age or culture that possessed symbols. Symbols are spirit from above, and under those conditions the spirit is above too. Therefore it would be a foolish and senseless undertaking for such people to wish to experience or investigate an unconscious that contains nothing but the silent, undisturbed sway of nature. Our unconscious, on the other hand, hides living water, spirit that has become nature, and that is why it is disturbed. Heaven has become for us the cosmic space of the physicists, and the divine empyrean a fair memory of things that once were. But "the heart glows," and a secret unrest gnaws at the roots of our being. In the words of the *Völuspa* we may ask:

What murmurs Wotan over Mimir's head?
Already the spring boils . . .

51 Our concern with the unconscious has become a vital question for us—a question of spiritual being or non-being. All those who have had an experience like that mentioned in the dream know that the treasure lies in the depths of the water and will try to salvage it. As they must never forget who they are, they must on no account imperil their consciousness. They will keep their standpoint firmly anchored to the earth, and will thus—to preserve the metaphor—become fishers who catch with hook and net what swims in the water. There may be consummate fools who do not understand what fishermen do, but the latter will not mistake the timeless meaning of their action, for the symbol of their craft is many centuries older than the still unfaded story of the Grail. But not every man is a fisherman. Sometimes this figure remains arrested at an early, instinctive level, and then it is an otter, as we know from Oskar Schmitz's fairytales.[27]

52 Whoever looks into the water sees his own image, but behind it living creatures soon loom up; fishes, presumably, harmless dwellers of the deep—harmless, if only the lake were not haunted. They are water-beings of a peculiar sort. Sometimes a nixie gets into the fisherman's net, a female, half-human fish.[28]

27 [The "Fischottermärchen" in *Märchen aus dem Unbewussten*, pp. 14ff., 43ff.—Editors.]
28 Cf. Paracelsus, *De vita longa* (1562), and my commentary in "Paracelsus as a Spiritual Phenomenon" [concerning Melusina, pars. 179f., 215ff.].

Nixies are entrancing creatures:

> Half drew she him,
> Half sank he down
> And nevermore was seen.

53   The nixie is an even more instinctive version of a magical feminine being whom I call the *anima*. She can also be a siren, *melusina* (mermaid),[29] wood-nymph, Grace, or Erlking's daughter, or a lamia or succubus, who infatuates young men and sucks the life out of them. Moralizing critics will say that these figures are projections of soulful emotional states and are nothing but worthless fantasies. One must admit that there is a certain amount of truth in this. But is it the whole truth? Is the nixie really nothing but a product of moral laxity? Were there not such beings long ago, in an age when dawning human consciousness was still wholly bound to nature? Surely there were spirits of forest, field, and stream long before the question of moral conscience ever existed. What is more, these beings were as much dreaded as adored, so that their rather peculiar erotic charms were only one of their characteristics. Man's consciousness was then far simpler, and his possession of it absurdly small. An unlimited amount of what we now feel to be an integral part of our psychic being disports itself merrily for the primitive in projections ranging far and wide.

54   The word "projection" is not really appropriate, for nothing has been cast out of the psyche; rather, the psyche has attained its present complexity by a series of acts of introjection. Its complexity has increased in proportion to the despiritualization of nature. An alluring nixie from the dim bygone is today called an "erotic fantasy," and she may complicate our psychic life in a most painful way. She comes upon us just as a nixie might; she sits on top of us like a succubus; she changes into all sorts of shapes like a witch, and in general displays an unbearable independence that does not seem at all proper in a psychic

[29] Cf. the picture of the adept in *Liber mutus* (1677) (fig. 13 in *The Practice of Psychotherapy*, p. 320). He is fishing, and has caught a nixie. His *soror mystica*, however, catches birds in her net, symbolizing the animus. The idea of the anima often turns up in the literature of the 16th and 17th cent., for instance in Richardus Vitus, Aldrovandus, and the commentator of the *Tractatus aureus*. Cf. "The Enigma of Bologna" in my *Mysterium Coniunctionis*, pars. 51ff.

content. Occasionally she causes states of fascination that rival the best bewitchment, or unleashes terrors in us not to be outdone by any manifestation of the devil. She is a mischievous being who crosses our path in numerous transformations and disguises, playing all kinds of tricks on us, causing happy and unhappy delusions, depressions and ecstasies, outbursts of affect, etc. Even in a state of reasonable introjection the nixie has not laid aside her roguery. The witch has not ceased to mix her vile potions of love and death; her magic poison has been refined into intrigue and self-deception, unseen though none the less dangerous for that.

55 But how do we dare to call this elfin being the "anima"? Anima means soul and should designate something very wonderful and immortal. Yet this was not always so. We should not forget that this kind of soul is a dogmatic conception whose purpose it is to pin down and capture something uncannily alive and active. The German word *Seele* is closely related, via the Gothic form *saiwalō*, to the Greek word αἰόλος, which means 'quick-moving,' 'changeful of hue,' 'twinkling,' something like a butterfly—ψυχή in Greek—which reels drunkenly from flower to flower and lives on honey and love. In Gnostic typology the ἄνθρωπος ψυχικός, 'psychic man,' is inferior to the πνευματικός, 'spiritual man,' and finally there are wicked souls who must roast in hell for all eternity. Even the quite innocent soul of the unbaptized newborn babe is deprived of the contemplation of God. Among primitives, the soul is the magic breath of life (hence the term "anima"), or a flame. An uncanonical saying of our Lord's aptly declares: "Whoso is near unto me is near to the fire." For Heraclitus the soul at the highest level is fiery and dry, because ψυχή as such is closely akin to "cool breath"—ψύχειν means 'to breathe,' 'to blow'; ψυχρός and ψῦχος mean 'cold,' 'chill,' 'damp.'

56 Being that has soul is living being. Soul is the living thing in man, that which lives of itself and causes life. Therefore God breathed into Adam a living breath, that he might live. With her cunning play of illusions the soul lures into life the inertness of matter that does not want to live. She makes us believe incredible things, that life may be lived. She is full of snares and traps, in order that man should fall, should reach the earth, entangle himself there, and stay caught, so that life should be

lived; as Eve in the garden of Eden could not rest content until she had convinced Adam of the goodness of the forbidden apple. Were it not for the leaping and twinkling of the soul, man would rot away in his greatest passion, idleness.[30] A certain kind of reasonableness is its advocate, and a certain kind of morality adds its blessing. But to have soul is the whole venture of life, for soul is a life-giving daemon who plays his elfin game above and below human existence, for which reason—in the realm of dogma—he is threatened and propitiated with superhuman punishments and blessings that go far beyond the possible deserts of human beings. Heaven and hell are the fates meted out to the soul and not to civilized man, who in his nakedness and timidity would have no idea of what to do with himself in a heavenly Jerusalem.

57   The anima is not the soul in the dogmatic sense, not an *anima rationalis*, which is a philosophical conception, but a natural archetype that satisfactorily sums up all the statements of the unconscious, of the primitive mind, of the history of language and religion. It is a "factor" in the proper sense of the word. Man cannot make it; on the contrary, it is always the *a priori* element in his moods, reactions, impulses, and whatever else is spontaneous in psychic life. It is something that lives of itself, that makes us live; it is a life behind consciousness that cannot be completely integrated with it, but from which, on the contrary, consciousness arises. For, in the last analysis, psychic life is for the greater part an unconscious life that surrounds consciousness on all sides—a notion that is sufficiently obvious when one considers how much unconscious preparation is needed, for instance, to register a sense-impression.

58   Although it seems as if the whole of our unconscious psychic life could be ascribed to the anima, she is yet only one archetype among many. Therefore, she is not characteristic of the unconscious in its entirety. She is only one of its aspects. This is shown by the very fact of her femininity. What is not-I, not masculine, is most probably feminine, and because the not-I is felt as not belonging to me and therefore as outside me, the anima-image is usually projected upon women. Either sex is inhabited by the opposite sex up to a point, for, biologically speaking, it is simply the greater number of masculine genes that tips the scales in

[30] La Rochefoucauld, Pensées DLX. Quoted in *Symbols of Transformation*, p. 174.

59 favour of masculinity. The smaller number of feminine genes seems to form a feminine character, which usually remains unconscious because of its subordinate position.

60 With the archetype of the anima we enter the realm of the gods, or rather, the realm that metaphysics has reserved for itself. Everything the anima touches becomes numinous—unconditional, dangerous, taboo, magical. She is the serpent in the paradise of the harmless man with good resolutions and still better intentions. She affords the most convincing reasons for not prying into the unconscious, an occupation that would break down our moral inhibitions and unleash forces that had better been left unconscious and undisturbed. As usual, there is something in what the anima says; for life in itself is not good only, it is also bad. Because the anima wants life, she wants both good and bad. These categories do not exist in the elfin realm. Bodily life as well as psychic life have the impudence to get along much better without conventional morality, and they often remain the healthier for it.

The anima believes in the καλὸν κἀγαθόν, the 'beautiful and the good,' a primitive conception that antedates the discovery of the conflict between aesthetics and morals. It took more than a thousand years of Christian differentiation to make it clear that the good is not always the beautiful and the beautiful not necessarily good. The paradox of this marriage of ideas troubled the ancients as little as it does the primitives. The anima is conservative and clings in the most exasperating fashion to the ways of earlier humanity. She likes to appear in historic dress, with a predilection for Greece and Egypt. In this connection we would mention the classic anima stories of Rider Haggard and Pierre Benoît. The Renaissance dream known as the *Ipnerotomachia* of Poliphilo,[31] and Goethe's *Faust*, likewise reach deep into antiquity in order to find "le vrai mot" for the situation. Poliphilo conjured up Queen Venus; Goethe, Helen of Troy. Aniela Jaffé[32] has sketched a lively picture of the anima in the age of Biedermeier and the Romantics. If you want to know what happens when the anima appears in modern society, I can warmly recommend John Erskine's *Private Life of Helen of*

31 Cf. *The Dream of Poliphilo*, ed. by Linda Fierz-David. [For Haggard and Benoît, see the bibliography.—EDITORS.]
32 "Bilder und Symbole aus E. T. A. Hoffmanns Märchen 'Der Goldne Topf.'"

Troy. She is not a shallow creation, for the breath of eternity lies over everything that is really alive. The anima lives beyond all categories, and can therefore dispense with blame as well as with praise. Since the beginning of time man, with his whole-some animal instinct, has been engaged in combat with his soul and its daemonism. If the soul were uniformly dark it would be a simple matter. Unfortunately this is not so, for the anima can appear also as an angel of light, a psychopomp who points the way to the highest meaning, as we know from *Faust*.

61   If the encounter with the shadow is the "apprentice-piece" in the individual's development, then that with the anima is the "master-piece." The relation with the anima is again a test of courage, an ordeal by fire for the spiritual and moral forces of man. We should never forget that in dealing with the anima we are dealing with psychic facts which have never been in man's possession before, since they were always found "outside" his psychic territory, so to speak, in the form of projections. For the son, the anima is hidden in the dominating power of the mother, and sometimes she leaves him with a sentimental attachment that lasts throughout life and seriously impairs the fate of the adult. On the other hand, she may spur him on to the highest flights. To the men of antiquity the anima appeared as a goddess or a witch, while for medieval man the goddess was replaced by the Queen of Heaven and Mother Church. The desymbolized world of the Protestant produced first an unhealthy sentimen-tality and then a sharpening of the moral conflict, which, be-cause it was so unbearable, led logically to Nietzsche's "beyond good and evil." In centres of civilization this state shows itself in the increasing insecurity of marriage. The American divorce rate has been reached, if not exceeded, in many European coun-tries, which proves that the anima projects herself by preference on the opposite sex, thus giving rise to magically complicated relationships. This fact, largely because of its pathological conse-quences, has led to the growth of modern psychology, which in its Freudian form cherishes the belief that the essential cause of all disturbances is sexuality—a view that only exacerbates the al-ready existing conflict.[33] There is a confusion here between cause and effect. The sexual disturbance is by no means the cause of neurotic difficulties, but is, like these, one of the patho-

33 I have expounded my views at some length in "Psychology of the Transference."

logical effects of a maladaptation of consciousness, as when consciousness is faced with situations and tasks to which it is not equal. Such a person simply does not understand how the world has altered, and what his attitude would have to be in order to adapt to it.

63   In dealing with the shadow or anima it is not sufficient just to know about these concepts and to reflect on them. Nor can we ever experience their content by feeling our way into them or by appropriating other people's feelings. It is no use at all to learn a list of archetypes by heart. Archetypes are complexes of experience that come upon us like fate, and their effects are felt in our most personal life. The anima no longer crosses our path as a goddess, but, it may be, as an intimately personal misadventure, or perhaps as our best venture. When, for instance, a highly esteemed professor in his seventies abandons his family and runs off with a young red-headed actress, we know that the gods have claimed another victim. This is how daemonic power reveals itself to us. Until not so long ago it would have been an easy matter to do away with the young woman as a witch.

64   In my experience there are very many people of intelligence and education who have no trouble in grasping the idea of the anima and her relative autonomy, and can also understand the phenomenology of the animus in women. Psychologists have more difficulties to overcome in this respect, probably because they are under no compulsion to grapple with the complex facts peculiar to the psychology of the unconscious. If they are doctors as well, their somato-psychological thinking gets in the way, with its assumption that psychological processes can be expressed in intellectual, biological, or physiological terms. Psychology, however, is neither biology nor physiology nor any other science than just this knowledge of the psyche.

The picture I have drawn of the anima so far is not complete. Although she may be the chaotic urge to life, something strangely meaningful clings to her, a secret knowledge or hidden wisdom, which contrasts most curiously with her irrational elfin nature. Here I would like to refer again to the authors already cited. Rider Haggard calls She "Wisdom's Daughter"; Benoît's Queen of Atlantis has an excellent library that even contains a lost book of Plato. Helen of Troy, in her reincarnation, is rescued from a Tyrian brothel by the wise Simon Magus and accompanies him on his travels. I purposely refrained from mentioning this thoroughly characteristic aspect of the anima earlier, because the first encounter with her usually leads one to infer anything rather than wisdom.[34] This aspect appears only to the person who gets to grips with her seriously. Only then, when this hard task has been faced,[35] does he come to realize more and more that behind all her cruel sporting with human fate there lies something like a hidden purpose which seems to reflect a superior knowledge of life's laws. It is just the most unexpected, the most terrifyingly chaotic things which reveal a deeper meaning. And the more this meaning is recognized, the more the anima loses her impetuous and compulsive character. Gradually breakwaters are built against the surging of chaos, and the meaningful divides itself from the meaningless. When sense and nonsense are no longer identical, the force of chaos is weakened by their subtraction; sense is then endued with the force of meaning, and nonsense with the force of meaninglessness. In this way a new cosmos arises. This is not a new discovery in the realm of medical psychology, but the age-old truth that out of the richness of a man's experience there comes a teaching which the father can pass on to the son.[36]

65   In elfin nature wisdom and folly appear as one and the same; and they *are* one and the same as long as they are acted out by the anima. Life is crazy and meaningful at once. And when we do not laugh over the one aspect and speculate about the other, life is exceedingly drab, and everything is reduced to the littlest scale. There is then little sense and little nonsense either. When you come to think about it, nothing has any meaning, for when there was nobody to think, there was nobody to interpret what happened. Interpretations are only for those who don't understand; it is only the things we don't understand that have any meaning. Man woke up in a world he did not understand, and that is why he tries to interpret it.

[34] I am referring here to literary examples that are generally accessible and not to clinical material. These are quite sufficient for our purpose.
[35] I.e., coming to terms with the contents of the collective unconscious in general. This is *the* great task of the integration process.
[36] A good example is the little book by Gustav Schmaltz, *Östliche Weisheit und Westliche Psychotherapie.*

66   Thus the anima and life itself are meaningless in so far as they offer no interpretation, for in all chaos there is a cosmos, in all disorder a secret order, in all caprice a fixed law, for everything that works is grounded on its opposite. It takes man's discriminating understanding, which breaks everything down, into antinomial judgments, to recognize this. Once he comes to grips with the anima, her chaotic capriciousness will give him cause to suspect a secret order, to sense a plan, a meaning, a purpose over and above her nature, or even—we might almost be tempted to say—to "postulate" such a thing, though this would not be in accord with the truth. For in actual reality we do not have at our command any power of cool reflection, nor does any science or philosophy help us, and the traditional teachings of religion do so only to a limited degree. We are caught and entangled in aimless experience, and the judging intellect with its categories proves itself powerless. Human interpretation fails, for a turbulent life-situation has arisen that refuses to fit any of the traditional meanings assigned to it. It is a moment of collapse. We sink into a final depth—Apuleius calls it "a kind of voluntary death." It is a surrender of our own powers, not artificially willed but forced upon us by nature; not a voluntary submission and humiliation decked in moral garb but an utter and unmistakable defeat crowned with the panic fear of demoralization. Only when all props and crutches are broken, and no cover from the rear offers even the slightest hope of security, does it become possible for us to experience an archetype that up till then had lain hidden behind the meaningful nonsense played out by the anima. This is the *archetype of meaning*, just as the anima is the *archetype of life itself.*

67   It always seems to us as if meaning—compared with life—were the younger event, because we assume, with some justification, that we assign it of ourselves, and because we believe, equally rightly no doubt, that the great world can get along without being interpreted. But how do we assign meaning? From what source, in the last analysis, do we derive meaning? The forms we use for assigning meaning are historical categories that reach back into the mists of time—a fact we do not take sufficiently into account. Interpretations make use of certain linguistic matrices that are themselves derived from primordial

328

68   images. From whatever side we approach this question, everywhere we find ourselves confronted with the history of language, with images and motifs that lead straight back to the primitive wonder-world.

Take, for instance, the word "idea." It goes back to the εἶδος concept of Plato, and the eternal ideas are primordial images stored up ἐν ὑπερουρανίῳ τόπῳ (in a supracelestial place) as eternal, transcendent forms. The eye of the seer perceives them as "imagines et lares," or as images in dreams and revelatory visions. Or let us take the concept of energy, which is an interpretation of physical events. In earlier times it was the secret fire of the alchemists, or phlogiston, or the heat-force inherent in matter, like the "primal warmth" of the Stoics, or the Heraclitean πῦρ ἀεὶ ζῶον (ever-living fire), which borders on the primitive notion of an all-pervading vital force, a power of growth and magic healing that is generally called *mana*.

69   I will not go on needlessly giving examples. It is sufficient to know that there is not a single important idea or view that does not possess historical antecedents. Ultimately they are all founded on primordial archetypal forms whose concreteness dates from a time when consciousness did not *think*, but only *perceived*. "Thoughts" were objects of inner perception, not thought at all, but sensed as external phenomena—seen or heard, so to speak. Thought was essentially revelation, not invented but forced upon us or bringing conviction through its immediacy and actuality. Thinking of this kind precedes the primitive ego-consciousness, and the latter is more its object than its subject. But we ourselves have not yet climbed the last peak of consciousness, so we also have a pre-existent thinking, of which we are not aware so long as we are supported by traditional symbols—or, to put it in the language of dreams, so long as the father or the king is not dead.

70   I would like to give you an example of how the unconscious "thinks" and paves the way for solutions. It is the case of a young theological student, whom I did not know personally. He was in great straits because of his religious beliefs, and about this time he dreamed the following dream: [37]

---

[37] I have already used this dream in "The Phenomenology of the Spirit in Fairytales," par. 398, infra, and in "Psychology and Education," pp. 117ff., as an example of a "big" dream, without commenting on it more closely.

71   *He was standing in the presence of a handsome old man dressed entirely in black. He knew it was the white magician. This personage had just addressed him at considerable length, but the dreamer could no longer remember what it was about. He had only retained the closing words: "And for this we need the help of the black magician." At that moment the door opened and in came another old man exactly like the first, except that he was dressed in white. He said to the white magician, "I need your advice," but threw a sidelong, questioning look at the dreamer, whereupon the white magician answered: "You can speak freely," he is an innocent." The black magician then began to relate his story. He had come from a distant land where something extraordinary had happened. The country was ruled by an old king who felt his death near. He—the king—had sought out a tomb for himself. For there were in that land a great number of tombs from ancient times, and the king had chosen the finest for himself. According to legend, a virgin had been buried in it. The king caused the tomb to be opened, in order to get it ready for use. But when the bones it contained were exposed to the light of day, they suddenly took on life and changed into a black horse, which at once fled into the desert and there vanished. The black magician had heard of this story and immediately set forth in pursuit of the horse. After a journey of many days, always on the tracks of the horse, he came to the desert and crossed to the other side, where the grasslands began again. There he met the horse grazing, and there also he came upon the find on whose account he now needed the advice of the white magician. For he had found the lost keys of paradise, and he did not know what to do with them. At this exciting moment the dreamer awoke.*

72   In the light of our earlier remarks the meaning of the dream is not hard to guess: the old king is the ruling symbol that wants to go to its eternal rest, and in the very place where similar "dominants" lie buried. His choice falls, fittingly enough, on the grave of anima, who lies in the death trance of a Sleeping Beauty so long as the king is alive—that is, so long as a valid principle (Prince or *princeps*) regulates and expresses life. But when the king draws to his end,[38] she comes to life again and changes into a black horse, which in Plato's parable stands for

[38] Cf. the motif of the "old king" in alchemy. *Psychology and Alchemy*, pars. 434ff.

the unruliness of the passions. Anyone who follows this horse comes into the desert, into a wild land remote from men—an image of spiritual and moral isolation. But there lie the keys of paradise.

73 Now what is paradise? Clearly, the Garden of Eden with its two-faced tree of life and knowledge and its four streams. In the Christian version it is also the heavenly city of the Apocalypse, which, like the Garden of Eden, is conceived as a mandala. But the mandala is a symbol of individuation. So it is the *black magician* who finds the keys to the solution of the problems of belief weighing on the dreamer, the keys that open the way of individuation. The contrast between desert and paradise therefore signifies isolation as contrasted with individuation, or the becoming of the self.

74 This part of the dream is a remarkable paraphrase of the Oxyrhynchus sayings of Jesus,[39] in which the way to the kingdom of heaven is pointed out by animals, and where we find the admonition: "Therefore know yourselves, for you are the city, and the city is the kingdom." It is also a paraphrase of the serpent of paradise who persuaded our first parents to sin, and who finally leads to the redemption of mankind through the Son of God. As we know, this causal nexus gave rise to the Ophitic identification of the serpent with the Σωτήρ (Saviour). The black horse and the black magician are half-evil elements whose relativity with respect to good is hinted at in the exchange of garments. The two magicians are, indeed, two aspects of the *wise old man*, the superior master and teacher, the archetype of the spirit, who symbolizes the pre-existent meaning hidden in the chaos of life. He is the father of the soul, and yet the soul, in some miraculous manner, is also his virgin mother, for which reason he was called by the alchemists the "first son of the mother." The black magician and the black horse correspond to the descent into darkness in the dreams mentioned earlier.

75 What an unbearably hard lesson for a young student of theology! Fortunately he was not in the least aware that the father of all prophets had spoken to him in the dream and placed a great secret almost within his grasp. One marvels at the inappropriateness of such occurrences. Why this prodigality? But I have to admit that we do not know how this dream

39 Cf. James, *The Apocryphal New Testament*, pp. 27f.

affected the student in the long run, and I must emphasize that to me, at least, the dream had a very great deal to say. It was not allowed to get lost, even though the dreamer did not understand it.

76   The old man in this dream is obviously trying to show how good and evil function together, presumably as an answer to the still unresolved moral conflict in the Christian psyche. With this peculiar relativization of opposites we find ourselves approaching nearer to the ideas of the East, to the *nirdvandva* of Hindu philosophy, the freedom from opposites, which is shown as a possible way of solving the conflict through reconciliation. How perilously fraught with meaning this Eastern relativity of good and evil is, can be seen from the Indian aphoristic question: "Who takes longer to reach perfection, the man who loves God, or the man who hates him?" And the answer is: "He who loves God takes seven reincarnations to reach perfection, and he who hates God takes only three, for he who hates God will think of him more than he who loves him." Freedom from opposites presupposes their functional equivalence, and this offends our Christian feelings. Nonetheless, as our dream example shows, the balanced co-operation of moral opposites is a natural truth which has been recognized just as naturally by the East. The clearest example of this is to be found in Taoist philosophy. But in the Christian tradition, too, there are various sayings that come very close to this standpoint. I need only remind you of the parable of the unjust steward.

77   Our dream is by no means unique in this respect, for the tendency to relativize opposites is a notable peculiarity of the unconscious. One must immediately add, however, that this is true only in cases of exaggerated moral sensibility; in other cases the unconscious can insist just as inexorably on the irreconcilability of the opposites. As a rule, the standpoint of the unconscious is relative to the conscious attitude. We can probably say, therefore, that our dream presupposes the specific beliefs and doubts of a theological consciousness of Protestant persuasion. This limits the statement of the dream to a definite set of problems. But even with this paring down of its validity the dream clearly demonstrates the superiority of its standpoint. Fittingly enough, it expresses its meaning in the opinion and voice of a wise magician, who goes back in direct line to the figure of the

medicine man in primitive society. He is, like the anima, an immortal daemon that pierces the chaotic darknesses of brute life with the light of meaning. He is the enlightener, the master and teacher, a psychopomp whose personification even Nietzsche, that breaker of tablets, could not escape—for he had called up his reincarnation in Zarathustra, the lofty spirit of an almost Homeric age, as the carrier and mouthpiece of his own "Dionysian" enlightenment and ecstasy. For him God was dead, but the driving daemon of wisdom became as it were his bodily double. He himself says:

> Then one was changed to two
> And Zarathustra passed me by.

78 Zarathustra is more for Nietzsche than a poetic figure; he is an involuntary confession, a testament. Nietzsche too had lost his way in the darknesses of a life that turned its back upon God and Christianity, and that is why there came to him the revealer and enlightener, the speaking fountainhead of his soul. Here is the source of the hieratic language of *Zarathustra*, for that is the style of this archetype.

79 Modern man, in experiencing this archetype, comes to know that most ancient form of thinking as an autonomous activity whose object he is. Hermes Trismegistus or the Thoth of Hermetic literature, Orpheus, the Poimandres (shepherd of men) and his near relation the Poimen of Hermes,[40] are other formulations of the same experience. If the name "Lucifer" were not prejudicial, it would be a very suitable one for this archetype. But I have been content to call it the *archetype of the wise old man*, or *of meaning*. Like all archetypes it has a positive and a negative aspect, though I don't want to enter into this here. The reader will find a detailed exposition of the two-facedness of the wise old man in "The Phenomenology of the Spirit in Fairytales."

80 The three archetypes so far discussed—the shadow, the anima, and the wise old man—are of a kind that can be directly experienced in personified form. In the foregoing I tried to indicate the general psychological conditions in which such an experience arises. But what I conveyed were only abstract

[40] Reitzenstein interprets the "Shepherd" of Hermas as a Christian rejoinder to the Poimandres writings.

generalizations. One could, or rather should, really give a description of the process as it occurs in immediate experience. In the course of this process the archetypes appear as active personalities in dreams and fantasies. But the process itself involves another class of archetypes which one could call the *archetypes of transformation*. They are not personalities, but are typical situations, places, ways and means, that symbolize the kind of transformation in question. Like the personalities, these archetypes are true and genuine symbols that cannot be exhaustively interpreted, either as signs or as allegories. They are genuine symbols precisely because they are ambiguous, full of half-glimpsed meanings, and in the last resort inexhaustible. The ground principles, the ἀρχαί, of the unconscious are indescribable because of their wealth of reference, although in themselves recognizable. The discriminating intellect naturally keeps on trying to establish their singleness of meaning and thus misses the essential point; for what we can above all establish as the one thing consistent with their nature is their *manifold meaning*, their almost limitless wealth of reference, which makes any unilateral formulation impossible. Besides this, they are in principle paradoxical, just as for the alchemists the spirit was conceived as "senex et iuvenis simul"—an old man and a youth at once.

81   If one wants to form a picture of the symbolic process, the series of pictures found in alchemy are good examples, though the symbols they contain are for the most part traditional despite their often obscure origin and significance. An excellent Eastern example is the Tantric *chakra* system,[41] or the mystical nerve system of Chinese yoga.[42] It also seems as if the set of pictures in the Tarot cards were distantly descended from the archetypes of transformation, a view that has been confirmed for me in a very enlightening lecture by Professor Bernoulli.[43]

82   The symbolic process is an experience *in images and of images*. Its development usually shows an enantiodromian structure like the text of the *I Ching*, and so presents a rhythm of negative and positive, loss and gain, dark and light. Its beginning is almost invariably characterized by one's getting stuck

---

41 Arthur Avalon, *The Serpent Power*.
42 Erwin Rousselle, "Spiritual Guidance in Contemporary Taoism."
43 R. Bernoulli, "Zur Symbolik geometrischer Figuren und Zahlen," pp. 397ff.

in a blind alley or in some impossible situation; and its goal is, broadly speaking, illumination or higher consciousness, by means of which the initial situation is overcome on a higher level. As regards the time factor, the process may be compressed into a single dream or into a short moment of experience, or it may extend over months and years, depending on the nature of the initial situation, the person involved in the process, and the goal to be reached. The wealth of symbols naturally varies enormously from case to case. Although everything is experienced in image form, i.e., symbolically, it is by no means a question of fictitious dangers but of very real risks upon which the fate of a whole life may depend. The chief danger is that of succumbing to the fascinating influence of the archetypes, and this is most likely to happen when the archetypal images are not made conscious. If there is already a predisposition to psychosis, it may even happen that the archetypal figures, which are endowed with a certain autonomy anyway on account of their natural numinosity, will escape from conscious control altogether and become completely independent, thus producing the phenomena of possession. In the case of an anima-possession, for instance, the patient will want to change himself into a woman through self-castration, or he is afraid that something of the sort will be done to him by force. The best-known example of this is Schreber's *Memoirs of My Nervous Illness.* Patients often discover a whole anima mythology with numerous archaic motifs. A case of this kind was published some time ago by Nelken.[44] Another patient has described his experiences himself and commented on them in a book.[45] I mention these examples because there are still people who think that the archetypes are subjective chimeras of my own brain.

The things that come to light brutally in insanity remain hidden in the background in neurosis, but they continue to influence consciousness nonetheless. When, therefore, the analysis penetrates the background of conscious phenomena, it discovers the same archetypal figures that activate the deliriums of psychotics. Finally, there is any amount of literary and historical evidence to prove that in the case of these archetypes we are dealing with normal types of fantasy that occur practically

44 "Analytische Beobachtungen über Phantasien eines Schizophrenen," pp. 504ff.
45 John Custance, *Wisdom, Madness, and Folly.*

everywhere and not with the monstrous products of insanity. The pathological element does not lie in the existence of these ideas, but in the dissociation of consciousness that can no longer control the unconscious. In all cases of dissociation it is therefore necessary to integrate the unconscious into consciousness. This is a synthetic process which I have termed the "individuation process."

84   As a matter of fact, this process follows the natural course of life—a life in which the individual becomes what he always was. Because man has consciousness, a development of this kind does not run very smoothly; often it is varied and disturbed, because consciousness deviates again and again from its archetypal, instinctual foundation and finds itself in opposition to it. There then arises the need for a synthesis of the two positions. This amounts to psychotherapy even on the primitive level, where it takes the form of restitution ceremonies. As examples I would mention the identification of the Australian aborigines with their ancestors in the *alcheringa* period, identification with the "sons of the sun" among the Pueblos of Taos, the Helios apotheosis in the Isis mysteries, and so on. Accordingly, the therapeutic method of complex psychology consists on the one hand in making as fully conscious as possible the constellated unconscious contents, and on the other hand in synthetizing them with consciousness through the act of recognition. Since, however, civilized man possesses a high degree of dissociability and makes continual use of it in order to avoid every possible risk, it is by no means a foregone conclusion that recognition will be followed by the appropriate action. On the contrary, we have to reckon with the singular ineffectiveness of recognition and must therefore insist on a meaningful application of it. Recognition by itself does not as a rule do this, nor does it imply, as such, any moral strength. In these cases it becomes very clear how much the cure of neurosis is a moral problem.

85   As the archetypes, like all numinous contents, are relatively autonomous, they cannot be integrated simply by rational means, but require a dialectical procedure, a real coming to terms with them, often conducted by the patient in dialogue form, so that, without knowing it, he puts into effect the alchemical definition of the *meditatio*: "an inner colloquy with

one's good angel." [46] Usually the process runs a dramatic course, with many ups and downs. It expresses itself in, or is accompanied by, dream symbols that are related to the "représentations collectives," which in the form of mythological motifs have portrayed psychic processes of transformation since the earliest times. [47]

86   In the short space of a lecture I must content myself with giving only a few examples of archetypes. I have chosen the ones that play the chief part in an analysis of the masculine psyche, and have tried to give you some idea of the transformation process in which they appear. Since this lecture was first published, the figures of the shadow, anima, and wise old man, together with the corresponding figures of the feminine unconscious, have been dealt with in greater detail in my contributions to the symbolism of the self, [48] and the individuation process in its relation to alchemical symbolism has also been subjected to closer investigation. [49]

[46] Ruland, *Lexicon alchemiae* (1612).
[47] Cf. *Symbols of Transformation*.

[48] *Aion*, Part II of this volume.
[49] *Psychology and Alchemy*.

PSYCHOLOGICAL ASPECTS OF THE MOTHER ARCHETYPE

On the Concept of the Archetype

148 The concept of the Great Mother belongs to the field of comparative religion and embraces widely varying types of mother-goddess. The concept itself is of no immediate concern to psychology, because the image of a Great Mother in this form is rarely encountered in practice, and then only under very special conditions. The symbol is obviously a derivative of the *mother archetype*. If we venture to investigate the background of the Great Mother image from the standpoint of psychology, then the mother archetype, as the more inclusive of the two, must form the basis of our discussion. Though lengthy discussion of the *concept* of an archetype is hardly necessary at this stage, some preliminary remarks of a general nature may not be out of place.

149 In former times, despite some dissenting opinion and the influence of Aristotle, it was not too difficult to understand Plato's conception of the Idea as supraordinate and pre-existent to all phenomena. "Archetype," far from being a modern term, was already in use before the time of St. Augustine, and was synonymous with "Idea" in the Platonic usage. When the *Corpus Hermeticum*, which probably dates from the third century, describes God as τὸ ἀρχέτυπον φῶς, the 'archetypal light,' it expresses the idea that he is the prototype of all light; that is to say, pre-existent and supraordinate to the phenomenon "light." Were I a philosopher, I should continue in this Platonic strain and say: Somewhere, in "a place beyond the skies," there is a prototype or primordial image of the mother that is pre-existent and supraordinate to all phenomena in which the "maternal," in the broadest sense of the term, is manifest. But I am an empiricist, not a philosopher; I cannot let myself presuppose that my peculiar temperament, my own attitude to intellectual problems, is universally valid. Apparently this is an assumption in which only the philosopher may indulge, who always takes it for granted that his own disposition and attitude are universal,

and will not recognize the fact, if he can avoid it, that his "personal equation" conditions his philosophy. As an empiricist, I must point out that there is a temperament which regards ideas as real entities and not merely as *nomina*. It so happens—by the merest accident, one might say—that for the past two hundred years we have been living in an age in which it has become unpopular or even unintelligible to suppose that ideas could be anything but *nomina*. Anyone who continues to think as Plato did must pay for his anachronism by seeing the "supracelestial," i.e., metaphysical, essence of the Idea relegated to the unverifiable realm of faith and superstition, or charitably left to the poet. Once again, in the age-old controversy over universals, the nominalistic standpoint has triumphed over the realistic, and the Idea has evaporated into a mere *flatus vocis*. This change was accompanied—and, indeed, to a considerable degree caused—by the marked rise of empiricism, the advantages of which were only too obvious to the intellect. Since that time the Idea is no longer something *a priori*, but is secondary and derived. Naturally, the new nominalism promptly claimed universal validity for itself in spite of the fact that it, too, is based on a definite and limited thesis coloured by temperament. This thesis runs as follows: we accept as valid anything that comes from outside and can be verified. The ideal instance is verification by experiment. The antithesis is: we accept as valid anything that comes from inside and cannot be verified. The hopelessness of this position is obvious. Greek natural philosophy with its interest in matter, together with Aristotelian reasoning, has achieved a belated but overwhelming victory over Plato.

150   Yet every victory contains the germ of future defeat. In our own day signs foreshadowing a change of attitude are rapidly increasing. Significantly enough, it is Kant's doctrine of categories, more than anything else, that destroys in embryo every attempt to revive metaphysics in the old sense of the word, but at the same time paves the way for a rebirth of the Platonic spirit. If it be true that there can be no metaphysics transcending human reason, it is no less true that there can be no empirical knowledge that is not already caught and limited by the *a priori* structure of cognition. During the century and a half that have elapsed since the appearance of the *Critique of Pure Reason*, the conviction has gradually gained ground that thinking, under-

340

standing, and reasoning cannot be regarded as independent processes subject only to the eternal laws of logic, but that they are *psychic functions* co-ordinated with the personality and subordinate to it. We no longer ask, "Has this or that been seen, heard, handled, weighed, counted, thought, and found to be logical?" We ask instead, "*Who saw, heard, or thought?*" Beginning with "the personal equation" in the observation and measurement of minimal processes, this critical attitude has gone on to the creation of an empirical psychology such as no time before ours has known. Today we are convinced that in all fields of knowledge psychological premises exist which exert a decisive influence upon the choice of material, the method of investigation, the nature of the conclusions, and the formulation of hypotheses and theories. We have even come to believe that Kant's personality was a decisive conditioning factor of his *Critique of Pure Reason*. Not only our philosophers, but our own predilections in philosophy, and even what we are fond of calling our "best" truths are affected, if not dangerously undermined, by this recognition of a personal premise. All creative freedom, we cry out, is taken away from us! What? Can it be possible that a man only thinks or says or does what he himself *is*?

151   Provided that we do not again exaggerate and so fall a victim to unrestrained "psychologizing," it seems to me that the critical standpoint here defined is inescapable. It constitutes the essence, origin, and method of modern psychology. There is an *a priori* factor in all human activities, namely the inborn, preconscious and unconscious individual structure of the psyche. The preconscious psyche—for example, that of a new-born infant—is not an empty vessel into which, under favourable conditions, practically anything can be poured. On the contrary, it is a tremendously complicated, sharply defined individual entity which appears indeterminate to us only because we cannot see it directly. But the moment the first visible manifestations of psychic life begin to appear, one would have to be blind not to recognize their individual character, that is, the unique personality behind them. It is hardly possible to suppose that all these details come into being only at the moment in which they appear. When it is a case of morbid predispositions already present in the parents, we infer hereditary transmission through

the germ-plasm; it would not occur to us to regard epilepsy in the child of an epileptic mother as an unaccountable mutation. Again, we explain by heredity the gifts and talents which can be traced back through whole generations. We explain in the same way the reappearance of complicated instinctive actions in animals that have never set eyes on their parents and therefore could not possibly have been "taught" by them.

152 Nowadays we have to start with the hypothesis that, so far as predisposition is concerned, there is no essential difference between man and all other creatures. Like every animal, he possesses a preformed psyche which breeds true to his species and which, on closer examination, reveals distinct features traceable to family antecedents. We have not the slightest reason to suppose that there are certain human activities or functions that could be exempted from this rule. We are unable to form any idea of what those dispositions or aptitudes are which make instinctive actions in animals possible. And it is just as impossible for us to know the nature of the preconscious psychic disposition that enables a child to react in a human manner. We can only suppose that his behaviour results from patterns of functioning, which I have described as *images*. The term "image" is intended to express not only the form of the activity taking place, but the typical situation in which the activity is released.[1] These images are "primordial" images in so far as they are peculiar to whole species, and if they ever "originated" their origin must have coincided at least with the beginning of the species. They are the "human quality" of the human being, the specifically human form his activities take. This specific form is hereditary and is already present in the germ-plasm. The idea that it is not inherited but comes into being in every child anew would be just as preposterous as the primitive belief that the sun which rises in the morning is a different sun from that which set the evening before.

153 Since everything psychic is preformed, this must also be true of the individual functions, especially those which derive directly from the unconscious predisposition. The most important of these is creative fantasy. In the products of fantasy the primordial images are made visible, and it is here that the concept of the archetype finds its specific application. I do not claim to

1 Cf. my "Instinct and the Unconscious," par. 277.

have been the first to point out this fact. The honour belongs to Plato. The first investigator in the field of ethnology to draw attention to the widespread occurrence of certain "elementary ideas" was Adolf Bastian. Two later investigators, Hubert and Mauss,[2] followers of Dürkheim, speak of "categories" of the imagination. And it was no less an authority than Hermann Usener[3] who first recognized unconscious preformation under the guise of "unconscious thinking." If I have any share in these discoveries, it consists in my having shown that archetypes are not disseminated only by tradition, language, and migration, but that they can rearise spontaneously, at any time, at any place, and without any outside influence.

154   The far-reaching implications of this statement must not be overlooked. For it means that there are present in every psyche forms which are unconscious but nonetheless active—living dispositions, ideas in the Platonic sense, that preform and continually influence our thoughts and feelings and actions.

155   Again and again I encounter the mistaken notion that an archetype is determined in regard to its content, in other words that it is a kind of unconscious idea (if such an expression be admissible). It is necessary to point out once more that archetypes are not determined as regards their content, but only as regards their form and then only to a very limited degree. A primordial image is determined as to its content only when it has become conscious and is therefore filled out with the material of conscious experience. Its form, however, as I have explained elsewhere, might perhaps be compared to the axial system of a crystal, which, as it were, preforms the crystalline structure in the mother liquid, although it has no material existence of its own. This first appears according to the specific way in which the ions and molecules aggregate. The archetype in itself is empty and purely formal, nothing but a *facultas praeformandi*, a possibility of representation which is given *a priori*. The representations themselves are not inherited, only the forms, and in that respect they correspond in every way to the instincts, which are also determined in form only. The existence of the instincts can no more be proved than the existence of the archetypes, so long as they do not manifest them-

2 [Cf. the previous paper, "Concerning the Archetypes," par. 137, n. 25.—EDITORS.]
3 Usener, *Das Weihnachtsfest*, p. 3.

selves concretely. With regard to the definiteness of the form, our comparison with the crystal is illuminating inasmuch as the axial system determines only the stereometric structure but not the concrete form of the individual crystal. This may be either large or small, and it may vary endlessly by reason of the different size of its planes or by the growing together of two crystals. The only thing that remains constant is the axial system, or rather, the invariable geometric proportions underlying it. The same is true of the archetype. In principle, it can be named and has an invariable nucleus of meaning—but always only in principle, never as regards its concrete manifestation. In the same way, the specific appearance of the mother-image at any given time cannot be deduced from the mother archetype alone, but depends on innumerable other factors.

2. THE MOTHER ARCHETYPE

156 Like any other archetype, the mother archetype appears under an almost infinite variety of aspects. I mention here only some of the more characteristic. First in importance are the personal mother and grandmother, stepmother and mother-in-law; then any woman with whom a relationship exists—for example, a nurse or governess or perhaps a remote ancestress. Then there are what might be termed mothers in a figurative sense. To this category belongs the goddess, and especially the Mother of God, the Virgin, and Sophia. Mythology offers many variations of the mother archetype, as for instance the mother who reappears as the maiden in the myth of Demeter and Kore; or the mother who is also the beloved, as in the Cybele-Attis myth. Other symbols of the mother in a figurative sense appear in things representing the goal of our longing for redemption, such as Paradise, the Kingdom of God, the Heavenly Jerusalem. Many things arousing devotion or feelings of awe, as for instance the Church, university, city or country, heaven, earth, the woods, the sea or any still waters, matter even, the underworld and the moon, can be mother-symbols. The archetype is often associated with things and places standing for fertility and fruitfulness: the cornucopia, a ploughed field, a garden. It can be attached to a rock, a cave, a tree, a spring, a deep well, or to various vessels such as the baptismal font, or to vessel-shaped flowers like the rose or the lotus. Because of the protection it implies, the magic circle or mandala can be a form of mother archetype. Hollow objects such as ovens and cooking vessels are associated with the mother archetype, and, of course, the uterus, *yoni*, and anything of a like shape. Added to this list there are many animals, such as the cow, hare, and helpful animals in general.

157 All these symbols can have a positive, favourable meaning or a negative, evil meaning. An ambivalent aspect is seen in the goddesses of fate (Moira, Graeae, Norns). Evil symbols are the

345

158 witch, the dragon (or any devouring and entwining animal, such as a large fish or a serpent), the grave, the sarcophagus, deep water, death, nightmares and bogies (Empusa, Lilith, etc.). This list is not, of course, complete; it presents only the most important features of the mother archetype.

The qualities associated with it are maternal solicitude and sympathy; the magic authority of the female; the wisdom and spiritual exaltation that transcend reason; any helpful instinct or impulse; all that is benign, all that cherishes and sustains, that fosters growth and fertility. The place of magic transformation and rebirth, together with the underworld and its inhabitants, are presided over by the mother. On the negative side the mother archetype may connote anything secret, hidden, dark; the abyss, the world of the dead, anything that devours, seduces, and poisons, that is terrifying and inescapable like fate. All these attributes of the mother archetype have been fully described and documented in my book *Symbols of Transformation*. There I formulated the ambivalence of these attributes as "the loving and the terrible mother." Perhaps the historical example of the dual nature of the mother most familiar to us is the Virgin Mary, who is not only the Lord's mother, but also, according to the medieval allegories, his cross. In India, "the loving and terrible mother" is the paradoxical Kali. Sankhya philosophy has elaborated the mother archetype into the concept of *prakṛti* (matter) and assigned to it the three *gunas* or fundamental attributes: *sattva, rajas, tamas*: goodness, passion, and darkness.[1] These are three essential aspects of the mother: her cherishing and nourishing goodness, her orgiastic emotionality, and her Stygian depths. The special feature of the philosophical myth, which shows Prakṛti dancing before Purusha in order to remind him of "discriminating knowledge," does not belong to the mother archetype but to the archetype of the anima, which in a man's psychology invariably appears, at first, mingled with the mother-image.

159 Although the figure of the mother as it appears in folklore is more or less universal, this image changes markedly when it appears in the individual psyche. In treating patients one is at

[1] This is the etymological meaning of the three *gunas*. See Weckerling, *Ananda-raya-makhi: Das Glück des Lebens*, pp. 21ff., and Garbe, *Die Samkhya Philosophie*, pp. 272ff. [Cf. also Zimmer, *Philosophies of India*, index, s.v.—Editors.]

first impressed, and indeed arrested, by the apparent significance of the personal mother. This figure of the personal mother looms so large in all personalistic psychologies that, as we know, they never got beyond it, even in theory, to other important aetiological factors. My own view differs from that of other medico-psychological theories principally in that I attribute to the personal mother only a limited aetiological significance. That is to say, all those influences which the literature describes as being exerted on the children do not come from the mother herself, but rather from the archetype projected upon her, which gives her a mythological background and invests her with authority and numinosity.[2] The aetiological and traumatic effects produced by the mother must be divided into two groups: (1) those corresponding to traits of character or attitudes actually present in the mother, and (2) those referring to traits which the mother only seems to possess, the reality being composed of more or less fantastic (i.e., archetypal) projections on the part of the child. Freud himself had already seen that the real aetiology of neuroses does not lie in traumatic effects, as he at first suspected, but in a peculiar development of infantile fantasy. This is not to deny that such a development can be traced back to disturbing influences emanating from the mother. I myself make it a rule to look first for the cause of infantile neuroses in the mother, as I know from experience that a child is much more likely to develop normally than neurotically, and that in the great majority of cases definite causes of disturbances can be found in the parents, especially in the mother. The contents of the child's abnormal fantasies can be referred to the personal mother only in part, since they often contain clear and unmistakable allusions which could not possibly have reference to human beings. This is especially true where definitely mythological products are concerned, as is frequently the case in infantile phobias where the mother may appear as a wild beast, a witch, a spectre, an ogre, a hermaphrodite, and so on. It must be borne in mind, however, that such fantasies are not always of unmistakably mythological origin, and even if they are, they may not always be rooted in the unconscious archetype but may have been occasioned by fairytales or accidental remarks. A

---

[2] American psychology can supply us with any amount of examples. A blistering but instructive lampoon on this subject is Philip Wylie's *Generation of Vipers*.

thorough investigation is therefore indicated in each case. For practical reasons, such an investigation cannot be made so readily with children as with adults, who almost invariably transfer their fantasies to the physician during treatment—or, to be more precise, the fantasies are projected upon him automatically.

160   When that happens, nothing is gained by brushing them aside as ridiculous, for archetypes are among the inalienable assets of every psyche. They form the "treasure in the realm of shadowy thoughts" of which Kant spoke, and of which we have ample evidence in the countless treasure motifs of mythology. An archetype is in no sense just an annoying prejudice; it becomes so only when it is in the wrong place. In themselves, archetypal images are among the highest values of the human psyche; they have peopled the heavens of all races from time immemorial. To discard them as valueless would be a distinct loss. Our task is not, therefore, to deny the archetype, but to dissolve the projections, in order to restore their contents to the individual who has involuntarily lost them by projecting them outside himself.

3. THE MOTHER-COMPLEX

161 The mother archetype forms the foundation of the so-called mother-complex. It is an open question whether a mother-complex can develop without the mother having taken part in its formation as a demonstrable causal factor. My own experience leads me to believe that the mother always plays an active part in the origin of the disturbance, especially in infantile neuroses or in neuroses whose aetiology undoubtedly dates back to early childhood. In any event, the child's instincts are disturbed, and this constellates archetypes which, in their turn, produce fantasies that come between the child and its mother as an alien and often frightening element. Thus, if the children of an over-anxious mother regularly dream that she is a terrifying animal or a witch, these experiences point to a split in the child's psyche that predisposes it to a neurosis.

I. THE MOTHER-COMPLEX OF THE SON

162 The effects of the mother-complex differ according to whether it appears in a son or a daughter. Typical effects on the son are homosexuality and Don Juanism, and sometimes also impotence.[1] In homosexuality, the son's entire heterosexuality is tied to the mother in an unconscious form; in Don Juanism, he unconsciously seeks his mother in every woman he meets. The effects of a mother-complex on the son may be seen in the ideology of the Cybele and Attis type: self-castration, madness, and early death. Because of the difference in sex, a son's mother-complex does not appear in pure form. This is the reason why in every masculine mother-complex, side by side with the mother archetype, a significant role is played by the image of the man's sexual counterpart, the anima. The mother is the first feminine being with whom the man-to-be comes in contact, and

[1] But the father-complex also plays a considerable part here.

she cannot help playing, overtly or covertly, consciously or unconsciously, upon the son's masculinity, just as the son in his turn grows increasingly aware of his mother's femininity, or unconsciously responds to it by instinct. In the case of the son, therefore, the simple relationships of identity or of resistance and differentiation are continually cut across by erotic attraction or repulsion, which complicates matters very considerably. I do not mean to say that for this reason the mother-complex of a son ought to be regarded as more serious than that of a daughter. The investigation of these complex psychic phenomena is still in the pioneer stage. Comparisons will not become feasible until we have some statistics at our disposal, and of these, so far, there is no sign.

163   Only in the daughter is the mother-complex clear and uncomplicated. Here we have to do either with an overdevelopment of feminine instincts indirectly caused by the mother, or with a weakening of them to the point of complete extinction. In the first case, the preponderance of instinct makes the daughter unconscious of her own personality; in the latter, the instincts are projected upon the mother. For the present we must content ourselves with the statement that in the daughter a mother-complex either unduly stimulates or else inhibits the feminine instinct, and that in the son it injures the masculine instinct through an unnatural sexualization.

164   Since a "mother-complex" is a concept borrowed from psychopathology, it is always associated with the idea of injury and illness. But if we take the concept out of its narrow psychopathological setting and give it a wider connotation, we can see that it has positive effects as well. Thus a man with a mother-complex may have a finely differentiated Eros [2] instead of, or in addition to, homosexuality. (Something of this sort is suggested by Plato in his *Symposium*.) This gives him a great capacity for friendship, which often creates ties of astonishing tenderness between men and may even rescue friendship between the sexes from the limbo of the impossible. He may have good taste and an aesthetic sense which are fostered by the presence of a feminine streak. Then he may be supremely gifted as a teacher because of his almost feminine insight and tact. He is likely to have a feeling for history, and to be conservative in the best

2 [Cf. *Two Essays on Analytical Psychology*, pars. 16ff.—EDITORS.]

sense and cherish the values of the past. Often he is endowed with a wealth of religious feelings, which help to bring the *ecclesia spiritualis* into reality; and a spiritual receptivity which makes him responsive to revelation.

165   In the same way, what in its negative aspect is Don Juanism can appear positively as bold and resolute manliness; ambitious striving after the highest goals; opposition to all stupidity, narrow-mindedness, injustice, and laziness; willingness to make sacrifices for what is regarded as right, sometimes bordering on heroism; perseverance, inflexibility and toughness of will; a curiosity that does not shrink even from the riddles of the universe; and finally, a revolutionary spirit which strives to put a new face upon the world.

166   All these possibilities are reflected in the mythological motifs enumerated earlier as different aspects of the mother archetype. As I have already dealt with the mother-complex of the son, including the anima complication, elsewhere, and my present theme is the archetype of the mother, in the following discussion I shall relegate masculine psychology to the background.

II. THE MOTHER-COMPLEX OF THE DAUGHTER [3]

167   (a) *Hypertrophy of the Maternal Element.*—We have noted that in the daughter the mother-complex leads either to a hypertrophy of the feminine side or to its atrophy. The exaggeration of the feminine side means an intensification of all female instincts, above all the maternal instinct. The negative aspect is seen in the woman whose only goal is childbirth. To her the husband is obviously of secondary importance; he is first and foremost the instrument of procreation, and she regards him merely as an object to be looked after, along with children, poor relations, cats, dogs, and household furniture. Even her own

[3] In the present section I propose to present a series of different "types" of mother-complex; in formulating them, I am drawing on my own therapeutic experiences. "Types" are not individual cases, neither are they freely invented schemata into which all individual cases have to be fitted. "Types" are ideal instances, or pictures of the average run of experience, with which no single individual can be identified. People whose experience is confined to books or psychological laboratories can form no proper idea of the cumulative experience of a practising psychologist.

personality is of secondary importance; she often remains entirely unconscious of it, for her life is lived in and through others, in more or less complete identification with all the objects of her care. First she gives birth to the children, and from then on she clings to them, for without them she has no existence whatsoever. Like Demeter, she compels the gods by her stubborn persistence to grant her the right of possession over her daughter. Her Eros develops exclusively as a maternal relationship while remaining unconscious as a personal one. An unconscious Eros always expresses itself as will to power.[4] Women of this type, though continually "living for others," are, as a matter of fact, unable to make any real sacrifice. Driven by ruthless will to power and a fanatical insistence on their own maternal rights, they often succeed in annihilating not only their own personality but also the personal lives of their children. The less conscious such a mother is of her own personality, the greater and the more violent is her unconscious will to power. For many such women Baubo rather than Demeter would be the appropriate symbol. The mind is not cultivated for its own sake but usually remains in its original condition, altogether primitive, unrelated, and ruthless, but also as true, and sometimes as profound, as Nature herself.[5] She herself does not know this and is therefore unable to appreciate the wittiness of her mind or to marvel philosophically at its profundity; like as not she will immediately forget what she has said.

(b) *Overdevelopment of Eros.*—It by no means follows that the complex induced in a daughter by such a mother must necessarily result in hypertrophy of the maternal instinct. Quite the contrary, this instinct may be wiped out altogether. As a substitute, an overdeveloped Eros results, and this almost invariably leads to an unconscious incestuous relationship with the father.[6] The intensified Eros places an abnormal emphasis on the personality of others. Jealousy of the mother and the desire to outdo her become the leitmotifs of subsequent undertakings, which

168

---

[4] This statement is based on the repeated experience that, where love is lacking, power fills the vacuum.

[5] In my English seminars [privately distributed] I have called this the "natural mind."

[6] Here the initiative comes from the daughter. In other cases the father's psychology is responsible; his projection of the anima arouses an incestuous fixation in the daughter.

are often disastrous. A woman of this type loves romantic and sensational episodes for their own sake, and is interested in married men, less for themselves than for the fact that they are married and so give her an opportunity to wreck a marriage, that being the whole point of her manoeuvre. Once the goal is attained, her interest evaporates for lack of any maternal instinct, and then it will be someone else's turn.[7] This type is noted for its remarkable unconsciousness. Such women really seem to be utterly blind to what they are doing,[8] which is anything but advantageous either for themselves or for their victims. I need hardly point out that for men with a passive Eros this type offers an excellent hook for anima projections.

169   (c) *Identity with the Mother.*—If a mother-complex in a woman does not produce an overdeveloped Eros, it leads to identification with the mother and to paralysis of the daughter's feminine initiative. A complete projection of her personality on to the mother then takes place, owing to the fact that she is unconscious both of her maternal instinct and of her Eros. Everything which reminds her of motherhood, responsibility, personal relationships, and erotic demands arouses feelings of inferiority and compels her to run away—to her mother, naturally, who lives to perfection everything that seems unattainable to her daughter. As a sort of superwoman (admired involuntarily by the daughter), the mother lives out for her beforehand all that the girl might have lived for herself. She is content to cling to her mother in selfless devotion, while at the same time unconsciously striving, almost against her will, to tyrannize over her, naturally under the mask of complete loyalty and devotion. The daughter leads a shadow-existence, often visibly sucked dry by her mother, and she prolongs her mother's life by a sort of continuous blood transfusion. These bloodless maidens are by no means immune to marriage. On the contrary, despite their shadowiness and passivity, they command a high price on the marriage market. First, they are so empty that a man is free to impute to them anything he fancies. In addition, they are so unconscious that the unconscious puts out countless invisible

---

[7] Herein lies the difference between this type of complex and the feminine father-complex related to it, where the "father" is mothered and coddled.
[8] This does not mean that they are unconscious of the *facts.* It is only their *meaning* that escapes them.

feelers, veritable octopus-tentacles, that suck up all masculine projections; and this pleases men enormously. All that feminine indefiniteness is the longed-for counterpart of male decisiveness and single-mindedness, which can be satisfactorily achieved only if a man can get rid of everything doubtful, ambiguous, vague, and muddled by projecting it upon some charming example of feminine innocence.[9] Because of the woman's characteristic passivity, and the feelings of inferiority which make her continually play the injured innocent, the man finds himself cast in an attractive role: he has the privilege of putting up with the familiar feminine foibles with real superiority, and yet with forbearance, like a true knight. (Fortunately, he remains ignorant of the fact that these deficiencies consist largely of his own projections.) The girl's notorious helplessness is a special attraction. She is so much an appendage of her mother that she can only flutter confusedly when a man approaches. She just doesn't know a thing. She is so inexperienced, so terribly in need of help, that even the gentlest swain becomes a daring abductor who brutally robs a loving mother of her daughter. Such a marvellous opportunity to pass himself off as a gay Lothario does not occur every day and therefore acts as a strong incentive. This was how Pluto abducted Persephone from the inconsolable Demeter. But, by a decree of the gods, he had to surrender his wife every year to his mother-in-law for the summer season. (The attentive reader will note that such legends do not come about by chance!)

170   (d) *Resistance to the Mother*.—These three extreme types are linked together by many intermediate stages, of which I shall mention only one important example. In the particular intermediate type I have in mind, the problem is less an over-development or an inhibition of the feminine instincts than an overwhelming resistance to maternal supremacy, often to the exclusion of all else. It is the supreme example of the negative mother-complex. The motto of this type is: Anything, so long as it is not like Mother! On one hand we have a fascination which never reaches the point of identification; on the other, an intensification of Eros which exhausts itself in jealous resist-

---

9 This type of woman has an oddly disarming effect on her husband, but only until he discovers that the person he has married and who shares his nuptial bed is his mother-in-law.

ance. This kind of daughter knows what she does *not* want, but is usually completely at sea as to what she would choose as her own fate. All her instincts are concentrated on the mother in the negative form of resistance and are therefore of no use to her in building her own life. Should she get as far as marrying, either the marriage will be used for the sole purpose of escaping from her mother, or else a diabolical fate will present her with a husband who shares all the essential traits of her mother's character. All instinctive processes meet with unexpected difficulties; either sexuality does not function properly, or the children are unwanted, or maternal duties seem unbearable, or the demands of marital life are responded to with impatience and irritation. This is quite natural, since none of it has anything to do with the realities of life when stubborn resistance to the power of the mother in every form has come to be life's dominating aim. In such cases one can often see the attributes of the mother archetype demonstrated in every detail. For example, the mother as representative of the family (or clan) causes either violent resistances or complete indifference to anything that comes under the head of family, community, society, convention, and the like. Resistance to the mother as *uterus* often manifests itself in menstrual disturbances, failure of conception, abhorrence of pregnancy, hemorrhages and excessive vomiting during pregnancy, miscarriages, and so on. The mother as *materia*, 'matter,' may be at the back of these women's impatience with objects, their clumsy handling of tools and crockery and bad taste in clothes.

171   Again, resistance to the mother can sometimes result in a spontaneous development of intellect for the purpose of creating a sphere of interest in which the mother has no place. This development springs from the daughter's own needs and not at all for the sake of a man whom she would like to impress or dazzle by a semblance of intellectual comradeship. Its real purpose is to break the mother's power by intellectual criticism and superior knowledge, so as to enumerate to her all her stupidities, mistakes in logic, and educational shortcomings. Intellectual development is often accompanied by the emergence of masculine traits in general.

4. POSITIVE ASPECTS OF THE MOTHER-COMPLEX

I. THE MOTHER

The positive aspect of the first type of complex, namely the overdevelopment of the maternal instinct, is identical with that well-known image of the mother which has been glorified in all ages and all tongues. This is the mother-love which is one of the most moving and unforgettable memories of our lives, the mysterious root of all growth and change; the love that means homecoming, shelter, and the long silence from which everything begins and in which everything ends. Intimately known and yet strange like Nature, lovingly tender and yet cruel like fate, joyous and untiring giver of life—*mater dolorosa* and mute implacable portal that closes upon the dead. Mother is mother-love, *my* experience and *my* secret. Why risk saying too much, too much that is false and inadequate and beside the point, about that human being who was our mother, the accidental carrier of that great experience which includes herself and myself and all mankind, and indeed the whole of created nature, the experience of life whose children we are? The attempt to say these things has always been made, and probably always will be; but a sensitive person cannot in all fairness load that enormous burden of meaning, responsibility, duty, heaven and hell, on to the shoulders of one frail and fallible human being—so deserving of love, indulgence, understanding, and forgiveness— who was our mother. He knows that the mother carries for us that inborn image of the *mater natura* and *mater spiritualis*, of the totality of life of which we are a small and helpless part. Nor should we hesitate for one moment to relieve the human mother of this appalling burden, for our own sakes as well as hers. It is just this massive weight of meaning that ties us to the mother and chains her to her child, to the physical and mental detriment of both. A mother-complex is not got rid of by blindly reducing the mother to human proportions. Besides that we run the risk of dissolving the experience "Mother" into atoms, thus destroying something supremely valuable and throwing away the golden key which a good fairy laid in our cradle. That is why mankind has always instinctively added the pre-existent divine pair to the personal parents—the "god"-father and "god"-mother of the newborn child—so that, from sheer unconsciousness or shortsighted rationalism, he should never forget himself so far as to invest his own parents with divinity.

¹⁷³   The archetype is really far less a scientific problem than an urgent question of psychic hygiene. Even if all proofs of the existence of archetypes were lacking, and all the clever people in the world succeeded in convincing us that such a thing could not possibly exist, we would have to invent them forthwith in order to keep our highest and most important values from disappearing into the unconscious. For when these fall into the unconscious the whole elemental force of the original experience is lost. What then appears in its place is fixation on the mother-imago; and when this has been sufficiently rationalized and "corrected," we are tied fast to human reason and condemned from then on to believe exclusively in what is rational. That is a virtue and an advantage on the one hand, but on the other a limitation and impoverishment, for it brings us nearer to the bleakness of doctrinairism and "enlightenment." This Déesse Raison emits a deceptive light which illuminates only what we know already, but spreads a darkness over all those things which it would be most needful for us to know and become conscious of. The more independent "reason" pretends to be, the more it turns into sheer intellectuality which puts doctrine in the place of reality and shows us man not as he is but how it wants him to be.

¹⁷⁴   Whether he understands them or not, man must remain conscious of the world of the archetypes, because in it he is still a part of Nature and is connected with his own roots. A view of the world or a social order that cuts him off from the primordial images of life not only is no culture at all but, in increasing degree, is a prison or a stable. If the primordial images remain conscious in some form or other, the energy that belongs to

them can flow freely into man. But when it is no longer possible to maintain contact with them, then the tremendous sum of energy stored up in these images, which is also the source of the fascination underlying the infantile parental complex, falls back into the unconscious. The unconscious then becomes charged with a force that acts as an irresistible *vis a tergo* to whatever view or idea or tendency our intellect may choose to dangle enticingly before our desiring eyes. In this way man is delivered over to his conscious side, and reason becomes the arbiter of right and wrong, of good and evil. I am far from wishing to belittle the divine gift of reason, man's highest faculty. But in the role of absolute tyrant it has no meaning—no more than light would have in a world where its counterpart, darkness, was absent. Man would do well to heed the wise counsel of the mother and obey the inexorable law of nature which sets limits to every being. He ought never to forget that the world exists only because opposing forces are held in equilibrium. So, too, the rational is counterbalanced by the irrational, and what is planned and purposed by what *is*.

175   This excursion into the realm of generalities was unavoidable, because the mother is the first world of the child and the last world of the adult. We are all wrapped as her children in the mantle of this great Isis. But let us now return to the different types of feminine mother-complex. It may seem strange that I am devoting so much more time to the mother-complex in woman than to its counterpart in man. The reason for this has already been mentioned: in a man, the mother-complex is never "pure," it is always mixed with the anima archetype, and the consequence is that a man's statements about the mother are always emotionally prejudiced in the sense of showing "animosity." Only in women is it possible to examine the effects of the mother archetype without admixture of animosity, and even this has prospects of success only when no compensating animus has developed.

II. THE OVERDEVELOPED EROS

176   I drew a very unfavourable picture of this type as we encounter it in the field of psychopathology. But this type, uninviting

as it appears, also has positive aspects which society could ill afford to do without. Indeed, behind what is possibly the worst effect of this attitude, the unscrupulous wrecking of marriages, we can see an extremely significant and purposeful arrangement of nature. This type often develops in reaction to a mother who is wholly a thrall of nature, purely instinctive and therefore all-devouring. Such a mother is an anachronism, a throw-back to a primitive state of matriarchy where the man leads an insipid existence as a mere procreator and serf of the soil. The reactive intensification of the daughter's Eros is aimed at some man who ought to be rescued from the preponderance of the female-maternal element in his life. A woman of this type instinctively intervenes when provoked by the unconsciousness of the marriage partner. She will disturb that comfortable ease so dangerous to the personality of a man but frequently regarded by him as marital faithfulness. This complacency leads to blank unconsciousness of his own personality and to those supposedly ideal marriages where he is nothing but Dad and she is nothing but Mom, and they even call each other that. This is a slippery path that can easily degrade marriage to the level of a mere breeding-pen.

¹⁷⁷ A woman of this type directs the burning ray of her Eros upon a man whose life is stifled by maternal solicitude, and by doing so she arouses a moral conflict. Yet without this there can be no consciousness of personality. "But why on earth," you may ask, "should it be necessary for man to achieve, by hook or by crook, a higher level of consciousness?" This is truly the crucial question, and I do not find the answer easy. Instead of a real answer I can only make a confession of faith: I believe that, after thousands and millions of years, someone had to realize that this wonderful world of mountains and oceans, suns and moons, galaxies and nebulae, plants and animals, *exists*. From a low hill in the Athi plains of East Africa I once watched the vast herds of wild animals grazing in soundless stillness, as they had done from time immemorial, touched only by the breath of a primeval world. I felt then as if I were the first man, the first creature, to know that all this *is*. The entire world round me was still in its primeval state; it did not know that it *was*. And then, in that one moment in which I came to know, the world sprang into being; without that moment it would never have

been. All Nature seeks this goal and finds it fulfilled in man, but only in the most highly developed and most fully conscious man. Every advance, even the smallest, along this path of conscious realization adds that much to the world.

178   There is no consciousness without discrimination of opposites. This is the paternal principle, the Logos, which eternally struggles to extricate itself from the primal warmth and primal darkness of the maternal womb; in a word, from unconsciousness. Divine curiosity yearns to be born and does not shrink from conflict, suffering, or sin. Unconsciousness is the primal sin, evil itself, for the Logos. Therefore its first creative act of liberation is matricide, and the spirit that dared all heights and all depths must, as Synesius says, suffer the divine punishment, enchainment on the rocks of the Caucasus. Nothing can exist without its opposite; the two were one in the beginning and will be one again in the end. Consciousness can only exist through continual recognition of the unconscious, just as everything that lives must pass through many deaths.

179   The stirring up of conflict is a Luciferian virtue in the true sense of the word. Conflict engenders fire, the fire of affects and emotions, and like every other fire it has two aspects, that of combustion and that of creating light. On the one hand, emotion is the alchemical fire whose warmth brings everything into existence and whose heat burns all superfluities to ashes (*omnes superfluitates comburit*). But on the other hand, emotion is the moment when steel meets flint and a spark is struck forth, for emotion is the chief source of consciousness. There is no change from darkness to light or from inertia to movement without emotion.

180   The woman whose fate it is to be a disturbing element is not solely destructive, except in pathological cases. Normally the disturber is herself caught in the disturbance; the worker of change is herself changed, and the glare of the fire she ignites both illuminates and enlightens all the victims of the entanglement. What seemed a senseless upheaval becomes a process of purification:

So that all that is vain
Might dwindle and wane.[1]

1 *Faust*, Part II, Act 5.

181 If a woman of this type remains unconscious of the meaning of her function, if she does not know that she is

Part of that power which would
Ever work evil but engenders good,[2]

she will herself perish by the sword she brings. But consciousness transforms her into a deliverer and redeemer.

III. THE "NOTHING-BUT" DAUGHTER

182 The woman of the third type, who is so identified with the mother that her own instincts are paralysed through projection, need not on that account remain a hopeless nonentity forever. On the contrary, if she is at all normal, there is a good chance of the empty vessel being filled by a potent anima projection. Indeed, the fate of such a woman depends on this eventuality; she can never find herself at all, not even approximately, without a man's help; she has to be literally abducted or stolen from her mother. Moreover, she must play the role mapped out for her for a long time and with great effort, until she actually comes to loathe it. In this way she may perhaps discover who she really is. Such women may become devoted and self-sacrificing wives of husbands whose whole existence turns on their identification with a profession or a great talent, but who, for the rest, are unconscious and remain so. Since they are nothing but masks themselves, the wife, too, must be able to play the accompanying part with a semblance of naturalness. But these women sometimes have valuable gifts which remained undeveloped only because they were entirely unconscious of their own personality. They may project the gift or talent upon a husband who lacks it himself, and then we have the spectacle of a totally insignificant man who seemed to have no chance whatsoever suddenly soaring as if on a magic carpet to the highest summits of achievement. *Cherchez la femme,* and you have the secret of his success. These women remind me—if I may be forgiven the impolite comparison—of hefty great bitches who turn tail before the smallest cur simply because he is a terrible male and it never occurs to them to bite him.

2 Ibid., Part I, Act 1.

183   Finally, it should be remarked that *emptiness* is a great feminine secret. It is something absolutely alien to man; the chasm, the unplumbed depths, the *yin*. The pitifulness of this vacuous nonentity goes to his heart (I speak here as a man), and one is tempted to say that this constitutes the whole "mystery" of woman. Such a female is fate itself. A man may say what he likes about it; be for it or against it, or both at once; in the end he falls, absurdly happy, into this pit, or, if he doesn't, he has missed and bungled his only chance of making a man of himself. In the first case one cannot disprove his foolish good luck to him, and in the second one cannot make his misfortune seem plausible. "The Mothers, the Mothers, how eerily it sounds!"[3] With this sigh, which seals the capitulation of the male as he approaches the realm of the Mothers, we will turn to the fourth type.

IV. THE NEGATIVE MOTHER-COMPLEX

184   As a pathological phenomenon this type is an unpleasant, exacting, and anything but satisfactory partner for her husband, since she rebels in every fibre of her being against everything that springs from natural soil. However, there is no reason why increasing experience of life should not teach her a thing or two, so that for a start she gives up fighting the mother in the personal and restricted sense. But even at her best she will remain hostile to all that is dark, unclear, and ambiguous, and will cultivate and emphasize everything certain and clear and reasonable. Excelling her more feminine sister in her objectivity and coolness of judgment, she may become the friend, sister, and competent adviser of her husband. Her own masculine aspirations make it possible for her to have a human understanding of the individuality of her husband quite transcending the realm of the erotic. The woman with this type of mother-complex probably has the best chance of all to make her marriage an outstanding success during the second half of life. But this is true only if she succeeds in overcoming the hell of "nothing but femininity," the chaos of the maternal womb, which is her greatest danger because of her negative complex. As we know, a com-

3 Ibid., Part II, Act 1.

plex can be really overcome only if it is lived out to the full. In other words, if we are to develop further we have to draw to us and drink down to the very dregs what, because of our complexes, we have held at a distance.

185   This type started out in the world with averted face, like Lot's wife looking back on Sodom and Gomorrah. And all the while the world and life pass by her like a dream—an annoying source of illusions, disappointments, and irritations, all of which are due solely to the fact that she cannot bring herself to look straight ahead for once. Because of her merely unconscious, reactive attitude toward reality, her life actually becomes dominated by what she fought hardest against—the exclusively maternal feminine aspect. But if she should later turn her face, she will see the world for the first time, so to speak, in the light of maturity, and see it embellished with all the colours and enchanting wonders of youth, and sometimes even of childhood. It is a vision that brings knowledge and discovery of truth, the indispensable prerequisite for consciousness. A part of life was lost, but the meaning of life has been salvaged for her.

186   The woman who fights against her father still has the possibility of leading an instinctive, feminine existence, because she rejects only what is alien to her. But when she fights against the mother she may, at the risk of injury to her instincts, attain to greater consciousness, because in repudiating the mother she repudiates all that is obscure, instinctive, ambiguous, and unconscious in her own nature. Thanks to her lucidity, objectivity, and masculinity, a woman of this type is frequently found in important positions in which her tardily discovered maternal quality, guided by a cool intelligence, exerts a most beneficial influence. This rare combination of womanliness and masculine understanding proves valuable in the realm of intimate relationships as well as in practical matters. As the spiritual guide and adviser of a man, such a woman, unknown to the world, may play a highly influential part. Owing to her qualities, the masculine mind finds this type easier to understand than women with other forms of mother-complex, and for this reason men often favour her with the projection of positive mother-complexes. The excessively feminine woman terrifies men who have a mother-complex characterized by great sensitivity. But this woman is not frightening to a man, because she builds bridges

363

for the masculine mind over which he can safely guide his feelings to the opposite shore. Her clarity of understanding inspires him with confidence, a factor not to be underrated and one that is absent from the relationship between a man and a woman much more often than one might think. The man's Eros does not lead upward only but downward into that uncanny dark world of Hecate and Kali, which is a horror to any intellectual man. The understanding possessed by this type of woman will be a guiding star to him in the darkness and seemingly unending mazes of life.

5. CONCLUSION

187   From what has been said it should be clear that in the last analysis all the statements of mythology on this subject as well as the observed effects of the mother-complex, when stripped of their confusing detail, point to the unconscious as their place of origin. How else could it have occurred to man to divide the cosmos, on the analogy of day and night, summer and winter, into a bright day-world and a dark night-world peopled with fabulous monsters, unless he had the prototype of such a division in himself, in the polarity between the conscious and the invisible and unknowable unconscious? Primitive man's perception of objects is conditioned only partly by the objective behaviour of the things themselves, whereas a much greater part is often played by intrapsychic facts which are not related to the external objects except by way of projection.[1] This is due to the simple fact that the primitive has not yet experienced that ascetic discipline of mind known to us as the critique of knowledge. To him the world is a more or less fluid phenomenon within the stream of his own fantasy, where subject and object are undifferentiated and in a state of mutual interpenetration. "All that is outside, also is inside," we could say with Goethe. But this "inside," which modern rationalism is so eager to derive from "outside," has an *a priori* structure of its own that antedates all conscious experience. It is quite impossible to conceive how "experience" in the widest sense, or, for that matter, anything psychic, could originate exclusively in the outside world. The psyche is part of the inmost mystery of life, and it has its own peculiar structure and form like every other organism. Whether this psychic structure and its elements, the archetypes, ever "originated" at all is a metaphysical question and therefore unanswerable. The structure is something given, the precondition that is found to be present in every case. And this is the *mother*, the matrix—the form into which all experience is

[1] [Cf. above, "Archetypes of the Collective Unconscious," par. 7.—Editors.]

365

poured. The *father*, on the other hand, represents the *dynamism* of the archetype, for the archetype consists of both—form and energy.

188   The carrier of the archetype is in the first place the personal mother, because the child lives at first in complete participation with her, in a state of unconscious identity. She is the psychic as well as the physical precondition of the child. With the awakening of ego-consciousness the participation gradually weakens, and consciousness begins to enter into opposition to the unconscious, its own precondition. This leads to differentiation of the ego from the mother, whose personal peculiarities gradually become more distinct. All the fabulous and mysterious qualities attaching to her image begin to fall away and are transferred to the person closest to her, for instance the grandmother. As the mother of the mother, she is "greater" than the latter; she is in truth the "grand" or "Great Mother." Not infrequently she assumes the attributes of wisdom as well as those of a witch. For the further the archetype recedes from consciousness and the clearer the latter becomes, the more distinctly does the archetype assume mythological features. The transition from mother to grandmother means that the archetype is elevated to a higher rank. This is clearly demonstrated in a notion held by the Bataks. The funeral sacrifice in honour of a dead father is modest, consisting of ordinary food. But if the son has a son of his own, then the father has become a grandfather and has consequently attained a more dignified status in the Beyond, and very important offerings are made to him.[2]

189   As the distance between conscious and unconscious increases, the grandmother's more exalted rank transforms her into a "Great Mother," and it frequently happens that the opposites contained in this image split apart. We then get a good fairy and a wicked fairy, or a benevolent goddess and one who is malevolent and dangerous. In Western antiquity and especially in Eastern cultures the opposites often remain united in the same figure, though this paradox does not disturb the primitive mind in the least. The legends about the gods are as full of contradictions as are their moral characters. In the West, the paradoxical behaviour and moral ambivalence of the gods scandalized people even in antiquity and gave rise to criticism that led

[2] Warneck, *Die Religion der Batak.*

366

finally to a devaluation of the Olympians on the one hand and to their philosophical interpretation on the other. The clearest expression of this is the Christian reformation of the Jewish concept of the Deity: the morally ambiguous Yahweh became an exclusively good God, while everything evil was united in the devil. It seems as if the development of the feeling function in Western man forced a choice on him which led to the moral splitting of the divinity into two halves. In the East the predominantly intuitive intellectual attitude left no room for feeling values, and the gods—Kali is a case in point—could retain their original paradoxical morality undisturbed. Thus Kali is representative of the East and the Madonna of the West. The latter has entirely lost the shadow that still distantly followed her in the allegories of the Middle Ages. It was relegated to the hell of popular imagination, where it now leads an insignificant existence as the devil's grandmother.[3] Thanks to the development of feeling-values, the splendour of the "light" god has been enhanced beyond measure, but the darkness supposedly represented by the devil has localized itself in man. This strange development was precipitated chiefly by the fact that Christianity, terrified of Manichaean dualism, strove to preserve its monotheism by main force. But since the reality of darkness and evil could not be denied, there was no alternative but to make man responsible for it. Even the devil was largely, if not entirely, abolished, with the result that this metaphysical figure, who at one time was an integral part of the Deity, was introjected into man, who thereupon became the real carrier of the *mysterium iniquitatis:* "omne bonum a Deo, omne malum ab homine." In recent times this development has suffered a diabolical reverse, and the wolf in sheep's clothing now goes about whispering in our ear that evil is really nothing but a misunderstanding of good and an effective instrument of progress. We think that the world of darkness has thus been abolished for good and all, and nobody realizes what a poisoning this is of man's soul. In this way he turns himself into the devil, for the devil is half of the archetype whose irresistible power makes even unbelievers ejaculate "Oh God!" on every suitable and unsuitable occasion. If one can possibly avoid it, one ought never to identify with an archetype, for, as psychopathology

[3] [A familiar figure of speech in German.—Editors.]

and certain contemporary events show, the consequences are terrifying.

190   Western man has sunk to such a low level spiritually that he even has to deny the apotheosis of untamed and untameable psychic power—the divinity itself—so that, after swallowing evil, he may possess himself of the good as well. If you read Nietzsche's *Zarathustra* with attention and psychological understanding, you will see that he has described with rare consistency and with the passion of a truly religious person the psychology of the "Superman," for whom God is dead, and who is himself burst asunder because he tried to imprison the divine paradox within the narrow framework of the mortal man. Goethe has wisely said: "What terror then shall seize the Superman!"—and was rewarded with a supercilious smile from the Philistines. His glorification of the Mother who is great enough to include in herself both the Queen of Heaven and Maria Aegyptiaca is supreme wisdom and profoundly significant for anyone willing to reflect upon it. But what can one expect in an age when the official spokesmen of Christianity publicly announce their inability to understand the foundations of religious experience! I extract the following sentence from an article by a Protestant theologian: "We understand ourselves—whether naturalistically or idealistically—to be *homogeneous creatures who are not so peculiarly divided that alien forces can intervene in our inner life*, as the New Testament supposes." [4] (Italics mine.) The author is evidently unacquainted with the fact that science demonstrated the lability and dissociability of consciousness more than half a century ago and proved it by experiment. Our conscious intentions are continually disturbed and thwarted, to a greater or lesser degree, by unconscious intrusions whose causes are at first strange to us. The psyche is far from being a homogeneous unit—on the contrary, it is a boiling cauldron of contradictory impulses, inhibitions, and affects, and for many people the conflict between them is so insupportable that they even wish for the deliverance preached by theologians. Deliverance from what? Obviously, from a highly questionable psychic state. The unity of consciousness or of the so-called personality is not a reality at all but a desideratum. I still have a vivid memory of a certain philosopher who also raved about this unity and

4 Buri, "Theologie und Philosophie," p. 117. [Quoting Rudolf Bultmann.—Eds.]

used to consult me about his neurosis: he was obsessed by the idea that he was suffering from cancer. I do not know how many specialists he had consulted already, and how many X-ray pictures he had had made. They all assured him that he had no cancer. He himself told me: "I know I have no cancer, but I still could have one." Who is responsible for this "imaginary" idea? He certainly did not make it himself; it was forced on him by an "alien" power. There is little to choose between this state and that of the man possessed in the New Testament. Now whether you believe in a demon of the air or in a factor in the unconscious that plays diabolical tricks on you is all one to me. The fact that man's imagined unity is menaced by alien powers remains the same in either case. Theologians would do better to take account for once of these psychological facts than to go on "demythologizing" them with rationalistic explanations that are a hundred years behind the times.

*

191   I have tried in the foregoing to give a survey of the psychic phenomena that may be attributed to the predominance of the mother-image. Although I have not always drawn attention to them, my reader will presumably have had no difficulty in recognizing those features which characterize the Great Mother mythologically, even when they appear under the guise of personalistic psychology. When we ask patients who are particularly influenced by the mother-image to express in words or pictures what "Mother" means to them—be it positive or negative—we invariably get symbolical figures which must be regarded as direct analogies of the mythological mother-image. These analogies take us into a field that still requires a great deal more work of elucidation. At any rate, I personally do not feel able to say anything definitive about it. If, nevertheless, I venture to offer a few suggestions, they should be regarded as altogether provisional and tentative.

192   Above all, I should like to point out that the mother-image in a man's psychology is entirely different in character from a woman's. For a woman, the mother typifies her own conscious life as conditioned by her sex. But for a man the mother typifies something alien, which he has yet to experience and which is filled with the imagery latent in the unconscious. For this

193   reason, if for no other, the mother-image of a man is essentially different from a woman's. The mother has from the outset a decidedly symbolical significance for a man, which probably accounts for his strong tendency to idealize her. Idealization is a hidden apotropaism; one idealizes whenever there is a secret fear to be exorcized. What is feared is the unconscious and its magical influence.[5]

194   Whereas for a man the mother is *ipso facto* symbolical, for a woman she becomes a symbol only in the course of her psychological development. Experience reveals the striking fact that the Urania type of mother-image predominates in masculine psychology, whereas in a woman the chthonic type, or Earth Mother, is the most frequent. During the manifest phase of the archetype an almost complete identification takes place. A woman can identify directly with the Earth Mother, but a man cannot (except in psychotic cases). As mythology shows, one of the peculiarities of the Great Mother is that she frequently appears paired with her male counterpart. Accordingly the man identifies with the son-lover on whom the grace of Sophia has descended, with a *puer aeternus* or a *filius sapientiae*. But the companion of the chthonic mother is the exact opposite: an ithyphallic Hermes (the Egyptian Bes) or a lingam. In India this symbol is of the highest spiritual significance, and in the West Hermes is one of the most contradictory figures of Hellenistic syncretism, which was the source of extremely important spiritual developments in Western civilization. He is also the god of revelation, and in the unofficial nature philosophy of the early Middle Ages he is nothing less than the world-creating Nous itself. This mystery has perhaps found its finest expression in the words of the *Tabula smaragdina:* "omne superius sicut inferius" (as it is above, so it is below).

    It is a psychological fact that as soon as we touch on these identifications we enter the realm of the syzygies, the paired opposites, where the One is never separated from the Other, its antithesis. It is a field of personal experience which leads directly to the experience of individuation, the attainment of the self. A vast number of symbols for this process could be mustered from the medieval literature of the West and even more

5 Obviously a daughter can idealize her mother too, but for this special circumstances are needed, whereas in a man idealization is almost the normal thing.

370

from the storehouses of Oriental wisdom, but in this matter words and ideas count for little. Indeed, they may become dangerous bypaths and false trails. In this still very obscure field of psychological experience, where we are in direct contact, so to speak, with the archetype, its psychic power is felt in full force. This realm is so entirely one of immediate experience that it cannot be captured by any formula, but can only be hinted at to one who already knows. He will need no explanations to understand what was the tension of opposites expressed by Apuleius in his magnificent prayer to the Queen of Heaven, when he associates "heavenly Venus" with "Proserpina, who strikest terror with midnight ululations": [6] it was the terrifying paradox of the primordial mother-image.

*

¹⁹⁵ When, in 1938, I originally wrote this paper, I naturally did not know that twelve years later the Christian version of the mother archetype would be elevated to the rank of a dogmatic truth. The Christian "Queen of Heaven" has, obviously, shed all her Olympian qualities except for her brightness, goodness, and eternality; and even her human body, the thing most prone to gross material corruption, has put on an ethereal incorruptibility. The richly varied allegories of the Mother of God have nevertheless retained some connection with her pagan prefigurations in Isis (Io) and Semele. Not only are Isis and the Horus-child iconological exemplars, but the ascension of Semele, the originally mortal mother of Dionysus. likewise anticipates the Assumption of the Blessed Virgin. Further, this son of Semele is a dying and resurgent god and the youngest of the Olympians. Semele herself seems to have been an earth-goddess, just as the Virgin Mary is the earth from which Christ was born. This being so, the question naturally arises for the psychologist: what has become of the characteristic relation of the mother-image to the earth, darkness, the abysmal side of the bodily man with his animal passions and instinctual nature, and to "matter" in general? The declaration of the dogma comes at a time when the achievements of science and technology, combined with a rationalistic and materialistic view of the world, threaten

⁶ "Nocturnis ululatibus horrenda Proserpina." Cf. *Symbols of Transformation*, par. 148.

the spiritual and psychic heritage of man with instant annihilation. Humanity is arming itself, in dread and fascinated horror, for a stupendous crime. Circumstances might easily arise when the hydrogen bomb would have to be used and the unthinkably frightful deed became unavoidable in legitimate self-defence. In striking contrast to this disastrous turn of events, the Mother of God is now enthroned in heaven; indeed, her Assumption has actually been interpreted as a deliberate counterstroke to the materialistic doctrinairism that provoked the chthonic powers into revolt. Just as Christ's appearance in his own day created a real devil and adversary of God out of what was originally a son of God dwelling in heaven, so now, conversely, a heavenly figure has split off from her original chthonic realm and taken up a counter-position to the titanic forces of the earth and the underworld that have been unleashed. In the same way that the Mother of God was divested of all the essential qualities of materiality, matter became completely de-souled, and this at a time when physics is pushing forward to insights which, if they do not exactly "de-materialize" matter, at least endue it with properties of its own and make its relation to the psyche a problem that can no longer be shelved. For just as the tremendous advancement of science led at first to a premature dethronement of mind and to an equally ill-considered deification of matter, so it is this same urge for scientific knowledge that is now attempting to bridge the huge gulf that has opened out between the two *Weltanschauungen*. The psychologist inclines to see in the dogma of the Assumption a symbol which, in a sense, anticipates this whole development. For him the relationship to the earth and to matter is one of the inalienable qualities of the mother archetype. So that when a figure that is conditioned by this archetype is represented as having been taken up into heaven, the realm of the spirit, this indicates a union of earth and heaven, or of matter and spirit. The approach of natural science will almost certainly be from the other direction: it will see in matter itself the equivalent of spirit, but this "spirit" will appear divested of all, or at any rate most, of its known qualities, just as earthly matter was stripped of its specific characteristics when it staged its entry into heaven. Nevertheless, the way will gradually be cleared for a union of the two principles.

196 Understood concretely, the Assumption is the absolute opposite of materialism. Taken in this sense, it is a counterstroke that does nothing to diminish the tension between the opposites, but drives it to extremes.

197 Understood symbolically, however, the Assumption of the body is a recognition and acknowledgment of matter, which in the last resort was identified with evil only because of an overwhelmingly "pneumatic" tendency in man. In themselves, spirit and matter are neutral, or rather, "utriusque capax"—that is, capable of what man calls good or evil. Although as names they are exceedingly relative, underlying them are very real opposites that are part of the energic structure of the physical and of the psychic world, and without them no existence of any kind could be established. There is no position without its negation. In spite or just because of their extreme opposition, neither can exist without the other. It is exactly as formulated in classical Chinese philosophy: *yang* (the light, warm, dry, masculine principle) contains within it the seed of *yin* (the dark, cold, moist, feminine principle), and vice versa. Matter therefore would contain the seed of spirit and spirit the seed of matter. The long-known "synchronistic" phenomena that have now been statistically confirmed by Rhine's experiments [7] point, to all appearances, in this direction. The "psychization" of matter puts the absolute immateriality of spirit in question, since this would then have to be accorded a kind of substantiality. The dogma of the Assumption, proclaimed in an age suffering from the greatest political schism history has ever known, is a compensating symptom that reflects the strivings of science for a uniform world-picture. In a certain sense, both developments were anticipated by alchemy in the *hieros gamos* of opposites, but only in symbolic form. Nevertheless, the symbol has the great advantage of being able to unite heterogeneous or even incommensurable factors in a *single* image. With the decline of alchemy the symbolical unity of spirit and matter fell apart, with the result that modern man finds himself "uprooted and alienated in a de-souled world.

198 The alchemist saw the union of opposites under the symbol of the tree, and it is therefore not surprising that the unconscious of present-day man, who no longer feels at home in his

[7] Cf. my "Synchronicity: An Acausal Connecting Principle."

world and can base his existence neither on the past that is no more nor on the future that is yet to be, should hark back to the symbol of the cosmic tree rooted in this world and growing up to heaven—the tree that is also man. In the history of symbols this tree is described as the way of life itself, a growing into that which eternally is and does not change; which springs from the union of opposites and, by its eternal presence, also makes that union possible. It seems as if it were only through an experience of symbolic reality that man, vainly seeking his own "existence" and making a philosophy out of it, can find his way back to a world in which he is no longer a stranger.

II

ON PATHOLOGY AND THERAPY

ON THE NATURE OF DREAMS[1]

530   Medical psychology differs from all other scientific disciplines in that it has to deal with the most complex problems without being able to rely on tested rules of procedure, on a series of verifiable experiments and logically explicable facts. On the contrary, it is confronted with a mass of shifting irrational happenings, for the psyche is perhaps the most baffling and unapproachable phenomenon with which the scientific mind has ever had to deal. Although we must assume that all psychic phenomena are somehow, in the broadest sense, causally dependent, it is advisable to remember at this point that causality is in the last analysis no more than a statistical truth. Therefore we should perhaps do well in certain cases to make allowance for absolute irrationality even if, on heuristic grounds, we approach each particular case by inquiring into its causality. Even then, it is advisable to bear in mind at least one of the classical distinctions, namely that between *causa efficiens* and *causa finalis*. In psychological matters, the question "Why does it happen?" is not necessarily more productive of results than the other question "To what purpose does it happen?"

531   Among the many puzzles of medical psychology there is one

1 [First published as "Vom Wesen der Träume," *Ciba-Zeitschrift* (Basel), IX : 99 (July, 1945). Revised and expanded in *Über psychische Energetik und das Wesen der Träume* (Psychologische Abhandlungen, II; Zurich, 1948).—Editors.]

532 problem-child, the dream. It would be an interesting, as well as difficult, task to examine the dream exclusively in its medical aspects, that is, with regard to the diagnosis and prognosis of pathological conditions. The dream does in fact concern itself with both health and sickness, and since, by virtue of its source in the unconscious, it draws upon a wealth of subliminal perceptions, it can sometimes produce things that are very well worth knowing. This has often proved helpful to me in cases where the differential diagnosis between organic and psychogenic symptoms presented difficulties. For prognosis, too, certain dreams are important.[2] In this field, however, the necessary preliminary studies, such as careful records of case histories and the like, are still lacking. Doctors with psychological training do not as yet make a practice of recording dreams systematically, so as to preserve material which would have a bearing on a subsequent outbreak of severe illness or a lethal issue—in other words, on events which could not be foreseen at the beginning of the record. The investigation of dreams in general is a life-work in itself, and their detailed study requires the co-operation of many workers. I have therefore preferred, in this short review, to deal with the fundamental aspects of dream psychology and interpretation in such a way that those who have no experience in this field can at least get some idea of the problem and the method of inquiry. Anyone who is familiar with the material will probably agree with me that a knowledge of fundamentals is more important than an accumulation of case histories, which still cannot make up for lack of experience.

The dream is a fragment of involuntary psychic activity, just conscious enough to be reproducible in the waking state. Of all psychic phenomena the dream presents perhaps the largest number of "irrational" factors. It seems to possess a minimum of that logical coherence and that hierarchy of values shown by the other contents of consciousness, and is therefore less transparent and understandable. Dreams that form logically, morally, or aesthetically satisfying wholes are exceptional. Usually a dream is a strange and disconcerting product distinguished by many "bad qualities," such as lack of logic, questionable morality, uncouth form, and apparent absurdity or nonsense. People are

2 Cf. "The Practical Use of Dream-Analysis," pars. 343ff.

therefore only too glad to dismiss it as stupid, meaningless, and worthless.

533   Every interpretation of a dream is a psychological statement about certain of its contents. This is not without danger, as the dreamer, like most people, usually displays an astonishing sensitiveness to critical remarks, not only if they are wrong, but even more if they are right. Since it is not possible, except under very special conditions, to work out the meaning of a dream without the collaboration of the dreamer, an extraordinary amount of tact is required not to violate his self-respect unnecessarily. For instance, what is one to say when a patient tells a number of indecent dreams and then asks: "Why should I have such disgusting dreams?" To this sort of question it is better to give no answer, since an answer is difficult for several reasons, especially for the beginner, and one is very apt under such circumstances to say something clumsy, above all when one thinks one knows what the answer is. So difficult is it to understand a dream that for a long time I have made it a rule, when someone tells me a dream and asks for my opinion, to say first of all to myself: "I have no idea what this dream means." After that I can begin to examine the dream.

534   Here the reader will certainly ask: "Is it worth while in any individual case to look for the meaning of a dream—supposing that dreams have any meaning at all and that this meaning can be proved?"

535   It is easy to prove that an animal is a vertebrate by laying bare the spine. But how does one proceed to lay bare the inner, meaningful structure of a dream? Apparently the dream follows no clearly determined laws or regular modes of behaviour, apart from the well-known "typical" dreams, such as nightmares. Anxiety dreams are not unusual but they are by no means the rule. Also, there are typical dream-motifs known to the layman, such as of flying, climbing stairs or mountains, going about with insufficient clothing, losing your teeth, crowds of people, hotels, railway stations, trains, aeroplanes, automobiles, frightening animals (snakes), etc. These motifs are very common but by no means sufficient to confirm the existence of any system in the organization of a dream.

536   Some people have recurrent dreams. This happens particularly in youth, but the recurrence may continue over several

decades. These are often very impressive dreams which convince one that they "must surely have a meaning." This feeling is justified in so far as one cannot, even taking the most cautious view, avoid the assumption that a definite psychic situation does arise from time to time which causes the dream. But a "psychic situation" is something that, if it can be formulated, is identical with a definite *meaning*—provided, of course, that one does not stubbornly hold to the hypothesis (certainly not proven) that all dreams can be traced back to stomach trouble or sleeping on one's back or the like. Such dreams do indeed tempt one to conjecture some kind of cause. The same is true of so-called typical motifs which repeat themselves frequently in longer series of dreams. Here again it is hard to escape the impression that they mean something.

537 But how do we arrive at a plausible meaning and how can we confirm the rightness of the interpretation? One method—which, however, is not scientific—would be to predict future happenings from the dreams by means of a dream-book and to verify the interpretation by subsequent events, assuming, of course that the meaning of dreams lies in their anticipation of the future.

538 Another way to get at the meaning of the dream directly might be to turn to the past and reconstruct former experiences from the occurrence of certain motifs in the dreams. While this is possible to a limited extent, it would have a decisive value only if we could discover in this way something which, though it had actually taken place, had remained unconscious to the dreamer, or at any rate something he would not like to divulge under any circumstances. If neither is the case, then we are dealing simply with memory-images whose appearance in the dream is (a) not denied by anyone, and (b) completely irrelevant so far as a meaningful dream function is concerned, since the dreamer could just as well have supplied the information consciously. This unfortunately exhausts the possible ways of proving the meaning of a dream directly.

539 It is Freud's great achievement to have put dream-interpretation on the right track. Above all, he recognized that no interpretation can be undertaken without the dreamer. The words composing a dream-narrative have not just *one* meaning, but many meanings. If, for instance, someone dreams of a table, we

are still far from knowing what the "table" of the dreamer signifies, although the word "table" sounds unambiguous enough. For the thing we do not know is that this "table" is the very one at which his father sat when he refused the dreamer all further financial help and threw him out of the house as a good-for-nothing. The polished surface of this table stares at him as a symbol of his lamentable worthlessness in his daytime consciousness as well as in his dreams at night. This is what our dreamer understands by "table." Therefore we need the dreamer's help in order to limit the multiple meanings of words to those that are essential and convincing. That the "table" stands as a mortifying landmark in the dreamer's life may be doubted by anyone who was not present. But the dreamer does not doubt it, nor do I. Clearly, dream-interpretation is in the first place an experience which has immediate validity for only two persons.

540   If, therefore, we establish that the "table" in the dream means just that fatal table, with all that this implies, then, although we have not explained the dream, we have at least interpreted one important motif of it; that is, we have recognized the subjective context in which the word "table" is embedded.

541   We arrived at this conclusion by a methodical questioning of the dreamer's own associations. The further procedures to which Freud subjects the dream-contents I have had to reject, for they are too much influenced by the preconceived opinion that dreams are the fulfilment of "repressed wishes." Although there are such dreams, this is far from proving that all dreams are wish-fulfilments, any more than are the thoughts of our conscious psychic life. There is no ground for the assumption that the unconscious processes underlying the dream are more limited and one-sided, in form and content, than conscious processes. One would rather expect that the latter could be limited to known categories, since they usually reflect the regularity or even monotony of the conscious way of life.

542   On the basis of these conclusions and for the purpose of ascertaining the meaning of the dream, I have developed a procedure which I call "taking up the context." This consists in making sure that every shade of meaning which each salient feature of the dream has for the dreamer is determined by the

543　associations of the dreamer himself. I therefore proceed in the same way as I would in deciphering a difficult text. This method does not always produce an immediately understandable result; often the only thing that emerges, at first, is a hint that looks significant. To give an example: I was working once with a young man who mentioned in his anamnesis that he was happily engaged, and to a girl of "good" family. In his dreams she frequently appeared in very unflattering guise. The context showed that the dreamer's unconscious connected the figure of his bride with all kinds of scandalous stories from quite another source—which was incomprehensible to him and naturally also to me. But, from the constant repetition of such combinations, I had to conclude that, despite his conscious resistance, there existed in him an unconscious tendency to show his bride in this ambiguous light. He told me that if such a thing were true it would be a catastrophe. His acute neurosis had set in a short time after his engagement. Although it was something he could not bear to think about, this suspicion of his bride seemed to me a point of such capital importance that I advised him to instigate some inquiries. These showed the suspicion to be well founded, and the shock of the unpleasant discovery did not kill the patient but, on the contrary, cured him of his neurosis and also of his bride. Thus, although the taking up of the context resulted in an "unthinkable" meaning and hence in an apparently nonsensical interpretation, it proved correct in the light of facts which were subsequently disclosed. This case is of exemplary simplicity, and it is superfluous to point out that only rarely do dreams have so simple a solution.

The examination of the context is, to be sure, a simple, almost mechanical piece of work which has only a preparatory significance. But the subsequent production of a readable text, i.e., the actual interpretation of the dream, is as a rule a very exacting task. It needs psychological empathy, ability to co-ordinate, intuition, knowledge of the world and of men, and above all a special "canniness" which depends on wide understanding as well as on a certain "intelligence du cœur." All these presupposed qualifications, including even the last, are valuable for the art of medical diagnosis in general. No sixth sense is needed to understand dreams. But more is required than routine recipes such as are found in vulgar little dream-books, or which invariably develop under the influence of preconceived notions. Stereotyped interpretation of dream-motifs is to be avoided; the only justifiable interpretations are those reached through a painstaking examination of the context. Even if one has great experience in these matters, one is again and again obliged, before each dream, to admit one's ignorance and, renouncing all preconceived ideas, to prepare for something entirely unexpected.

511   Even though dreams refer to a definite attitude of consciousness and a definite psychic situation, their roots lie deep in the unfathomably dark recesses of the conscious mind. For want of a more descriptive term we call this unknown background the unconscious. We do not know its nature in and for itself, but we observe certain effects from whose qualities we venture certain conclusions in regard to the nature of the unconscious psyche. Because dreams are the most common and most normal expression of the unconscious psyche, they provide the bulk of the material for its investigation.

545   Since the meaning of most dreams is *not* in accord with the tendencies of the conscious mind but shows peculiar deviations, we must assume that the unconscious, the matrix of dreams, has an independent function. This is what I call the autonomy of the unconscious. The dream not only fails to obey our will but very often stands in flagrant opposition to our conscious intentions. The opposition need not always be so marked; sometimes the dream deviates only a little from the conscious attitude and introduces only slight modifications; occasionally it may even coincide with conscious contents and tendencies. When I attempted to express this behaviour in a formula, the concept of *compensation* seemed to me the only adequate one, for it alone is capable of summing up all the various ways in which a dream behaves. Compensation must be strictly distinguished from *complementation.* The concept of a complement is too narrow and too restricting; it does not suffice to explain the function of dreams, because it designates a relationship in which two things supplement one another more or less mechanically.[3] Compensation, on the other hand, as the term implies, means balancing

[3] This is not to deny the principle of *complementarity*. "Compensation" is simply a psychological refinement of this concept.

and comparing different data or points of view so as to produce an adjustment or a rectification.

546 In this regard there are three possibilities. If the conscious attitude to the life situation is in large degree one-sided, then the dream takes the opposite side. If the conscious has a position fairly near the "middle," the dream is satisfied with variations. If the conscious attitude is "correct" (adequate), then the dream coincides with and emphasizes this tendency, though without forfeiting its peculiar autonomy. As one never knows with certainty how to evaluate the conscious situation of a patient, dream-interpretation is naturally impossible without question-ing the dreamer. But even if we know the conscious situation we know nothing of the attitude of the unconscious. As the uncon-scious is the matrix not only of dreams but also of psychogenic symptoms, the question of the attitude of the unconscious is of great practical importance. The unconscious, not caring whether I and those about me feel my attitude to be right, may—so to speak—be of "another mind." This, especially in the case of a neurosis, is not a matter of indifference, as the unconscious is quite capable of bringing about all kinds of unwelcome dis-turbances "by mistake," often with serious consequences, or of provoking neurotic symptoms. These disturbances are due to lack of harmony between conscious and unconscious. "Nor-mally," as we say, such harmony should be present. The fact is, however, that very frequently it is simply not there, and this is the reason for a vast number of psychogenic misfortunes rang-ing from severe accidents and illness to harmless slips of the tongue. We owe our knowledge of these relationships to the work of Freud.[4]

547 Although in the great majority of cases compensation aims at establishing a normal psychological balance and thus appears as a kind of self-regulation of the psychic system, one must not forget that under certain circumstances and in certain cases (for instance, in latent psychoses) compensation may lead to a fatal outcome owing to the preponderance of destructive tendencies. The result is suicide or some other abnormal action, apparently preordained in the life-pattern of certain hereditarily tainted individuals.

[4] *The Psychopathology of Everyday Life.*

548   In the treatment of neurosis, the task before us is to re-establish an approximate harmony between conscious and unconscious. This, as we know, can be achieved in a variety of ways: from "living a natural life," persuasive reasoning, strengthening the will, to analysis of the unconscious.

549   Because the simpler methods so often fail and the doctor does not know how to go on treating the patient, the compensatory function of dreams offers welcome assistance. I do not mean that the dreams of modern people indicate the appropriate method of healing, as was reported of the incubation-dreams dreamt in the temples of Aesculapius.[5] They do, however, illuminate the patient's situation in a way that can be exceedingly beneficial to health. They bring him memories, insights, experiences, awaken dormant qualities in the personality, and reveal the unconscious element in his relationships. So it seldom happens that anyone who has taken the trouble to work over his dreams with qualified assistance for a longer period of time remains without enrichment and a broadening of his mental horizon. Just because of their compensatory behaviour, a methodical analysis of dreams discloses new points of view and new ways of getting over the dreaded impasse.

550   The term "compensation" naturally gives us only a very general idea of the function of dreams. But if, as happens in long and difficult treatments, the analyst observes a series of dreams often running into hundreds, there gradually forces itself upon him a phenomenon which, in an isolated dream, would remain hidden behind the compensation of the moment. This phenomenon is a kind of developmental process in the personality itself. At first it seems that each compensation is a momentary adjustment of one-sidedness or an equalization of disturbed balance. But with deeper insight and experience, these apparently separate acts of compensation arrange themselves into a kind of plan. They seem to hang together and in the deepest sense to be subordinated to a common goal, so that a long dream-series no longer appears as a senseless string of incoherent and isolated happenings, but resembles the successive steps in a planned and orderly process of development. I have called this unconscious process spontaneously expressing

5 [Cf. Meier, *Ancient Incubation and Modern Psychotherapy.*—EDITORS.]

itself in the symbolism of a long dream-series the individuation process.

551 Here, more than anywhere else in a discussion of dream psychology, illustrative examples would be desirable. Unfortunately, this is quite impossible for technical reasons. I must therefore refer the reader to my book *Psychology and Alchemy*, which contains an investigation into the structure of a dream-series with special reference to the individuation process.

552 The question whether a long series of dreams recorded outside the analytical procedure would likewise reveal a development aiming at individuation is one that cannot be answered at present for lack of the necessary material. The analytical procedure, especially when it includes a systematic dream-analysis, is a "process of quickened maturation," as Stanley Hall once aptly remarked. It is therefore possible that the motifs accompanying the individuation process appear chiefly and predominantly in dream-series recorded under analysis, whereas in "extra-analytical" dream-series they occur only at much greater intervals of time.

553 I have mentioned before that dream-interpretation requires, among other things, specialized knowledge. While I am quite ready to believe that an intelligent layman with some psychological knowledge and experience of life could, with practice, diagnose dream-compensation correctly, I consider it impossible for anyone without knowledge of mythology and folklore and without some understanding of the psychology of primitives and of comparative religion to grasp the essence of the individuation process, which, according to all we know, lies at the base of psychological compensation.

554 Not all dreams are of equal importance. Even primitives distinguish between "little" and "big" dreams, or, as we might say, "insignificant" and "significant" dreams. Looked at more closely, "little" dreams are the nightly fragments of fantasy coming from the subjective and personal sphere, and their meaning is limited to the affairs of everyday. That is why such dreams are easily forgotten, just because their validity is restricted to the day-to-day fluctuations of the psychic balance. Significant dreams, on the other hand, are often remembered for a lifetime, and not infrequently prove to be the richest jewel in the treasure-house of psychic experience. How many people have I

encountered who at the first meeting could not refrain from saying: "I once had a dream!" Sometimes it was the first dream they could ever remember, and one that occurred between the ages of three and five. I have examined many such dreams, and often found in them a peculiarity which distinguishes them from other dreams: they contain symbolical images which we also come across in the mental history of mankind. It is worth noting that the dreamer does not need to have any inkling of the existence of such parallels. This peculiarity is characteristic of dreams of the individuation process, where we find the mythological motifs or mythologems I have designated as archetypes. These are to be understood as specific forms and groups of images which occur not only at all times and in all places but also in individual dreams, fantasies, visions, and delusional ideas. Their frequent appearance in individual case material, as well as their universal distribution, prove that the human psyche is unique and subjective or personal only in part, and for the rest is collective and objective.[6]

555 Thus we speak on the one hand of a *personal* and on the other of a *collective* unconscious, which lies at a deeper level and is further removed from consciousness than the personal unconscious. The "big" or "meaningful" dreams come from this deeper level. They reveal their significance—quite apart from the subjective impression they make—by their plastic form, which often has a poetic force and beauty. Such dreams occur mostly during the critical phases of life, in early youth, puberty, at the onset of middle age (thirty-six to forty), and within sight of death. Their interpretation often involves considerable difficulties, because the material which the dreamer is able to contribute is too meagre. For these archetypal products are no longer concerned with personal experiences but with general ideas, whose chief significance lies in their intrinsic meaning and not in any personal experience and its associations. For example, a young man dreamed of *a great snake that guarded a golden bowl in an underground vault.* To be sure, he had once seen a huge snake in a zoo, but otherwise he could suggest nothing that might have prompted such a dream, except perhaps the reminiscence of fairytales. Judging by this unsatisfactory

[6] Cf. *Two Essays on Analytical Psychology,* I, chs. V–VII.

context the dream, which actually produced a very powerful effect, would have hardly any meaning. But that would not explain its decided emotionality. In such a case we have to go back to mythology, where the combination of snake or dragon with treasure and cave represents an ordeal in the life of the hero. Then it becomes clear that we are dealing with a collective emotion, a typical situation full of affect, which is not primarily a personal experience but becomes one only secondarily. Primarily it is a universally human problem which, because it has been overlooked subjectively, forces itself objectively upon the dreamer's consciousness.[7]

556   A man in middle life still feels young, and age and death lie far ahead of him. At about thirty-six he passes the zenith of life, without being conscious of the meaning of this fact. If he is a man whose whole make-up and nature do not tolerate excessive unconsciousness, then the import of this moment will be forced upon him, perhaps in the form of an archetypal dream. It would be in vain for him to try to understand the dream with the help of a carefully worked out context, for it expresses itself in strange mythological forms that are not familiar to him. The dream uses collective figures because it has to express an eternal human problem that repeats itself endlessly, and not just a disturbance of personal balance.

557   All these moments in the individual's life, when the universal laws of human fate break in upon the purposes, expectations, and opinions of the personal consciousness, are stations along the road of the individuation process. This process is, in effect, the spontaneous realization of the whole man. The ego-conscious personality is only a part of the whole man, and its life does not yet represent his total life. The more he is merely "I," the more he splits himself off from the collective man, of whom he is also a part, and may even find himself in opposition to him. But since everything living strives for wholeness, the inevitable one-sidedness of our conscious life is continually being corrected and compensated by the universal human being in us, whose goal is the ultimate integration of conscious and unconscious, or better, the assimilation of the ego to a wider personality.

7 Cf. my and C. Kerényi's Essays on (or Introduction to) a Science of Mythology. [Also, Symbols of Transformation, pars. 572ff., 577ff.]

558 Such reflections are unavoidable if one wants to understand the meaning of "big" dreams. They employ numerous mythological motifs that characterize the life of the hero, of that greater man who is semi-divine by nature. Here we find the dangerous adventures and ordeals such as occur in initiations. We meet dragons, helpful animals, and demons; also the Wise Old Man, the animal-man, the wishing tree, the hidden treasure, the well, the cave, the walled garden, the transformative processes and substances of alchemy, and so forth—all things which in no way touch the banalities of everyday. The reason for this is that they have to do with the realization of a part of the personality which has not yet come into existence but is still in the process of becoming.

559 How such mythologems get "condensed" in dreams, and how they modify one another, is shown by the picture of the Dream of Nebuchadnezzar (Daniel 4 : 7ff.) [*frontispiece*]. Although purporting to be no more than a representation of that dream, it has, so to speak, been dreamed over again by the artist, as is immediately apparent if one examines the details more closely. The tree is growing (in a quite unbiblical manner) out of the king's navel: it is therefore the genealogical tree of Christ's ancestors, that grows from the navel of Adam, the tribal father.[8] For this reason it bears in its branches the pelican, who nourishes its young with its blood—a well-known allegory of Christ. Apart from that the pelican, together with the four birds that take the place of the four symbols of the evangelists, form a quincunx, and this quincunx reappears lower down in the stag, another symbol of Christ,[9] with the four animals looking

---

[8] The tree is also an alchemical symbol. Cf. *Psychology and Alchemy*, index, *s.v.* "tree"; and "The Philosophical Tree."

[9] The stag is an allegory of Christ because legend attributes to it the capacity for self-renewal. Thus Honorius of Autun writes in his *Speculum de Mysteriis Ecclesiae* (Migne, *P.L.*, vol. 172, col. 847): "They say that the deer, after he has swallowed a serpent, hastens to the water, that by a draught of water he may eject the poison, and then cast his horns and his hair and so take new." In the *Sant-Graal* (III, pp. 219 and 224), it is related that Christ sometimes appeared to the disciples as a white stag with four lions (= four evangelists). In alchemy, Mercurius is allegorized as the stag (Manget, *Bibl. chem.*, Tab. IX, fig. XIII, and elsewhere) because the stag can renew itself. "Les os du cuer du serf vault moult pour conforter le cuer humain" (Delatte, *Textes latins et vieux français relatifs aux Cyranides*, p. 346).

expectantly upwards. These two quaternities have the closest connections with alchemical ideas: above the *volatilia*, below the *terrena*, the former traditionally represented as birds, the latter as quadrupeds. Thus not only has the Christian conception of the genealogical tree and of the evangelical idea insinuated itself into the picture, but also the alchemical idea of the double quaternity ("superius est sicut quod inferius"). This contamination shows in the most vivid way how individual dreams make use of archetypes. The archetypes are condensed, interwoven, and blended not only with one another (as here), but also with unique individual elements.

560   But if dreams produce such essential compensations, why are they not understandable? I have often been asked this question. The answer must be that the dream is a natural occurrence, and that nature shows no inclination to offer her fruits gratis or according to human expectations. It is often objected that the compensation must be ineffective unless the dream is understood. This is not so certain, however, for many things can be effective without being understood. But there is no doubt that we can enhance its effect considerably by understanding the dream, and this is often necessary because the voice of the unconscious so easily goes unheard. "What nature leaves imperfect is perfected by the art," says an alchemical dictum.

561   Coming now to the form of dreams, we find everything from lightning impressions to endlessly spun out dream-narrative. Nevertheless there are a great many "average" dreams in which a definite structure can be perceived, not unlike that of a drama. For instance, the dream begins with a STATEMENT OF PLACE, such as, "I was in a street, it was an avenue" (1), or, "I was in a large building like a hotel" (2). Next comes a statement about the PROTAGONISTS, for instance, "I was walking with my friend X in a city park. At a crossing we suddenly ran into Mrs. Y." (3), or, "I was sitting with Father and Mother in a train compartment" (4), or, "I was in uniform with many of my comrades" (5). Statements of time are rarer. I call this phase of the dream the EXPOSITION. It indicates the scene of action, the people involved, and often the initial situation of the dreamer.

562   In the second phase comes the DEVELOPMENT of the plot. For instance: "I was in a street, it was an avenue. In the distance a car appeared, which approached rapidly. It was being driven

very unsteadily, and I thought the driver must be drunk" (1). Or: *"Mrs. Y seemed to be very excited and wanted to whisper something to me hurriedly, which my friend X was obviously not intended to hear"* (3). The situation is somehow becoming complicated, and a definite tension develops because one does not know what will happen.

563   The third phase brings the CULMINATION or *peripeteia*. Here something decisive happens or something changes completely: *"Suddenly I was in the car and seemed to be myself this drunken driver. Only I was not drunk, but strangely insecure and as if without a steering-wheel. I could no longer control the fast moving car, and crashed into a wall"* (1). Or: *"Suddenly Mrs. Y turned deathly pale and fell to the ground"* (3).

564   The fourth and last phase is the *lysis*, the SOLUTION or RESULT produced by the dream-work. (There are certain dreams in which the fourth phase is lacking, and this can present a special problem, not to be discussed here.) Examples: *"I saw that the front part of the car was smashed. It was a strange car that I did not know. I myself was unhurt. I thought with some uneasiness of my responsibility"* (1). *"We thought Mrs. Y was dead, but it was evidently only a faint. My friend X cried out: 'I must fetch a doctor'"* (3). The last phase shows the final situation, which is at the same time the solution "sought" by the dreamer. In dream 1 a new reflectiveness has supervened after a kind of rudderless confusion, or rather, should supervene, since the dream is compensatory. The upshot of dream 3 is the thought that the help of a competent third person is indicated.

565   The first dreamer was a man who had rather lost his head in difficult family circumstances and did not want to let matters go to extremes. The other dreamer wondered whether he ought to obtain the help of a psychiatrist for his neurosis. Naturally these statements are not an interpretation of the dream, they merely outline the initial situation. This division into four phases can be applied without much difficulty to the majority of dreams met with in practice—an indication that dreams generally have a "dramatic" structure.

566   The essential content of the dream-action, as I have shown above, is a sort of finely attuned compensation of the one-sidedness, errors, deviations, or other shortcomings of the conscious attitude. An hysterical patient of mine, an aristocratic lady who

seemed to herself no end distinguished, met in her dreams a whole series of dirty fishwives and drunken prostitutes. In extreme cases the compensation becomes so menacing that the fear of it results in sleeplessness.

567   Thus the dream may either repudiate the dreamer in a most painful way, or bolster him up morally. The first is likely to happen to people who, like the last-mentioned patient, have too good an opinion of themselves; the second to those whose self-valuation is too low. Occasionally, however, the arrogant person is not simply humiliated in the dream, but is raised to an altogether improbable and absurd eminence, while the all-too-humble individual is just as improbably degraded, in order to "rub it in," as the English say.

568   Many people who know something, but not enough, about dreams and their meaning, and who are impressed by their subtle and apparently intentional compensation, are liable to succumb to the prejudice that the dream actually has a moral purpose, that it warns, rebukes, comforts, foretells the future, etc. If one believes that the unconscious always knows best, one can easily be betrayed into leaving the dreams to take the necessary decisions, and is then disappointed when the dreams become more and more trivial and meaningless. Experience has shown me that a slight knowledge of dream psychology is apt to lead to an overrating of the unconscious which impairs the power of conscious decision. The unconscious functions satisfactorily only when the conscious mind fulfils its tasks to the very limit. A dream may perhaps supply what is then lacking, or it may help us forward where our best efforts have failed. If the unconscious really were superior to consciousness it would be difficult to see wherein the advantage of consciousness lay, or why it should ever have come into being as a necessary element in the scheme of evolution. If it were nothing but a *lusus naturae*, the fact of our conscious awareness of the world and of our own existence would be without meaning. The idea that consciousness is a freak of nature is somehow difficult to digest, and for psychological reasons we should avoid emphasizing it, even if it were correct—which, by the way, we shall luckily never be in a position to prove (any more than we can prove the contrary). It is a question that belongs to the realm of metaphysics, where no criterion of truth exists. However, this is in

569 no way to underestimate the fact that metaphysical views are of the utmost importance for the well-being of the human psyche.

In the study of dream psychology we encounter far-reaching philosophical and even religious problems to the understanding of which the phenomenon of dreams has already made decisive contributions. But we cannot boast that we are, at present, in possession of a generally satisfying theory or explanation of this complicated phenomenon. We still know far too little about the nature of the unconscious psyche for that. In this field there is still an infinite amount of patient and unprejudiced work to be done, which no one will begrudge. For the purpose of research is not to imagine that one possesses the theory which alone is right, but, doubting all theories, to approach gradually nearer to the truth.

ON THE PSYCHOGENESIS OF SCHIZOPHRENIA[1]

504   It is just twenty years since I read a paper on "The Problem of Psychogenesis in Mental Disease"[2] before this Society. William McDougall, whose recent death we all deplore, was in the chair. What I said then about psychogenesis could safely be repeated today, for it has left no visible traces, or other noticeable consequences, either in text-books or in clinics. Although I hate to repeat myself, it is almost impossible to say anything wholly new and different about a subject which has not changed its face in the many years that have gone by. My experience has increased and some of my views have matured, but I could not say that my standpoint has had to undergo any radical change. I am therefore in the somewhat uncomfortable situation of one who believes that he has a well-founded conviction, and yet on the other hand is afraid to indulge in the habit of repeating old stories. Psychogenesis has long been discussed, but it is still a modern, even an ultra-modern, problem.

505   There is little doubt nowadays about the psychogenesis of hysteria and other neuroses, although thirty years ago some brain enthusiasts still vaguely suspected that at bottom "there was something organically wrong in the neuroses." Nevertheless the *consensus doctorum* in their vast majority has admitted the psychic causation of hysteria and similar neuroses. Concerning the mental diseases, however, and especially concerning schizophrenia, they agreed unanimously upon an essentially organic aetiology, although for a long time specific destruction of the brain-cells could not be proved. Even today the question of how far schizophrenia itself can destroy the brain-cells has not been satisfactorily answered, much less the more specific question of how far primary organic disintegrations account for the symp-

1 [Written in English and read at a meeting of the Section of Psychiatry, Royal Society of Medicine, London, April 4, 1939. Published in the *Journal of Mental Science* (London), LXXXV (1939), 999–1011.—Editors.]
2 [Cf. supra, pars. 466ff.]

tomatology of schizophrenia. I fully agree with Bleuler that the great majority of symptoms are of a secondary nature and are due chiefly to psychic causes. For the primary symptoms, however, Bleuler assumes the existence of an organic cause. As *the* primary symptom he points to a peculiar disturbance of the association-process. According to his description, some kind of disintegration is involved, inasmuch as the associations seem to be peculiarly mutilated and disjointed. He refuses to accept Wernicke's concept of "sejunction," because of its anatomical implications. He prefers the term "schizophrenia," obviously understanding by this a *functional* disturbance. Such disturbances, or at least very similar ones, can be observed in delirious states of various kinds. Bleuler himself points out the remarkable similarity between schizophrenic associations and the association-phenomena in dreams and half-waking states. From his description it is sufficiently clear that the primary symptom coincides with the condition which Pierre Janet termed *abaissement du niveau mental*. It is caused by a peculiar *faiblesse de la volonté*. If the main guiding and controlling force of our mental life is will-power, then we can agree that Janet's concept of *abaissement* explains a psychic condition in which a train of thought is not carried through to its logical conclusion, or is interrupted by strange contents that are insufficiently inhibited. Though Bleuler does not mention Janet, I think that Janet's *abaissement* aptly formulates Bleuler's views on the primary symptoms.

506   It is true that Janet uses his hypothesis chiefly to explain the symptomatology of hysteria and other neuroses, which are indubitably psychogenic and quite different from schizophrenia. Yet there are certain noteworthy analogies between the neurotic and the schizophrenic mental condition. If you study the association tests of neurotics, you will find that their normal associations are disturbed by the spontaneous intervention of complex contents typical of an *abaissement*. The dissociation can even go so far as to create one or more secondary personalities, each, apparently, with a separate consciousness of its own. But the fundamental difference between neurosis and schizophrenia lies in the maintenance of the potential unity of the personality. Despite the fact that consciousness can be split up into several personal consciousnesses, the unity of all the dissociated frag-

ments is not only visible to the professional eye but can be re-established by means of hypnosis. This is not the case with schizophrenia. The general picture of an association test of a schizophrenic may be very similar to that of a neurotic, but closer examination shows that in a schizophrenic patient the connection between the ego and some of the complexes is more or less completely lost. The split is not relative, it is absolute. An hysterical patient might suffer from a persecution-mania very similar to real paranoia, but the difference is that in the former case one can bring the delusion back under the control of consciousness, whereas it is virtually impossible to do this in paranoia. A neurosis, it is true, is characterized by the relative autonomy of its complexes, but in schizophrenia the complexes have become disconnected and autonomous fragments, which either do not reintegrate back to the psychic totality, or, in the case of a remission, are unexpectedly joined together again as if nothing had happened.

507   The dissociation in schizophrenia is not only far more serious, but very often it is irreversible. The dissociation is no longer fluid and changeable as it is in a neurosis, it is more like a mirror broken up into splinters. The unity of personality which, in a case of hysteria, lends a humanly understandable character to its own secondary personalities is definitely shattered into fragments. In hysterical multiple personality there is a fairly smooth, even tactful, co-operation between the different persons, who keep to their respective roles and, if possible, do not bother each other. One feels the presence of an invisible *spiritus rector*, a central manager who arranges the stage for the different figures in an almost rational way, often in the form of a more or less sentimental drama. Each figure has a suggestive name and an admissible character, and they are just as nicely hysterical and just as sentimentally biased as the patient's own consciousness.

508   The picture of a personality dissociation in schizophrenia is quite different. The split-off figures assume banal, grotesque, or highly exaggerated names and characters, and are often objectionable in many other ways. They do not, moreover, co-operate with the patient's consciousness. They are not tactful and they have no respect for sentimental values. On the contrary, they break in and make a disturbance at any time, they torment the

509

ego in a hundred ways; all are objectionable and shocking, either in their noisy and impertinent behaviour or in their grotesque cruelty and obscenity. There is an apparent chaos of incoherent visions, voices, and characters, all of an overwhelmingly strange and incomprehensible nature. If there is a drama at all, it is certainly far beyond the patient's understanding. In most cases it transcends even the physician's comprehension, so much so that he is inclined to suspect the mental sanity of anybody who sees more than plain madness in the ravings of a lunatic.

510

The autonomous figures have broken away from the control of the ego so thoroughly that their original participation in the patient's mental make-up has vanished. The *abaissement* has reached a degree unheard of in the sphere of neurosis. An hysterical dissociation is bridged over by a unity of personality which still functions, whereas in schizophrenia the very foundations of the personality are impaired.

511

The *abaissement*

(1) Causes the loss of whole regions of normally controlled contents.

(2) Produces split-off fragments of the personality.

(3) Hinders normal trains of thought from being consistently carried through and completed.

(4) Decreases the responsibility and the adequate reaction of the ego.

(5) Causes incomplete realizations and thus gives rise to insufficient and inadequate emotional reactions.

(6) Lowers the threshold of consciousness, thereby allowing normally inhibited contents of the unconscious to enter consciousness in the form of autonomous invasions.

512

We find all these effects of *abaissement* in neurosis as well as in schizophrenia. But in neurosis the unity of personality is at least potentially preserved, whereas in schizophrenia it is almost irreparably damaged. Because of this fundamental injury the cleavage between dissociated psychic elements amounts to a real destruction of their former connections.

The psychogenesis of schizophrenia therefore prompts us to ask, first of all: Can the primary symptom, the extreme *abaissement*, be considered an effect of psychological conflicts and other disorders of an emotional nature, or not? I do not think it necessary to discuss in detail whether or not the *secondary symptoms*, as described by Bleuler, owe their existence and their specific form to psychological determination. Bleuler himself is fully convinced that their form and content, i.e., their individual phenomenology, are derived entirely from emotional complexes. I agree with Bleuler, whose experience of the psychogenesis of secondary symptoms coincides with my own, for we were collaborating in the years which preceded his famous book on dementia praecox. As a matter of fact, I began as early as 1903 to analyse cases of schizophrenia for therapeutic purposes. There can, indeed, be no doubt about the psychological determination of secondary symptoms. Their structure and origin are in no way different from those of neurotic symptoms, with, of course, the important exception that they exhibit all the characteristics of mental contents no longer subordinated to the supreme control of a complete personality. There is, as a matter of fact, hardly one secondary symptom which does not show some signs of a typical *abaissement*. This characteristic, however, does not depend upon psychogenesis but derives entirely from the primary symptom. Psychological causes, in other words, produce secondary symptoms exclusively on the basis of the primary condition.

513 In dealing with the question of psychogenesis in schizophrenia, therefore, we can dismiss the secondary symptoms altogether. There is only one problem, and that is the psychogenesis of the primary condition, i.e., the extreme *abaissement*, which is, from the psychological point of view, the root of the schizophrenic disorder. We therefore ask: Is there any reason to believe that the *abaissement* can be due to causes which are strictly psychological? An *abaissement* can be produced—as we well know—by many causes: by fatigue, normal sleep, intoxication, fever, anaemia, intense affects, shocks, organic diseases of the central nervous system; likewise it can be induced by mass-psychology or a primitive mentality, or by religious and political fanaticism, etc. It can also be caused by constitutional and hereditary factors.

514 The more common form of *abaissement* does not affect the unity of the personality, at least not seriously. Thus all dissociations and other psychic phenomena derived from this general form of *abaissement* bear the stamp of the integral personality.

515 Neuroses are specific consequences of an *abaissement*; as a rule they arise from a habitual or chronic form of it. Where they appear to be the effect of an acute form, a more or less latent psychological disposition always existed prior to the *abaissement*, so that the latter is no more than a conditional cause.

516 Now there is no doubt that an *abaissement* which leads to a neurosis is produced either by exclusively psychological factors or by these in conjunction with other, perhaps more physical, conditions. Any *abaissement*, particularly one that leads to a neurosis, means in itself that there is a weakening of the supreme control. A neurosis is a relative dissociation, a conflict between the ego and a resistant force based upon unconscious contents. These contents have more or less lost their connection with the psychic totality. They form themselves into fragments, and the loss of them means a depotentiation of the conscious personality. The intense conflict, on the other hand, expresses an equally intense desire to re-establish the severed connection. There is no co-operation, but at least there is a violent conflict, which functions instead of a positive connection. Every neurotic fights for the maintenance and supremacy of his ego-consciousness and for the subjugation of the resistant unconscious forces. But a patient who allows himself to be swayed by the intrusion of strange contents from the unconscious, a patient who does not fight, who even identifies with the morbid elements, immediately exposes himself to the suspicion of schizophrenia. His *abaissement* has reached the fatal, extreme degree, when the ego loses all power to resist the onslaught of an apparently more powerful unconscious.

517 Neurosis lies on this side of the critical point, schizophrenia on the other. We do not doubt that psychological motives can bring about an *abaissement* which eventually results in a neurosis. A neurosis approaches the danger line, yet somehow it manages to remain on the hither side. If it should transgress the line it would cease to be a neurosis. Yet are we quite certain that a neurosis never steps beyond the danger-line? You know that there are such cases, neuroses to all appearances for many years, and then it suddenly happens that the patient steps beyond the line and clearly transforms himself into a real psychotic.

518 Now, what do we say in such a case? We say that it has always

been a psychosis, a "latent" one, or one concealed or camouflaged by an ostensible neurosis. But what has really happened? For many years the patient fought for the maintenance of his ego, for the supremacy of his control and for the unity of his personality. But at last he gave in—he succumbed to the invader he could no longer suppress. He is not just overcome by a violent emotion, he is actually drowned in a flood of insurmountably strong forces and thought-forms which go far beyond any ordinary emotion, no matter how violent. These unconscious forces and contents have long existed in him and he has wrestled with them successfully for years. As a matter of fact, these strange contents are not confined to the patient alone, they exist in the unconscious of normal people as well, who, however, are fortunate enough to be profoundly ignorant of them. These forces did not originate in our patient out of nowhere. They are most emphatically not the result of poisoned brain-cells, but are normal constituents of our unconscious psyche. They appeared in numberless dreams, in the same or a similar form, at a time of life when seemingly nothing was wrong. And they appear in the dreams of normal people who never get anywhere near a psychosis. But if a normal individual should suddenly undergo a dangerous *abaissement*, his dreams would instantly seize hold of him and make him think, feel, and act exactly like a lunatic. And he would be a lunatic, like the man in one of Andreyev's stories, who thought he could safely bark at the moon because he knew that he was perfectly normal. But when he barked he lost consciousness of the little bit of difference between normal and crazy, so that the other side overwhelmed him and he became mad.

519   What happened was that our patient succumbed to an attack of weakness—in reality it is often just a sudden panic—it made him hopeless or desperate, and then all the suppressed material welled up and drowned him.

520   In my experience of almost forty years I have seen quite a number of cases who developed either a psychotic interval or a lasting psychosis out of a neurotic condition. Let us assume for the moment that they were really suffering from a latent psychosis, concealed under the cloak of a neurosis. What, then, is a latent psychosis exactly? It is obviously nothing but the possibility that an individual may become mentally deranged at

401

some period of his life. The existence of strange unconscious material proves nothing. You find the same material in neurotics, modern artists, and poets, and also in fairly normal people who have submitted to a careful investigation of their dreams. Moreover, you find most suggestive parallels in the mythology and symbolism of all races and times. The possibility of a future psychosis has nothing to do with the peculiar contents of the unconscious. But it has everything to do with whether the individual can stand a certain panic, or the chronic strain of a psyche at war with itself. Very often it is simply a matter of a little bit too much, of the drop that falls into a vessel already full, or of the spark that accidentally lands on a heap of gunpowder.

521   Under the stress of an extreme *abaissement* the psychic totality falls apart and splits up into complexes, and the ego-complex ceases to play the important role among these. It is just one among several complexes which are all equally important, or perhaps even more important than the ego. All these complexes assume a personal character although they remain fragments. It is understandable that people should get panicky, or that they eventually become demoralized under a chronic strain, or despair of their hopes and expectations. It is also understandable that their will-power weakens and their self-control becomes slack and begins to lose its grip upon circumstances, moods, and thoughts. It is quite consistent with such a state of mind if some particularly unruly parts of the patient's psyche then acquire a certain degree of autonomy.

522   Thus far schizophrenia does not behave in any way differently from a purely psychological disorder. We would search in vain for anything characteristic of the disease in this part of the symptomatology. The real trouble begins with the disintegration of the personality and the divestment of the ego-complex of its habitual supremacy. As I have already pointed out, not even multiple personality, or certain religious or "mystical" phenomena, can be compared to what happens in schizophrenia. The primary symptom seems to have no analogy with any kind of functional disturbance. It is as if the very foundations of the psyche were giving way, as if an explosion or an earthquake were tearing asunder the structure of a normally built house. I use this analogy on purpose, because it is suggested by the symptomatology of the initial stages. Sollier has given us a vivid

523 description of these *troubles cénesthésiques*,[3] which are compared to explosions, pistol-shots, and other violent noises in the head. They appear in projection as earthquakes, cosmic catastrophes, as the fall of the stars, the splitting of the sun, the falling asunder of the moon, the transformation of people into corpses, the freezing of the universe, and so on.

524 I have just said that the primary symptom appears to have no analogy with any kind of functional disturbance, yet I have omitted to mention the phenomena of the *dream*. Dreams can produce similar pictures of great catastrophes. They can manifest all stages of personal disintegration, so it is no exaggeration to say that the dreamer is normally insane, or that insanity is a dream which has replaced normal consciousness. To say that insanity is a dream which has become real is no metaphor. The phenomenology of the dream and of schizophrenia are almost identical, with a certain difference, of course; for the one occurs normally under the condition of sleep, while the other upsets the waking or conscious state. Sleep, too, is an *abaissement du niveau mental* which leads to more or less complete oblivion of the ego. The psychic mechanism that brings about the normal extinction and disintegration of consciousness in sleep is therefore a normal function which almost obeys our will. In schizophrenia it seems as if this function were set in motion in order to bring about that sleep-like condition in which consciousness is reduced to the level of dreams, or in which dreams are intensified to a degree equalling that of consciousness.

Yet even if we knew that the primary symptom is produced with the aid of an ever-present normal function, we should still have to explain why a pathological condition ensues instead of the normal effect, which is sleep. It must, however, be emphasized that it is not exactly sleep which is produced, but something which disturbs sleep, namely, the dream. Dreams are due to an incomplete extinction of consciousness, or to a somewhat excited state of the unconscious which interferes with sleep. Sleep is disturbed if too many remnants of consciousness go on stirring, or if there are unconscious contents with too great an energy-charge, for then they rise above the threshold and create a relatively conscious state. Hence it is better to explain many

3 [Cf. *Le Mécanisme des émotions*, ch. IV, esp. p. 208.—EDITORS.]

403

dreams as the remnants of conscious impressions, while others derive directly from unconscious sources which have never been conscious. Dreams of the first type have a personal character and conform to the rules of a personalistic psychology; those of the second type have a collective character, inasmuch as they contain peculiarly mythological, legendary, or generally archaic imagery. One must turn to historical or primitive symbology in order to explain such dreams.

525 Both types of dream are reflected in the symptomatology of schizophrenia. There is a mixture of personal and collective material just as there is in dreams. But in contradistinction to normal dreams, the collective material seems to predominate. This is particularly evident in the so-called "dream-states" or delirious intervals and in paranoid conditions. It seems also to predominate in the catatonic phases, so far as we can get any insight into the inner experiences of such patients. Whenever collective material prevails under normal conditions, it produces important dreams. Primitives call them "big dreams" and consider them of tribal significance. You find the same thing in the Greek and Roman civilizations, where such dreams were reported to the Areopagus or to the Senate. One meets these dreams frequently in the decisive moments or periods of life: in childhood from the third to the sixth year; at puberty, from fourteen to sixteen; in the period of maturity from twenty to twenty-five; in middle life from thirty-five to forty; and before death. They also occur in particularly important psychological situations. It seems that such dreams come chiefly at those moments or periods when the man of antiquity or the primitive would deem it necessary to perform certain religious or magic rites, in order to procure favourable results or to propitiate the gods for the same end.

526 We may safely assume that important personal matters and worries account for personal dreams. We are not so sure of our ground when we come to collective dreams, with their often weird and archaic imagery, which cannot be traced back to personal sources. The history of symbols, however, yields the most surprising and enlightening parallels, without which we could never follow up the remarkable meaning of such dreams.

527 This fact makes one realize how inadequate the psychological training of the psychiatrist is. It is, of course, impossible to

528 appreciate the importance of comparative psychology for the theory of delusions without a detailed knowledge of historical and ethnic symbols. No sooner did we begin with the qualitative analysis of schizophrenia at the Psychiatric Clinic in Zurich than we realized the need of such additional information. We naturally started with an entirely personalistic medical psychology, mainly as presented by Freud. But we soon came up against the fact that, in its basic structure, the human psyche is as little personalistic as the body. It is far rather something inherited and universal. The logic of the intellect, the *raison du cœur*, the emotions, the instincts, the basic images and forms of imagination, have in a way more resemblance to Kant's table of *a priori* categories or to Plato's *eida* than to the scurrilities, circumstantialities, whims, and tricks of our personal minds. Schizophrenia in particular yields an immense harvest of collective symbols, the neuroses yield far less, for with few exceptions they show a predominantly personal psychology. The fact that schizophrenia disrupts the foundations of the psyche accounts for the abundance of collective symbols, because it is the latter material that constitutes the basic structure of the personality.

From this point of view we might conclude that the schizophrenic state of mind, so far as it yields archaic material, has all the characteristics of a "big dream"—in other words, that it is an important event, exhibiting the same "numinous" quality which in primitive cultures is attributed to a magic ritual. As a matter of fact, the insane person has always enjoyed the prerogative of being the one who is possessed by spirits or haunted by a demon. This is, by the way, a correct interpretation of his psychic condition, for he is invaded by autonomous figures and thoughtforms. The primitive valuation of insanity, moreover, lays stress on a special characteristic which we should not overlook: it ascribes personality, initiative, and wilful intention to the unconscious—again a true interpretation of the obvious facts. From the primitive standpoint it is perfectly clear that the unconscious, of its own volition, has taken possession of the ego. According to this view it is not the ego that is enfeebled; on the contrary, it is the unconscious that is strengthened through the presence of a demon. The primitive, therefore, does not seek the cause of insanity in a primary weakness of consciousness but rather in an inordinate strength of the unconscious.

529   I must admit it is exceedingly difficult to decide the intricate question of whether it is a matter of a primary weakness and corresponding dissociability of consciousness, or of the primary strength of the unconscious. The latter possibility cannot easily be dismissed, since it is conceivable that the abundant archaic material in schizophrenia is the expression of a still existing infantile and therefore primitive mentality. It might be a question of *atavism*. I seriously consider the possibility of a so-called "arrested development," in which a more than normal amount of primitive psychology remains intact and does not become adapted to modern conditions. It is natural that under such conditions a considerable part of the psyche should not catch up with the normal progress of consciousness. In the course of years the distance between the unconscious and the conscious mind increases and produces a conflict—latent at first. But when a special effort at adaptation is needed, and when consciousness should draw upon its unconscious instinctive resources, the conflict becomes manifest; the hitherto latent primitive mind suddenly bursts forth with contents that are too incomprehensible and too strange for assimilation to be possible. Indeed, such a moment marks the beginning of the psychosis in a great number of cases.

530   It should not be overlooked that many patients seem quite capable of exhibiting a modern and sufficiently developed consciousness, sometimes of a particularly concentrated, rational, obstinate kind. However, one must quickly add that such a consciousness shows early signs of a defensive nature. This is a symptom of weakness, not of strength.

531   It may be that in schizophrenia a normal consciousness is confronted with an unusually strong unconscious: it may also be that the patient's consciousness is just weak and therefore unable to keep back the inrush of unconscious material. In practice I must allow for the existence of two groups of schizophrenia: one with a weak consciousness and the other with a strong unconscious. We have here a certain analogy with the neuroses, where we also find plenty of patients with a markedly weak consciousness and little will-power, and others who possess remarkable energy but are subjected to an almost overwhelm-

532   ingly strong unconscious determination. This is particularly the case when creative impulses (artistic or otherwise) are coupled with unconscious incompatibilities.

If we now return to our original question, the psychogenesis of schizophrenia, we reach the conclusion that the problem itself is rather complicated. At all events we ought to make it clear that the term "psychogenesis" means two different things: (1) an exclusively psychological origin, (2) a number of psychological conditions. We have dealt with the second point, but we have not yet touched upon the first. This envisages psychogenesis from the standpoint of a *causa efficiens*. The question is: Is the sole and absolute cause of schizophrenia a psychological one or not?

533   Over the whole field of medicine such a question is, as you know, more than embarrassing. Only in a very few cases can it be answered positively. The usual aetiology consists in a competition between various conditions. It has therefore been urged that the word *causality* or *cause* should be expunged from the medical vocabulary and replaced by the term "conditionalism." I am absolutely in favour of such a measure, since it is well-nigh impossible to prove, even approximately, that schizophrenia is an organic disease to begin with. It is equally impossible to make its exclusively psychological origin evident. We may have strong suspicions as to the organic nature of the primary symptom, but we cannot ignore the well-established fact that there are many cases which developed out of an emotional shock, a disappointment, a difficult situation, a reversal of fortune, etc.; and also that many relapses as well as improvements are due to psychological conditions. What are we to say about a case like the following? A young student experiences a great disappointment in a love-affair. He has a catatonic attack, from which he recovers after several months. He then finishes his studies and becomes a successful professional man. After a number of years he returns to Zurich, where he had experienced his love-affair. Instantly he is seized by a new and very similar attack. He says that he believes he saw the girl somewhere. He recovers and avoids Zurich for several years. Then he returns and in a few days he is back in the clinic with a catatonic attack, again because he is under the impression that he has seen the girl, who by that time was married and had children.

534   My teacher, Eugen Bleuler, used to say that a psychological cause can produce only the symptoms of the disease, but not the disease itself. This statement may be profound or the reverse. At all events it shows the psychiatrist's dilemma. One could say, for instance, that our patient returned to Zurich when he felt the disease coming on, and one thinks one has said something clever. He denies it—naturally, you will say. But it is a fact that this man was still deeply in love with his girl. He never went near another woman and his thoughts kept on returning to Zurich. What could be more natural than that once in a while he should give way to his unconquered longing to see the streets, the houses, the walks again, where he had met her, insanity or not? We do not know, moreover, what ecstasies and adventures he experienced in his insanity and what thrilling expectations tempted him to seek the experience once more. I once treated a schizophrenic girl who told me that she hated me because I had made it impossible for her to return into her beautiful psychosis. I have heard my psychiatric colleagues say, "That was no schizophrenia." But they did not know that they, together with at least three other specialists, had made the diagnosis themselves, for they were ignorant of the fact that my patient was identical with the one they had diagnosed.

535   Shall we now say that our patient became ill before he fell in love and before he returned to Zurich? If that is so, then we are bound to make the paradoxical statement that when he was still normal he was already ill and on account of his illness he fell in love, and for the same reason he returned to the fatal place. Or shall we say that the shock of his passionate love was too much for him and instead of committing suicide he became insane, and that it was his longing which brought him back again to the place of the fatal memories?

536   But surely, it will be objected, not everybody becomes insane on account of a disappointment in love. Certainly not, just as little as everyone commits suicide, falls so passionately in love, or remains true to the first love for ever. Shall we lay more stress on the assumption of an organic weakness, for which we have no tangible evidence, or on his passion, for which we have all the symptoms?

537   The far-reaching consequences of the initial *abaissement*, however, constitute a serious objection to the hypothesis of pure

538 psychogenesis. Unfortunately nearly all that we know of the primary symptom, and its supposedly organic nature, amounts to a series of question marks, whereas our knowledge of possibly psychogenic conditions consists of many carefully observed facts. There are indeed organic cases with brain-oedema and lethal outcome. But they are a small minority and it is not certain whether such a disease should be called schizophrenia.

A serious objection against the psychogenesis of schizophrenia is the bad prognosis, the incurability, and the ultimate dementia. But, as I pointed out twenty years ago,[4] the hospital statistics are based chiefly upon a selection of the worst cases; all the milder cases are excluded.

539 Two facts have impressed themselves on me during my career as a psychiatrist and psychotherapist. One is the enormous change that the average mental hospital has undergone in my lifetime. That whole desperate crowd of utterly degenerate catatonics has practically disappeared, simply because they have been given something to do. The other fact that impressed me is the discovery I made when I began my psychotherapeutic practice: I was amazed at the number of schizophrenics whom we almost never see in psychiatric hospitals. These cases are partially camouflaged as obsessional neuroses, compulsions, phobias, and hysterias, and they are very careful never to go near an asylum. These patients insist upon treatment, and I found myself, Bleuler's loyal disciple, trying my hand on cases we never would have dreamed of touching if we had had them in the clinic, cases unmistakably schizophrenic even before treatment—I felt hopelessly unscientific in treating them at all—and after the treatment I was told that they could never have been schizophrenic in the first place. There are numbers of latent psychoses—and quite a few that are not so latent—which, under favourable conditions, can be subjected to psychological analysis, sometimes with quite decent results. Even if I am not very hopeful about a patient, I try to give him as much psychology as he can stand, because I have seen plenty of cases where the later attacks were less severe, and the prognosis was better, as a result of increased psychological understanding. At least so it seemed to me. You know how difficult it is to judge these things

4 Cf. supra, "On the Problem of Psychogenesis in Mental Disease."

correctly. In such doubtful matters, where you have to work as a pioneer, you must be able to put some trust in your intuition and to follow your feeling even at the risk of going wrong. To make a correct diagnosis, and to nod your head gravely at a bad prognosis, is the less important aspect of the medical art. It can even cripple your enthusiasm, and in psychotherapy enthusiasm is the secret of success.

540   The results of occupational therapy in mental hospitals have clearly shown that the status of hopeless cases can be enormously improved. And the much milder cases not in hospitals sometimes show encouraging results under psychotherapeutic treatment. I do not want to appear overoptimistic. Often enough one can do little or nothing at all; or again, one can have unexpected results. For about fourteen years I have been seeing a woman, who is now sixty-four years of age. I never see her more than fifteen times in the course of a year. She is a schizophrenic and has twice spent a number of months in hospital with an acute psychosis. She suffers from numberless voices distributed all over her body. I found one voice which was fairly reasonable and helpful. I tried to cultivate that voice, with the result that for about two years the right side of the body has been free of voices. Only the left side is still under the domination of the unconscious. No further attacks have occurred. Unfortunately, the patient is not intelligent. Her mentality is early medieval, and I was able to establish a fairly good rapport with her only by adapting my terminology to that of the early Middle Ages. There were no hallucinations then; it was all devils and witchcraft.

541   This is not a brilliant case, but I have found that I always learn most from difficult and even impossible patients. I treat such cases as if they were not organic, as if they were psychogenic and as if one could cure them by purely psychological means. I admit that I cannot imagine how something "merely" psychic can cause an *abaissement* which destroys the unity of personality, only too often beyond repair. But I know from long experience not only that the overwhelming majority of symptoms are psychologically determined, but that in an unspecified number of cases the onset of the disease is influenced by, or at least coupled with, psychic facts which one would not hesitate to declare causal in a case of neurosis. Statistics in this respect prove nothing to me, for I know that even in a neurosis one is

likely to discover the true anamnesis only after months of careful analysis. In psychiatric anamnesis there is a lack of psychological knowledge which is sometimes appalling. I do not say that the general practitioner should have a knowledge of psychology, but if the psychiatrist wants to practise psychotherapy at all he certainly ought to have a proper psychological training. What we call "medical psychology" is unfortunately a very one-sided affair. It may give you some knowledge of everyday complexes, but far too little is known of anything outside the medical department. Psychology does not consist of medical rules of thumb. It has far more to do with the history of civilization, of philosophy, of religion, and quite particularly with the primitive mentality. The pathological mind is a vast, almost unexplored region and comparatively little has been done in this field, whereas the biology, anatomy, and physiology of schizophrenia have had all the attention they want. And with all this work, what exact knowledge have we of the heredity or of the nature of the primary symptom? I should say: Let us discuss the question of psychogenesis once more when the psychic side of schizophrenia has had a square deal.

THE PSYCHOLOGY OF THE TRANSFERENCE

INTRODUCTION

1

Bellica pax, vulnus dulce, suave malum.
(A warring peace, a sweet wound, a mild evil.)
—JOHN GOWER, *Confessio amantis*, II, p. 35

353   The fact that the idea of the mystic marriage plays such an important part in alchemy is not so surprising when we remember that the term most frequently employed for it, *coniunctio*, referred in the first place to what we now call chemical combination, and that the substances or "bodies" to be combined were drawn together by what we would call affinity. In days gone by, people used a variety of terms which all expressed a human, and more particularly an erotic, relationship, such as *nuptiae, matrimonium, coniugium, amicitia, attractio, adulatio.* Accordingly the bodies to be combined were thought of as *agens et patiens*, as *vir* or *masculus*, and as *femina, mulier, femineus;* or they were described more picturesquely as dog and bitch,[1] horse (stallion) and donkey,[2] cock and hen,[3] and as the winged and wingless dragon.[4] The more anthropomorphic and theriomorphic the terms become, the more obvious is the part played by creative fantasy and thus by the unconscious, and

1 "Accipe canem corascenum masculum et caniculum Armeniae" ("Take a Corascene dog and an Armenian bitch").—"De alchimiae difficultatibus," *Theatrum chemicum*, I, p. 163. A quotation from Kalid (in the *Rosarium, Artis auriferae,* II, p. 248) runs: "Accipe canem coetaneum et catulam Armeniae" ("Take a Coetanean dog and an Armenian bitch). In a magic papyrus, Selene (moon) is called κύων (bitch).—Paris MS. Z 2280, in Preisendanz, *Papyri Graecae Magicae,* I, p. 142. In Zosimos, dog and wolf.—Berthelot, *Alchimistes grecs,* III, xii, 9. [No translation of the words *corascenum* and *coetaneum* has been attempted, as we are advised that they are probably corrupt, or may indicate geographical names. —EDITORS.]

2 Zosimos, in Berthelot, *Alch. grecs,* III, xii, 9.

3 The classical passage is to be found in Senior, *De chemia,* p. 8: "Tu mei indiges, sicut gallus gallinae indiget" (You need me as the cock needs the hen).

4 Numerous pictures exist in the literature.

413

the more we see how the natural philosophers of old were tempted, as their thoughts explored the dark, unknown qualities of matter, to slip away from a strictly chemical investigation and to fall under the spell of the "myth of matter." Since there can never be absolute freedom from prejudice, even the most objective and impartial investigator is liable to become the victim of some unconscious assumption upon entering a region where the darkness has never been illuminated and where he can recognize nothing. This need not necessarily be a misfortune, since the idea which then presents itself as a substitute for the unknown will take the form of an archaic though not inapposite analogy. Thus Kekulé's vision of the dancing couples,[5] which first put him on the track of the structure of certain carbon compounds, namely the benzene ring, was surely a vision of the *coniunctio*, the mating that had preoccupied the minds of the alchemists for seventeen centuries. It was precisely this image that had always lured the mind of the investigator away from the problem of chemistry and back to the ancient myth of the royal or divine marriage; but in Kekulé's vision it reached its chemical goal in the end, thus rendering the greatest imaginable service both to our understanding of organic compounds and to the subsequent unprecedented advances in synthetic chemistry. Looking back, we can say that the alchemists had keen noses when they made this *arcanum arcanorum*,[6] this *donum Dei et secretum altissimi*,[7] this inmost mystery of the art of gold-making, the climax of their work. The subsequent confirmation of the other idea central to gold-making—the transmutability of chemical elements—also takes a worthy place in this belated triumph of alchemical thought. Considering the eminently practical and theoretical importance of these two key ideas, we might well conclude that they were intuitive anticipations whose fascination can be explained in the light of later developments.[8]

5 Kekulé, *Lehrbuch der organischen Chemie*, I, pp. 624f., and Fierz-David, *Die Entwicklungsgeschichte der Chemie*, pp. 235ff.

6 Zacharius, "Opusculum," *Theatr. chem.*, I, p. 826.

7 "Consilium coniugii," *Ars chemica*, p. 259. Cf. *Aurora consurgens*, I, Ch. II: "Est namque donum et sacramentum Dei atque res divina" (For she [Wisdom] is a gift and sacrament of God and a divine matter).

8 This does not contradict the fact that the *coniunctio* motif owes its fascination primarily to its archetypal character.

354   We find, however, that alchemy did not merely change into chemistry by gradually discovering how to break away from its mythological premises, but that it also became, or had always been, a kind of mystic philosophy. The idea of the *coniunctio* served on the one hand to shed light on the mystery of chemical combination, while on the other it became the symbol of the *unio mystica*, since, as a mythologem, it expresses the archetype of the union of opposites. Now the archetypes do not represent anything external, non-psychic, although they do of course owe the concreteness of their imagery to impressions received from without. Rather, independently of, and sometimes in direct contrast to, the outward forms they may take, they represent the life and essence of a non-individual psyche. Although this psyche is innate in every individual it can neither be modified not possessed by him personally. It is the same in the individual as it is in the crowd and ultimately in everybody. It is the precondition of each individual psyche, just as the sea is the carrier of the individual wave.

355   The alchemical image of the *coniunctio*, whose practical importance was proved at a later stage of development, is equally valuable from the psychological point of view: that is to say, it plays the same role in the exploration of the darkness of the psyche as it played in the investigation of the riddle of matter. Indeed, it could never have worked so effectively in the material world had it not already possessed the power to fascinate and thus to fix the attention of the investigator along those lines. The *coniunctio* is an *a priori* image that occupies a prominent place in the history of man's mental development. If we trace this idea back we find it has two sources in alchemy, one Christian, the other pagan. The Christian source is unmistakably the doctrine of Christ and the Church, *sponsus* and *sponsa*, where Christ takes the role of Sol and the Church that of Luna.[9] The pagan source is on the one hand the hierosgamos,[10] on the other the marital union of the mystic with God.[11] These psychic experiences and the traces they have left behind in tradition explain much that would otherwise

9 Cf. the detailed account in Rahner, "Mysterium lunae."

10 A collection of the classical sources is to be found in Klinz, Ἱερὸς γάμος.

11 Bousset, *Hauptprobleme der Gnosis*, pp. 69ff., 263f., 315ff.; Leisegang, *Der heilige Geist*, I, p. 235.

356 be totally unintelligible in the strange world of alchemy and its secret language.

As we have said, the image of the *coniunctio* has always occupied an important place in the history of the human mind. Recent developments in medical psychology have, through observation of the mental processes in neuroses and psychoses, forced us to become more and more thorough in our investigation of the psychic background, commonly called the unconscious. It is psychotherapy above all that makes such investigations necessary, because it can no longer be denied that morbid disturbances of the psyche are not to be explained exclusively by the changes going on in the body or in the conscious mind; we must adduce a third factor by way of explanation, namely hypothetical unconscious processes.[12]

357 Practical analysis has shown that unconscious contents are invariably projected at first upon concrete persons and situations. Many projections can ultimately be integrated back into the individual once he has recognized their subjective origin; others resist integration, and although they may be detached from their original objects, they thereupon transfer themselves to the doctor. Among these contents the relation to the parent of opposite sex plays a particularly important part, i.e., the relation of son to mother, daughter to father, and also that of brother to sister.[13] As a rule this complex cannot be integrated completely, since the doctor is nearly always put in the place of the father, the brother, and even (though naturally more rarely) the mother. Experience has shown that this projection persists with all its original intensity (which Freud regarded as aetiological), thus creating a bond that corresponds in every respect to the initial infantile relationship, with a tendency to recapitulate all the experiences of childhood on the doctor. In other words, the neurotic maladjustment of the patient is now

12 I call unconscious processes "hypothetical" because the unconscious is by definition not amenable to direct observation and can only be inferred.

13 I am not considering the so-called homosexual forms, such as father-son, mother-daughter, etc. In alchemy, as far as I know, this variation is alluded to only once, in the "Visio Arislei" (*Art. aurif.*, I, p. 147): "Domine, quamvis rex sis, male tamen imperas et regis: masculos namque masculis coniunxisti, sciens quod masculi non gignunt" (Lord, though thou art king, yet thou rulest and governest badly; for thou hast joined males with males, knowing that males do not produce offspring).

transferred to him.[14] Freud, who was the first to recognize and describe this phenomenon, coined the term "transference neurosis."[15]

358   This bond is often of such intensity that we could almost speak of a "combination." When two chemical substances combine, both are altered. This is precisely what happens in the transference. Freud rightly recognized that this bond is of the greatest therapeutic importance in that it gives rise to a *mixtum compositum* of the doctor's own mental health and the patient's maladjustment. In Freudian technique the doctor tries to ward off the transference as much as possible—which is understandable enough from the human point of view, though in certain cases it may considerably impair the therapeutic effect. It is inevitable that the doctor should be influenced to a certain extent and even that his nervous health should suffer.[16]

14 Freud says (*Introductory Lectures*, Part III, p. 455): "The decisive part of the work is achieved by creating in the patient's relation to the doctor—in the 'transference'—new editions of the old conflicts; in these the patient would like to behave in the same way as he did in the past. . . . In place of the patient's true illness there appears the artificially constructed transference illness, in place of the various unreal objects of his libido there appears a single, and once more imaginary, object in the person of the doctor." It is open to doubt whether the transference is always constructed artificially, since it is a phenomenon that can take place quite apart from any treatment, and is moreover a very frequent natural occurrence. Indeed, in any human relationship that is at all intimate, certain transference phenomena will almost always operate as helpful or disturbing factors.

15 "Provided only that the patient shows compliance enough to respect the necessary conditions of the analysis, we regularly succeed in giving all the symptoms of the illness a new transference meaning and in replacing his ordinary neurosis by a 'transference-neurosis'. . . ." ("Remembering, Repeating, and Working-Through," p. 154.) Freud puts down a little too much to his own account here. A transference is not by any means always the work of the doctor. Often it is in full swing before he has even opened his mouth. Freud's conception of the transference as a "new edition of the old disorder," a "newly created and transformed neurosis," or a "new, artificial neurosis" (*Introductory Lectures*, III, p. 444), is right in so far as the transference of a neurotic patient is equally neurotic, but this neurosis is neither new nor artificial nor created: it is the same old neurosis, and the only new thing about it is that the doctor is now drawn into the vortex, more as its victim than as its creator.

16 Freud had already discovered the phenomenon of the "counter-transference." Those acquainted with his technique will be aware of its marked tendency to keep the person of the doctor as far as possible beyond the reach of this effect.

He quite literally "takes over" the sufferings of his patient and shares them with him. For this reason he runs a risk—and must run it in the nature of things.[17] The enormous importance that Freud attached to the transference phenomenon became clear to me at our first personal meeting in 1907. After a conversation lasting many hours there came a pause. Suddenly he asked me out of the blue, "And what do you think about the transference?" I replied with the deepest conviction that it was the alpha and omega of the analytical method, whereupon he said, "Then you have grasped the main thing."

359   The great importance of the transference has often led to the mistaken idea that it is absolutely indispensable for a cure, that it must be demanded from the patient, so to speak. But a thing like that can no more be demanded than faith, which is only valuable when it is spontaneous. Enforced faith is nothing but spiritual cramp. Anyone who thinks that he must "demand" a transference is forgetting that this is only one of the therapeutic factors, and that the very word "transference" is closely akin to "projection"—a phenomenon that cannot possibly be demanded.[18] I personally am always glad when there is only a

Hence the doctor's preference for sitting behind the patient, also his pretence that the transference is a product of his technique, whereas in reality it is a perfectly natural phenomenon that can happen to him just as it can happen to the teacher, the clergyman, the general practitioner, and—last but not least—the husband. Freud also uses the expression "transference-neurosis" as a collective term for hysteria, hysterical fears, and compulsion neuroses (Ibid., p. 445).

[17] The effects of this on the doctor or nurse can be very far-reaching. I know of cases where, in dealing with borderline schizophrenics, short psychotic intervals were actually "taken over," and during these periods it happened that the patients were feeling more than ordinarily well. I have even met a case of induced paranoia in a doctor who was analysing a woman patient in the early stages of latent persecution mania. This is not so astonishing since certain psychic disturbances can be extremely infectious if the doctor himself has a latent predisposition in that direction.

[18] Freud himself says ("Observations on Transference-Love," p. 380) of this: "I can hardly imagine a more senseless proceeding. In doing so, an analyst robs the phenomenon of the element of spontaneity which is so convincing and lays up obstacles for himself in the future which are hard to overcome." Here Freud stresses the "spontaneity" of the transference, in contrast to his views quoted above. Nevertheless those who "demand" the transference can fall back on the following cryptic utterance of their master ("Fragment of an Analysis of a Case of Hysteria," p. 116): "If the theory of analytic technique is gone into, it becomes

mild transference or when it is practically unnoticeable. Far less claim is then made upon one as a person, and one can be satisfied with other therapeutically effective factors. Among these the patient's own insight plays an important part, also his good-will, the doctor's authority, suggestion,[19] good advice,[20] under-standing, sympathy, encouragement, etc. Naturally the more serious cases do not come into this category.

360 Careful analysis of the transference phenomenon yields an extremely complicated picture with such startlingly pronounced features that we are often tempted to pick out one of them as the most important and then exclaim by way of explanation: "Of course, it's nothing but . . . !" I am referring chiefly to the erotic or sexual aspect of transference fantasies. The ex-istence of this aspect is undeniable, but it is not always the only one and not always the essential one. Another is the will to power (described by Adler), which proves to be coexistent with sexuality, and it is often very difficult to make out which of the two predominates. These two aspects alone offer sufficient grounds for a paralysing conflict.

361 There are, however, other forms of instinctive *concupis-centia* that come more from "hunger," from wanting to pos-sess; others again are based on the instinctive negation of desire, so that life seems to be founded on fear or self-destruction. A certain *abaissement du niveau mental*, i.e., a weakness in the hierarchical order of the ego, is enough to set these instinctive urges and desires in motion and bring about a dissociation of personality—in other words, a multiplication of its centres of gravity. (In schizophrenia there is an actual fragmentation of personality.) These dynamic components must be regarded as real or symptomatic, vitally decisive or merely syndromal, ac-cording to the degree of their predominance. Although the strongest instincts undoubtedly demand concrete realization

evident that transference is [something necessarily demanded]." [". . . that trans-ference is an inevitable necessity," as in the authorized translation, is to stretch the meaning of Freud's "etwas notwendig Gefordertes."—TRANS.]

[19] Suggestion happens of its own accord, without the doctor's being able to pre-vent it or taking the slightest trouble to produce it.

[20] "Good advice" is often a doubtful remedy, but generally not dangerous because it has so little effect. It is one of the things the public expects in the *persona medici.*

and generally enforce it, they cannot be considered exclusively biological since the course they actually follow is subject to powerful modifications coming from the personality itself. If a man's temperament inclines him to a spiritual attitude, even the concrete activity of the instincts will take on a certain symbolical character. This activity is no longer the mere satisfaction of instinctual impulses, for it is now associated with or complicated by "meanings." In the case of purely syndromal instinctive processes, which do not demand concrete realization to the same extent, the symbolical character of their fulfilment is all the more marked. The most vivid examples of these complications are probably to be found in erotic phenomenology. Four stages of eroticism were known in the late classical period: Hawwah (Eve), Helen (of Troy), the Virgin Mary, and Sophia. The series is repeated in Goethe's *Faust:* in the figures of Gretchen as the personification of a purely instinctual relationship (Eve); Helen as an anima figure; [21] Mary as the personification of the "heavenly," i.e., Christian or religious, relationship; and the "eternal feminine" as an expression of the alchemical *Sapientia.* As the nomenclature shows, we are dealing with the heterosexual Eros or anima-figure in four stages, and consequently with four stages of the Eros cult. The first stage—Hawwah, Eve, earth—is purely biological; woman is equated with the mother and only represents something to be fertilized. The second stage is still dominated by the sexual Eros, but on an aesthetic and romantic level where woman has already acquired some value as an individual. The third stage raises Eros to the heights of religious devotion and thus spiritualizes him: Hawwah has been replaced by spiritual motherhood. Finally, the fourth stage illustrates something which unexpectedly goes beyond the almost unsurpassable third stage: *Sapientia.* How can wisdom transcend the most holy and the most pure?—Presumably only by virtue of the truth that the less sometimes means the more. This stage represents a spiritualization of Helen and consequently of Eros as such. That is why *Sapientia* was regarded as a parallel to the Shulamite in the Song of Songs.

[21] Simon Magus' Helen (Selene) is another excellent example.

362 Not only are there different instincts which cannot forcibly be reduced to one another, there are also different levels on which they move. In view of this far from simple situation, it is small wonder that the transference—also an instinctive process, in part—is very difficult to interpret and evaluate. The instincts and their specific fantasy-contents are partly concrete, partly symbolical (i.e., "unreal"), sometimes one, sometimes the other, and they have the same paradoxical character wheu they are projected. The transference is far from being a simple phenomenon with only one meaning, and we can never make out beforehand what it is all about. The same applies to its specific content, commonly called incest. We know that it is possible to interpret the fantasy-contents of the instincts either as *signs*, as self-portraits of the instincts, i.e., reductively; or as *symbols*, as the spiritual meaning of the natural instinct. In the former case the instinctive process is taken to be "real" and in the latter "unreal."

363 In any particular case it is often almost impossible to say what is "spirit" and what is "instinct." Together they form an impenetrable mass, a veritable magma sprung from the depths of primeval chaos. When one meets such contents one immediately understands why the psychic equilibrium of the neurotic is disturbed, and why the whole psychic system is broken up in schizophrenia. They emit a fascination which not only grips—and has already gripped—the patient, but can also have an inductive effect on the unconscious of the impartial spectator, in this case the doctor. The burden of these unconscious and chaotic contents lies heavy on the patient; for, although they are present in everybody, it is only in him that they have become active, and they isolate him in a spiritual loneliness which neither he nor anybody else can understand and which is bound to be misinterpreted. Unfortunately, if we do not feel our way into the situation and approach it purely from the outside, it is only too easy to dismiss it with a light word or to push it in the wrong direction. This is what the patient has long been doing on his own account, giving the doctor every opportunity for misinterpretation. At first the secret seems to lie with his

parents, but when this tie has been loosed and the projection withdrawn, the whole weight falls upon the doctor, who is faced with the question: "What are *you* going to do about the transference?"

364   The doctor, by voluntarily and consciously taking over the psychic sufferings of the patient, exposes himself to the overpowering contents of the unconscious and hence also to their inductive action. The case begins to "fascinate" him. Here again it is easy to explain this in terms of personal likes and dislikes, but one overlooks the fact that this would be an instance of *ignotum per ignotius.* In reality these personal feelings, if they exist at all in any decisive degree, are governed by those same unconscious contents which have become activated. An unconscious tie is established and now, in the patient's fantasies, it assumes all the forms and dimensions so profusely described in the literature. The patient, by bringing an activated unconscious content to bear upon the doctor, constellates the corresponding unconscious material in him, owing to the inductive effect which always emanates from projections in greater or lesser degree. Doctor and patient thus find themselves in a relationship founded on mutual unconsciousness.

365   It is none too easy for the doctor to make himself aware of this fact. One is naturally loath to admit that one could be affected in the most personal way by just any patient. But the more unconsciously this happens, the more the doctor will be tempted to adopt an "apotropaic" attitude, and the *persona medici* he hides behind is, or rather seems to be, an admirable instrument for this purpose. Inseparable from the *persona* is the doctor's routine and his trick of knowing everything beforehand, which is one of the favourite props of the well-versed practitioner and of all infallible authority. Yet this lack of insight is an ill counsellor, for the unconscious infection brings with it the therapeutic possibility—which should not be underestimated—of the illness being transferred to the doctor. We must suppose as a matter of course that the doctor is the better able to make the constellated contents conscious, otherwise it would only lead to mutual imprisonment in the same state of unconsciousness. The greatest difficulty here is that contents are often activated in the doctor which might normally remain latent. He might perhaps be so normal as not to need any such

unconscious standpoints to compensate his conscious situation. At least this is often how it looks, though whether it is so in a deeper sense is an open question. Presumably he had good reasons for choosing the profession of psychiatrist and for being particularly interested in the treatment of the psychoneuroses; and he cannot very well do that without gaining some insight into his own unconscious processes. Nor can his concern with the unconscious be explained entirely by a free choice of interests, but rather by a fateful disposition which originally inclined him to the medical profession. The more one sees of human fate and the more one examines its secret springs of action, the more one is impressed by the strength of unconscious motives and by the limitations of free choice. The doctor knows—or at least he should know—that he did not choose this career by chance; and the psychotherapist in particular should clearly understand that psychic infections, however superfluous they seem to him, are in fact the predestined concomitants of his work, and thus fully in accord with the instinctive disposition of his own life. This realization also gives him the right attitude to his patient. The patient then means something to him personally, and this provides the most favourable basis for treatment.

3

366   In the old pre-analytical psychotherapy, going right back to the doctors of the Romantic Age, the transference was already defined as "rapport." It forms the basis of therapeutic influence once the patient's initial projections are dissolved. During this work it becomes clear that the projections can also obscure the judgment of the doctor—to a lesser extent, of course, for otherwise all therapy would be impossible. Although we may justifiably expect the doctor at the very least to be acquainted with the effects of the unconscious on his own person, and may therefore demand that anybody who intends to practise psychotherapy should first submit to a training analysis, yet even the best preparation will not suffice to teach him everything about the unconscious. A complete "emptying" of the unconscious is out of the question, if only because its creative powers are continually producing new formations.

367 Consciousness, no matter how extensive it may be, must always remain the smaller circle within the greater circle of the unconscious, an island surrounded by the sea; and, like the sea itself, the unconscious yields an endless and self-replenishing abundance of living creatures, a wealth beyond our fathoming. We may long have known the meaning, effects, and characteristics of unconscious contents without ever having fathomed their depths and potentialities, for they are capable of infinite variation and can never be depotentiated. The only way to get at them in practice is to try to attain a conscious attitude which allows the unconscious to co-operate instead of being driven into opposition.

368 Even the most experienced psychotherapist will discover again and again that he is caught up in a bond, a combination resting on mutual unconsciousness. And though he may believe himself to be in possession of all the necessary knowledge concerning the constellated archetypes, he will in the end come to realize that there are very many things indeed of which his academic knowledge never dreamed. Each new case that requires thorough treatment is pioneer work, and every trace of routine then proves to be a blind alley. Consequently the higher psychotherapy is a most exacting business and sometimes it sets tasks which challenge not only our understanding or our sympathy, but the whole man. The doctor is inclined to demand this total effort from his patient, yet he must realize that this same demand only works if he is aware that it applies also to himself.

I said earlier that the contents which enter into the transference were as a rule originally projected upon the parents or other members of the family. Owing to the fact that these contents seldom or never lack an erotic aspect or are genuinely sexual in substance (apart from the other factors already mentioned), an incestuous character does undoubtedly attach to them, and this has given rise to the Freudian theory of incest. Their exogamous transference to the doctor does not alter the situation. He is merely drawn into the peculiar atmosphere of family incest through the projection. This necessarily leads to an unreal intimacy which is highly distressing to both doctor and patient and arouses resistance and doubt on both sides. The violent repudiation of Freud's original discoveries gets us nowhere, for we are dealing with an empirically demonstrable fact which meets with such universal confirmation that only the ignorant still try to oppose it. But the interpretation of this fact is, in the very nature of the case, highly controversial. Is it a genuine incestuous instinct or a pathological variation? Or is the incest one of the "arrangements" (Adler) of the will to power? Or is it regression of normal libido [22] to the infantile level, from fear of an apparently impossible task in life? [23] Or is all incest-fantasy purely symbolical, and thus a reactivation of the incest archetype, which plays such an important part in the history of the human mind?

369   For all these widely differing interpretations we can marshal more or less satisfactory arguments. The view which probably causes most offence is that incest is a genuine instinct. But, considering the almost universal prevalence of the incest taboo, we may legitimately remark that a thing which is not liked and desired generally requires no prohibition. In my opinion, each of these interpretations is justified up to a point, because all the corresponding shades of meaning are present in individual cases, though with varying intensity. Sometimes one aspect predominates and sometimes another. I am far from asserting that the above list could not be supplemented further.

370   In practice, however, it is of the utmost importance how the incestuous aspect is interpreted. The explanation will vary according to the nature of the case, the stage of treatment, the perspicacity of the patient, and the maturity of his judgment.

371   The existence of the incest element involves not only an intellectual difficulty but, worst of all, an emotional complication of the therapeutic situation. It is the hiding place for all the most secret, painful, intense, delicate, shamefaced, timorous, grotesque, unmoral, and at the same time the most sacred feelings which go to make up the indescribable and inexplicable wealth of human relationships and give them their compelling power. Like the tentacles of an octopus they twine themselves invisibly round parents and children and, through the trans-

22 The reader will know that I do not understand *libido* in the original Freudian sense as *appetitus sexualis*, but as an *appetitus* which can be defined as psychic energy. See "On Psychic Energy."

23 This is the view I have put forward as an explanation of certain processes in "The Theory of Psychoanalysis."

ference, round doctor and patient. This binding force shows itself in the irresistible strength and obstinacy of the neurotic symptom and in the patient's desperate clinging to the world of infancy or to the doctor. The word "possession" describes this state in a way that could hardly be bettered.

372   The remarkable effects produced by unconscious contents allow us to infer something about their energy. All unconscious contents, once they are activated—i.e., have made themselves felt—possess as it were a specific energy which enables them to manifest themselves everywhere (like the incest motif, for instance). But this energy is normally not sufficient to thrust the content into consciousness. For that there must be a certain predisposition on the part of the conscious mind, namely a deficit in the form of loss of energy. The energy so lost raises the psychic potency of certain compensating contents in the unconscious. The *abaissement du niveau mental*, the energy lost to consciousness, is a phenomenon which shows itself most drastically in the "loss of soul" among primitive peoples, who also have interesting psychotherapeutic methods for recapturing the soul that has gone astray. This is not the place to go into these matters in detail, so a bare mention must suffice.[24] Similar phenomena can be observed in civilized man. He too is liable to a sudden loss of initiative for no apparent reason. The discovery of the real reason is no easy task and generally leads to a somewhat ticklish discussion of things lying in the background. Carelessness of all kinds, neglected duties, tasks postponed, wilful outbursts of defiance, and so on, all these can dam up his vitality to such an extent that certain quanta of energy, no longer finding a conscious outlet, stream off into the unconscious, where they activate other, compensating contents, which in turn begin to exert a compulsive influence on the conscious mind. (Hence the very common combination of extreme neglect of duty and a compulsion neurosis.)

373   This is one way in which loss of energy may come about. The other way causes loss not through a malfunctioning of the conscious mind but through a "spontaneous" activation of unconscious contents, which react secondarily upon consciousness. There are moments in human life when a new page is turned.

24 Cf. Frazer, *Taboo and the Perils of the Soul*, pp. 54ff.

374 New interests and tendencies appear which have hitherto received no attention, or there is a sudden change of personality (a so-called mutation of character). During the incubation period of such a change we can often observe a loss of conscious energy: the new development has drawn off the energy it needs from consciousness. This lowering of energy can be seen most clearly before the onset of certain psychoses and also in the empty stillness which precedes creative work.[25]

The remarkable potency of unconscious contents, therefore, always indicates a corresponding weakness in the conscious mind and its functions. It is as though the latter were threatened with impotence. For primitive man this danger is one of the most terrifying instances of "magic." So we can understand why this secret fear is also to be found among civilized people. In serious cases it is the secret fear of going mad; in less serious, the fear of the unconscious—a fear which even the normal person exhibits in his resistance to psychological views and explanations. This resistance borders on the grotesque when it comes to scouting all psychological explanations of art, philosophy, and religion, as though the human psyche had, or should have, absolutely nothing to do with these things. The doctor knows these well-defended zones from his consulting hours: they are reminiscent of island fortresses from which the neurotic tries to ward off the octopus. ("Happy neurosis island," as one of my patients called his conscious state!) The doctor is well aware that the patient needs an island and would be lost without it. It serves as a refuge for his consciousness and as the last stronghold against the threatening embrace of the unconscious. The same is true of the normal person's taboo regions which psychology must not touch. But since no war was ever won on the defensive, one must, in order to terminate hostilities, open negotiations with the enemy and see what his terms really are. Such is the intention of the doctor who volunteers to act as a mediator. He is far from wishing to disturb the somewhat precarious island idyll or pull down the fortifications. On the contrary, he is thankful that somewhere a firm foothold exists that does not first have to be fished up out of

[25] The same phenomenon can be seen on a smaller scale, but no less clearly, in the apprehension and depression which precede any special psychic exertion, such as an examination, a lecture, an important interview, etc.

the chaos, always a desperately difficult task. He knows that the island is a bit cramped and that life on it is pretty meagre and plagued with all sorts of imaginary wants because too much life has been left outside, and that as a result a terrifying monster is created, or rather is roused out of its slumbers. He also knows that this seemingly alarming animal stands in a secret compensatory relationship to the island and could supply everything that the island lacks.

375   The transference, however, alters the psychological stature of the doctor, though this is at first imperceptible to him. He too becomes affected, and has as much difficulty in distinguishing between the patient and what has taken possession of him as has the patient himself. This leads both of them to a direct confrontation with the daemonic forces lurking in the darkness. The resultant paradoxical blend of positive and negative, of trust and fear, of hope and doubt, of attraction and repulsion, is characteristic of the initial relationship. It is the νεῖκος καὶ φιλία (hate and love) of the elements, which the alchemists likened to the primeval chaos. The activated unconscious appears as a flurry of unleashed opposites and calls forth the attempt to reconcile them, so that, in the words of the alchemists, the great panacea, the *medicina catholica*, may be born.

4

376   It must be emphasized that in alchemy the dark initial state of *nigredo* is often regarded as the product of a previous operation, and that it therefore does not represent the absolute beginning.[26] Similarly, the psychological parallel to the *nigredo* is the result of the foregoing preliminary talk which, at a certain moment, sometimes long delayed, "touches" the uncon-

26 Where the *nigredo* is identified with the *putrefactio* it does not come at the beginning, as for example in fig. 6 of our series of pictures from the *Rosarium philosophorum* (*Art. aurif.*, II, p. 254). In Mylius, *Philosophia reformata*, p. 116, the *nigredo* appears only in the fifth grade of the work, during the "putrefactio, quae in umbra purgatorii celebratur" (putrefaction which is celebrated in the darkness of Purgatory): but further on (p. 118), we read in contradiction to this: "Et haec denigratio est operis initium, putrefactionis indicium" etc. (And this *denigratio* is the beginning of the work, an indication of the putrefaction).

scious and establishes the unconscious identity[27] of doctor and patient. This moment *may* be perceived and registered consciously, but generally it happens outside consciousness and the bond thus established is recognized only later and indirectly by its results. Occasionally dreams occur about this time, announcing the appearance of the transference. For instance, a dream may say that a fire has started in the cellar, or that a burglar has broken in, or that the patient's father has died, or it may depict an erotic or some other ambiguous situation.[28] From the moment when such a dream occurs there may be initiated a queer unconscious time-reckoning, lasting for months or even longer. I have often observed this process and will give a practical instance of it:

377   When treating a lady of over sixty, I was struck by the following passage in a dream she had on October 21, 1938: "*A beautiful little child, a girl of six months old, is playing in the kitchen with her grandparents and myself, her mother. The grandparents are on the left of the room and the child stands on the square table in the middle of the kitchen. I stand by the table and play with the child. The old woman says she can hardly believe we have known the child for only six months. I say that it is not so strange because we knew and loved the child long before she was born.*"

378   It is immediately apparent that the child is something special, i.e., a child hero or divine child. The father is not mentioned; his absence is part of the picture.[29] The kitchen, as the scene of the happening, points to the unconscious. The square table is the quaternity, the classical basis of the "special" child,[30]

27 "Unconscious identity" is the same as Lévy-Bruhl's *participation mystique*. Cf. *How Natives Think*.

28 A pictorial representation of this moment, in the form of a flash of lightning and a "stone-birth," is to be found in my "A Study in the Process of Individuation," Picture 2.

29 Because he is the "unknown father," a theme to be met with in Gnosticism. See Bousset, *Hauptprobleme der Gnosis*, Ch. II, pp. 58–91.

30 Cf. Nicholas of Flüe's vision of the threefold fountain arising in the square container (Lavaud, *Vie profonde de Nicolas de Flue*, p. 67, and Stöckli, *Die Visionen des seligen Bruder Klaus*, p. 19). A Gnostic text says: "In the second Father[hood] the five trees are standing and in their midst is a trapeza [τράπεζα]. Standing on the trapeza is an Only-begotten word [λόγος μονογενής]." (Baynes, *A Coptic Gnostic Treatise*, p. 70.) The trapeza is an abbreviation of

379 for the child is a symbol of the self and the quaternity is a symbolical expression of this. The self as such is timeless and existed before any birth.[31] The dreamer was strongly influenced by Indian writings and knew the Upanishads well, but not the medieval Christian symbolism which is in question here. The precise age of the child made me ask the dreamer to look in her notes to see what had happened in the unconscious six months earlier. Under April 20, 1938, she found the following dream:

"*With some other women I am looking at a piece of tapestry, a square with symbolical figures on it. Immediately afterwards I am sitting with some women in front of a marvellous tree. It is magnificently grown, at first it seems to be some kind of conifer, but then I think—in the dream—that it is a monkey-puzzle* [a tree of genus *Araucaria*] *with the branches growing straight up like candles* [a confusion with *Cereus candelabrum*]. *A Christmas tree is fitted into it in such a way that at first it looks like one tree instead of two.*"—As the dreamer was writing down this dream immediately on waking, with a vivid picture of the tree before her, she suddenly had a vision of a tiny golden child lying at the foot of the tree (tree-birth motif). She had thus gone on dreaming the sense of the dream. It undoubtedly depicts the birth of the divine ("golden") child.

380 But what had happened nine months previous to April 20, 1938? Between July 19 and 22, 1937, she had painted a picture showing, on the left, a heap of coloured and polished (precious) stones surmounted by a silver serpent, winged and crowned. In the middle of the picture there stands a naked female figure from whose genital region the same serpent rears up towards the heart, where it bursts into a five-pointed, gor-

τετράπεζα, a four-legged table or podium (ibid., p. 71). Cf. Irenaeus, *Contra haereses*, III, 11, where he compares the "fourfold gospel" with the four cherubim in the vision of Ezekiel, the four regions of the world, and the four winds: "ex quibus manifestum est, quoniam qui est omnium artifex Verbum, qui sedet super Cherubim et continet omnia, dedit nobis quadriforme Evangelium, quod uno spiritu continetur" (from which it is clear that He who is the Maker of all things, the Word [Logos] who sits above the Cherubim and holds all things together, gave unto us the fourfold gospel, which is contained in one spirit). Concerning the kitchen, cf. Lavaud, *Vie profonde*, p. 66, and Stöckli, *Die Visionen*, p. 18.

31 This is not a metaphysical statement but a psychological fact.

381 geously flashing golden star. A coloured bird flies down on the right with a little twig in its beak. On the twig five flowers are arranged in a *quaternio*, one yellow, one blue, one red, one green, but the topmost is golden—obviously a mandala structure.[32] The serpent represents the hissing ascent of Kundalini, and in the corresponding yoga this marks the first moment in a process which ends with deification in the divine Self, the syzygy of Shiva and Shakti.[33] It is obviously the moment of symbolical conception, which is both Tantric and—because of the bird—Christian in character, being a contamination of the symbolism of the Annunciation with Noah's dove and the sprig of olive.

This case, and more particularly the last image, is a classical example of the kind of symbolism which marks the onset of the transference. Noah's dove (the emblem of reconciliation), the *incarnatio Dei*, the union of God with matter for the purpose of begeting the redeemer, the serpent path, the Sushumna representing the line midway between sun and moon—all this is the first, anticipatory stage of an as-yet-unfulfilled programme that culminates in the union of opposites. This union is analogous to the "royal marriage" in alchemy. The prodromal events signify the meeting or collision of various opposites and can therefore appropriately be called chaos and blackness. As mentioned above, this may occur at the beginning of the treatment, or it may have to be preceded by a lengthy analysis, a stage of *rapprochement*. Such is particularly the case when the patient shows violent resistances coupled with fear of the activated contents of the unconscious.[34]

32 As regards the bird with the flowering twig, see Figs. 2 and 3 infra.

33 Avalon, *The Serpent Power*, pp. 345f.

34 Freud, as we know, observes the transference problem from the standpoint of a personalistic psychology and thus overlooks the very essence of the transference—the collective contents of an archetypal nature. The reason for this is his notoriously negative attitude to the psychic reality of archetypal images, which he dismisses as "illusion." This materialistic bias precludes strict application of the phenomenological principle without which an objective study of the psyche is absolutely impossible. My handling of the transference problem, in contrast to Freud's, includes the archetypal aspect and thus gives rise to a totally different picture. Freud's rational treatment of the problem is quite logical as far as his purely personalistic premises go, but both in theory and in practice they do not go far enough, since they fail to do justice to the obvious admixture of archetypal data.

There is good reason and ample justification for these resistances and they should never, under any circumstances, be ridden over roughshod or otherwise argued out of existence. Neither should they be belittled, disparaged, or made ridiculous; on the contrary, they should be taken with the utmost seriousness as a vitally important defence mechanism against overpowering contents which are often very difficult to control. The general rule should be that the weakness of the conscious attitude is proportional to the strength of the resistance. When, therefore, there are strong resistances, the conscious rapport with the patient must be carefully watched, and—in certain cases—his conscious attitude must be supported to such a degree that, in view of later developments, one would be bound to charge oneself with the grossest inconsistency. That is inevitable, because one can never be too sure that the weak state of the patient's conscious mind will prove equal to the subsequent assault of the unconscious. In fact, one must go on supporting his conscious (or, as Freud thinks, "repressive") attitude until the patient can let the "repressed" contents rise up spontaneously. Should there by any chance be a latent psychosis [35] which cannot be detected beforehand, this cautious procedure may prevent the devastating invasion of the unconscious or at least catch it in time. At all events the doctor then has a clear conscience, knowing that he has done everything in his power to avoid a fatal outcome.[36] Nor is it beside the point to add that consistent support of the conscious attitude has in itself a high therapeutic value and not infrequently serves to bring about satisfactory results. It would be a dangerous prejudice to imagine that analysis of the unconscious is the one and only panacea which should therefore be employed in every case. It is rather like a surgical operation and we should only resort to the knife when other methods have failed. So long as it does not obtrude itself the unconscious is best left alone. The reader

35 The numerical proportion of latent to manifest psychoses is about equal to that of latent to active cases of tuberculosis.

36 The violent resistance, mentioned by Freud, to the rational resolution of the transference is often due to the fact that in some markedly sexual forms of transference there are concealed collective unconscious contents which defy all rational resolution. Or, if this resolution is successful, the patient is cut off from the collective unconscious and comes to feel this as a loss.

382 should be quite clear that my discussion of the transference problem is not an account of the daily routine of the psychotherapist, but far more a description of what happens when the check normally exerted on the unconscious by the conscious mind is disrupted, though this need not necessarily occur at all.

Cases where the archetypal problem of the transference becomes acute are by no means always "serious" cases, i.e., grave states of illness. There are of course such cases among them, but there are also mild neuroses, or simply psychological difficulties which we would be at a loss to diagnose. Curiously enough, it is these latter cases that present the doctor with the most difficult problems. Often the persons concerned endure unspeakable suffering without developing any neurotic symptoms that would entitle them to be called ill. We can only call it an intense suffering, a passion of the soul but not a disease of the mind.

5

383 Once an unconscious content is constellated, it tends to break down the relationship of conscious trust between doctor and patient by creating, through projection, an atmosphere of illusion which either leads to continual misinterpretations and misunderstandings, or else produces a most disconcerting impression of harmony. The latter is even more trying than the former, which at worst (though it is sometimes for the best!) can only hamper the treatment, whereas in the other case a tremendous effort is needed to discover the points of difference. But in either case the constellation of the unconscious is a troublesome factor. The situation is enveloped in a kind of fog, and this fully accords with the nature of the unconscious content: it is a "black blacker than black" (nigrum, nigrius nigro),[37] as the alchemists rightly say, and in addition is charged with dangerous polar tensions, with the *inimicitia elementorum*. One finds oneself in an impenetrable chaos, which is indeed one of the synonyms for the mysterious *prima materia*. The latter corresponds to the nature of the unconscious content in every respect, with one exception: this time it does not appear in the

37 Cf. Lully, "Testamentum," *Bibliotheca chemica curiosa*, I, pp. 790ff., and Maier, *Symbola aureae mensae*, pp. 379f.

384 alchemical substance but in man himself. In the case of alchemy it is quite evident that the unconscious content is of human origin, as I have shown in *Psychology and Alchemy*.[38] Hunted for centuries and never found, the *prima materia* or *lapis philosophorum* is, as a few alchemists rightly suspected, to be discovered in man himself. But it seems that this content can never be found and integrated directly, but only by the circuitous route of projection. For as a rule the unconscious first appears in projected form. Whenever it appears to obtrude itself directly, as in visions, dreams, illuminations, psychoses, etc., these are always preceded by psychic conditions which give clear proof of projection. A classical example of this is Saul's fanatical persecution of the Christians before Christ appeared to him in a vision.

The elusive, deceptive, ever-changing content that possesses the patient like a demon now flits about from patient to doctor and, as the third party in the alliance, continues its game, sometimes impish and teasing, sometimes really diabolical. The alchemists aptly personified it as the wily god of revelation, Hermes or Mercurius; and though they lament over the way he hoodwinks them, they still give him the highest names, which bring him very near to deity.[39] But for all that, they deem themselves good Christians whose faithfulness of heart is never in doubt, and they begin and end their treatises with pious invocations.[40] Yet it would be an altogether unjustifiable suppression of the truth were I to confine myself to the negative

38 Pars. 342f.
39 Cf. "The Spirit Mercurius," Part II, sec. 6.
40 Thus *Aurora consurgens*, II (*Art. aurif.*, I, pp. 185–246) closes with the words: "Et sic probata est medicina Philosophorum, quam omni [investiganti] fideli et pio praestare dignetur Deus omnipotens, unigenitusque filius Dei Dominus noster Jesus Christus, qui cum Patre et Spiritu sancto vivit et regnat, unus Deus per infinita saeculorum. Amen" (And this is the approved medicine of the philosophers, which may our Lord Jesus Christ, who liveth and reigneth with the Father and the Holy Ghost, one God for ever and ever, deign to give to every searcher who is faithful, pious, and of good will, Amen). This conclusion no doubt comes from the Offertorium (prayer during the *commixtio*), where it says: ". . . qui humanitatis nostrae fieri dignatus est particeps, Jesus Christus, Filius tuus, Dominus noster: qui tecum vivit et regnat in unitate Spiritus Sancti Deus per omnia saecula saeculorum. Amen." (. . . who vouchsafed to become partaker of our humanity, Jesus Christ, Thy Son, our Lord: who liveth and reigneth with Thee in the unity of the Holy Ghost, one God, world without end. Amen.)

385   description of Mercurius' impish drolleries, his inexhaustible invention, his insinuations, his intriguing ideas and schemes, his ambivalence and—often—his unmistakable malice. He is also capable of the exact opposite, and I can well understand why the alchemists endowed their Mercurius with the highest spiritual qualities, although these stand in flagrant contrast to his exceedingly shady character. The contents of the unconscious are indeed of the greatest importance, for the unconscious is after all the matrix of the human mind and its inventions. Wonderful and ingenious as this other side of the unconscious is, it can be most dangerously deceptive on account of its numinous nature. Involuntarily one thinks of the devils mentioned by St Athanasius in his life of St Anthony, who talk very piously, sing psalms, read the holy books, and—worst of all—speak the truth. The difficulties of our psychotherapeutic work teach us to take truth, goodness, and beauty where we find them. They are not always found where we look for them: often they are hidden in the dirt or are in the keeping of the dragon. "In stercore invenitur" (it is found in filth) [41] runs an alchemical dictum—nor is it any the less valuable on that account. But, it does not transfigure the dirt and does not diminish the evil, any more than these lessen God's gifts. The contrast is painful and the paradox bewildering. Sayings like

ουρανο ανω
ουρανο κατω
αστρα ανω
αστρα κατω
παν ο ανω
τουτο κατω
ταντα λαβε
κε ευτυχε [42]

(Heaven above
Heaven below
Stars above
Stars below
All that is above
Also is below
Grasp this
And rejoice) [42]

are too optimistic and superficial; they forget the moral torment occasioned by the opposites, and the importance of ethical values.

The refining of the *prima materia*, the unconscious con-

41 Cf. "Tractatus aureus," *Ars chemica*, p. 21.
42 Kircher, "Oedipus Aegyptiacus," II, Class X. Ch. V, p. 414. There is a connection between this text and the "Tabula smaragdina"; cf. Ruska, *Tabula smaragdina*, p. 217.

tent, demands endless patience, perseverance,[43] equanimity, knowledge, and ability on the part of the doctor; and, on the part of the patient, the putting forth of his best powers and a capacity for suffering which does not leave the doctor altogether unaffected. The deep meaning of the Christian virtues, especially the greatest among these, will become clear even to the unbeliever; for there are times when he needs them all if he is to rescue his consciousness, and his very life, from this pocket of chaos, whose final subjugation, without violence, is no ordinary task. If the work succeeds, it often works like a miracle, and one can understand what it was that prompted the alchemists to insert a heartfelt *Deo concedente* in their recipes, or to allow that only if God wrought a miracle could their procedure be brought to a successful conclusion.

6

386 It may seem strange to the reader that a "medical procedure" should give rise to such considerations. Although in illnesses of the body there is no remedy and no treatment that can be said to be infallible in all circumstances, there are still a great many which will probably have the desired effect without either doctor or patient having the slightest need to insert a *Deo concedente*. But we are not dealing here with the body —we are dealing with the psyche. Consequently we cannot speak the language of body-cells and bacteria; we need another language commensurate with the nature of the psyche, and equally we must have an attitude which measures the danger and can meet it. And all this must be genuine or it will have no effect; if it is hollow, it will damage both doctor and patient. The *Deo concedente* is not just a rhetorical flourish; it expresses the firm attitude of the man who does not imagine that he knows better on every occasion and who is fully aware that the un-

43 The *Rosarium* (*Art. aurif.*, II, p. 230) says: "Et scias, quod haec est longissima via, ergo patientia et mora sunt necessariae in nostro magisterio" (And you must know that this is a very long road; therefore patience and deliberation are needful in our magistery). Cf. *Aurora consurgens*, I, Ch. 10: "Tria sunt necessaria videlicet patientia mora et aptitudo instrumentorum" (Three things are necessary, namely: patience, deliberation, and skill with the instruments).

conscious material before him is something *alive*, a paradoxical Mercurius of whom an old master says: "Et est ille quem natura paululum operata est et in metallicam formam formavit, tamen imperfectum relinquit." (And he is that on whom nature hath worked but a little, and whom she hath wrought into metallic form yet left unfinished) [44]—a natural being, therefore, that longs for integration within the wholeness of a man. It is like a fragment of primeval psyche into which no consciousness has as yet penetrated to create division and order, a "united dual nature," as Goethe says—an abyss of ambiguities.

387   Since we cannot imagine—unless we have lost our critical faculties altogether—that mankind today has attained the highest possible degree of consciousness, there must be some potential unconscious psyche left over whose development would result in a further extension and a higher differentiation of consciousness. No one can say how great or small this "remnant" might be, for we have no means of measuring the possible range of conscious development, let alone the extent of the unconscious. But there is not the slightest doubt that a *massa confusa* of archaic and undifferentiated contents exists, which not only manifests itself in neuroses and psychoses but also forms the "skeleton in the cupboard" of innumerable people who are not really pathological. We are so accustomed to hear that everybody has his "difficulties and problems" that we simply accept it as a banal fact, without considering what these difficulties and problems really mean. Why is one never satisfied with oneself? Why is one unreasonable? Why is one not always good and why must one ever leave a cranny for evil? Why does one sometimes say too much and sometimes too little? Why does one do foolish things which could easily be avoided with a little forethought? What is it that is always frustrating us and thwarting our best intentions? Why are there people who never notice these things and cannot even admit their existence? And finally, why do people in the mass beget the historical lunacy of the last thirty years? Why couldn't Pythagoras, twenty-four hundred years ago, have established the rule of wisdom once and for all, or Christianity have set up the Kingdom of Heaven upon earth?

44 *Rosarium*, p. 231. What the alchemist sees in "metallic form" the psychotherapist sees in man.

388   The Church has the doctrine of the devil, of an evil principle, whom we like to imagine complete with cloven hoofs, horns, and tail, half man, half beast, a chthonic deity apparently escaped from the rout of Dionysus, the sole surviving champion of the sinful joys of paganism. An excellent picture, and one which exactly describes the grotesque and sinister side of the unconscious; for we have never really come to grips with it and consequently it has remained in its original savage state. Probably no one today would still be rash enough to assert that the European is a lamblike creature and not possessed by a devil. The frightful records of our age are plain for all to see, and they surpass in hideousness everything that any previous age, with its feeble instruments, could have hoped to accomplish.

389   If, as many are fain to believe, the unconscious were only nefarious, only evil, then the situation would be simple and the path clear: to do good and to eschew evil. But what is "good" and what is "evil"? The unconscious is not just evil by nature, it is also the source of the highest good:[45] not only dark but also light, not only bestial, semi-human, and demonic but superhuman, spiritual, and, in the classical sense of the word, "divine." The Mercurius who personifies the unconscious[46] is essentially "duplex," paradoxically dualistic by nature, fiend, monster, beast, and at the same time panacea, "the philosophers' son," *sapientia Dei,* and *donum Spiritus Sancti.*[47]

390   Since this is so, all hope of a simple solution is abolished. All definitions of good and evil become suspect or actually invalid. As moral forces, good and evil remain unshaken, and —as the simple verities for which the penal code, the ten commandments, and conventional Christian morality take them— undoubted. But conflicting loyalties are much more subtle and

---

45 Here I must expressly emphasize that I am not dabbling in metaphysics or discussing questions of faith, but am speaking of psychology. Whatever religious experience or metaphysical truth may be in themselves, looked at empirically they are essentially psychic phenomena, that is, they manifest themselves as such and must therefore be submitted to psychological criticism, evaluation, and investigation. Science comes to a stop at its *own* borders.

46 Cf. "The Spirit Mercurius," Part II, sec. 10.

47 The alchemists also liken him to Lucifer ("bringer of light"), God's fallen and most beautiful angel. Cf. Mylius, *Phil. ref.,* p. 18.

dangerous things, and a conscience sharpened by worldly wisdom can no longer rest content with precepts, ideas, and fine words. When it has to deal with that remnant of primeval psyche, pregnant with the future and yearning for development, it grows uneasy and looks round for some guiding principle or fixed point. Indeed, once this stage has been reached in our dealings with the unconscious, these desiderata become a pressing necessity. Since the only salutary powers visible in the world today are the great psychotherapeutic systems which we call the religions, and from which we expect the soul's salvation, it is quite natural that many people should make the justifiable and often successful attempt to find a niche for themselves in one of the existing creeds and to acquire a deeper insight into the meaning of the traditional saving verities.

391 This solution is normal and satisfying in that the dogmatically formulated truths of the Christian Church express, almost perfectly, the nature of psychic experience. They are the repositories of the secrets of the soul, and this matchless knowledge is set forth in grand symbolical images. The unconscious thus possesses a natural affinity with the spiritual values of the Church, particularly in their dogmatic form, which owes its special character to centuries of theological controversy—absurd as this seemed in the eyes of later generations—and to the passionate efforts of many great men.

7

392 The Church would be an ideal solution for anyone seeking a suitable receptacle for the chaos of the unconscious were it not that everything man-made, however refined, has its imperfections. The fact is that a return to the Church, i.e., to a particular creed, is not the general rule. Much the more frequent is a better understanding of, and a more intense relation to, religion as such, which is not to be confused with a creed.[48] This, it seems to me, is mainly because anyone who appreciates the legitimacy of the two viewpoints, of the two branches into which Christianity has been split, cannot maintain the exclu-

48 Cf. "Psychology and Religion," pars. 6f.

sive validity of either of them, for to do so would be to deceive himself. As a Christian, he has to recognize that the Christendom he belongs to has been split for four hundred years and that his Christian beliefs, far from redeeming him, have exposed him to a conflict and a division that are still rending the body of Christ. These are the facts, and they cannot be abolished by each creed pressing for a decision in its favour, as though each were perfectly sure it possessed the absolute truth. Such an attitude is unfair to modern man; he can see very well the advantages that Protestantism has over Catholicism and *vice versa*, and it is painfully clear to him that this sectarian insistence is trying to corner him against his better judgment—in other words, tempting him to sin against the Holy Ghost. He even understands why the churches are bound to behave in this way, and knows that it must be so lest any joyful Christian should imagine himself already reposing in Abraham's anticipated bosom, saved and at peace and free from all fear. Christ's passion continues—for the life of Christ in the *corpus mysticum*, or Christian life in both camps, is at loggerheads with itself and no honest man can deny the split. We are thus in the precise situation of the neurotic who must put up with the painful realization that he is in the midst of conflict. His repeated efforts to repress the other side have only made his neurosis worse. The doctor must advise him to accept the conflict just as it is, with all the suffering this inevitably entails, otherwise the conflict will never be ended. Intelligent Europeans, if at all interested in such questions, are consciously or semiconsciously protestant Catholics and catholic Protestants, nor are they any the worse for that. It is no use telling me that no such people exist: I have seen both sorts, and they have considerably raised my hopes about the European of the future.

But the negative attitude of the public at large to all credos seems to be less the result of religious convictions than one symptom of the general mental sloth and ignorance of religion. We can wax indignant over man's notorious lack of spirituality, but when one is a doctor one does not invariably think that the disease is malevolent or the patient morally inferior; instead, one supposes that the negative results may possibly be due to the remedy applied. Although it may reasonably be doubted whether man has made any marked or even percep-

394 tible progress in morality during the known five thousand years of human civilization, it cannot be denied that there has been a notable development of consciousness and its functions. Above all, there has been a tremendous extension of consciousness in the form of *knowledge*. Not only have the individual functions become differentiated, but to a large extent they have been brought under the control of the ego—in other words, man's will has developed. This is particularly striking when we compare our mentality with that of primitives. The security of our ego has, in comparison with earlier times, greatly increased and has even taken such a dangerous leap forward that, although we sometimes speak of "God's will," we no longer know what we are saying, for in the same breath we assert, "Where there's a will there's a way." And who would ever think of appealing to God's help rather than to the goodwill, the sense of responsibility and duty, the reason or intelligence, of his fellow men?

395 Whatever we may think of these changes of outlook, we cannot alter the fact of their existence. Now when there is a marked change in the individual's state of consciousness, the unconscious contents which are thereby constellated will also change. And the further the conscious situation moves away from a certain point of equilibrium, the more forceful and accordingly the more dangerous become the unconscious contents that are struggling to restore the balance. This leads ultimately to a dissociation: on the one hand, ego-consciousness makes convulsive efforts to shake off an invisible opponent (if it does not suspect its next-door neighbour of being the devil!), while on the other hand it increasingly falls victim to the tyrannical will of an internal "Government opposition" which displays all the characteristics of a dæmonic subman and superman combined.

396 When a few million people get into this state, it produces the sort of situation which has afforded us such an edifying object-lesson every day for the last ten years. These contemporary events betray their psychological background by their very singularity. The insensate destruction and devastation are a reaction against the deflection of consciousness from the point of equilibrium. For an equilibrium does in fact exist between the psychic ego and non-ego, and that equilibrium is a *religio,*

441

396

a "careful consideration" [49] of ever-present unconscious forces which we neglect at our peril. The present crisis has been brewing for centuries because of this shift in man's conscious situation.

Have the Churches adapted themselves to this secular change? Their truth may, with more right than we realize, call itself "eternal," but its temporal garment must pay tribute to the evanescence of all earthly things and should take account of psychic changes. Eternal truth needs a human language that alters with the spirit of the times. The primordial images undergo ceaseless transformation and yet remain ever the same, but only in a new form can they be understood anew. Always they require a new interpretation if, as each formulation becomes obsolete, they are not to lose their spellbinding power over that *fugax Mercurius* [50] and allow that useful though dangerous enemy to escape. What is that about "new wine in old bottles"? Where are the answers to the spiritual needs and troubles of a new epoch? And where has eternal truth been faced with such a hybris of will and power.

8

397

Here, apart from motives of a more personal nature, probably lie the deeper reasons for the fact that the greater part of Europe has succumbed to neo-paganism and anti-Christianity, and has set up a religious ideal of worldly power in opposition to the metaphysical ideal founded on love. But the individual's decision not to belong to a Church does not necessarily denote an anti-Christian attitude; it may mean exactly the reverse: a reconsidering of the kingdom of God in the human heart where, in the words of St. Augustine,[51] the *mysterium paschale* is accomplished "in its inward and higher meanings." The ancient and long obsolete idea of man as a microcosm contains a supreme psychological truth that has yet to be discov-

[49] I use the classical etymology of *religio* and not that of the Church Fathers.
[50] Maier, *Symb. aur. mens.*, p. 386.
[51] *Epistula LV* (Migne, *P.L.*, vol. 33, cols. 208–09).

ered. In former times this truth was projected upon the body, just as alchemy projected the unconscious psyche upon chemical substances. But it is altogether different when the microcosm is understood as that interior world whose inward nature is fleetingly glimpsed in the unconscious. An inkling of this is to be found in the words of Origen: "Intellige te alium mundum esse in parvo et esse intra te Solem, esse Lunam, esse etiam stellas" (Understand that thou art a second little world and that the sun and the moon are within thee, and also the stars).[52] And just as the cosmos is not a dissolving mass of particles, but rests in the unity of God's embrace, so man must not dissolve into a whirl of warring possibilities and tendencies imposed on him by the unconscious, but must become the unity that embraces them all. Origen says pertinently: "Vides, quomodo ille, qui putatur unus esse, non est unus, sed tot in eo personae videntur esse, quot mores" (Thou seest that he who seemeth to be one is yet not one, but as many persons appear in him as he hath velleities).[53] Possession by the unconscious means being torn apart into many people and things, a *disiunctio*. That is why, according to Origen, the aim of the Christian is to become an inwardly united human being.[54] The blind insistence on the outward community of the Church naturally fails to fulfil this aim; on the contrary, it inadvertently provides the inner disunity with an outward vessel without really changing the *disiunctio* into a *coniunctio*.

398   The painful conflict that begins with the *nigredo* or *tenebrositas* is described by the alchemists as the *separatio* or *divisio elementorum*, the *solutio*, *calcinatio*, *incineratio*, or as dismemberment of the body, excruciating animal sacrifices, amputation of the mother's hands or the lion's paws, atomization of the bridegroom in the body of the bride, and so on.[55] While this extreme form of *disiunctio* is going on, there is a transformation of that arcanum—be it substance or spirit—which invariably turns out to be the mysterious Mercurius. In other words, out of the monstrous animal forms there gradually emerges a *res simplex*, whose nature is one and the same and yet consists

[52] *Homiliae in Leviticum*, V, 2 (Migne, *P.G.*, vol. 12, col. 449).
[53] Ibid.
[54] *Hom. in Librum Regnorum*, 1, 4.
[55] "Hounded from one bride-chamber to the next."—*Faust*, Part I.

9

399   Alchemy describes, not merely in general outline but often in the most astonishing detail, the same psychological phenomenology which can be observed in the analysis of unconscious processes. The individual's specious unity that emphatically says "*I want*, *I think*" breaks down under the impact of the unconscious. So long as the patient can think that somebody else (his father or mother) is responsible for his difficulties, he can save some semblance of unity (*putatur unus esse*). But once he realizes that he himself has a shadow, that his enemy is in his own heart, then the conflict begins and one becomes two. Since the "other" will eventually prove to be yet another duality, a compound of opposites, the ego soon becomes a shuttlecock tossed between a multitude of "velleities," with the result that there is an "obfuscation of the light," i.e., consciousness is depotentiated and the patient is at a loss to know where his personality begins or ends. It is like passing through the valley of the shadow, and sometimes the patient has to cling to

of a duality (Goethe's "united dual nature"). The alchemist tries to get round this paradox or antinomy with his various procedures and formulae, and to make one out of two.[56] But the very multiplicity of his symbols and symbolic processes proves that success is doubtful. Seldom do we find symbols of the goal whose dual nature is not immediately apparent. His *filius philosophorum*, his *lapis*, his *rebis*, his homunculus, are all hermaphroditic. His gold is *non vulgi*, his *lapis* is spirit and body, and so is his tincture, which is a *sanguis spiritualis*—a spiritual blood.[57] We can therefore understand why the *nuptiae chymicae*, the royal marriage, occupies such an important place in alchemy as a symbol of the supreme and ultimate union, since it represents the magic-by-analogy which is supposed to bring the work to its final consummation and bind the opposites by love, for "love is stronger than death."

56 For the same process in the individual psyche, see *Psychology and Alchemy*, pars. 44ff.

57 Cf. Ruska, *Turba*, Sermo XIX, p. 129. The term comes from the Book of El-Habib (ibid., p. 43).

the doctor as the last remaining shred of reality. This situation is difficult and distressing for both parties; often the doctor is in much the same position as the alchemist who no longer knew whether he was melting the mysterious amalgam in the crucible or whether he was the salamander glowing in the fire. Psychological induction inevitably causes the two parties to get involved in the transformation of the third and to be themselves transformed in the process, and all the time the doctor's knowledge, like a flickering lamp, is the one dim light in the darkness. Nothing gives a better picture of the psychological state of the alchemist than the division of his work-room into a "laboratory," where he bustles about with crucibles and alembics, and an "oratory," where he prays to God for the much needed illumination—"purge the horrible darknesses of our mind,"[58] as the author of *Aurora* quotes.

400   "Ars requirit totum hominem," we read in an old treatise.[59] This is in the highest degree true of psychotherapeutic work. A genuine participation, going right beyond professional routine, is absolutely imperative, unless of course the doctor prefers to jeopardize the whole proceeding by evading his own problems, which are becoming more and more insistent. The doctor must go to the limits of his subjective possibilities, otherwise the patient will be unable to follow suit. Arbitrary limits are no use, only real ones. It must be a genuine process of purification where "all superfluities are consumed in the fire" and the basic facts emerge. Is there anything more fundamental than the realization, "This is what I am"? It reveals a unity which nevertheless is—or was—a diversity. No longer the earlier ego with its make-believes and artificial contrivances, but another, "objective" ego, which for this reason is better called the "self." No longer a mere selection of suitable fictions, but a string of hard facts, which together make up the cross we all have to carry or the fate we ourselves are. These first indications of a future synthesis of personality, as I have shown in my earlier publications, appear in dreams or in "active imagination," where they

[58] "Spiritus alme,/illustrator hominum,/horridas nostrae/mentis purga tenebras." (Sublime spirit, enlightener of mankind, purge the horrible darknesses of our mind.)—Notker Balbulus, *Hymnus in Die Pentecostes* (Migne, *P.L.*, vol. 131, cols. 1012–13).

[59] Hoghelande, "De alchemiae difficultatibus," p. 139.

take the form of the mandala symbols which were also not unknown in alchemy. But the first signs of this symbolism are far from indicating that unity has been attained. Just as alchemy has a great many very different procedures, ranging from the sevenfold to the thousandfold distillation, or from the "work of one day" to "the errant quest" lasting for decades, so the tensions between the psychic pairs of opposites ease off only gradually; and, like the alchemical end-product, which always betrays its essential duality, the united personality will never quite lose the painful sense of innate discord. Complete redemption from the sufferings of this world is and must remain an illusion. Christ's earthly life likewise ended, not in complacent bliss, but on the cross. (It is a remarkable fact that in their hedonistic aims materialism and a certain species of "joyful" Christianity join hands like brothers.) The goal is important only as an idea; the essential thing is the *opus* which leads to the goal: *that* is the goal of a lifetime. In its attainment "left and right" [60] are united, and conscious and unconscious work in harmony.

401   The *coniunctio oppositorum* in the guise of Sol and Luna, the royal brother-sister or mother-son pair, occupies such an important place in alchemy that sometimes the entire process takes the form of the *hierosgamos* and its mystic consequences. The most complete and the simplest illustration of this is perhaps the series of pictures contained in the *Rosarium philosophorum* of 1550, which series I reproduce in what follows. Its psychological importance justifies closer examination. Everything that the doctor discovers and experiences when analysing the unconscious of his patient coincides in the most remarkable way with the content of these pictures. This is not likely to be mere chance, because the old alchemists were often doctors as

60 *Acta Joannis*, 98 (cf. James, *Apocryphal New Testament*, p. 255): . . . καὶ ἁρμονία σοφίας· σοφία δὲ οὖσα ἐν ἁρμονίᾳ ὑπάρχουσιν δεξιοὶ καὶ ἀριστεροί, δυνάμεις, ἐξουσίαι, ἀρχαὶ καὶ δαίμονες, ἐνέργειαι . . . (". . . Harmony of wisdom, but when there is wisdom the left and the right are in harmony; powers, principalities, archons, daemons, forces . . .").

10

well, and thus had ample opportunity for such experiences if, like Paracelsus, they worried about the psychological well-being of their patients or inquired into their dreams (for the purpose of diagnosis, prognosis, and therapy). In this way they could collect information of a psychological nature, not only from their patients but also from themselves, i.e., from the observation of their own unconscious contents which had been activated by induction.[61] Just as the unconscious expresses itself even today in a picture series, often drawn spontaneously by the patient, so those earlier pictures, such as we find in the Codex Rhenoviensis 172, in Zurich, and in other treatises, were no doubt produced in a similar way, that is, as the deposit of impressions collected during the work and then interpreted or modified in the light of traditional factors.[62] In the modern pictures, too, we find not a few traces of traditional themes side by side with spontaneous repetitions of archaic or mythological ideas. In view of this close connection between picture and psychic content, it does not seem to me out of place to examine a medieval series of pictures in the light of modern discoveries, or even to use them as an Ariadne thread in our account of the latter. These curiosities of the Middle Ages contain the seeds of much that emerged in clearer form only many centuries later.

[61] Cardan (*Somniorum synesiorum . . .*) is an excellent example of one who examined his own dreams.

[62] As regards the work of reinterpretation, see my "Brother Klaus." Also Lavaud, *Vie profonde*, Ch. III, "La Grande Vision."

III

ON THE RELIGIOUS FUNCTION

2. A pair of alchemists, kneeling by the furnace and praying for God's blessing.
—*Mutus liber* (1702)

INTRODUCTION TO THE RELIGIOUS AND PSYCHOLOGICAL PROBLEMS OF ALCHEMY

1   For the reader familiar with analytical psychology, there is no need of any introductory remarks to the subject of the following study. But for the reader whose interest is not professional and who comes to this book unprepared, some kind of preface will probably be necessary. The concepts of alchemy and the individuation process are matters that seem to lie very far apart, so that the imagination finds it impossible at first to conceive of any bridge between them. To this reader I owe an explanation, more particularly as I have had one or two experiences since the publication of my recent lectures which lead me to infer a certain bewilderment in my critics.

2   What I now have to put forward as regards the nature of the human psyche is based first and foremost on my observations of people. It has been objected that these observations deal with experiences that are either unknown or barely accessible. It is a remarkable fact, which we come across again and again, that absolutely everybody, even the most unqualified layman, thinks he knows all about psychology as though the psyche were something that enjoyed the most universal understanding. But anyone who really knows the human psyche will agree with me

when I say that it is one of the darkest and most mysterious regions of our experience. There is no end to what can be learned in this field. Hardly a day passes in my practice but I come across something new and unexpected. True enough, my experiences are not commonplaces lying on the surface of life. They are, however, within easy reach of every psychotherapist working in this particular field. It is therefore rather absurd, to say the least, that ignorance of the experiences I have to offer should be twisted into an accusation against me. I do not hold myself responsible for the shortcomings in the lay public's knowledge of psychology.

3   There is in the analytical process, that is to say in the dialectical discussion between the conscious mind and the unconscious, a development or an advance towards some goal or end, the perplexing nature of which has engaged my attention for many years. Psychological treatment may come to an *end* at any stage in the development without one's always or necessarily having the feeling that a *goal* has also been reached. Typical and temporary terminations may occur (1) after receiving a piece of good advice; (2) after making a fairly complete but nevertheless adequate confession; (3) after having recognized some hitherto unconscious but essential psychic content whose realization gives a new impetus to one's life and activity; (4) after a hard-won separation from the childhood psyche; (5) after having worked out a new and rational mode of adaptation to perhaps difficult or unusual circumstances and surroundings; (6) after the disappearance of painful symptoms; (7) after some positive turn of fortune such as an examination, engagement, marriage, divorce, change of profession, etc.; (8) after having found one's way back to the church or creed to which one previously belonged, or after a conversion; and finally, (9) after having begun to build up a practical philosophy of life (a "philosophy" in the classical sense of the word).

4   Although the list could admit of many more modifications and additions, it ought to define by and large the main situations in which the analytical or psychotherapeutic process reaches a temporary or sometimes even a definitive end. Experience shows, however, that there is a relatively large number of patients for whom the outward termination of work with the doctor is far from denoting the end of the analytical process. It is rather the

case that the dialectical discussion with the unconscious still continues, and follows much the same course as it does with those who have not given up their work with the doctor. Occasionally one meets such patients again after several years and hears the often highly remarkable account of their subsequent development. It was experiences of this kind which first confirmed me in my belief that there is in the psyche a process that seeks its own goal independently of external factors, and which freed me from the worrying feeling that I myself might be the sole cause of an unreal—and perhaps unnatural—process in the psyche of the patient. This apprehension was not altogether misplaced inasmuch as no amount of argument based on any of the nine categories mentioned above—not even a religious conversion or the most startling removal of neurotic symptoms—can persuade certain patients to give up their analytical work. It was these cases that finally convinced me that the treatment of neurosis opens up a problem which goes far beyond purely medical considerations and to which medical knowledge alone cannot hope to do justice.

5   Although the early days of analysis now lie nearly half a century behind us, with their pseudo-biological interpretations and their depreciation of the whole process of psychic development, memories die hard and people are still very fond of describing a lengthy analysis as "running away from life," "unresolved transference," "auto-eroticism"—and by other equally unpleasant epithets. But since there are two sides to everything, it is legitimate to condemn this so-called "hanging on" as negative to life only if it can be shown that it really does contain nothing positive. The very understandable impatience felt by the doctor does not prove anything in itself. Only through infinitely patient research has the new science succeeded in building up a profounder knowledge of the nature of the psyche, and if there have been certain unexpected therapeutic results, these are due to the self-sacrificing perseverance of the doctor. Unjustifiably negative judgments are easily come by and at times harmful; moreover they arouse the suspicion of being a mere cloak for ignorance if not an attempt to evade the responsibility of a thorough-going analysis. For since the analytical work must inevitably lead sooner or later to a fundamental discussion between "I" and "You," and "You" and "I" on a plane stripped of

all human pretences, it is very likely, indeed it is almost certain, that not only the patient but the doctor as well will find the situation "getting under his skin." Nobody can meddle with fire or poison without being affected in some vulnerable spot; for the true physician does not stand outside his work but is always in the thick of it.

6   This "hanging on," as it is called, may be something undesired by both parties, something incomprehensible and even unendurable, without necessarily being negative to life. On the contrary, it can easily be a positive "hanging on," which, although it constitutes an apparently insurmountable obstacle, represents just for that reason a unique situation that demands the maximum effort and therefore enlists the energies of the whole man. In fact, one could say that while the patient is unconsciously and unswervingly seeking the solution to some ultimately insoluble problem, the art and technique of the doctor are doing their best to help him towards it. "Ars totum requirit hominem!" exclaims an old alchemist. It is just this *homo totus* whom we seek. The labours of the doctor as well as the quest of the patient are directed towards that hidden and as yet unmanifest "whole" man, who is at once the greater and the future man. But the right way to wholeness is made up, unfortunately, of fateful detours and wrong turnings. It is a *longissima via*, not straight but snakelike, a path that unites the opposites in the manner of the guiding caduceus, a path whose labyrinthine twists and turns are not lacking in terrors. It is on this *longissima via* that we meet with those experiences which are said to be "inaccessible." Their inaccessibility really consists in the fact that they cost us an enormous amount of effort: they demand the very thing we most fear, namely the "wholeness" which we talk about so glibly and which lends itself to endless theorizing, though in actual life we give it the widest possible berth.[1] It is infinitely more popular to go in for "compartment psychology," where the left-hand pigeon-hole does not know what is in the right.

7   I am afraid that we cannot hold the unconsciousness and

---

[1] It is worth noting that a Protestant theologian, writing on homiletics, had the courage to demand wholeness of the preacher from the ethical point of view. He substantiates his argument by referring to my psychology. See Händler, *Die Predigt*.

impotence of the individual entirely responsible for this state of affairs: it is due also to the general psychological education of the European. Not only is this education the proper concern of the ruling religions, it belongs to their very nature—for religion excels all rationalistic systems in that it alone relates to the outer and inner man in equal degree. We can accuse Christianity of arrested development if we are determined to excuse our own shortcomings; but I do not wish to make the mistake of blaming religion for something that is due mainly to human incompetence. I am speaking therefore not of the deepest and best understanding of Christianity but of the superficialities and disastrous misunderstandings that are plain for all to see. The demand made by the *imitatio Christi*—that we should follow the ideal and seek to become like it—ought logically to have the result of developing and exalting the inner man. In actual fact, however, the ideal has been turned by superficial and formalistically-minded believers into an external object of worship, and it is precisely this veneration for the object that prevents it from reaching down into the depths of the psyche and giving the latter a wholeness in keeping with the ideal. Accordingly the divine mediator stands outside as an image, while man remains fragmentary and untouched in the deepest part of him. Christ can indeed be imitated even to the point of stigmatization without the imitator coming anywhere near the ideal or its meaning. For it is not a question of an imitation that leaves a man unchanged and makes him into a mere artifact, but of realizing the ideal on one's own account—*Deo concedente*—in one's own individual life. We must not forget, however, that even a mistaken imitation may sometimes involve a tremendous moral effort which has all the merits of a total surrender to some supreme value, even though the real goal may never be reached and the value is represented externally. It is conceivable that by the virtue of this total effort a man may even catch a fleeting glimpse of his wholeness, accompanied by the feeling of grace that always characterizes this experience.

8   The mistaken idea of a merely outward *imitatio Christi* is further exacerbated by a typically European prejudice which distinguishes the Western attitude from the Eastern. Western man is held in thrall by the "ten thousand things"; he sees only particulars, he is ego-bound and thing-bound, and unaware of

455

the deep root of all being. Eastern man, on the other hand, experiences the world of particulars, and even his own ego, like a dream; he is rooted essentially in the "Ground," which attracts him so powerfully that his relations with the world are relativized to a degree that is often incomprehensible to us. The Western attitude, with its emphasis on the object, tends to fix the ideal—Christ—in its outward aspect and thus to rob it of its mysterious relation to the inner man. It is this prejudice, for instance, which impels the Protestant interpreters of the Bible to interpret ἐντὸς ὑμῶν (referring to the Kingdom of God) as "among you" instead of "within you." I do not mean to say anything about the validity of the Western attitude: we are sufficiently convinced of its rightness. But if we try to come to a real understanding of Eastern man—as the psychologist must—we find it hard to rid ourselves of certain misgivings. Anyone who can square it with his conscience is free to decide this question as he pleases, though he may be unconsciously setting himself up as an *arbiter mundi*. I for my part prefer the precious gift of doubt, for the reason that it does not violate the virginity of things beyond our ken.

9   Christ the ideal took upon himself the sins of the world. But if the ideal is wholly outside then the sins of the individual are also outside, and consequently he is more of a fragment than ever, since superficial misunderstanding conveniently enables him, quite literally, to "cast his sins upon Christ" and thus to evade his deepest responsibilities—which is contrary to the spirit of Christianity. Such formalism and laxity were not only one of the prime causes of the Reformation, they are also present within the body of Protestantism. If the supreme value (Christ) and the supreme negation (sin) are outside, then the soul is void: its highest and lowest are missing. The Eastern attitude (more particularly the Indian) is the other way about: everything, highest and lowest, is in the (transcendental) Subject. Accordingly the significance of the Atman, the Self, is heightened beyond all bounds. But with Western man the value of the self sinks to zero. Hence the universal depreciation of the soul in the West. Whoever speaks of the reality of the soul or psyche[2] is accused

---

[2] [The translation of the German word *Seele* presents almost insuperable difficulties on account of the lack of a single English equivalent and because it combines the two words "psyche" and "soul" in a way not altogether familiar to the Eng-

456

of "psychologism." Psychology is spoken of as if it were "only" psychology and nothing else. The notion that there can be psychic factors which correspond to divine figures is regarded as a devaluation of the latter. It smacks of blasphemy to think that a religious experience is a psychic process; for, so it is argued, a religious experience "is not *only* psychological." Anything psychic is *only* Nature and therefore, people think, nothing religious can come out of it. At the same time such critics never hesitate to derive all religions—with the exception of their own—from the nature of the psyche. It is a telling fact that two theological reviewers of my book *Psychology and Religion*—one of them Catholic, the other Protestant—assiduously overlooked my demonstration of the psychic origin of religious phenomena.

10   Faced with this situation, we must really ask: How do we know so much about the psyche that we can say "only" psychic? For this is how Western man, whose soul is evidently "of little worth," speaks and thinks. If much were in his soul he would speak of it with reverence. But since he does not do so we can only conclude that there is nothing of value in it. Not that this is necessarily so always and everywhere, but only with people who put nothing into their souls and have "all God outside." (A

---

lish reader. For this reason some comment by the Editors will not be out of place.

[In previous translations, and in this one as well, "psyche"—for which Jung in the German original uses either *Psyche* or *Seele*—has been used with reference to the totality of *all* psychic processes (cf. Jung, *Psychological Types*, Def. 48); i.e., it is a comprehensive term. "Soul," on the other hand, as used in the technical terminology of analytical psychology, is more restricted in meaning and refers to a "function complex" or partial personality and never to the whole psyche. It is often applied specifically to "anima" and "animus"; e.g., in this connection it is used in the composite word "soul-image" (*Seelenbild*). This conception of the soul is more primitive than the Christian one with which the reader is likely to be more familiar. In its Christian context it refers to "the transcendental energy in man" and "the spiritual part of man considered in its moral aspect or in relation to God." (Cf. definition in *The Shorter Oxford English Dictionary*.)

[In the above passage in the text (and in similar passages), "soul" is used in a non-technical sense (i.e., it does not refer to "animus" or "anima"), nor does it refer to the transcendental conception, but to a psychic (phenomenological) fact of a highly numinous character. This usage is adhered to except when the context shows clearly that the term is used in the Christian or Neoplatonic sense.—Editors.]

little more Meister Eckhart would be a very good thing sometimes!)

11   An exclusively religious projection may rob the soul of its values so that through sheer inanition it becomes incapable of further development and gets stuck in an unconscious state. At the same time it falls victim to the delusion that the cause of all misfortune lies outside, and people no longer stop to ask themselves how far it is their own doing. So insignificant does the soul seem that it is regarded as hardly capable of evil, much less of good. But if the soul no longer has any part to play, religious life congeals into externals and formalities. However we may picture the relationship between God and soul, one thing is certain: that the soul cannot be "nothing but." [3] On the contrary it has the dignity of an entity endowed with consciousness of a relationship to Deity. Even if it were only the relationship of a drop of water to the sea, that sea would not exist but for the multitude of drops. The immortality of the soul insisted upon by dogma exalts it above the transitoriness of mortal man and causes it to partake of some supernatural quality. It thus infinitely surpasses the perishable, conscious individual in significance, so that logically the Christian is forbidden to regard the soul as a "nothing but." [4] As the eye to the sun, so the soul corresponds to God. Since our conscious mind does not comprehend the soul it is ridiculous to speak of the things of the soul in a patronizing or depreciatory manner. Even the believing Christian does not know God's hidden ways and must leave him to decide whether he will work on man from outside or from within, through the soul. So the believer should not boggle at the fact that there are *somnia a Deo missa* (dreams sent by God) and illuminations of the soul which cannot be traced back to any external causes. It would be blasphemy to assert that God can manifest himself everywhere save only in the human soul. Indeed the very intimacy of the relationship between God and

3 [The term "nothing but" (*nichts als*), which occurs frequently in Jung to denote the habit of explaining something unknown by reducing it to something apparently known and thereby devaluing it, is borrowed from William James, *Pragmatism*, p. 16: "What is higher is explained by what is lower and treated for ever as a case of 'nothing but'—nothing but something else of a quite inferior sort."]
4 The dogma that man is formed in the likeness of God weighs heavily in the scales in any assessment of man—not to mention the Incarnation.

458

the soul precludes from the start any devaluation of the latter.[5] It would be going perhaps too far to speak of an affinity; but at all events the soul must contain in itself the faculty of relationship to God, i.e., a correspondence, otherwise a connection could never come about.[6] *This correspondence is, in psychological terms, the archetype of the God-image.*

12   Every archetype is capable of endless development and differentiation. It is therefore possible for it to be more developed or less. In an outward form of religion where all the emphasis is on the outward figure (hence where we are dealing with a more or less complete projection), the archetype is identical with externalized ideas but remains unconscious as a psychic factor. When an unconscious content is replaced by a projected image to that extent, it is cut off from all participation in and influence on the conscious mind. Hence it largely forfeits its own life, because prevented from exerting the formative influence on consciousness natural to it; what is more, it remains in its original form—unchanged, for nothing changes in the unconscious. At a certain point it even develops a tendency to regress to lower and more archaic levels. It may easily happen, therefore, that a Christian who believes in all the sacred figures is still undeveloped and unchanged in his inmost soul because he has "all God outside" and does not experience him in the soul. His deciding motives, his ruling interests and impulses, do not spring from the sphere of Christianity but from the unconscious and undeveloped psyche, which is as pagan and archaic as ever. Not the individual alone but the sum total of individual lives in a nation proves the truth of this contention. The great events of our world as planned and executed by man do not breathe the spirit of Christianity but rather of unadorned paganism. These things originate in a psychic condition that has remained archaic and has not been even remotely touched by Christianity. The Church assumes, not altogether without reason, that the fact

[5] The fact that the devil too can take possession of the soul does not diminish its significance in the least.

[6] It is therefore psychologically quite unthinkable for God to be simply the "wholly other," for a "wholly other" could never be one of the soul's deepest and closest intimacies—which is precisely what God is. The only statements that have psychological validity concerning the God-image are either paradoxes or antinomies.

of *semel credidisse* (having once believed) leaves certain traces behind it; but of these traces nothing is to be seen in the broad march of events. Christian civilization has proved hollow to a terrifying degree: it is all veneer, but the inner man has remained untouched and therefore unchanged. His soul is out of key with his external beliefs; in his soul the Christian has not kept pace with external developments. Yes, everything is to be found outside—in image and in word, in Church and Bible—but never inside. Inside reign the archaic gods, supreme as of old; that is to say the inner correspondence with the outer God-image is undeveloped for lack of psychological culture and has therefore got stuck in heathenism. Christian education has done all that is humanly possible, but it has not been enough. Too few people have experienced the divine image as the innermost possession of their own souls. Christ only meets them from without, never from within the soul; that is why dark paganism still reigns there, a paganism which, now in a form so blatant that it can no longer be denied and now in all too threadbare disguise, is swamping the world of so-called Christian civilization.

13   With the methods employed hitherto we have not succeeded in Christianizing the soul to the point where even the most elementary demands of Christian ethics can exert any decisive influence on the main concerns of the Christian European. The Christian missionary may preach the gospel to the poor naked heathen, but the spiritual heathen who populate Europe have as yet heard nothing of Christianity. Christianity must indeed begin again from the very beginning if it is to meet its high educative task. So long as religion is only faith and outward form, and the religious function is not experienced in our own souls, nothing of any importance has happened. It has yet to be understood that the *mysterium magnum* is not only an actuality but is first and foremost rooted in the human psyche. The man who does not know this from his own experience may be a most learned theologian, but he has no idea of religion and still less of education.

14   Yet when I point out that the soul possesses by nature a religious function,[7] and when I stipulate that it is the prime task of all education (of adults) to convey the archetype of the God-

7 Tertullian, *Apologeticus*, XVII: "Anima naturaliter christiana."

image, or its emanations and effects, to the conscious mind, then it is precisely the theologian who seizes me by the arm and accuses me of "psychologism." But were it not a fact of experience that supreme values reside in the soul (quite apart from the ἀντίμιμον πνεῦμα who is also there), psychology would not interest me in the least, for the soul would then be nothing but a miserable vapour. I know, however, from hundredfold experience that it is nothing of the sort, but on the contrary contains the equivalents of everything that has been formulated in dogma and a good deal more, which is just what enables it to be an eye destined to behold the light. This requires limitless range and unfathomable depth of vision. I have been accused of "deifying the soul." Not I but God himself has deified it! I did not attribute a religious function to the soul, I merely produced the facts which prove that the soul is *naturaliter religiosa*, i.e., possesses a religious function. I did not invent or insinuate this function, it produces itself of its own accord without being prompted thereto by any opinions or suggestions of mine. With a truly tragic delusion these theologians fail to see that it is not a matter of proving the existence of the light, but of blind people who do not know that their eyes could see. It is high time we realized that it is pointless to praise the light and preach it if nobody can see it. It is much more needful to teach people the art of seeing. For it is obvious that far too many people are incapable of establishing a connection between the sacred figures and their own psyche: they cannot see to what extent the equivalent images are lying dormant in their own unconscious. In order to facilitate this inner vision we must first clear the way for the faculty of seeing. How this is to be done without psychology, that is, without making contact with the psyche, is frankly beyond my comprehension.[8]

15   Another equally serious misunderstanding lies in imputing to psychology the wish to be a new and possibly heretical doctrine. If a blind man can gradually be helped to see it is not to be expected that he will at once discern new truths with an eagle eye. One must be glad it he sees anything at all, and if he begins to understand what he sees. Psychology is concerned with the act of seeing and not with the construction of new religious

[8] Since it is a question here of human effort, I leave aside acts of grace which are beyond man's control.

truths, when even the existing teachings have not yet been perceived and understood. In religious matters it is a well-known fact that we cannot understand a thing until we have experienced it inwardly, for it is in the inward experience that the connection between the psyche and the outward image or creed is first revealed as a relationship or correspondence like that of *sponsus* and *sponsa*. Accordingly when I say as a psychologist that God is an archetype, I mean by that the "type" in the psyche. The word "type" is, as we know, derived from τύπος, "blow" or "imprint"; thus an archetype presupposes an imprinter. Psychology as the science of the soul has to confine itself to its subject and guard against overstepping its proper boundaries by metaphysical assertions or other professions of faith. Should it set up a God, even as a hypothetical cause, it would have implicitly claimed the possibility of proving God, thus exceeding its competence in an absolutely illegitimate way. Science can only be science; there are no "scientific" professions of faith and similar *contradictiones in adiecto*. We simply do not know the ultimate derivation of the archetype any more than we know the origin of the psyche. The competence of psychology as an empirical science only goes so far as to establish, on the basis of comparative research, whether for instance the imprint found in the psyche can or cannot reasonably be termed a "God-image." Nothing positive or negative has thereby been asserted about the possible existence of God, any more than the archetype of the "hero" posits the actual existence of a hero.

Now if my psychological researches have demonstrated the existence of certain psychic types and their correspondence with well-known religious ideas, then we have opened up a possible approach to those experienceable contents which manifestly and undeniably form the empirical foundations of all religious experience. The religious-minded man is free to accept whatever metaphysical explanations he pleases about the origin of these images; not so the intellect, which must keep strictly to the principles of scientific interpretation and avoid trespassing beyond the bounds of what can be known. Nobody can prevent the believer from accepting God, Purusha, the Atman, or Tao as the Prime Cause and thus putting an end to the fundamental disquiet of man. The scientist is a scrupulous worker; he cannot take heaven by storm. Should he allow himself to be seduced

16

17 into such an extravagance he would be sawing off the branch on which he sits.

The fact is that with the knowledge and actual experience of these inner images a way is opened for reason and feeling to gain access to those other images which the teachings of religion offer to mankind. Psychology thus does just the opposite of what it is accused of: it provides possible approaches to a better understanding of these things, it opens people's eyes to the real meaning of dogmas, and, far from destroying, it throws open an empty house to new inhabitants. I can corroborate this from countless experiences: people belonging to creeds of all imaginable kinds, who had played the apostate or cooled off in their faith, have found a new approach to their old truths, not a few Catholics among them. Even a Parsee found the way back to the Zoroastrian fire-temple, which should bear witness to the objectivity of my point of view.

18 But this objectivity is just what my psychology is most blamed for: it is said not to decide in favour of this or that religious doctrine. Without prejudice to my own subjective convictions I should like to raise the question: Is it not thinkable that when one refrains from setting oneself up as an *arbiter mundi* and, deliberately renouncing all subjectivism, cherishes on the contrary the belief, for instance, that God has expressed himself in many languages and appeared in divers forms and that all these statements are *true*—is it not thinkable, I say, that this too is a decision? The objection raised, more particularly by Christians, that it is impossible for contradictory statements to be true, must permit itself to be politely asked: Does one equal three? How can three be one? Can a mother be a virgin? And so on. Has it not yet been observed that all religious statements contain logical contradictions and assertions that are impossible in principle, that this is in fact the very essence of religious assertion? As witness to this we have Tertullian's avowal: "And the Son of God is dead, which is worthy of belief because it is absurd. And when buried He rose again, which is certain because it is impossible." [9] If Christianity demands faith in such contradictions it does not seem to me that it can very well condemn those who assert a few paradoxes more. Oddly enough the paradox is one of our most valuable spiritual possessions, while

[9] Tertullian, *De carne Christi*, 5 (Migne, *P.L.*, vol. 2, col. 751).

uniformity of meaning is a sign of weakness. Hence a religion becomes inwardly impoverished when it loses or waters down its paradoxes; but their multiplication enriches because only the paradox comes anywhere near to comprehending the fulness of life. Non-ambiguity and non-contradiction are one-sided and thus unsuited to express the incomprehensible.

Not everyone possesses the spiritual strength of a Tertullian. It is evident not only that he had the strength to sustain paradoxes but that they actually afforded him the highest degree of religious certainty. The inordinate number of spiritual weaklings makes paradoxes dangerous. So long as the paradox remains unexamined and is taken for granted as a customary part of life, it is harmless enough. But when it occurs to an insufficiently cultivated mind (always, as we know, the most sure of itself) to make the paradoxical nature of some tenet of faith the object of its lucubrations, as earnest as they are impotent, it is not long before such a one will break out into iconoclastic and scornful laughter, pointing to the manifest absurdity of the mystery. Things have gone rapidly downhill since the Age of Enlightenment, for, once this petty reasoning mind, which cannot endure any paradoxes, is awakened, no sermon on earth can keep it down. A new task then arises: to lift this still undeveloped mind step by step to a higher level and to increase the number of persons who have at least some inkling of the scope of paradoxical truth. If this is not possible, then it must be admitted that the spiritual approaches to Christianity are as good as blocked. We simply do not understand any more what is meant by the paradoxes contained in dogma; and the more external our understanding of them becomes the more we are affronted by their irrationality, until finally they become completely obsolete, curious relics of the past. The man who is stricken in this way cannot estimate the extent of his spiritual loss, because he has never experienced the sacred images as his inmost possession and has never realized their kinship with his own psychic structure. But it is just this indispensable knowledge that the psychology of the unconscious can give him, and its scientific objectivity is of the greatest value here. Were psychology bound to a creed it would not and could not allow the unconscious of the individual that free play which is the basic condition for the production of archetypes. It is precisely the spontaneity of archetypal contents that convinces, whereas any prejudiced intervention is a bar to genuine experience. If the theologian really believes in the almighty power of God on the one hand and in the validity of dogma on the other, why then does he not trust God to speak in the soul? Why this fear of psychology? Or is, in complete contradiction to dogma, the soul itself a hell from which only demons gibber? Even if this were really so it would not be any the less convincing; for as we all know the horrified perception of the reality of evil has led to at least as many conversions as the experience of good.

20   The archetypes of the unconscious can be shown empirically to be the equivalents of religious dogmas. In the hermeneutic language of the Fathers the Church possesses a rich store of analogies with the individual and spontaneous products to be found in psychology. What the unconscious expresses is far from being merely arbitrary or opinionated: it is something that happens to be "just-so," as is the case with every other natural being. It stands to reason that the expressions of the unconscious are natural and not formulated dogmatically; they are exactly like the patristic allegories which draw the whole of nature into the orbit of their amplifications. If these present us with some astonishing *allegoriae Christi*, we find much the same sort of thing in the psychology of the unconscious. The only difference is that the patristic allegory *ad Christum spectat*—refers to Christ—whereas the psychic archetype is simply itself and can therefore be interpreted according to time, place, and milieu. In the West the archetype is filled out with the dogmatic figure of Christ; in the East, with Purusha, the Atman, Hiranyagarbha, the Buddha, and so on. The religious point of view, understandably enough, puts the accent on the imprinter, the imprint—the only thing it can understand. The religious point of view understands the imprint as the working of an imprinter; the scientific point of view understands it as the symbol of an unknown and incomprehensible content. Since the *typos* is less definite and more variegated than any of the figures postulated by religion, psychology is compelled by its empirical material to express the *typos* by means of a terminology not bound by time, place, or milieu. If, for example, the *typos* agreed in every detail with the dogmatic figure of Christ, and if it contained no determinant that went beyond

21 that figure, we would be bound to regard the *typos* as at least a faithful copy of the dogmatic figure, and to name it accordingly. The *typos* would then coincide with Christ. But as experience shows, this is not the case, seeing that the unconscious, like the allegories employed by the Church Fathers, produces countless other determinants that are not explicitly contained in the dogmatic formula; that is to say, non-Christian figures such as those mentioned above are included in the *typos*. But neither do these figures comply with the indeterminate nature of the archetype. It is altogether inconceivable that there could be any definite figure capable of expressing archetypal indefiniteness. For this reason I have found myself obliged to give the corresponding archetype the psychological name of the "self"—a term on the one hand definite enough to convey the essence of human wholeness and on the other hand indefinite enough to express the indescribable and indeterminable nature of this wholeness. The paradoxical qualities of the term are a reflection of the fact that wholeness consists partly of the conscious man and partly of the unconscious man. But we cannot define the latter or indicate his boundaries. Hence in its scientific usage the term "self" refers neither to Christ nor to the Buddha but to the totality of the figures that are its equivalent, and each of these figures is a symbol of the self. This mode of expression is an intellectual necessity in scientific psychology and in no sense denotes a transcendental prejudice. On the contrary, as we have said before, this objective attitude enables one man to decide in favour of the determinant Christ, another in favour of the Buddha, and so on. Those who are irritated by this objectivity should reflect that science is quite impossible without it. Consequently by denying psychology the right to objectivity they are making an untimely attempt to extinguish the life-light of a science. Even if such a preposterous attempt were to succeed, it would only widen the already catastrophic gulf between the secular mind on the one hand and Church and religion on the other.

It is quite understandable for a science to concentrate more or less exclusively on its subject—indeed, that is its absolute *raison d'être*. Since the concept of the self is of central interest in psychology, the latter naturally thinks along lines diametrically opposed to theology: for psychology the religious figures point to the self, whereas for theology the self points to its—theology's

—own central figure. In other words, theology might possibly take the psychological self as an allegory of Christ. This opposition is, no doubt, very irritating, but unfortunately inevitable, unless psychology is to be denied the right to exist at all. I therefore plead for tolerance. Nor is this very hard for psychology since as a science it makes no totalitarian claims.

22 The Christ-symbol is of the greatest importance for psychology in so far as it is perhaps the most highly developed and differentiated symbol of the self, apart from the figure of the Buddha. We can see this from the scope and substance of all the pronouncements that have been made about Christ: they agree with the psychological phenomenology of the self in unusually high degree, although they do not include all aspects of this archetype. The almost limitless range of the self might be deemed a disadvantage as compared with the definiteness of a religious figure, but it is by no means the task of science to pass value judgments. Not only is the self indefinite but—paradoxically enough—it also includes the quality of definiteness and even of uniqueness. This is probably one of the reasons why precisely those religions founded by historical personages have become world religions, such as Christianity, Buddhism, and Islam. The inclusion in a religion of a unique human personality —especially when conjoined to an indeterminable divine nature —is consistent with the absolute individuality of the self, which combines uniqueness with eternity and the individual with the universal. The self is a union of opposites *par excellence*, and this is where it differs essentially from the Christ-symbol. The androgyny of Christ is the utmost concession the Church has made to the problem of opposites. The opposition between light and good on the one hand and darkness and evil on the other is left in a state of open conflict, since Christ simply represents good, and his counterpart the devil, evil. This opposition is the real world problem, which at present is still unsolved. The self, however, is absolutely paradoxical in that it represents in every respect thesis and antithesis, and at the same time synthesis. (Psychological proofs of this assertion abound, though it is impossible for me to quote them here *in extenso*. I would refer the knowledgeable reader to the symbolism of the mandala.)

23 Once the exploration of the unconscious has led the conscious mind to an experience of the archetype, the individual is con-

467

fronted with the abysmal contradictions of human nature, and this confrontation in turn leads to the possibility of a direct experience of light and darkness, of Christ and the devil. For better or worse there is only a bare possibility of this, and not a guarantee; for experiences of this kind cannot of necessity be induced by any human means. There are factors to be considered which are not under our control. Experience of the opposites has nothing whatever to do with intellectual insight or with empathy. It is more what we would call fate. Such an experience can convince one person of the truth of Christ, another of the truth of the Buddha, to the exclusion of all other evidence.

Without the experience of the opposites there is no experience of wholeness and hence no inner approach to the sacred figures. For this reason Christianity rightly insists on sinfulness and original sin, with the obvious intent of opening up the abyss of universal opposition in every individual—at least from the outside. But this method is bound to break down in the case of a moderately alert intellect: dogma is then simply no longer believed and on top of that is thought absurd. Such an intellect is merely one-sided and sticks at the *ineptia mysterii*. It is miles from Tertullian's antinomies; in fact, it is quite incapable of enduring the suffering such a tension involves. Cases are not unknown where the rigorous exercises and proselytizings of the Catholics, and a certain type of Protestant education that is always sniffing out sin, have brought about psychic damage that leads not to the Kingdom of Heaven but to the consulting room of the doctor. Although insight into the problem of opposites is absolutely imperative, there are very few people who can stand it in practice—a fact which has not escaped the notice of the confessional. By way of a reaction to this we have the palliative of "moral probabilism," a doctrine that has suffered frequent attack from all quarters because it tries to mitigate the crushing effect of sin.[10] Whatever one may think of this phe-

10 Zöckler ("Probabilismus," p. 67) defines it as follows: "Probabilism is the name generally given to that way of thinking which is content to answer scientific questions with a greater or lesser degree of probability. The moral probabilism with which alone we are concerned here consists in the principle that acts of ethical self-determination are to be guided not by conscience but according to what is probably right, i.e., according to whatever has been recommended by any representative or doctrinal authority." The Jesuit probabilist Escobar (d. 1669) was, for instance, of the opinion that if the penitent should plead a probable opinion

nomenon one thing is certain: that apart from anything else it holds within it a large humanity and an understanding of human weakness which compensate for the world's unbearable antinomies. The tremendous paradox implicit in the insistence on original sin on the one hand and the concession made by probabilism on the other is, for the psychologist, a necessary consequence of the Christian problem of opposites outlined above —for in the self good and evil are indeed closer than identical twins! The reality of evil and its incompatibility with good cleave the opposites asunder and lead inexorably to the crucifixion and suspension of everything that lives. Since "the soul is by nature Christian," this result is bound to come as infallibly as it did in the life of Jesus: we all have to be "crucified with Christ," i.e., suspended in a moral suffering equivalent to veritable crucifixion. In practice this is only possible up to a point, and apart from that is so unbearable and inimical to life that the ordinary human being can afford to get into such a state only occasionally, in fact as seldom as possible. For how could he remain ordinary in face of such suffering! A more or less probabilistic attitude to the problem of evil is therefore unavoidable. Hence the truth about the self—the unfathomable union of good and evil—comes out concretely in the paradox that although sin is the gravest and most pernicious thing there is, it is still not so serious that it cannot be disposed of with "probabilist" arguments. Nor is this necessarily a lax or frivolous proceeding but simply a practical necessity of life. The confessional proceeds like life itself, which successfully struggles against being engulfed in an irreconcilable contradiction. Note that at the same time the conflict remains in full force, as is once more consistent with the antinomial character of the self, which is itself both conflict and unity.

as the motive of his action, the father-confessor would be obliged to absolve him even if he were not of the same opinion. Escobar quotes a number of Jesuit authorities on the question of how often one is bound to love God in a lifetime. According to one opinion, loving God once shortly before death is sufficient; another says once a year or once every three or four years. He himself comes to the conclusion that it is sufficient to love God once at the first awakening of reason, then once every five years, and finally once in the hour of death. In his opinion the large number of different moral doctrines forms one of the main proofs of God's kindly providence, "because they make the yoke of Christ so light" (Zöckler, p. 68). Cf. also Harnack, *History of Dogma*, VII, pp. 101ff.

Christianity has made the antinomy of good and evil into a world problem and, by formulating the conflict dogmatically, raised it to an absolute principle. Into this as yet unresolved conflict the Christian is cast as a protagonist of good, a fellow player in the world drama. Understood in its deepest sense, being Christ's follower involves a suffering that is unendurable to the great majority of mankind. Consequently the example of Christ is in reality followed either with reservation or not at all, and the pastoral practice of the Church even finds itself obliged to "lighten the yoke of Christ." This means a pretty considerable reduction in the severity and harshness of the conflict and hence, in practice, a relativism of good and evil. Good is equivalent to the unconditional imitation of Christ and evil is its hindrance. Man's moral weakness and sloth are what chiefly hinder the imitation, and it is to these that probabilism extends a practical understanding which may sometimes, perhaps, come nearer to Christian tolerance, mildness, and love of one's neighbour than the attitude of those who see in probabilism a mere laxity. Although one must concede a number of cardinal Christian virtues to the probabilist endeavour, one must still not overlook the fact that it obviates much of the suffering involved in the imitation of Christ and that the conflict of good and evil is thus robbed of its harshness and toned down to tolerable proportions. This brings about an approach to the psychic archetype of the self, where even these opposites seem to be united—though, as I say, it differs from the Christian symbolism, which leaves the conflict open. For the latter there is a rift running through the world: light wars against night and the upper against the lower. The two are not one, as they are in the psychic archetype. But, even though religious dogma may condemn the idea of two being one, religious practice does, as we have seen, allow the natural psychological symbol of the self at one with itself an approximate means of expression. On the other hand, dogma insists that three are one, while denying that four are one. Since olden times, not only in the West but also in China, uneven numbers have been regarded as masculine and even numbers as feminine. The Trinity is therefore a decidedly masculine deity, of which the androgyny of Christ and the special position and veneration accorded to the Mother of God are not the real equivalent.

26   With this statement, which may strike the reader as peculiar, we come to one of the central axioms of alchemy, namely the saying of Maria Prophetissa: "One becomes two, two becomes three, and out of the third comes the one as the fourth." As the reader has already seen from its title, this book is concerned with the psychological significance of alchemy and thus with a problem which, with very few exceptions, has so far eluded scientific research. Until quite recently science was interested only in the part that alchemy played in the history of chemistry, concerning itself very little with the part it played in the history of philosophy and religion. The importance of alchemy for the historical development of chemistry is obvious, but its cultural importance is still so little known that it seems almost impossible to say in a few words wherein that consisted. In this introduction, therefore, I have attempted to outline the religious and psychological problems which are germane to the theme of alchemy. The point is that alchemy is rather like an undercurrent to the Christianity that ruled on the surface. It is to this surface as the dream is to consciousness, and just as the dream compensates the conflicts of the conscious mind, so alchemy endeavours to fill in the gaps left open by the Christian tension of opposites. Perhaps the most pregnant expression of this is the axiom of Maria Prophetissa quoted above, which runs like a *leitmotiv* throughout almost the whole of the lifetime of alchemy, extending over more than seventeen centuries. In this aphorism the even numbers which signify the feminine principle, earth, the regions under the earth, and evil itself are interpolated between the uneven numbers of the Christian dogma. They are personified by the *serpens mercurii*, the dragon that creates and destroys itself and represents the *prima materia*. This fundamental idea of alchemy points back to the םוֹהְּת (Tehom),[11] to Tiamat with her dragon attribute, and thus to the primordial matriarchal world which, in the theomachy of the Marduk myth,[12] was overthrown by the masculine world of the father. The historical shift in the world's consciousness towards the masculine is compensated at first by the chthonic femininity of the

11 Cf. Genesis 1 : 2.
12 The reader will find a collection of these myth motifs in Lang, *Hat ein Gott die Welt erschaffen?* Unfortunately philological criticism will have much to take exception to in this book, interesting though it is for its Gnostic trend.

unconscious. In certain pre-Christian religions the differentiation of the masculine principle had taken the form of the father-son specification, a change which was to be of the utmost importance for Christianity. Were the unconscious merely complementary, this shift of consciousness would have been accompanied by the production of a mother and daughter, for which the necessary material lay ready to hand in the myth of Demeter and Persephone. But, as alchemy shows, the unconscious chose rather the Cybele-Attis type in the form of the *prima materia* and the *filius macrocosmi*, thus proving that it is not complementary but compensatory. This goes to show that the unconscious does not simply act *contrary* to the conscious mind but *modifies* it more in the manner of an opponent or partner. The son type does not call up a daughter as a complementary image from the depths of the "chthonic" unconscious—it calls up another son. This remarkable fact would seem to be connected with the incarnation in our earthly human nature of a purely spiritual God, brought about by the Holy Ghost impregnating the womb of the Blessed Virgin. Thus the higher, the spiritual, the masculine inclines to the lower, the earthly, the feminine; and accordingly, the mother, who was anterior to the world of the father, accommodates herself to the masculine principle and, with the aid of the human spirit (alchemy or "the philosophy"), produces a son —not the antithesis of Christ but rather his chthonic counterpart, not a divine man but a fabulous being conforming to the nature of the primordial mother. And just as the redemption of man the microcosm is the task of the "upper" son, so the "lower" son has the function of a *salvator macrocosmi*.

27   This, in brief, is the drama that was played out in the obscurities of alchemy. It is superfluous to remark that these two sons were never united, except perhaps in the mind and innermost experience of a few particularly gifted alchemists. But it is not very difficult to see the "purpose" of this drama: in the Incarnation it looked as though the masculine principle of the father-world were approximating to the feminine principle of the mother-world, with the result that the latter felt impelled to approximate in turn to the father-world. What it evidently amounted to was an attempt to bridge the gulf separating the two worlds as compensation for the open conflict between them.

28   I hope the reader will not be offended if my exposition

29 sounds like a Gnostic myth. We are moving in those psychological regions where, as a matter of fact, Gnosis is rooted. The message of the Christian symbol is Gnosis, and the compensation effected by the unconscious is Gnosis in even higher degree. Myth is the primordial language natural to these psychic processes, and no intellectual formulation comes anywhere near the richness and expressiveness of mythical imagery. Such processes are concerned with the primordial images, and these are best and most succinctly reproduced by figurative language.

30 The process described above displays all the characteristic features of psychological compensation. We know that the mask of the unconscious is not rigid—it reflects the face we turn towards it. Hostility lends it a threatening aspect, friendliness softens its features. It is not a question of mere optical reflection but of an autonomous answer which reveals the self-sufficing nature of that which answers. Thus the *filius philosophorum* is not just the reflected image, in unsuitable material, of the son of God; on the contrary, this son of Tiamat reflects the features of the primordial maternal figure. Although he is decidedly hermaphroditic he has a masculine name—a sign that the chthonic underworld, having been rejected by the spirit and identified with evil, has a tendency to compromise. There is no mistaking the fact that he is a concession to the spiritual and masculine principle, even though he carries in himself the weight of the earth and the whole fabulous nature of primordial animality.

This answer of the mother-world shows that the gulf between it and the father-world is not unbridgeable, seeing that the unconscious holds the seed of the unity of both. The essence of the conscious mind is discrimination; it must, if it is to be aware of things, separate the opposites, and it does this *contra naturam*. In nature the opposites seek one another—*les extrêmes se touchent*—and so it is in the unconscious, and particularly in the archetype of unity, the self. Here, as in the deity, the opposites cancel out. But as soon as the unconscious begins to manifest itself they split asunder, as at the Creation; for every act of dawning consciousness is a creative act, and it is from this psychological experience that all our cosmogonic symbols are derived.

31 Alchemy is pre-eminently concerned with the seed of unity which lies hidden in the chaos of Tiamat and forms the counterpart to the divine unity. Like this, the seed of unity has a trini-

tarian character in Christian alchemy and a triadic character in pagan alchemy. According to other authorities it corresponds to the unity of the four elements and is therefore a quaternity. The overwhelming majority of modern psychological findings speaks in favour of the latter view. The few cases I have observed which produced the number three were marked by a systematic deficiency in consciousness, that is to say, by an unconsciousness of the "inferior function." The number three is not a natural expression of wholeness, since four represents the minimum number of determinants in a whole judgment. It must nevertheless be stressed that side by side with the distinct leanings of alchemy (and of the unconscious) towards quaternity there is always a vacillation between three and four which comes out over and over again. Even in the axiom of Maria Prophetissa the quaternity is muffled and alembicated. In alchemy there are three as well as four *regimina* or procedures, three as well as four colours. There are always four elements, but often three of them are grouped together, with the fourth in a special position—sometimes earth, sometimes fire. Mercurius[13] is of course *quadratus*, but he is also a three-headed snake or simply a triunity. This uncertainty has a duplex character—in other words, the central ideas are ternary as well as quaternary. The psychologist cannot but mention the fact that a similar puzzle exists in the psychology of the unconscious: the least differentiated or "inferior" function is so much contaminated with the collective unconscious that, on becoming conscious, it brings up among others the archetype of the self as well—τὸ ἕν τέταρτον, as Maria Prophetissa says. Four signifies the feminine, motherly, physical; three the masculine, fatherly, spiritual. Thus the uncertainty as

13 In alchemical writings the word "Mercurius" is used with a very wide range of meaning, to denote not only the chemical element mercury or quicksilver, Mercury (Hermes) the god, and Mercury the planet, but also—and primarily—the secret "transforming substance" which is at the same time the "spirit" indwelling in all living creatures. These different connotations will become apparent in the course of the book. It would be misleading to use the English "Mercury" and "mercury," because there are innumerable passages where neither word does justice to the wealth of implications. It has therefore been decided to retain the Latin "Mercurius" as in the German text, and to use the personal pronoun (since "Mercurius" is personified), the word "quicksilver" being employed only where the chemical element (Hg) is plainly meant. [*Author's note for the English edn.*]

to three or four amounts to a wavering between the spiritual and the physical—a striking example of how every human truth is a last truth but one.

32   I began my introduction with human wholeness as the goal to which the psychotherapeutic process ultimately leads. This question is inextricably bound up with one's philosophical or religious assumptions. Even when, as frequently happens, the patient believes himself to be quite unprejudiced in this respect, the assumptions underlying his thought, mode of life, morale, and language are historically conditioned down to the last detail, a fact of which he is often kept unconscious by lack of education combined with lack of self-criticism. The analysis of his situation will therefore lead sooner or later to a clarification of his general spiritual background going far beyond his personal determinants, and this brings up the problems I have attempted to sketch in the preceding pages. This phase of the process is marked by the production of symbols of unity, the so-called mandalas, which occur either in dreams or in the form of concrete visual impressions, often as the most obvious compensation of the contradictions and conflicts of the conscious situation. It would hardly be correct to say that the gaping "rift" [14] in the Christian order of things is responsible for this, since it is easy to show that Christian symbolism is particularly concerned with healing, or attempting to heal, this very wound. It would be more correct to take the open conflict as a symptom of the psychic situation of Western man, and to deplore his inability to assimilate the whole range of the Christian symbol. As a doctor I cannot demand anything of my patients in this respect, also I lack the Church's means of grace. Consequently I am faced with the task of taking the only path open to me: the archetypal images—which in a certain sense correspond to the dogmatic images—must be brought into consciousness. At the same time I must leave my patient to decide in accordance with his assumptions, his spiritual maturity, his education, origins, and temperament, so far as this is possible without serious conflicts. As a doctor it is my task to help the patient to cope with life. I cannot presume to pass judgment on his final decisions, because I know from experience that all coercion—be it suggestion, insinuation, or any other method of persuasion—ultimately

14 Przywara, *Deus semper maior*, I, pp. 71ff.

proves to be nothing but an obstacle to the highest and most decisive experience of all, which is to be alone with his own self, or whatever else one chooses to call the objectivity of the psyche. The patient must be alone if he is to find out what it is that supports him when he can no longer support himself. Only this experience can give him an indestructible foundation.

33 I would be only too delighted to leave this anything but easy task to the theologian, were it not that many of my patients come. They ought to have hung on to the community of the Church, but they were shed like dry leaves from the great tree and now find themselves "hanging on" to the treatment. Something in them clings, often with the strength of despair, as if they or the thing they cling to would drop off into the void the moment they relaxed their hold. They are seeking firm ground on which to stand. Since no outward support is of any use to them they must finally discover it in themselves—admittedly the most unlikely place from the rational point of view, but an altogether possible one from the point of view of the unconscious. We can see this from the archetype of the "lowly origin of the redeemer."

34 The way to the goal seems chaotic and interminable at first, and only gradually do the signs increase that it is leading anywhere. The way is not straight but appears to go round in circles. More accurate knowledge has proved it to go in spirals: the dream-motifs always return after certain intervals to definite forms, whose characteristic it is to define a centre. And as a matter of fact the whole process revolves about a central point or some arrangement round a centre, which may in certain circumstances appear even in the initial dreams. As manifestations of unconscious processes the dreams rotate or circumambulate round the centre, drawing closer to it as the amplifications increase in distinctness and in scope. Owing to the diversity of the symbolical material it is difficult at first to perceive any kind of order at all. Nor should it be taken for granted that dream sequences are subject to any governing principle. But, as I say, the process of development proves on closer inspection to be cyclic or spiral. We might draw a parallel between such spiral courses and the processes of growth in plants; in fact the plant motif (tree, flower, etc.) frequently recurs in these dreams and

fantasies and is also spontaneously drawn or painted.[15] In alchemy the tree is the symbol of Hermetic philosophy.

35   The first of the following two studies—that which composes Part II—deals with a series of dreams which contain numerous symbols of the centre or goal. The development of these symbols is almost the equivalent of a healing process. The centre or goal thus signifies *salvation* in the proper sense of the word. The justification for such a terminology comes from the dreams themselves, for these contain so many references to religious phenomena that I was able to use some of them as the subject of my book *Psychology and Religion*. It seems to me beyond all doubt that these processes are concerned with the religion-creating archetypes. Whatever else religion may be, those psychic ingredients of it which are empirically verifiable undoubtedly consist of unconscious manifestations of this kind. People have dwelt far too long on the fundamentally sterile question of whether the assertions of faith are true or not. Quite apart from the impossibility of ever proving or refuting the truth of a metaphysical assertion, the very existence of the assertion is a self-evident fact that needs no further proof, and when a *consensus gentium* allies itself thereto the validity of the statement is proved to just that extent. The only thing about it that we can verify is the psychological phenomenon, which is incommensurable with the category of objective rightness or truth. No phenomenon can ever be disposed of by rational criticism, and in religious life we have to deal with phenomena and facts and not with arguable hypotheses.

36   During the process of treatment the dialectical discussion leads logically to a meeting between the patient and his shadow, that dark half of the psyche which we invariably get rid of by means of projection: either by burdening our neighbours—in a wider or narrower sense—with all the faults which we obviously have ourselves, or by casting our sins upon a divine mediator with the aid of *contritio* or the milder *attritio*.[16] We know of

---

[15] See the illustrations in Jung, "Concerning Mandala Symbolism."

[16] *Contritio* is "perfect" repentance; *attritio* "imperfect" repentance (*contritio imperfecta*, to which category *contritio naturalis* belongs). The former regards sin as the opposite of the highest good; the latter reprehends it not only on account of its wicked and hideous nature but also from fear of punishment.

course that without sin there is no repentance and without repentance no redeeming grace, also that without original sin the redemption of the world could never have come about; but we assiduously avoid investigating whether in this very power of evil God might not have placed some special purpose which it is most important for us to know. One often feels driven to some such view when, like the psychotherapist, one has to deal with people who are confronted with their blackest shadow.[17] At any rate the doctor cannot afford to point, with a gesture of facile moral superiority, to the tables of the law and say, "Thou shalt not." He has to examine things objectively and weigh up possibilities, for he knows, less from religious training and education than from instinct and experience, that there is something very like a *felix culpa*. He knows that one can miss not only one's happiness but also one's final guilt, without which a man will never reach his wholeness. Wholeness is in fact a charisma which one can manufacture neither by art nor by cunning; one can only grow into it and endure whatever its advent may bring. No doubt it is a great nuisance that mankind is not uniform but compounded of individuals whose psychic structure spreads them over a span of at least ten thousand years. Hence there is absolutely no truth that does not spell salvation to one person and damnation to another. All universalisms get stuck in this terrible dilemma. Earlier on I spoke of Jesuit probabilism: this gives a better idea than anything else of the tremendous catholic task of the Church. Even the best-intentioned people have been horrified by probabilism, but, when brought face to face with the realities of life, many of them have found their horror evaporating or their laughter dying on their lips. The doctor too must weigh and ponder, not whether a thing is for or against the Church but whether it is for or against life and health. On paper the moral code looks clear and neat enough;

17 A religious terminology comes naturally, as the only adequate one in the circumstances, when we are faced with the tragic fate that is the unavoidable concomitant of wholeness. "My fate" means a daemonic will to precisely that fate—a will not necessarily coincident with my own (the ego will). When it is opposed to the ego, it is difficult not to feel a certain "power" in it, whether divine or infernal. The man who submits to his fate calls it the will of God; the man who puts up a hopeless and exhausting fight is more apt to see the devil in it. In either event this terminology is not only universally understood but meaningful as well.

478

but the same document written on the "living tables of the heart" is often a sorry tatter, particularly in the mouths of those who talk the loudest. We are told on every side that evil is evil and that there can be no hesitation in condemning it, but that does not prevent evil from being the most problematical thing in the individual's life and the one which demands the deepest reflection. What above all deserves our keenest attention is the question "Exactly *who* is the doer?" For the answer to this question ultimately decides the value of the deed. It is true that society attaches greater importance at first to what is done, because it is immediately obvious; but in the long run the right deed in the hands of the wrong man will also have a disastrous effect. No one who is far-sighted will allow himself to be hoodwinked by the right deed of the wrong man, any more than by the wrong deed of the right man. Hence the psychotherapist must fix his eye not on what is done but on how it is done, because therein is decided the whole character of the doer. Evil needs to be pondered just as much as good, for good and evil are ultimately nothing but ideal extensions and abstractions of doing, and both belong to the chiaroscuro of life. In the last resort there is no good that cannot produce evil and no evil that cannot produce good.

37 The encounter with the dark half of the personality, or "shadow," comes about of its own accord in any moderately thorough treatment. This problem is as important as that of sin in the Church. The open conflict is unavoidable and painful. I have often been asked, "And what do you *do* about it?" I do nothing; there is nothing I can do except wait, with a certain trust in God, until, out of a conflict borne with patience and fortitude, there emerges the solution destined—although I cannot foresee it—for that particular person. Not that I am passive or inactive meanwhile: I help the patient to understand all the things that the unconscious produces during the conflict. The reader may believe me that these are no ordinary products. On the contrary, they are among the most significant things that have ever engaged my attention. Nor is the patient inactive; he must do the right thing, and do it with all his might, in order to prevent the pressure of evil from becoming too powerful in him. He needs "justification by works," for "justification by faith" alone has remained an empty sound for him as for so many

others. Faith can sometimes be a substitute for lack of experience. In these cases what is needed is real work. Christ espoused the sinner and did not condemn him. The true follower of Christ will do the same, and, since one should do unto others as one would do unto oneself, one will also take the part of the sinner who is oneself. And as little as we would accuse Christ of fraternizing with evil, so little should we reproach ourselves that to love the sinner who is oneself is to make a pact with the devil. Love makes a man better, hate makes him worse—even when that man is oneself. The danger in this point of view is the same as in the imitation of Christ; but the Pharisee in us will never allow himself to be caught talking to publicans and whores. I must emphasize of course that psychology invented neither Christianity nor the imitation of Christ. I wish everybody could be freed from the burden of their sins by the Church. But he to whom she cannot render this service must bend very low in the imitation of Christ in order to take the burden of his cross upon him. The ancients could get along with the Greek wisdom of the ages: Μηδὲν ἄγαν, τῷ καιρῷ πάντα πρόσεστι καλά (Exaggerate nothing, all good lies in right measure). But what an abyss still separates us from reason!

38   Apart from the moral difficulty there is another danger which is not inconsiderable and may lead to complications, particularly with individuals who are pathologically inclined. This is the fact that the contents of the personal unconscious (i.e., the shadow) are indistinguishably merged with the archetypal contents of the collective unconscious and drag the latter with them when the shadow is brought into consciousness. This may exert an uncanny influence on the conscious mind; for activated archetypes have a disagreeable effect even—or I should perhaps say, particularly—on the most cold-blooded rationalist. He is afraid that the lowest form of conviction, namely superstition, is, as he thinks, forcing itself on him. But superstition in the truest sense only appears in such people if they are pathological, not if they can keep their balance. It then takes the form of the fear of "going mad"—for everything that the modern mind cannot define it regards as insane. It must be admitted that the archetypal contents of the collective unconscious can often assume grotesque and horrible forms in dreams and fantasies, so that even the most hard-boiled rationalist is not immune from shattering nightmares and haunting fears. The

psychological elucidation of these images, which cannot be passed over in silence or blindly ignored, leads logically into the depths of religious phenomenology. The history of religion in its widest sense (including therefore mythology, folklore, and primitive psychology) is a treasure-house of archetypal forms from which the doctor can draw helpful parallels and enlightening comparisons for the purpose of calming and clarifying a consciousness that is all at sea. It is absolutely necessary to supply these fantastic images that rise up so strange and threatening before the mind's eye with some kind of context so as to make them more intelligible. Experience has shown that the best way to do this is by means of comparative mythological material.

39   Part II of this volume gives a large number of such examples. The reader will be particularly struck by the numerous connections between individual dream symbolism and medieval alchemy. This is not, as one might suppose, a prerogative of the case in question, but a general fact which only struck me some ten years ago when first I began to come to grips with the ideas and symbolism of alchemy.

40   Part III contains an introduction to the symbolism of alchemy in relation to Christianity and Gnosticism. As a bare introduction it is naturally far from being a complete exposition of this complicated and obscure subject—indeed, most of it is concerned only with the *lapis*-Christ parallel. True, this parallel gives rise to a comparison between the aims of the *opus alchymicum* and the central ideas of Christianity, for both are of the utmost importance in understanding and interpreting the images that appear in dreams and in assessing their psychological effect. This has considerable bearing on the practice of psychotherapy, because more often than not it is precisely the more intelligent and cultured patients who, finding a return to the Church impossible, come up against archetypal material and thus set the doctor problems which can no longer be mastered by a narrowly personalistic psychology. Nor is a mere knowledge of the psychic structure of a neurosis by any means sufficient; for once the process has reached the sphere of the collective unconscious we are dealing with healthy material, i.e., with the universal basis of the individually varied psyche. Our understanding of these deeper layers of the psyche is helped not only by a knowledge of primitive psychology and mythology, but to an even greater extent by some familiarity with the history of our

modern consciousness and the stages immediately preceding it. On the one hand it is a child of the Church; on the other, of science, in whose beginnings very much lies hid that the Church was unable to accept—that is to say, remnants of the classical spirit and the classical feeling for nature which could not be exterminated and eventually found refuge in the natural philosophy of the Middle Ages. As the "spiritus metallorum" and the astrological components of destiny the old gods of the planets lasted out many a Christian century.[18] Whereas in the Church the increasing differentiation of ritual and dogma alienated consciousness from its natural roots in the unconscious, alchemy and astrology were ceaselessly engaged in preserving the bridge to nature, i.e., to the unconscious psyche, from decay. Astrology led the conscious mind back again and again to the knowledge of Heimarmene, that is, the dependence of character and destiny on certain moments in time; and alchemy afforded numerous "hooks" for the projection of those archetypes which could not be fitted smoothly into the Christian process. It is true that alchemy always stood on the verge of heresy and that certain decrees leave no doubt as to the Church's attitude towards it,[19] but on the other hand it was effectively protected by the obscurity of its symbolism, which could always be explained as harmless allegory. For many alchemists the allegorical aspect undoubtedly occupied the foreground to such an extent that they were firmly convinced that their sole concern was with chemical substances. But there were always a few for whom laboratory work was primarily a matter of symbols and their psychic effect. As the texts show, they were quite conscious of this, to the point of condemning the naïve goldmakers as liars, frauds, and dupes. Their own standpoint they proclaimed with propositions like "Aurum nostrum non est aurum vulgi." Although their labours over the retort were a serious effort to elicit the secrets of chemical transformation, it was at the same time —and often in overwhelming degree—the reflection of a parallel psychic process which could be projected all the more easily into the unknown chemistry of matter since that process is an uncon-

18 Paracelsus still speaks of the "gods" enthroned in the *mysterium magnum* (*Philosophia ad Athenienses*, p. 403), and so does the 18th-cent. treatise of Abraham Eleazar, *Uraltes chymisches Werk*, which was influenced by Paracelsus.
19 Cf. Sanchez, *Opus morale*, Decalog. 2, 49m, 51; and Pignatelli, *Consultationes canonicae*, canon ix.

scious phenomenon of nature, just like the mysterious alteration of substances. What the symbolism of alchemy expresses is the whole problem of the evolution of personality described above, the so-called individuation process.

41   Whereas the Church's great buttress is the imitation of Christ, the alchemist, without realizing it and certainly without wanting it, easily fell victim, in the loneliness and obscure problems of his work, to the promptings and unconscious assumptions of his own mind, since, unlike the Christians, he had no clear and unmistakable models on which to rely. The authors he studied provided him with symbols whose meaning he thought he understood in his own way; but in reality they touched and stimulated his unconscious. Ironical towards themselves, the alchemists coined the phrase "obscurum per obscurius." But with this method of explaining the obscure by the more obscure they only sank themselves deeper in the very process from which the Church was struggling to redeem them. While the dogmas of the Church offered analogies to the alchemical process, these analogies, in strict contrast to alchemy, had become detached from the world of nature through their connection with the historical figure of the Redeemer. The alchemical four in one, the philosophical gold, the *lapis angularis*, the *aqua divina*, became, in the Church, the four-armed cross on which the Only-Begotten had sacrificed himself once in history and at the same time for all eternity. The alchemists ran counter to the Church in preferring to seek through knowledge rather than to find through faith, though as medieval people they never thought of themselves as anything but good Christians. Paracelsus is a classical example in this respect. But in reality they were in much the same position as modern man, who prefers immediate personal experience to belief in traditional ideas, or rather has it forced upon him. Dogma is not arbitrarily invented nor is it a unique miracle, although it is often described as miraculous with the obvious intent of lifting it out of its natural context. The central ideas of Christianity are rooted in Gnostic philosophy, which, in accordance with psychological laws, simply *had* to grow up at a time when the classical religions had become obsolete. It was founded on the perception of symbols thrown up by the unconscious individuation process which always sets in when the collective dominants of human life fall into decay. At such a time there is bound to

be a considerable number of individuals who are possessed by archetypes of a numinous nature that force their way to the surface in order to form new dominants. This state of possession shows itself almost without exception in the fact that the possessed identify themselves with the archetypal contents of their unconscious, and, because they do not realize that the role which is being thrust upon them is the effect of new contents still to be understood, they exemplify these concretely in their own lives, thus becoming prophets and reformers. In so far as the archetypal content of the Christian drama was able to give satisfying expression to the uneasy and clamorous unconscious of the many, the *consensus omnium* raised this drama to a universally binding truth—not of course by an act of judgment, but by the irrational fact of possession, which is far more effective. Thus Jesus became the tutelary image or amulet against the archetypal powers that threatened to possess everyone. The glad tidings announced: "It has happened, but it will not happen to you inasmuch as you believe in Jesus Christ, the Son of God." Yet it could and it can and it will happen to everyone in whom the Christian dominant has decayed. For this reason there have always been people who, not satisfied with the dominants of conscious life, set forth—under cover and by devious paths, to their destruction or salvation—to seek direct experience of the eternal roots, and, following the lure of the restless unconscious psyche, find themselves in the wilderness where, like Jesus, they come up against the son of darkness, the ἀντίμιμον πνεῦμα. Thus an old alchemist—and he a cleric!—prays: "Horridas nostrae mentis purga tenebras, accende lumen sensibus!" (Purge the horrible darknesses of our mind, light a light for our senses!) The author of this sentence must have been undergoing the experience of the *nigredo*, the first stage of the work, which was felt as "melancholia" in alchemy and corresponds to the encounter with the shadow in psychology.

42   When, therefore, modern psychotherapy once more meets with the activated archetypes of the collective unconscious, it is merely the repetition of a phenomenon that has often been observed in moments of great religious crisis, although it can also occur in individuals for whom the ruling ideas have lost their meaning. An example of this is the *descensus ad inferos* depicted in *Faust*, which, consciously or unconsciously, is an *opus alchymicum*.

43   The problem of opposites called up by the shadow plays a great—indeed, the decisive—role in alchemy, since it leads in the ultimate phase of the work to the union of opposites in the archetypal form of the *hierosgamos* or "chymical wedding." Here the supreme opposites, male and female (as in the Chinese *yang* and *yin*), are melted into a unity purified of all opposition and therefore incorruptible. The prerequisite for this, of course, is that the artifex should not identify himself with the figures in the work but should leave them in their objective, impersonal state. So long as the alchemist was working in his laboratory he was in a favourable position, psychologically speaking, for he had no opportunity to identify himself with the archetypes as they appeared, since they were all projected immediately into the chemical substances. The disadvantage of this situation was that the alchemist was forced to represent the incorruptible substance as a chemical product—an impossible undertaking which led to the downfall of alchemy, its place in the laboratory being taken by chemistry. But the psychic part of the work did not disappear. It captured new interpreters, as we can see from the example of *Faust*, and also from the signal connection between our modern psychology of the unconscious and alchemical symbolism.

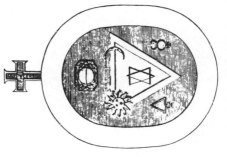

3. Symbol of the alchemical work.
—*Hermaphroditisches Sonn- und Mondskind* (1752)

485

FROM *PSYCHOLOGY AND RELIGION*

The Autonomy of the Unconscious

1   As it seems to be the intention of the founder of the Terry Lectures to enable representatives of science, as well as of philosophy and other spheres of human knowledge, to contribute to the discussion of the eternal problem of religion, and since Yale University has bestowed upon me the great honour of delivering the Terry Lectures for 1937, I assume that it will be my task to show what psychology, or rather that special branch of medical psychology which I represent, has to do with or to say about religion. Since religion is incontestably one of the earliest and most universal expressions of the human mind, it is obvious that any psychology which touches upon the psychological structure of human personality cannot avoid taking note of the fact that religion is not only a sociological and historical phenomenon, but also something of considerable personal concern to a great number of individuals.

2   Although I have often been called a philosopher, I am an empiricist and adhere as such to the phenomenological standpoint. I trust that it does not conflict with the principles of scientific empiricism if one occasionally makes certain reflections which go beyond a mere accumulation and classification of experience. As a matter of fact I believe that experience is not even possible without reflection, because "experience" is a process of assimilation without which there could be no under-

3 standing. As this statement indicates, I approach psychological matters from a scientific and not from a philosophical standpoint. Inasmuch as religion has a very important psychological aspect, I deal with it from a purely empirical point of view, that is, I restrict myself to the observation of phenomena and I eschew any metaphysical or philosophical considerations. I do not deny the validity of these other considerations, but I cannot claim to be competent to apply them correctly.

  I am aware that most people believe they know all there is to be known about psychology, because they think that psychology is nothing but what they know of themselves. But I am afraid psychology is a good deal more than that. While having little to do with philosophy, it has much to do with empirical facts, many of which are not easily accessible to the experience of the average man. It is my intention to give you a few glimpses of the way in which practical psychology comes up against the problem of religion. It is self-evident that the vastness of the problem requires far more than three lectures, as the necessary elaboration of concrete detail takes a great deal of time and explanation. My first lecture will be a sort of introduction to the problem of practical psychology and religion. The second is concerned with facts which demonstrate the existence of an authentic religious function in the unconscious. The third deals with the religious symbolism of unconscious processes.

4 Since I am going to present a rather unusual argument, I cannot assume that my audience will be fully acquainted with the methodological standpoint of the branch of psychology I represent. This standpoint is exclusively phenomenological, that is, it is concerned with occurrences, events, experiences—in a word, with facts. Its truth is a fact and not a judgment. When psychology speaks, for instance, of the motif of the virgin birth, it is only concerned with the fact that there is such an idea, but it is not concerned with the question whether such an idea is true or false in any other sense. The idea is psychologically true inasmuch as it exists. Psychological existence is subjective in so far as an idea occurs in only one individual. But it is objective in so far as that idea is shared by a society—by a *consensus gentium*.

5 This point of view is the same as that of natural science. Psychology deals with ideas and other mental contents as zool-

488

ogy, for instance, deals with the different species of animals. An elephant is "true" because it exists. The elephant is neither an inference nor a statement nor the subjective judgment of a creator. It is a phenomenon. But we are so used to the idea that psychic events are wilful and arbitrary products, or even the inventions of a human creator, that we can hardly rid ourselves of the prejudiced view that the psyche and its contents are nothing but our own arbitrary invention or the more or less illusory product of supposition and judgment. The fact is that certain ideas exist almost everywhere and at all times and can even spontaneously create themselves quite independently of migration and tradition. They are not made by the individual, they just happen to him—they even force themselves on his consciousness. This is not Platonic philosophy but empirical psychology.

6   In speaking of religion I must make clear from the start what I mean by that term. Religion, as the Latin word denotes, is a careful and scrupulous observation of what Rudolf Otto [1] aptly termed the *numinosum*, that is, a dynamic agency or effect not caused by an arbitrary act of will. On the contrary, it seizes and controls the human subject, who is always rather its victim than its creator. The *numinosum*—whatever its cause may be—is an experience of the subject independent of his will. At all events, religious teaching as well as the *consensus gentium* always and everywhere explain this experience as being due to a cause external to the individual. The *numinosum* is either a quality belonging to a visible object or the influence of an invisible presence that causes a peculiar alteration of consciousness. This is, at any rate, the general rule.

7   There are, however, certain exceptions when it comes to the question of religious practice or ritual. A great many ritualistic performances are carried out for the sole purpose of producing at will the effect of the *numinosum* by means of certain devices of a magical nature, such as invocation, incantation, sacrifice, meditation and other yoga practices, self-inflicted tortures of various descriptions, and so forth. But a religious belief in an external and objective divine cause is always prior to any such performance. The Catholic Church, for instance, administers the sacraments for the purpose of bestowing their spiritual blessings upon the believer; but since this act would amount to

1 *The Idea of the Holy.*

enforcing the presence of divine grace by an indubitably magical procedure, it is logically argued that nobody can compel divine grace to be present in the sacramental act, but that it is nevertheless inevitably present since the sacrament is a divine institution which God would not have caused to be if he had not intended to lend it his support.[2]

8   Religion appears to me to be a peculiar attitude of mind which could be formulated in accordance with the original use of the word *religio*, which means a careful consideration and observation of certain dynamic factors that are conceived as "powers": spirits, daemons, gods, laws, ideas, ideals, or whatever name man has given to such factors in his world as he has found powerful, dangerous, or helpful enough to be taken into careful consideration, or grand, beautiful, and meaningful enough to be devoutly worshipped and loved. In colloquial speech one often says of somebody who is enthusiastically interested in a certain pursuit that he is almost "religiously devoted" to his cause; William James, for instance, remarks that a scientist often has no creed, but his "temper is devout."[3]

9   I want to make clear that by the term "religion"[4] I do not mean a creed. It is, however, true that every creed is originally based on the one hand upon the experience of the *numinosum* and on the other hand upon πίστις, that is to say, trust or loyalty, faith and confidence in a certain experience of a numinous nature and in the change of consciousness that ensues. The conversion of Paul is a striking example of this. We might say, then, that the term "religion" designates the attitude peculiar to a consciousness which has been changed by experience of the *numinosum*.

---

2 *Gratia adiuvans* and *gratia sanctificans* are the effects of the *sacramentum ex opere operato*. The sacrament owes its undoubted efficacy to the fact that it is directly instituted by Christ himself. The Church is powerless to connect the rite with grace in such a way that the sacramental act would produce the presence and effect of grace. Consequently the rite performed by the priest is not a *causa instrumentalis*, but merely a *causa ministerialis*.

3 "But our esteem for facts has not neutralized in us all religiousness. It is itself almost religious. Our scientific temper is devout." *Pragmatism*, p. 14.

4 "Religion is that which gives reverence and worship to some higher nature [which is called divine]." Cicero, *De inventione rhetorica*, II, 53, 161. For "testimony given under the sanction of religion on the faith of an oath" cf. Cicero, *Pro Coelio*, 55.

10   Creeds are codified and dogmatized forms of original religious experience.[5] The contents of the experience have become sanctied and are usually congealed in a rigid, often elaborate, structure of ideas. The practice and repetition of the original experience have become a ritual and an unchangeable institution. This does not necessarily mean lifeless petrifaction. On the contrary, it may prove to be a valid form of religious experience for millions of people for thousands of years, without there arising any vital necessity to alter it. Although the Catholic Church has often been accused of particular rigidity, she nevertheless admits that dogma is a living thing and that its formulation is therefore capable of change and development. Even the number of dogmas is not limited and can be multiplied in the course of time. The same holds true of the ritual. Yet all changes and developments are determined within the framework of the facts as originally experienced, and this sets up a special kind of dogmatic content and emotional value. Even Protestantism, which has abandoned itself apparently to an almost unlimited emancipation from dogmatic tradition and codified ritual and has thus split into more than four hundred denominations—even Protestantism is bound at least to be Christian and to express itself within the framework of the belief that God revealed himself in Christ, who suffered for mankind. This is a definite framework with definite contents which cannot be combined with or supplemented by Buddhist or Islamic ideas and feelings. Yet it is unquestionably true that not only Buddha and Mohammed, Confucius and Zarathustra, represent religious phenomena, but also Mithras, Attis, Cybele, Mani, Hermes, and the deities of many other exotic cults. The psychologist, if he takes up a scientific attitude, has to disregard the claim of every creed to be the unique and eternal truth. He must keep his eye on the human side of the religious problem, since he is concerned with the original religious experience quite apart from what the creeds have made of it.

11   As I am a doctor and a specialist in nervous and mental diseases, my point of departure is not a creed but the psychology of the *homo religiosus*, that is, of the man who takes into account and carefully observes certain factors which influence him and

5 Heinrich Scholz (*Die Religionsphilosophie des Als-Ob*) insists on a similar standpoint. Cf. also Pearcy, *A Vindication of Paul.*

his general condition. It is easy to designate and define these factors in accordance with historical tradition or ethnological knowledge, but to do the same thing from the standpoint of psychology is an uncommonly difficult task. What I can contribute to the question of religion is derived entirely from my practical experience, both with my patients and with so-called normal persons. As our experience with people depends to a large extent upon what we do with them, I can see no other way of proceeding than to give you at least a general idea of the line I take in my professional work.

Since every neurosis is connected with man's most intimate life, there will always be some hesitation when a patient has to give a complete account of all the circumstances and complications which originally led him into a morbid condition. But why shouldn't he be able to talk freely? Why should he be afraid or shy or prudish? The reason is that he is "carefully observing" certain external factors which together constitute what one calls public opinion or respectability or reputation. And even if he trusts his doctor and is no longer shy of him, he will be reluctant or even afraid to admit certain things to *himself*, as if it were dangerous to become conscious of himself. One is usually afraid of things that seem to be overpowering. But is there anything in man that is stronger than himself? We should not forget that every neurosis entails a corresponding amount of demoralization. If a man is neurotic, he has lost confidence in himself. A neurosis is a humiliating defeat and is felt as such by people who are not entirely unconscious of their own psychology. And one is defeated by something "unreal." Doctors may have assured the patient, long ago, that there is nothing the matter with him, that he does not suffer from a real heart-disease or from a real cancer. His symptoms are quite imaginary. The more he believes that he is a *malade imaginaire*, the more a feeling of inferiority permeates his whole personality. "If my symptoms are imaginary," he will say, "where have I picked up this confounded imagination and why should I put up with such a perfect nuisance?" It is indeed pathetic to have an intelligent man almost imploringly assure you that he is suffering from an intestinal cancer and declare at the same time in a despondent voice that of course he knows his cancer is a purely imaginary affair.

Our usual materialistic conception of the psyche is, I am

afraid, not particularly helpful in cases of neurosis. If only the soul were endowed with a subtle body, then one could at least say that this breath- or vapour-body was suffering from a real though somewhat ethereal cancer, in the same way as the gross material body can succumb to a cancerous disease. That, at least, would be something real. Medicine therefore feels a strong aversion for anything of a psychic nature—either the body is ill or there is nothing the matter. And if you cannot prove that the body is really ill, that is only because our present techniques do not enable the doctor to discover the true nature of the undoubtedly organic trouble.

14 But what, actually, is the psyche? Materialistic prejudice explains it as a mere epiphenomenal by-product of organic processes in the brain. Any psychic disturbance must therefore be an organic or physical disorder which is undiscoverable only because of the inadequacy of our present methods of diagnosis. The undeniable connection between psyche and brain gives this point of view a certain weight, but not enough to make it an unshakable truth. We do not know whether there is a real disturbance of the organic processes in the brain in a case of neurosis, and if there are disorders of an endocrine nature it is impossible to say whether they might not be effects rather than causes.

15 On the other hand, it cannot be doubted that the real causes of neurosis are psychological. Not so long ago it was very difficult to imagine how an organic or physical disorder could be relieved by quite simple psychological means, yet in recent years medical science has recognized a whole class of diseases, the psychosomatic disorders, in which the patient's psychology plays the essential part. Since my readers may not be familiar with these medical facts I may instance a case of hysterical fever, with a temperature of 102°, which was cured in a few minutes through confession of the psychological cause. A patient with psoriasis extending over practically the whole body was told that I did not feel competent to treat his skin trouble, but that I should concentrate on his psychological conflicts, which were numerous. After six weeks of intense analysis and discussion of his purely psychological difficulties, there came about as an unexpected by-product the almost complete disappearance of the skin disease. In another case, the patient had recently undergone an

operation for distention of the colon. Forty centimetres of it had been removed, but this was followed by another extraordinary distention. The patient was desperate and refused to permit a second operation, though the surgeon thought it vital. As soon as certain intimate psychological facts were discovered, the colon began to function normally again.

16   Such experiences make it exceedingly difficult to believe that the psyche is nothing, or that an imaginary fact is unreal. Only, it is not there where a near-sighted mind seeks it. It exists, but not in physical form. It is an almost absurd prejudice to suppose that existence can only be physical. As a matter of fact, the only form of existence of which we have immediate knowledge is psychic. We might well say, on the contrary, that physical existence is a mere inference, since we know of matter only in so far as we perceive psychic images mediated by the senses.

17   We are surely making a great mistake when we forget this simple yet fundamental truth. Even if a neurosis had no cause at all other than imagination, it would, none the less, be a very real thing. If a man imagined that I was his arch-enemy and killed me, I should be dead on account of mere imagination. Imaginary conditions do exist and they may be just as real and just as harmful or dangerous as physical conditions. I even believe that psychic disturbances are far more dangerous than epidemics or earthquakes. Not even the medieval epidemics of bubonic plague or smallpox killed as many people as certain differences of opinion in 1914 or certain political "ideals" in Russia.

18   Although the mind cannot apprehend its own form of existence, owing to the lack of an Archimedean point outside, it nevertheless exists. Not only does the psyche exist, it is existence itself.

19   What, then, shall we say to our patient with the imaginary cancer? I would tell him: "Yes, my friend, you are really suffering from a cancer-like thing, you really do harbour in yourself a deadly evil. However, it will not kill your body, because it is imaginary. But it will eventually kill your soul. It has already spoilt and even poisoned your human relations and your personal happiness and it will go on growing until it has swallowed your whole psychic existence. So that in the end you will not be a human being any more, but an evil destructive tumour."

20 It is obvious to our patient that he is not the author of his morbid imagination, although his theoretical turn of mind will certainly suggest that he is the owner and maker of his own imaginings. If a man is suffering from a real cancer, he never believes himself to be responsible for such an evil, despite the fact that the cancer is in his own body. But when it comes to the psyche we instantly feel a kind of responsibility, as if we were the makers of our psychic conditions. This prejudice is of relatively recent date. Not so very long ago even highly civilized people believed that psychic agencies could influence our minds and feelings. There were ghosts, wizards, and witches, daemons and angels, and even gods, who could produce certain psychological changes in human beings. In former times the man with the idea that he had cancer might have felt quite differently about his idea. He would probably have assumed that somebody had worked witchcraft against him or that he was possessed. He never would have thought of himself as the originator of such a fantasy.

21 As a matter of fact, I take his cancer to be a spontaneous growth, which originated in the part of the psyche that is not identical with consciousness. It appears as an autonomous formation intruding upon consciousness. Of consciousness one might say that it is our own psychic existence, but the cancer has *its* own psychic existence, independent of ourselves. This statement seems to formulate the observable facts completely. If we submit such a case to an association experiment,[6] we soon discover that he is not master in his own house. His reactions will be delayed, altered, suppressed, or replaced by autonomous intruders. There will be a number of stimulus-words which cannot be answered by his conscious intention. They will be answered by certain autonomous contents, which are very often unconscious even to himself. In our case we shall certainly discover answers that come from the psychic complex at the root of the cancer idea. Whenever a stimulus-word touches something connected with the hidden complex, the reaction of the conscious ego will be disturbed, or even replaced, by an answer coming from the complex. It is just as if the complex were an autonomous being capable of interfering with the intentions of

[6] Cf. my "Studies in Word Association."

22

the ego. Complexes do indeed behave like secondary or partial personalities possessing a mental life of their own.

23

Many complexes are split off from consciousness because the latter preferred to get rid of them by repression. But there are others that have never been in consciousness before and therefore could never have been arbitrarily repressed. They grow out of the unconscious and invade the conscious mind with their weird and unassailable convictions and impulses. Our patient belonged to the latter category. Despite his culture and intelligence, he was a helpless victim of something that obsessed and possessed him. He was unable to help himself in any way against the demonic power of his morbid idea. It proliferated in him like a carcinoma. One day the idea appeared and from then on it remained unshakable; there were only short intervals when he was free from it.

The existence of such cases does something to explain why people are afraid of becoming conscious of themselves. There might really be something behind the screen—one never knows —and so people prefer "to consider and observe carefully" the factors external to their consciousness. In most people there is a sort of primitive δεισιδαιμονία with regard to the possible contents of the unconscious. Beneath all natural shyness, shame, and tact, there is a secret fear of the unknown "perils of the soul." Of course one is reluctant to admit such a ridiculous fear. But one should realize that this fear is by no means unjustified; on the contrary, it is only too well founded. We can never be sure that a new idea will not seize either upon ourselves or upon our neighbours. We know from modern as well as from ancient history that such ideas are often so strange, indeed so bizarre, that they fly in the face of reason. The fascination which is almost invariably connected with ideas of this sort produces a fanatical obsession, with the result that all dissenters, no matter how well meaning or reasonable they are, get burnt alive or have their heads cut off or are disposed of in masses by the more modern machine-gun. We cannot even console ourselves with the thought that such things belong to the remote past. Unfortunately they seem to belong not only to the present, but, quite particularly, to the future. "Homo homini lupus" is a sad yet eternal truism. There is indeed reason enough for man to be afraid of the impersonal forces lurking in his unconscious. We

24 are blissfully unconscious of these forces because they never, or almost never, appear in our personal relations or under ordinary circumstances. But if people crowd together and form a mob, then the dynamisms of the collective man are let loose—beasts or demons that lie dormant in every person until he is part of a mob. Man in the mass sinks unconsciously to an inferior moral and intellectual level, to that level which is always there, below the threshold of consciousness, ready to break forth as soon as it is activated by the formation of a mass.

25 It is, to my mind, a fatal mistake to regard the human psyche as a purely personal affair and to explain it exclusively from a personal point of view. Such a mode of explanation is only applicable to the individual in his ordinary everyday occupations and relationships. If, however, some slight trouble occurs, perhaps in the form of an unforeseen and somewhat unusual event, instantly instinctual forces are called up, forces which appear to be wholly unexpected, new, and strange. They can no longer be explained in terms of personal motives, being comparable rather to certain primitive occurrences like panics at solar eclipses and the like. To explain the murderous outbreak of Bolshevism, for instance, as a personal father-complex appears to me singularly inadequate.

26 The change of character brought about by the uprush of collective forces is amazing. A gentle and reasonable being can be transformed into a maniac or a savage beast. One is always inclined to lay the blame on external circumstances, but nothing could explode in us if it had not been there. As a matter of fact, we are constantly living on the edge of a volcano, and there is, so far as we know, no way of protecting ourselves from a possible outburst that will destroy everybody within reach. It is certainly a good thing to preach reason and common sense, but what if you have a lunatic asylum for an audience or a crowd in a collective frenzy? There is not much difference between them because the madman and the mob are both moved by impersonal, overwhelming forces.

As a matter of fact, it only needs a neurosis to conjure up a force that cannot be dealt with by rational means. Our cancer case shows clearly how impotent man's reason and intellect are against the most palpable nonsense. I always advise my patients to take such obvious but invincible nonsense as the manifesta-

497

tion of a power and a meaning they have not yet understood. Experience has taught me that it is much more effective to take these things seriously and then look for a suitable explanation. But an explanation is suitable only when it produces a hypothesis equal to the morbid effect. Our patient is confronted with a power of will and suggestion more than equal to anything his consciousness can put against it. In this precarious situation it would be bad strategy to convince him that in some incomprehensible way he is at the back of his own symptom, secretly inventing and supporting it. Such a suggestion would instantly paralyse his fighting spirit, and he would get demoralized. It is far better for him to understand that his complex is an autonomous power directed against his conscious personality. Moreover, such an explanation fits the actual facts much better than a reduction to personal motives. An apparently personal motivation does exist, but it is not made by his will, it just happens to him.

27   When in the Babylonian epic Gilgamesh's arrogance and hybris defy the gods, they create a man equal in strength to Gilgamesh in order to check the hero's unlawful ambition. The very same thing has happened to our patient: he is a thinker who has settled, or is always going to settle, the world by the power of his intellect and reason. His ambition has at least succeeded in forging his own personal fate. He has forced everything under the inexorable law of his reason, but somewhere nature escaped and came back with a vengeance in the form of an unassailable bit of nonsense, the cancer idea. This was the clever device of the unconscious to keep him on a merciless and cruel leash. It was the worst blow that could be dealt to all his rational ideals and especially to his belief in the all-powerful human will. Such an obsession can occur only in a person who makes habitual misuse of reason and intellect for egotistical power purposes.

28   Gilgamesh, however, escaped the vengeance of the gods. He had warning dreams to which he paid attention. They showed him how he could overcome his enemy. Our patient, living in an age when the gods have become extinct and have fallen into bad repute, also had such dreams, but he did not listen to them. How could an intelligent man be so superstitious as to take dreams seriously! The very common prejudice against dreams is

29 but one symptom of a far more serious undervaluation of the human psyche in general. The marvellous development of science and technics is counterbalanced by an appalling lack of wisdom and introspection. It is true that our religion speaks of an immortal soul; but it has very few kind words to say for the human psyche as such, which would go straight to eternal damnation were it not for a special act of Divine Grace. These two important factors are largely responsible for the general undervaluation of the psyche, but not entirely so. Older by far than these relatively recent developments are the primitive fear of and aversion to everything that borders on the unconscious.

Consciousness must have been a very precarious thing in its beginnings. In relatively primitive societies we can still observe how easily consciousness gets lost. One of the "perils of the soul," [7] for instance, is the loss of a soul. This is what happens when part of the psyche becomes unconscious again. Another example is "running amok," [8] the equivalent of "going berserk" in Germanic saga. [9] This is a more or less complete trance-state, often accompanied by devastating social effects. Even a quite ordinary emotion can cause considerable loss of consciousness. Primitives therefore cultivate elaborate forms of politeness, speaking in a hushed voice, laying down their weapons, crawling on all fours, bowing the head, showing the palms. Even our own forms of politeness still exhibit a "religious" consideration of possible psychic dangers. We propitiate fate by magically wishing one another a good day. It is not good form to keep the left hand in your pocket or behind your back when shaking hands. If you want to be particularly ingratiating you use both hands. Before people of great authority we bow with uncovered head, i.e., we offer our head unprotected in order to propitiate the powerful one, who might quite easily fall sudden prey to a fit of uncontrollable violence. In war-dances primitives can become so excited that they may even shed blood.

30 The life of the primitive is filled with constant regard for the ever-lurking possibility of psychic danger, and the procedures employed to diminish the risks are very numerous. The setting up of tabooed areas is an outward expression of this fact. The

[7] Frazer, *Taboo and the Perils of the Soul*, pp. 30ff.; Crawley, *The Idea of the Soul*, pp. 82ff.; Lévy-Bruhl, *Primitive Mentality*.   [8] Fenn, *Running Amok*.
[9] Ninck, *Wodan und germanischer Schicksalsglaube*.

innumerable taboos are delimited psychic areas which are meticulously and fearfully observed. I once made a terrific mistake when I was with a tribe on the southern slopes of Mount Elgon, in East Africa. I wanted to inquire about the ghosthouses I frequently found in the woods, and during a palaver I mentioned the word *selelteni*, meaning 'ghost.' Instantly everybody was silent and painfully embarrassed. They all looked away from me because I had spoken aloud a carefully hushed-up word, and had thus invited most dangerous consequences. I had to change the subject in order to be able to continue the meeting. The same men assured me that they never had dreams; they were the prerogative of the chief and of the medicine man. The medicine man then confessed to me that he no longer had any dreams either, they had the District Commissioner instead. "Since the English are in the country we have no dreams any more," he said. "The District Commissioner knows everything about war and diseases, and about where we have got to live." This strange statement is based on the fact that dreams were formerly the supreme political guide, the voice of *Mungu*, 'God.' Therefore it would have been unwise for an ordinary man to suggest that he had dreams.

³¹   Dreams are the voice of the Unknown, ever threatening new schemes, new dangers, sacrifices, warfare, and other troublesome things. An African Negro once dreamt that his enemies had taken him prisoner and burnt him alive. The next day he called his relatives together and implored them to burn him. They consented so far as to bind his feet together and put them in the fire. He was of course badly crippled but had escaped his foes.[10]

³²   There are any amount of magical rites that exist for the sole purpose of erecting a defence against the unexpected, dangerous tendencies of the unconscious. The peculiar fact that the dream is a divine voice and messenger and yet an unending source of trouble does not disturb the primitive mind in the least. We find obvious remnants of this primitive thinking in the psychology of the Hebrew prophets.[11] Often enough they hesitate to listen to the voice. And it was, we must admit, rather hard on a pious man like Hosea to marry a harlot in order to obey the

10 Lévy-Bruhl, *How Natives Think*, and *Primitive Mentality*, ch. 3, "Dreams," pp. 97ff.

11 Haeussermann, *Wortempfang und Symbol in der alttestamentlichen Prophetie*.

Lord's command. Since the dawn of humanity there has been a marked tendency to limit this unruly and arbitrary "supernatural" influence by means of definite forms and laws. And this process has continued throughout history in the form of a multiplication of rites, institutions, and beliefs. During the last two thousand years we find the institution of the Christian Church taking over a mediating and protective function between these influences and man. It is not denied in medieval ecclesiastical writings that a divine influx may occur in dreams, but this view is not exactly encouraged, and the Church reserves the right to decide whether a revelation is to be considered authentic or not.[12] In spite of the Church's recognition that

[12] In his excellent treatise on dreams and their functions, Benedictus Pererius, S.J. (*De Magia; De Observatione Somniorum et de Divinatione Astrologica libri tres*, 1598) says. "For God is not constrained by such laws of time, nor does he await opportune moments for his operation; for he inspires dreams where he will, when he will, and in whomsoever he will" (p. 147). The following passage throws an interesting light on the relation of the Church to the problem of dreams: "For we read in Cassian's 22nd Collation, that the old governors and directors of the monks were well versed in seeking out and testing the causes of certain dreams" (p. 142). Pererius classifies dreams as follows: "Many [dreams] are natural, some are of human origin, and some are even divine" (p. 145). There are four causes of dreams: (1) An affection of the body. (2) An affect or vehement commotion of the mind caused by love, hope, fear, or hatred (pp. 126ff.). (3) The power and cunning of the demon, i.e. of a heathen god or the Christian devil. ("For the devil is able to know natural effects which will needs come about at some future time from fixed causes; he can know those things which he himself is going to bring about at a later time; he can know things, both present and past, which are hidden from men, and make them known to men in dreams" [p. 129]. Concerning the diagnosis of demonic dreams, the author says: "It can be surmised that dreams are sent by the devil, firstly if dreams often occur which signify future or hidden events, knowledge whereof is advantageous not to any useful end whether for oneself or for others, but only for the vain display of curious information, or even for the doing of some evil act . . ." [p. 130].) (4) Dreams sent by God. Concerning the signs indicating the divine nature of a dream, the author says: ". . . from the importance of the matters made known by the dream, especially if, in the dream, those things are made known to a man of which certain knowledge can come to him only by God's leave and bounty. Of such sort are those things which in the schools of the theologians are called contingent future events; further, the secrets of the heart which are wholly hidden from all men's understanding; and lastly, those highest mysteries of our faith which are known to no man unless he be taught them by God [!] . . . That this [is divine] is especially declared by a certain enlightenment and moving of the spirits, whereby God so illumines the mind, so acts upon the will, and so assures the dreamer of the

certain dreams are sent by God, she is disinclined, and even averse, to any serious concern with dreams, while admitting that some might conceivably contain an immediate revelation. Thus the change of mental attitude that has taken place in recent centuries is, from this point of view at least, not wholly unwelcome to the Church," because it effectively discouraged the earlier introspective attitude which favoured a serious consideration of dreams and inner experiences.

credibility and authority of his dream that he so clearly recognizes and so certainly judges God to be its author that he not only desires to believe it, but must believe it without any doubt whatsoever" (pp. 131ff). Since the demon, as stated above, is also capable of producing dreams accurately predicting future events, the author adds a quotation from Gregory the Great (*Dialogorum Libri IV*, cap. 48, in Migne, *P.L.*, vol. 77, col. 412): "Holy men discern between illusions and revelations, the very words and images of visions, by a certain inward sensibility, so that they know what they receive from the good spirit and what they endure from the deceiver. For if a man's mind were not careful in this regard, it would plunge itself into many vanities through the deceiving spirit, who is sometimes wont to foretell many true things, in order that he may entirely prevail to ensnare the soul by some one single falsity" (p. 132). It seemed to be a welcome safeguard against this uncertainty if dreams were concerned with the "highest mysteries of our faith." Athanasius, in his biography of St. Anthony, gives us some idea of how clever the devils are in foretelling future events. (Cf. Budge, *The Book of Paradise*, I, pp. 37ff.) The same author says they sometimes appear even in the shape of monks, singing psalms, reading the Bible aloud, and making disturbing remarks about the moral conduct of the brethren (pp. 33ff. and 47). Pererius, however, seems to trust his own criterion, for he continues: "As therefore the natural light of our minds enables us clearly to discern the truth of first principles, so that they are embraced by our assent immediately and without any argument; so in dreams sent by God the divine light shining upon our minds brings it about that we understand and believe with certainty that those dreams are true and of God." He does not touch on the delicate question of whether every unshakable conviction derived from a dream necessarily proves the divine origin of the dream. He merely takes it for granted that a dream of this sort would naturally exhibit a character consistent with the "highest mysteries of our faith," and not perchance with those of another one. The humanist Kaspar Peucer (in his *Commentarius de praecipuis generibus divinationum*, 1560) is far more definite and restrictive in this respect. He says (p. 270): "Those dreams are of God which the sacred scriptures affirm to be sent from on high, not to every one promiscuously, nor to those who strive after and expect revelations of their own opinion, but to the Holy Patriarchs and Prophets by the will and judgment of God. [Such dreams are concerned] not with light matters, or with trifles and ephemeral things, but with Christ, the governance of the Church, with empires and their well ordering, and other remarkable events; and to these God always adds sure testimonies, such as the gift of interpretation and other things, by

33   Protestantism, having pulled down so many walls carefully erected by the Church, immediately began to experience the disintegrating and schismatic effect of individual revelation. As soon as the dogmatic fence was broken down and the ritual lost its authority, man had to face his inner experience without the protection and guidance of dogma and ritual, which are the very quintessence of Christian as well as of pagan religious experience. Protestantism has, in the main, lost all the finer shades of traditional Christianity: the mass, confession, the greater part of the liturgy, and the vicarious function of priesthood.

34   I must emphasize that this statement is not a value-judgment and is not intended to be one. I merely state the facts. Protestantism has, however, intensified the authority of the Bible as a substitute for the lost authority of the Church. But as history has shown, one can interpret certain biblical texts in many ways. Nor has scientific criticism of the New Testament been very helpful in enhancing belief in the divine character of the holy scriptures. It is also a fact that under the influence of a so-called

which it is clear that they are not rashly to be objected to, nor are they of natural origin, but are divinely inspired." His crypto-Calvinism is palpably manifest in his words, particularly when one compares them with the natural theology of his Catholic contemporaries. It is probable that Peucer's hint about "revelations" refers to certain heretical innovations. At any rate, in the next paragraph, where he deals with dreams of diabolical origin, he says these are the dreams "which the devil shows nowadays to Anabaptists, and at all times to Enthusiasts and suchlike fanatics." Pererius with more perspicacity and human understanding devotes one chapter to the question "Whether it be lawful for a Christian man to observe dreams?" (pp. 142ff.) and another to the question "To what kind of man does it belong to interpret dreams aright?" (pp. 245ff.). In the first he reaches the conclusion that important dreams should be considered. I quote his words: "Finally, to consider whether the dreams which ofttimes disturb us and move us to evil courses are put before us by the devil, as likewise on the other hand to ponder whether those by which we are aroused and incited to good, as for example to celibacy, almsgiving, and entering the religious life, are sent us by God, is the part not of a superstitious mind, but of one that is religious, prudent, and careful and solicitous for its salvation." Only stupid people would observe all the other futile dreams. In the second chapter, he answers that nobody should or could interpret dreams "unless he be divinely inspired and instructed." "Even so," he adds, "the things of God knoweth no man, but the Spirit of God" (I Cor. 2:11). This statement, eminently true in itself, reserves the art of interpretation to such persons as are endowed by their office with the gift of the Holy Spirit. It is obvious, however, that a Jesuit author could not envisage a descent of the Holy Spirit outside the Church.

scientific enlightenment great masses of educated people have either left the Church or become profoundly indifferent to it. If they were all dull rationalists or neurotic intellectuals the loss would not be regrettable. But many of them are religious people, only incapable of agreeing with the existing forms of belief. Otherwise, one could hardly explain the remarkable effect of the Buchman movement on the more-or-less educated Protestant classes. The Catholic who has turned his back on the Church usually develops a secret or manifest leaning towards atheism, whereas the Protestant follows, if possible, a sectarian movement. The absolutism of the Catholic Church seems to demand an equally absolute negation, whereas Protestant relativism permits of variations.

35   It may perhaps be thought that I have gone a bit too far into the history of Christianity, and for no other purpose than to explain the prejudice against dreams and inner experiences. But what I have just said might have been part of my conversation with our cancer patient. I told him that it would be better to take his obsession seriously instead of reviling it as pathological nonsense. But to take it seriously would mean acknowledging it as a sort of diagnostic statement of the fact that, in a psyche which really existed, trouble had arisen in the form of a cancer-like growth. "But," he will certainly ask, "what could that growth be?" And I shall answer: "I do not know," as indeed I do not. Although, as I mentioned before, it is surely a compensatory or complementary unconscious formation, nothing is yet known about its specific nature or about its content. It is a spontaneous manifestation of the unconscious, based on contents which are not to be found in consciousness.

36   My patient is now very curious how I shall set about getting at the contents that form the root of the obsession. I then inform him, at the risk of shocking him severely, that his dreams will provide us with all the necessary information. We will take them as if they issued from an intelligent, purposive, and, as it were, personal source. This is of course a bold hypothesis and at the same time an adventure, because we are going to give extraordinary credit to a discredited entity—the psyche—whose very existence is still denied by not a few contemporary psychologists as well as by philosophers. A famous anthropologist, when I showed him my way of proceeding, made the typical remark:

504

"That's all very interesting indeed, but dangerous." Yes, I admit it is dangerous, just as dangerous as a neurosis. If you want to cure a neurosis you have to risk something. To do something without taking a risk is merely ineffectual, as we know only too well. A surgical operation for cancer is a risk too, and yet it has to be done. For the sake of better understanding I have often felt tempted to advise my patients to think of the psyche as a subtle body in which subtle tumours can grow. The prejudiced belief that the psyche is unimaginable and consequently less than air, or that it is a more or less intellectual system of logical concepts, is so great that when people are not conscious of certain contents they assume these do not exist. They have no confidence and no belief in a reliable psychic functioning outside consciousness, and dreams are thought to be only ridiculous. Under such conditions my proposal arouses the worst suspicions. And indeed I have heard every argument under the sun used against the vague spectres of dreams.

37   Yet in dreams we find, without any profound analysis, the same conflicts and complexes whose existence can also be demonstrated by the association test. Moreover, these complexes form an integral part of the existing neurosis. We have, therefore, reason to believe that dreams can give us at least as much information as the association test can about the content of a neurosis. As a matter of fact, they give very much more. The symptom is like the shoot above ground, yet the main plant is an extended rhizome underground. The rhizome represents the content of a neurosis; it is the matrix of complexes, of symptoms, and of dreams. We have every reason to believe that dreams mirror exactly the underground processes of the psyche. And if we get there, we literally get at the "roots" of the disease.

38   As it is not my intention to go any further into the psychopathology of neuroses, I propose to choose another case as an example of how dreams reveal the unknown inner facts of the psyche and of what these facts consist. The dreamer was another intellectual, of remarkable intelligence and learning. He was neurotic and was seeking my help because he felt that his neurosis had become overpowering and was slowly but surely undermining his morale. Fortunately his intellectual integrity had not yet suffered and he had the free use of his fine intelligence. For this reason I set him the task of observing and recording his

dreams himself. The dreams were not analysed or explained to him and it was only very much later that we began their analysis. Thus the dreams I am going to relate have not been tampered with at all. They represent an entirely uninfluenced natural sequence of events. The patient had never read any psychology, much less any analytical psychology.

39   Since the series consists of over four hundred dreams, I could not possibly convey an impression of the whole material; but I have published elsewhere a selection of seventy-four dreams containing motifs of special religious interest.[13] The dreamer, it should be said, was a Catholic by education, but no longer a practising one, nor was he interested in religious problems. He was one of those scientifically minded intellectuals who would be simply amazed if anybody should saddle them with religious views of any kind. If one holds that the unconscious has a psychic existence independent of consciousness, a case such as that of our dreamer might be of particular interest, provided we are not mistaken in our conception of the religious character of certain dreams. And if one lays stress on the conscious mind alone and does not credit the unconscious with an independent existence, it will be interesting to find out whether or not the dreams really derive their material from conscious contents. Should the facts favour the hypothesis of the unconscious, one could then use dreams as possible sources of information about the religious tendencies of the unconscious.

40   One cannot expect dreams to speak of religion as we know it. There are, however, two dreams among the four hundred that obviously deal with religion. I will now give the text which the dreamer himself had taken down:

All the houses have something theatrical about them, with stage scenery and decorations. The name of Bernard Shaw is mentioned. The play is supposed to take place in the distant future. There is a notice in English and German on one of the sets:

13 "Dream Symbols of the Individuation Process." [Orig. in *Eranos-Jahrbuch 1935*. A revised and expanded version of this appears in *Psychology and Alchemy*, as Part II.—EDITORS.] Although the dreams cited here are mentioned in the above publication, they are examined there from a different standpoint. Since dreams have many aspects they can be studied from various angles.

This is the universal Catholic Church.
It is the Church of the Lord.
All those who feel that they are the instruments of the Lord may enter.

Under this is printed in smaller letters: *"The Church was founded by Jesus and Paul"*—like a firm advertising its long standing.

I say to my friend, *"Come on, let's have a look at this."* He replies, *"I do not see why a lot of people have to get together when they're feeling religious."* I answer, *"As a Protestant you will never understand."* A woman nods emphatic approval. Then I see a sort of proclamation on the wall of the church. It runs:

Soldiers'

When you feel you are under the power of the Lord, do not address him directly. The Lord cannot be reached by words. We also strongly advise you not to indulge in any discussions among yourselves concerning the attributes of the Lord. It is futile, for everything valuable and important is ineffable.

(Signed) Pope . . . (Name illegible)

Now we go in. The interior resembles a mosque, more particularly the Hagia Sophia: no seats—wonderful effect of space; no images, only framed texts decorating the walls (like the Koran texts in the Hagia Sophia). One of the texts reads *"Do not flatter your benefactor."* The woman who had nodded approval bursts into tears and cries, *"Then there's nothing left!"* I reply, *"I find it quite right!"* but she vanishes. At first I stand with a pillar in front of me and can see nothing. Then I change my position and see a crowd of people. I do not belong to them and stand alone. But they are quite clear, so that I can see their faces. They all say in unison, *"We confess that we are under the power of the Lord. The Kingdom of Heaven is within us."* They repeat this three times with great solemnity. Then the organ starts to play and they sing a Bach fugue with chorale. But the original text is omitted; sometimes there is only a sort of coloratura singing, then the words are repeated: *"Everything else is paper"* (meaning that it does not make a living impression on me), When the chorale has faded away the gemütlich part of the ceremony begins; it is almost like a students' party. The people are all cheerful and equable. We move about, converse, and greet one another, and wine (from an episcopal seminary) is served with other refreshments. The health of the Church is drunk and, as if to express everybody's pleasure at the increase in membership, a loudspeaker blares a ragtime melody with the refrain, "Charles is also with us now." Thereupon I awake with a feeling of great relief.

"These somewhat trivial amusements are officially approved and permitted. We must adapt a little to American methods. With a large crowd such as we have here this is inevitable. But we differ in principle from the American churches by our decidedly anti-ascetic tendency)." A priest explains to me: "Charles is also with us now."

41   There are, as you know, numerous works on the phenomenology of dreams, but very few that deal with their psychology. This for the obvious reason that a psychological interpretation of dreams is an exceedingly ticklish and risky business. Freud has made a courageous attempt to elucidate the intricacies of dream psychology with the help of views which he gathered in the field of psychopathology.[14] Much as I admire the boldness of his attempt, I cannot agree either with his method or with its results. He explains the dream as a mere façade behind which something has been carefully hidden. There is no doubt that neurotics hide disagreeable things, probably just as much as normal people do. But it is a serious question whether this category can be applied to such a normal and world-wide phenomenon as the dream. I doubt whether we can assume that a dream is something other than it appears to be. I am rather inclined to quote another Jewish authority, the Talmud, which says: "The dream is its own interpretation." In other words I take the dream for what it is. The dream is such a difficult and complicated thing that I do not dare to make any assump-

[14] Freud, The Interpretation of Dreams. Silberer (Der Traum, 1919) presents a more cautious and more balanced point of view. As to the difference between Freud's and my own views, I would refer the reader to my little essay on this subject, "Freud and Jung: Contrasts." Further material in Two Essays on Analytical Psychology, pars. 16ff.; Kranefeldt, Secret Ways of the Mind; Gerhard Adler, Entdeckung der Seele; and Toni Wolff, "Einführung in die Grundlagen der komplexen Psychologie," in Die kulturelle Bedeutung der komplexen Psychologie.

42 tions about its possible cunning or its tendency to deceive. The dream is a natural occurrence, and there is no earthly reason why we should assume that it is a crafty device to lead us astray. It occurs when consciousness and will are to a large extent extinguished. It seems to be a natural product which is also found in people who are not neurotic. Moreover, we know so little about the psychology of the dream process that we must be more than careful when we introduce into its explanation elements that are foreign to the dream itself.

42 For all these reasons I hold that our dream really is speaking of religion and that it intends to do so. Since the dream has a coherent and well designed structure, it suggests a certain logic and a certain intention, that is, it has a meaningful motivation which finds direct expression in the dream-content.

43 The first part of the dream is a serious statement in favour of the Catholic Church. A certain Protestant point of view—that religion is just an individual experience—is discouraged by the dreamer. The second, more grotesque part is the Church's adaptation to a decidedly worldly standpoint, and the end is a statement in favour of an anti-ascetic tendency which would not and could not be backed up by the real Church. Nevertheless the dreamer's anti-ascetic priest makes it a matter of principle. Spiritualization and sublimation are essentially Christian principles, and any insistence upon the contrary would amount to blasphemous paganism. Christianity has never been worldly nor has it ever looked with favour on good food and wine, and it is more than doubtful whether the introduction of jazz into the cult would be a particular asset. The "cheerful and equable" people who peripatetically converse with each other in more or less Epicurean style remind one much more of an ancient philosophical ideal which is rather distasteful to the contemporary Christian. In the first and second part the importance of masses or crowds of people is emphasized.

44 Thus the Catholic Church, though highly recommended, appears coupled with a strange pagan point of view which is irreconcilable with a fundamentally Christian attitude. The actual irreconcilability does not appear in the dream. It is hushed up as it were by a cosy ("gemütlich") atmosphere in which dangerous contrasts are blurred and blended. The Protestant conception of an individual relationship to God is swamped by mass organiza-

tion and a correspondingly collective religious feeling. The insistence on crowds and the insinuation of a pagan ideal are remarkable parallels to things that are actually happening in Europe today. Everybody was astonished at the pagan tendencies of modern Germany because nobody knew how to interpret Nietzsche's Dionysian experience. Nietzsche was but one of the thousands and millions of Germans yet unborn in whose unconscious the Teutonic cousin of Dionysus—Wotan—came to birth during the Great War.[15] In the dreams of the Germans whom I treated then I could clearly see the Wotanistic revolution coming on, and in 1918 I published an article in which I pointed out the peculiar kind of new development to be expected in Germany.[16] Those Germans were by no means people who had studied *Thus Spake Zarathustra*, and certainly the young people who resurrected the pagan sacrifices of sheep knew nothing of Nietzsche's experience.[17] That is why they called their god Wotan and not Dionysus. In Nietzsche's biography you will find irrefutable proof that the god he originally meant was really Wotan, but, being a philologist and living in the seventies and eighties of the nineteenth century, he called him Dionysus. Looked at from a comparative point of view, the two gods have much in common.

45   There is apparently no opposition to collective feeling, mass religion, and paganism anywhere in the dream of my patient, except for the Protestant friend who is soon reduced to silence. One curious incident merits our attention, and that is the unknown woman who at first backs up the eulogy of Catholicism and then suddenly bursts into tears, saying: "Then there's nothing left," and vanishes without returning.

15 Cf. the relation of Odin as the god of poets, seers, and raving enthusiasts, and of Mimir, the Wise One, to Dionysus and Silenus. The word Odin has a root-connection with Gall. *oûāteis*, Ir. *faith*, L. *vates*, similar to μάντις and μαίνομαι. Ninck, *Wodan und germanischer Schicksalsglaube*, pp. 30ff.

16 "The Role of the Unconscious."

17 Cf. my "Wotan," *Neue Schweizer Rundschau*, 1936 [an abbreviated version in the *Saturday Review of Literature*, Oct. 16, 1937; subsequently published in *Essays on Contemporary Events*, 1947; now in *Coll. Works*, vol. 10]. The Wotan parallels in Nietzsche's work are to be found in the poem "To the Unknown God" (*Werke*, ed. Baeumler, V, p. 457); *Thus Spake Zarathustra*, trans. by Thomas Common, pp. 293ff, 150, and 185f.; and the Wotan dream of 1859 in Elisabeth Foerster-Nietzsche, *Der werdende Nietzsche*, pp. 84ff.

46   Who is this woman? To the dreamer she is a vague and unknown person, but when he had that dream he was already well acquainted with her as the "unknown woman" who had frequently appeared in previous dreams.

47   As this figure plays a great role in men's dreams, it bears the technical name of the "anima," [18] with reference to the fact that, from time immemorial, man in his myths has expressed the idea of a male and female coexisting in the same body. Such psychological intuitions were usually projected in the form of the divine syzygy, the divine pair, or in the idea of the hermaphroditic nature of the creator. [19] Edward Maitland, the biographer of Anna Kingsford, relates in our own day an inner experience of the bisexual nature of the Deity. [20] Then there is Hermetic philosophy with its hermaphrodite and its androgynous inner man, [21] the *homo Adamicus*, who, "although he appears in

---

[18] Cf. my *Two Essays*, pars. 296ff.; *Psychological Types*, Defs. 48, 49: "Archetypes of the Collective Unconscious," pars. 52ff.; and "Concerning the Archetypes."

[19] Cf. my "Concerning the Archetypes," pars. 120ff.

[20] Maitland, *Anna Kingsford*, I, pp. 129ff. [Cf. "Comm. on *Golden Flower*," par. 40.]

[21] The statement about the hermaphroditic nature of the Deity in *Corpus Hermeticum*, Lib. I (ed. Scott, *Hermetica*, I, p. 118): "For the first Mind was bisexual," is probably taken from Plato, *Symposium*, XIV. It is questionable whether the later medieval representations of the hermaphrodite stem from "Poimandres" (*Hermetica*, I), since the hermaphrodite figure was practically unknown in the West before the *Poimander* was printed by Marsilio Ficino in 1471. It is possible, however, that one of the few scholars of those days who understood Greek got the idea from one of the Greek codices then extant, as for instance the Codex Laurentianus 71, 33, the Codex Parisinus Graecus 1220, or the Codices Vaticanus Graecus 237 and 951, all from the 14th century. There are no older codices. The first Latin translation by Marsilio Ficino had a sensational effect. But before that date we have the hermaphroditic symbols from the Codex Germanicus Monacensis 598, dated 1417. It seems to me more probable that the hermaphrodite symbol derives from Arabic or Syriac MSS. translated in the 11th or 12th century. In the old Latin "Tractatulus Avicennae," which is strongly influenced by Arabic tradition, we find: "[The elixir] is a voluptuous serpent impregnating itself" (*Artis auriferae*, I, 1593, p. 406). Although the author was a Pseudo-Avicenna and not the authentic Ibn Sina (970–1037), he is one of the Arabic-Latin sources for medieval Hermetic literature. We find the same passage in "Rosinus ad Sarratantam" (*Artis aurif.*, I, p. 303). "Rosinus" is an Arabic-Latin corruption of "Zosimos," a Greek neo-Platonic philosopher of the 3rd century. His treatise "Ad Sarratantam" belongs to the same class of literature, and since the history of these texts is still shrouded in darkness, nobody can say who copied from whom. The *Turba philosophorum*, Sermo LXV, a Latin text of Arabic

masculine form, always carries about with him Eve, or his wife, hidden in his body," as a medieval commentator on the *Hermetis Tractatus aureus* says.[22]

48   The anima is presumably a psychic representation of the minority of female genes in a man's body. This is all the more probable since the same figure is not to be found in the imagery of a woman's unconscious. There is a corresponding figure, however, that plays an equivalent role, yet it is not a woman's image but a man's. This masculine figure in a woman's psychology has been termed the "animus."[23] One of the most typical manifestations of both figures is what has long been called "animosity." The anima causes illogical moods, and the animus produces irritating platitudes and unreasonable opinions. Both are frequent dream-figures. As a rule they personify the unconscious and give it its peculiarly disagreeable or irritating character. The unconscious in itself has no such negative qualities. They appear only when it is personified by these figures and when they begin to influence consciousness. Being only partial personalities, they have the character either of an inferior woman or of an inferior man—hence their irritating effect. A man experiencing this influence will be subject to unaccountable

22 The "Tractatus aureus Hermetis" is of Arabic origin and does not belong to the *Corpus Hermeticum*. Its history is unknown (first printed in *Ars chemica*, 1566). Dominicus Gnosius wrote a commentary on the text in his *Hermetis Trismegisti Tractatus vere Aureus de Lapide philosophici secreto* (1610). On p. 101 he says: "As a shadow continually follows the body of one who walks in the sun . . . so our Adamic hermaphrodite, though he appears in masculine form, nevertheless always carries about with him Eve, or his feminine part, hidden in his body." This commentary, together with the text, is reproduced in Manget, *Bibliotheca chemica curiosa*, I (1702), pp. 401ff.

origin, makes the same allusion: "The composite brings itself forth." (Ruska, *Turba philosophorum*, 1931, p. 165.) So far as I can judge, the first text that definitely mentions the hermaphrodite is the "Liber de arte chymica" of the 16th century (*Artis aurif.*, I, pp. 575ff.). On p. 610 it says: "For that Mercurius is all metals, male and female, and an hermaphroditic monster even in the marriage of soul and body." Of the later literature I mention only Hieronymus Reusner, *Pandora* (1588); "Splendor Solis" (*Aureum vellus*, 1598); Michael Maier, *Symbola aureae mensae* (1617) and *Atalanta fugiens* (1618); J. D. Mylius, *Philosophia reformata* (1622).

23 There is a description of both these figures in *Two Essays*, Part II, pars. 296ff. See also *Psychological Types*, Def. 48, and Emma Jung, "On the Nature of the Animus." [Cf. also *Aion*, ch. III.]

49   moods, and a woman will be argumentative and produce opinions that are beside the mark.[24]

50   The negative reaction of the anima to the church dream indicates that the dreamer's feminine side, his unconscious, disagrees with his conscious attitude. The disagreement started with the text on the wall: "Do not flatter your benefactor," which the dreamer agreed with. The meaning of the text seems sound enough, so that one does not understand why the woman should feel so desperate about it. Without delving further into this mystery, we must content ourselves for the time being with the statement that there is a contradiction in the dream and that a very important minority has left the stage under vivid protest and pays no more attention to the proceedings.

51   We gather, then, from the dream that the unconscious functioning of the dreamer's mind has produced a pretty flat compromise between Catholicism and pagan *joie de vivre*. The product of the unconscious is manifestly not expressing a fixed point of view or a definite opinion, rather it is a dramatic exposition of an act of reflection. It could be formulated perhaps as follows: "Now what about this religious business? You are a Catholic, are you not? Is that not good enough? But asceticism—well, well, even the church has to adapt a little—movies, radio, spiritual five o'clock tea and all that—why not some ecclesiastical wine and gay acquaintances?" But for some secret reason this awkward mystery woman, well known from many former dreams, seems to be deeply disappointed and quits.

     I must confess that I find myself in sympathy with the anima. Obviously the compromise is too cheap and too superficial, but it is characteristic of the dreamer as well as of many other people to whom religion does not matter very much. Religion was of no concern to my patient and he certainly never expected that it would concern him in any way. But he had come to me because of a very alarming experience. Being highly rationalistic and intellectual he had found that his attitude of mind and his philosophy forsook him completely in the face of his neurosis and its demoralizing forces. He found nothing in his whole

24 Anima and animus do not only occur in negative form. They may sometimes appear as a source of enlightenment, as messengers (ἄγγελοι), and as mystagogues. [Cf. Jung, *Aion* (*Coll. Works*, Vol. 9, pt. II), p. 16; "Psychology of the Transference," par. 504.—EDITORS.]

Weltanschauung that would help him to gain sufficient control of himself. He was therefore very much in the situation of a man deserted by his hitherto cherished convictions and ideals. It is by no means extraordinary that under such conditions a man should return to the religion of his childhood in the hope of finding something helpful there. It was, however, not a conscious attempt or decision to revivify his earlier religious beliefs. He merely dreamed it; that is, his unconscious produced a peculiar statement about his religion. It is just as if the spirit and the flesh, the eternal enemies in a Christian consciousness, had made peace with each other in the form of a curious mitigation of their contradictory nature. Spirituality and worldliness come together in unexpected amity. The effect is slightly grotesque and comical. The inexorable severity of the spirit seems to be undermined by an almost antique gaiety perfumed with wine and roses. At all events the dream describes a spiritual and worldly atmosphere that dulls the sharpness of a moral conflict and swallows up in oblivion all mental pain and distress.

53   If this was a wish-fulfilment it was surely a conscious one, for it was precisely what the patient had already done to excess. And he was not unconscious of this either, since wine was one of his most dangerous enemies. The dream, on the other hand, is an impartial statement of the patient's spiritual condition. It gives a picture of a degenerate religion corrupted by worldliness and mob instincts. There is religious sentimentality instead of the *numinosum* of divine experience. This is the well-known characteristic of a religion that has lost its living mystery. It is readily understandable that such a religion is incapable of giving help or of having any other moral effect.

The over-all aspect of the dream is definitely unfavourable, although certain other aspects of a more positive nature are dimly visible. It rarely happens that dreams are either exclusively positive or exclusively negative. As a rule one finds both aspects, but usually one is stronger than the other. It is obvious that such a dream provides the psychologist with enough material to raise the problem of a religious attitude. If our dream were the only one we possess we could hardly hope to unlock its innermost meaning, but we have quite a number of dreams in our series which point to a remarkable religious problem. I never, if I can help it, interpret one dream by itself. As a rule a

54   dream belongs in a series. Since there is a continuity of consciousness despite the fact that it is regularly interrupted by sleep, there is probably also a continuity of unconscious processes—perhaps even more than with the events of consciousness. In any case my experience is in favour of the probability that dreams are the visible links in a chain of unconscious events. If we want to shed any light on the deeper reasons for the dream, we must go back to the series and find out where it is located in the long chain of four hundred dreams.

54   We find our dream wedged in between two important dreams of an uncanny quality. The dream before reports that there is a gathering of many people and that a peculiar ceremony is taking place, apparently of magical character, for the purpose of "reconstructing the gibbon." The dream after is concerned with a similar theme—the magical transformation of animals into human beings.[25]

55   Both dreams are intensely disagreeable and very alarming to the patient. Whereas the church dream manifestly moves on the surface and expresses opinions which in other circumstances could just as well have been thought consciously, these two dreams are strange and remote in character and their emotional effect is such that the dreamer would avoid them if possible. As a matter of fact, the text of the second dream says: "If one runs away, all is lost." Curiously enough, this remark coincides with that of the unknown woman: "Then there's nothing left." The inference to be drawn from these remarks is that the church dream was an attempt to escape from other dream ideas of a much deeper significance. These ideas appear in the dreams occurring immediately before and after it.

[25] [Cf. *Psychology and Alchemy*, pars. 164ff., 183ff.—Editors.]

56   The first of these dreams—the one preceding the church dream—speaks of a ceremony whereby an ape is to be reconstructed. To explain this point sufficiently would require too many details. I must, therefore, restrict myself to the mere statement that the "ape" refers to the dreamer's instinctual personality,[1] which he had completely neglected in favour of an exclusively intellectual attitude. The result had been that his instincts got the better of him and attacked him at times in the form of uncontrollable outbursts. The "reconstruction" of the ape means the rebuilding of the instinctual personality within the framework of the hierarchy of consciousness. Such a reconstruction is only possible if accompanied by important changes in the conscious attitude. The patient was naturally afraid of the tendencies of the unconscious, because hitherto they had revealed themselves to him in their most unfavourable form. The church dream that followed represents an attempt to seek refuge from this fear in the shelter of a church religion. The third dream, in speaking of the "transformation of animals into human beings," obviously continues the theme of the first one; that is, the ape is reconstructed solely for the purpose of being transformed later into a human being. In other words, the pa-

1 [Cf. *Psychology and Alchemy*, par. 175.—EDITORS.]

tient has to undergo an important change through the reintegration of his hitherto split-off instinctuality, and is thus to be made over into a new man. The modern mind has forgotten those old truths that speak of the death of the old man and the making of a new one, of spiritual rebirth and such-like old-fashioned "mystical absurdities." My patient, being a scientist of today, was more than once seized by panic when he realized how much he was gripped by such thoughts. He was afraid he was going mad, whereas the man of two thousand years ago would have welcomed such dreams and rejoiced in the hope of a magical rebirth and renewal of life. But our modern attitude looks back arrogantly upon the mists of superstition and of medieval or primitive credulity, entirely forgetting that we carry the whole living past in the lower storeys of the skyscraper of rational consciousness. Without the lower storeys our mind is suspended in mid air. No wonder it gets nervous. The true history of the mind is not preserved in learned volumes but in the living psychic organism of every individual.

57 I must admit, however, that the idea of renewal took on shapes that could easily shock a modern mind. It is indeed difficult, if not impossible, to connect "rebirth," as we understand it, with the way it is depicted in the dreams. But before we discuss the strange and unexpected transformation there hinted at, we should turn our attention to the other manifestly religious dream to which I alluded before.

58 While the church dream comes relatively early in the long series, the following dream belongs to the later stages of the process.[2] This is the literal text:

I come to a strange, solemn house—the "House of the Gathering." Many candles are burning in the background, arranged in a peculiar pattern with four points running upward. Outside, at the door of the house, an old man is posted. People are going in. They say nothing and stand motionless in order to collect themselves inwardly. The man at the door says of the visitors to the house, "When they come out again they are cleansed." I go into the house myself and find I can concentrate perfectly. Then a voice says: "What you are doing is dangerous. Religion is not a tax to be paid so that you can rid yourself of the woman's

2 [Cf. ibid., par. 293.—Editors.]

image, for this image cannot be got rid of. Woe unto them who use religion as a substitute for the other side of the soul's life; they are in error and will be accursed. Religion is no substitute; it is to be added to the other activities of the soul as the ultimate completion. Out of the fullness of life shall you bring forth your religion; only then shall you be blessed!" While the last sentence is being spoken in ringing tones I hear distant music, simple chords on an organ. Something about it reminds me of Wagner's Fire Music. As I leave the house I see a burning mountain and I feel: "The fire that is not put out is a holy fire" (Shaw, Saint Joan).

59   The patient was deeply impressed by this dream. It was a solemn and powerful experience for him, one of several which produced a far-reaching change in his attitude to life and humanity.

60   It is not difficult to see that this dream forms a parallel to the church dream. Only this time the church has become a house of solemnity and self-collection. There are no indications of ceremonies or of any other known attributes of the Catholic Church, with the sole exception of the burning candles, which are arranged in a symbolic form probably derived from the Catholic cult.[3] They form four pyramids or points, which perhaps anticipate the final vision of the flaming mountain. The appearance of the number four is, however, a regular feature in the patient's dreams and plays a very important role. The holy fire refers to Bernard Shaw's *Saint Joan*, as the dreamer himself observes. The unquenchable fire, on the other hand, is a well-known attribute of the Deity, not only in the Old Testament, but also as an *allegoria Christi* in an uncanonical logion cited in Origen's *Homilies*:[4] "Ait ipse salvator: qui iuxta me est, iuxta ignem est, qui longe est a me, longe est a regno" (the Saviour himself says: Whoever is near to me is near to the fire; whoever is far from me is far from the kingdom). Since the time of Heraclitus life has been conceived as a πῦρ ἀεὶ ζῶν, an ever-

3 A bishop is allowed four candles for a private mass. Some of the more solemn forms of the Mass, such as the *Missa cantata*, also have four. Still higher forms have six or seven.

4 Origen, *In Jeremiam homiliae*, XX, 3, in Migne, P.G., vol. 13, col. 532. Also in James, *The Apocryphal New Testament*, p. 35.

living fire; and as Christ calls himself "The Life," the uncanonical saying is quite understandable. The fire signifying "life" fits into the frame of the dream, for it emphasizes that "fulness of life" is the only legitimate source of religion. Thus the four fiery points function almost as an icon denoting the presence of the Deity or an equivalent being. In the system of Barbelo-Gnosis, four lights surround the Autogenes (the Self-Born, or Uncreated).[5] This strange figure may correspond to the Monogenes of Coptic Gnosis, mentioned in the Codex Brucianus. There too the Monogenes is characterized as a quaternity symbol.

61   As I said before, the number four plays an important role in these dreams, always alluding to an idea akin to the Pythagorean tetraktys.[6]

62   The *quaternarium* or quaternity has a long history. It appears not only in Christian iconology and mystical speculation[7] but plays perhaps a still greater role in Gnostic philosophy[8]

---

[5] Irenaeus, *Against Heresies*, trans. by Keble, p. 81.

[6] Cf. Zeller, *Die Philosophie der Griechen*, where all the sources are collected. "Four is the origin and root of eternal nature" (I, p. 291). Plato derives the human body from the four. According to the Neoplatonists, Pythagoras himself called the soul a square (Zeller, III, II, p. 120).

[7] The "four" in Christian iconography appears chiefly in the form of the four evangelists and their symbols, arranged in a rose, circle, or melothesia, or as a tetramorph, as for instance in the *Hortus deliciarum* of Herrad of Landsberg and in works of mystical speculation. Of these I mention only: (1) Jakob Böhme, XL *Questions concerning the Soule* (1647). (2) Hildegard of Bingen, Codex Luccensis, fol. 372, and Codex Heidelbergensis, "Scivias," representations of the mystic universe; cf. Singer, *Studies in the History and Method of Science*. (3) The remarkable drawings of Opicinus de Canistris in the Codex Palatinus Latinus 1993, Vatican; cf. Salomon, *Weltbild und Bekenntnisse eines avignonesischen Klerikers des 14. Jahrhunderts*. (4) Heinrich Khunrath, *Vom hylealischen, das ist, pri-materialischen catholischen, oder algemeinen natürlichen Chaos* (1597), pp. 204 and 281, where he says the "Monas catholica" arises from the rotation of the "Quaternarium" and interprets it as an image and allegory of Christ (further material in Khunrath, *Amphitheatrum sapientiae aeternae*, 1604). (5) The speculations about the cross: "It is said . . . that the cross was made of four kinds of wood," St. Bernard, *Vitis mystica*, cap. XLVI, in Migne, *P.L.*, vol. 184, col. 752; cf. W. Meyer, *Die Geschichte des Kreuzholzes vor Christus*, p. 7. For the quaternity see also Dunbar, *Symbolism in Mediaeval Thought and Its Consummation in the Divine Comedy*.

[8] Cf. the systems of Isidorus, Valentinus, Marcus, and Secundus. A most instructive example is the symbolism of the Monogenes in the Codex Brucianus (Bodleian Library, Oxford, MS. Bruce 96), trans. by C. A. Baynes, *A Coptic Gnostic Treatise*, pp. 59ff., 70ff. [Cf. *Psychology and Alchemy*, pars. 138ff.]

63   and from then on down through the Middle Ages until well into the eighteenth century.[9]

In the dream under discussion, the quaternity appears as the most significant exponent of the religious cult created by the unconscious.[10] The dreamer enters the "House of the Gathering" alone, instead of with a friend as in the church dream. Here he meets an old man, who had already appeared in an earlier dream as the sage who had pointed to a particular spot on the earth where the dreamer belonged. The old man explains the character of the cult as a purification ritual. It is not clear from the dream-text what kind of purification is meant, or from what it should purify. The only ritual that actually takes place seems to be a concentration or meditation, leading up to the ecstatic phenomenon of the voice. The voice is a frequent occurrence in this dream-series. It always utters an authoritative declaration or command, either of astonishing common sense or of profound philosophic import. It is nearly always a final statement, usually coming toward the end of a dream, and it is, as a rule, so clear and convincing that the dreamer finds no argument against it. It has, indeed, so much the character of indisputable truth that it can hardly be understood as anything except a final and trenchant summing up of a long process of unconscious deliberation and weighing of arguments. Fre-

[9] I am thinking of the mystical speculations about the four "roots" (the rhizomata of Empedocles), i.e., the four elements or four qualities (wet, dry, warm, cold), peculiar to Hermetic or alchemical philosophy. Descriptions in Petrus Bonus, Pretiosa margarita novella (1546); Joannes Pantheus, Ars transmutationis metallicae (1519) p. 5, based on a quaternario; Raymond Lully, "Theorica et practica" (Theatrum chemicum, IV, 1613, p. 174), a quaternio elementorum and of chemical processes; Michael Maier, Scrutinium chymicum (1687), symbols of the four elements. The last-named author wrote an interesting treatise called De circulo physico quadrato (1616). There is much the same symbolism in Mylius, Philosophia reformata (1622). Pictures of the Hermetic redemption in the form of a tetrad with symbols of the four evangelists (from Reusner's Pandora and the Codex Germanicus Monacensis 598) are reproduced in Psychology and Alchemy, figs. 231 and 232; quaternity symbolism, ibid., par. 327. Further material in Kuekelhaus, Urzahl und Gebärde. Eastern parallels in Zimmer, Kunstform und Yoga im indischen Kultbild; Wilhelm and Jung, The Secret of the Golden Flower. The literature on the symbolism of the cross is also relevant here.

[10] This sentence may sound presumptuous, for I seem to be forgetting that we are concerned here with a single and unique dream from which no far-reaching conclusions can be drawn. My conclusions, however, are based not on this dream alone but on many similar experiences to which I have alluded elsewhere.

quently the voice issues from an authoritative figure, such as a military commander, or the captain of a ship, or an old physician. Sometimes, as in this case, there is simply a voice coming apparently from nowhere. It was interesting to see how this very intellectual and sceptical man accepted the voice; often it did not suit him at all, yet he accepted it unquestioningly, even humbly. Thus the voice revealed itself, in the course of several hundred carefully recorded dreams, as an important and even decisive spokesman of the unconscious. Since this patient is by no means the only one I have observed who exhibited the phenomenon of the voice in dreams and in other peculiar states of consciousness, I am forced to admit that the unconscious is capable at times of manifesting an intelligence and purposiveness superior to the actual conscious insight. There can be no doubt that this is a basic religious phenomenon, observed here in a person whose conscious mental attitude certainly seemed most unlikely to produce religious phenomena. I have not infrequently made similar observations in other cases and I must confess that I am unable to formulate the facts in any other way. I have often met with the objection that the thoughts which the voice represents are no more than the thoughts of the individual himself. That may be; but I would call a thought my own only when *I* have thought it, just as I would call money my own only when I have earned or acquired it in a conscious and legitimate manner. If somebody gives me the money as a present, then I shall certainly not say to my benefactor, "Thank you for my money," although to a third person I might say afterwards: "This is my own money." With the voice I am in a similar situation. The voice gives me certain contents, exactly as if a friend were informing me of his ideas. It would be neither decent nor truthful to suggest that what he says are my own ideas.

This is the reason why I differentiate between what I have produced or acquired by my own conscious effort and what is clearly and unmistakably a product of the unconscious. Someone may object that the so-called unconscious mind is merely my own mind and that, therefore, such a differentiation is superfluous. But I am not at all convinced that the unconscious mind is merely *my* mind, because the term "unconscious" means that I am not even conscious of it. As a matter of fact, the concept of the unconscious is an assumption for the sake of convenience.

64

In reality I am totally unconscious of—or, in other words, I do not know at all—where the voice comes from. Not only am I incapable of producing the phenomenon at will, I am unable to anticipate what the voice will say. Under such conditions it would be presumptuous to refer to the factor that produces the voice as *my* unconscious or *my* mind. This would not be accurate, to say the least. The fact that you perceive the voice in your dream proves nothing at all, for you can also hear the noises in the street, which you would never think of calling your own.

65   There is only one condition under which you might legitimately call the voice your own, and that is when you assume your conscious personality to be a part of a whole or to be a smaller circle contained in a bigger one. A little bank-clerk, showing a friend around town, who points to the bank building with the words, "And this is *my* bank," is making use of the same privilege.

66   We may suppose that human personality consists of two things: first, consciousness and whatever this covers, and second, an indefinitely large hinterland of unconscious psyche. So far as the former is concerned, it can be more or less clearly defined and delimited; but as for the sum total of human personality, one has to admit the impossibility of a complete description or definition. In other words, there is bound to be an illimitable and indefinable addition to every personality, because the latter consists of a conscious and observable part which does not contain certain factors whose existence, however, we are forced to assume in order to explain certain observable facts. The unknown factors form what we call the unconscious part of the personality.

67   Of what those factors consist we have no idea, since we can observe only their effects. We may assume that they are of a psychic nature comparable to that of conscious contents, yet there is no certainty about this. But if we suppose such a likeness we can hardly refrain from going further. Since psychic contents are conscious and perceivable only when they are associated with an ego, the phenomenon of the voice, having a strongly personal character, may also issue from a centre—but a centre which is not identical with the conscious ego. Such reasoning is permissible if we conceive of the ego as being subordi-

68   nated to, or contained in, a supraordinate self as centre of the total, illimitable, and indefinable psychic personality.

  I do not enjoy philosophical arguments that amuse by their own complications. Although my argument may seem abstruse, it is at least an honest attempt to formulate the observed facts. To put it simply one could say: Since we do not know everything, practically every experience, fact, or object contains something unknown. Hence, if we speak of the totality of an experience, the word "totality" can refer only to the conscious part of it. As we cannot assume that our experience covers the totality of the object, it is clear that its absolute totality must necessarily contain the part that has not been experienced. The same holds true, as I have mentioned, of every experience and also of the psyche, whose absolute totality covers a greater area than consciousness. In other words, the psyche is no exception to the general rule that the universe can be established only so far as our psychic organism permits.

69   My psychological experience has shown time and again that certain contents issue from a psyche that is more complete than consciousness. They often contain a superior analysis or insight or knowledge which consciousness has not been able to produce. We have a suitable word for such occurrences—intuition. In uttering this word most people have an agreeable feeling, as if something had been settled. But they never consider that you do not *make* an intuition. On the contrary, it always comes to you; you *have* a hunch, it has come of itself, and you only catch it if you are clever or quick enough.

70   Consequently, I explain the voice, in the dream of the sacred house, as a product of the more complete personality of which the dreamer's conscious self is a part, and I hold that this is the reason why the voice shows an intelligence and a clarity superior to the dreamer's actual consciousness. This superiority is the reason for the absolute authority of the voice.

71   The message of the voice contains a strange criticism of the dreamer's attitude. In the church dream, he made an attempt to reconcile the two sides of life by a kind of cheap compromise. As we know, the unknown woman, the anima, disagreed and left the scene. In the present dream the voice seems to have taken the place of the anima, making not a merely emotional protest but a masterful statement on two kinds of religion. According

to this statement, the dreamer is inclined to use religion as a substitute for the "woman's image," as the text says. The "woman" refers to the anima. This is borne out by the next sentence, which speaks of religion being used as a substitute for "the other side of the soul's life." The anima is the "other side," as I explained before. She is the representative of the female minority hidden below the threshold of consciousness, that is to say, in the unconscious. The criticism, therefore, would read as follows: "You try religion in order to escape from your unconscious. You use it as a substitute for a part of your soul's life. But religion is the fruit and culmination of the completeness of life, that is, of a life which contains both sides."

72   Careful comparison with other dreams of the same series shows unmistakably what the "other side" is. The patient always tried to evade his emotional needs. As a matter of fact he was afraid they might get him into trouble, for instance into marriage, and into other responsibilities such as love, devotion, loyalty, trust, emotional dependence, and general submission to the soul's needs. All this had nothing to do with science or an academic career; moreover, the word "soul" was nothing but an intellectual obscenity, not fit to be touched with a barge pole.

73   The "mystery" of the anima is the mysterious allusion to religion. This was a great puzzle to my patient, who naturally enough knew nothing of religion except as a creed. He also knew that religion can be a substitute for certain awkward emotional demands which one might circumvent by going to church. The prejudices of our age are visibly reflected in the dreamer's apprehensions. The voice, on the other hand, is unorthodox, indeed shockingly unconventional: it takes religion seriously, puts it on the very apex of life, a life containing "both sides," and thus upsets his most cherished intellectual and rationalistic prejudices. This was such a revolution that my patient was often afraid he would go crazy. Well, I should say that we—knowing the average intellectual of today and yesterday—can easily sympathize with his predicament. To take the "woman's image"—in other words, the unconscious—seriously into account, what a blow to enlightened common sense! [11]

11 Cf. the *Hypnerotomachia Poliphili* (1499). This book is supposed to have been written by a monk of the 15th century. It is an excellent example of an anima-romance. [Fierz-David's study *The Dream of Poliphilo* treats it as such.—Editors.]

74   I began his personal treatment only after he had observed the first series of about three hundred and fifty dreams. Then I got the whole backwash of his upsetting experiences. No wonder he wanted to run away from his adventure! But, fortunately, the man had *religio*, that is, he "carefully took account of" his experience and he had enough πίστις, or loyalty to his experience, to enable him to hang on to it and continue it. He had the *great advantage of being neurotic* and so, whenever he tried to be disloyal to his experience or to deny the voice, the neurotic condition instantly came back. He simply could not "quench the fire" and finally he had to admit the incomprehensibly numinous character of his experience. He had to confess that the unquenchable fire was "holy." This was the *sine qua non* of his cure.

75   One might, perhaps, consider this case an exception inasmuch as fairly complete human beings are exceptions. It is true that an overwhelming majority of educated people are fragmentary personalities and have a lot of substitutes instead of the genuine goods. But being like that meant a neurosis for this man, and it means the same for a great many other people too. What is ordinarily called "religion," is a substitute to such an amazing degree that I ask myself seriously whether this kind of "religion," which I prefer to call a creed, may not after all have an important function in human society. The substitute has the obvious purpose of replacing *immediate experience* by a choice of suitable symbols tricked out with an organized dogma and ritual. The Catholic Church maintains them by her indisputable authority, the Protestant "church" (if this term is still applicable) by insistence on belief in the evangelical message. So long as these two principles work, people are effectively protected against immediate religious experience.[12] Even if something of the sort should happen to them, they can refer to the Church, for she would know whether the experience came from God or from the devil, and whether it is to be accepted or rejected.

76   In my profession I have encountered many people who have had immediate experience and who would not and could not submit to the authority of ecclesiastical decision. I had to go

---

12 Ecclesiastical vestments are not for adornment only, they also serve to protect the officiating priest. "Fear of God" is no groundless metaphor, for at the back of it there is a very real phenomenology. Cf. Exodus 20: 18f.

with them through the crises of passionate conflicts, through the panics of madness, through desperate confusions and depressions which were grotesque and terrible at the same time, so that I am fully aware of the extraordinary importance of dogma and ritual, at least as methods of mental hygiene. If the patient is a practising Catholic, I invariably advise him to confess and to receive communion in order to protect himself from immediate experience, which might easily prove too much for him. With Protestants it is usually not so easy, because dogma and ritual have become so pale and faint that they have lost their efficacy to a very great extent. There is also, as a rule, no confession, and the clergy share the common dislike of psychological problems and also, unfortunately, the common ignorance of psychology. The Catholic "director of conscience" often has infinitely more psychological skill and insight. Protestant parsons, moreover, have gone through a scientific training at a theological faculty which, with its critical spirit, undermines naïveté of faith, whereas the powerful historical tradition in a Catholic priest's training is apt to strengthen the authority of the institution.

77   As a doctor I might, of course, espouse a so-called "scientific" creed, holding that the contents of a neurosis are nothing but repressed infantile sexuality or will to power. By thus depreciating these contents, it would be possible, up to a point, to shield a number of patients from the risk of immediate experience. But I know that this theory is only partially true, which means that it formulates only certain aspects of the neurotic psyche. And I cannot tell my patients what I myself do not fully believe.

78   Now people may ask me: "But if you tell your practising Catholic to go to the priest and confess, you are telling him something you do not believe"—that is, assuming that I am a Protestant.

79   In order to answer this critical question I must first of all explain that, if I can help it, I never preach my belief. If asked I shall certainly stand by my convictions, but these do not go beyond what I consider to be my actual knowledge. I believe only what I *know*. Everything else is hypothesis and beyond that I can leave a lot of things to the Unknown. They do not bother me. But they would begin to bother me, I am sure, if I felt that I *ought* to know about them. If, therefore, a patient is convinced

of the exclusively sexual origin of his neurosis, I would not disturb him in his opinion because I know that such a conviction, particularly if it is deeply rooted, is an excellent defence against an onslaught of immediate experience with its terrible ambiguity. So long as such a defence works I shall not break it down, since I know that there must be cogent reasons why the patient has to think in such a narrow circle. But if his dreams should begin to destroy the protective theory, I have to support the wider personality, as I have done in the case of the dream described. In the same way and for the same reason I support the hypothesis of the practising Catholic while it works for him. In either case, I reinforce a means of defence against a grave risk, without asking the academic question whether the defence is an ultimate truth. I am glad when it works and so long as it works.

80   With our patient, the Catholic defence had broken down long before I ever touched the case. He would have laughed at me if I had advised him to confess or anything of that sort, just as he laughed at the sexual theory, which he had no use for either. But I always let him see that I was entirely on the side of the voice, which I recognized as part of his future greater personality, destined to relieve him of his one-sidedness.

81   For a certain type of intellectual mediocrity characterized by enlightened rationalism, a scientific theory that simplifies matters is a very good means of defence because of the tremendous faith modern man has in anything which bears the label "scientific." Such a label sets your mind at rest immediately, almost as well as *Roma locuta causa finita*: "Rome has spoken, the matter is settled." In itself any scientific theory, no matter how subtle, has, I think, less value than religious dogma, for the simple reason that a theory is necessarily highly abstract and exclusively rational, whereas dogma expresses an irrational whole by means of imagery. This guarantees a far better rendering of an irrational fact like the psyche. Moreover, dogma owes its continued existence and its form on the one hand to so-called "revealed" or immediate experiences of the "Gnosis" [13]—for instance, the Godman, the Cross, the Virgin Birth, the Immaculate Conception,

13 Gnosis, as a special kind of knowledge, should not be confused with "Gnosticism."

the Trinity, and so on, and on the other hand to the ceaseless collaboration of many minds over many centuries. It may not be quite clear why I call certain dogmas "immediate experiences," since in itself a dogma is the very thing that precludes immediate experience. Yet the Christian images I have mentioned are not peculiar to Christianity alone (although in Christianity they have undergone a development and intensification of meaning not to be found in any other religion). They occur just as often in pagan religions, and besides that they can reappear spontaneously in all sorts of variations as psychic phenomena, just as in the remote past they originated in visions, dreams, or trances. Ideas like these are never invented. They came into being before man had learned to use his mind purposively. Before man learned to produce thoughts, thoughts came to him. *He did not think—he perceived his mind functioning.* Dogma is like a dream, reflecting the spontaneous and autonomous activity of the objective psyche, the unconscious. Such an expression of the unconscious is a much more efficient means of defence against further immediate experiences than any scientific theory. The theory has to disregard the emotional values of the experience. The dogma, on the other hand, is extremely eloquent in just this respect. One scientific theory is soon superseded by another. Dogma lasts for untold centuries. The suffering God-Man may be at least five thousand years old and the Trinity is probably even older.

82   Dogma expresses the psyche more completely than a scientific theory, for the latter gives expression to and formulates the conscious mind alone. Furthermore, a theory can do nothing except formulate a living thing in abstract terms. Dogma, on the contrary, aptly expresses the living process of the unconscious in the form of the drama of repentance, sacrifice, and redemption. It is rather astonishing, from this point of view, that the Protestant schism could not have been avoided. But since Protestantism became the creed of the adventurous Germanic tribes with their characteristic curiosity, acquisitiveness, and recklessness, it seems possible that their peculiar nature was unable to endure the peace of the Church, at least not for any length of time. It looks as if they were not yet advanced enough to suffer a process of salvation and to submit to a deity who was made visible in the magnificent structure of the Church.

There was, perhaps, too much of the Imperium Romanum or of the Pax Romana in the Church—too much, at least, for their energies, which were and still are insufficiently domesticated. It is quite likely that they needed an unmitigated and less controlled experience of God, as often happens to adventurous and restless people who are too youthful for any form of conservatism or domestication. They therefore did away with the intercession of the Church between God and man, some more and some less. With the demolition of protective walls, the Protestant lost the sacred images that expressed important unconscious factors, together with the ritual which, from time immemorial, has been a safe way of dealing with the unpredictable forces of the unconscious. A vast amount of energy was thus liberated and instantly went into the old channels of curiosity and acquisitiveness. In this way Europe became the mother of dragons that devoured the greater part of the earth.

83   Since those days Protestantism has become a hotbed of schisms and, at the same time, of rapid advances in science and technics which cast such a spell over man's conscious mind that it forgot the unpredictable forces of the unconscious. The catastrophe of the first World War and the extraordinary manifestations of profound spiritual malaise that came afterwards were needed to arouse a doubt as to whether all was well with the white man's mind. Before the war broke out in 1914 we were all quite certain that the world could be righted by rational means. Now we behold the amazing spectacle of states taking over the age-old totalitarian claims of theocracy, which are inevitably accompanied by suppression of free opinion. Once more we see people cutting each other's throats in support of childish theories of how to create paradise on earth. It is not very difficult to see that the powers of the underworld—not to say of hell—which in former times were more or less successfully chained up in a gigantic spiritual edifice where they could be of some use, are now creating, or trying to create, a State slavery and a State prison devoid of any mental or spiritual charm. There are not a few people nowadays who are convinced that mere human reason is not entirely up to the enormous task of putting a lid on the volcano.

84   This whole development is fate. I would not lay the blame either on Protestantism or on the Renaissance. But one thing is

529

certain—that modern man, Protestant or otherwise, has lost the protection of the ecclesiastical walls erected and reinforced so carefully since Roman days, and because of this loss has approached the zone of world-destroying and world-creating fire. Life has become quickened and intensified. Our world is shot through with waves of uneasiness and fear.

85   Protestantism was, and still is, a great risk and at the same time a great opportunity. If it goes on disintegrating as a church, it must have the effect of stripping man of all his spiritual safeguards and means of defence against immediate experience of the forces waiting for liberation in the unconscious. Look at all the incredible savagery going on in our so-called civilized world: it all comes from human beings and the spiritual condition they are in! Look at the devilish engines of destruction! They are invented by completely innocuous gentlemen, reasonable, respectable citizens who are everything we could wish. And when the whole thing blows up and an indescribable hell of destruction is let loose, nobody seems to be responsible. It simply happens, and yet it is all man-made. But since everybody is blindly convinced that he is nothing more than his own extremely unassuming and insignificant conscious self, which performs its duties decently and earns a moderate living, nobody is aware that this whole rationalistically organized conglomeration we call a state or a nation is driven on by a seemingly impersonal, invisible but terrifying power which nobody and nothing can check. This ghastly power is mostly explained as fear of the neighbouring nation, which is supposed to be possessed by a malevolent fiend. Since nobody is capable of recognizing just where and how much he himself is possessed and unconscious, he simply projects his own condition upon his neighbour, and thus it becomes a sacred duty to have the biggest guns and the most poisonous gas. The worst of it is that he is quite right. All one's neighbours are in the grip of some uncontrolled and uncontrollable fear, just like oneself. In lunatic asylums it is a well-known fact that patients are far more dangerous when suffering from fear than when moved by rage or hatred.

86   The Protestant is left to God alone. For him there is no confession, no absolution, no possibility of an expiatory *opus divinum* of any kind. He has to digest his sins by himself; and, because the absence of a suitable ritual has put it beyond his

reach, he is none too sure of divine grace. Hence the present alertness of the Protestant conscience—and this bad conscience has all the disagreeable characteristics of a lingering illness which makes people chronically uncomfortable. But, for this very reason, the Protestant has a unique chance to make himself conscious of sin to a degree that is hardly possible for a Catholic mentality, as confession and absolution are always at hand to ease excess of tension. The Protestant, however, is left to his tensions, which can go on sharpening his conscience. Conscience, and particularly a bad conscience, can be a gift from heaven, a veritable grace if used in the interests of the higher self-criticism. And self-criticism, in the sense of an introspective, discriminating activity, is indispensable in any attempt to understand your own psychology. If you have done something that puzzles you and you ask yourself what could have prompted you to such an action, you need the sting of a bad conscience and its discriminating faculty in order to discover the real motive of your behaviour. It is only then that you can see what motives are governing your actions. The sting of a bad conscience even spurs you on to discover things that were unconscious before, and in this way you may be able to cross the threshold of the unconscious and take cognizance of those impersonal forces which make you an unconscious instrument of the wholesale murderer in man. If a Protestant survives the complete loss of his church and still remains a Protestant, that is to say a man who is defenceless against God and no longer shielded by walls or communities, he has a unique spiritual opportunity for immediate religious experience.

87   I do not know whether I have succeeded in conveying what the experience of the unconscious meant to my patient. There is, however, no objective criterion by which such an experience can be valued. We have to take it for what it is worth to the person who has the experience. Thus you may be impressed by the fact that the apparent futility of certain dreams should mean something to an intelligent person. But if you cannot accept what he says, or if you cannot put yourself in his place, you should not judge his case. The *genius religiosus* is a wind that bloweth where it listeth. There is no Archimedean point from which to judge, since the psyche is indistinguishable from its manifestations. The psyche is the object of psychology, and—

88 fatally enough—also its subject. There is no getting away from this fact.

89 The few dreams I have chosen as examples of what I call "immediate experience" certainly look very insignificant to the unpractised eye. They are not spectacular, and are only modest witnesses to an individual experience. They would cut a better figure if I could present them in their sequence, together with the wealth of symbolic material that was brought up in the course of the entire process. But even the sum total of the dreams in the series could not compare in beauty and expressiveness with any part of a traditional religion. A dogma is always the result and fruit of many minds and many centuries, purified of all the oddities, shortcomings, and flaws of individual experience. But for all that, the individual experience, by its very poverty, is immediate life, the warm red blood pulsating today. It is more convincing to a seeker after truth than the best tradition. Immediate life is always individual since the carrier of life is the individual, and whatever emanates from the individual is in a way unique, and hence transitory and imperfect, particularly when it comes to spontaneous psychic products such as dreams and the like. No one else will have the same dreams, although many have the same problem. But just as no individual is differentiated to the point of absolute uniqueness, so there are no individual products of absolutely unique quality. Even dreams are made of collective material to a very high degree, just as, in the mythology and folklore of different peoples, certain motifs repeat themselves in almost identical form. I have called these motifs "archetypes," [14] and by this I mean forms or images of a collective nature which occur practically all over the earth as constituents of myths and at the same time as autochthonous, individual products of unconscious origin. The archetypal motifs presumably derive from patterns of the human mind that are transmitted not only by tradition and migration but also by heredity. The latter hypothesis is indispensable, since even complicated archetypal images can be reproduced spontaneously without there being any possibility of direct tradition.

The theory of preconscious primordial ideas is by no means my own invention, as the term "archetype," which stems from

14 Cf. *Psychological Types*, Def. 26. [Also "On the Nature of the Psyche," *Coll. Works*, Vol. 8, pp. 212ff.—Editors.]

the first centuries of our era, proves.[15] With special reference to psychology we find this theory in the works of Adolf Bastian[16] and then again in Nietzsche.[17] In French literature Hubert and Mauss,[18] and also Lévy-Bruhl,[19] mention similar ideas. I only gave an empirical foundation to the theory of what were formerly called primordial or elementary ideas, "catégories" or "habitudes directrices de la conscience," "représentations collectives," etc., by setting out to investigate certain details.

In the second of the dreams discussed above, we met with an archetype which I have not yet considered. This is the peculiar arrangement of the burning candles in four pyramid-like points. The arrangement emphasizes the symbolic importance of the number four by putting it in place of the altar or iconostasis where one would expect to find the sacred images. Since the temple is called the "House of the Gathering," we may assume that this character is expressed if the image or symbol appears

15 The term "archetypus" is used by Cicero, Pliny, and others. It appears in the Corpus Hermeticum, Lib. I (Scott, Hermetica, I, p. 116, 8a) as a definitely philosophical concept: "Thou knowest in thy mind the archetypal form [τὸ ἀρχέτυπον εἶδος], the beginning before the beginning, the unbounded."

16 Das Beständige in den Menschenrassen, p. 75; Die Vorstellungen von der Seele, p. 306; Der Völkergedanke im Aufbau einer Wissenschaft vom Menschen; Ethnische Elementargedanken in der Lehre vom Menschen.

17 "In sleep and in dreams we pass through the whole thought of earlier humanity. . . . I mean, as a man now reasons in dreams, so humanity also reasoned for many thousands of years when awake: the first cause which occurred to the mind as an explanation of anything that required explanation was sufficient and passed for truth. . . . This atavistic element in man's nature continues to manifest itself in our dreams, for it is the foundation upon which the higher reason has developed and still develops in every individual. Dreams carry us back to remote conditions of human culture and afford us a ready means of understanding it better." Nietzsche, Human All-Too-Human, I, pp. 24-25, trans. by Zimmern and Cohn, modified.

18 Hubert and Mauss, Mélanges d'Histoire des Religions, p. xxix: "Constantly set before us in language, though not necessarily explicit in it, . . . the categories . . . generally exist rather under the form of habits that guide consciousness, themselves remaining unconscious. The notion of mana is one of these principles; it is a datum of language; it is implied in a whole series of judgments and reasonings concerned with attributes that are those of mana. We have described mana as a category, but it is a category not confined to primitive thought; and today, in a weakened degree, it is still the primal form that certain other categories which always function in our minds have covered over: those of substance, cause . . ." etc.

19 Lévy-Bruhl, How Natives Think.

in the place of worship. The tetraktys—to use the Pythagorean term—does indeed refer to an "inner gathering," as our patient's dream clearly demonstrates. The symbol appears in other dreams, usually in the form of a circle divided into four or containing four main parts. In other dreams of the same series it takes the form of an undivided circle, a flower, a square place or room, a quadrangle, a globe, a clock, a symmetrical garden with a fountain in the centre, four people in a boat, in an aeroplane, or at a table, four chairs round a table, four colours, a wheel with eight spokes, an eight-rayed star or sun, a round hat divided into eight parts, a bear with four eyes, a square prison cell, the four seasons, a bowl containing four nuts, the world clock with a disc divided into $4 \times 8 = 32$ partitions, and so on.[20]

91 These quaternity symbols occur no less than seventy-one times in a series of four hundred dreams.[21] My case is no exception in this respect. I have observed many cases where the number four occurred and it always had an unconscious origin, that is, the dreamer got it first from a dream and had no idea of its meaning, nor had he ever heard of the symbolic importance of the number four. It would of course be a different thing with the number three, since the Trinity represents a symbolic number known to everybody. But for us, and particularly for a modern scientist, four conveys no more than any other number. Number symbolism and its venerable history is a field of knowledge completely outside our dreamer's intellectual interests. If under such conditions dreams insist upon the importance of four, we have every right to call its origin an unconscious one. The numinous character of the quaternity is obvious in the second dream. From this we must conclude that it points to a meaning which we have to call "sacred." Since the dreamer was unable to trace this peculiar character to any conscious source, I apply a comparative method in order to elucidate the meaning of the symbolism. It is of course impossible to give a complete account of this procedure here, so I must restrict myself to the barest hints.

20 For the psychology of the *tetraktys*, see my "Commentary on *The Secret of the Golden Flower*," par. 31: ["Dogma of the Trinity," pars. 246, 268ff.]; and Hauer, "Symbole und Erfahrung des Selbstes in der Indo-Arischen Mystik."
21 [For a tabulation of these dreams, see *Psychology and Alchemy*, par. 329, n.—EDITORS.]

92   Since many unconscious contents seem to be remnants of historical states of mind, we need only go back a few hundred years in order to reach the conscious level that forms the parallel to our dreams. In our case we step back not quite three hundred years and find ourselves among scientists and natural philosophers who were seriously discussing the enigma of squaring the circle.[22] This abstruse problem was itself a psychological projection of something much older and completely unconscious. But they knew in those days that the circle signified the Deity: "God is an intellectual figure whose centre is everywhere and the circumference nowhere,"[23] as one of these philosophers said, repeating St. Augustine. A man as introverted and introspective as Emerson[24] could hardly fail to touch on the same idea and likewise quote St. Augustine. The image of the circle—regarded as the most perfect form since Plato's *Timaeus*, the prime authority for Hermetic philosophy—was assigned to the most perfect substance, to the gold, also to the *anima mundi* or *anima media natura*, and to the first created light. And because the macrocosm, the Great World, was made by the creator "in a form round and globose,"[25] the smallest part of the whole, the point, also possesses this perfect nature. As the philosopher says: "Of all shapes the simplest and most perfect is the sphere, which rests in a point."[26] This image of the Deity dormant and

---

[22] There is an excellent presentation of the problem in Maier, *De circulo* (1616).

[23] [On the source of this saying, see par. 229, n. 6, below.—EDITORS.]

[24] Cf. his essay "Circles" (*Essays*, Everyman edn., p. 167).

[25] Plato, *Timaeus*, 7; Steeb, *Coelum Sephiroticum Hebraeorum* (1679), p. 15.

[26] Steeb, p. 19. Maier (*De circulo*, p. 27) says: "The circle is a symbol of eternity or an indivisible point." Concerning the "round element," see *Turba philosophorum*, Sermo XLI (ed. Ruska, p. 148), where the "rotundum which turns copper into four" is mentioned. Ruska says there is no similar symbol in the Greek sources. This is not quite correct, since we find a στοιχεῖον στρογγύλον (round element) in the περὶ ὀργάνων of Zosimos (Berthelot, *Alch. grecs*, III, xlix, 1). The same symbolism may also occur in his τόλμα (Berthelot, III, v bis), in the form of the περηκουσμένον, which Berthelot translates as "objet circulaire." (The correctness of this translation, however, is doubtful.) [Cf. "The Visions of Zosimos," par. 86, n. 12.] A better parallel might be Zosimos' "omega element." He himself describes it as "round" (Berthelot, III, xlix, 1).

The idea of the creative point in matter is mentioned in Sendivogius, "Novum lumen" (*Musaeum hermeticum*, 1678, p. 559); cf. *The Hermetic Museum Restored and Enlarged*, trans. by A. E. Waite, II, p. 89: "For there is in every body a centre, the seeding-place or spermatic point." This point is a "point born of God" (p. 59). Here we encounter the doctrine of the "panspermia" (all-embracing

concealed in matter was what the alchemists called the original chaos, or the earth of paradise, or the round fish in the sea,[27] or the egg, or simply the *rotundum*. That round thing was in possession of the magical key which unlocked the closed doors of matter. As is said in the *Timaeus*, only the demiurge, the perfect being, is capable of dissolving the tetraktys, the embrace of the four elements.[28] One of the great authorities since the thirteenth century, the *Turba philosophorum*, says that the *rotundum* can turn copper into four.[29] Thus the much-sought-for *aurum philosophicum* was round.[30] Opinions were divided as to the procedure for procuring the dormant demiurge. Some hoped to lay hold of him in the form of a *prima materia* containing a particular concentration or a particularly suitable variety of this substance. Others endeavoured to produce the round substance by a sort of synthesis, called the *coniunctio*; the anonymous author of the *Rosarium philosophorum* says: "Make a round circle of man and woman, extract therefrom a quadrangle and from it a triangle. Make the circle round, and you will have the Philosophers' Stone."[31]

seed-bed), about which Athanasius Kircher, S.J. (*Mundus subterraneus*, 1678, II, p. 347) says: "Thus from the holy words of Moses . . . it appears that God, the creator of all things, in the beginning created from nothing a certain Matter, which we not unfittingly call Chaotic . . . within which something . . . confused lay hidden as if in a kind of panspermia . . . as though he brought forth afterward from the underlying material all things which had already been fecundated and incubated by the divine Spirit. . . . But he did not forthwith destroy the Chaotic Matter, but willed it to endure until the consummation of the world, as at the first beginning of things so to this very day, a panspermia replete with all things. . . ." These ideas lead us back to the "descent" or "fall of the deity" in the Gnostic systems. Cf. Bussell, *Religious Thought and Heresy in the Middle Ages*, pp. 554ff.; Reitzenstein, *Poimandres*, p. 50; Mead, *Pistis Sophia*, pp. **36ff.**, and *Fragments of a Faith Forgotten*, p. 470.

27 "There is in the sea a round fish, lacking bones and scales, and having in itself a fatness" (the *humidum radicale*—the *anima mundi* imprisoned in matter). From "Allegoriae super Turbam," *Art. aurif.*, I (1593), p. 141. [Cf. *Aion*, pars. 195ff.]

28 *Timaeus* 7.   29 See above, n. 26.

30 "For as the heaven which is visible is round in form and motion . . . so is the Gold" (Maier, *De circulo*, p. 39).

31 *Rosarium philosophorum* (*Art. aurif.*, II, p. 261). This treatise is ascribed to Petrus Toletanus, who lived in Toledo about the middle of the 13th century. He is said to have been either an older contemporary or a brother of Arnold of Villanova, the famous physician and philosopher. The present form of the *Rosarium*, based on the first printing of 1550, is a compilation and probably does not date

93   This marvellous stone was symbolized as a perfect living being of hermaphroditic nature corresponding to the Empedoclean σφαῖρος, the εὐδαιμονέστατος θεός and all-round bisexual being in Plato.[32] As early as the beginning of the fourteenth century, the *lapis* was compared by Petrus Bonus to Christ, as an *allegoria Christi*.[33] In the *Aurea hora*, a Pseudo-Thomist tract from the thirteenth century, the mystery of the stone is rated even higher than the mysteries of the Christian religion.[34] I mention these facts merely to show that the circle or globe containing the four was an allegory of the Deity for not a few of our learned forefathers.

94   From the Latin treatises it is also evident that the latent demiurge, dormant and concealed in matter, is identical with the so-called *homo philosophicus*, the second Adam.[35] He is the spiritual man, Adam Kadmon, often identified with Christ. Whereas the original Adam was mortal, because he was made of the corruptible four elements, the second Adam is immortal, because he consists of one pure and incorruptible essence. Thus Pseudo-Thomas says: "The Second Adam . . . from pure elements entered into eternity. Therefore, what is composed of simple and pure essence remaineth forever."[36] The same treatise quotes a Latinized Arabic author called Senior, a famous author-

back further than the 15th century, though certain parts may have originated early in the 13th century.   [32] *Symposium* XIV.

[33] Petrus Bonus in Janus Lacinius, *Pretiosa margarita novella* (1946). For the *allegoria Christi*, see *Psychology and Alchemy*, "The Lapis-Christ Parallel."

[34] *Beati Thomae de Aquino Aurora sive Aurea hora*. Complete text in the rare printing of 1625: *Harmoniae Inperscrutabilis Chymico-philosophicae sive Philosophorum Antiquorum Consentientium Decas I* (Francofurti apud Conrad Eifridum. Anno MDCXXV). (British Museum 1033 d.11.) The interesting part of this treatise is the first part, "Tractatus parabolarum," which was omitted on account of its "blasphemous" character from the printings of *Artis auriferae* in 1572 and 1593. In the so-called Codex Rhenoviensis (Zurich Central Library), about four chapters of the "Parabolarum" are missing. The Codex Parisinus Fond. Lat. 14006 (Bibl. nat.) contains a complete text, [For English translation, see *Aurora Consurgens*, edited by M.-L. von Franz.—EDITORS.]

[35] A good example is the commentary of Gnosius on the "Tractatus aureus Hermetis," *Theatr. chem.*, IV, pp. 672ff.; Manget, *Bibl. chem.*, I, pp. 400ff.

[36] *Aurora Consurgens* (ed. von Franz) p. 129. Zosimos (Berthelot, *Alch grecs*, III, xlix, 4–5), quoting from a Hermetic writing, says that ὁ θεοῦ υἱὸς παντογενόμενος was Adam or Thoth, who was made of the four elements and the four cardinal points. Cf. *Psychology and Alchemy*, par. 456, sec. 6.

95 ity throughout the Middle Ages, as saying: "There is One thing that never dieth, for it continueth by perpetual increase," and interprets this One thing as the second Adam.[37]

It is clear from these quotations that the round substance searched for by the philosophers was a projection very similar to our own dream symbolism. We have historical documents which prove that dreams, visions, and even hallucinations were often mixed up with the great philosophic opus.[38] Our forefathers, being even more naïvely constituted than ourselves, projected their unconscious contents directly into matter. Matter, however, could easily take up such projections, because at that time it was a practically unknown and incomprehensible entity. And whenever man encounters something mysterious he projects his own assumptions into it without the slightest self-criticism. But since chemical matter nowadays is something we know fairly well, we can no longer project as freely as our ancestors. We have, at last, to admit that the quaternity is something psychic; and we do not yet know whether, in a more or less distant future, this too may not prove to be a projection. For the time being we must be satisfied with the fact that an idea of God which is entirely absent from the conscious mind of modern man returns in a form known consciously three hundred or four hundred years ago.

96 I do not need to emphasize that this piece of history was completely unknown to my dreamer. One could say with the classical poet: "Naturam expelles furca tamen usque recurret" (Drive out nature with a pitchfork and she always turns up again).[39]

97 The idea of those old philosophers was that God manifested himself first in the creation of the four elements. They were symbolized by the four partitions of the circle. Thus we read in a Coptic treatise of the Codex Brucianus[40] concerning the Only-Begotten (Monogenes or Anthropos):

This same is he who dwelleth in the Monad, which is in the Setheus [creator], and which came from the place of which none can say where it is. . . . From Him it is the Monad came, in the manner of a ship, laden with all good things, and in the manner of a field, filled or planted with every kind of tree, and in the manner of a city,

37 *Aurora Consurgens* (ed. von Franz), p. 129.
38 Cf. *Psychology and Alchemy*, pars. 347ff.   39 Horace, *Epistles*, I, x, 24.
40 Baynes, ed., *A Coptic Gnostic Treatise*, pp. 22, 89, 94.

filled with all races of mankind . . . And to its veil which surround-
eth it in the manner of a defence there are twelve Gates . . . This
same is the Mother-City (μητρόπολις) of the Only-Begotten.

98   In another place the Anthropos himself is the city and his members are the four gates. The Monad is a spark of light (σπινθήρ),
an atom of the Deity. The Monogenes is thought of as standing
upon a τετράπεζα, a platform supported by four pillars, corresponding to the Christian quaternarium of the Evangelists, or
to the Tetramorph, the symbolic steed of the Church, composed
of the symbols of the four evangelists: the angel, eagle, ox or
calf, and lion. The analogy with the New Jerusalem of the Apocalypse is obvious.

99   The division into four, the synthesis of the four, the miraculous appearance of the four colours, and the four stages of the
work—*nigredo, dealbatio, rubefactio,* and *citrinitas*—are constant preoccupations of the old philosophers.[41] Four symbolizes
the parts, qualities, and aspects of the One. But why should my
patient recapitulate these old speculations?

100   I do not know why he should. I only know that this is not an
isolated case; many others under my observation or under that
of my colleagues have spontaneously produced the same symbolism. I naturally do not think that it originated three or four
hundred years ago. That was simply another epoch when this
same archetypal idea was very much in the foreground. As a
matter of fact, it is much older than the Middle Ages, as the
Timaeus proves. Nor is it a classical or an Egyptian heritage,
since it is to be found practically everywhere and in all ages.
One has only to remember, for instance, how great an importance was attributed to the quaternity by the American In-
dians.[42]

101   Although the quaternity is an age-old and presumably
prehistoric symbol,[43] always associated with the idea of a
world-creating deity, it is—curiously enough—rarely understood as such by those moderns in whom it occurs, I have always
been particularly interested to see how people, if left to their

41 The *Rosarium philosophorum* is one of the first attempts at a synopsis and
gives a fairly comprehensive account of the medieval quaternity.
42 Cf., for instance, the 5th and 8th Annual Reports of the Smithsonian Institution, Bureau of Ethnology, Washington (1887 and 1892).
43 Cf. the paleolithic (?) "sun wheels" of Rhodesia. [But see infra, par. 484, n. 9.]

own devices and not informed about the history of the symbol, would interpret it to themselves. I was careful, therefore, not to disturb them with my own opinions, and as a rule I discovered that they took it to symbolize *themselves* or rather *something in themselves*. They felt it belonged intimately to themselves as a sort of creative background, a life-producing sun in the depths of the unconscious. Though it was easy to see that certain mandala-drawings were almost an exact replica of Ezekiel's vision, it very seldom happened that people recognized the analogy even when they knew the vision—which knowledge, by the way, is pretty rare nowadays. What one could almost call a systematic blindness is simply the effect of the prejudice that God is *outside* man. Although this prejudice is not exclusively Christian, there are certain religions which do not share it at all. On the contrary they insist, as do certain Christian mystics, on the essential identity of God and man, either in the form of an *a priori* identity or of a goal to be attained by certain practices or initiations, as known to us, for instance, from the metamorphoses of Apuleius, not to speak of certain yoga methods.

101   The use of the comparative method shows without a doubt that the quaternity is a more or less direct representation of the God who is manifest in his creation. We might, therefore, conclude that the symbol spontaneously produced in the dreams of modern people means something similar—*the God within*. Although the majority of the persons concerned do not recognize this analogy, the interpretation might nevertheless be correct. If we consider the fact that the idea of God is an "unscientific" hypothesis, we can easily explain why people have forgotten to think along such lines. And even if they do cherish a certain belief in God they would be deterred from the idea of a God within by their religious education, which has always depreciated this idea as "mystical." Yet it is precisely this "mystical" idea which is forced upon the conscious mind by dreams and visions. I myself, as well as my colleagues, have seen so many cases developing the same kind of symbolism that we cannot doubt its existence any longer. My observations, moreover, date back to 1914, and I waited fourteen years before alluding to them publicly.[44]

102   It would be a regrettable mistake if anybody should take my

44 [In his commentary to *The Secret of the Golden Flower*, first pub. (in German) in 1929.—Editors.]

103 observations as a kind of proof of the existence of God. They prove only the existence of an archetypal God-image, which to my mind is the most we can assert about God psychologically. But as it is a very important and influential archetype, its relatively frequent occurrence seems to be a noteworthy fact for any *theologia naturalis*. And since experience of this archetype has the quality of numinosity, often in very high degree, it comes into the category of religious experiences.

104 I cannot refrain from calling attention to the interesting fact that whereas the central Christian symbolism is a Trinity, the formula presented by the unconscious is a quaternity. In reality the orthodox Christian formula is not quite complete, because the dogmatic aspect of the evil principle is absent from the Trinity and leads a more or less awkward existence on its own as the devil. Nevertheless, it seems that the Church does not exclude an inner relationship between the devil and the Trinity. A Catholic authority expresses himself on this question as follows: "The existence of Satan, however, can only be understood in relation to the Trinity." "Any theological treatment of the devil that is not related to God's trinitarian consciousness is a falsification of the actual position." [45] According to this view, the devil possesses personality and absolute freedom. That is why he can be the true, personal "counterpart of Christ." "Herein is revealed a new freedom in God's being: he freely allows the devil to subsist beside him and permits his kingdom to endure for ever." "The idea of a mighty devil is incompatible with the conception of Yahweh, but not with the conception of the Trinity. The mystery of one God in Three Persons opens out a new freedom in the depths of God's being, and this even makes possible the thought of a personal devil existing alongside God and in opposition to him." [46] The devil, accordingly, possesses an autonomous personality, freedom, and eternality, and he has these metaphysical qualities so much in common with God that he can actually subsist in opposition to him. Hence the relationship or even the (negative) affinity of the devil with the Trinity can no longer be denied as a Catholic idea.

The inclusion of the devil in the quaternity is by no means a modern speculation or a monstrous fabrication of the unconscious. We find in the writings of the sixteenth-century natural

45 Koepgen, *Die Gnosis des Christentums*, pp. 189, 190.   46 Ibid., pp. 185ff.

philosopher and physician, Gerard Dorn, a detailed discussion of the symbols of the Trinity and the quaternity, the latter being attributed to the devil. Dorn breaks with the whole alchemical tradition inasmuch as he adopts the rigidly Christian standpoint that Three is One but Four is not, because Four attains to unity in the *quinta essentia*. According to this author the quaternity is in truth a "diabolical fraud" or "deception of the devil," and he holds that at the fall of the angels the devil "fell into the realm of quaternity and the elements" (*in quaternariam et elementariam regionem decidit*). He also gives an elaborate description of the symbolic operation whereby the devil produced the "double serpent" (the number 2) "with the four horns" (the number 4). Indeed, the number 2 is the devil himself, the *quadricornutus binarius*.[47]

105   Since a God identical with the individual man is an exceedingly complex assumption bordering on heresy,[48] the "God

---

47 Dorn thinks that God created the *binarius* on the second day of Creation, when he separated the upper waters from the lower, and that this was the reason why he omitted to say on the evening of the second day what he said on all the others, namely that "it was good." The emancipation of the *binarius*, Dorn holds, was the cause of "confusion, division, and strife." From the *binarius* issued "its quaternary offspring" (*sua proles quaternaria*). Since the number 2 is feminine, it also signified Eve, whereas the number 3 was equated with Adam. Therefore the devil tempted Eve first: "For [the devil] knew, being full of all guile, that Adam was marked with the *unarius*, and for this cause he did not at first attack him, for he greatly doubted whether he could do anything against him. Moreover, he was not ignorant that Eve was divided from her husband as a natural binary from the unity of its ternary [*tanquam naturalem binarium ab unario sui ternarii*]. Accordingly, armed with a certain likeness of binary to binary, he made his attack on the woman. For all even numbers are feminine, of which two, Eve's proper and original number, is the first." (Dorn, "De tenebris contra naturam et vita brevi," *Theat. chem.*, 1602, I, p. 527. In this treatise and the one that follows it, "De Duello Animi cum Corpore," pp. 535ff., the reader will find everything I have mentioned here.) The reader will have noticed how Dorn, with great cunning, discovers in the *binarius* a secret affinity between the devil and woman. He was the first to point out the discord between threeness and fourness, between God as Spirit and Empedoclean nature, thus—albeit unconsciously—cutting the thread of alchemical projection. Accordingly, he speaks of the *quaternarius* as "fundamental to the medicine of the infidels." We must leave it an open question whether by "infidels" he meant the Arabs or the pagans of antiquity. At any rate Dorn suspected that there was something ungodly in the quaternity, which was intimately associated with the nature of woman. Cf. my remarks concerning the "virgo terra," pars. 107, n. 52, 123, 126.

48 I am not referring here to the dogma of the human nature of Christ.

within" also presents a dogmatic difficulty. But the quaternity as produced by the modern psyche points directly not only to the God within, but to the identity of God and man. Contrary to the dogma, there are not three, but four aspects. It could easily be inferred that the fourth represents the devil. Though we have the logion "I and the Father are one: who seeth me seeth the Father," it would be considered blasphemy or madness to stress Christ's dogmatic humanity to such a degree that man could identify himself with Christ and his homoousia.[49] But this is precisely what seems to be meant by the natural symbol. From an orthodox standpoint, therefore, the natural quaternity could be declared a *diabolica fraus*, and the chief proof of this would be its assimilation of the fourth aspect which represents the reprehensible part of the Christian cosmos. The Church, it seems to me, probably has to repudiate any attempt to take such conclusions seriously. She may even have to condemn any approach to these experiences, since she cannot admit that nature unites what she herself has divided. The voice of nature is clearly audible in all experiences of the quaternity, and this arouses all the old mistrust of anything even remotely connected with the unconscious. Scientific investigation of dreams is simply the old oneiromancy in new guise and therefore just as objectionable as any other of the "occult" arts. Close parallels to the symbolism of dreams can be found in the old alchemical treatises, and these are quite as heretical as dreams.[50] Here, it would seem, was reason enough for secrecy and protective metaphors.[51] The symbolic statements of the old alchemists issue from the same unconscious as modern dreams and are just as much the voice of nature.

106   If we were still living in a medieval setting where there was not much doubt about the ultimate things and where every history of the world began with Genesis, we could easily brush

[40] This identification has nothing to do with the Catholic conception of the assimilation of the individual's life to the life of Christ and his absorption into the *corpus mysticum* of the Church. It is rather the opposite of this view.
[50] I am thinking chiefly of works that contain alchemical legends and didactic tales. A good example would be Maier's *Symbola aureae mensae* (1617), with its symbolic *peregrinatio* (pp. 569ff.).
[51] So far as I know, there are no complaints in alchemical literature of persecution by the Church. The authors allude usually to the tremendous secret of the magistery as a reason for secrecy.

aside dreams and the like. Unfortunately we live in a modern setting where all the ultimate things are doubtful, where there is a prehistory of enormous extension, and where people are fully aware that if there is any numinous experience at all, it is the experience of the psyche. We can no longer imagine an empyrean world revolving round the throne of God, and we would not dream of seeking for him somewhere behind the galactic systems. Yet the human soul seems to harbour mysteries, since to an empiricist all religious experience boils down to a peculiar psychic condition. If we want to know anything of what religious experience means to those who have it, we have every chance nowadays of studying it in every imaginable form. And if it means anything, it means everything to those who have it. This is at any rate the inevitable conclusion one reaches by a careful study of the evidence. One could even define religious experience as that kind of experience which is accorded the highest value, no matter what its contents may be. The modern mind, so far as it stands under the verdict "extra ecclesiam nulla salus," will turn to the psyche as the last hope. Where else could one obtain experience? And the answer will be more or less of the kind which I have described. The voice of nature will answer and all those concerned with the spiritual problem of man will be confronted with new and baffling problems. Because of the spiritual need of my patients I have been forced to make a serious attempt to understand some of the symbols produced by the unconscious. As it would lead much too far to embark on a discussion of the intellectual and ethical consequences, I shall have to content myself with a mere sketch.

107 The main symbolic figures of a religion are always expressive of the particular moral and mental attitude involved. I would mention, for instance, the cross and its various religious meanings. Another main symbol is the Trinity. It is of exclusively masculine character. The unconscious, however, transforms it into a quaternity, which is at the same time a unity, just as the three persons of the Trinity are one and the same God. The natural philosophers of antiquity represented the Trinity, so far as it was *imaginata in natura*, as the three ἀσώματα or "spirits," also called "volatilia," namely water, air, and fire. The fourth constituent, on the other hand, was τὸ σῶματον, the earth or the body.

They symbolized the latter by the Virgin.[52] In this way they added the feminine element to their physical Trinity, thereby producing the quaternity or *circulus quadratus*, whose symbol was the hermaphroditic *rebis*,[53] the *filius sapientiae*. The natural philosophers of the Middle Ages undoubtedly meant earth and woman by the fourth element. The principle of evil was not openly mentioned, but it appears in the poisonous quality of the *prima materia* and in other allusions. The quaternity in modern dreams is a creation of the unconscious. As I explained in the first chapter, the unconscious is often personified by the anima, a feminine figure. Apparently the symbol of the quaternity issues from her. She would be the matrix of the quaternity, a Θεοτόκος or Mater Dei, just as the earth was understood to be the Mother of God. But since woman, as well as evil, is excluded from the Deity in the dogma of the Trinity, the element of evil would form part of the religious symbol if the latter should be a quaternity. It needs no particular effort of imagination to guess the far-reaching spiritual consequences of such a development.

---

[52] Cf. *Psychology and Alchemy*, fig. 232, showing the glorification of the body in the form of the Assumption of the Virgin (from Reusner, *Pandora*, 1588). St. Augustine used the earth to symbolize the Virgin: "Truth is arisen from the earth, for Christ is born of a virgin" (*Sermones*, 189, II, in Migne, *P.L.*, vol. 38, col. 1006). Likewise Tertullian: "That virgin earth, not yet watered by the rains nor fertilized by the showers" (*Adversus Judaeos*, 13, in Migne, *P.L.*, vol. 2, col. 655).

[53] The *rebis* ("made of two") is the philosophers' stone, for in it the masculine and the feminine nature are united. [Cf. *Psychology and Alchemy*, fig. 125, and "The Psychology of the Transference," pars. 525ff.—EDITORS]

IV

ON HUMAN DEVELOPMENT

MARRIAGE AS A PSYCHOLOGICAL RELATIONSHIP [1]

324   Regarded as a psychological relationship, marriage is a highly complex structure made up of a whole series of subjective and objective factors, mostly of a very heterogeneous nature. As I wish to confine myself here to the purely psychological problems of marriage, I must disregard in the main the objective factors of a legal and social nature, although these cannot fail to have a pronounced influence on the psychological relationship between the marriage partners.

325   Whenever we speak of a "psychological relationship" we presuppose one that is *conscious*, for there is no such thing as a psychological relationship between two people who are in a state of unconsciousness. From the psychological point of view they would be wholly without relationship. From any other point of view, the physiological for example, they could be regarded as related, but one could not call their relationship psychological. It must be admitted that though such total unconsciousness as I have assumed does not occur, there is nevertheless a not inconsiderable degree of partial unconsciousness, and the psychological relationship is limited in the degree to which that unconsciousness exists.

1 [First published as "Die Ehe als psychologische Beziehung," in *Das Ehebuch* (Celle, 1925), a volume edited by Count Hermann Keyserling; translated by Theresa Duerr in the English version, *The Book of Marriage* (New York, 1926). The original was reprinted in *Seelenprobleme der Gegenwart* (Zurich, 1931). The essay was again translated into English by H. G. and Cary F. Baynes in *Contributions to Analytical Psychology* (London and New York, 1928), and this version has been freely consulted in the present translation.—EDITORS.]

326 In the child, consciousness rises out of the depths of unconscious psychic life, at first like separate islands, which gradually unite to form a "continent," a continuous land-mass of consciousness. Progressive mental development means, in effect, extension of consciousness. With the rise of a continuous consciousness, and not before, psychological relationship becomes possible. So far as we know, consciousness is always ego-consciousness. In order to be conscious of myself, I must be able to distinguish myself from others. Relationship can only take place where this distinction exists. But although the distinction may be made in a general way, normally it is incomplete, because large areas of psychic life still remain unconscious. As no distinction can be made with regard to unconscious contents, on this terrain no relationship can be established; here there still reigns the original unconscious condition of the ego's primitive identity with others, in other words a complete absence of relationship.

327 The young person of marriageable age does, of course, possess an ego-consciousness (girls more than men, as a rule), but, since he has only recently emerged from the mists of original unconsciousness, he is certain to have wide areas which still lie in the shadow and which preclude to that extent the formation of psychological relationship. This means, in practice, that the young man (or woman) can have only an incomplete understanding of himself and others, and is therefore imperfectly informed as to his, and their, motives. As a rule the motives he acts from are largely unconscious. Subjectively, of course, he thinks himself very conscious and knowing, for we constantly overestimate the existing content of consciousness, and it is a great and surprising discovery when we find that what we had supposed to be the final peak is nothing but the first step in a very long climb. The greater the area of unconsciousness, the less is marriage a matter of free choice, as is shown subjectively in the fatal compulsion one feels so acutely when one is in love. The compulsion can exist even when one is not in love, though in less agreeable form.

328 Unconscious motivations are of a personal and of a general nature. First of all, there are the motives deriving from parental influence. The relationship of the young man to his mother, and of the girl to her father, is the determining factor in this respect.

It is the strength of the bond to the parents that unconsciously influences the choice of husband or wife, either positively or negatively. Conscious love for either parent favours the choice of a like mate, while an unconscious tie (which need not by any means express itself consciously as love) makes the choice difficult and imposes characteristic modifications. In order to understand them, one must know first of all the cause of the unconscious tie to the parents, and under what conditions it forcibly modifies, or even prevents, the conscious choice. Generally speaking, all the life which the parents could have lived, but of which they thwarted themselves for artificial motives, is passed on to the children in substitute form. That is to say, the children are driven unconsciously in a direction that is intended to compensate for everything that was left unfulfilled in the lives of their parents. Hence it is that excessively moral-minded parents have what are called "unmoral" children, or an irresponsible wastrel of a father has a son with a positively morbid amount of ambition, and so on. The worst results flow from parents who have kept themselves artificially unconscious. Take the case of a mother who deliberately keeps herself unconscious so as not to disturb the pretence of a "satisfactory" marriage. Unconsciously she will bind her son to her, more or less as a substitute for a husband. The son, if not forced directly into homosexuality, is compelled to modify his choice in a way that is contrary to his true nature. He may, for instance, marry a girl who is obviously inferior to his mother and therefore unable to compete with her; or he will fall for a woman of a tyrannical and overbearing disposition, who may perhaps succeed in tearing him away from his mother. The choice of a mate, if the instincts have not been vitiated, may remain free from these influences, but sooner or later they will make themselves felt as obstacles. A more or less instinctive choice might be considered the best from the point of view of maintaining the species, but it is not always fortunate psychologically, because there is often an uncommonly large difference between the purely instinctive personality and one that is individually differentiated. And though in such cases the race might be improved and invigorated by a purely instinctive choice, individual happiness would be bound to suffer. (The idea of "instinct" is of course nothing more than a collec-

329 tive term for all kinds of organic and psychic factors whose nature is for the most part unknown.)

If the individual is to be regarded solely as an instrument for maintaining the species, then the purely instinctive choice of a mate is by far the best. But since the foundations of such a choice are unconscious, only a kind of impersonal liaison can be built upon them, such as can be observed to perfection among primitives. If we can speak here of a "relationship" at all, it is, at best, only a pale reflection of what we mean, a very distant state of affairs with a decidedly impersonal character, wholly regulated by traditional customs and prejudices, the prototype of every conventional marriage.

330 So far as reason or calculation or the so-called loving care of the parents does not arrange the marriage, and the pristine instincts of the children are not vitiated either by false education or by the hidden influence of accumulated and neglected parental complexes, the marriage choice will normally follow the unconscious motivations of instinct. Unconsciousness results in non-differentiation, or unconscious identity. The practical consequence of this is that one person presupposes in the other a psychological structure similar to his own. Normal sex life, as a shared experience with apparently similar aims, further strengthens the feeling of unity and identity. This state is described as one of complete harmony, and is extolled as a great happiness ("one heart and one soul")—not without good reason, since the return to that original condition of unconscious oneness is like a return to childhood. Hence the childish gestures of all lovers. Even more is it a return to the mother's womb, into the teeming depths of an as yet unconscious creativity. It is, in truth, a genuine and incontestable experience of the Divine, whose transcendent force obliterates and consumes everything individual; a real communion with life and the impersonal power of fate. The individual will for self-possession is broken: the woman becomes the mother, the man the father, and thus both are robbed of their freedom and made instruments of the life urge.

331 Here the relationship remains within the bounds of the biological instinctive goal, the preservation of the species. Since this goal is of a collective nature, the psychological link between husband and wife will also be essentially collective, and cannot

be regarded as an individual relationship in the psychological sense. We can only speak of this when the nature of the unconscious motivations has been recognized and the original identity broken down. Seldom or never does a marriage develop into an individual relationship smoothly and without crises. There is no birth of consciousness without pain.

331a   The ways that lead to conscious realization are many, but they follow definite laws. In general, the change begins with the onset of the second half of life. The middle period of life is a time of enormous psychological importance. The child begins its psychological life within very narrow limits, inside the magic circle of the mother and the family. With progressive maturation it widens its horizon and its own sphere of influence; its hopes and intentions are directed to extending the scope of personal power and possessions; desire reaches out to the world in ever-widening range; the will of the individual becomes more and more identical with the natural goals pursued by unconscious motivations. Thus man breathes his own life into things, until finally they begin to live of themselves and to multiply; and imperceptibly he is overgrown by them. Mothers are overtaken by their children, men by their own creations, and what was originally brought into being only with labour and the greatest effort can no longer be held in check. First it was passion, then it became duty, and finally an intolerable burden, a vampire that battens on the life of its creator. Middle life is the moment of greatest unfolding, when a man still gives himself to his work with his whole strength and his whole will. But in this very moment evening is born, and the second half of life begins. Passion now changes her face and is called duty; "I want" becomes the inexorable "I must," and the turnings of the pathway that once brought surprise and discovery become dulled by custom. The wine has fermented and begins to settle and clear. Conservative tendencies develop if all goes well; instead of looking forward one looks backward, most of the time involuntarily, and one begins to take stock, to see how one's life has developed up to this point. The real motivations are sought and real discoveries are made. The critical survey of himself and his fate enables a man to recognize his peculiarities. But these insights do not come to him easily; they are gained only through the severest shocks.

331b Since the aims of the second half of life are different from those of the first, to linger too long in the youthful attitude produces a division of the will. Consciousness still presses forward, in obedience, as it were, to its own inertia, but the unconscious lags behind, because the strength and inner resolve needed for further expansion have been sapped. This disunity with oneself begets discontent, and since one is not conscious of the real state of things one generally projects the reasons for it upon one's partner. A critical atmosphere thus develops, the necessary prelude to conscious realization. Usually this state does not begin simultaneously for both partners. Even the best of marriages cannot expunge individual differences so completely that the state of mind of the partners is absolutely identical. In most cases one of them will adapt to marriage more quickly than the other. The one who is grounded on a positive relationship to the parents will find little or no difficulty in adjusting to his or her partner, while the other may be hindered by a deep-seated unconscious tie to the parents. He will therefore achieve complete adaptation only later, and, because it is won with greater difficulty, it may even prove the more durable.

331c These differences in tempo, and in the degree of spiritual development, are the chief causes of a typical difficulty which makes its appearance at critical moments. In speaking of "the degree of spiritual development" of a personality, I do not wish to imply an especially rich or magnanimous nature. Such is not the case at all. I mean, rather, a certain complexity of mind or nature, comparable to a gem with many facets as opposed to the simple cube. There are many-sided and rather problematical natures burdened with hereditary traits that are sometimes very difficult to reconcile. Adaptation to such natures, or their adaptation to simpler personalities, is always a problem. These people, having a certain tendency to dissociation, generally have the capacity to split off irreconcilable traits of character for considerable periods, thus passing themselves off as much simpler than they are; or it may happen that their many-sidedness, their very versatility, lends them a peculiar charm. Their partners can easily lose themselves in such a labyrinthine nature, finding in it such an abundance of possible experiences that their personal interests are completely absorbed, sometimes in a not very agreeable way, since their sole occupation then consists in tracking the other through all the twists and turns of his character. There is always so much experience available that the simpler personality is surrounded, if not actually swamped, by it; he is swallowed up in his more complex partner and cannot see his way out. It is an almost regular occurrence for a woman to be wholly contained, spiritually, in her husband, and for a husband to be wholly contained, emotionally, in his wife. One could describe this as the problem of the "contained" and the "container."

332 The one who is contained feels himself to be living entirely within the confines of his marriage; his attitude to the marriage partner is undivided; outside the marriage there exist no essential obligations and no binding interests. The unpleasant side of this otherwise ideal partnership is the disquieting dependence upon a personality that can never be seen in its entirety, and is therefore not altogether credible or dependable. The great advantage lies in his own undividedness, and this is a factor not to be underrated in the psychic economy.

333 The container, on the other hand, who in accordance with his tendency to dissociation has an especial need to unify himself in undivided love for another, will be left far behind in this effort, which is naturally very difficult for him, by the simpler personality. While he is seeking in the latter all the subtleties and complexities that would complement and correspond to his own facets, he is disturbing the other's simplicity. Since in normal circumstances simplicity always has the advantage over complexity, he will very soon be obliged to abandon his efforts to arouse subtle and intricate reactions in a simpler nature. And soon enough his partner, who in accordance with her [2] simpler nature expects simple answers from him, will give him plenty to do by constellating his complexities with her everlasting insistence on simple answers. Willynilly, he must withdraw into himself before the suasions of simplicity. Any mental effort, like the conscious process itself, is so much of a strain for the ordinary man that he invariably prefers the simple, even when it does not

[2] [In translating this and the following passages, I have, for the sake of clarity, assumed that the container is the man and the contained the woman. This assumption is due entirely to the exigencies of English grammar, and is not implied in the German text. Needless to say, the situation could just as easily be reversed.—TRANS.]

happen to be the truth. And when it represents at least a half-truth, then it is all up with him. The simpler nature works on the more complicated like a room that is too small, that does not allow him enough space. The complicated nature, on the other hand, gives the simpler one too many rooms with too much space, so that she never knows where she really belongs. So it comes about quite naturally that the more complicated contains the simpler. The former cannot be absorbed in the latter, but encompasses it without being itself contained. Yet, since the more complicated has perhaps a greater need of being contained than the other, he feels himself outside the marriage and accordingly always plays the problematical role. The more the contained clings, the more the container feels shut out of the relationship. The contained pushes into it by her clinging, and the more she pushes, the less the container is able to respond. He therefore tends to spy out of the window, no doubt unconsciously at first; but with the onset of middle age there awakens in him a more insistent longing for that unity and undividedness which is especially necessary to him on account of his dissociated nature. At this juncture things are apt to occur that bring the conflict to a head. He becomes conscious of the fact that he is seeking completion, seeking the contentedness and undividedness that have always been lacking. For the contained this is only a confirmation of the insecurity she has always felt so painfully; she discovers that in the rooms which apparently belonged to her there dwell other, unwished-for guests. The hope of security vanishes, and this disappointment drives her in on herself, unless by desperate and violent efforts she can succeed in forcing her partner to capitulate, and in extorting a confession that his longing for unity was nothing but a childish or morbid fantasy. If these tactics do not succeed, her acceptance of failure may do her a real good, by forcing her to recognize that the security she was so desperately seeking in the other is to be found in herself. In this way she finds herself and discovers in her own simpler nature all those complexities which the container had sought for in vain.

334

If the container does not break down in face of what we are wont to call "unfaithfulness," but goes on believing in the inner justification of his longing for unity, he will have to put up with his self-division for the time being. A dissociation is not healed by being split off, but by more complete disintegration. All the powers that strive for unity, all healthy desire for selfhood, will resist the disintegration, and in this way he will become conscious of the possibility of an inner integration, which before he had always sought outside himself. He will then find his reward in an undivided self.

335   This is what happens very frequently about the midday of life, and in this wise our miraculous human nature enforces the transition that leads from the first half of life to the second. It is a metamorphosis from a state in which man is only a tool of instinctive nature, to another in which he is no longer a tool, but himself: a transformation of nature into culture, of instinct into spirit.

336   One should take great care not to interrupt this necessary development by acts of moral violence, for any attempt to create a spiritual attitude by splitting off and suppressing the instincts is a falsification. Nothing is more repulsive than a furtively prurient spirituality; it is just as unsavoury as gross sensuality. But the transition takes a long time, and the great majority of people get stuck in the first stages. If only we could, like the primitives, leave the unconscious to look after this whole psychological development which marriage entails, these transformations could be worked out more completely and without too much friction. So often among so-called "primitives" one comes across spiritual personalities who immediately inspire respect, as though they were the fully matured products of an undisturbed fate. I speak here from personal experience. But where among present-day Europeans can one find people not deformed by acts of moral violence? We are still barbarous enough to believe both in asceticism and its opposite. But the wheel of history cannot be put back; we can only strive towards an attitude that will allow us to live out our fate as undisturbedly as the primitive pagan in us really wants. Only on this condition can we be sure of not perverting spirituality into sensuality, and vice versa; for both must live, each drawing life from the other.

337   The transformation I have briefly described above is the very essence of the psychological marriage relationship. Much could be said about the illusions that serve the ends of nature and bring about the transformations that are characteristic of middle life. The peculiar harmony that characterizes mar-

riage during the first half of life—provided the adjustment is successful—is largely based on the projection of certain archetypal images, as the critical phase makes clear.

338   Every man carries within him the eternal image of woman, not the image of this or that particular woman, but a definite feminine image. This image is fundamentally unconscious, an hereditary factor of primordial origin engraved in the living organic system of the man, an imprint or "archetype" of all the ancestral experiences of the female, a deposit, as it were, of all the impressions ever made by woman—in short, an inherited system of psychic adaptation. Even if no women existed, it would still be possible, at any given time, to deduce from this unconscious image exactly how a woman would have to be constituted psychically. The same is true of the woman: she too has her inborn image of man. Actually, we know from experience that it would be more accurate to describe it as an image of *men*, whereas in the case of the man it is rather the image of *woman*. Since this image is unconscious, it is always unconsciously projected upon the person of the beloved, and is one of the chief reasons for passionate attraction or aversion. I have called this image the "anima," and I find the scholastic question *Habet mulier animam?* especially interesting, since in my view it is an intelligent one inasmuch as the doubt seems justified. Woman has no anima, no soul, but she has an *animus*. The anima has an erotic, emotional character, the animus a rationalizing one. Hence most of what men say about feminine eroticism, and particularly about the emotional life of women, is derived from their own anima projections and distorted accordingly. On the other hand, the astonishing assumptions and fantasies that women make about men come from the activity of the animus, who produces an inexhaustible supply of illogical arguments and false explanations.

339   Anima and animus are both characterized by an extraordinary many-sidedness. In a marriage it is always the contained who projects this image upon the container, while the latter is only partially able to project his unconscious image upon his partner. The more unified and simple this partner is, the less complete the projection. In which case, this highly fascinating image hangs as it were in mid air, as though waiting to be filled out by a living person. There are certain types of women who

seem to be made by nature to attract anima projections; indeed one could almost speak of a definite "anima type." The so-called "sphinx-like" character is an indispensable part of their equipment, also an equivocalness, an intriguing elusiveness—not an indefinite blur that offers nothing, but an indefiniteness that seems full of promises, like the speaking silence of a Mona Lisa. A woman of this kind is both old and young, mother and daughter, of more than doubtful chastity, childlike, and yet endowed with a naïve cunning that is extremely disarming to men.[3] Not every man of real intellectual power can be an animus, for the animus must be a master not so much of fine ideas as of fine words—words seemingly full of meaning which purport to leave a great deal unsaid. He must also belong to the "misunderstood" class, or be in some way at odds with his environment, so that the idea of self-sacrifice can insinuate itself. He must be a rather questionable hero, a man with possibilities, which is not to say that an animus projection may not discover a real hero long before he has become perceptible to the sluggish wits of the man of "average intelligence."[4]

340   For man as well as for woman, in so far as they are "containers," the filling out of this image is an experience fraught with consequences, for it holds the possibility of finding one's own complexities answered by a corresponding diversity. Wide vistas seem to open up in which one feels oneself embraced and contained. I say "seem" advisedly, because the experience may be two-faced. Just as the animus projection of a woman can often pick on a man of real significance who is not recognized by the mass, and can actually help him to achieve his true destiny with her moral support, so a man can create for himself a *femme inspiratrice* by his anima projection. But more often it turns out to be an illusion with destructive consequences, a failure because his faith was not sufficiently strong. To the pessimists I would say that these primordial psychic images have an extraordinarily positive value, but I must warn the optimists against

3 There are excellent descriptions of this type in H. Rider Haggard's *She* (London, 1887) and Pierre Benoît's *L'Atlantide* (Paris, 1920; trans. by Mary C. Tongue and Mary Ross as *Atlantida*, New York, 1920).

4 A passably good account of the animus is to be found in Marie Hay's book *The Evil Vineyard* (New York, 1923), also in Elinor Wylie's *Jennifer Lorn* (New York, 1923) and Selma Lagerlöf's *Gösta Berlings Saga* (1891; English trans. by P. B. Flach, *The Story of Gösta Berling*, 1898).

341   blinding fantasies and the likelihood of the most absurd aberrations.

One should on no account take this projection for an individual and conscious relationship. In its first stages it is far from that, for it creates a compulsive dependence based on unconscious motives other than the biological ones. Rider Haggard's *She* gives some indication of the curious world of ideas that underlies the anima projection. They are in essence spiritual contents, often in erotic disguise, obvious fragments of a primitive mythological mentality that consists of archetypes, and whose totality constitutes the collective unconscious. Accordingly, such a relationship is at bottom collective and not individual. (Benoît, who created in *L'Atlantide* a fantasy figure similar even in details to "She," denies having plagiarized Rider Haggard.)

342   If such a projection fastens on to one of the marriage partners, a collective spiritual relationship conflicts with the collective biological one and produces in the container the division or disintegration I have described above. If he is able to hold his head above water, he will find himself through this very conflict. In that case the projection, though dangerous in itself, will have helped him to pass from a collective to an individual relationship. This amounts to full conscious realization of the relationship that marriage brings. Since the aim of this paper is a discussion of the psychology of marriage, the psychology of projection cannot concern us here. It is sufficient to mention it as a fact.

343   One can hardly deal with the psychological marriage relationship without mentioning, even at the risk of misunderstanding, the nature of its critical transitions. As is well known, one understands nothing psychological unless one has experienced it oneself. Not that this ever prevents anyone from feeling convinced that his own judgment is the only true and competent one. This disconcerting fact comes from the necessary overvaluation of the momentary content of consciousness, for without this concentration of attention one could not be conscious at all. Thus it is that every period of life has its own psychological truth, and the same applies to every stage of psychological development. There are even stages which only the few can reach, it being a question of race, family, education, talent, and passion. Nature is aristocratic. The normal man is a fiction, al-

though certain generally valid laws do exist. Psychic life is a development that can easily be arrested on the lowest levels. It is as though every individual had a specific gravity, in accordance with which he either rises, or sinks down, to the level where he reaches his limit. His views and convictions will be determined accordingly. No wonder, then, that by far the greater number of marriages reach their upper psychological limit in fulfilment of the biological aim, without injury to spiritual or moral health. Relatively few people fall into deeper disharmony with themselves. Where there is a great deal of pressure from outside, the conflict is unable to develop much dramatic tension for sheer lack of energy. Psychological insecurity, however, increases in proportion to social security, unconsciously at first, causing neuroses, then consciously, bringing with it separations, discord, divorces, and other marital disorders. On still higher levels, new possibilities of psychological development are discerned, touching on the sphere of religion where critical judgment comes to a halt.

344   Progress may be permanently arrested on any of these levels, with complete unconsciousness of what might have followed at the next stage of development. As a rule graduation to the next stage is barred by violent prejudices and superstitious fears. This, however, serves a most useful purpose, since a man who is compelled by accident to live at a level too high for him becomes a fool and a menace.

345   Nature is not only aristocratic, she is also esoteric. Yet no man of understanding will thereby be induced to make a secret of what he knows, for he realizes only too well that the secret of psychic development can never be betrayed, simply because that development is a question of individual capacity.

The Collected Works of C. G. Jung

Editors: Sir Herbert Read, Michael Fordham, and Gerhard Adler; executive editor, William McGuire. Translated by R.F.C. Hull, except where noted.

In the following list, dates of original publication are given in parentheses (of original composition, in brackets). Multiple dates indicate revisions.

1. PSYCHIATRIC STUDIES (1957; 2d ed., 1970)

On the Psychology and Pathology of So-Called Occult Phenomena (1902)
On Hysterical Misreading (1904)
Cryptomnesia (1905)
On Manic Mood Disorder (1903)
A Case of Hysterical Stupor in a Prisoner in Detention (1902)
On Simulated Insanity (1903)
A Medical Opinion on a Case of Simulated Insanity (1904)
A Third and Final Opinion on Two Contradictory Psychiatric Diagnoses (1906)
On the Psychological Diagnosis of Facts (1905)

2. EXPERIMENTAL RESEARCHES (1973)

Translated by Leopold Stein in collaboration with Diana Riviere

STUDIES IN WORD ASSOCIATION (1904–7, 1910)

The Associations of Normal Subjects (by Jung and F. Riklin)
An Analysis of the Associations of an Epileptic
The Reaction-Time Ratio in the Association Experiment
Experimental Observations on the Faculty of Memory
Psychoanalysis and Association Experiments
The Psychological Diagnosis of Evidence
Association, Dream, and Hysterical Symptom
The Psychopathological Significance of the Association Experiment
Disturbances in Reproduction in the Association Experiment
The Association Method
The Family Constellation

PSYCHOPHYSICAL RESEARCHES (1907–8)

On the Psychophysical Relations of the Association Experiment

Related Publications

THE BASIC WRITINGS OF C. G. JUNG
Selected and introduced by Violet S. de Laszlo

C. G. JUNG: LETTERS
Selected and edited by Gerhard Adler, in collaboration with Aniela Jaffé.
Translations from the German by R. F. C. Hull
 VOL. 1: 1906–1950
 VOL. 2: 1951–1961

C. G. JUNG SPEAKING: Interviews and Encounters
Edited by William McGuire and R. F. C. Hull

C. G. JUNG: Word and Image
Edited by Aniela Jaffé

THE ESSENTIAL JUNG
Selected and introduced by Anthony Storr

THE GNOSTIC JUNG
Selected and introduced by Robert A. Segal

PSYCHE AND SYMBOL
Selected and introduced by Violet S. de Laszlo

Notes of C. G. Jung's Seminars

DREAM ANALYSIS ([1928–30] 1984)
Edited by William McGuire

NIETZSCHE'S *ZARATHUSTRA* ([1934–39] 1988)
Edited by James L. Jarrett (2 vols.)

ANALYTICAL PSYCHOLOGY ([1925] 1989)
Edited by William McGuire

THE PSYCHOLOGY OF KUNDALINI YOGA ([1932] 1996)
Edited by Sonu Shamdasani

VISIONS ([1930–34] 1997)
Edited by Claire Douglas (2 vols.)

PRINCETON / BOLLINGEN PAPERBACK EDITIONS
FROM THE COLLECTED WORKS OF C. G. JUNG

Aion (CW 9,ii)
Alchemical Studies (CW 13)
Analytical Psychology
Answer to Job
Archetypes and the Collective Unconscious (CW 9,i)
Aspects of the Feminine
Aspects of the Masculine
Basic Writings of C. G. Jung
The Development of Personality (CW 17)
Dreams
Essay on Contemporary Events
Essays on a Science of Mythology
The Essential Jung
Experimental Researches (CW 2)
Flying Saucers
Four Archetypes
Freud and Psychoanalysis (CW 4)
The Gnostic Jung
Mandala Symbolism
Mysterium Coniunctionis (CW 14)
On the Nature of the Psyche
The Practice of Psychotherapy (CW 16)
Psyche and Symbol
Psychiatric Studies (CW 1)
Psychogenesis of Mental Disease (CW 3)
Psychological Types (CW 6)
Psychology and Alchemy (CW 12)
Psychology and the East
Psychology and the Occult
Psychology and Western Religion
The Psychology of the Transference
The Spirit in Man, Art, and Literature (CW 15)
Symbols of Transformation (CW 5)
Synchronicity
Two Essays on Analytical Psychology (CW 7)
The Undiscovered Self

OTHER BOLLINGEN PAPERBACKS DEVOTED TO C. G. JUNG

C. G. Jung Speaking
Complex/Archetype/Symbol in the Psychology of C. G. Jung
Psychological Reflections
Selected Letters
C. G. Jung: Word & Image

Library of Congress Cataloging-in-Publication Data

Jung, C. G. (Carl Gustav), 1875–1961.
 [Selections. English. 1990]
 The basic writings of C. G. Jung/selected and introduced by Violet S. de Laszlo;
translated by R.F.C. Hull.
  p. cm.—(Bollingen series; 20)
 Includes bibliographical references.
 ISBN 0-691-01902-9 (alk. paper)
 1. Psychoanalysis. I. De Laszlo, Violet, 1900–1988. II. Hull, R.F.C. (Richard
Francis Carrington), 1913–1974. III. Title.
IV. Series.
BF173.J6623 1990
150.19′54—dc20

90-39712
CIP